Lecture Notes in Computer Science 8257

Michel Abdalla Cristina Nita-Rotaru
Ricardo Dahab (Eds.)

Cryptology and Network Security

12th International Conference, CANS 2013
Paraty, Brazil, November 20-22, 2013
Proceedings

Springer

Volume Editors

Michel Abdalla
École Normale Supérieure and CNRS
45 rue d'Ulm, 75005 Paris, France
E-mail: michel.abdalla@ens.fr

Cristina Nita-Rotaru
Purdue University, Department of Computer Science, LWSN 2142J
305 N. University Street, West Lafayette, IN 47907, USA
E-mail: cnitarot@purdue.edu

Ricardo Dahab
University of Campinas, Institute of Computing
Avenida Albert Einstein 1251, Campinas, SP 13083-852, Brazil
E-mail: rdahab@ic.unicamp.br

ISSN 0302-9743 e-ISSN 1611-3349
ISBN 978-3-319-02936-8 e-ISBN 978-3-319-02937-5
DOI 10.1007/978-3-319-02937-5
Springer Cham Heidelberg New York Dordrecht London

Library of Congress Control Number: 2013950915

CR Subject Classification (1998): E.3, K.6.5, C.2, D.4.6, E.4

LNCS Sublibrary: SL 4 – Security and Cryptology

Typesetting: Camera-ready by author, data conversion by Scientific Publishing Services, Chennai, India

Printed on acid-free paper

Springer is part of Springer Science+Business Media (www.springer.com)

Preface

The International Conference on Cryptology and Network Security (CANS) is a recognized annual conference, focusing on all aspects of cryptology and network security and attracting cutting-edge results from world-renowned scientists in the area. The 12th edition of the conference was held at Casa da Cultura, Paraty, Brazil, during November 20–22, 2013, and was organized by the Institute of Computing of the University of Campinas (UNICAMP) in cooperation with the International Association for Cryptologic Research (IACR).

CANS 2013 received 57 submissions and each submission was assigned to at least three committee members. Submissions co-authored by members of the Program Committee were assigned to at least five committee members. After careful deliberation, the Program Committee selected 18 submissions for presentation. The authors of the accepted papers had three weeks for revision and preparation of final versions. The revised papers were not subject to editorial review and the authors bear full responsibility for their contents.

The conference also featured four invited talks in addition to the regular papers. These talks were given by George Cox (Intel), Rosario Gennaro (CUNY), Jacques Stern (ENS), and Gene Tsudik (UCI), and covered a wide range of topics in cryptography and network security. The abstracts of these invited talks are also included in this volume.

The reviewing process was run using the iChair software, written by Thomas Baignères from CryptoExperts, France, and Matthieu Finiasz from EPFL, LASEC, Switzerland. We are grateful to them for letting us use their software.

There are many people who contributed to the success of CANS 2013. First, we would like to thank the authors of all papers (both accepted and rejected) for submitting their results to the conference. Second, we are grateful to the committee members and external reviewers for their outstanding work in thoroughly reviewing all papers in a timely manner. Special thanks to Angelo De Caro, Orr Dunkelman, Anderson Nascimento, and Damien Vergnaud, for their extra work as shepherds. Third, we are also indebted to the CANS Steering Committee members for their guidance. Last, but not least, we thank our sponsors, CAPES and CGI.br, for their generous support.

November 2013

Michel Abdalla
Cristina Nita-Rotaru
Ricardo Dahab

CANS 2013

The 12th International Conference on Cryptology and Network Security

Paraty, Brazil
November 20–22, 2013

Organized by

Institute of Computing
University of Campinas (UNICAMP)

In Cooperation with
The International Association for Cryptologic Research (IACR)

General Chair

Ricardo Dahab	University of Campinas, Brazil

Program Chairs

Michel Abdalla	École Normale Supérieure and CNRS, France
Cristina Nita-Rotaru	Purdue University, USA

Steering Committee

Yvo Desmedt	University of Texas at Dallas, USA
Juan Garay	Yahoo! Research, USA
Yi Mu	University of Wollongong, Australia
David Pointcheval	École Normale Supérieure and CNRS, France

Program Committee

Nuttapong Attrapadung	AIST, Japan
Paulo S.L.M. Barreto	University of São Paulo, Brazil
Jean-Luc Beuchat	ELCA Informatique SA, Switzerland
Alexandra Boldyreva	Georgia Tech, USA
Ioana Boureanu	EPFL, Switzerland
Colin Boyd	NTNU, Norway
Bogdan Carbunar	Florida International University, USA

David Cash	Rutgers University, USA
Reza Curtmola	New Jersey Institute of Technology, USA
Angelo De Caro	NTT Secure Platform Laboratories, Japan
Emiliano De Cristofaro	Palo Alto Research Center, USA
Roberto Di Pietro	Università di Roma Tre, Italy
Orr Dunkelman	University of Haifa, Israel
Alejandro Hevia	Universidad de Chile, Chile
Dennis Hofheinz	Karlsruher Institute of Technology, Germany
Seny Kamara	Microsoft Research, USA
Taekyoung Kwon	Yonsei University, Korea
Gaëtan Leurent	Université Catholique de Louvain, Belgium
Julio López	University of Campinas, Brazil
Ivan Martinovic	University of Oxford, UK
Jelena Mircovic	University of Southern California, USA
Refik Molva	Eurecom, France
Michael Naehrig	Microsoft Research, USA
Anderson Nascimento	Universidade de Brasília, Brazil
Claudio Orlandi	Aarhus University, Denmark
Thomas Peyrin	Nanyang Technological University, Singapore
Bart Preneel	Katholieke Universiteit Leuven, Belgium
Emmanuel Prouff	ANSSI, France
Kasper Rasmussen	University of California, Irvine, USA
Francisco Rodríguez-Henríquez	CINVESTAV-IPN, Mexico
Jeff Seibert	MIT Lincoln Labs, USA
Radu State	University of Luxembourg, Luxembourg
Angelos Stavrou	George Mason University, USA
Willy Susilo	University of Wollongong, Australia
Damien Vergnaud	École Normale Supérieure, France
Andrew White	University of North Carolina, USA
David Zage	Sandia National Laboratories, USA
Xinwen Zhang	Huawei Research Center, USA
Jianying Zhou	Institute for Infocomm Research, Singapore

Additional Reviewers

Jean-Philippe Aumasson
Monir Azraoui
Joppe W. Bos
Melissa Chase
Donald Chen
Craig Costello
Alexandre Duc
Simon Eberz
Nadia El Mrabet
Kaoutar Elkhiyaoui
Liming Fang
Matthieu Finiasz
Thomas Fuhr
Jinguang Han
Jungyeon Hwang
Vincenzo Iovino
Haiqing Jiang
Orhun Kara
Taechan Kim
JongHyup Lee

Jooyoung Lee
Yoonho Lee
Wang Lei
Kaitai Liang
Atul Luykx
Marine Minier
Aziz Mohaisen
Satsuya Ohata
Christopher Peikert
Christiane Peters
Thomas Roche
Rodrigo Roman
Yusuke Sakai
Ismail San
Martin Schlaffer
Peter Schwabe
Yannick Seurin
Ji Sun Shin
Wu Shuang
Emil Stefanov
Martin Strohmeier
Katsuyuki Takashima
Serge Vaudenay
Antonio Villani
Jia Xu
Lei Xu
Naoto Yanai

Sponsoring Institutions

Brazilian Government Agency for the Development of Higher Education (CAPES)
Brazilian Internet Steering Committee (CGI.br)

Invited Talks

Solving the Platform Entropy Problem – Phase 2

George Cox

Intel Corporation
JF3-224, 2111 NE 25th Street, Hillsboro, OR 97124
cox@intel.com

Abstract. In this talk, we discuss the need for high quality "seeding" material for software pseudorandom number generators (SW PRNGs), the resultant development of NIST SP800-90 B/C, and Intel's product response to it with evolution of our existing Digital Random Number Generator (DRNG) and addition of our new RdSeed instruction.

A Survey of Verifiable Delegation of Computations

Rosario Gennaro

The City College of New York
rosario@ccny.cuny.edu

Abstract. In this talk, I will give an overview of past and recent research on the area of Verifiable Delegation of Computation. The goal is to enable a computationally weak client to "outsource" the computation of a function F on various inputs $x_1, \ldots, x_k$ to one or more powerful servers. The server must return the result of the function evaluation, e.g., $y_i = F(x_i)$, as well as a proof that the computation of F was carried out correctly on the given value x_i. A crucial requirement is that the verification of the proof should require substantially less computational effort than computing $F(x_i)$ from scratch.

For the "general purpose" case (protocols that work for any function F), I will discuss the different ways this problem has been approached theoretically, particularly the line of research that links Interactive Proofs, to Probabilistic Checkable Proofs, to Succinct Non-Interactive Arguments. I will also survey recent exciting experimental results that show how these techniques are on the verge of becoming practical.

I will also talk about "ad hoc" protocols that aim to verify specific computations of particular importance in practice.

What Is Public-Key Cryptanalysis?

Jacques Stern

École Normale Supérieure, France
jacques.stern@ens.fr

Abstract. Traditionally, cryptanalysis has been based on statistical analysis. This remains true for conventional secret key cryptosystems. In the area of public key however, the picture is quite different. On one hand, there is usually some mathematical structure hidden in the public data; on the other hand, the cryptographic security is more or less tightly related with some well identified computational problem which is believed to be hard to solve. The talk will give several examples where the cryptanalyst was able to recover the hidden mathematical structure through a purely algebraic approach, and to break schemes that might otherwise have appeared promising, such as the S-FLASH signature scheme. It will also discuss surprising changes of perspective that have recently occurred: algorithmic progress have lowered the asymptotic complexity of problems underlying the so-called HFE signature, as well as the complexity of the discrete logarithm in fields of small characteristic, thus questioning the security of related cryptographic schemes. In another direction, problems such as the approximate GCD, which had long been known to be easily solvable by lattice reduction, at least in small dimensions, now form the basis for a large number of successful homomorphic schemes.

Security and Privacy in Named-Data Networking

Gene Tsudik

Computer Science Department
University of California, Irvine (UCI)
gts@ics.uci.edu

Abstract. With the growing realization that current Internet protocols are reaching the limits of their senescence, a number of ongoing research efforts aim to design potential next-generation Internet architectures. Although they vary in maturity and scope, in order to avoid past pitfalls, these efforts seek to treat security and privacy as key initial requirements. The Named Data Networking (NDN) is an Internet architecture that avoids IP's host-based, point-to-point networking approach in order to better accommodate new and emerging patterns of communication. NDN treats data as a first class object, explicitly naming it instead of its location. While the current Internet secures the "pipe" that carries data between hosts, NDN secures data – a design choice that decouples trust in data from trust in hosts, enabling scalable communication mechanisms, such as automatic caching of data in routers to optimize bandwidth. The NDN project poses numerous technical challenges that must be addressed to validate it as a future Internet architecture: routing scalability, fast forwarding, trust models, network security, content protection and privacy, and fundamental communication theory.

This talk will overview NDN and then turn to security and privacy issues. By stressing content dissemination, NDN is an attractive and viable approach to many types of current and emerging communication models. It also incorporates some useful security and privacy features. We will first consider communication privacy and anonymity in NDN and describe an NDN add-on (called ANDANA) that offers the functionality similar to TOR on today's Internet.

Since resilience to Denial of Service (DoS) attacks that plague todays Internet is a major issue for any new architecture, we will discuss some initial research towards assessment and mitigation of DoS in NDN. Next, we will consider privacy implications of router-side content caching. Finally, we will discuss how to adapt NDN and its security features to environments other than content distribution, using the example of building automation.

Table of Contents

Cryptanalysis I

Zero-Knowledge Protocols

Distributed Protocols

Network Security and Applications

Advanced Cryptographic Primitives

Cryptanalysis II

Verifiable Computation

Differential Attacks on Generalized Feistel Schemes

Valérie Nachef[1], Emmanuel Volte[1], and Jacques Patarin[2]

[1] Department of Mathematics, University of Cergy-Pontoise, CNRS UMR 8088
2 Avenue Adolphe Chauvin, 95011 Cergy-Pontoise Cedex, France
[2] PRISM, University of Versailles
45 avenue des Etats-Unis, 78035 Versailles Cedex, France
valerie.nachef@u-cergy.fr

Abstract. While generic attacks on classical Feistel schemes and unbalanced Feistel schemes have been studied a lot, generic attacks on several generalized Feistel schemes like type-1, type-2 and type-3 and alternating Feistel schemes, as defined in [8], have not been systematically investigated. These generalized Feistel schemes are used in well known block cipher networks that use generalized Feistel schemes: CAST-256 (type-1), RC-6 (type-2), MARS (type-3) and BEAR/LION (alternating). Also, type-1 and type-2 Feistel schemes are respectively used in the construction of the hash functions Lesamnta and SHAvite $-\ 3_{512}$.In this paper, we give our best Known Plaintext Attacks and non-adaptive Chosen Plaintext Attacks on these schemes. We determine the maximal number of rounds that we can attack when we want to distinguish a permutation produced by the scheme from a permutation chosen randomly in the set of permutations.

Keywords: generalized Feistel schemes, generic attacks on encryption schemes, block ciphers.

1 Introduction

Classical Feistel schemes have been extensively studied since the seminal work of Luby and Rackoff [14]. These schemes allow to construct permutations from $\{0,1\}^{2n}$ to $\{0,1\}^{2n}$ by using round functions from n bits to n bits (DES is an example of a classical Feistel scheme). For 3 and 4 rounds, there are attacks with $\sqrt{2^n}$ inputs in [1] and [18]. For 5 rounds, an attack with $O(2^n)$ inputs is given in [19,20]. When the round functions are permutations, attacks are studied in [12,13,25]. Security results on classical Feistel schemes are given in [8,20,17].

We define generalized Feistel schemes as follows: the input belongs to $\{0,1\}^{kn}$ and we apply different kinds of round functions on some parts of the input in order to construct permutations from kn bits to kn bits.

When the round functions are from $(k-1)n$ bits to n bits, we obtain an unbalanced Feistel scheme with contracting functions. Attacks on these schemes were studied in [22]. When the round functions are from n bits to $(k-1)n$

M. Abdalla, C. Nita-Rotaru, and R. Dahab (Eds.): CANS 2013, LNCS 8257, pp. 1–19, 2013.

bits, we have unbalanced Feistel schemes with expanding functions. Attacks on these schemes are given in [10,23,24,26]. Alternating Feistel schemes alternate contracting and expanding rounds. They are described in [2] and are used in the BEAR/LION block cipher. There are also type-1, type-2 and type-3 Feistel schemes (they are described in Section 2, see also [9,29]). These schemes are used respectively in the block ciphers CAST-256, RC6 and MARS. In [4], the authors provide attacks on the hash functions Lesamnta and $SHAvite-3_{512}$ whose construction is based on type-1 and type-2 Feistel schemes. Some attacks on instances of generalized Feistel schemes are also given in [3]. Impossible differential attacks on generalized Feistel schemes are studied in [5] when there is no condition on the round functions, and in [6,13,27] when the round functions are permutations.

Security results have been obtained for most of these schemes. For classical Feistel schemes the different results are given in [8,20,17]. Unbalanced Feistel schemes with contracting functions have been studied in [8,15,17,28] and for unbalanced Feistel schemes with expanding functions, alternating, type-1, type-2 and type-3 Feistel schemes, the results are in [8].

This paper is devoted to the study of generic attacks on type-1, type-2, type-3 and alternating generalized Feistel schemes. Our attacks are distinguishers that allow to distinguish a permutation produced by a scheme from a permutation chosen randomly in the set of permutations. The round functions are chosen at random and are not known to the adversary. Moreover, we assume that the round functions are independent of each other.

Our attacks will use differential characteristics. We provide Known Plaintext Attacks (KPA) and non-adaptive Chosen Plaintext Attacks (CPA-1). For each kind of scheme, we will give the maximal number of rounds that we can attack in KPA and CPA-1 and we will describe our best attacks up to the maximal number of rounds. Table 1 gives the maximal number of rounds attacked by either KPA, CPA-1 that we have obtained and the comparison with impossible differential attacks for type-1, type-2 and type-3 Feistel schemes when the round functions are bijective or not. In this table, we consider that we want to distinguish permutations kn bits to kn bits either produced by the scheme or chosen randomly from the set of permutations.

Table 1. Maximal number of rounds reached by our attacks and impossible differential attacks

Structure	KPA	CPA-1	Impossible Differential	
			bijective	any
Type-1	$2k^2+2k-2$ (Sec. 4.1)	$2k^2+k-1$ (Sec. 4.1)	k^2+2 [6,27]	k^2 [4]
Type-2	$2k+2$ (Sec. 4.2)	$2k+1$ (Sec. 4.2)	$2k+1$ [27]	N/A
Type-3	$k+\lfloor \frac{k}{2} \rfloor+1$ (Sec. 4.3)	$k+1$ (Sec. 4.3)	$2k+3$ [27]	$2k$ [4]
Alternating	$3k$ (Sec. 4.4)	$3k$ (Sec. 4.4)	N/A	N/A

The paper is organized as follows. In Section 2, we give the notations and define type-1, type-2, type-3 and alternating Feistel schemes. Section 3 is devoted to an overview of the attacks. In Section 4 we detail the attacks. For type-1 Feistel schemes, we also provide the results of our simulations. In the Appendices, we give examples of computations of the variances, needed to get the complexity of our attacks.

2 Notations - Definitions of the Schemes

The input is always denoted by $[I_1, I_2, \ldots, I_k]$ and the output by $[S_1, S_2, \ldots, S_k]$ where each I_s, S_s is an element of $\{0,1\}^n$. When we have m messages, $I_s(i)$ represents part s of the input of message number i. The same notation is used for the outputs as well. We use differential attacks, i.e. attacks where we study how differences on pairs of input variables will propagate following a differential characteristic, and give relations between pairs of input/output variables. The number of rounds is denoted by r. We now define our schemes.

1. *Type-1 Feistel schemes (Fig. 1)*
   After one round, the output is given by $[I_2 \oplus F^1(I_1), I_3, I_4, \ldots, I_k, I_1]$ where F^1 is a function from n bits to n bits.
2. *Type-2 Feistel schemes (Fig. 1)*
   Here k is even. After one round, the output is given by $[I_2 \oplus F_1^1(I_1), I_3, I_4 \oplus F_2^1(I_3), \ldots, I_k \oplus F_{\frac{k}{2}}^1(I_{k-1}), I_1]$ where each F_s^1, $1 \le s \le \frac{k}{2}$ is a function from n bits to n bits.
3. *Type-3 Feistel schemes (Fig. 2)*
   After one round, the output is given by $[I_2 \oplus F_1^1(I_1), I_3 \oplus F_2^1(I_2), I_4 \oplus F_3^1(I_3), \ldots, I_k \oplus F_{k-1}^1(I_{k-1}), I_1]$ where each F_s^1, $1 \le s \le k-1$ is a function from n bits to n bits.
4. *Alternating Feistel schemes (Fig. 2)*
   On the input $[I_1, I_2, \ldots, I_k]$, for the first round, we apply a contracting function F^1 from $(k-1)n$ bits to n. Let $X^1 = I_1 \oplus F^1([I_2, \ldots, I_k])$. After one round, the output is given by $[X^1, I_2, \ldots, I_k]$ and X^1 is called an internal variable. For the second round, we apply an expanding function $G^2 = (G_1^2, G_2^2, \ldots, G_k^2)$ where each G_s^2 is a function from n bits to n bits. The output after the second round is given by $[X^1, I_2 \oplus G_1^2(X^1), \ldots, I_k \oplus G_k^2(X^1)]$. Then we alternate contracting and expanding rounds. We can also start with an expanding round. In this paper, we will always begin with a contracting round.

We now explain the differential notation. We use plaintext/ciphertexts pairs. In KPA, on the input variables, the notation $[\mathbf{0}, \mathbf{0}, \Delta_3^0, \Delta_4^0, \ldots, \Delta_k^0]$ means that the pair of messages (i, j) satisfies $I_1(i) = I_1(j)$, $I_2(i) = I_2(j)$, and $I_s(i) \oplus I_s(j) = \Delta_s^0$, $3 \le s \le k$. In CPA-1, the notation $[\underline{\mathbf{0}}, \underline{\mathbf{0}}, \Delta_3^0, \Delta_4^0, \ldots, \Delta_k^0]$ means that we choose I_1 and I_2 to be constants. The differential of the outputs i and j after round r is denoted by $[\Delta_1^r, \Delta_2^r, \ldots, \Delta_k^r]$. At each round, internal variables are defined by the structure of the scheme. In our attacks, we determine

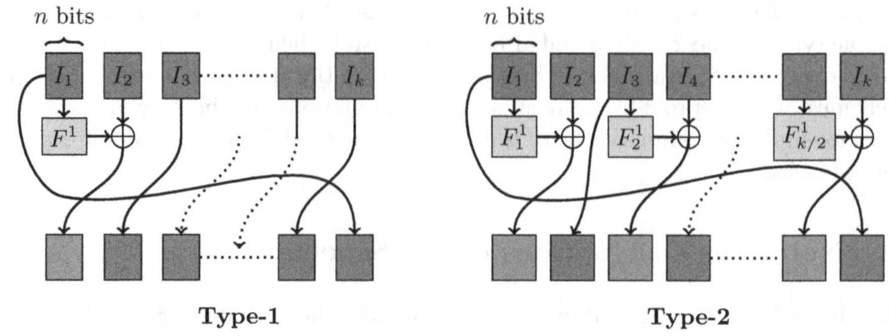

Fig. 1. First round for type-1 and type-2 Feistel schemes

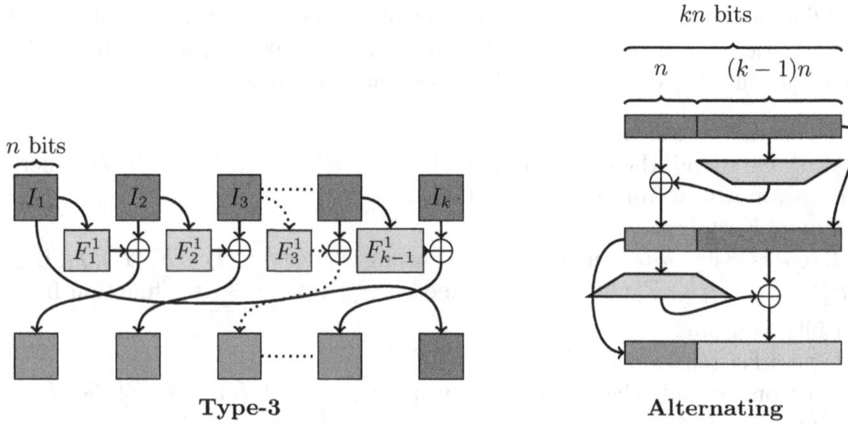

Fig. 2. First round for type-3 Feistel scheme and first two rounds of alternating Feistel scheme

conditions that have to be satisfied by the outputs. When we have a scheme, these conditions are satisfied either at random or because the internal variables verify some equalities. Thus, we will impose conditions on the internal variables on some chosen rounds. When we impose conditions on the internal variables in order to get a differential characteristic, we use the notation $\boxed{0}$ to mean that the corresponding internal variables are equal in messages i and j.

3 Overview of the Attacks

We present attacks that allow us to distinguish a permutation computed by the scheme from a random permutation. Depending on the number of rounds, it is possible to find some relations between the input and output variables. These relations hold conditionally to equalities of some internal variables due to the structure of the Feistel scheme. Our attacks consist of using m plaintext/ciphertexts pairs and in counting the number $\mathcal{N}$ of couples of these pairs that satisfy the relations between the input and output variables. We then compare $\mathcal{N}_{scheme}$, the number of such couples we obtain with a generalized scheme, with $\mathcal{N}_{perm}$, the corresponding number for a random permutation. The attack is successful, i.e. we are able to distinguish a permutation generated by a generalized Feistel scheme from a random permutation if the difference $|E(\mathcal{N}_{scheme}) - E(\mathcal{N}_{perm})|$ is larger than both standard deviations $\sigma(\mathcal{N}_{perm})$ and $\sigma(\mathcal{N}_{scheme})$, where E denotes the expectancy function. In order to compute these values, we need to take into account the fact that the structures obtained from the m plaintext/ciphertext tuples are not independent. However, their mutual dependence is very small. To compute $\sigma(\mathcal{N}_{perm})$ and $\sigma(\mathcal{N}_{scheme})$, we will use this well-known formula (see [7], p.97), that we will call the "Covariance Formula": if $x_1, \ldots x_n$, are random variables, then if V represents the variance, we have $V(\sum_{i=1}^{n} x_i) = \sum_{i=1}^{n} V(x_i) + 2\sum_{i=1}^{n-1}\sum_{j=i+1}^{n}\left[E(x_i\, x_j) - E(x_i)E(x_j)\right]$. Similar computation are also performed in [22].

As we will see in our computations, in this paper, we will always have $\sigma(\mathcal{N}_{perm}) \simeq \sqrt{E(\mathcal{N}_{perm})}$ and $\sigma(\mathcal{N}_{scheme}) \simeq \sqrt{E(\mathcal{N}_{scheme})} \simeq \sqrt{E(\mathcal{N}_{perm})}$. In Appendices A and B, this is explained on an example.

4 Description of Our Attacks on the Schemes

For each scheme, we give examples of attacks and describe more precisely KPA and CPA-1 that allow to attack the maximal number of rounds. We always assume that $k \geq 3$.

4.1 Type-1 Feistel Schemes

For 1 to $k-1$ rounds, one message is enough, since after r rounds, $1 \leq r \leq k-1$, we have $S_{k-r+1} = I_1$. This condition is satisfied with probability 1 with a type-1 Feistel scheme and with probability $\frac{1}{2^n}$ when we deal with a random permutation. Thus with one message we can distinguish a type-1 Feistel scheme from a random permutation in KPA and CPA-1.

We now consider KPA for $r \geq k$. In Table 2 (left part), we give the general pattern of the differential characteristics used in our KPA.

The conditions after $rk-2$ rounds ($r \geq 3$) are given by

$$\begin{cases} S_2(i) = S_2(j) \\ I_1(i) \oplus I_1(j) = S_3(i) \oplus S_3(j) \end{cases} \tag{1}$$

We count the number of indices (i, j) such that these conditions are satisfied. Let $\mathcal{N}_{perm}$ be the number obtained when we have permutation chosen randomly and uniformly from the set of permutations from kn bits to kn bits. Similarly, $\mathcal{N}_{scheme}$ represents the number obtained with a permutation produced by the scheme. For $\mathcal{N}_{perm}$, the conditions appear at random and we obtain $E(\mathcal{N}_{perm}) \simeq \frac{m^2}{2.2^{2n}}$. For $\mathcal{N}_{scheme}$, the conditions appear at random or because some conditions are satisfied by the internal variables and we get $E(\mathcal{N}_{scheme}) \simeq \frac{m^2}{2.2^{2n}} + O(\frac{m^2}{2^{(r-1)n}})$.

Table 2. Differential characteristic used in our attacks on type-1 Feistel schemes

round	Δ_1^0	Δ_2^0	Δ_3^0	...	Δ_{k-1}^0	Δ_k^0
1				...		Δ_1^0
2				...	Δ_1^0	
$\vdots$						
$k-1$	$\boxed{0}$	Δ_1^0		...		
k	Δ_1^0			...		0
$k+1$				...		Δ_1^0
$\vdots$						
$rk-2$		0	Δ_1^0	...		
$rk-1$	$\boxed{0}$	Δ_1^0		...		
rk	Δ_1^0			...		0
$\vdots$						
$(r+1)k-2$		0	Δ_1^0	...		

KPA

round	$\underline{0}$	Δ_2^0	Δ_3^0	...	Δ_{k-1}^0	Δ_k^0
1	Δ_2^0	Δ_3^0		...		0
2				...	0	Δ_2^0
$\vdots$						
$k-1$		0	Δ_2^0	...		
k	$\boxed{0}$	Δ_2^0		...		
$k+1$	Δ_2^0			...		0
$k+2$				...	0	Δ_2^0
$\vdots$						
$rk-1$		0	Δ_2^0	...		
rk	$\boxed{0}$	Δ_2^0		...		
$\vdots$						
$(r+1)k-1$		0	Δ_2^0	...		

CPA-1

The O function comes from the conditions $\boxed{0}$ that we impose on the differential characteristic. In Appendix B, we will explain on an example how to estimate this O function. Both standard deviations satisfy $\sigma(\mathcal{N}_{perm}) \simeq \sqrt{E(\mathcal{N}_{perm})}$ and $\sigma(\mathcal{N}_{scheme}) \simeq \sqrt{E(\mathcal{N}_{scheme})} \simeq \sqrt{E(\mathcal{N}_{perm})}$ when $r \geq 4$. This means that we can distinguish between a random permutation and a type-1 Feistel scheme as soon as $\frac{m^2}{2^{(r-1)n}} \geq \frac{m}{2^n}$. This gives the condition $m \geq 2^{(r-2)n}$. Since the maximal number of messages is 2^{kn}, these attacks work for $r-2 \leq k$ and then with $r = k+2$, we can attack up to $(k+2)k-2 = k^2+2k-2$ rounds.

The analysis of all the attacks will be very similar. We first choose the differential characteristics. Then, we compute $E(\mathcal{N}_{perm})$, $E(\mathcal{N}_{scheme})$, $\sigma(\mathcal{N}_{perm})$ and $\sigma(\mathcal{N}_{scheme})$ as define previously. Again, $E(\mathcal{N}_{perm})$ will be greater than $E(\mathcal{N}_{scheme})$ because there are conditions on the internal variables that will imply conditions on the outputs. Moreover, we have $\sigma(\mathcal{N}_{perm}) \simeq \sqrt{E(\mathcal{N}_{perm})}$ and $\sigma(\mathcal{N}_{scheme}) \simeq \sqrt{E(\mathcal{N}_{scheme})} \simeq \sqrt{E(\mathcal{N}_{perm})}$. Then, we compare the difference of the mean values with the standard deviation and we obtain the number of messages needed for the attack. The previous attack is summarized by the Table 3, where σ denotes either $\sigma(\mathcal{N}_{perm})$ or $\sigma(\mathcal{N}_{scheme})$.

We study CPA-1 for $r \geq k$. For k to $2k-1$ rounds, we have a CPA-1 with 2 messages such that $\forall s, 1 \leq s \leq k-1$, $I_s(1) = I_s(2)$. Then, at round r ($k \leq r \leq 2k-1$), with a type-1 Feistel scheme, we obtain with probability 1 that $S_{2k-r}(1) \oplus S_{2k-r}(2) = I_k(1) \oplus I_k(2)$. If we are not dealing with a type-1 Feistel scheme, the probability to obtain this equality is $\frac{1}{2^n}$.

Table 3. Type-1 Feistel scheme: KPA on $rk-2$ rounds

Differential	$E(\mathcal{N}_{perm})$	$E(\mathcal{N}_{scheme})$	σ	m
$\Delta_2^{rk-2} = 0$ $\Delta_3^{rk-2} = \Delta_1^0$	$\frac{m^2}{2.2^{2n}}$	$\frac{m^2}{2.2^{2n}} + O(\frac{m^2}{2^{(r-1)n}})$	$\frac{m}{\sqrt{2}2^n}$	$2^{(r-2)n}$

On round r (with $r \geq 2k$), we will have to consider different conditions on the input variables. We explain now a CPA-1 on $rk-1$ rounds (with $r \geq 3$) in Table 2 (right part) and Table 4, where we choose the messages such that I_1 takes only one value for all messages. Here, we have $m \geq 2^{(r-2)n}$. Since the maximal number of messages is $2^{(k-1)n}$, these attacks work as long as $r-2 \leq k-1$. Thus with $r = k+1$, we can attack up to $(k+1)k-1 = k^2+k-1$ rounds.

Table 6 summarizes the complexities for type-1 Feistel schemes. We also give the results of our simulations in Table 5.

Table 4. Type-1 Feistel scheme: CPA-1 on $rk-1$ rounds

Differential	$E(\mathcal{N}_{perm})$	$E(\mathcal{N}_{scheme})$	σ	m
$\Delta_2^{rk-2} = 0$ $\Delta_3^{rk-2} = \Delta_2^0$	$\frac{m^2}{2.2^{2n}}$	$\frac{m^2}{2.2^{2n}} + O(\frac{m^2}{2^{(r-1)n}})$	$\frac{m}{\sqrt{2}2^n}$	$2^{(r-2)n}$

Table 5. Experimental results for CPA-1 against type-1 Feistel scheme with k^2+k-1 rounds

k	n	% of success −% of false alarm	# iterations
6	2	67%	10000
8	2	66,5%	10000
9	2	66%	10000
6	4	95%	10000
8	4	96%	10000
4	6	99,5%	10000

Table 6. Complexities of the attacks on type-1 Feistel schemes

r rounds	KPA
$1 \to k-1$	1
$k \to 2k-1$	$2^{n/2}$
$2k \to 3k-2$	2^n
… $rk-2$ $rk-1$	$2^{(r-2)n}$ $2^{(r-3/2)n}$
rk … $(r+1)k-2$ … k^2+2k-2	$2^{(r-1)n}$ 2^{kn}

r rounds	CPA-1	r	CPA-1
1 … $k-1$	1	…	
k … $2k-2$	2	$pk-(p-2)$ … $(p+1)k-p$	$2^{(p-2)n}$
$2k-1$ … $3k-2$	$2^{n/2}$	…	
$3k-1$ … $4k-3$	2^n	k^2+1 … k^2+k-1	$2^{(k-1)n}$

4.2 Type-2 Feistel Schemes

For type-2 Feistel schemes, k is always even. Table 7 and Table 8 represent a KPA on $2k + 2$ rounds.

Table 7. Differential characteristic used in our attacks on type-2 Feistel schemes (KPA)

round	$\mathbf{0}$	Δ_2^0	Δ_3^0	Δ_4^0	...	Δ_{k-3}^0	Δ_{k-2}^0	Δ_{2k-1}^0	Δ_k^0
1	Δ_2^0				...				0
2					...			$\boxed{0}$	Δ_2^0
3					...		0	Δ_2^0	
⋮									
$k-1$		0	Δ_2^0		...				
k	$\boxed{0}$	Δ_2^0			...				
$k+1$	Δ_2^0				...				0
$k+2$					...			$\boxed{0}$	Δ_2^0
⋮									
$2k-1$		0	Δ_2^0		...				
$2k$	$\boxed{0}$	Δ_2^0			...				
$2k+1$	Δ_2^0				...				0
$2k+2$					...				Δ_2^0

Table 8. Type-2 Feistel scheme: KPA on $2k + 2$ rounds

Differential	$E(\mathcal{N}_{perm})$	$E(\mathcal{N}_{scheme})$	m
$\Delta_1^0 = 0$ $\Delta_k^k = \Delta_2^0$	$\frac{m^2}{2.2^{2n}}$	$\frac{m^2}{2.2^{2n}} + O(\frac{m^2}{2^{(k+1)n}})$	2^{kn}

We explain how to get attacks on intermediate rounds. After $2r$ rounds, $r \geq 1$, we have in Table 9:

Table 9. Type-2 Feistel scheme: KPA on $2r$ rounds

Differential	$E(\mathcal{N}_{perm})$	$E(\mathcal{N}_{scheme})$	σ	m
$\Delta_1^0 = 0$ $\Delta_s^{2r} = \Delta_2^0$	$\frac{m^2}{2.2^{2n}}$	$\frac{m^2}{2.2^{2n}} + O(\frac{m^2}{2^{rn}})$	$\frac{m}{\sqrt{2}2^n}$	$2^{(r-1)n}$

where $1 \leq s \leq k$ and $s \equiv 2 - 2r \pmod{k}$.

In this attack, $m = 2^{(r-1)n}$. Thus, for $r = k+1$, we have reached the maximal number of rounds with $2^{(k-1)n}$ messages.

After $2r + 1$ rounds, $r \geq 1$, the attack is represented in Table 10:

where $1 \leq t \leq k$ and $t \equiv 1 - 2r \pmod{k}$.

For CPA-1, we can impose conditions on a given number of input variables. We give in Table 11 and Table 12 an example of an attack on $2k - 1$ rounds for which we consider messages where I_1, I_2, I_3 are given constant values. Then we will generalize.

Table 10. Type-2 Feistel scheme: KPA on $2r+1$ rounds

Differential	$E(\mathcal{N}_{perm})$	$E(\mathcal{N}_{scheme})$	σ	m
$\Delta_1^0 = 0$ $\Delta_t^{2r+1} = \Delta_2^0$ $\Delta_{t-1}^{2r+1} = 0$	$\frac{m^2}{2.2^{3n}}$	$\frac{m^2}{2.2^{3n}} + O(\frac{m^2}{2^{(r+1)n}})$	$\frac{m}{\sqrt{22^n}}$	$2^{(r-\frac{1}{2})n}$

For round $2k-2$, the attack is represented in Table 13.

More generally, if we suppose that for the input variables, we have $I_1, \ldots, I_r$ are constants ($r \leq k-1$), we can perform the same kind of attacks. It is easy to check that we can attack up to $2k-r+2$ rounds and we need exactly $2^{(k-r)n}$ messages. In order to get the best CPA-1 for each round, we will change the conditions on the input variables. For example, for $k+1$, $k+2$ and $k+3$ rounds, we choose $I_1, \ldots I_{k-1}$ to be constant values, then we will have $I_1, \ldots I_{k-2}$ constants, and so on.

Table 14 summarizes the complexities for type-2 Feistel schemes.

4.3 Type-3 Feistel Schemes

We will present our attacks when k is even. For k odd, the computations are similar. The results are summarized in Table 18. We begin with KPA. For one round, we need one message, we just have to check if $I_1 = S_k$. With a random permutation, this happens with probability $\frac{1}{2^n}$ and with a scheme with probability one. Suppose we want to attack r rounds with $2 \leq r \leq k$. We wait until

Table 11. Differential characteristic used in our attacks on type-2 Feistel schemes (CPA-1)

round	$\underline{0}$	$\underline{0}$	$\underline{0}$	Δ_4^0	Δ_5^0	Δ_6^0	...	Δ_{k-3}^0	Δ_{k-2}^0	Δ_{k-1}^0	Δ_k^0
1	0	0	Δ_4^0				...				0
2	0	Δ_4^0					...				0
3	Δ_4^0						...				0
4							...			$\boxed{0}$	Δ_4^0
5							...		0	Δ_4^0	
⋮											
k			$\boxed{0}$	Δ_4^0			...				
$k+1$		0	Δ_4^0				...				
$k+2$	$\boxed{0}$	Δ_4^0					...				
$k+3$	Δ_4^0						...				0
⋮											
$2k-2$					$\boxed{0}$	Δ_4^0	...				
$2k-1$				0	Δ_2^0		...				

Table 12. Type-2 Feistel scheme: CPA-1 on $2k-1$ rounds

Differential	$E(\mathcal{N}_{perm})$	$E(\mathcal{N}_{scheme})$	σ	m
$\Delta_4^{2k-1} = 0$ $\Delta_5^{2k-1} = \Delta_4^0$	$\frac{m^2}{2.2^{2n}}$	$\frac{m^2}{2.2^{2n}} + O(\frac{m^2}{2^{(k-2)n}})$	$\frac{m}{\sqrt{22^n}}$	$2^{(k-3)n}$

Table 13. Type-2 Feistel scheme: CPA-1 on $r = 2k - 2$ rounds

Differential	$E(\mathcal{N}_{perm})$	$E(\mathcal{N}_{scheme})$	σ	m
$\Delta_6^{2k-2} = 0$	$\frac{m^2}{2.2^n}$	$\frac{m^2}{2.2^n} + O(\frac{m^2}{2^{(k-3)n}})$	$\frac{m}{\sqrt{2}2^{\frac{n}{2}}}$	$2^{(k-\frac{7}{2})n}$

Table 14. Complexities of the attacks on type-2 Feistel schemes

r	KPA	CPA-1
1	1	1
2	$2^{n/2}$	2
$3 \leq r \leq k$	$2^{\frac{r-2}{2}n}$	2
$k+1$	$2^{(k-1/2)n}$	$2^{n/2}$
$k+1$	$2^{\frac{k}{2}n}$	$2^{n/2}$
$k+3 \leq r \leq 2k+2$	$2^{\frac{r-2}{2}n}$	$2^{(r-k-2)n}$

we have 2 messages such that $I_1(1) = I_1(2), \ldots, I_{r-1}(1) = I_{r-1}(2)$. Then we test if $I_{r-1}(1) \oplus I_{r-1}(2) = S_k(1) \oplus S_k(2)$. With a random permutation, this happens with probability $\frac{1}{2^n}$ and with a scheme with probability one. Moreover, from the birthday paradox, if we have $2^{\frac{(r-1)n}{2}}$ messages, we get 2 messages with the given conditions with a high probability. We give in Table 15 (left part) a KPA on $k+4$ rounds, where we suppose that $4 \leq \frac{k}{2} + 1$.

Table 15. Differential characteristics used in our attacks on type-3 Feistel schemes

round	**0**	...	**0**	**0**	**0**	**0**	Δ_0^k
1	0	...	0	0	0	Δ_k^0	0
2	0	..	0	0	Δ_k^0		0
3	0	..	0	Δ_k^0			0
$\vdots$							
$k-1$	Δ_k^0	...					0
k		...	[0]	[0]	[0]	[0]	Δ_k^0
$k+1$		...	0	0	0	Δ_k^0	
$k+2$		...	0	0	Δ_k^0		
$k+3$		...	0	Δ_k^0			
$k+4$		...	Δ_k^0				

KPA

round	**0**	**0**	...	**0**	**0**	**0**	**0**	Δ_k^0
1	0	0	...	0	0	0	Δ_k^0	0
2	0	0	..	0	0	Δ_k^0		0
3	0	0	..	0	Δ_k^0			0
$\vdots$								
$k-1$	Δ_k^0		...					0
k			...				[0]	Δ_k^0
$k+1$			...				Δ_k^0	

CPA-1

For this KPA on $k+4$ rounds, we have in Table 16:

Since $m = 2^{(\frac{k}{2}+3)n}$, we can perform the same kind of attack for $k+r$ rounds, with $r \leq \frac{k}{2} + 1$. We can attack up to $k + \frac{k}{2} + 1$ rounds. For $k + \frac{k}{2} + 1$, we need the maximal number of messages i.e. 2^{kn}.

For CPA-1, it is easy to see that after one round, one message is sufficient. We just have to check if $S_k = I_1$. For 2 rounds, we choose 2 messages such that $I_1(1) = I_1(2)$ and we check if $S_k(1) \oplus S_k(2) = I_2(1) \oplus I_2(2)$. With a random

Table 16. Type-3 Feistel scheme: KPA on $r = k + 4$ rounds

Differential	$E(\mathcal{N}_{perm})$	$E(\mathcal{N}_{scheme})$	σ	m
$\Delta_1^0 = 0$ $\Delta_2^0 = 0$ $\vdots$ $\Delta_{k-1}^0 = 0$ $\Delta_k^0 = \Delta_{k-5}^{k+4}$	$\frac{m^2}{2.2^{kn}}$	$\frac{m^2}{2.2^{kn}} + O(\frac{m^2}{2^{(k+3)n}})$	$\frac{m}{\sqrt{2}2^{\frac{kn}{2}}}$	$2^{(\frac{k}{2}+3)n}$

permutation this happens with probability $\frac{1}{2^n}$, but with a scheme, the probability is one. Thus, we can distinguish between the two permutations with only 2 messages. More generally, for r rounds with $r \leq k$, we choose 2 messages such that $I_s(1) = I_s(2)$ for $1 \leq s \leq k-1$ and then we check if $S_k(1) \oplus S_k(2) = I_d(1) \oplus I_d(2)$. With a random permutation this happens with probability $\frac{1}{2^n}$, but with a scheme, the probability is one. Thus, we can distinguish between the two permutations with only 2 messages. We can attack up to k rounds.

For $k+1$ rounds,We choose m messages such that $I_1, I_2, \dots, I_{k-1}$ have a constant value. We have the following CPA-1 described in Table 15 (right part) and Table 17:

Table 17. Type-3 Feistel scheme: CPA-1 on $k+1$ rounds

Differential	$E(\mathcal{N}_{perm})$	$E(\mathcal{N}_{scheme})$	σ	m
$\Delta_{k-1}^{k+1} = \Delta_k^0$	$\frac{m^2}{2.2^n}$	$\frac{m^2}{2.2^n} + O(\frac{m^2}{2^n})$	$\frac{m}{\sqrt{2}2^{\frac{n}{2}}}$	$2^{\frac{n}{2}}$

Table 18 gives KPA and CPA-1 complexities.

Table 18. Complexities of the attacks on type-3 Feistel schemes

r	KPA	CPA-1
1	1	1
2	$2^{n/2}$	2
3	2^n	2
$\vdots$		
k	$2^{(k-1)n/2}$	2
$k+1$	$2^{\frac{k}{2}n}$	$2^{n/2}$
$k+2 \leq r \leq k + \lfloor \frac{k}{2} \rfloor + 1$	$2^{(r-\lfloor \frac{k}{2} \rfloor -1)n}$	$2^{(r-\lfloor \frac{k}{2} \rfloor -1)n}$

4.4 Alternating Feistel Schemes

Here we will describe our best attacks on alternating Feistel schemes. After one round, we have $[I_2, I_3, \dots, I_k] = [S_2, S_3, \dots, S_k]$. Thus, we choose one message and we check if this condition is satisfied. With a random permutation, this happens with probability $\frac{1}{2^{(k-1)n}}$ and with a scheme the probability is one. Thus, with one message we can distinguish a random permutation from a permutation obtained with an alternating scheme. After 2 rounds, in CPA-1, we choose 2 messages such that $\forall s$, $2 \leq s \leq k$, $I_s(1) = I_s(2)$ and then we check if $I_1(1) \oplus I_1(2) = S_1(1) \oplus S_1(2)$. The probability to have this condition satisfied is $\frac{1}{2^n}$ with a random permutation and 1 with an alternating scheme. We can transform this CPA-1 into a KPA. We generate m messages and from the birthday paradox, when $m \simeq 2^{\frac{(k-1)n}{2}}$ with a good probability, we can find (i, j) such that $\forall s$, $2 \leq s \leq k$, $I_s(i) = I_s(j)$ and then we test if $I_1(i) \oplus I_1(j) = S_1(i) \oplus S_1(j)$.

But there are better KPA, as we now show. We have the following KPA on $2r$ ($r \leq k$) rounds, described in Table 19 and Table 20, where Δ^0 denotes $[\Delta_2^0, \Delta_3^0, \Delta_4^0, \ldots, \Delta_k^0]$.

Table 19. Differential characteristic of our attacks on alternating Feistel schemes (KPA)

round	Δ_1^0	Δ^0
1	$\boxed{0}$	Δ^0
2	0	Δ^0
3	$\boxed{0}$	Δ^0
4	0	Δ^0
$\vdots$	$\vdots$	
$2r-1$	$\boxed{0}$	Δ^0
$2r$	0	Δ^0

Table 20. Alternating Feistel scheme: KPA on $2r$ rounds $r \leq k$

Differential	$E(\mathcal{N}_{perm})$	$E(\mathcal{N}_{scheme})$	m
$\Delta_1^0 = 0$ $\Delta^{2r} = \Delta^0$	$\frac{m^2}{2.2^{kn}}$	$\frac{m^2}{2.2^{kn}} + O(\frac{m^2}{2^{rn}})$	$2^{\frac{r}{2}n}$

Here we obtain, $m = 2^{\frac{r}{2}}$, since when $r \leq k$, $E(\mathcal{N}_{perm})$ is greater than or equal to twice $E(\mathcal{N}_{scheme})$ and we can distinguish when $m = 2^{\frac{r}{2}}$. Notice that in this case, we do not need to use the standard deviation. Thus, after 2 rounds we get a KPA with $2^{\frac{n}{2}}$ messages (notice that the CPA-1 complexity of the previous attack was better). After 2 rounds, KPA are the best attacks. We do not have better attack if we fix some part on the inputs.

After $2r$ rounds with $r > k$, in KPA, we keep the same differential characteristics and the attack is given in Table 21.

Table 21. Alternating Feistel scheme: KPA on $2r$ rounds $r > k$

Differential	$E(\mathcal{N}_{perm})$	$E(\mathcal{N}_{scheme})$	σ	m
$\Delta_1^0 = 0$ $\Delta^{2r} = \Delta^0$	$\frac{m^2}{2.2^{kn}}$	$\frac{m^2}{2.2^{kn}} + O(\frac{m^2}{2^{rn}})$	$\frac{m}{\sqrt{2}2^{\frac{kn}{2}}}$	$2^{(r-\frac{k}{2})n}$

Here since $r > k$, we need to compute the standard deviation and we get $m = 2^{(r-\frac{k}{2})n}$. Since the number of messages cannot exceed 2^{kn}, we obtain the condition $r \leq 3k/2$. Here we have given the complexity for even rounds. If we want to attack the odd round $2r+1$, we will only impose $\Delta^{2r+1} = \Delta^0$. We can attack up to $3k$ rounds. The complexities are summarized in Table 22.

Table 22. Complexities of the attacks on alternating Feistel schemes

r rounds	KPA
1	1
2	$2^{n/2}$
3	$2^{n/2}$
$\vdots$	
$3 \leq r \leq 2k+1$	$2^{(\frac{\lfloor \frac{r}{2} \rfloor}{2})n}$
$\vdots$	
$2k+1$	$2^{\frac{kn}{2}}$
$\vdots$	
$2k+1 \leq r \leq 3k$	$2^{(\frac{(r-k)}{2})n}$
$\vdots$	
$3k$	2^{kn}

5 Conclusion

In this paper, we have given our best differential generic attacks (KPA and CPA-1) on different kinds of generalized Feistel schemes: type-1, type-2, type-3 and alternating Feistel schemes. Since these schemes are used in well known block ciphers, it is interesting to find the maximal number of rounds that we can attack. We also gave the complexity of attacks on intermediate rounds. In our attacks, the computations of the mean values and the standard deviations are very useful. We generally stop attacking schemes, when we need the maximal number of possible messages to perform the attack. A way to overcome this problem is to attack permutation generators instead of a single permutation. Impossible differential attacks are better on type-3 Feistel schemes. For type-2 Feistel schemes, we can attack the same number of rounds as impossible attacks but here the internal functions are not necessarily bijective. For type-1 Feistel schemes, our attacks can reach more rounds as impossible differential attacks.

References

1. Aiello, W., Venkatesan, R.: Foiling Birthday Attacks in Length-Doubling Transformations - Benes: A Non-Reversible Alternative to Feistel. In: EUROCRYPT 1996. LNCS, vol. 1070, pp. 307–320. Springer, Heidelberg (1996)
2. Anderson, R.J., Biham, E.: Two Practical and Provably Secure Block Ciphers: BEAR and LION. In: Gollmann, D. (ed.) FSE 1996. LNCS, vol. 1039, pp. 113–120. Springer, Heidelberg (1996)
3. Bogdanov, A., Rijmen, V.: Zero-Correlation Linear Cryptanalysis on Block Cipher. Cryptology ePrint archive: 2011/123: Listing for 2011 (2011)
4. Bouillaguet, C., Dunkelman, O., Leurent, G., Fouque, P.-A.: Attacks on Hash Functions Based on Generalized Feistel: Application to Reduced-Round *Lesamnta* and *SHAvite-3*$_{512}$. In: Biryukov, A., Gong, G., Stinson, D.R. (eds.) SAC 2010. LNCS, vol. 6544, pp. 18–35. Springer, Heidelberg (2011)
5. Bouillaguet, C., Dunkelman, O., Fouque, P.-A., Leurent, G.: New Insights on Impossible Differential Cryptanalysis. In: Miri, A., Vaudenay, S. (eds.) SAC 2011. LNCS, vol. 7118, pp. 243–259. Springer, Heidelberg (2012)
6. Choy, J., Yap, H.: Impossible Boomerang Attack for Block Cipher Structures. In: Takagi, T., Mambo, M. (eds.) IWSEC 2009. LNCS, vol. 5824, pp. 22–37. Springer, Heidelberg (2009)
7. Hoel, P.G., Port, S.C., Stone, C.J.: Introduction to Probability Theory. Houghton Mifflin Company (1971)
8. Hoang, V.T., Rogaway, P.: On Generalized Feistel Networks. In: Rabin, T. (ed.) CRYPTO 2010. LNCS, vol. 6223, pp. 613–630. Springer, Heidelberg (2010)
9. Ibrahim, S., Mararof, M.A.: Diffusion Analysis of Scalable Feistel Networks. World Academy of Science, Engineering and Technology 5, 98–101 (2005)
10. Jutla, C.S.: Generalized Birthday Attacks on Unbalanced Feistel Networks. In: Krawczyk, H. (ed.) CRYPTO 1998. LNCS, vol. 1462, pp. 186–199. Springer, Heidelberg (1998)
11. Kim, J., Hong, S., Lim, J.: Impossible Differential Cryptanalysis Using Matrix Method. Discrete Mathematics 310(5), 988–1002 (2010)
12. Knudsen, L.R.: DEAL - A 128-bit Block Cipher. Technical Report 151, University of Bergen, Department of Informatics, Norway (February 1998)
13. Knudsen, L.R., Rijmen, V.: On the Decorrelated Fast Cipher (DFC) and Its Theory. In: Knudsen, L.R. (ed.) FSE 1999. LNCS, vol. 1636, pp. 81–94. Springer, Heidelberg (1999)
14. Luby, M., Rackoff, C.: How to Construct Pseudorandom Permutations from Pseudorandom Functions. SIAM J. Comput. 17(2), 373–386 (1988)
15. Naor, M., Reingold, O.: On the Construction of Pseudorandom Permutations: Luby-Rackoff Revisited. J. Cryptology 12(1), 29–66 (1999)
16. Patarin, J.: Generic Attacks on Feistel Schemes - Extended version. In: Cryptology ePrint archive: 2008/036: Listing for 2008 (2008)
17. Patarin, J.: Security of balanced and unbalanced Feistel schemes with linear non equalities. In: Cryptology ePrint archive: 2010/293: Listing for (2010)
18. Patarin, J.: New Results on Pseudorandom Permutation Generators Based on the DES Scheme. In: Feigenbaum, J. (ed.) CRYPTO 1991. LNCS, vol. 576, pp. 301–312. Springer, Heidelberg (1992)
19. Patarin, J.: Generic Attacks on Feistel Schemes. In: Boyd, C. (ed.) ASIACRYPT 2001. LNCS, vol. 2248, pp. 222–238. Springer, Heidelberg (2001)

20. Patarin, J.: Security of Random Feistel Schemes with 5 or More Rounds. In: Franklin, M. (ed.) CRYPTO 2004. LNCS, vol. 3152, pp. 106–122. Springer, Heidelberg (2004)
21. Patarin, J., Nachef, V., Berbain, C.: Generic Attacks on Unbalanced Feistel Schemes with Expanding Functions - Extended version. Cryptology ePrint archive: 2007/449: Listing for 2007 (2007)
22. Patarin, J., Nachef, V., Berbain, C.: Generic Attacks on Unbalanced Feistel Schemes with Contracting Functions. In: Lai, X., Chen, K. (eds.) ASIACRYPT 2006. LNCS, vol. 4284, pp. 396–411. Springer, Heidelberg (2006)
23. Patarin, J., Nachef, V., Berbain, C.: Generic Attacks on Unbalanced Feistel Schemes with Expanding Functions. In: Kurosawa, K. (ed.) ASIACRYPT 2007. LNCS, vol. 4833, pp. 325–341. Springer, Heidelberg (2007)
24. Schneier, B., Kelsey, J.: Unbalanced Feistel Networks and Block Cipher Design. In: Gollmann, D. (ed.) FSE 1996. LNCS, vol. 1039, pp. 121–144. Springer, Heidelberg (1996)
25. Treger, J., Patarin, J.: Generic Attacks on Feistel Networks with Internal Permutations. In: Preneel, B. (ed.) AFRICACRYPT 2009. LNCS, vol. 5580, pp. 41–59. Springer, Heidelberg (2009)
26. Volte, E., Nachef, V., Patarin, J.: Improved Generic Attacks on Unbalanced Feistel Schemes with Expanding Functions. In: Abe, M. (ed.) ASIACRYPT 2010. LNCS, vol. 6477, pp. 94–111. Springer, Heidelberg (2010)
27. Lai, X., Luo, Y., Wu, Z., Gong, G.: A Unified Method for Finding Impossible Differentials of Block Cipher Structures (2009), `http://eprint.iacr.org/`
28. Yun, A., Park, J.H., Lee, J.: Lai-Massey Scheme and Quasi-Feistel Networks. Cryptology ePrint archive: 2007/347: Listing for 2007 (2007)
29. Zheng, Y., Matsumoto, T., Imai, H.: On the Construction of Block Ciphers Provably Secure and Not Relying on Any Unproved Hypotheses. In: Brassard, G. (ed.) CRYPTO 1989. LNCS, vol. 435, pp. 461–480. Springer, Heidelberg (1990)

A An Example of Computation of the Mean Value and the Variance for Random Permutations

Very often in cryptographic attacks based on the computations of variance V and mean value E we have $V \simeq E$, particularly when we deal with differential attacks. We will prove this precisely here for the CPA-1 given in section 4.1. This is an attack on $pk-1$ rounds with $3 \leq p \leq k+1$ Similar proofs have also been done for other cases.

First we compute the mean value denoted by $E(\mathcal{N}_{perm})$. We have $\forall i,\ 1 \leq i \leq m,\ I_1(i) = 0$. Here $m \simeq 2^{(p-2)n}$. The inputs are pairwise distinct. Let $\delta_{ij} = 1$ if (2) is satisfied $\delta_{ij} = 0$ otherwise. Then $\mathcal{N}_{perm} = \sum_{i<j} \delta_{ij}$,
$E(\mathcal{N}_{perm}) = \sum_{i<j} E(\delta_{ij})$ and
$E(\delta_{ij}) = Pr[S_2(i) = S_2(j) \text{ and } I_2(i) \oplus I_2(j) = S_3(i) \oplus S_3(j)]$
Case 1: $I_2(i) = I_2(j)$.
$E(\delta_{ij}) = Pr[S_2(i) = S_2(j) \text{ and } S_3(i) = S_3(j)] = \frac{2^{(k-2)n}-1}{2^{kn}-1} = (\frac{1}{2^{2n}})(\frac{1-\frac{1}{2^{(k-2)n}}}{1-\frac{1}{2^{kn}}})$
Case 2: $I_2(i) \neq I_2(j)$.
$E(\delta_{ij}) = Pr[S_2(i) = S_2(j) \text{ and } I_2(i) \oplus I_2(j) = S_3(i) \oplus S_3(j)] = \frac{2^{(k-2)n}}{2^{kn}-1} = (\frac{1}{2^{2n}})(\frac{1}{1-\frac{1}{2^{kn}}})$.
Let α be the number of (i,j) such that $I_2(i) = I_2(j)$. Then
$E(\mathcal{N}_{perm}) = \alpha\left(\frac{2^{(k-2)n}-1}{2^{kn}-1}\right) + \left(\frac{m(m-1)}{2} - \alpha\right)\left(\frac{2^{(k-2)n}}{2^{kn}-1}\right) = [\frac{m(m-1)}{2\cdot 2^{2n}} - \frac{\alpha}{2^{kn}}](\frac{1}{1-\frac{1}{2^{kn}}})$.
We can assume that $\alpha = \frac{m(m-1)}{2\cdot 2^n} + O(\frac{m}{\sqrt{2^n}})$. Then we get
$E(\mathcal{N}_{perm}) = [\frac{m(m-1)}{2\cdot 2^{2n}} - \frac{1}{2^{kn}}\left(\frac{m(m-1)}{2\cdot 2^n} + 0(\frac{m}{\sqrt{2^n}})\right)](\frac{1}{1-\frac{1}{2^{kn}}}) =$
$(\frac{m(m-1)}{2\cdot 2^{2n}}) \times (\frac{1-\frac{1}{2^{(k-1)n}}}{1-\frac{1}{2^{kn}}}) + O(\frac{m}{2^{k+\frac{1}{2}}})$.
Finally, this gives
$\frac{m(m-1)}{2\cdot 2^{2n}}\left(1 - \frac{1}{2^{(k-1)n}} + \frac{1}{2^{kn}}\right) + O(\frac{m}{2^{(k+\frac{1}{2})n}}) \leq E(\mathcal{N}_{perm}) \leq \frac{m(m-1)}{2\cdot 2^{2n}} + O(\frac{m}{2^{(k+\frac{1}{2})n}})$.

We now gives the main steps in order to compute the standard deviation. We will use the "covariance formula " given in Section 3 in order to compute $V(\mathcal{N}_{perm})$. We have: $V(\delta_{ij}) = E(\delta_{ij}^2) - E(\delta_{ij})^2 = E(\delta_{ij}) - E(\delta_{ij})^2$.
Case 1: $I_2(i) = I_2(j)$.
$V(\delta_{ij}) = \frac{1}{2^{2n}} \times \frac{1-\frac{1}{2^{(k-2)n}}}{1-\frac{1}{2^{kn}}} - \left(\frac{1}{2^{2n}} \times \frac{1-\frac{1}{2^{(k-2)n}}}{1-\frac{1}{2^{kn}}}\right)^2$.
This gives:
$V(\delta_{ij}) = \frac{1}{2^{2n}}\Big[1 - \frac{1}{2^{2n}} - \frac{1}{2^{(k-2)n}} + \frac{3}{2^{kn}} - \frac{2}{2^{(k+2)n}} - \frac{2}{2^{(2k-2)n}} + \frac{5}{2^{2kn}} - \frac{3}{2^{(2k+2)n}} - \frac{3}{2^{(3k-2)n}}\Big] + O(\frac{1}{2^{3kn}})$
Case 2: $I_2(i) \neq I_2(j)$.
$V(\delta_{ij}) = \frac{1}{2^{2n}} \times \frac{1}{1-\frac{1}{2^{kn}}} - \left(\frac{1}{2^{2n}} \times \frac{1}{1-\frac{1}{2^{kn}}}\right)^2$. We obtain
$V(\delta_{ij}) = \frac{1}{2^{2n}}\Big[1 - \frac{1}{2^{2n}} + \frac{1}{2^{kn}} - \frac{2}{2^{(k+2)n}} + \frac{1}{2^{2kn}} - \frac{3}{2^{(2k+2)n}}\Big] + O(\frac{1}{2^{3kn}})$.
Since we want to use the covariance formula, we have to evaluate $E(\delta_{ij})E(\delta_{qv})$ and $E(\delta_{ij}\delta_{qv})$. We explain the case where i, j, q, v are pairwise distinct. The case

where in $\{i, j, q, v\}$ we have exactly 3 values is similar. The total number of outputs is given by
$A = 2^{kn}(2^{kn}-1)(2^{kn}-2)(2^{kn}-3) = 2^{4kn}(1-\frac{6}{2^{kn}}+\frac{11}{2^{2kn}}-\frac{6}{2^{3kn}})$.
Then
$\frac{1}{A} = \frac{1}{2^{4kn}}\left(1+\frac{6}{2^{kn}}+\frac{25}{2^{2kn}}+O(\frac{1}{2^{3kn}})\right)$.
We first evaluate $E(\delta_{ij})E(\delta_{qv})$. We have to study several cases:

1. $I_2(i) \neq I_2(j)$ and $I_2(q) \neq I_2(v)$. Then
$E(\delta_{ij})E(\delta_{qv}) = \frac{1}{2^{4n}}\left(\frac{1}{1-\frac{1}{2^{kn}}}\right)^2 = \frac{1}{2^{4n}}(1+\frac{2}{2^{kn}}+\frac{3}{2^{2kn}}+O(\frac{1}{2^{3kn}}))$.
2. $(I_2(i) = I_2(j)$ and $I_2(q) \neq I_2(v))$ or $(I_2(i) \neq I_2(j)$ and $I_2(q) = I_2(v))$. Then
$E(\delta_{ij})E(\delta_{qv}) = \frac{1}{2^{4n}}\left(\frac{1-\frac{1}{2^{(k-2)n}}}{(1-\frac{1}{2^{kn}})^2}\right)$.
$E(\delta_{ij})E(\delta_{qv}) = \frac{1}{2^{4n}}(1-\frac{1}{2^{(k-2)n}}+\frac{2}{2^{kn}}-\frac{2}{2^{(2k-2)n}}+\frac{3}{2^{2kn}}-\frac{3}{2^{(3k-2)n}}+O(\frac{1}{2^{3kn}}))$.
3. $I_2(i) = I_2(j)$ and $I_2(q) = I_2(v)$. Then $E(\delta_{ij})E(\delta_{qv}) = \frac{1}{2^{4n}} \times \frac{(1-\frac{1}{2^{(k-2)n}})^2}{(1-\frac{1}{2^{kn}})^2}$
$= \frac{1}{2^{4n}}(1-\frac{2}{2^{(k-2)n}}+\frac{2}{2^{kn}}+\frac{1}{2^{(2k-4)n}}-\frac{4}{2^{(2k-2)n}}+\frac{3}{2^{2kn}}+\frac{2}{2^{(3k-4)n}}-\frac{6}{2^{(3k-2)n}}+O(\frac{1}{2^{3kn}}))$.

We compute $E(\delta_{ij}\delta_{qv})$. Again we have to consider several cases. We give the main case: $I_2(i) \neq I_2(j)$, $I_2(q) \neq I_2(v)$ and $I_2(i) \oplus I_2(j) \oplus I_2(q) \oplus I_2(v) \neq 0$.
In that case, $S_3(j) = I_2(i) \oplus I_2(j) \oplus S_3(i) \neq S_3(i)$. There are 2^{kn} possibilities for $S(i)$. When $S(i)$ is fixed, there are $2^{(k-2)n}$ possibilities for $S(j)$, since $S_2(j)$ and $S_3(j)$ are fixed. Now for $S(q)$ there are 6 possibilities:
1) $S_2(q) \neq S_2(i)$ (we have $S_2(i) = S_2(j)$).
Then $S_2(v) = S_2(q) \neq S_2(i)$. Since $S_3(v) = S_3(q) \oplus I_2(q) \oplus I_2(v)$, we have $S_3(q) \neq S_3(v)$. Thus there are
$(2^n-1)2^{(k-1)n}$ possibilities for $S(q)$ and $2^{(k-2)n}$ possibilities for $S(v)$ This gives $(2^n-1)2^{(2k-3)n}$ possibilities for $(S(q), S(v))$.
2) $S_2(q) = S_2(i) = S_2(j)$ and $S_3(q) = S_3(i) \oplus I_2(q) \oplus I_2(v)$.
Then $S_3(v) = S_3(i)$ and $S_2(v) = S_2(q)) = S_2(i)$. There are $2^{(k-2)n}$ possibilities for $S(p)$ and $(2^{(k-2)n}-1)$ possibilities for $S(v)$. This gives $2^{2(k-2)n}(2^{2(k-2)n}-1)$ possibilities for $(S(q), S(v))$.
3) $S_2(q) = S_2(i) = S_2(j)$ and $S_3(q) = S_3(j) \oplus I_2(q) \oplus I_2(v)$.
There are $2^{(k-2)n}$ possibilities for $S(p)$ and $2^{(k-2)n}-1$ possibilities for $S(v)$. This gives $2^{2(k-2)n}(2^{2(k-2)n}-1)$ possibilities for $(S(q), S(v))$
4) $S_2(q) = S_2(i) = S_2(j)$ and $S_3(q) = S_3(i)$.
This gives $(2^{2(k-2)n}-1)2^{2(k-2)n}$ possibilities for $(S(q), S(v))$
5) $S_2(q) = S_2(i) = S_2(j)$ and $S_3(q) = S_3(j)$.
This gives again $(2^{2(k-2)n}-1)2^{2(k-2)n}$ possibilities for $(S(q), S(v))$
6) $S_2(q) = S_2(i) = S_2(j)$ and we are not in cases 2), 3), 4), 5). This gives $(2^{2(k-2)n}-4)2^{2(k-2)n}$ possibilities for $(S(q), S(v))$
Finally, the number of possible outputs for $S(i), S(j), S(q), S(v)$ in this case 1 is given by $B = 2^{(4k-4)n}\left(1-\frac{4}{2^{kn}}\right)$ and $E(\delta_{ij}\delta_{qv}) = \frac{B}{A} = \frac{1}{2^{4n}}\left(1+\frac{2}{2^{kn}}+\frac{1}{2^{2kn}}+O(\frac{1}{2^{3kn}})\right)$. Thus $E(\delta_{ij})E(\delta_{qv}) - E(\delta_{ij}\delta_{qv}) = \frac{1}{2^{4n}}\left(-\frac{2}{2^{2kn}}+O(\frac{1}{2^{3kn}})\right)$. The term $\frac{-2m^4}{4\cdot 2^{4n}.2^{2kn}} \ll \frac{m^2}{2^{2n}}$ since $m \ll 2^{kn}$ The other cases are $I_2(i) = (j)$, $I_2(q) \neq I_2(v)$,

$I_2(i) \neq I_2(j)$, $I_2(q) \neq I_2(v)$ and $I_2(i) \oplus I_2(j) \oplus I_2(q) \oplus I_2(v) = 0$ and $I_2(i) = I_2(j)$ and $I_2(q) = I_2(v)$. The study is similar to the main case.
All the computations show that $V(\mathcal{N}_{perm}) = \frac{m(m-1)}{2 \cdot 2^{2n}}(1 - \frac{1}{2^{2n}} + O(\frac{1}{2^{kn}}))$.
Thus $V(\mathcal{N}_{perm}) \simeq E(\mathcal{N}_{perm})$ as claimed.

B Computation of the Mean Value and the Variance for Feistel Type-1 Schemes

Here we suppose that $p = 4$. For any p the computations are similar. We introduce the internal variables X^i where X^i is the first block of the output after round i.
After $4k - 1$ rounds the output is given by:

$$[S_1, S_2, S_3, \ldots, S_k] = [X^{4k-1}, X^{3k}, X^{3k+1}, \ldots, X^{4k-2}]$$

where $S_3 = I_2 \oplus f^1(I_1) \oplus F^{k+1}(X^k) \oplus F^{2k+1}(X^{2k}) \oplus F^{3k+1}(X^{3k})$. Thus the following conditions:
$(*)$ $\quad S_2(i) = S_2(j)$, and $I_2(i) \oplus I_2(j) = S_3(i) \oplus S_3(j)$ are equivalent to
$(**) X^{3k}(i) = X^{3k}(j)$ and $F^{k+1}(X^k(i)) \oplus F^{2k+1}(X^{2k}(i)) = F^{k+1}(X^k(j))$
$\oplus F^{2k+1}(X^{2k}(j))$
In order to compute $E(\delta_{ij})$, we consider 2 cases:

1. $X^{3k}(i) = X^{3k}(j)$ and $(X^k(i), X^{2k}(i)) = (X^k(j), X^{2k}(j))$.
2. $X^{3k}(i) = X^{3k}(j)$, $(X^k(i), X^{2k}(i)) \neq X^k(j), X^{2k}(j))$ and $F^{k+1}(X^k(i)) \oplus F^{2k+1}(X^{2k}(i)) = F^{k+1}(X^k(j)) \oplus F^{2k+1}(X^{2k}(j))$.

Let

$$p_1 = Pr[X^{3k}(i) = X^{3k}(j) / (X^k(i), X^{2k}(i)) = (X^k(j), X^{2k}(j))$$
$$p_1' = Pr[X^{3k}(i) = X^{3k}(j) / (X^k(i), X^{2k}(i)) \neq (X^k(j), X^{2k}(j))$$
$$p_2 = Pr[(X^k(i), X^{2k}(i)) = (X^k(j), X^{2k}(j))$$

The the probability of the first case is $p_1 p_2$ and the probability of the second case is $\frac{1}{2^n} p_1'(1 - p_2)$. Finally $E(\delta_{ij}) = p_1 p_2 + \frac{1}{2^n} p_1'(1 - p_2)$, and $E(\mathcal{N}_{type1}) = \frac{m(m-1)}{2}\left(p_1 p_2 + \frac{1}{2^n} p_1'(1 - p_2)\right)$. We have $p_1' \simeq \frac{1}{2^n}$. In p_2 the dominant term is in $O(\frac{1}{2^{2n}})$. Indeed, according to Lemma 24 of [8], we have $\frac{1}{2^n} \leq Pr[X^k(i) = X^k(j)] \leq \frac{k-1}{2^n}$. Using the same arguments, we obtain $\frac{1}{2^{2n}} \leq p_2 \leq \frac{(k-1)^2}{2^{2n}}$ and $\frac{1}{2^n} \leq p_1 \leq \frac{k-1}{2^n}$.
We want to show that the variance behaves like the mean value. For this, we will use the covariance formula:

$$V(\mathcal{N}_{type1}) = \sum_{i<j} V(\delta_{ij}) + \sum_{\substack{1<j \\ q<v \\ (i,j) \neq (q,v)}} [E(\delta_{ij}\delta_{qv}) - E(\delta_{ij})E(\delta_{qv})]$$

We now compute $E(\delta_{ij}\delta_{qv})$. We explain the case where i, j, q, v are pairwise distinct. The case where in $\{i, j, q, v\}$ we have exactly 3 values is similar.
When i, j, q, v are pairwise distinct, the conditions $(**)$ are satisfied for the pairs (i, j) and (q, v). Then we have to study several cases.

1. $X^{3k}(i) = X^{3k}(j)$, $X^{3k}(q) = X^{3k}(v)$, $(X^k(i), X^{2k}(i)) = (X^k(j), X^{2k}(j))$ and $(X^k(q), X^{2k}(q)) = (X^k(v), X^{2k}(v))$. The probability is $(p_1p_2)^2$.
2. $X^{3k}(i) = X^{3k}(j)$, $X^{3k}(q) = X^{3k}(v)$, $(X^k(i), X^{2k}(i)) = (X^k(j), X^{2k}(j))$ and $(X^k(q), X^{2k}(q)) \neq (X^k(v), X^{2k}(v))$ and $F^{k+1}(X^k(q)) \oplus F^{2k+1}(X^{2k}(q)) = F^{k+1}(X^k(v)) \oplus F^{2k+1}(X^{2k}(v))$. Then the probability is given by $\frac{1}{2^n}p_1p_1'p_2(1-p_2)$.
3. $X^{3k}(i) = X^{3k}(j)$, $X^{3k}(q) = X^{3k}(v)$, $(X^k(i), X^{2k}(i)) \neq (X^k(j), X^{2k}(j))$ and $(X^k(q), X^{2k}(q)) = (X^k(v), X^{2k}(v))$ and $F^{k+1}(X^k(i) \oplus F^{2k+1}(X^{2k}(i)) = F^{k+1}(X^k(j)) \oplus F^{2k+1}(X^{2k}(j))$. As in the previous case, the probability is given by $\frac{1}{2^n}p_1p_1'p_2(1-p_2)$.
4. $X^{3k}(i) = X^{3k}(j)$, $X^{3k}(q) = X^{3k}(v)$, $(X^k(i), X^{2k}(i)) \neq (X^k(j), X^{2k}(j))$, $(X^k(q), X^{2k}(q)) = (X^k(i), X^{2k}(i))$, $(X^k(v), X^{2k}(v)) = (X^k(j), X^{2k}(j))$ $F^{k+1}(X^k(i) \oplus F^{2k+1}(X^{2k}(i)) = F^{k+1}(X^k(j)) \oplus F^{2k+1}(X^{2k}(j))$. The probability is given by $\frac{1}{2^n}(p_1')^2p_2^2(1-p_2)$.
5. $X^{3k}(i) = X^{3k}(j)$, $X^{3k}(q) = X^{3k}(v)$, $(X^k(i), X^{2k}(i)) \neq (X^k(j), X^{2k}(j))$, $(X^k(v), X^{2k}(v)) = (X^k(i), X^{2k}(i))$, $(X^k(q), X^{2k}(q)) = (X^k(j), X^{2k}(j))$, $F^{k+1}(X^k(i) \oplus F^{2k+1}(X^{2k}(i)) = F^{k+1}(X^k(j)) \oplus F^{2k+1}(X^{2k}(j))$. Again the probability is given by $\frac{1}{2^n}(p_1')^2p_2^2(1-p_2)$.
6. $X^{3k}(i) = X^{3k}(j)$, $X^{3k}(q) = X^{3k}(v)$, $(X^k(i), X^{2k}(i)) \neq (X^k(j), X^{2k}(j))$ and $(X^k(q), X^{2k}(q)) \neq (X^k(v), X^{2k}(v))$, we are not in cases 4 and 5 and $F^{2k+1}(X^{2k}(i)) = F^{k+1}(X^k(j)) \oplus F^{2k+1}(X^{2k}(j))$ and $F^{k+1}(X^k(q))$ $\oplus F^{2k+1}(X^{2k}(q)) = F^{k+1}(X^k(v)) \oplus F^{2k+1}(X^{2k}(v))$. Then the probability is $\frac{1}{2^{2n}}(p_1')^2[(1-p_2)^2 - 2(1-p_2)p_2^2]$.

Finally we obtain when i, j, q, v are pairwise distinct

$$E(\delta_{ij}\delta_{qv}) - E(\delta_{ij})E(\delta_{qv}) = 2\frac{1}{2^n}(p_1')^2p_2^2(1-p_2) - 2\frac{1}{2^{2n}}(p_1')^2p_2^2(1-p_2)$$

Using the dominant term in p_1' and p_2, we get that the dominant term in $\sum_{\substack{1<j\\ q<v\\ (i,j)\neq(q,v)}} [E(\delta_{ij}\delta_{qv}) - E(\delta_{ij})E(\delta_{qv})]$ is in $O(\frac{m^4}{2^{7n}})$ and $\frac{m^4}{2^{7n}} \ll \frac{m^2}{2^{2n}}$ since $m \simeq 2^{2n}$ in our attack.
Similarly, in the case where we have exactly 3 values in $\{i, j, q, v\}$, the dominant term in $\sum_{\substack{1<j\\ q<v\\ (i,j)\neq(q,v)}} [E(\delta_{ij}\delta_{qv}) - E(\delta_{ij})E(\delta_{qv})]$ is in $O(\frac{m^3}{2^{5n}})$ and $\frac{m^3}{2^{5n}} \ll \frac{m^2}{2^{2n}}$ since $m \simeq 2^{2n}$ in our attack.
Thus the dominant term in the $V(\mathcal{N}_{type1})$ is in $O(\frac{m^2}{2^{2n}})$.

More generally, our computations show that the CPA-1 on $pk-1$ rounds with $p \leq k+2$, we have: $E(\mathcal{N}_{perm}) \simeq \frac{m^2}{2.2^{2n}}$, $E(\mathcal{N}_{type1}) \simeq \frac{m^2}{2.2^{2n}} + O(\frac{m^2}{2^{(p-1)n}})$, $V(\mathcal{N}_{perm}) \simeq \frac{m^2}{2^{2n}}$ and, $\sigma(\mathcal{N}_{perm}) \simeq \frac{m}{2^n}$, $V(\mathcal{N}_{type1}) \simeq \frac{m^2}{2^{2n}}$, and $\sigma(\mathcal{N}_{type1}) \simeq \frac{m}{2^n}$. Thus we can distinguish a permutation obtained by a type-1 Feistel scheme from a random permutation as soon as $|E(\mathcal{N}_{perm}) - E(\mathcal{N}_{type1})| \geq \sigma(\mathcal{N}_{perm})$, $|E(\mathcal{N}_{perm}) - E(\mathcal{N}_{type1})| \geq \sigma(\mathcal{N}_{type1})$ i.e. as soon as $\frac{m^2}{2^{(p-1)n}} \geq \frac{m}{2^n}$ i.e. $m \geq 2^{(p-2)n}$.

Revisiting MAC Forgeries, Weak Keys and Provable Security of Galois/Counter Mode of Operation

Bo Zhu, Yin Tan, and Guang Gong

Department of Electrical and Computer Engineering
University of Waterloo
Waterloo, Ontario N2L 3G1, Canada
{bo.zhu,y24tan,ggong}@uwaterloo.ca

Abstract. Galois/Counter Mode (GCM) is a block cipher mode of operation widely adopted in many practical applications and standards, such as IEEE 802.1AE and IPsec. We demonstrate that to construct successful forgeries of GCM-like polynomial-based MAC schemes, hash collisions are not necessarily required and any polynomials could be used in the attacks, which removes the restrictions of attacks previously proposed by Procter and Cid. Based on these new discoveries on forgery attacks, we show that all subsets with no less than two authentication keys are weak key classes, if the final block cipher masking is computed additively. In addition, by utilizing a special structure of GCM, we turn these forgery attacks into birthday attacks, which will significantly increase their success probabilities. Furthermore, we provide a method to fix GCM in order to avoid the security proof flaw discovered by Iwata, Ohashi and Minematsu. By applying the method, the security bounds of GCM can be improved by a factor of around 2^{20}. Lastly, we show that these forgery attacks will still succeed if GCM adopts MAC-then-Enc paradigm to protect its MAC scheme as one of the options mentioned in previous papers.

Keywords: Galois/Counter Mode, GCM, MAC forgery, weak key, birthday attack, provable security, MAC-then-Enc.

1 Introduction

Information security plays an increasingly important role due to the fast growth of computer networks. How to prevent personal data from unauthorized access by third parties is one of the fundamental problems of any system design, and it highly depends on the security levels of underlying algorithms to protect confidentiality and authentication. However, in practice, system designers and software developers may have restrained time and resources to learn and understand the detailed designs and principles of sophisticated cryptographic algorithms and protocols, and may make poor decisions in their system or software development and put users' personal data in danger. Therefore, bridging

M. Abdalla, C. Nita-Rotaru, and R. Dahab (Eds.): CANS 2013, LNCS 8257, pp. 20–38, 2013.

the gap between academic research and practical developments and introducing unified interfaces for both confidentiality and authentication are very important tasks for researchers. We believe these can serve as some of the goals of the CAESAR competition calling for authenticated encryption designs [3].

Generally, block ciphers are used with various modes of operation, such as CCM, GCM and OCB, to compute ciphertexts and message authentication codes to provide confidentiality and authentication respectively. It would be very important to better investigate and understand existing designs of modes of operation when designing new authenticated encryption schemes. Galois/Counter Mode (GCM) [4,12] is an Authenticated Encryption with Associated Data (AEAD) mode [18] for block ciphers, which possesses many excellent features. GCM can be easily and efficiently implemented in both software and hardware. The computations of GCM can be done in parallel, and only small portions need to be recomputed if one block of input is changed. The theoretical proofs of GCM are given by its designers McGrew and Viega in the paper [13]. GCM is included in NSA Suite B Cryptography [15], and is widely adopted by many standards and protocols, such as IEEE 802.1AE [7] and IPsec [21].

The design of GCM is based on Counter Mode for encryption and a polynomial-based MAC scheme for authentication. The security of GCM has been assessed by many researchers [5,6,10]. Recently, the algebraic structures of its underlying polynomial-based MAC scheme were analyzed by Saarinen [19], and by Procter and Cid [16,17]. Procter and Cid showed that almost all subsets of these kinds of polynomial-based MAC schemes are weak key classes. In 2012, Iwata *et al.* found a flaw in GCM's original security proofs, and presented new security bounds for it [8,9]. Under such circumstance, further investigation on these attacks and the security bounds would be very important for usage of GCM and future designs of authenticated ciphers.

Our Contributions. The main contributions of this paper are as follows.

- We reveal (and demonstrate by practical examples) that hash collisions are not necessarily required for forgeries of GCM-like polynomial-based MAC schemes, and polynomials with non-zero constant terms can be used for the attacks. These remove certain restrictions of MAC forgery attacks proposed by Procter and Cid.
- Based on the above discoveries on MAC forgeries, we show that all non-singleton subsets (i.e. with more than one element) of authentication keys are weak key classes, if the final masking by block ciphers is computed additively. This is an extension to previous analysis of Procter and Cid.
- Based on a special structure of GCM, we show how to turn these forgery attacks into birthday-bound based attacks by attacking the encryption oracle instead of the verification or decryption oracle. This can significantly increase success probabilities and avoid certain countermeasures.
- We provide a method to fix GCM in order to avoid the security proofs' flaw discovered by Iwata *et al.* By applying this method, the security bounds of GCM can be improved by a factor of around 2^{20}.

– We indicate that even if GCM is changed to MAC-then-Enc paradigm to make adversaries more difficult to attack MAC schemes (one of the options mentioned in [16,17]), these forgery attacks can still work.

The rest of this paper is organized as follows. The next section gives the background knowledge and notation used throughout the paper. Section 3 presents our improved forgery attacks on polynomial-based MAC schemes, and studies weak key classes of GCM-like schemes. Section 4 shows how to turn these forgery attacks on GCM into birthday attacks to improve the success probabilities. The method to fix GCM and the new security bounds are given in Section 5. The attacks on the revised version of GCM in MAC-then-Enc paradigm are discussed in Section 6. The last section concludes the paper and mentions potential future work. The appendix provides several computational examples to demonstrate the MAC forgery attacks proposed in this paper.

2 Preliminaries

This section firstly clarifies the notation that will be used throughout the paper. Secondly, the design of GCM and adversarial models will be briefly introduced.

2.1 Notation

Following the notation in [8], $\mathsf{str}_n(x)$ denotes the n-bit binary representation of the integer x, where the leftmost bits are interpreted as the most significant bits (MSB) of x, and $\mathsf{int}(s)$ returns the integer converted from the bit-string s.

The operator $||$ concatenates two bit-strings, e.g. $s_1||s_2$. $\mathsf{len}(s)$ returns the bit-length of s. $\mathsf{msb}_n(s)$ represents the leftmost n bits of s, and $\mathsf{lsb}_n(s)$ is the rightmost n bits. 0^l is used to denote a bit-string with l-bit 0's, and $0^{31}1$ is the concatenation of 0^{31} with one 1. For a set $\mathcal{S}$, the number of elements in $\mathcal{S}$ is denoted as $|\mathcal{S}|$.

The function $\mathsf{inc}(s)$, where $\mathsf{len}(s) = 128$, is defined as

$$\mathsf{inc}(s) = \mathsf{msb}_{96}(s)||\mathsf{str}_{32}(\mathsf{int}(\mathsf{lsb}_{32}(s)) + 1 \bmod 2^{32}),$$

and inc^n denotes applying inc for n times.

2.2 A Brief Introduction to GCM

GCM is an AEAD scheme who adopts Counter Mode for encryption, and a polynomial-based hash algorithm for message authentication. In this paper, we concentrate on the version of GCM based on a 128-bit block cipher, which is the major usage case proposed in its specification. The finite field $\mathrm{GF}(2^{128})$ adopted in GCM uses the generating polynomial $1 + x + x^2 + x^7 + x^{128}$.

The authenticated encryption of GCM requires four bit-string inputs, an initialization vector (IV, or nonce) N, a master key K, a plaintext P and an associated data A, and then produces a pair (C, T), where C is the ciphertext which has the same length as P and T is a t-bit authentication tag, where $t \leq 128$. The authenticated decryption algorithm takes N, K, C and T, and returns P if T is valid or *FAIL* if T does not pass the verification. The lengths of these variables should meet the following requirements [13]:

$$0 \le \mathsf{len}(N) \le 2^{64},$$
$$0 \le \mathsf{len}(P) \le 128(2^{32}-2),$$
$$0 \le \mathsf{len}(A) \le 2^{64}.$$

We use $E_K(x)$ to denote the block cipher encryption with the master key K. Suppose $\mathsf{len}(P) = 128(n-1) + m$, where $1 \le m \le 128$. Segment P into a sequence of message blocks $P_1||P_2||\cdots||P_n$, where $\mathsf{len}(P_i) = 128$ for $1 \le i \le n-1$ and $\mathsf{len}(P_n) = m$. The authentication key H is derived from the master key by computing $H = E_K(0^{128})$.

Algorithm 1 ([13]). *The steps of GCM encryption are described as follows.*

$$N_0 = \begin{cases} N||0^{31}1 & \textit{if } \mathsf{len}(N) = 96, \\ \mathsf{GHASH}_H(N) & \textit{if } \mathsf{len}(N) \ne 96, \end{cases}$$
$$N_i = \mathsf{inc}(N_{i-1}) \textit{ for } 1 \le i \le n,$$
$$C_i = P_i \oplus E_K(N_i) \textit{ for } 1 \le i \le n-1,$$
$$C_n = P_n \oplus \mathsf{msb}_m(E_K(N_n))$$
$$C = C_1||C_2||\cdots||C_n,$$

where GHASH is a keyed hash function that will be described later.

GCM follows the Enc-then-MAC (EtM) paradigm, i.e. computing authentication tags from ciphertexts. The authentication tag T is computed by GMAC, defined as

$$T = \mathsf{GMAC}_{H,t}(A, C) = \mathsf{msb}_t(\mathsf{GHASH}_H(A, C) \oplus E_K(N_0)). \tag{1}$$

$\mathsf{GHASH}_H(\cdot,\cdot)$ is a polynomial-based hash function defined over $GF(2^{128})$, and $\mathsf{GHASH}_H(s)$ denotes $\mathsf{GHASH}_H(0^0, s)$, i.e. the first parameter is an empty bit-string. Suppose w and v are two bit-strings, $\mathsf{len}(w) = 128(n_1-1) + m_1$ and $\mathsf{len}(v) = 128(n_2-1) + m_2$ for $1 \le m_1, m_2 \le 128$. Segment w and v into $w_1||w_2||\cdots||w_{m_1}$ and $v = v_1||v_2||\cdots||v_{m_2}$ respectively, where $\mathsf{len}(w_i) = 128$ for $1 \le i \le n_1-1$, $\mathsf{len}(v_i) = 128$ for $1 \le i \le n_2-1$, $\mathsf{len}(w_{n_1}) = m_1$, and $\mathsf{len}(v_{n_2}) = m_2$. By using the following notation,

$$B_i = \begin{cases} w_i & \text{for } 1 \le i \le n_1 - 1, \\ w_i||0^{128-m_1} & \text{for } i = n_1, \\ v_i & \text{for } n_1+1 \le i \le n_1+n_2-1, \\ v_i||0^{128-m_2} & \text{for } i = n_1+n_2, \\ \mathsf{str}_{64}(\mathsf{len}(w))||\mathsf{str}_{64}(\mathsf{len}(v)) & \text{for } i = n_1+n_2+1, \end{cases}$$

the computation of $\mathsf{GHASH}_H(w, v)$ is defined as

$$\sum_{i=1}^{n_1+n_2+1} B_i H^{n_1+n_2+2-i}.$$

One important requirement when using GCM is that nonces must be distinct. Once an IV is reused, the counter numbers N_i used in the Counter Mode of encryption will be the same, and thus exclusive-oring two ciphertexts will eliminate the key stream and get information about plaintexts. Another reason of forbidding IV reuse is well explained in Joux's *forbidden attack* [10], i.e. same nonces will result in identical $E_K(N_0)$ used in the equation (1) and by exclusive-oring two authentication tags we will get an equation on H over finite fields that may be easily solved.

For simplicity, in the following content, A, P and C are considered being multiples of 128 bits, and N is also a multiple of 128 bits if $\mathsf{len}(N) \neq 96$, such that all inputs do not need to be padded. If not stated explicitly, A is regarded as an empty bit-string. Moreover, as in [17], the indices of input blocks are reversed, e.g. $P = P_n || P_{n-1} || \cdots || P_1$ instead of $P = P_1 || P_2 || \cdots || P_n$, for convenience of polynomial representations.

2.3 Security Definitions

For a fixed but unknown master key K of GCM, adversaries are given two oracles, *encryption oracle* and *decryption oracle*. Adversaries can feed a tuple (N, P) to the encryption oracle to get (C, T), or query the decryption oracle with (N, C, T). The decryption oracle will return P if T passes verification, or *FAIL* otherwise. Adversaries are assumed to be nonce-respecting, i.e. no repeating nonces are queried to the encryption oracle, which is not allowed in GCM or Counter Mode.

One of adversaries' goals is to construct *MAC forgeries*. In this case, adversaries aim to create a valid authentication tag T for (N, C), which has not been queried yet. Adversaries can make any queries except (N, C) to the encryption and decryption oracles. If adversaries target only MAC schemes, they can be given two oracles, *authentication oracle* and *verification oracle*. The authentication oracle produces T for queried (N, C); while the verification oracle returns *FAIL* if T is not valid for (N, C), or returns *PASS* otherwise.

Analysis of a cryptographic algorithm's *weak keys* is a very important assessment. Handschuh and Preneel give a theoretical definition of weak keys for symmetric cryptosystems in [6]: "A class of keys is called *weak* if for members of the class the algorithm behaves in an unexpected way and if it is easy to detect whether a particular key belongs to this class." For example, for a MAC scheme, the unexpected behavior may be that MAC forgeries can be made in a very high probability. Moreover, to determine whether a key is in the class $\mathcal{K}$, the number of queries has to be fewer than exhaustive search's, i.e. $|\mathcal{K}|$.

3 Revisiting Weak Keys of Polynomial-Based MACs

In [16,17], Procter and Cid study the weak keys and MAC forgeries of polynomial-based MAC schemes, including the one used in GCM. This is a more general model upon Saarinen's cycling attack [19].

The main framework of MACs, in which they are interested, is based on *evaluation hash* [20]. Let $\mathbb{F}$ be a finite field of characteristic 2, $H \in \mathbb{F}$ be the authentication key, and $M = M_m||M_{m-1}||\cdots||M_1$ be a message to be authenticated, where $M_i \in \mathbb{F}$. Define a polynomial $g_M(x) \in \mathbb{F}[x]$ as

$$g_M(x) = \sum_{i=1}^{m} M_i x^i.$$

Then the function $h_H(M) = g_M(H)$ is called *evaluation hash.* The hash function outputs are masked by block cipher encryptions to produce the authentication tags, such as $E_K(N) \oplus h_H(M)$ and $E_K(h_H(M))$. Poly1305-AES [2], and the MAC schemes in GCM and SGCM [19] are all within this framework.

We summarize the main observation by Procter and Cid in [17] as follows. For the convenience of the readers, we include a short proof of their result.

Result 1 ([17]). *With the same notation as above, if there exists a polynomial $f(x) \in \mathbb{F}[x]$ without a constant term, such that $f(H) = 0$, then forgeries of MAC schemes based on the evaluation hash $h_H(x)$ can be made.*

Proof. Assume

$$f(x) = \sum_{i=1}^{n} F_i x^i,$$

and $F = F_n||F_{n-1}||\cdots||F_1$. Given a message M, we have

$$h_H(M \oplus F) = g_{M\oplus F}(H) = g_M(H) \oplus f(H) = g_M(H) = h_H(M),$$

where the shorter one of M and F in $M \oplus F$ is padded with zeros. We obtain a collision on the evaluation hash, and thus a MAC forgery of the MAC scheme. □

After obtaining a valid tuple (N, C, T) by eavesdropping or active querying, the adversaries query the verification oracle about $(N, C \oplus F, T)$. If the result is not *FAIL*, then a valid MAC is forged. Please note that the polynomial $f(x)$ always has x as its factor, and is in the ideal $\langle x^2 \oplus Hx \rangle$.

For an unknown H, the success probability of MAC forgery is directly related to the choice of $f(x)$. Procter and Cid propose three ways to select $f(x)$: (1) The first way is to use $f(x) = x\prod_i(x \oplus H_i)$ to involve as many H_i as desired; (2) The second way is based on irreducible factors of $x^{2^{128}} \oplus x$, which includes Saarinen's cycling attack as a special case; (3) The third is just using random polynomials.

In the next section, we will show that, a MAC forgery can also be made for any polynomial $f(x) \in \mathbb{F}[x]$, which is an extension of Result 1.

Moreover, based on these analyses, Procter and Cid point out that almost any subset of the key space of these polynomial-based MAC schemes is a weak key class.

Result 2 ([17]). *Let $\mathcal{H}$ be a subset of the authentication key space of the MAC scheme based on evaluation hash. If $0 \in \mathcal{H}$ and $|\mathcal{H}| \geq 2$, or $|\mathcal{H}| \geq 3$, then $\mathcal{H}$ is weak.*

Proof. If $|\mathcal{H}| \geq 2$ and $0 \in \mathcal{H}$, one query forged by $f(x) = x\prod_i(x \oplus H_i)$ can be fed into the verification oracle, where $H_i \in \mathcal{H}$. To further determine whether 0 is in the set $\mathcal{H}$, two queries by distinct $f(x) \in \langle x^2 \oplus Hx \rangle$ have to be made, so all elements in a subset $|\mathcal{H}| \geq 3$ can be detected by using two queries. □

3.1 New Improved MAC Forgery Attacks

The MAC forgery attacks proposed by Procter and Cid are constructed upon hash collisions, and one of the attacks' restrictions is that the chosen polynomial $f(x)$ should always have x as a factor, or equivalently do not have a constant term. We will demonstrate below how to create MAC forgeries not based on hash collisions, and without the zero constant term restriction.

For the MAC schemes as in GCM and SGCM, whose final masking by block ciphers is computed additively, we give the following theorem, where the notation is the same as above.

Theorem 1. *Given any polynomial $q(x) \in \mathbb{F}[x]$ such that $q(H) = 0$, for the evaluation hash based MAC scheme $T = E_K(N) \oplus h_H(M)$, a MAC forgery can be constructed.*

Proof. Let Q^* be the concatenation of coefficients $Q_n||Q_{n-1}||\cdots||Q_1$ without Q_0, and $q(x) = q^*(x) \oplus Q_0$. Since $q(H) = 0$, we have

$$T = h_H(M) \oplus E_k(N) = h_H(M) \oplus E_k(N) \oplus q(H),$$

which implies

$$\begin{aligned} T \oplus Q_0 &= E_k(N) \oplus h_H(M) \oplus q^*(H) \\ &= E_k(N) \oplus g_M(H) \oplus q^*(H) \\ &= E_k(N) \oplus g_{M \oplus Q^*}(H). \end{aligned}$$

This means if we know a polynomial $q(x)$ such that $q(H) = 0$, we can exclusive-or coefficients of $q(x)$'s non-constant terms with the captured message, to obtain a valid tuple as $(N, M \oplus Q^*, T \oplus Q_0)$, if the authentication tag T is computed as $E_k(N) \oplus h_H(M)$. □

Please note that the method in the above proof does not rely on a hash collision, and the constant term Q_0 is not required to be zero. We also want to mention that Theorem 1 leads us to an extension to the original analysis of Procter and Cid on weak keys, which will be discussed in the next subsection.

A practical attack example on GCM, by using the method in Theorem 1 (along with a length extension technique), is given in Appendix A.1.

For the sake of completeness, we also give the following theorem, which works for both $E_K(N) \oplus h_H(M)$ and $E_K(h_H(M))$.

Theorem 2. *Given any polynomial $q(x) \in \mathbb{F}[x]$ such that $q(H) = 0$, a forgery can be made on the MAC schemes based on evaluation hash by using $\alpha(x)q(x)$, where $\alpha(x)$ is a polynomial without a constant term.*

Proof. Since $q(H) = 0$, we have $\alpha(H)q(H) = 0$. Because $\alpha(0) = 0$, $\alpha(0)q(0) = 0$. Therefore, we can apply the same method in Result 1 to construct hash collisions and thus MAC forgeries. □

Theorem 2 can be seen as covered by the analysis of Procter and Cid, since $\alpha(x)q(x)$ is still in the ideal $\langle x^2 \oplus Hx\rangle$. However, Theorem 2 is insufficient to deduce the result about weak key classes (Theorem 3 in the next subsection) supported by Theorem 1.

3.2 All Non-singleton Subsets of Keys are Weak

To detect whether an authentication key H is in a subset $\mathcal{H}$ of the key space, the number of queries should be less than $|\mathcal{H}|$. If $|\mathcal{H}| = 2$, only one query can be made, and thus whether zero is in $\mathcal{H}$ cannot be determined by using polynomials in $\langle x^2 \oplus Hx\rangle$, since it will need at least two queries. However, based on the analysis of Theorem 1, we may use polynomials in $\langle x \oplus H\rangle$ instead of $\langle x^2 \oplus Hx\rangle$ to make one query and determine whether the authentication key is in $\mathcal{H}$.

Theorem 3. *For an evaluation hash based MAC scheme, $T = E_K(N) \oplus h_H(M)$, if given a valid tuple (N, M, T), then making one query to the verification oracle is enough to determine whether the authentication key $H \in \mathbb{F}$ in use is in a subset of keys $\mathcal{H} = \{H_1, H_2, \cdots, H_n\} \subseteq \mathbb{F}$.*

Proof. First define a polynomial

$$q(x) = \sum_{i=0}^{n} Q_i x^i = \prod_{i=1}^{n} (x \oplus H_i),$$

where $Q_i \in \mathbb{F}$ for $0 \le i \le n$. Let $M' = M \oplus Q^*$ and $T' = T \oplus Q_0$ with zero pre-padding for shorter strings, where $Q^* = Q_n || Q_{n-1} || \cdots || Q_1$. Query the verification oracle with the tuple (N, M', T'). If the verification oracle does not return *FAIL*, the authentication key H in use is known to be in $\mathcal{H}$. H is not in $\mathcal{H}$ if *FAIL* is returned.

It is easy to see H is in $\mathcal{H}$ if and only if (N, M', T') passes. If H is in $\mathcal{H}$, then $q(H) = 0$, and thus (N, M', T') is valid. On the other hand, the validity of (N, M', T') implies $q(H) = 0$, so H must be a root of $q(x) = 0$, which is among all the elements of $\mathcal{H}$. □

The steps in Theorem 3 are similar to those in [17], except the absence of the steps to determine whether 0 is in $\mathcal{H}$.

Based on Theorem 3, we have the following corollary about weak key classes.

Corollary 1. *For an evaluation hash based MAC scheme, $T = E_K(N) \oplus h_H(M)$, any subset of authentication key space, $\mathcal{H}$, is weak if $|\mathcal{H}| \ge 2$.*

Proof. Due to Theorem 3, after obtaining a valid tuple (N, M, T) by passive eavesdropping, whether the authentication key H in use is the subset $\mathcal{H}$ can be determined by only one query, which is efficient compared to the size of the subset, i.e. $1 < |\mathcal{H}|$.

On the other hand, once H is known to be in the subset $\mathcal{H}$, H is a solution for $q(x) = \prod_{i=1}^{n}(x \oplus H_i) = 0$, where H_i's are all elements of $\mathcal{H}$. Then the polynomial $\alpha(x)q(x)$ with an arbitrary non-zero $\alpha(x)$ can be used to construct more MAC forgeries. □

4 Turning MAC Forgeries into Birthday Attacks

In [8], Iwata *et al.* find a flaw in the security proofs of GCM given by McGrew and Viega in [13]. The main problem is that inc may be translated to multiple distinct forms in terms of exclusive-ors, such that the equation

$$\mathsf{inc}^{r_1}(\mathsf{GHASH}_H(N^a)) = \mathsf{inc}^{r_2}(\mathsf{GHASH}_H(N^b)) \tag{2}$$

may have many more solutions than the desired $l_N + 1$ for any given r_1, r_2, N^a and N^b, where $0 \leq r_1, r_2 \leq 2^{32} - 2$, $N^a \neq N^b$, and l_N is the maximum number of blocks for nonces.

Result 3 ([8]). *For a randomly chosen H, the probability for the equation (2) to hold is at most*

$$2^{22}(l_N + 1)/2^{128}.$$

Furthermore, for n queries to the encryption oracle with the nonces N^i's, where $1 \leq i \leq n$, the probability of having a collision on counter numbers, i.e. $N^a_{r_1} = N^b_{r_2}$ for certain r_1, r_2, a and b, is at most

$$\frac{2^{22}(n-1)(\sigma + n)(l_N + 1)}{2^{128}}, \tag{3}$$

where $0 \leq r_1, r_2 \leq 2^{32} - 2$, $1 \leq a, b \leq n$, the total length of plaintexts is at most σ blocks, and N^a and N^b are the corresponding nonces for the counter numbers $N^a_{r_1}$ and $N^b_{r_2}$ respectively.

4.1 New Birthday-Bound-Based MAC Forgery Attacks on GCM

The original forgery attacks on polynomial-based MAC schemes, including our attacks described in Section 3.1, are targeting algebraic properties of underlying evaluation hash functions, e.g., GHASH in the case of GCM. The forged queries cannot be fed to the encryption oracle directly because two queries with identical nonces are forbidden.

The work by Iwata *et al.* reminds us that GCM has a very special design, in which GHASH is reused for generating initial counter numbers if $\mathsf{len}(N) \neq 96$. This makes GHASH attackable in the encryption oracle. Precisely, assuming $H \neq 0$, the attack consists of the following three steps:

1. Either passively or actively obtain a valid tuple (N, P, C), where $\mathsf{len}(N) \neq 96$. Please note that we do not need the authentication tag T here.
2. Construct a polynomial $q(x)$, and properly apply $x^d q(x)$ to N to derive N', where $d \geq 1$. Feed the pair (N', P) to the encryption oracle, and get the corresponding ciphertext C'. If $C' = C$, we know that $q(H) = 0$.
3. Apply $q(x)$ to other captured messages and tags to construct more forgeries, or recover the authentication key by binary search or solving $q(x) = 0$.

If $H = 0$, the outputs of GMAC will be the same, and thus it can be easily detected.

One advantage of targeting the encryption oracle is that we can collect all query results into a set to perform birthday attacks. For any query to the encryption oracle, we can always get corresponding ciphertext and tag as long as the nonce is not previously queried. Using the same notation in the specification of GCM in Algorithm 1, collect $E_K(N_1)$'s, which are derived from exclusive-oring P_1's with C_1's, into a set $\mathcal{S}$. If a collision occurs in $\mathcal{S}$, e.g. $E_K(N_1^a) = E_K(N_1^b)$, where N_1^a and N_1^b are the corresponding first counter numbers for the nonces N^a and N^b, then we have $N_1^a = N_1^b$ as well. Hence a collision $\mathsf{GHASH}_H(N^a) = \mathsf{GHASH}_H(N^b)$ is found. This birthday collision attack can have a significantly higher success probability than the original attacks on the verification or decryption oracle.

Assume the polynomial $q(x)$ is chosen randomly and independently, and $H \neq 0$. The success probability for the original trial-and-error method on the verification or decryption oracle is

$$n(l_N + 1)/2^{128}, \tag{4}$$

where n is the number of queries that have been made; while the upper bound for the probability of the birthday attack is (see Lemma A.9 in Section A.4 of [11])

$$0.5 \cdot n^2(l_N + 1)/2^{128}. \tag{5}$$

In addition to the first encrypted counter blocks, we can also collect the following blocks into $\mathcal{S}$, in which way we may achieve even larger collision probabilities. For example, $E_K(N_i^a)$ may be equal to $E_K(N_j^b)$ for certain i and j. The collision probability for this case can be obtained from the equation (3) in Result 3. Although the success probability of this case is higher than the previous methods of trial-and-error and birthday attacks, the collision $N_i^a = N_j^b$ may need more time complexity to be utilized for MAC forgery attacks. One naive way is to try every polynomial over the finite field that can be converted from inc^r with the specific r, and this will cost 2^{22} time at most.

Moreover, if certain countermeasures on the decryption or verification oracle are carried out, such as forbidding nonce reuse, the original attacks would fail or be detected, but the attacks on the encryption oracle will be unaffected.

A practical attack example on non-96-bit nonces is given in Appendix A.2.

5 Revisiting Provable Security of GCM

After pointing out the flaw in GCM's original security proofs, Iwata *et al.* give new security bounds, which are characterized by *privacy advantage* and *authenticity advantage.* Please refer to [13,8,9] for the detailed definitions of privacy and authenticity advantages.

Result 4 ([16,17]). *The privacy advantage of GCM is at most*

$$\frac{0.5(\sigma+q+1)^2}{2^{128}}+\frac{2^{22}q(\sigma+q)(l_N+1)}{2^{128}}, \tag{6}$$

and the upper bound for the authenticity advantage is

$$\frac{0.5(\sigma+q+q'+1)^2}{2^{128}}+\frac{2^{22}(q+q'+1)(\sigma+q)(l_N+1)}{2^{128}}+\frac{q'(l_A+1)}{2^t}, \tag{7}$$

where the total length of plaintexts is at most σ blocks, q and q' are numbers of encryption and decryption queries respectively, and l_N and l_A are the maximum numbers of blocks for nonces and inputs respectively.

Generally, the values of the equations (6) and (7) are dominated by their second terms, since they have a large constant 2^{22}.

5.1 Repairing GCM and Its Security Bounds

Here we propose a method to fix the design of GCM such that the large constant 2^{22} in the equations (6) and (7) can be reduced to 2^2. Since the flaw of the GCM's security proofs originates from the operation inc as explained in the previous section, we aim to replace the functionality of inc with operations in the finite field.

Consider $w \cdot x$, where w is a primitive element of $\mathbb{F}_{2^n}$. It is clear that the outputs of $w \cdot x$ consist of two cycles, namely (0) and $(1, w, \ldots, w^{2^n-2})$. Now define a new function L_w as

$$L_w(x) = \begin{cases} w \cdot x & \text{if } x = w^i,\ 0 \le i \le 2^n-3, \\ 0 & \text{if } x = w^{2^n-2}, \\ 1 & \text{if } x = 0. \end{cases} \tag{8}$$

The following theorem is important for our discussions in this subsection.

Theorem 4. *Let L_w be the function defined above, and f, g be two functions defined on $\mathbb{F}_{2^n}$ with $f(0), g(0) \neq 0$. Denoting $\deg(f) = d_1, \deg(g) = d_2$ and $d = \max(d_1, d_2)$, we have*

$$\max_{0 \le r \le 2^n-1} |\{x : x \in \mathbb{F}_{2^n} | L_w^r(f(x)) + g(x) = 0\}| \le 4d.$$

Proof. Now we consider the number of solutions of the equation

$$L_w^r(f(x)) + g(x) = 0, \tag{9}$$

where $0 \le r \le 2^n - 1$. The equation (9) can be divided into the following cases.

1. If $f(x) = 0$,
   (a) If $L_w^r(f(x)) = 0$, then $g(x) = 0$.
   (b) If $L_w^r(f(x)) \neq 0$, then $g(x) = w^{r-1}$.
2. If $f(x) \neq 0$,
   (a) If $L_w^r(f(x)) = 0$, then $g(x) = 0$.
   (b) If $L_w^r(f(x)) \neq 0$, let $f(x) = w^{r_1}$ and $L_w^r(f(x)) = w^{r_2}$, where $0 \le r_1, r_2 < 2^n - 1$. Then we have
      i. If $r_1 \le r_2$, then $w^r f(x) = g(x)$.
      ii. If $r_1 > r_2$, then $w^{r-1} f(x) = g(x)$.

Therefore, for a given r, any solution of the equation $L_w^r(f(x)) + g(x) = 0$ must be one of the solutions of the four equations

$$\begin{cases} g(x) = 0, \\ g(x) = w^{r-1}, \\ w^r f(x) = g(x), \\ w^{r-1} f(x) = g(x). \end{cases}$$

The total number of solutions for these four equations are at most $2d_2 + 2d \le 4d$. □

It is known that the detailed design of the next counter function of Counter Mode is not important as long as counter numbers are produced uniquely [14]. If the underlying block cipher is ideal, i.e. treated as a pseudorandom permutation PRP for randomly chosen encryption key, $\mathsf{PRP}(L_w^r(s))$ is indistinguishable from $\mathsf{PRP}(\mathsf{inc}^r(s))$. Therefore, the Counter Mode encryption in GCM will have same security properties as original if inc is replaced by L_w defined over $\mathbb{F}$. We propose the following revised design of GCM.

Algorithm 2. *The encryption steps of the revised GCM, denoted by LGCM, are as follows.*

$$\begin{aligned} N_0 &= \mathit{GHASH}_H(N), \\ N_i &= L_w^i(N_0) \text{ for } 1 \le i \le n, \\ C_i &= P_i \oplus E_K(N_i) \text{ for } 1 \le i \le n-1, \\ C_n &= P_n \oplus \mathit{msb}_m(E_K(N_n)), \\ C &= C_1 || C_2 || \cdots || C_n, \end{aligned}$$

where the notation is the same as in Algorithm 1.

Please note that nonces are always processed by GHASH regardless of nonces' lengths, for simplicity of security proofs.

Based on Theorem 4, we can have the following lemma.

Lemma 1. *Randomly choosing an authentication key H, the probability to have*

$$L_w^{r_1}(\mathsf{GHASH}_H(N_1)) = L_w^{r_2}(\mathsf{GHASH}_H(N_2)) \tag{10}$$

is no more than $4(l_N + 1)/2^{128}$ for any given r_1, r_2, N_1 and N_2, where $0 \leq r_1, r_2 \leq 2^{32} - 2$, $N_1 \neq N_2$, and l_N is the maximum number of blocks for nonces.

Proof. Without loss of generality, assume $r_2 \leq r_1$, then the equation (10) is equivalent to

$$L_w^{r_1 - r_2}(\mathsf{GHASH}_H(N_1)) = \mathsf{GHASH}_H(N_2). \tag{11}$$

The maximum degree of $\mathsf{GHASH}_H(N_1)$ and $\mathsf{GHASH}_H(N_2)$ is $l_N + 1$, so by applying Theorem 4 we know the probability for the equation (11) to hold is $4(l_N + 1)/2^{128}$ for a randomly chosen H. □

Now we can give the security bounds of LGCM as follows.

Theorem 5. *For LGCM, the revised GCM algorithm defined in Algorithm 2, the privacy advantage is at most*

$$\frac{0.5(\sigma + q + 1)^2}{2^{128}} + \frac{4q(\sigma + q)(l_N + 1)}{2^{128}}, \tag{12}$$

and the new upper bound for the authenticity advantage is

$$\frac{0.5(\sigma + q + q' + 1)^2}{2^{128}} + \frac{4(q + q' + 1)(\sigma + q)(l_N + 1)}{2^{128}} + \frac{q'(l_A + 1)}{2^t}, \tag{13}$$

where the notation is the same as in Result 4.

Proof. The proofs of Theorems 1 and 2 in [9] can be carried over by using Lemma 1 in the paper to replace the original probability statement of counter number collisions. □

Implementation against Timing-Based Side-Channel Attacks

The functions defined in (8) have vulnerabilities for timing-based side-channel attacks since the computations will have inconsistent times for different inputs. To minimize such effects, we may use the following equations in practical implementations.

$$y = w \cdot x,$$
$$L_w(x) = \begin{cases} 1 & \text{if } y = 0, \\ 0 & \text{if } y = 1, \\ y & \text{otherwise.} \end{cases} \tag{14}$$

The equations (14) would have very close computational time costs for different branches.

We want to make a note here that it might be possible to directly adopt $w \cdot x$ instead of $L_w(x)$ to generate counter numbers since the probability for GHASH to output zero is low, but the security proofs for GCM may require to be largely rewritten and new bounds might have different formats as existing ones. We leave this as an open problem for interested readers.

6 Attacking GCM in MAC-then-Enc Mode

GCM follows the Enc-then-MAC paradigm, i.e. authentication tag is computed based on ciphertexts. It is known that once the integrity of the system is compromised, the whole system including privacy will not be trustworthy. For GCM, if we successfully perform a MAC forgery attack described in previous sections, e.g., a forged tuple (N, C', T'), based on a valid (N, C, T), is fed to the decryption oracle and passes verification, the oracle will return P' that may have a known linear difference with P. In this way, P can be obtained even without any knowledge of the encryption key. Therefore, the message authentication algorithm must be well protected.

One potential and straightforward option, which is indicated in [16,17], is to change GCM to a MAC-then-Enc scheme (MtE GCM, thereafter). More precisely, in MtE GCM, GMAC is computed based on plaintexts instead of ciphertexts, and the authentication tag is encrypted by block ciphers in Counter Mode.

However, we find that the MAC forgery attacks described in previous sections may still work on MtE GCM. These attacks are based on the linear properties of the polynomial-based MAC schemes. Assuming no length extension is needed, applying $q(x)$ directly to ciphertexts and encrypted tags may successfully result in MAC forgeries. Consider the simplified case with

$$\begin{aligned} ET &= h_H(P) \oplus E_K(N) \oplus E_K(N_t) \\ &= h_H(P) \oplus \mathsf{Mask} \\ &= h_H(C \oplus S) \oplus \mathsf{Mask}, \end{aligned}$$

where ET is the encrypted authentication tag, $E_K(N_t)$ is to encrypt the authentication tag, $\mathsf{Mask} = E_K(N) \oplus E_K(N_t)$, S is the key stream produced by Counter Mode, and the other variables are the same as in previous analyses. If we know a function $q(x)$ such that $q(H) = 0$, then

$$\begin{aligned} ET' = ET \oplus Q_0 &= h_H(C \oplus S) \oplus q^*(H) \oplus \mathsf{Mask} \\ &= g_{C \oplus S}(H) \oplus g_{Q^*}(H) \oplus \mathsf{Mask} \\ &= g_{C \oplus Q^* \oplus S}(H) \oplus \mathsf{Mask} \\ &= h_H(C \oplus Q^* \oplus S) \oplus \mathsf{Mask} \\ &= h_H(C' \oplus S) \oplus \mathsf{Mask}. \end{aligned}$$

This implies the tuple (N, C', ET'), where $C' = C \oplus Q^*$ and $ET' = ET \oplus Q_0$, will pass the verification oracle of MtE GCM. A computational example is given in Appendix A.3.

If $\mathsf{len}(Q^*) > \mathsf{len}(C)$, i.e. length extension is needed, the above attack on MtE GCM may not work. To decrypt $C \oplus Q^*$, where $\mathsf{len}(C \oplus Q^*) > \mathsf{len}(C)$, the verification oracle will produce longer key stream $S' = S || S_u$ with an unknown portion S_u, so outputs of the oracle will become unpredictable. However, adversaries may avoid this by trying to attack GHASH in the encryption oracle as discussed in Section 4.1, or simply waiting for longer ciphertexts.

Therefore, we can see that changing GCM into MAC-then-Enc paradigm would add little strength against these MAC forgery attacks.

7 Concluding Remarks

This paper revisits weak key classes of polynomial-based MAC schemes and provable security of GCM. We demonstrate that hash collisions are not necessary to construct successful MAC forgeries and any polynomials can be used in these attacks, which removes the restrictions in Procter and Cid's attacks. Based on these new discoveries on MAC forgeries, we prove that all subsets of keys with no less than two elements are weak key classes for GCM-like polynomial-based MAC schemes, which is an extension to Procter and Cid's analysis on weak keys. Moreover, we present a novel approach to transform these MAC forgery attacks into birthday attacks to increase their success probabilities. The success probabilities of these attacks are summarized in Table 1. Furthermore, we provide a method to fix GCM in order to avoid the security proof flaw discovered by Iwata *et al.* and significantly improve the security bounds. In addition, we show that these MAC forgeries attacks would still succeed if GCM is modified to MAC-then-Enc paradigm, as one of the options mentioned in [16,17], such that authentication tags are protected by Counter Mode encryptions.

Table 1. Comparisons of success probabilities of MAC forgery attacks

Method	Success Probability	Reference
Trial-and-Error	$n(l_N+1)/2^{128}$	[16,17]
Birthday Attack	$\leq 0.5 \cdot n^2(l_N+1)/2^{128}$	Section 4.1
Birthday Attack with inc	$\leq 2^{22}(n-1)(n+\sigma)(l_N+1)/2^{128}$	Section 4.1

Future work may include improving the probability analyses in Section 4.1. Certain probabilities for collisions and MAC forgeries are characterized by upper bounds rather than average estimations. If more accurate probabilities can be derived, this work may also, in return, improve the security bounds given by Iwata *et al.* on the original GCM design.

As recommended in [8,9], we further suggest that GCM may preferably be used with 96-bit nonces. For example, an altered version of GCM was introduced by Aoki and Yasuda in [1], which only accepts a fixed-length nonce. Reusing GHASH in both generating initial counter numbers and computing authentication tags may help attackers to amplify their success probabilities for MAC forgeries as we discussed in Section 4.1. For practical applications that have to use non-96-bit nonces, we suggest applying the fix to GCM proposed in Section 5.1, i.e. using LGCM defined in Algorithm 2, which could tighten the security bounds by a factor of around 2^{20}.

Acknowledgments. The authors would like to thank the anonymous reviewer for the helpful comments. This work is supported by NSERC Discovery Grant and ORF-RE Grant.

References

1. Aoki, K., Yasuda, K.: The security and performance of "GCM" when short multiplications are used instead. In: Kutyłowski, M., Yung, M. (eds.) Inscrypt 2012. LNCS, vol. 7763, pp. 225–245. Springer, Heidelberg (2013)
2. Bernstein, D.J.: The Poly1305-AES message-authentication code. In: Gilbert, H., Handschuh, H. (eds.) FSE 2005. LNCS, vol. 3557, pp. 32–49. Springer, Heidelberg (2005)
3. CAESAR. Competition for Authenticated Encryption: Security, Applicability, and Robustness, `http://competitions.cr.yp.to/caesar.html`
4. Dworkin, M.J.: SP 800-38D. Recommendation for block cipher modes of operation: Galois/Counter Mode (GCM) and GMAC. Technical report, Gaithersburg, MD, United States (2007)
5. Ferguson, N.: Authentication weaknesses in GCM. Comments Submitted to NIST Modes of Operation Process (2005)
6. Handschuh, H., Preneel, B.: Key-recovery attacks on universal hash function based MAC algorithms. In: Wagner, D. (ed.) CRYPTO 2008. LNCS, vol. 5157, pp. 144–161. Springer, Heidelberg (2008)
7. IEEE 802.1AE. Media access control (MAC) security (2006), `http://www.ieee802.org/1/pages/802.1ae.html`
8. Iwata, T., Ohashi, K., Minematsu, K.: Breaking and repairing GCM security proofs. In: Safavi-Naini, R., Canetti, R. (eds.) CRYPTO 2012. LNCS, vol. 7417, pp. 31–49. Springer, Heidelberg (2012)
9. Iwata, T., Ohashi, K., Minematsu, K.: Breaking and repairing GCM security proofs. Cryptology ePrint Archive, Report 2012/438 (2012), `http://eprint.iacr.org/`
10. Joux, A.: Authentication failures in NIST version of GCM. NIST Comment (2006)
11. Katz, J., Lindell, Y.: Introduction to modern cryptography. Chapman & Hall (2008)
12. McGrew, D., Viega, J.: The Galois/Counter Mode of operation (GCM). Submission to NIST Modes of Operation Process (2004)
13. McGrew, D.A., Viega, J.: The security and performance of the Galois/Counter Mode (GCM) of operation. In: Canteaut, A., Viswanathan, K. (eds.) INDOCRYPT 2004. LNCS, vol. 3348, pp. 343–355. Springer, Heidelberg (2004)
14. McGrew, D.A.: Counter mode security: Analysis and recommendations (2002), `http://www.mindspring.com/~dmcgrew/ctr-security.pdf`
15. NSA. Suite B Cryptography (2005), `http://www.nsa.gov/ia/programs/suiteb_cryptography/`
16. Procter, G., Cid, C.: On weak keys and forgery attacks against polynomial-based MAC schemes. In: Fast Software Encryption.LNCS. Springer (to appear, 2013)
17. Procter, G., Cid, C.: On weak keys and forgery attacks against polynomial-based MAC schemes. Cryptology ePrint Archive, Report 2013/144 (2013), `http://eprint.iacr.org/`
18. Rogaway, P.: Authenticated-encryption with associated-data. In: Proceedings of the 9th ACM Conference on Computer and Communications Security, CCS 2002, pp. 98–107. ACM, New York (2002)
19. Saarinen, M.-J.O.: Cycling attacks on GCM, GHASH and other polynomial MACs and hashes. In: Canteaut, A. (ed.) FSE 2012. LNCS, vol. 7549, pp. 216–225. Springer, Heidelberg (2012)

20. Shoup, V.: On fast and provably secure message authentication based on universal hashing. In: Koblitz, N. (ed.) CRYPTO 1996. LNCS, vol. 1109, pp. 313–328. Springer, Heidelberg (1996)
21. Viega, J., McGrew, D.A.: The use of Galois/Counter Mode (GCM) in IPsec encapsulating security payload, ESP (2005), `http://tools.ietf.org/html/rfc4106.html`

Appendix A Practical Attack Examples

A.1 A Example for Forgeries by Polynomials with Non-zero Constant Terms

This example is for GCM with AES-128 and 128-bit authentication tags, and the associated data A is always considered as empty. We use the same representations as the test vectors in GCM's specification [12], e.g. 1 in GF(2^{128}) is represented as 80000000000000000000000000000000, and longer strings will written in multiple lines.

We take the following values for the encryption of GCM. The lengths of P and C are 128 bits, i.e. one block.

K	71eebc49c8fb773b2224eaff3ad68714
N	07e961e67784011f72faafd95b0eb640
	89c8de15ad685ec57e63d56e679d3e20
	2b18b75fcbbec3185ffc41653bc2ac4a
	e6ae8be8c85636f353a9d19a86100d0b
P	705da82292143d2c949dc4ba014f6396
H	d27430c121f14d4ddfecb38acaffec53
C	251ccc6d2c45540cac4fde8b1e36802d
T	be2da05993fbde00421c1d8eaaaea373

Suppose we have a subset of authentication keys $\mathcal{H} = \{H_1, H_2, H_3\}$, whose values are as follows.

H_1	d27430c121f14d4ddfecb38acaffec53
H_2	00000000000000000000000000000001
H_3	00000000000000000000000000000002

Construct the polynomial

$$q(x) = \sum_{i=0}^{3} Q_i x^i = \prod_{i=1}^{3} (x \oplus H_i),$$

we can get the values for Q_i's.

Q_3	80000000000000000000000000000000
Q_2	d27430c121f14d4ddfecb38acaffec50
Q_1	c488aa211ab5dccec9c440bc33fc47b3
Q_0	5bb5716dc4b4687a06f15f10d62613ee

Please note $q(x)$ is a polynomial with non-zero constant term, i.e. $Q_0 \neq 0$.

Then compute $\alpha = (1 \oplus 2)/Q_0 =$ 7ef05dd871ead7e7f8e79d7d9343a170, such that $\alpha \cdot Q_1 \oplus 1$ will match the length of new message, i.e. 2. Construct the new ciphertext $C' = (\alpha \cdot Q_3)||(C \oplus \alpha \cdot Q_2)$, and the authentication tag $T' = T \oplus \alpha \cdot Q_0$.

C'	7ef05dd871ead7e7f8e79d7d9343a170
	7ccbd8dbfca54d785f5662d48c7eef81
T'	8b53b318750a2e948459b204e47629b4

(N, C', T') passes the verification, and thus we complete a MAC forgery with length extension by using a polynomial with a non-zero constant term.

A.2 MAC Forgeries by Attacking Non-96-bit Nonces of GCM

We only give a basic example for this case. The values and the polynomial $q(x)$ computed in the previous example are reused here.

Construct the polynomial $q'(x) = x^2 q(x)$, and apply $q'(x)$ to N to get a new 512-bit nonce N', i.e. $N' = (N_4 \oplus Q_3)||(N_3 \oplus Q_2)||(N_2 \oplus Q_1)||(N_1 \oplus Q_0)$.

N'	87e961e67784011f72faafd95b0eb640
	5bbceed48c991388a18f66e4ad62d270
	ef901d7ed10b1fd6963801d9083eebf9
	bd1bfa850ce25e8955588e8a50361ee5

Feeding (N', P) to the encryption oracle will result in the same ciphertext as C, so we are sure that the authentication H is the set $\mathcal{H}$, and further MAC forgeries can be carried out by using $q(x)$.

A.3 MAC Forgeries for GCM in MAC-then-Enc Mode

The same K, N, H_1, and H_2 as in the previous examples are used. In order to avoid length extension, P is chosen to be longer and H_3 is explicitly chosen to be $H_1 \cdot H_2/(H_1 \oplus H_2)$.

P	705da82292143d2c949dc4ba014f6396
	705da82292143d2c949dc4ba014f6396
C	a51ccc6d2c45540cac4fde8b1e36802d
	a4bd55da5dcde1d763021d44f5fb3ab8
ET	5aba7c39516a4a90f738eaf61b02514a
H_3	6e0b0d1eaf109b0f26926be82780085c

Constructing the polynomial $q(x)$, we can have its coefficients as follows.

Q_3	80000000000000000000000000000000
Q_2	bc7f3ddf8ee1d642f97ed862ed7fe40e
Q_1	00000000000000000000000000000000
Q_0	c52222258b2614c4c6f5981c65f15acd

Please note $Q_1 = 0$, so the length padding block in GHASH can stay unchanged.
The new ciphertext and encrypted authentication tag are $C' = (C_2 \oplus Q_3)||(C_1 \oplus Q_2)$ and $ET' = ET \oplus Q_0$.

C'	a51ccc6d2c45540cac4fde8b1e36802d
	a4bd55da5dcde1d763021d44f5fb3ab8
ET'	5aba7c39516a4a90f738eaf61b02514a

(N, C', ET') passes the verification oracle of MtE GCM.

Padding Oracle Attack on PKCS#1 v1.5: Can Non-standard Implementation Act as a Shelter?

Si Gao, Hua Chen, and Limin Fan

Trusted Computing and Information Assurance Laboratory,
Institute of Software, Chinese Academy of Sciences
{gaosi,chenhua,fanlimin}@tca.iscas.ac.cn

Abstract. In the past decade, Padding Oracle Attacks (POAs) have become a major threat to PKCS#1 v1.5. Although the updated scheme (OAEP) has solved this problem, PKCS#1 v1.5 is still widely deployed in various real-life applications. Among these applications, it is not hard to find that some implementations do not follow PKCS#1 v1.5 step-by-step. Some of these non-standard implementations provide different padding oracles, which causes standard POA to fail. In this paper, we show that although these implementations can avoid the threat of standard POA, they may still be vulnerable to POA in some way. Our study mainly focuses on two cases of non-standard implementations. The first one only performs the "0x00 separator" check in the decryption process; while the other one does not check for the second byte. Although standard POA cannot be directly applied, we can still build efficient padding oracle attacks on these implementations. Moreover, we give the mathematical analysis of the correctness and performance of our attacks. Experiments show that, one of our attacks only takes about 13 000 oracle calls to crack a valid ciphertext under a 1024-bit RSA key, which is even more efficient than attacks on standard PKCS#1 v1.5 implementation. We hope our work could serve as a warning for security engineers: secure implementation requires joint efforts from all participants, rather than simple implementation tricks.

1 Introduction

PKCS#1 is the standard for the implementation of public-key cryptography based on the RSA algorithm. The current version v2.2 [1], published by RSA in 2012, contains two encryption schemes: RSAES_PKCS1_v1.5 and RSAES_OAEP. For simplicity's sake, we denote them as PKCS#1 v1.5 and OAEP respectively. OAEP is required to be supported for new applications, while PKCS#1 v1.5 is included only for compatibility with existing applications.

Padding Oracle Attack. In the past decade, Padding Oracle Attacks (POAs) [2] have become a major threat to PKCS#1 v1.5. Padding Oracle Attack is a type of chosen ciphertext attack, which takes advantage of whether cryptographic operation is successfully executed. Usually, we assume the attacker can

M. Abdalla, C. Nita-Rotaru, and R. Dahab (Eds.): CANS 2013, LNCS 8257, pp. 39–56, 2013.

trick an honest user to decrypt the ciphertext he chose. In the decryption process, a format check is performed after decryption. Although the attacker does not have access to the decryption result, he can detect whether the ciphertext he chose passes the format check. We call such decryption process a "Padding Oracle" (PO) [3]. By collecting thousands of PO's responses, the original message can be extracted. In the past decade, POAs have drawn major attention from both symmetric and asymmetric cryptography research. In symmetric cryptography, CBC Padding Oracle has been used to build plaintext-recovery attacks on various network protocols [4–9]. In asymmetric cryptography, PKCS#1 v1.5 is the main target. The first POA on PKCS#1 v1.5, published by Bleichenbacher in 1998 [10], took about 1 million PO calls to recover a 1024-bit RSA plaintext. Bleichenbacher's attack has been extensively studied ever since, applied to SSL [11], PIN encryption in EMV [12], USB token [2] and XML encryption [13]. Recently, Bardou, Focardi, Kawamoto, Simionato, Steel and Tsay claim that using their improved version of Bleichenbacher's attack, a wrapped secret key can be recovered from RSA Securid 800 in only 13 minutes [2].

Other Attacks on PKCS#1 v1.5. Other non-POA attacks also exist for PKCS#1 v1.5: Coron, Joye, Naccache and Paillier proposed two brilliant attacks in 2000 [14], which can efficiently recover the plaintext, if the public exponent is small enough, or most message bits are zeros. Bauer, Coron, Naccache, Tibouchi and Vergnaud proposed a broadcast attack [15], which could reveal the identical plaintext when the public exponent is small. However, none of these attacks works for the commonly used public exponent 65537 with a random message. Bauer et al. also proposed a reliable distinguish attack [15]. Using one PO query, it predicts which of two chosen plaintexts corresponds to a challenge ciphertext. Although we only focus on full-plaintext-recovery attacks without requirements on exponent or plaintext, whether POAs can combine with these non-POA attacks may be an interesting topic for further study.

Does PKCS#1 v1.5 Still Matters in Today's Application? To avoid POA, RSA introduced OAEP as the new recommended encoding scheme in PKCS#1 v2.0. However, according to ECRYPT's "Yearly Report on Algorithms and Keysizes", PKCS#1 v1.5 is still widely deployed in today's application ((W)TLS, S/MME, XML, JSON, etc.) [16, 17]. Take USB tokens for instance: most tokens today support PKCS#1 v1.5, while only a few can support OAEP [2]. In software deployment, OAEP is widely supported today; while for backward compatibility reasons, PKCS#1 v1.5 is still mandatory. Jager and Paterson suggest that in such scenario [17], the attacker can trick the honest user to use legacy scheme (PKCS#1 v1.5) , and undermine the security of the up-to-date scheme (OAEP).

Motivation. Despite the fact that detailed implementation instructions are given in [1], implementations do not always follow them. For efficiency or other reasons, they tend to simplify the standard decryption process as long as valid ciphertexts can be decrypted correctly. For instance, in most of Microsoft's Cryptographic Service Providers (CSP), PKCS #1 v1.5 decryption does not check padding string's length. Non-standard implementations also exist in many widely used cryptographic libraries (PGP, Boton, etc.) . Some may ignore padding string length check; others may not check the first byte of decryption result. For cryptographic devices, where the source code may not be available for public review, the situation is worse. In their full paper, Bardou et al. have already addressed this problem [2]. Bleichenbacher's attack can cover several non-standard implementations; while for the others, current POA on PKCS #1 v1.5 fails. Such implementations include Sata DKey (session key) [2] and perhaps many other devices that have not been studied yet. Since no POA works for them, non-standard implementations provide a "shelter" for cryptographic device vendors. In practice, such shelter can be pretty attractive: they only require minimal changes, which will not cause any compatibility trouble.

But can these non-standard implementations really prevent POA? Unfortunately, the answer remains unclear so far. All previous works mainly focus on standard implementation, leaving a lot of non-standard implementations in a "grey zone".

Our Contribution. In this paper, we focus on two types of non-standard implementations. The first one only checks if there is an byte with hexadecimal value 0x00 to separate padding string from the real message. The other one performs a thorough check, except for whether the second byte has hexadecimal value 0x02. Recalls that Bleichenbacher's attack mainly takes advantage of the leading 0x0002 in the conforming check [10]. Clearly, Bleichenbacher's attack cannot apply to these cases.

Our attack on the second implementation is even more efficient than standard POA (it requires a mean of 13 000 oracle calls, while standard POA [2] needs 49 001 oracle calls). Our attack on the first implementation requires about 0.1 million oracle calls, which is still practical in application [13]. We give detailed correctness proof and complexity analysis of our attacks, as well as experiments to show their practical validity. Moreover, each attack can cover several non-standard implementations: together with Bleichenbacher's attack, we can see that secure "shelter" is indeed hard to find.

The rest of this paper is organized as follows. We first recall PKCS#1 v1.5 standard and Bleichenbacher's attack in Section 2. In Section 3, we present two case studies on certain implementation, and show that most of non-standard implementations are vulnerable to POA in some way. Experimental results are given in Section 4.

2 Padding Oracle Attacks on Standard PKCS#1 v1.5

2.1 PKCS#1 v1.5

We briefly recall PKCS#1 v1.5 standard in this section. For clarity, we use the same notations as [10]. PKCS#1 v1.5 encryption block format is given in Fig.1.

Encryption process takes the original message, pads it with pseudo-randomly generated non-zero bytes, then uses RSA to encrypt. Decryption process simply uses RSA to decrypt, then checks whether the padded message is valid. For valid padded message, the message in the data block is returned as decryption result. Otherwise, decryption fails with a "decryption error".

00	02	Padding String	00	Data Block

Fig. 1. PKCS#1 v1.5 block format for encryption

A valid "padded message" must satisfy all following conditions [1]:

a) The first byte has hexadecimal value `0x00`
b) The second byte has hexadecimal value `0x02`
c) The length of non-zero padding string (PS) is at least 8 bytes
d) There is an byte with hexadecimal value `0x00` to separate PS from data block

In the standard decryption process, all above conditions must be checked. However, some implementations simplify this process, only check part of these conditions. We call such implementations "non-standard implementations".

2.2 Bleichenbacher's Attack

Bleichenbacher shows that if the attacker can decide whether a chosen ciphertext is valid, the whole padded message can be recovered [10]. Following the notations of [10], we have (n, e) as the RSA public key; (p, q, d) as the corresponding secret key; k as the byte length of n. Let $B = 2^{8(k-2)}$, according to condition a) and b), for any valid ciphertext c, the corresponding padded plaintext m must satisfy

$$2B \leq m \bmod n < 3B$$

Bleichenbacher's attack takes full advantage of this interval, while ignoring other conditions. For more details on Bleichenbacher's attack, we refer to [10].

3 Padding Oracle Attacks on Non-standard PKCS#1 v1.5 Implementations

Through this section, attacks take a valid ciphertext c as input, and try to find the corresponding padded plaintext m through padding oracle calls. We use s as the multiplier of m, which is used in $c' = cs^e \bmod n$ to build the ciphertext for sm. The integer i represents the round counter, and $[a,b]$ represents the current m's interval.

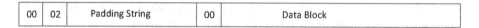

3.1 Case 1: Implementation only Checks "the 0x00 Separator"

In this case, after RSA decryption, implementation searches for a 0x00 byte, from the most significant byte to the least significant byte. Whenever a 0x00 byte is found, PO returns 'True'; otherwise, PO returns 'False'. Take the need of real-life application into consideration, this PO may also have some other features:

- A 0x00 in the first or second byte does not count. For any valid padded message, the first two bytes are set to 0x0002. The most reasonable check is to ignore these bytes, start from the third byte and search for 0x00.
- If the only 0x00 exists in the last byte, decryption will fail. No message can be extracted from this ciphertext.

These additional conditions cause some trouble in our analysis, as we shall see soon.

Basic Idea. The "0x00 separator check" is rather complicated. Unlike condition a) and b) ("0x0002 ") , it does not have a clear mathematical expression. Luckily, certain multipliers can bridge this gap. For example, $256m$'s binary representation is the binary representation of m shifted left for 1 byte. On $\mathbb{Z}_n^*$, if $256m < n$, m passes the "0x00 separator check", $256m$ should pass the check as well; while if $256m > n$, since n is a random modular, $256m \bmod n$ could fail. Similar property holds for the messages that fail the check. Notice here we consider the second additional condition, otherwise PO will always returns 'True' for the ciphertext of $256m$ when $256m < n$. Suppose we have a randomly-generated padded message m_1 on $\mathbb{Z}_n^*$, with corresponding ciphertext $c_1 = {m_1}^e \bmod n$. Let PO(c_1) represent padding oracle's reply when input c_1. Let $m_2 = 256m_1 \bmod n$, $c_2 = {m_2}^e \bmod n$. In general, if we get different replies from PO(c_1) and PO(c_2), we can conclude that $256m_1 > n$.

However, considering the "additional conditions", a few abnormal points appear: for instance, when $256m_1 < n$, if m_1 has only one 0x00 byte in the third byte, PO(c_1) returns 'True' while PO(c_2) returns 'False' .

Formally, $PO(c_1) = F$ means m_1 contains no 0x00 from the third byte to the second to last byte. Since m_1 is picked uniformly on $\mathbb{Z}_n^*$, $Pr(PO(c_1) = F) = \left(\frac{255}{256}\right)^{k-3}$. Thus, the following proposition holds.

Proposition 1. *Assume m_1 is picked uniformly on $\mathbb{Z}_n^*$, $m_2 = 256m_1 \bmod n$, $c_1 = {m_1}^e \bmod n$, $c_2 = {m_2}^e \bmod n$. For commonly used RSA modulus length, $Pr(PO(c_1) \neq PO(c_2)|256m_1 < n)$ and $Pr(PO(c_1) \neq PO(c_2)|256m_1 > n)$ are distinguishable.*

Proof. When $256m_1 > n$, $PO(c_1)$ and $PO(c_2)$ are nearly independent. Notice that $256m_1 > n$ merely adds constraint condition on the first two bytes of m_1, $Pr(PO(c_1) = F) = Pr(PO(c_1) = F|256m_1 > n)$. Thus, we have

$$Pr(PO(c_1) \neq PO(c_2)|256m_1 > n) = 2\left(1 - \left(\frac{255}{256}\right)^{k-3}\right)\left(\frac{255}{256}\right)^{k-3}$$

When $256m_1 < n$, $Pr(PO(c_1) = T, PO(c_2) = F)$ means the only 0x00 appears in the third byte of m_1. Thus, we have $Pr(PO(c_1) = T, PO(c_2) = F|256m_1 < n) = \frac{1}{256}\left(\frac{255}{256}\right)^{k-4}$. Similarly, we also have $Pr(PO(c_1) = F, PO(c_2) = T|256m_1 < n) = \frac{1}{256}\left(\frac{255}{256}\right)^{k-3}$. Thus,

$$Pr(PO(c_1) \neq PO(c_2)|256m_1 < n) = \frac{1}{256}\left(\frac{255}{256}\right)^{k-4} + \frac{1}{256}\left(\frac{255}{256}\right)^{k-3}$$
$$Pr(PO(c_1) \neq PO(c_2)|256m_1 > n) = 2\left(1 - \left(\frac{255}{256}\right)^{k-3}\right)\left(\frac{255}{256}\right)^{k-3}$$

For $k = 128$,

$$Pr(PO(c_1) \neq PO(c_2)|256m_1 < n) \approx 0.0048$$
$$Pr(PO(c_1) \neq PO(c_2)|256m_1 > n) \approx 0.4744$$

Larger k leads to smaller $Pr(PO(c_1) \neq PO(c_2))$, although the probabilities above are still distinguishable. □

Since the probability difference here is quite significant, we can simply calculate $Pr(PO(c_1) \neq PO(c_2))$ in a small block near m_1, and use a threshold to decide whether $256m_1 > n$. With m's current interval, we can easily find a pair of (s_{max}, s_{min}) which can guarantee $s_{max}m \bmod n > \frac{n}{256}$ and $s_{min}m \bmod n < \frac{n}{256}$. Use $sm \bmod n$ as the m_1 in the procedure above, a tighter bound for s can be found, which leads to a smaller interval for m. This procedure can be extended to $[rn, (r+1)n)$, as in Algorithm 1.

It is worth mentioning that 256 is not the only multiplier that causes probability difference. Similar proposition also holds for the multiplier 2.

Proposition 2. *Assume m_1 is picked uniformly on $\mathbb{Z}_n^*$, $m_2 = 2m_1 \bmod n$, $c_1 = {m_1}^e \bmod n$, $c_2 = {m_2}^e \bmod n$. For commonly used RSA modulus length, $Pr(PO(c_1) \neq PO(c_2)|2m_1 < n)$ and $Pr(PO(c_1) \neq PO(c_2)|2m_1 > n)$ are distinguishable.*

Proof. When $2m_1 > n$, the probability will be exactly the same as before. For $2m_1 < n$, if $PO(c_2) = T$ and $PO(c_1) = F$, there must exist a position $p \in [2, k-2]$ which satisfies $m_1[p] = 128$ and $0 < m_1[p+1] < 128$. Therefore,

$$Pr(PO(c_2) = T, PO(c_1) = F|2m_1 < n) = \left(1 - \left(1 - \frac{127}{255^2}\right)^{k-3}\right)\left(\frac{255}{256}\right)^{k-3}$$

Similarly, we also have

$$Pr(PO(c_2) = F, PO(c_1) = T|2m_1 < n) = \frac{127}{128}\left(1 - \left(\frac{509}{510}\right)^{k-3}\right)\left(\frac{255}{256}\right)^{k-3}$$

Algorithm 1. Multiply 256 method with additional condition, on $[rn, (r+1)n)$

Require: Padding Oracle PO, ciphertext c, m's current interval $[a, b]$, r
  compute the possible interval of s $[s_{min}, s_{max}]$
  $s_{min} = \left\lfloor \frac{(r+\frac{1}{256})n}{b} \right\rfloor, s_{max} = \left\lceil \frac{(r+\frac{1}{256})n}{a} \right\rceil$
  while $s < s_{max}$ **do**
    collect some sample points near current s, $c_1 = s^e c \bmod n$, $c_2 = (256s)^e c \bmod n$
    call PO to calculate $Pr(PO(c_1) \neq PO(c_2))$
    if $Pr(PO(c_1) \neq PO(c_2)) < threadhold$ **then**
      break
    else
      $s{+}{+}$
    end if
  end while
  $a' = \left\lceil \frac{r+\frac{1}{256}n}{s+block+1} \right\rceil, b' = \left\lfloor \frac{r+\frac{1}{256}n}{s-block} \right\rfloor$
  return $[a', b']$

For k=128,

$$Pr(PO(c_1) \neq PO(c_2)|2m_1 < n) \approx 0.2653$$
$$Pr(PO(c_1) \neq PO(c_2)|2m_1 > n) \approx 0.4744$$

Larger k leads to smaller $Pr(PO(c_1) \neq PO(c_2))$, although the probabilities above are still distinguishable. □

The probability difference here is not as significant as before. In order to decide whether $2m_1 > n$, better statistical tools should be applied. The multiply 2 version of Algorithm 1 is denoted as Algorithm 2. The initial interval of s in Algorithm 2 is quite large, a binary search can be applied here.

Attack Algorithm. Both Algorithm 1 and 2 can narrow down m's interval with different r, thus, we can keep running them until there's only one possible m. In some cases, keep using Algorithm 1 leads to a "stuck problem" (no available r can be found for Algorithm 1). For this reason, we introduce Algorithm 2. Since the probability difference in Algorithm 2 isn't as significant as Algorithm 1, for efficiency, Algorithm 2 is only used when Algorithm 1 is "stuck" . The full-plaintext-recovery attack is presented in Algorithm 3.

Analysis

Correctness Proof. First, we prove the correct padded message m always stays in interval $[a, b]$. In this section, assume that Algorithm 1 and 2 can always succeed. In round 0, we have $m \in [2B, 3B-1]$. If in round $i-1$,we have $m \in [a, b]$, in round i, the process can go to either Step 2.b or Step 2.c. Define s_{exact} as the

Algorithm 2. Multiply 2 method with additional condition,on $[rn, (r+1)n)$

Require: Padding Oracle PO, ciphertext c, m's current interval $[a, b]$, r
compute the possible interval of s $[s_{min}, s_{max}]$
$s_{min} = \left\lfloor \frac{(r+\frac{1}{2})n}{b} \right\rfloor$, $s_{max} = \left\lceil \frac{(r+\frac{1}{2})n}{a} \right\rceil$
$sl = s_{min}, su = s_{max}$
while $su > sl$ **do**
  $s = \lfloor \frac{su+sl}{2} \rfloor$
  collect some sample points near current s, call PO to get $Pr(PO(c_1) \neq PO(c_2))$
  if $Pr(PO(c_1) \neq PO(c_2))$ suggest $2m_1 < n$ **then**
    $sl = s$
  else
    $su = s$
  end if
end while
$a' = \left\lceil \frac{r+\frac{1}{2}n}{s+block+1} \right\rceil, b' = \left\lfloor \frac{r+\frac{1}{2}n}{s-block} \right\rfloor$
return $[a', b']$

s satisfying both $256r_i n < 256 s_{exact} m \leq (256r_i + 1)\, n$ and $256\,(s_{exact} + 1)\, m > (256r_i + 1)\, n$. For Step 2.b, the initial interval of s we chose in Algorithm 1 always contains s_{exact}. After a round of Algorithm 1, $s_{exact} \in [s - block, s + block]$, thus:

$$a' = \left\lceil \frac{r_i + \frac{1}{256}n}{s + block + 1} \right\rceil \leq \left\lceil \frac{r_i + \frac{1}{256}n}{s_{exact} + 1} \right\rceil < m$$

$$b' = \left\lfloor \frac{r_i + \frac{1}{256}n}{s - block} \right\rfloor \geq \left\lfloor \frac{r_i + \frac{1}{256}n}{s_{exact}} \right\rfloor \geq m$$

Hence, if Step 2.b is chosen,we always have $m \in [a', b']$ when round i ends. Same analysis works for Step 2.c, as long as we change multiplier 256 above to 2. Therefore, in this attack, the interval $[a, b]$ in each round always contains m.

Next, we prove our attack always narrows down m's interval in each round. Obviously, for m in $[2B, 3B - 1]$, round 0 runs Step 2.b with $r_0 = 0$ successfully. Suppose after round $i - 1$, m's interval is $[a, b]$, denote $t = \frac{b}{a}$. In round i, we need to prove m's new interval $[a', b']$ is smaller than $[a, b]$. Roughly speaking, this means in Algorithm 1 and 2, the length of $[s_{min}, s_{max}]$ should be larger than $2block + 1$. We use $block_{256}$, $block_2$ to denote the parameter $block$ in Algorithm 1 and 2.

If in round i, Step 2.b runs, we have

$$\begin{aligned} s_{max} - s_{min} &\geq (r_i + \frac{1}{256})n \times \frac{b-a}{ab} \\ &> \frac{n}{256} \times \left(1 + \frac{1}{t-1}\right) \times \frac{t-1}{at} - n \times \frac{b-a}{ab} \\ &= \frac{n}{256a} - n \times \frac{b-a}{ab} \end{aligned} \tag{1}$$

Algorithm 3. Full plaintext recovery attack for case 1

Require: ciphertext c, RSA modulus n and public exponent e
Step 1: Attack Start
Set $i = 1$,$r = -1$,$[a,b]$=$[2B,3B-1]$
Step 2: Using Padding Oracle to narrow down m's interval
while $b - a >$"Ending Parameter" **do**
Step 2.a: Check if multiply 256 method can be used. Compute $r_i = \left\lfloor \frac{1}{256(\frac{b}{a}-1)} \right\rfloor$
if $r_i > r_{i-1}$ **then**
Step 2.b: Multiply 256 method. Using Algorithm 1 with r_i
else
$r_i = r_{i-1}$
Step 2.c: Multiply 2 method. Using Algorithm 2 with $r = \left\lfloor \frac{1}{2(\frac{b}{a}-1)} \right\rfloor$,
end if
end while
Step 3: Exhaustive search to find m
return m

In Step 2.b we have $r_i > r_{i-1}$, thus

$$\begin{aligned} s_{max} - s_{min} &\geq (r_i + \frac{1}{256})n \times \frac{b-a}{ab} \\ &\geq (r_{i-1} + \frac{1}{256})n \times \frac{b-a}{ab} + n \times \frac{b-a}{ab} \end{aligned} \tag{2}$$

In experiment, $block_{256} = 8$ can ensure Algorithm 1 will success with high probability. It is easy to see $\frac{n}{256a} > 4block_{256} + 2$, thus from (1)(2) we can always prove $s_{max} - s_{min} > 2block_{256} + 1$.

Otherwise, if in round i, Step 2.c runs

$$\begin{aligned} s_{max} - s_{min} &\geq (r + \frac{1}{2})n \times \frac{b-a}{ab} \\ &> \frac{n}{2} \times \left(1 + \frac{1}{t-1}\right) \times \frac{t-1}{at} - n \times \frac{b-a}{ab} \\ &= \frac{n}{a} \times \left(\frac{1}{t} - \frac{1}{2}\right) \end{aligned} \tag{3}$$

In experiment, we find $block_2 = 200$ can ensure Algorithm 2 will success with high probability. Since $1 < t < 1.5$, $\frac{1}{6} < \frac{1}{t} - \frac{1}{2} < \frac{1}{2}$, we can always prove $s_{max} - s_{min} > 2block_2 + 1$ from (3). Thus, our attack always narrows down m's interval in each round. □

Complexity Analysis. In round i, Step 2.b will always be chosen when $r_i - r_{i-1} \geq 1$. Suppose in the beginning of round $i-1$, m exists in $[a_1, b_1]$, denote $t_1 = \frac{b_1}{a_1}$. Let $len = b - a$, $len_1 = b_1 - a_1$, $d = \frac{len}{len_1}$. No matter which method runs in round $i-1$, we always have $r_{i-1} \leq \frac{1}{256(t_1-1)}$. Therefore,

$$r_i - r_{i-1} > \frac{1}{256} \times \left(\frac{1}{t-1} - \frac{1}{t_1 - 1}\right) - 1 = \frac{1}{256} \times \left(\frac{a}{len} - \frac{a_1}{len_1}\right) - 1$$
$$\geq \frac{a}{256} \times \left(\frac{1}{len} - \frac{d}{len}\right) - 1 = \frac{1}{256} \times \frac{1}{t-1} \times (1-d) - 1 \quad (4)$$

From above, it is not hard to see for Step 2.b $1 - \mathrm{d} \geq \frac{1}{2block_{256}+2}$, while for Step 2.c,$1 - \mathrm{d} \geq 1 - \frac{2block_2+1}{\frac{n}{6a}}$. Notice $\frac{1}{t-1}$ keeps growing in our attack. Therefore, after some rounds, we will reach a situation where $\frac{1}{t-1}$ is large enough to ensure $r_i - r_{i-1} \geq 1$. From this point, Step 2.b will always be chosen until we find m. For $k = 128$, after 3 rounds of Step 2.c, $\frac{1}{t-1}$ will be large enough to ensure this. Roughly speaking, if round $i-1$ and i both runs Step 2.b, $d \approx \frac{2block_{256}+1}{\frac{n}{256a}} \approx 0.24$, while in Step 2.c d is close to 0.04. In practice, binary search is used for Step 2.c, which leads to complexity close to $2\text{block}_2 \times \log_2 |s_{max} - s_{min}| = 2\text{block}_2 \times \log_2 \frac{n}{2a} \approx 5300$. In Step 2.b, the interval of s is rather small (most times less than 100) ; we have to search for all of s between s_{max} and s_{min}, which leads to nearly 170 times oracle calls. We give an overall complexity approximation as $5300 \times 3 + 170 \times \left(\log_{0.24}\left(\frac{EndParam}{B} \div 0.04^3\right) + 1\right)$. For EndParam=100000, the overall complexity is close to 0.1 million oracle calls.

3.2 Case 2: PO Checks All Conditions Expect for the Second Byte

In this case, PO checks condition a) (the `0x00` prefix) . This seems to be a pleasant condition, since it has a perfect mathematical expression. Let $T = 256B = 2^{8(k-1)}$, condition a) equals to $sm \bmod n < T$. This condition alone results in a very efficient attack [18], although condition c) and d) (PS length and the `0x00` separator) have complicated the case.

Basic Idea. With condition c) and d), oracle will not return 'True' for every $sm \bmod n < T$. Thus, highly efficient binary search from [18] cannot be applied. However, the framework of our attack in Section 3.1 still works. In fact, now we have a better situation: one side of the interval is deterministic. Whenever get a 'True' from oracle, we know for sure $sm \bmod n < T$.

Attack Algorithm. With the same notation, the "narrow down process" for this case is as follow. Search from the lower bound, whenever get a 'True' from PO, set the new lower bound of s to current s. If after a while no more $sm \bmod n$ causes a 'True' reply from PO, we can conclude that we have passed s_{exact}, and set the new upper bound of s to current s. As in the previous section, a parameter *block* is used to describe this interval. This process is presented in Algorithm 4 in Appendix C. Note that we can also search from the upper side, like Algorithm 5 in Appendix C.

Full-plaintext-recovery attack can be built from Algorithm 4 and 5, like we did in the previous section. Step 1 and 3 are exactly the same as before, here we only presents Step 2 in detail.

Step 2: Using Padding Oracle to narrow down m's interval
while $b - a >$ "Ending Parameter" **do**
Step 2.a: Check if Algorithm 4 can be used. Compute $r_i = \left\lfloor \frac{1}{\frac{b}{a}-1} \times \frac{T}{n} \right\rfloor$
if $r_i > r_{i-1}$ **then**
Step 2.b: use Algorithm 4 with r_i
else
$r_i = r_{i-1}$
Step 2.c: use Algorithm 5 with $r = \left\lfloor \frac{1}{\frac{b}{a}-1} \left(1 - \frac{T}{n}\right) - \frac{T}{n} \right\rfloor$
end if
end while

Analysis. Since attack for this case has the same skeleton as before, correctness proof and complexity analysis is quite similar. Due to the length limitation, we present this part in Appendix B.

3.3 Other Non-standard Implementations

According to Section 2.1, standard PO returns 'True' if the RSA decryption result satisfies all four conditions. Therefore, we describe the type of implementations as a four bits integer. The most significant bit represents whether condition a) is checked in PKCS#1 v1.5 decryption. If condition a) is checked, this bit is 1; otherwise, it is 0. The other three bits (from the second most significant to the least significant) , represents whether condition b), c), d) is checked, respectively. Thus, type 15 stands for standard implementation, while type 1 represents the case in Section 3.1. Based on the two most significant bits, implementations can be further divided into four groups:

Group I (Both the `0x00` prefix and the `0x02` are ignored) : We ignore type 0, because it can not separate padding string from the data block. Our attack in Section 3.1 is designed for type 1. Unlike Bleichenbacher's attack, our attack is insensitive to subtle condition changes. Since condition c) (PS length check) has limited influence on the overall probability distribution, our attack also works on type 3. Type 2 does not seem to be a reasonable implementation in practice: there is no separator between data and padding string. Without such separator, the implementation should have a fixed length for the data block. In that case, checking the length of padding string seems unnecessary.

Group II (The `0x02` is checked while the `0x00` prefix is ignored) : In this group, implementations check condition b) (`0x02`) while ignore condition a) (the `0x00` prefix) . Unlike other groups, the distribution of m that causes a 'True' reply from PO is "partly-discrete" . It is not as discrete as Group I, neither does it have a neat mathematical expression like Group III or IV. We suspect this group could be vulnerable to a simple variant[1] of Bleichenbacher's attack, although some adjustment is needed for Step 3.

Group III (The `0x00` prefix is checked while the `0x02` is ignored) : Our attack in Section 3.2 is designed for type 11 (with PS length and `0x00` separator check). For the same reason, it also works for type 9 (without PS length check). Type 8 forms a perfect PO for Manger's attack [18], which is the most efficient attack in all non-standard implementations. For type 10, the situation is similar to type 2.

Group IV (Both the `0x00` prefix and the `0x02` are checked) : Bleichenbacher's attack can be applied to all implementations in this group. Type 15 is the standard implementation. Type 12, 13, 14 corresponds to the "TTT" , "FTT" and "TFT" oracle in [2], respectively.

4 Experimental Results

With discussion in Section 3.3, implementation types with corresponding attacks is given in Table 1, along with the complexity in terms of oracle calls. In this section, all experiments use 1024-bit RSA modulus n, e=65537, with PKCS#1 v1.5 encryption. Each experiment runs 1000 times, with 16 bytes of randomly generated messages. For Bleichenbacher's attack, we use Bardou el al.'s improved version[2] [2].

Table 1. Implementation types with corresponding attack algorithm

Type	Conditions				Group	Available Attack Algorithm	Performance	
	a)	b)	c)	d)			Median	Mean
1				✓	Group I	Group I Attack	113 520	115 978
2			✓			Unnecessary	—	—
3			✓	✓		Group I Attack	111 890	114 331
4		✓			Group II	Variant of Bleichenbacher's attack	—	—
5		✓		✓				
6		✓	✓					
7		✓	✓	✓				
8	✓				Group III	Manger's attack	1 168	1 174
9	✓			✓		Group III Attack	12 843	12 878
10	✓		✓			Unnecessary	—	—
11	✓		✓	✓		Group III Attack	13 047	13 058
12	✓	✓			Group IV	Bleichenbacher's attack	4 762	14 532
13	✓	✓		✓		Bleichenbacher's attack	15 315	92 820
14	✓	✓	✓			Unnecessary	—	—
15	✓	✓	✓	✓		Bleichenbacher's attack	17 473	104 839

[1] In this paper, "variant" means simply adjust some of the parameters in the original algorithm, while the basic skeleton and the core unit remains the same.

[2] Notice our results here are worse than [2]. This is probably caused by the *Parallel thread method.* However, even if we use the performance in [2], the performance order remains the same.

Condition c) (PS length check) alone has rather limited influence: type 1 and 3 share the same attack algorithm, and have similar complexity. Same property holds for type 9 and 11, type 13 and 15. Compare with others, Group IV Attack's (Bleichenbacher's attack) performance varies a lot. Their density distribution curves have longer "tails", which is given in Fig.2 (Appendix A) . All attacks above run in different situations, it is not fair to compare their performance with each other. Nonetheless, from Table 1, we can easily conclude that most of the non-standard implementations are insecure against POA.

5 Conclusion

In the last decade, Padding Oracle Attacks (POAs) have become a major threat to PKCS#1 v1.5 [2, 10]. To our knowledge, all previous works mainly focus on the standard implementation. However, in today's application, some implementations do not always follow the standard step-by-step. Since the padding oracles in these non-standard implementations are quite different from the standard padding oracle, Bleichenbacher's attack cannot cover all of them. Using the similar idea as Bleichenbacher's attack, we propose two attacks for certain non-standard implementations: one requires about 0.1 million oracle calls, while the other requires only 13 000 oracle calls. Together with Bleichenbacher's attack, we can see that most of the "non-standard implementations" are vulnerable to POA in some way. We hope our work could convince industry engineers that the threat of POA can not be prevented by some simple implementation tricks.

Acknowledgements. We would like to thank the anonymous reviewers for providing valuable comments. We would also like to thank Damien Vergnaud for his generous help and valuable advice. This work is supported by the National Natural Science Foundation of China (No.91118006) and the National Basic Research Program of China (No.2013CB338002).

References

1. RSA Laboratories: PKCS #1 v2.2: RSA Cryptography Standard (October 27, 2012)
2. Bardou, R., Focardi, R., Kawamoto, Y., Simionato, L., Steel, G., Tsay, J.-K.: Efficient Padding Oracle Attacks on Cryptographic Hardware. In: Safavi-Naini, R., Canetti, R. (eds.) CRYPTO 2012. LNCS, vol. 7417, pp. 608–625. Springer, Heidelberg (2012)
3. Vaudenay, S.: Security Flaws Induced by CBC Padding - Applications to SSL, IPSEC, WTLS... In: Knudsen, L.R. (ed.) EUROCRYPT 2002. LNCS, vol. 2332, pp. 534–545. Springer, Heidelberg (2002)
4. Canvel, B., Hiltgen, A.P., Vaudenay, S., Vuagnoux, M.: Password Interception in a SSL/TLS Channel. In: Boneh, D. (ed.) CRYPTO 2003. LNCS, vol. 2729, pp. 583–599. Springer, Heidelberg (2003)
5. Paterson, K.G., Yau, A.K.L.: Cryptography in Theory and Practice: The Case of Encryption in IPsec. In: Vaudenay, S. (ed.) EUROCRYPT 2006. LNCS, vol. 4004, pp. 12–29. Springer, Heidelberg (2006)

6. Degabriele, J., Paterson, K.: Attacking the IPsec Standards in Encryption-only Configurations. In: IEEE Symposium on Security and Privacy, SP 2007, pp. 335–349 (2007)
7. Albrecht, M., Paterson, K., Watson, G.: Plaintext Recovery Attacks against SSH. In: 2009 30th IEEE Symposium on Security and Privacy, pp. 16–26 (2009)
8. Degabriele, J.P., Paterson, K.G.: On the (in)security of IPsec in MAC-then-encrypt configurations. In: Proceedings of the 17th ACM Conference on Computer and Communications Security, CCS 2010, pp. 493–504. ACM, New York (2010)
9. Rizzo, J., Duong, T.: Practical Padding Oracle Attacks. In: WOOT 2010: 4th USENIX Workshop on Offensive Technologies. USENIX Association (2010)
10. Bleichenbacher, D.: Chosen ciphertext attacks against protocols based on the RSA encryption standard PKCS #1. In: Krawczyk, H. (ed.) CRYPTO 1998. LNCS, vol. 1462, pp. 1–12. Springer, Heidelberg (1998)
11. Klíma, V., Rosa, T.: Further Results and Considerations on Side Channel Attacks on RSA. In: Kaliski Jr., B.S., Koç, Ç.K., Paar, C. (eds.) CHES 2002. LNCS, vol. 2523, pp. 244–259. Springer, Heidelberg (2003)
12. Smart, N.P.: Errors Matter: Breaking RSA-Based PIN Encryption with Thirty Ciphertext Validity Queries. In: Pieprzyk, J. (ed.) CT-RSA 2010. LNCS, vol. 5985, pp. 15–25. Springer, Heidelberg (2010)
13. Jager, T., Schinzel, S., Somorovsky, J.: Bleichenbacher's Attack Strikes again: Breaking PKCS#1 v1.5 in XML Encryption. In: Foresti, S., Yung, M., Martinelli, F. (eds.) ESORICS 2012. LNCS, vol. 7459, pp. 752–769. Springer, Heidelberg (2012)
14. Coron, J.-S., Joye, M., Naccache, D., Paillier, P.: New Attacks on PKCS#1 v1.5 Encryption. In: Preneel, B. (ed.) EUROCRYPT 2000. LNCS, vol. 1807, pp. 369–381. Springer, Heidelberg (2000)
15. Bauer, A., Coron, J.-S., Naccache, D., Tibouchi, M., Vergnaud, D.: On the Broadcast and Validity-Checking Security of PKCS#1 v1.5 Encryption. In: Zhou, J., Yung, M. (eds.) ACNS 2010. LNCS, vol. 6123, pp. 1–18. Springer, Heidelberg (2010)
16. European Network of Excellence in Cryptology II: ECRYPT II Yearly Report on Algorithms and Keysizes (2009-2010). Technical report, European Network of Excellence in Cryptology II (March 30, 2010)
17. Jager, T., Paterson, K.G., Somorovsky, J.: One Bad Apple: Backwards Compatibility Attacks on State-of-the-Art Cryptography. In: NDSS Symposium 2013 (2013)
18. Manger, J.: A Chosen Ciphertext Attack on RSA Optimal Asymmetric Encryption Padding (OAEP) as Standardized in PKCS #1 v2.0. In: Kilian, J. (ed.) CRYPTO 2001. LNCS, vol. 2139, pp. 230–238. Springer, Heidelberg (2001)

A Density Distribution of Oracle Calls of the Attacks in Table 1

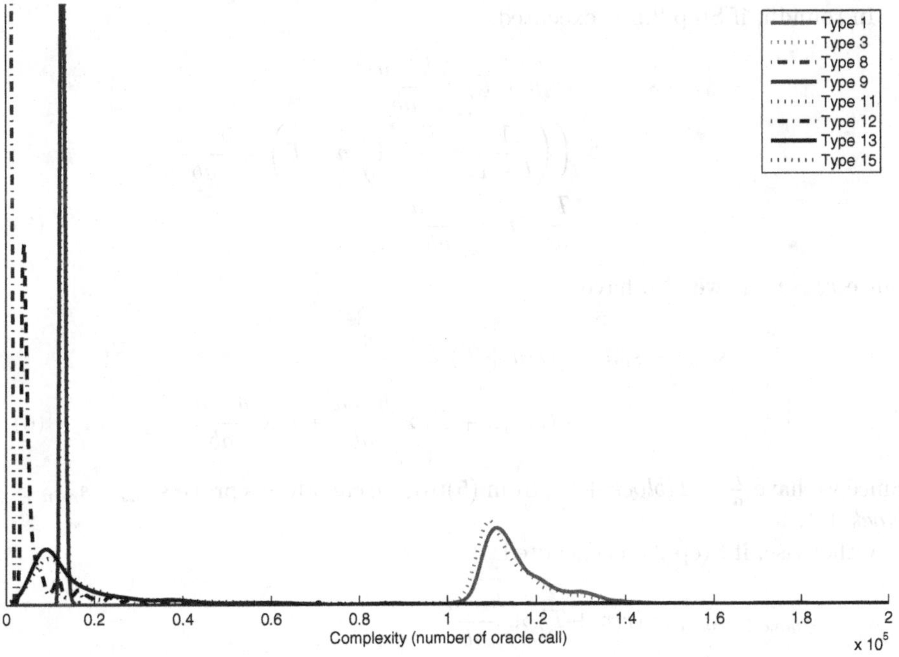

Fig. 2. Distribution of oracle calls of attacks in Table 1, each attack runs 1000 times

B Analysis of the Attack for Case 2

Correctness Proof. Assume *block* is chosen to ensure Algorithm 4 and 5 always succeed. Since Algorithm 5 has a more clear form, we start with Algorithm 5.

First, we prove m always stays in the interval $[a, b]$. Initially, we have $m \in [2B, 3B - 1]$, which means the proposition holds for round 0. Suppose in round i-1, we have $m \in [a, b]$; according to Algorithm 5, after Step 2, we have $s_{\text{exact}} \in [s, s + block]$. s_{exact} is defined as the s satisfies , $s_{exact}m \leq r_i n + T$ and $(s_{exact} + 1)m > r_i n + T$. Obviously such s_{exact} exist in $[s_{min}, s_{max}]$. Thus, in Algorithm 5 we have:

$$a' = \left\lceil \frac{r_i n + T}{s + block + 1} \right\rceil \leq \left\lceil \frac{r_i n + T}{s_{exact} + 1} \right\rceil < m$$

$$b' = \left\lfloor \frac{r_i n + T}{s} \right\rfloor \geq \left\lfloor \frac{r_i n + T}{s_{exact}} \right\rfloor \geq m$$

Proof for Algorithm 4 works exactly the same way.

Then we show in each round of our attack, m's interval is narrowed down as expected. In experiment, we find $block = 17$ provide a success rate larger than 90%. Obviously, for m in $[2B, 3B-1]$, round 0 runs Step 2.b with $r_0 = 0$ successfully. Suppose after round i-1, m's interval is $[a, b]$, denote $t = \frac{b}{a}$. In round i, we need to prove s's initial interval $[s_{min}, s_{max}]$ is always larger than $block + 1$.

In round i, if Step 2.b is executed,

$$\begin{aligned} s_{max} - s_{min} &\geq (r_i n + T) \times \frac{b-a}{ab} \\ &> \left(\left(\frac{1}{t-1} \times \frac{T}{n} - 1 \right) n + T \right) \times \frac{b-a}{ab} \\ &= \frac{T}{a} - n \times \frac{b-a}{ab} \end{aligned} \tag{5}$$

Since $r_i > r_{i-1}$, we also have

$$\begin{aligned} s_{max} - s_{min} &\geq (r_i n + T) \times \frac{b-a}{ab} \\ &> (r_{i-1} n + T) \times \frac{b-a}{ab} + n \times \frac{b-a}{ab} \end{aligned} \tag{6}$$

Since we have $\frac{T}{a} > 2\,(block + 1)$, from (5)(6), we can always prove $s_{max} - s_{min} > block + 1$.

Otherwise, if Step 2.c is executed

$$\begin{aligned} s_{max} - s_{min} &\geq (r_i n + T) \times \frac{b-a}{ab} \\ &> \left(\left(\frac{1}{t-1} \times \left(1 - \frac{T}{n}\right) - \frac{T}{n} - 1 \right) n + T \right) \times \frac{b-a}{ab} \\ &= \frac{n-T}{b} - n \times \frac{t-1}{b} = \frac{(2-t) \times n - T}{b} \end{aligned} \tag{7}$$

Since $t < 1.5$, $(2-t)n > 0.5n$,$s_{max} - s_{min} > \frac{63T}{3B} > block + 1$.This completes our correctness proof. □

Complexity Analysis Complexity approximation is similar to our analysis in Section 3.3. To make sure in round i Step 2.b is executed, we need $r_i - r_{i-1} > 1$.

$$\begin{aligned} r_i - r_{i-1} &> \frac{T}{n} \times \left(\frac{1}{t-1} - \frac{1}{t_1 - 1} \right) - 1 = \frac{T}{n} \times \left(\frac{a}{len} - \frac{a_1}{len_1} \right) - 1 \\ &> \frac{aT}{n} \times \left(\frac{1}{len} - \frac{d}{len} \right) - 1 = \frac{T}{n} \times \frac{1}{t-1} \times (1-d) - 1 \end{aligned} \tag{8}$$

Since $\frac{T}{n} \in \left(\frac{1}{256}, \frac{1}{128}\right)$, in Step 2.b we have $1 - d \geq \frac{1}{block+2}$, while for Step 2.c,d $< \frac{block+1}{\frac{0.5n-T}{b}} < 0.003$, $1 - d > 0.997$. $\frac{1}{t-1}$ keeps increasing in our attack. Thus, we have the same "turning point" as before, after which only Step 2.b will be executed. Normally, only 1 or 2 round of Algorithm 5 is need.

Now let's consider how many oracle calls is needed for each round. Noted in Section 3.1, both multiply 2 method and multiply 256 method have a "balanced" interval. Roughly speaking, in narrow down process, s_{exact} is most likely to appear in the middle part of $[s_{min}, s_{max}]$. Duo to the facts that Algorithm 4 and 5 is "one-side-deterministic", now s_{exact} is most likely to appear in somewhere near s_{min}. Suppose for round i-1, we got new bounds for s as $[s_{newmin}, s_{newmax}]$. For a random m, condition c) and d) can be satisfied with probability $Pr\,(c\&d) = \left(\frac{255}{256}\right)^8 \left(1 - \left(\frac{255}{256}\right)^{k-10}\right)$. For $k = 128$, this probability is close to 0.36. Thus, the distribution sequence of s_{exact}'s position should follow Table 2. Clearly this is a

Table 2. The distribution sequence of s_{exact}'s position

$s_{exact} - s_{newmin}$	0	1	2	...	q	...
Probability	0.36	$0.36 \cdot 0.64$	$0.36 \cdot 0.64^2$	...	$0.36 \cdot 0.64^q$	...

geometric distribution, with expectation of $\frac{1-0.36}{0.36} = 1.78$. We use $slen$ denoted the length of $[s_{min}, s_{max}]$. If in round i, $slen$ is exactly the same as the length of $[s_{newmin}, s_{newmax}]$(a.k.a, $block$) in round i-1, at the most times, we only need to search for less than $1.78 + 1 + block$ points for Algorithm 4 to find s_{exact}'s new lower bound. For Algorithm 4, roughly speaking, we have

$$slen = s_{max} - s_{min} \approx (r_i n + T) \times \frac{b-a}{ab} = \left(\frac{T}{t-1} + T\right) \times \frac{t-1}{at} = \frac{T}{a}$$

which means $slen$ is almost stable. In that case, $d = \frac{block}{\frac{T}{a}}$ is also stable. Choosing the r_i in Algorithm 4 enlarge $[s_{newmin}, s_{newmax}]$ of round i-1 to $[s_{min}, s_{max}]$ in round i. This means the number of oracle calls in round i is roughly $1.78 \times \frac{1}{d} + d \times \frac{T}{a} + 1$. In fact, this is why we favor Algorithm 4 over Algorithm 5. Although Algorithm 4 has a neat form and larger r, we can see above that it always starts searching for s_{exact} from the "unlikely" upper side, which causes complexity waste. For complexity approximation, we simply ignore the several rounds of Algorithm 5 in the beginning. Thus, the overall complexity should be:

$$C\,(d) = \left(1.78 \times \frac{1}{d} + d \times \frac{T}{a} + 1\right) \times \log_d \frac{1}{B}$$

$C(d)$ reaches its minimal at $d = 0.08$, increases for $d > 0.08$. In Algorithm 3, for $block = 17$, even if we choose the largest r possible (like we did in our attack),we cannot get a $d = 0.08$. Thus, the minimal of d lead to the minimal of the complexity of our attack. With $d = 0.175$, we have $C(d)$ around 11 thousands.

C Pseudo-code for Algorithms in the Text

Algorithm 4. Narrow down process for PO that does not check the second byte

Require: Padding Oracle PO, ciphertext c, m's current interval $[a, b]$, r
  compute the possible interval of s $[s_{min}, s_{max}]$
  $s_{\min} = \lfloor \frac{rn+T}{b} \rfloor$, $s_{\max} = \lceil \frac{rn+T}{a} \rceil$
  $fcount = 0, s = s_{min}$
  while $s \leq s_{max}$ **do**
    $c_1 = s^e \bmod n$;
    if PO(c_1)==T **then**
      $fcount \leftarrow 0$;
    else
      $fcount$++;
    end if
    if $fcount > block$ **then**
      break;
    end if
    s++;
  end while
  $a' = \lceil \frac{rn+T}{s} \rceil, b' = \left\lfloor \frac{rn+T}{s-block-1} \right\rfloor$
  return $[a', b']$

Algorithm 5. Another narrow down process for PO that does not check the second byte

Require: Padding Oracle PO, ciphertext c, m's current interval $[a, b]$, r
  compute the possible interval of s $[s_{min}, s_{max}]$
  $s_{\min} = \lfloor \frac{rn+T}{b} \rfloor$, $s_{\max} = \lceil \frac{rn+T}{a} \rceil$
  $s = s_{max}$
  while PO(c_1)==T **do**
    $s = s - 1$;
    $c_1 = s^e \bmod n$;
  end while
  $a' = \left\lceil \frac{rn+T}{s+block+1} \right\rceil, b' = \lfloor \frac{rn+T}{s} \rfloor$
  return $[a', b']$

Zero Knowledge Proofs from Ring-LWE

Xiang Xie[1], Rui Xue[2], and Minqian Wang[1]

[1] Trusted Computing and Information Assurance Laboratory
Institute of Software, Chinese Academy of Sciences
[2] The State Key Laboratory of Information Security
Institute of Information Engineering, Chinese Academy of Sciences
{xiexiang,wangminqian}@tca.iscas.ac.cn, xuerui@iie.ac.cn

Abstract. Zero-Knowledge proof is a very basic and important primitive, which allows a prover to prove some statement without revealing anything else. Very recently, Jain et al. proposed very efficient zero-knowledge proofs to prove any polynomial relations on bits, based on the Learning Parity with Noise (LPN) problem (Asiacrypt'12).

In this work, we extend analogous constructions whose security is based on the Ring Learning with Errors (RLWE) problem by adapting the techniques presented by Ling et al. (PKC'13). Specifically, we show a simple zero-knowledge proof of knowledge (Σ-protocol) for committed values, and prove any polynomial relations in the underlying ring. I.e. proving committed ring elements $m, m_1, ..., m_t$ satisfying $m = f(m_1, ..., m_t)$ for any polynomial f. Comparing to other existing Σ-protocols, the extracted witness (error vector) has length only small constant times than the one possessed by the prover. When representing ring element as elements in $\mathbb{Z}_q$, our protocol has amortized communication complexity $\tilde{O}(\lambda \cdot |f|)$ with exponentially small soundness in security parameter λ, where $|f|$ is the size of the circuit in $\mathbb{Z}_q$ computing f.

Keywords: zero-knowledge proofs of knowledge, ring learning with errors, lattices.

1 Introduction

The notions of commitment schemes and zero-knowledge proofs are fundamental primitives in the theory and practice of cryptographic protocols. Intuitively, a commitment scheme provides a way for a prover to commit a value x by putting it in a locked box. Later, the prover can open the box by sending the key of it. The commitment must be hiding and binding. Hiding means that the commitment will not leak any information of x, binding means that the prover can not open one commitment to two different values. Zero-knowledge proofs, introduced in [12], allow a prover to convince a verifier that some statement is true, without revealing anything to the verifier except for what is already contained in the claim. A zero-knowledge proof of knowledge needs additionally the prover to convince a verifier that it indeed has some secret information.

Zero-knowledge proofs have been studied in many works, e.g., [2,5,6,11,13,15,18]. The wonderful work of Ishai et al. [15] shows how to construct zero-knowledge proofs

M. Abdalla, C. Nita-Rotaru, and R. Dahab (Eds.): CANS 2013, LNCS 8257, pp. 57–73, 2013.

for all NP relations from multiparty computation by using the "MPC-in-the-head" technique. Although a zero-knowledge for any NP relation can be used to prove any relations among the committed values, in general this would be rather expensive, especially the description of the relation is part of the computation. More direct constructions to prove relations on the committed values has been considered, e.g.,[6,7]. These works give efficient proofs for algebraic circuit over large fields or integers. However, their schemes make exclusively use of homomorphic commitments, which are constructed based on number theoretical assumptions. These assumptions turn out to be inadequate under quantum computers. Very recently, Jain et al. [16] propose a very efficient zero-knowledge proof under the learning parity with noise (LPN) problem and also prove any relations over $\mathbb{Z}_2$ of the committed messages. Ling et al. [20] showed an identification scheme (essentially a Σ-protocol) under weaker lattice assumptions. Although they focus on the Small Integer Solution (SIS) problem, we remark that it's easy to extend it to Learning with Errors (LWE) problem. We remark that it's non-trivial to extend the work of Ling et at. to the Ring-LWE setting, especially to prove any relations on the underlying ring.

1.1 Our Results

In this paper, we first give a "natural" commitment scheme which is analogous to the one in [16], whose security is based on RLWE assumption. Informally, in a ring $R = \mathbb{Z}[X]/(f(X))$ for monic irreducible $f(X)$ with degree d, and for an integer modulus q defining $R_q := R/qR$, the commitment with message space R_q^ℓ is in the form $\mathbf{A} \cdot (\mathbf{s} \| \mathbf{m}) + \mathbf{e} \mod q$, where $\mathbf{A} = (\mathbf{A}_1 \| \mathbf{A}_2) \in R_q^{m \times (n+\ell)}$ is a public random matrix, $\mathbf{s} \in R_q^\ell$ is a uniformly random vector, and $\mathbf{e} \in R^m$ is "short". The commitment scheme becomes computationally hiding and (almost) perfectly binding. The hiding property follows directly from the RLWE assumption. The binding property is due to the fact that the shortest non-zero vector in the q-ary lattice defined by $\mathbf{A}$ will not be too small with overwhelming probability.

We construct a zero-knowledge proof, which is essentially a Σ-protocol, that proves the knowledge of the message hidden in our commitment schemes. Furthermore, we show Σ-protocols to prove linear and multiplicative relations of the message, i.e. $\mathbf{m}_3 = \mathbf{m}_1 \circ \mathbf{m}_2$, where $\circ$ denotes component-wise addition or multiplication on the underlying ring. By representing elements in R_q to vectors in $\mathbb{Z}_q$, our protocol allows to simultaneously prove any polynomial relations in $\mathbb{Z}_q$. The soundness of our protocol is $2/3$, to get exponentially small soundness, we need to repeat the execution. The best amortized communication complexity is $\tilde{O}(\lambda \cdot |f|)$, where $2^{-\lambda}$ is the soundness error, and $|f|$ is the size of the circuit in $\mathbb{Z}_q$ computing the polynomial f. Actually, the Σ-protocol in our paper is the weaker version defined in [8,1] called gap Σ-protocol. Intuitively, the extracted witness is in a larger relation set, which may lead to stronger assumptions when we view it as a zero-knowledge proof. Most existing Σ-protocols [1,17,21,22,25] for hard lattice relations (say,LWE,SIS,CVP,SVP) are gap Σ-protocols, i.e., the extracted short vectors (witness) are at least $O(\sqrt{n})$, which we call the gap factor, longer than the original one. Our protocol has an almost optimal gap factor

(< 2) as the zero-knowledge proof for ISIS relation in [20], which means that we almost do not need to strength the underlying lattice assumption in the zero-knowledge proof. The gap factor can even achieve to 1, with the cost of larger communication complexity.

1.2 Difficulties and Our Techniques

We first roughly review the main ideas in [16] and [20]. The LPN based Σ-protocol in [16] extends Stern's [27] zero-knowledge proof of knowledge for the syndrome decoding problem. Informally, the prover generates three encapsulation commitments to the verifier, then the verifier randomly chooses a uniformly challenge in $\{1, 2, 3\}$, and the prover opens two commitments according to the challenge. The first two openings proves the public inputs $\mathbf{A}, \mathbf{c}$ have the form $\mathbf{c} = \mathbf{A}(\mathbf{s}\|\mathbf{m}) + \mathbf{e}$. The third opening proves that $\mathbf{e}$ is "short". The major difficulty here is how to convince the verifier that $\mathbf{e}$ is "short" without revealing anything else of $\mathbf{e}$. In [16], for bit string $\mathbf{e}$ has low Hamming weight, the prover sends $\pi(\mathbf{e})$ for uniformly chosen and hidden permutation π to the verifier. In order not to leak other information of $\mathbf{e}$, they insist that $\mathbf{e}$ has exact Hamming, say β. Now $\pi(\mathbf{e})$ only leaks the Hamming weight of $\mathbf{e}$ (but the verifier already knows it) with uniformly random and hidden π. This restriction leads to a variant of the LPN assumption which they call the exact LPN or xLPN assumption. The standard LPN assumption which only needs the Hamming weight of $\mathbf{e}$ is less than β could not work here, because $\pi(\mathbf{e})$ leaks information, at least the weight (the verifier does not know), of $\mathbf{e}$.

When dealing with $\mathbf{e}$ does not have exact weight. Ling et al. introduced a Decomposition-Extension technique in [20]. Taking LWE for example, consider the infinity norm of $\mathbf{e} \in \mathbb{Z}^m$, i.e., $\|\mathbf{e}\|_\infty \leq \beta$, they first decompose $\mathbf{e}$ to k vectors $\tilde{\mathbf{e}}_i$ for $0 \leq i \leq k-1$, where $\tilde{\mathbf{e}}_i \in \{-1, 0, 1\}^m$, such that $\mathbf{e} = \sum_{i=0}^{k-1} 2^i \tilde{\mathbf{e}}_i$, where $k = \lfloor \log \beta \rfloor + 1$. In order to prove $\tilde{\mathbf{e}}_i$ belongs to $\{-1, 0, 1\}^m$ without revealing. Since $\pi(\tilde{\mathbf{e}}_i)$ leaks the information of $\tilde{\mathbf{e}}$, extend $\tilde{\mathbf{e}}$ to $\mathbf{e}_i$ with larger dimension by appending $2m$ elements in $\{-1, 0, 1\}$ such that the numbers of $-1, 0, 1$ in $\mathbf{e}_i$ are exactly m. The prover sends $\pi'(\mathbf{e}_i)$ to the verifier, and the verifier can only check that $\tilde{\mathbf{e}}_i \in \{-1, 0, 1\}^m$ without knowing anything else. This is because $\pi'(\mathbf{e}_i)$ is uniformly random and independent of $\tilde{\mathbf{e}}_i$ with random and hidden π'. Let's turn back to the standard LPN based Σ-protocol. For bit string $\mathbf{e} \in \{0, 1\}^m$ has small Hamming weight, i.e., $\|\mathbf{e}\|_1 \leq \beta$. Extend $\mathbf{e}$ to $\hat{\mathbf{e}} \in \{0, 1\}^{m+\beta}$ by appending bits to $\mathbf{e}$ such that $\|\mathbf{e}\|_1 = \beta$. The prover then sends $\pi'(\hat{\mathbf{e}})$ to the verifier. As before, the verifier can check that $\|\mathbf{e}\|_1 \leq \beta$ without knowing anything else.

The major difficulty to prove polynomial relations is to handle the multiplicative relation, i.e., prove that the committed messages $\mathbf{m}_1, \mathbf{m}_2, \mathbf{m}_3$ satisfying $\mathbf{m}_3 = \mathbf{m}_1 \circ \mathbf{m}_2$, where $\circ$ denotes the component-wise multiplication. Our technique to address this difficulty is a generalization but in a more direct way of the method used in [16] to prove bitwise relations. We first consider a "naive" case for LWE with polynomial q, where $\mathbf{m}_i \in \mathbb{Z}_q^\ell$ for $1 \leq i \leq 3$. In the proof, the prover first extends $\mathbf{m}_1, \mathbf{m}_2$ to $\hat{\mathbf{m}}_1, \hat{\mathbf{m}}_2$ with dimension $q^2\ell$ by setting $\hat{\mathbf{m}}_i = (\mathbf{m}_i\|\bar{\mathbf{m}}_i)$, where $\bar{\mathbf{m}}_i \leftarrow \mathbb{Z}_q^{(q^2-1)\ell}$ for $i = 1, 2$ such that for any pair $(a, b) \in \mathbb{Z}_q \times \mathbb{Z}_q$, the number of j satisfying $(a, b) = (\hat{\mathbf{m}}_1[j], \hat{\mathbf{m}}_2[j])$ is exactly ℓ. Then let $\hat{\mathbf{m}}_3 = \hat{\mathbf{m}}_1 \circ \hat{\mathbf{m}}_2$. Denote $\hat{\mathbf{I}}$ to be the ℓ dimension identity matrix appended by $(q^2 - 1)\ell$ column 0. It's easy to see that $\mathbf{m}_i = \hat{\mathbf{I}} \cdot \hat{\mathbf{m}}_i$, for $i = 1, 2, 3$. Although $\hat{\mathbf{m}}_i$ leaks all the information of $\mathbf{m}_i$, $\pi(\hat{\mathbf{m}}_i)$ is independent of $\mathbf{m}_i$ except for the multiplicative relation for uniformly and hidden π. The communication complexity here is very large, but this simple proof system enjoys another property. If the encapsulation commitment is statistically hiding, we get statistical zero-knowledge. Theoretically, we can use the result in [14] to obtain statistically hiding commitment schemes from RLWE assumption. However the protocol in [16] only achieves computational zero-knowledge.

To get small communication complexity zero-knowledge proof, we look into the techniques used in the "naive" method. The reason we get large dimension is that the committed message is from large $\mathbb{Z}_q$, this brings to dimension q^2. The method we use here is to convince the verifier that the committed value is actually from $\mathbb{Z}_2$, this only brings to dimension by a constant factor 4. More concretely, we first propose a Σ-protocol to prove that the committed value is in $\mathbb{Z}_2$. Then, by using this basic protocol, the prover decomposes $\mathbf{m}_i = \sum_{j=0}^{\lfloor \log q \rfloor} 2^j \cdot \mathbf{m}_{ij}$ for $i = 1, 2$, and commits each $\mathbf{m}_{jk} = \mathbf{m}_{1j} \diamond \mathbf{m}_{2k}$ and $\mathbf{m}_{1j}, \mathbf{m}_{2k}$ along with $\mathbf{m}_1, \mathbf{m}_2, \mathbf{m}_3$ to the verifier, $\diamond$ means component-wise bit multiplication. Then the prover convince that the $\mathbf{m}_{1j}$ and $\mathbf{m}_{1k}$ are in $\mathbb{Z}_2$ and satisfy that

$$\mathbf{m}_1 = \sum_{j=0}^{\lfloor \log q \rfloor} 2^j \cdot \mathbf{m}_{1j};\ \mathbf{m}_2 = \sum_{k=0}^{\lfloor \log q \rfloor} 2^k \cdot \mathbf{m}_{2k};\ \mathbf{m}_{jk} = \mathbf{m}_{1j} \diamond \mathbf{m}_{2k};\ \mathbf{m}_3 = \sum_{j,k} 2^{j+k} \cdot \mathbf{m}_{jk}.$$

This method only extends the dimension from ℓ to 4ℓ (instead of $q^2\ell$), hence has low communication complexity. However, it needs extra $O(\log^2 q)$ commitments, and only achieves computational zero-knowledge.

In the RLWE case, actually we can not directly use the above techniques, this is because the number of elements in the polynomial ring R_q is exponential which results undesirable exponential large dimension. To address this problem, we apply the Chinese Remainder Theorem (CRT) representation of ring elements. The important property is that the multiplication of ring elements under CRT is just component-wise multiplication under $\mathbb{Z}_q$. This helps us to construct Σ-protocol in the RLWE case, and also brings better amortized communication complexity.

1.3 Other Related Works

Several zero-knowledge proofs of knowledge based on lattice have been proposed. Kawachi et al. [17] construct an identification scheme based on the SIS problem, and very recently Ling et al. [20] improve the efficiency and weaken the assumption. Cayrel et al. [3,4] give an identification scheme with 5 round and soundness error 1/2. Asharov et al. [1] propose Σ-protocols for various LWE problems.

However, their construction exclusively use the "smudge out" technique, which only works for super-polynomial size module.

2 Preliminaries

Notations A function negl(λ) is *negligible*, if it vanishes faster than the inverse of any polynomial in λ. For a vector $\mathbf{v}$, we denote $\|\mathbf{v}\|_\infty$ as the infinity norm. We denote $R = \mathbb{Z}[X]/(\Phi_M(X))$, where $\Phi_M(X)$ is the M-th cyclotomic polynomial. For simplicity, we only consider power of 2 cyclotomic rings, i.e. $M = 2^k$ for some positive integer k. We note that our results can be easily extended to any cyclomotic rings by using the techniques in [24]. Denote $R_q = R/qR$. For a prime integer $q = 1 \mod M$, the field $\mathbb{Z}_q$ contains a primitive M-th root of unity ζ, because the multiplicative group of $\mathbb{Z}_q$ is cyclic with order $q-1$. Indeed, there are $\phi(M)$ distinct such roots of unity $\zeta^i \in \mathbb{Z}_q$, for $i \in \mathbb{Z}_M^*$, where $\phi(\cdot)$ is Euler's totient function. Therefore, $f(x)$ splits into linear terms modulo q, $\Phi_M(X) = \prod_{i\in\mathbb{Z}_M^*}(X - \zeta^i) \mod q$.

Coefficient and Chinese Remaindering (CRT) *Representation.* For an element $a \in R_q$, let $d = \phi(M)$, we consider two ways of representing it: Viewing a as a degree $d-1$ polynomial $a(X) = \sum_{i=0}^{d-1} a_i X^i$, we can list all the coefficients in order $\mathbf{a} = (a_0, ..., a_{d-1}) \in \mathbb{Z}_q^d$. We call $\mathbf{a}$ the coefficient representation of a. For the other representation, we consider the value that the polynomial $a(X)$ assigns on all primitive M-th roots of unity modulo q, $\hat{a}_i = a(\zeta^i) \mod q$ for $i \in \mathbb{Z}_M^*$. The $\hat{a}_i$ in order also yield a vector $\hat{\mathbf{a}} \in \mathbb{Z}_q^d$, which we call it the CRT representation. These two representations are related via $\hat{\mathbf{a}} = \mathbf{V} \cdot \mathbf{a}$, where $\mathbf{V}$ is the Vandermonde matrix over the primitive M-th root of unity modulo q. For a ring element $a \in R_q$, we view it either a single element in R_q or a vector in $\mathbb{Z}_q^d$ by the coefficient representation, and we define the bijective map σ, such that $\sigma(a)$ is either the same ring element in R_q, or a vector in $\mathbb{Z}_q^d$ by the CRT representation. The CRT representation has very nice property, the addition and multiplication in R_q can be computed as component-wise addition and multiplication of the entries of CRT form. I.e. for $a, b \in R_q$, we have $\sigma(a+b) = \sigma(a) + \sigma(b)$ and $\sigma(a \cdot b) = \sigma(a) \odot \sigma(b)$, where $\odot$ denotes the component-wise multiplication in $\mathbb{Z}_q$ of the vector in the CRT form.

A distribution χ from $\mathbb{Z}$ is called β-bounded if $\Pr_{e\leftarrow\chi}[|e| > \beta] = \text{negl}(n)$. Denote $\mathcal{B}^{3m} \in \{-1, 0, 1\}^{3dm}$ as the set of vectors with the numbers of -1,0, and 1 are exactly dm, and denote $\mathcal{B}^{2\ell} \in \{0,1\}^{2d\ell}$ as the set of vectors with the numbers of 0, 1 are exactly $d\ell$. Denote $\mathcal{S}_k$ be the set of all permutations on k elements. For a vector $\mathbf{a} \in R_q^n$ and $\pi \in \mathcal{S}_{dn}$, we denote $\pi(\mathbf{a})$ and $\pi(\sigma(\mathbf{a}))$ to permute the elements in $\mathbb{Z}_q$ when we view $\mathbf{a}$ and $\sigma(\mathbf{a})$ as vectors in $\mathbb{Z}_q^{dn}$.

2.1 Commitment Schemes

A commitment scheme consists of three algorithms (KGen, Com, Ver). Where KGen on input security parameter λ, outputs a public key pk. Com on input a message m, a public key pk, outputs a commitment/opening pair (c, d). Ver on input a public key pk, a message m, and pair commitment/opening pair (c, d), output 1 or 0.

The commitment scheme satisfies the three security properties: *Correctness* needs Ver evaluates to 1 when the inputs are computed honestly. I.e. $\mathsf{Ver}(pk, m, c, d) = 1$, where $pk \leftarrow \mathsf{KGen}(1^\lambda)$, $(c, d) \leftarrow \mathsf{Com}(pk, m)$. *Hiding* needs the commitment c hiding the information of the message. I.e. the distributions of c_0, c_1 are computational or statistically indistinguishable, where $(c_0, d_0) \leftarrow \mathsf{Com}(pk, m_0)$, $(c_1, d_1) \leftarrow \mathsf{Com}(pk, m_1)$ for any m_0, m_1. *Binding* requires that any commitment c can not be opened to two different messages. I.e. the probability of $m \neq m'$ is negligible, if $\mathsf{Ver}(pk, c, m, d) = \mathsf{Ver}(pk, c, m', d') = 1$.

2.2 Σ-Protocols

In this subsection, we adopt the definition of Σ-protocols as in [16]. Let $(\mathcal{P}, \mathcal{V})$ be a two party protocol, where $\mathcal{V}$ is PPT, and let $\mathcal{R}$ be a binary relation. A Σ-protocol $(\mathcal{P}, \mathcal{V})$ for $\mathcal{R}$ with challenge set $\mathcal{C}$, public input y and private input ω is a three rounds protocol with transcript (t, c, s). t is a commitment sent from $\mathcal{P}$ to $\mathcal{V}$, c is randomly chosen from $\mathcal{C}$ by the verifier $\mathcal{V}$, and $\mathcal{P}$ responds s to $\mathcal{V}$. Finally, $\mathcal{V}$ accepts or reject the proof according to (t, c, s). Besides, a Σ-protocol requires other three properties:

Completeness : The verifier $\mathcal{V}$ accepts whenever $(y, \omega) \in \mathcal{R}$.

Special Soundness : There exists a PPT algorithm Ext which takes as input a set $\{(t, c, s_c) : c \in \mathcal{C}\}$ of accepting transcripts with the same commitment, outputs ω' such that $(y, \omega') \in \mathcal{R}$.

Special honest-verifier zero-knowledge : There exists a PPT simulator $\mathcal{S}$ takes as input y and $c \in \mathcal{C}$, outputs triples (t, c, s) whose distribution is indistinguishable from accepting protocol transcriptions generated by the real protocol runs.

It's well known that a Σ-protocol can be extended to a proof of knowledge for the same relation [9,10]. Here the definition of Σ-protocol (as in [16]) is a little different from the standard one defined in [9]. We loose the special soundness by only requiring ω' can be computed given valid responses to *all* challenges for a fixed commitment. As discussed in [16], the knowledge error of the resulting proof of knowledge is given by $1 - 1/|\mathcal{C}|$ instead of $1/|\mathcal{C}|$ in the standard definition.

We remark that, the Σ-protocols in this paper are slightly different from the the definition above. The extracted witness lies in a slightly larger space. This is weaker version called Gap Σ-protocol, which is already considered in [8,1]. In this paper, the original witness space is integer vectors with norm no more that β, and the norm of the extracted witness is no more that β'. We call the ratio β'/β the gap factor. The protocols in this paper achieves constant gap factor which is almost optimal.

2.3 Lattices and Hard Problems

A m-dimensional lattice Λ is a discrete additive subgroup whose linear span is $\mathbb{R}^m$. Every lattice is generated as the $\mathbb{Z}$-linear combination of some basis of linearly independent vectors $\mathbf{B} = \{\mathbf{b}_1, ..., \mathbf{b}_m\} \subset \mathbb{R}^m$, i.e.,$\Lambda = \{\sum_{i=1}^m z_i \mathbf{b}_i : z_i \in \mathbb{Z}\}$. Denote $\lambda_1^\infty(\Lambda)$ be the infinity norm of the shortest non-zero vector in Λ. We define "q-ary" lattices. For a matrix $\mathbf{A} \in R_q^{m\times n}$, define the integer lattice

$$\Lambda_q(\mathbf{A}) = \{\mathbf{y} \in R^m : \exists \mathbf{x} \in R_q^n, \text{ s.t. } \mathbf{A}\mathbf{x} = \mathbf{y} \mod q\}.$$

The Ring Learning with Errors (RLWE) Problem. The Ring Learning with Errors (RLWE) problem is introduced by Lyubaskevsky, Peikert and Regev [23] which extends the Learning with Errors (LWE) problem proposed by Regev [26] to the ring case. For a security parameter λ, let $d = \phi(M)$, M is a power of 2. Let $q \geq 2$ be an integer. Let $R = \mathbb{Z}[X]/(\Phi_M(X))$ and $R_q = R/qR$. Let χ be a distribution over R. The $\mathsf{RLWE}_{d,q,\chi}$ problem is to distinguish the following two distributions: In the first distribution, one samples (a_i, b_i) uniformly from $R_q \times R_q$. In the second distribution, one first draws $s \leftarrow R_q$ uniformly and then samples $(a_i, b_i) \in R_q \times R_q$ by sampling $a_i \leftarrow R_q$ uniformly, $e_i \leftarrow \chi$, and setting $b_i = a_i \cdot s + e_i$. The $\mathsf{RLWE}_{d,q,\chi}$ assumption is that the $\mathsf{RLWE}_{d,q,\chi}$ problem is infeasible. Denote the assumption by $\mathsf{RLWE}_{d,q,\chi}^{(m)}$ when we require the indistinguishability to hold given only m samples. We state the hardness of the special case of $\mathsf{RLWE}_{d,q,\chi}^{(m)}$ described in [23] as follows.

Theorem 1 ([23]). *For ring $R = \mathbb{Z}[X]/(\Phi_M(X))$, $d = \phi(M)$, M is a power of 2, and prime integer $q = q(d) = 1 \mod M$, and $\beta = \omega(\sqrt{d \log d})$, there is an efficiently samplable distribution χ that outputs elements of R with norm at most β with overwhelming probability, such that if there exists an efficient algorithm that solves $\mathsf{RLWE}_{d,q,\chi}^{(m)}$, then there is an efficient quantum algorithm for solving $d^{2.5} \cdot (q/\beta) \cdot (dm/\log(dm))^{1/4}$-approximate worst-case* SVP *for ideal lattices over R.*

3 Commitment Scheme from RLWE Assumption

The message space is R_q^ℓ, where $\ell = \ell(\lambda)$. Let χ be a β-bounded distribution over R. The algorithms are given as follows:

KGen : Chooses $\mathbf{a}_1 \leftarrow R_q^m$ and $\mathbf{A}_2 \leftarrow R_q^{m\times\ell}$. Set $pk = \mathbf{A} = [\mathbf{a}_1 \| \mathbf{A}_2]$.

Com : For a message $\mathbf{m} \in R_q^\ell$, choose a uniformly random vector $s \leftarrow R_q$, and choose a vector $\mathbf{e} \leftarrow \chi^m$. Output the commitment $\mathbf{c} = \mathbf{A}(s\|\mathbf{m}) + \mathbf{e}$.

Ver : Given a commitment $\mathbf{c}$, the message $\mathbf{m}'$ and the randomness s', the verifier accepts iff $\|\mathbf{c} - \mathbf{A}(s'\|\mathbf{m}')\|_\infty \leq \beta$.

Theorem 2. *Let $m = (\ell + 1) \cdot \omega(\log \lambda)$, $\beta < q/2d$. If $\mathsf{RLWE}_{d,q,\chi}^{(m)}$ is hard. Then the above commitment scheme is perfectly binding (with overwhelming probability over the public key) and computationally hiding.*

Proof. The correctness is obvious, we show the binding and hiding properties.

Perfect binding . Assume that $\mathbf{m}_i, s_i, i = 1, 2$ are two different openings for a commitment $\mathbf{c}$. That is $\mathbf{e}_i = \mathbf{c} - \mathbf{A}(s_i \| \mathbf{m}_i)$ has infinity norm at most β for $i = 1, 2$. Thus, we have $\mathbf{e}_1 - \mathbf{e}_2 = \mathbf{A}(s_2 - s_1 \| \mathbf{m}_2 - \mathbf{m}_1)$ with infinity norm $\|\mathbf{e}_1 - \mathbf{e}_2\|_\infty \leq \|\mathbf{e}_1\|_\infty + \|\mathbf{e}_2\|_\infty < 2\beta$. Since $\mathbf{A}$ is uniformly random, by applying Lemma 1 showed below, with overwhelming probability over the choice of $\mathbf{A}$, for every non-zero vector $\mathbf{x} \in R_q^n$, $\|\mathbf{A}\mathbf{x}\|_\infty \geq 2\beta$ for nonzero $\mathbf{x}$. Since $\mathbf{m}_1, \mathbf{m}_2$ are different, there is a contradiction.

Computational hiding . Since $\mathbf{c} = \mathbf{a}_1 \cdot s + \mathbf{e} + \mathbf{A}_2\mathbf{m}$, and by the $\mathsf{RLWE}_{d,q,\chi}^{(m)}$ assumption, $\mathbf{c}$ is pseudorandom. □

Theoretically, the length of the message ℓ can be arbitrary, but for efficiency reasons it's better to choose $\ell = O(1)$, and $m = \omega(\log \lambda)$.

Lemma 1 ([19] Lemma 21). *Let n, m, d, q be positive integers with $n \leq m$. We have:* $\Pr_{\mathbf{A} \leftarrow R_q^{m \times n}}[\lambda_1^\infty(\Lambda_q(\mathbf{A})) \geq \frac{1}{8\sqrt{d}} q^{1-\frac{n}{m}}] \geq 1 - (\frac{1}{2\sqrt{d}})^{nd}$.

4 Zero-Knowledge Proofs of Knowledge

In this section, we construct Σ-protocols to prove knowledge of valid openings, linear relations and multiplicative relations.

4.1 Proving Knowledge of a Valid Opening

We propose a Σ-protocol analogous to the ones presented in [20,16]. The structure is essentially the same, and we extend its security to base on the RLWE assumption. We construct a Σ-protocol for the following relation:

$$\mathcal{R}_{\mathsf{RLWE}} = \{((\mathbf{A}, \mathbf{c}), (s, \mathbf{m}, \mathbf{e})) \ : \ \mathbf{c} = \mathbf{A}(s \| \mathbf{m}) + \mathbf{e} \mod q \ \wedge \ \|\mathbf{e}\|_\infty \leq \beta\}.$$

We adapt the techniques in [20], and we note that the ISIS proof in [20] implicitly implies this protocol. The common inputs to prover $\mathcal{P}$ and verifier $\mathcal{V}$ is $\mathbf{A} \in R_q^{m \times (1+\ell)}$ and $\mathbf{c} \in R_q^m$, $\mathcal{P}$ has secret input $(s, \mathbf{m}, \mathbf{e})$ where $s \in R_q$, $\mathbf{m} \in R_q^\ell$, $\mathbf{e} \in R^m$. $\mathcal{P}$ and $\mathcal{V}$ first define a common matrix $\hat{\mathbf{I}} \in R^{m \times 3m}$ by appending $2m$ zero columns to identity matrix $\mathbf{I}_m \in R^m$. $\mathcal{P}$ first decomposes $\mathbf{e} \in R^m$ to $k = \lfloor \log \beta \rfloor + 1$ vectors $\tilde{\mathbf{e}}_i \in R^m$ with coefficients in $\{-1, 0, 1\}$ such that $\mathbf{e} = \sum_{i=0}^{k-1} 2^i \cdot \tilde{\mathbf{e}}_i$. Then $\mathcal{P}$ extends each $\tilde{\mathbf{e}}_i$ to a vector $\mathbf{e}_i = (\tilde{\mathbf{e}}_i \| \bar{\mathbf{e}}_i) \in \mathcal{B}^{3m}$, where $\bar{\mathbf{e}}_i$ is randomly chosen from $\{-1, 0, 1\}^{2dm}$. We have:

$$\mathbf{c} = \mathbf{A}(s \| \mathbf{m}) + \mathbf{e} \Leftrightarrow \mathbf{c} = \mathbf{A}(s \| \mathbf{m}) + \hat{\mathbf{I}}(\sum_{i=0}^{k-1} 2^i \cdot \mathbf{e}_i)$$

The protocol is given as follows, where the commitment scheme $\mathsf{Com}(\cdot)$ is a string commitment scheme, and can be instantiated from the RLWE based one.

$\mathcal{P}$ samples k uniformly random vector $(\mathbf{r}_0, ..., \mathbf{r}_{k-1}) \leftarrow (R_q^{3m})^k$, a uniformly random vector $\mathbf{v} \leftarrow R_q^{1+\ell}$, and k random permutations $(\pi_0, ..., \pi_{k-1}) \leftarrow (\mathcal{S}_{3dm})^k$. It sends the following commitments to the verifier $\mathcal{V}$:

$$\begin{cases} C_1 = \mathsf{Com}\Big(\{\pi_i\}_{i=0}^{k-1}, \mathbf{t}_1 = \mathbf{A}\mathbf{v} + \hat{\mathbf{I}}(\sum_{i=0}^{k-1} 2^i \cdot \mathbf{r}_i)\Big) \\ C_2 = \mathsf{Com}\Big(\{\mathbf{t}_{2i} = \pi_i(\mathbf{r}_i)\}_{i=0}^{k-1}\Big) \\ C_3 = \mathsf{Com}\Big(\{\mathbf{t}_{3i} = \pi_i(\mathbf{r}_i + \mathbf{e}_i)\}_{i=0}^{k-1}\Big) \end{cases}$$

The verifier $\mathcal{V}$ draws $Ch \leftarrow \{1, 2, 3\}$, and sends it to $\mathcal{P}$.

Depending on the value of Ch, $\mathcal{P}$ opens the following commitments:

$Ch = 1$: $\mathcal{P}$ opens C_1, C_2 by sending $\{\pi_i\}_{i=0}^{k-1}, \mathbf{t}_1, \{\mathbf{t}_{2i}\}_{i=0}^{k-1}$ and the associated random coins of the commitment.

$Ch = 2$: $\mathcal{P}$ opens C_1, C_3 by sending $\{\pi_i\}_{i=0}^{k-1}, \mathbf{t}_1, \{\mathbf{t}_{3i}\}_{i=0}^{k-1}$ and the associated random coins of the commitment.

$Ch = 3$: $\mathcal{P}$ opens C_2, C_3 by sending $\{\mathbf{t}_{2i}\}_{i=0}^{k-1}, \{\mathbf{t}_{3i}\}_{i=0}^{k-1}$ and the associated random coins of the commitment.

The verifier $\mathcal{V}$ checks the correctness of the opening from the prover $\mathcal{P}$, and additionally performs the following checks depending on the challenge Ch:

$Ch = 1$: $\mathcal{V}$ accepts, iff $\mathbf{t}_1 - \hat{\mathbf{I}} \cdot (\sum_{i=0}^{k-1} 2^i \cdot \pi_i^{-1}(\mathbf{t}_{2i})) \in \Lambda_q(\mathbf{A})$ and $\{\pi_i\}_{i=0}^{k-1} \in (\mathcal{S}_{3dm})^k$.

$Ch = 2$: $\mathcal{V}$ accepts, iff $\mathbf{t}_1 + \mathbf{c} - \hat{\mathbf{I}} \cdot (\sum_{i=0}^{k-1} 2^i \cdot \pi_i^{-1}(\mathbf{t}_{3i})) \in \Lambda_q(\mathbf{A})$ and $\{\pi_i\}_{i=0}^{k-1} \in (\mathcal{S}_{3dm})^k$.

$Ch = 3$: $\mathcal{V}$ accepts, iff $\mathbf{t}_{3i} - \mathbf{t}_{2i} \in \mathcal{B}^{3m}$ for all $0 \leq i \leq k-1$.

Theorem 3. *The above protocol is a Σ-protocol for the $\mathcal{R}_{\mathsf{RLWE}}$ relation, where*

$$\mathcal{R}_{\mathsf{RLWE}} = \Big\{ \Big((\mathbf{A}, \mathbf{c}), (s, \mathbf{m}, \mathbf{e})\Big) : \Big(\mathbf{c} = \mathbf{A}(s \| \mathbf{m}) + \mathbf{e}\Big) \wedge \|\mathbf{e}\|_\infty \leq \beta \Big\}.$$

Proof. The correctness is obvious, we show the other properties hold.

Special Soundness. Assume that we have fixed values C_1, C_2, C_3 and openings for all challenges $Ch \in \{1, 2, 3\}$, such that the verifier accepts on all of them. Then by the binding property of the underlying commitment scheme $\mathsf{Com}(\cdot)$, we know that the openings to identical commitments must be identical for different challenges.

By the verification equations for $Ch = 1$ and $Ch = 2$, we get that $\mathbf{t}_1 - \hat{\mathbf{I}} \cdot (\sum_{i=0}^{k-1} 2^i \cdot \pi_i^{-1}(\mathbf{t}_{2i})) = \mathbf{A}(s_1 \| \mathbf{m}_1)$, and $\mathbf{t}_1 + \mathbf{c} - \hat{\mathbf{I}} \cdot (\sum_{i=0}^{k-1} 2^i \cdot \pi_i^{-1}(\mathbf{t}_{3i})) = \mathbf{A}(s_2 \| \mathbf{m}_2)$, for some $s_1, s_2 \in R_q$, $\mathbf{m}_1, \mathbf{m}_2 \in R_q^\ell$. Therefore, $\mathbf{c} = \mathbf{A}(s_2 - s_1 \| \mathbf{m}_2 - \mathbf{m}_1) + \hat{\mathbf{I}} \cdot (\sum_{i=0}^{k-1} 2^i \cdot \pi_i^{-1}(\mathbf{t}_{3i} - \mathbf{t}_{2i})) \mod q$. From $Ch = 3$ we get $\mathbf{t}_{3i} - \mathbf{t}_{2i} \in \mathcal{B}^{3dm}$ for all $0 \leq i \leq k-1$, then also $\pi_i^{-1}(\mathbf{t}_{3i} - \mathbf{t}_{2i}) \in \mathcal{B}^{3dm}$ for all $0 \leq i \leq k-1$. By the definition of $\hat{\mathbf{I}}$, we get that $\|\hat{\mathbf{I}} \cdot (\sum_{i=0}^{k-1} 2^i \cdot \pi_i^{-1}(\mathbf{t}_{3i} - \mathbf{t}_{2i}))\|_\infty \leq 2\beta - 1$. Therefore, we have a valid witness $\Big(s_2 - s_1, \mathbf{m}_2 - \mathbf{m}_1, \hat{\mathbf{I}} \cdot (\sum_{i=0}^{k-1} 2^i \cdot \pi_i^{-1}(\mathbf{t}_{3i} - \mathbf{t}_{2i}))\Big)$.

Special Honest-Verifier Zero-Knowledge. We now describe an efficient simulator S, which for each challenge $Ch \in \{1, 2, 3\}$ outputs an accepting protocol transcript. The distribution of the transcript is indistinguishable from the real protocol transcript with an honest prover for challenge Ch.

$Ch = 1$: The simulator S computes C_1, C_2 like an honest prover, and computes C_3 as a commitment to 0. Clearly, the distribution of $C_1, C_2, \{\pi_i\}_{i=0}^{k-1}, \mathbf{t}_1, \{\mathbf{t}_{2i}\}_{i=0}^{k-1}$ is identical to that in real protocol. By the hiding property of the commitment, the distribution of C_3 is computationally indistinguishable to the real protocol.

$Ch = 2$: The simulator S first chooses uniformly random vector $\mathbf{u} \leftarrow R_q^{1+\ell}$, $\{\mathbf{f}_i\}_{i=0}^{k-1} \leftarrow (R_q^{3m})^k$, and k random permutations $\{\pi_i\}_{i=0}^{k} \leftarrow (\mathcal{S}_{3dm})^k$. It sets $C_1 = \mathsf{Com}(\{\pi_i\}_{i=0}^{k-1}, \mathbf{Au} + \hat{\mathbf{I}} \cdot (\sum_{i=0}^{k-1} 2^i \cdot \mathbf{f}_i) - \mathbf{c})$, and $C_3 = \mathsf{Com}(\{\pi_i(\mathbf{f}_i)\}_{i=0}^{k-1})$, and computes C_2 as a commitment to 0. It's easy to see that the opening of C_1, C_3 pass the verification. To see the correctness of the distribution, in the simulated content of C_1, the first part (permutations) are randomly chosen which are identical to the real protocol. The second part is $\mathbf{A}(\mathbf{u}-s\|\mathbf{m}) + \hat{\mathbf{I}} \cdot (\sum_{i=0}^{k-1} 2^i(\mathbf{f}_i - \mathbf{e}_i))$, we can view $\mathbf{r}_i = \mathbf{f}_i - \mathbf{e}_i$ for $0 \le i \le k-1$. Since $\mathbf{f}_i$ are uniformly random in R_q^{3m}, and so are $\mathbf{r}_i$. We know that $\mathbf{f}_i = \mathbf{r}_i + \mathbf{e}_i$, therefore, the content of C_3 is $\{\pi_i(\mathbf{r}_i + \mathbf{e}_i)\}_{i=0}^{k-1}$. Thus, the distribution of C_1, C_3 and their opening are perfectly simulated, and the distribution of C_2 is indistinguishable from the real protocol by the hiding property of the commitment scheme.

$Ch = 3$: The simulator chooses uniformly random vectors $\{\mathbf{r}'_i\}_{i=0}^{k-1} \leftarrow (R_q^{3m})^k$, and $\{\mathbf{e}'_i\}_{i=0}^{k-1} \leftarrow (\mathcal{B}_{3m})^k$. It then computes C_1 as a commitment to 0, $C_2 = \mathsf{Com}(\{\mathbf{r}'_i\}_{i=0}^{k-1})$, and $C_3 = \mathsf{Com}(\{\mathbf{r}'_i + \mathbf{e}'_i\}_{i=0}^{k-1})$. As before, the distribution of C_1 is indistinguishable to the real protocol by the hiding property of the commitment scheme, and C_2, C_3 as well as their openings can easily be seen to perfectly simulate the behavior of an honest prover. □

4.2 Component-Wise Relations

In this section, we describe Σ-protocols to prove component-wise relations of the committed messages of $\mathbf{c}_1, \mathbf{c}_2, \mathbf{c}_3$. That is, it allows one to prove the messages satisfy $\mathbf{m}_3 = \mathbf{m}_1 \circ \mathbf{m}_2$, where $\circ$ denotes the component-wise addition or multiplicative in R_q. Our techniques are simpler and more direct than [16]. We remark that by using the CRT representation, the component-wise addition and multiplication on R_q^ℓ can be seen as component-wise addition and multiplication in $\mathbb{Z}_q$ respectively, when we take $\sigma(\mathbf{m}_i)$ as a vector in $\mathbb{Z}_q^{d\ell}$. We give two protocols to prove this relation, the first one is simpler but with larger communication complexity, the other one is more involved but with small complexity.

In the first protocol, the prover with secret inputs $\mathbf{m}_1, \mathbf{m}_2, \mathbf{m}_3 \in R_q^\ell$ first views the messages as vectors in $\mathbb{Z}_q^{d\ell}$ by using the CRT representation. I.e. $\sigma(\mathbf{m}_1), \sigma(\mathbf{m}_2), \sigma(\mathbf{m}_3)$. We note that $\mathbf{m}_3 = \mathbf{m}_1 \circ \mathbf{m}_2 \Leftrightarrow \sigma(\mathbf{m}_3) = \sigma(\mathbf{m}_1) \odot \sigma(\mathbf{m}_2)$. Where $\odot$ denotes component-wise addition and multiplication in $\mathbb{Z}_q^{d\ell}$. It then extends $\sigma(\mathbf{m}_1), \sigma(\mathbf{m}_2)$ to $\hat{\mathbf{m}}_1$, $\hat{\mathbf{m}}_2$ with $\hat{\mathbf{m}}_1 = (\sigma(\mathbf{m}_1)\|\bar{\mathbf{m}}_1) \in \mathbb{Z}_q^{dq^2\ell}$, $\hat{\mathbf{m}}_2 = (\sigma(\mathbf{m}_2)\|\bar{\mathbf{m}}_2) \in \mathbb{Z}_q^{dq^2\ell}$ by randomly choosing $\bar{\mathbf{m}}_1, \bar{\mathbf{m}}_2 \in \mathbb{Z}_q^{d(q^2-1)\ell}$ such that for any pair $(a, b) \in \mathbb{Z}_q^2$ the number of index $j \in \{1, ..., dq^2\ell\}$ satisfying $\hat{\mathbf{m}}_1[j] = \hat{\mathbf{m}}_2[j]$ is exactly $d\ell$, here we assume $q = \text{poly}(\lambda)$. $\hat{\mathbf{m}}_1, \hat{\mathbf{m}}_2$ also can be seen as vectors in $R_q^{q^2\ell}$ according to the CRT representation. Then set $\hat{\mathbf{m}}_3 = \hat{\mathbf{m}}_1 \odot \hat{\mathbf{m}}_2$. Denote $\hat{\mathbf{I}}_2 \in R^{\ell \times q^2\ell}$ by appending $(q^2-1)\ell$ zero columns to identity matrices $\mathbf{I}_\ell \in R^{\ell\times\ell}$, then $\mathbf{m}_i = \hat{\mathbf{I}}_2 \cdot (\sigma^{-1}(\hat{\mathbf{m}}_i))$. Although $\hat{\mathbf{m}}_i$ leaks information of $\mathbf{m}_i$, we note that $\pi(\hat{\mathbf{m}}_i)$ is completely random and independent of $\mathbf{m}_i$, for uniformly random permutations in $\mathcal{S}_{dq^2\ell}$. $\mathcal{P}$ and $\mathcal{V}$ now run the basic protocol from the previous section to prove the validity of $\mathbf{m}_i$ simultaneously, and $\mathcal{P}$ proves the relation $\pi(\hat{\mathbf{m}}_3) = \pi(\hat{\mathbf{m}}_1) \odot \pi(\hat{\mathbf{m}}_2)$. The special soundness from the fact that $\hat{\mathbf{I}}_2 \cdot \pi(\hat{\mathbf{m}}_3) = \hat{\mathbf{I}}_2 \cdot \pi(\hat{\mathbf{m}}_1) \odot \hat{\mathbf{I}}_2 \cdot \pi(\hat{\mathbf{m}}_2)$.

The common inputs to prover $\mathcal{P}$ and verifier $\mathcal{V}$ is $\mathbf{A} = (\mathbf{A}_1\|\mathbf{A}_2) \in R_q^{m\times(1+\ell)}$ and $\mathbf{c}_i \in R_q^m$ for $1 \le i \le 3$, $\mathcal{P}$ has secret input $(\mathbf{s}_i, \mathbf{m}_i, \mathbf{e}_i)$. $\mathcal{P}$ and $\mathcal{V}$ first define two common matrices $\hat{\mathbf{I}}_2$ as above and $\hat{\mathbf{I}}_1 \in R^{m\times 3m}$ by appending $2m$ zero columns to identity matrix $\mathbf{I}_m \in R^{m\times m}$. $\mathcal{P}$ decomposes $\mathbf{e}_i \in R^m$ for $1 \le i \le 3$ to $k = \lfloor \log\beta \rfloor + 1$ vectors $\tilde{\mathbf{e}}_{ij}$ in R^m with coefficients in $\{-1, 0, 1\}$ such that $\mathbf{e}_i = \sum_{j=0}^{k-1} 2^j \cdot \tilde{\mathbf{e}}_{ij}$. Then $\mathcal{P}$ extends each $\tilde{\mathbf{e}}_{ij}$ to a vector $\mathbf{e}_{ij} \in \mathcal{B}_{3m}$. Finally, $\mathcal{P}$ extends $\mathbf{m}_i$ to $\hat{\mathbf{m}}_i$ in $\mathbb{Z}_q^{dq^2\ell}$ (equivalently, $R_q^{q^2\ell}$) as described above. We define $0 \le j \le k-1$ and $1 \le i \le 3$. The protocol is as follows.

$\mathcal{P}$ samples $3k$ uniformly random vectors $(\mathbf{r}_{i0}, ..., \mathbf{r}_{i(k-1)}) \leftarrow (R_q^{3m})^k$, uniformly random vectors $u_i \leftarrow R_q$, $\mathbf{v}_i \leftarrow R_q^{q^2\ell}$, together with $3k$ random permutations $(\pi_{i0}, ..., \pi_{i(k-1)}) \leftarrow (\mathcal{S}_{3dm})^k$, and a uniformly random permutations $\pi' \leftarrow \mathcal{S}_{dq^2\ell}$. It sends the following commitments for $i = 1, 2, 3$ to the verifier $\mathcal{V}$:

$$\begin{cases} C_0 = \mathsf{Com}(\pi') \\ C_{i1} = \mathsf{Com}\Big(\{\pi_{ij}\}_{j=0}^{k-1}, \mathbf{t}_{i1} = \mathbf{A}(u_i\|\hat{\mathbf{I}}_2 \cdot \mathbf{v}_i) + \hat{\mathbf{I}}_1(\sum_{j=0}^{k-1} 2^j \cdot \mathbf{r}_{ij})\Big) \\ C_{i2} = \mathsf{Com}\Big(\{\mathbf{t}_{i2}^j = \pi_{ij}(\mathbf{r}_{ij})\}_{j=0}^{k-1}, \mathbf{t}'_{i2} = \pi'(\sigma(\mathbf{v}_i))\Big) \\ C_{i3} = \mathsf{Com}\Big(\{\mathbf{t}_{i3}^j = \pi_{ij}(\mathbf{r}_{ij} + \mathbf{e}_{ij})\}_{j=0}^{k-1}, \mathbf{t}'_{i3} = \pi'(\sigma(\mathbf{v}_i) + \hat{\mathbf{m}}_i)\Big) \end{cases}$$

The verifier $\mathcal{V}$ draws $Ch \leftarrow \{1, 2, 3\}$, and sends it to $\mathcal{P}$.

Depending on the value of Ch, $\mathcal{P}$ opens the following commitments:

$Ch = 1$: $\mathcal{P}$ opens C_0, C_{i1}, C_{i2} by sending $\pi', \{\pi_{ij}\}_{j=0}^{k-1}, \mathbf{t}_{i1}, \{\mathbf{t}_{i2}^j\}_{j=0}^{k-1}, \mathbf{t}'_{2i}$ and the associated random coins of the commitment.

$Ch = 2$: $\mathcal{P}$ opens C_0, C_{i1}, C_{i3} by sending $\pi', \{\pi_{ij}\}_{j=0}^{k-1}, \mathbf{t}_{i1}, \{\mathbf{t}_{i3}^j\}_{j=0}^{k-1}, \mathbf{t}'_{3i}$ and the associated random coins of the commitment.

$Ch = 3$: $\mathcal{P}$ opens C_{i2}, C_{i3} by sending $\{\mathbf{t}_{i2}^j\}_{j=0}^{k-1}, \mathbf{t}'_{i2}, \{\mathbf{t}_{i3}^j\}_{j=0}^{k-1}, \mathbf{t}'_{i3}$ and the associated random coins of the commitment.

The verifier $\mathcal{V}$ checks the correctness of the opening from the prover $\mathcal{P}$, and additionally performs the following checks depending the challenge Ch:

1. $\mathcal{V}$ accepts, iff $\mathbf{t}_{i1} - \mathbf{A}_2\hat{\mathbf{I}}_2 \cdot \sigma^{-1}(\pi'^{-1}(\mathbf{t}'_{i2})) - \hat{\mathbf{I}}_1 \cdot \left(\sum_{j=0}^{k-1} 2^j \cdot \pi_{ij}^{-1}(\mathbf{t}_{i2}^j)\right) \in \Lambda_q(\mathbf{a}_1)$, $\{\pi_{ij}\}_{j=0}^{k-1} \in \mathcal{S}_{3dm}^k$, and $\pi' \in \mathcal{S}_{dq^2\ell}$.
2. $\mathcal{V}$ accepts, iff $\mathbf{t}_{i1} + \mathbf{c}_i - \mathbf{A}_2\hat{\mathbf{I}}_2 \cdot \sigma^{-1}(\pi'^{-1}(\mathbf{t}'_{i3})) - \hat{\mathbf{I}}_1 \cdot \left(\sum_{j=0}^{k-1} 2^j \cdot \pi_{ij}^{-1}(\mathbf{t}_{i3}^j)\right) \in \Lambda_q(\mathbf{a}_1)$, $\{\pi_{ij}\}_{j=0}^{k-1} \in \mathcal{S}_{3dm}^k$, and $\pi' \in \mathcal{S}_{dq^2\ell}$.
3. $\mathcal{V}$ accepts, iff $\mathbf{t}_{i3}^j - \mathbf{t}_{i2}^j \in \mathcal{B}^{3m}$ and $\mathbf{t}'_{33} - \mathbf{t}'_{32} = (\mathbf{t}'_{23} - \mathbf{t}'_{22}) \odot (\mathbf{t}'_{13} - \mathbf{t}'_{12})$, for all $0 \le j \le k-1, 1 \le i \le 3$.

Theorem 4. *The above protocol is a Σ-protocol for the $\mathcal{R}_{\mathsf{CWRLWE}}$ relation, where*

$$\mathcal{R}_{\mathsf{CWRLWE}} = \Big\{ \Big((\mathbf{A}, \mathbf{c}_1, \mathbf{c}_2, \mathbf{c}_3), (s_1, s_2, s_3, \mathbf{m}_1, \mathbf{m}_2, \mathbf{m}_3, \mathbf{e}_1, \mathbf{e}_2, \mathbf{e}_3) \Big) : \bigwedge_{i=1}^{3} \Big(\mathbf{c}_i = \mathbf{A}(s_i \| \mathbf{m}_i) + \mathbf{e}_i \mod q \wedge \|\mathbf{e}_i\|_\infty \le \beta \Big) \wedge \mathbf{m}_3 = \mathbf{m}_1 \circ \mathbf{m}_2 \Big\}.$$

Proof. The correctness is easy. We show how the other properties hold.

Special Soundness. Assume that we have fixed values $C_0, C_{i1}, C_{i2}, C_{i3}$ and openings for all challenges $Ch \in \{1,2,3\}$, such that the verifier accepts on all of them. Then by the perfect binding property of the underlying commitment scheme $\mathsf{Com}(\cdot)$, we know that the openings to identical commitments must be identical for different challenges. By the verification equation for $Ch = 1$ and $Ch = 2$, we get that $\mathbf{c}_i - \mathbf{A}_2\hat{\mathbf{I}}_2 \cdot \sigma^{-1}(\pi'^{-1}(\mathbf{t}'_{i3} - \mathbf{t}'_{i2})) - \hat{\mathbf{I}}_1 \cdot (\sum_{j=0}^{k-1} 2^j \pi_{ij}^{-1}(\mathbf{t}_{i3} - \mathbf{t}_{i2}) \in \Lambda_q(\mathbf{a}_1)$. Thus exists computable $s'_i \in R_q$, such that $\mathbf{c}_i = \mathbf{a}_1 \cdot s'_i + \mathbf{A}_2\mathbf{m}'_i + \mathbf{e}'_i$, where $\mathbf{m}'_i = \hat{\mathbf{I}}_2 \cdot \sigma^{-1}(\pi'^{-1}(\mathbf{t}'_{i3} - \mathbf{t}'_{i2}))$ and $\mathbf{e}'_i = \hat{\mathbf{I}}_1 \cdot (\sum_{j=0}^{k-1} 2^j \pi_{ij}^{-1}(\mathbf{t}_{i3} - \mathbf{t}_{i2})$. From $Ch = 3$ we know that $\mathbf{t}_{i3} - \mathbf{t}_{i2} \in \mathcal{B}^{3m}$ and $\mathbf{t}'_{33} - \mathbf{t}'_{32} = (\mathbf{t}'_{23} - \mathbf{t}'_{22}) \odot (\mathbf{t}'_{13} - \mathbf{t}'_{12})$. By the special form of $\hat{\mathbf{I}}_1, \hat{\mathbf{I}}_2$, we infer that $\|\mathbf{e}'_i\|_1 \le 2\beta - 1$, $\mathbf{m}'_3 = \mathbf{m}'_2 \circ \mathbf{m}'_1$ and output $(s'_i, \mathbf{m}'_i, \mathbf{e}'_i)$ as valid witnesses.

Special Honest-Verifier Zero-knowledge . We now describe an efficient simulator S, which for each challenge $Ch \in \{1,2,3\}$ outputs an accepting protocol transcript. The distribution of the transcript is indistinguishable from the real protocol transcript with an honest prover for challenge Ch.

$Ch = 1$: the simulator S computes C_0, C_{i1}, C_{i2} like an honest prover, and computes C_{i3} as commitments to 0. Then clearly, the distributions of C_0, C_{i1}, C_{i2}, $\pi', \pi_{ij}, \mathbf{t}_{i1}, \mathbf{t}_{i2}^j, \mathbf{t}'_{i2}$ are identical to that in real protocol. By the hiding property of the commitment, the distributions of C_{i3} are indistinguishable to the real protocol.

$Ch = 2$: the simulator S first chooses uniformly random vector $u_1, u_2, u_3 \leftarrow R_q$, $\mathbf{v}_1, \mathbf{v}_2, \mathbf{v}_3 \leftarrow R_q^{q^2\ell}$, $3k$ random vectors $\mathbf{r}_{ij} \leftarrow R_q^{3m}$, $3k$ random permutations $\pi_{ij} \leftarrow S_{3dm}$, and a uniformly permutation $\pi' \leftarrow \mathcal{S}_{dq^2\ell}$. It sets $C_0 = \mathsf{Com}(\pi')$, $C_{i1} = \mathsf{Com}(\{\pi_{ij}\}_{j=0}^{k-1}, \mathbf{t}_{i1} = \mathbf{A}(u_i \| \hat{\mathbf{I}}_2 \cdot \mathbf{v}_i) + \hat{\mathbf{I}}_1 \cdot \sum_{j=0}^{k-1} 2^j \mathbf{r}_{ij} - \mathbf{c}_i)$, and $C_{i3} = \mathsf{Com}(\mathbf{t}_{i3} = \pi_i(\mathbf{r}_i), \mathbf{t}'_{i3} = \pi'(\sigma(\mathbf{v}_i)))$, and computes C_{i2} as commitments to 0. It's easy to see that the openings of C_0, C_{i1}, C_{i3} pass the verification. To see the correctness of the distribution we only need to consider the openings of C_{i1} and C_{i3}. Note that now $\mathbf{t}_{i1} = \mathbf{A}(u_i - s_i \| \hat{\mathbf{I}}_2 \cdot (\mathbf{v}_i - \sigma^{-1}(\hat{\mathbf{m}}_i))) +$

$\hat{\mathbf{I}}_1 \cdot \sum_{j=0}^{k-1} 2^j(\mathbf{r}_{ij} - \mathbf{e}_{ij})$, because we can rewrite $\mathbf{c}_i = \mathbf{A}(s_i \| \hat{\mathbf{I}}_2 \cdot \sigma^{-1}(\hat{\mathbf{m}}_i)) + \hat{\mathbf{I}}_1 \cdot \sum_{j=0}^{k-1} 2^j \mathbf{e}_{ij}$, and the special form of $\hat{\mathbf{I}}_2$. Set $\mathbf{v}'_i = \mathbf{v}_i - \sigma^{-1}(\hat{\mathbf{m}}_i)$, and $\mathbf{r}'_{ij} = \mathbf{r}_{ij} - \mathbf{e}_{ij}$. Since $\mathbf{v}_i$ and $\mathbf{r}_{ij}$ are uniformly in $R_q^{q^2\ell}$ and R_q^{3m} respectively, then also $\mathbf{v}'_i, \mathbf{r}'_{ij}$. Therefore, $\sigma(\mathbf{v}_i) = \sigma(\mathbf{v}'_i) + \hat{\mathbf{m}}_i$, $\mathbf{r}_{ij} = \mathbf{r}'_{ij} + \mathbf{e}_{ij}$, and the distribution of the simulated $(\mathbf{t}_{i1}, \mathbf{t}_{i3}, \mathbf{t}'_{i3})$ is identical to the real protocol, and the distributions of C_{i2} are computationally indistinguishable from the real protocol by the hiding property of the commitment scheme.

$Ch = 3$: the simulator chooses uniformly random vectors $\mathbf{r}_{ij} \leftarrow R_q^{3m}$, $\mathbf{v}_i \leftarrow \mathbb{Z}_q^{dq^2\ell}$. It then chooses uniformly random vectors $\mathbf{e}'_{1j}, \mathbf{e}'_{2j}, \mathbf{e}'_{3j} \leftarrow \mathcal{B}^{3m}$. It also chooses $\hat{\mathbf{m}}'_1, \hat{\mathbf{m}}'_2 \leftarrow \mathbb{Z}_q^{dq^2\ell}$ such that for any $(a,b) \in \mathbb{Z}_q^2$ the number of $j \in \{1, ..., dq^2\ell\}$ satisfying $(\hat{\mathbf{m}}'_1[j], \hat{\mathbf{m}}'_2[j]) = (a,b)$ is exactly dl, and set $\hat{\mathbf{m}}'_3 = \hat{\mathbf{m}}'_1 \odot \hat{\mathbf{m}}'_2$. Finally, it computes C_0, C_{i1} as commitments to 0, $C_{i2} = \mathsf{Com}(\mathbf{t}^j_{i2} = \mathbf{r}_{ij}, \mathbf{t}'_{i2} = \mathbf{v}_i)$, $C_{i3} = \mathsf{Com}(\mathbf{t}_{i3} = \mathbf{r}_{ij} + \mathbf{e}'_{ij}, \mathbf{t}'_{i3} = \mathbf{v}_i + \hat{\mathbf{m}}'_i)$. As before, the distributions of C_0, C_{i1} are computationally indistinguishable to the real protocol by the hiding property of the commitment scheme, and C_{i2}, C_{i3} as well as their openings can easily be seen to perfectly simulate the behavior of an honest prover. □

Remark 1. There exists simpler protocols to prove linear relations. The technique is very similar to the one in [16]. Furthermore, one can prove the committed value $\mathbf{m}_1, \mathbf{m}_2, \mathbf{m}_3$ satisfies $\mathbf{m}_3 = \mathbf{X}_1\mathbf{m}_1 + \mathbf{X}_2\mathbf{m}_2$, for any matrices $\mathbf{X}_1, \mathbf{X}_2 \in R_q^{\ell\times\ell}$.

Remark 2. Clearly, this protocol only works for polynomial size q, and the communication complexity is large since it chooses vectors with dimension q^2, this is undesirable in practice. In the positive side, if the underlying commitment scheme Com is statistically hiding, it brings statistically hiding zero-knowledge in spite of the RLWE one is only computationally hiding. Next, we describe another protocol to prove the component-wise relations with communication complexity only expand with factor $O(\log^2 q)$, which works even for sub-exponential q, but only achieves computationally zero-knowledge property.

4.3 Component-Wise Relations with Small Communication Complexity

Let's see why the above protocol brings large communication complexity. From now on, we only discuss the multiplicative relation for simplicity. In order to prove multiplicative relation, we randomize $\sigma(\mathbf{m}_1), \sigma(\mathbf{m}_2)$ to $\pi'(\hat{\mathbf{m}}_1), \pi'(\hat{\mathbf{m}}_2)$. To make the later terms be independent of the messages, we have to append $(a,b) \in \mathbb{Z}_q^2$ pairs and guarantee all possible pairs has exactly the same number, this expands the dimension of vector with factor q^2. Assume that if the CRT representation of the messages are guaranteed to be in $\{0,1\}^{d\ell}$, then we only need to expand the dimension with factor 4 which is much smaller. Our technique first decomposes each $\sigma(\mathbf{m}_1), \sigma(\mathbf{m}_2)$ to vectors in $\{0,1\}^{d\ell}$. I.e. $\sigma(\mathbf{m}_i) = \sum_{j=0}^{h-1} 2^j \mathbf{m}_{ij}$, where

$i = 1, 2$, $h = \lfloor \log q \rfloor + 1$ and $\mathbf{m}_{ij} \in \{0,1\}^{d\ell}$. We know $\sigma(\mathbf{m}_3) = (\sum_{j=0}^{h-1} 2^j \mathbf{m}_{1j}) \odot (\sum_{j=0}^{h-1} 2^j \mathbf{m}_{2j})$, unfold the later term, it turns to $\sigma(\mathbf{m}_3) = \sum_{j=0}^{h-1}\sum_{k=0}^{h-1} 2^{j+k}\mathbf{m}_{1j} \odot \mathbf{m}_{2k}$, denote $\tilde{\mathbf{m}}_{jk} = \mathbf{m}_{1j} \odot \mathbf{m}_{2k}$. Then the prover computes RLWE based commitments $\mathbf{c}_{1j}, \mathbf{c}_{2k}, \tilde{\mathbf{c}}_{jk}$ for $\sigma^{-1}(\mathbf{m}_{1j}), \sigma^{-1}(\mathbf{m}_{1k}), \sigma^{-1}(\tilde{\mathbf{m}}_{jk})$, and simultaneously proves $\tilde{\mathbf{m}}_{jk} = \mathbf{m}_{1j} \odot \mathbf{m}_{2k}$, $\sigma(\mathbf{m}_1) = \sum_{j=0}^{h-1} 2^j \mathbf{m}_{1j}$, $\sigma(\mathbf{m}_2) = \sum_{k=0}^{h-1} 2^k \mathbf{m}_{2k}$. It finally proves the linear relation $\sigma(\mathbf{m}_3) = \sum_{j=0}^{h-1}\sum_{k=0}^{h-1} 2^{j+k}\tilde{\mathbf{m}}_{jk} \mod q$. The multiplication relation here only expands dimension with constant factor, and the protocol needs another $\log^2 q + 2\log q$ commitments. When simulating, the simulator have to compute commitments $\mathbf{c}_{1j}, \mathbf{c}_{2k}, \tilde{\mathbf{c}}_{jk}$, but the simulator does not know the underlying contents, this does not matter due to the computational hiding property of the RLWE based commitment scheme. Therefore, the protocol only achieves computational zero-knowledge. However, we need to handle another problem, in the argument above, we assume that the $\mathbf{m}_{1j}, \mathbf{m}_{1k}$ in $\{0,1\}^{d\ell}$, so the prover has to convince the verifier that the CRT representation of the messages under $\mathbf{c}_{1j}, \mathbf{c}_{2k}$ are in $\{0,1\}^{d\ell}$. Due to the space limit, the entire construction is given in the full version. Here we only show a Σ-protocol for the following relation:

$$\mathcal{R}_{\mathsf{bRLWE}} = \{((\mathbf{A}, \mathbf{c}), (s, \mathbf{m}, \mathbf{e})) \ : \ \mathbf{c} = \mathbf{A}(s\|\mathbf{m}) + \mathbf{e} \mod q \\ \wedge \sigma(\mathbf{m}) \in \{0,1\}^{d\ell} \wedge \|\mathbf{e}\|_\infty \leq \beta\}$$

The common inputs to prover $\mathcal{P}$ and verifier $\mathcal{V}$ is $\mathbf{A} = (\mathbf{a}_1\|\mathbf{A}_2) \in R_q^{m\times(1+\ell)}$ and $\mathbf{c} \in R_q^m$, $\mathcal{P}$ has secret input $(s, \mathbf{m}, \mathbf{e})$ where $s \in R_q$, $\mathbf{m} \in R_q^\ell$, $\mathbf{e} \in R^m$, $\sigma(\mathbf{m}) \in \{0,1\}^{d\ell}$. $\mathcal{P}$ and $\mathcal{V}$ first define a common matrix $\hat{\mathbf{I}}_2 \in R^{\ell\times 2\ell}$ and $\hat{\mathbf{I}}_1 \in R^{m\times 3m}$ by appending ℓ, $2m$ zero columns to identity matrix $\mathbf{I}_\ell, \mathbf{I}_m \in R^m$ respectively. $\mathcal{P}$ first decomposes $\mathbf{e} \in R^m$ to $k = \lfloor \log \beta \rfloor + 1$ vectors $\tilde{\mathbf{e}}_i \in R^m$ with coefficients in $\{-1, 0, 1\}$ such that $\mathbf{e} = \sum_{i=0}^{k-1} 2^i \cdot \tilde{\mathbf{e}}_i$. Then $\mathcal{P}$ extends each $\tilde{\mathbf{e}}_i$ to a vector $\mathbf{e}_i \in \mathcal{B}^{3m}$. Meanwhile, $\mathcal{P}$ extends $\sigma(\mathbf{m}) \in \{0,1\}^{d\ell}$ to $\hat{\mathbf{m}} = (\sigma(\mathbf{m})\|\bar{\mathbf{m}}) \in \{0,1\}^{2d\ell}$ such that the coefficients of $\hat{\mathbf{m}}$ has exactly $d\ell$ 0's and 1's, i.e.,$\hat{\mathbf{m}} \in \mathcal{B}^{2\ell}$.

The protocol is given as follows, where the commitment scheme $\mathsf{Com}(\cdot)$ is a string commitment scheme.

$\mathcal{P}$ samples k uniformly random vector $(\mathbf{r}_0, ..., \mathbf{r}_{k-1}) \leftarrow (R_q^{3m})^k$, a uniformly random vector $u \leftarrow R_q$, $\mathbf{v} \leftarrow R_q^{2\ell}$, k random permutations $(\pi_0, ..., \pi_{k-1}) \leftarrow (\mathcal{S}_{3dm})^k$, and a random permutation $\pi' \leftarrow \mathcal{S}_{2d\ell}$. It sends the following commitments to the verifier $\mathcal{V}$:

$$\begin{cases} C_1 = \mathsf{Com}\Big(\pi', \{\pi_i\}_{i=0}^{k-1}, \mathbf{t}_1 = \mathbf{A}(u\|\hat{\mathbf{I}}_2\mathbf{v}) + \hat{\mathbf{I}}_1(\sum_{i=0}^{k-1} 2^i \cdot \mathbf{r}_i)\Big) \\ C_2 = \mathsf{Com}\Big(\{\mathbf{t}_{2i} = \pi_i(\mathbf{r}_i)\}_{i=0}^{k-1}, \mathbf{t}_2' = \pi'(\sigma(\mathbf{v}))\Big) \\ C_3 = \mathsf{Com}\Big(\{\mathbf{t}_{3i} = \pi_i(\mathbf{r}_i + \mathbf{e}_i)\}_{i=0}^{k-1}, \mathbf{t}_3' = \pi'(\sigma(\mathbf{v}) + \hat{\mathbf{m}})\Big) \end{cases}$$

The verifier $\mathcal{V}$ draws $Ch \leftarrow \{1, 2, 3\}$, and sends it to $\mathcal{P}$

Depending on the value of Ch, $\mathcal{P}$ opens the following commitments:

$Ch = 1$: $\mathcal{P}$ opens C_1, C_2 by sending $\pi', \{\pi_i\}_{i=0}^{k-1}, \mathbf{t}_1, \{\mathbf{t}_{2i}\}_{i=0}^{k-1}$ and the associated random coins of the commitment.
$Ch = 2$: $\mathcal{P}$ opens C_1, C_3 by sending $\pi', \{\pi_i\}_{i=0}^{k-1}, \mathbf{t}_1, \{\mathbf{t}_{3i}\}_{i=0}^{k-1}$ and the associated random coins of the commitment.
$Ch = 3$: $\mathcal{P}$ opens C_2, C_3 by sending $\mathbf{t}'_2, \{\mathbf{t}_{2i}\}_{i=0}^{k-1}, \mathbf{t}'_3, \{\mathbf{t}_{3i}\}_{i=0}^{k-1}$ and the associated random coins of the commitment.

The verifier $\mathcal{V}$ checks the correctness of the opening from the prover $\mathcal{P}$, and additionally performs the following checks depending the challenge Ch:

1. $\mathcal{V}$ accepts, iff $\mathbf{t}_1 - \mathbf{A}_2\hat{\mathbf{I}}_2 \cdot \sigma^{-1}(\pi'^{-1}(\mathbf{t}'_2)) - \hat{\mathbf{I}}_1 \cdot \left(\sum_{i=0}^{k-1} 2^i \cdot \pi_i^{-1}(\mathbf{t}_{2i})\right) \in \Lambda_q(\mathbf{a}_1)$ and $\{\pi_i\}_{i=0}^{k-1} \in \mathcal{S}_{3dm}^k$, $\pi' \in \mathcal{S}_{2d\ell}$.
2. $\mathcal{V}$ accepts, iff $\mathbf{t}_1 + \mathbf{c} - \mathbf{A}_2\hat{\mathbf{I}}_2 \cdot \sigma^{-1}(\pi'^{-1}(\mathbf{t}'_3)) - \hat{\mathbf{I}}_1 \cdot \left(\sum_{i=0}^{k-1} 2^i \cdot \pi_i^{-1}(\mathbf{t}_{3i})\right) \in \Lambda_q(\mathbf{a}_1)$ and $\{\pi_i\}_{i=0}^{k-1} \in \mathcal{S}_{3dm}^k$, $\pi' \in \mathcal{S}_{2d\ell}$.
3. $\mathcal{V}$ accepts, iff $\mathbf{t}_{3i} - \mathbf{t}_{2i} \in \mathcal{B}^{3m}$ for all $0 \le i \le k-1$ and $\mathbf{t}'_3 - \mathbf{t}'_2 \in \mathcal{B}^{2\ell}$.

Theorem 5. *The above protocol is a Σ-protocol for the $\mathcal{R}_{\mathsf{bRLWE}}$ relation.*

Proof. We do not give the full proof here. It's easy to check the correctness, and special soundness. The proof of Special honest-verifier zero-knowledge is similar to Theorem 3, except that when handling $Ch = 3$ the simulator additionally chooses uniformly random vectors $\hat{\mathbf{m}}' \leftarrow \{0,1\}^{2d\ell}$. □

Efficiency. To prove arbitrary functions in R_q is now straight by the above protocols. We now consider communication complexity of arbitrary function f based on the second protocol. The communication complexity of the protocol for f is $O(km \cdot |R_q| \cdot \log^2 q \cdot |f|)$ with soundness error 2/3. When instantiating using RLWE, we remark that an element in R_q represents d elements in $\mathbb{Z}_q$. Therefore, the protocol can simultaneously prove $d\ell$ inputs in $\mathbb{Z}_q$ satisfies the function f in $\mathbb{Z}_q$. This brings amortized complexity $O(km \cdot |R_q| \cdot \log^2 q \cdot |f|/(d\ell)) = O(k \log^3 q \cdot |f|)$. To achieve $2^{-\lambda}$ soundness error, we repeat the protocol λ times, which result communication complexity $O(\lambda k \log^3 q \cdot |f|)$. Since $k = \lfloor \log \beta \rfloor + 1$. The amortized complexity is $\tilde{O}(\lambda |f|)$, where $\tilde{O}$ hides polylogorithmic factors.

Acknowledgements. This work is supported by the National Basic Research Program of China (No. 2013CB338003). Xiang Xie and Rui Xue are supported by the Fund of the National Natural Science Foundation of China under Grant No. 61170280, the Strategic Priority Research Program of the Chinese Academy of Sciences under Grant No. XDA06010701, and IIE's Cryptography Research Project. Xiang Xie would like to thank Stephan Krenn, Chris Peikert, Krzysztof Pietrzak, Damien Stehlé for their helpful discussion at the early stage of this paper, and the authors are grateful to the reviewers for their valuable comments.

References

1. Asharov, G., Jain, A., López-Alt, A., Tromer, E., Vaikuntanathan, V., Wichs, D.: Multiparty computation with low communication, computation and interaction via threshold FHE. In: Pointcheval, D., Johansson, T. (eds.) EUROCRYPT 2012. LNCS, vol. 7237, pp. 483–501. Springer, Heidelberg (2012)

2. Boyar, J., Damgård, I., Peralta, R.: Short non-interactive cryptographic proofs. J. Cryptology 13(4), 449–472 (2000)
3. Cayrel, P.-L., Lindner, R., Rückert, M., Silva, R.: Improved zero-knowledge identification with lattices. In: Heng, S.-H., Kurosawa, K. (eds.) ProvSec 2010. LNCS, vol. 6402, pp. 1–17. Springer, Heidelberg (2010)
4. Cayrel, P.-L., Véron, P., El Yousfi Alaoui, S.M.: A zero-knowledge identification scheme based on the q-ary syndrome decoding problem. In: Biryukov, A., Gong, G., Stinson, D.R. (eds.) SAC 2010. LNCS, vol. 6544, pp. 171–186. Springer, Heidelberg (2011)
5. Cramer, R., Damgård, I.: Zero-knowledge proofs for finite field arithmetic, or: Can zero-knowledge be for free? In: Krawczyk, H. (ed.) CRYPTO 1998. LNCS, vol. 1462, pp. 424–441. Springer, Heidelberg (1998)
6. Cramer, R., Damgård, I.: On the amortized complexity of zero-knowledge protocols. In: Halevi, S. (ed.) CRYPTO 2009. LNCS, vol. 5677, pp. 177–191. Springer, Heidelberg (2009)
7. Cramer, R., Damgård, I., Pastro, V.: On the amortized complexity of zero knowledge protocols for multiplicative relations. In: Smith, A. (ed.) ICITS 2012. LNCS, vol. 7412, pp. 62–79. Springer, Heidelberg (2012)
8. Cramer, R., Damgård, I., Schoenmakers, B.: Proofs of partial knowledge and simplified design of witness hiding protocols. In: Desmedt, Y.G. (ed.) CRYPTO 1994. LNCS, vol. 839, pp. 174–187. Springer, Heidelberg (1994)
9. Damgård, I.: On σ-protocol. In: Lecture on Cryptologic Protocol Theory (2004)
10. Damgård, I., Goldreich, O., Okamoto, T., Wigderson, A.: Honest verifier vs dishonest verifier in public coin zero-knowledge proofs. In: Coppersmith, D. (ed.) CRYPTO 1995. LNCS, vol. 963, pp. 325–338. Springer, Heidelberg (1995)
11. Feige, U., Shamir, A.: Zero knowledge proofs of knowledge in two rounds. In: Brassard, G. (ed.) CRYPTO 1989. LNCS, vol. 435, pp. 526–544. Springer, Heidelberg (1990)
12. Goldwasser, S., Micali, S., Rackoff, C.: The knowledge complexity of interactive proof-systems. In: STOC, pp. 291–304 (1985)
13. Groth, J., Sahai, A.: Efficient non-interactive proof systems for bilinear groups. In: Smart, N.P. (ed.) EUROCRYPT 2008. LNCS, vol. 4965, pp. 415–432. Springer, Heidelberg (2008)
14. Haitner, I., Reingold, O.: Statistically-hiding commitment from any one-way function. In: STOC, pp. 1–10 (2007)
15. Ishai, Y., Kushilevitz, E., Ostrovsky, R., Sahai, A.: Zero-knowledge from secure multiparty computation. In: STOC, pp. 21–30 (2007)
16. Jain, A., Krenn, S., Pietrzak, K., Tentes, A.: Commitments and efficient zero-knowledge proofs from learning parity with noise. Cryptology ePrint Archive, Report 2012/513 (2012), `http://eprint.iacr.org/`
17. Kawachi, A., Tanaka, K., Xagawa, K.: Concurrently secure identification schemes based on the worst-case hardness of lattice problems. In: Pieprzyk, J. (ed.) ASIACRYPT 2008. LNCS, vol. 5350, pp. 372–389. Springer, Heidelberg (2008)
18. Kilian, J., Petrank, E.: An efficient noninteractive zero-knowledge proof system for np with general assumptions. J. Cryptology 11(1), 1–27 (1998)
19. Langlois, A., Stehle, D.: Worst-case to average-case reductions for module lattices. Cryptology ePrint Archive, Report 2012/090 (2012), `http://eprint.iacr.org/`
20. Ling, S., Nguyen, K., Stehle, D., Wang, H.: Improved zero-knowledge proofs of knowledge for the isis problem, and applications. Cryptology ePrint Archive, Report 2012/569 (2012), `http://eprint.iacr.org/`

21. Lyubashevsky, V.: Lattice-based identification schemes secure under active attacks. In: Cramer, R. (ed.) PKC 2008. LNCS, vol. 4939, pp. 162–179. Springer, Heidelberg (2008)
22. Lyubashevsky, V.: Lattice signatures without trapdoors. In: Pointcheval, D., Johansson, T. (eds.) EUROCRYPT 2012. LNCS, vol. 7237, pp. 738–755. Springer, Heidelberg (2012)
23. Lyubashevsky, V., Peikert, C., Regev, O.: On ideal lattices and learning with errors over rings. In: Gilbert, H. (ed.) EUROCRYPT 2010. LNCS, vol. 6110, pp. 1–23. Springer, Heidelberg (2010)
24. Lyubashevsky, V., Peikert, C., Regev, O.: A toolkit for ring-LWE cryptography. In: Johansson, T., Nguyen, P.Q. (eds.) EUROCRYPT 2013. LNCS, vol. 7881, pp. 35–54. Springer, Heidelberg (2013)
25. Micciancio, D., Vadhan, S.: Statistical zero-knowledge proofs with efficient provers: Lattice problems and more. In: Boneh, D. (ed.) CRYPTO 2003. LNCS, vol. 2729, pp. 282–298. Springer, Heidelberg (2003)
26. Regev, O.: On lattices, learning with errors, random linear codes, and cryptography. In: STOC, pp. 84–93. ACM (2005)
27. Stern, J.: A new identification scheme based on syndrome decoding. In: Stinson, D.R. (ed.) CRYPTO 1993. LNCS, vol. 773, pp. 13–21. Springer, Heidelberg (1994)

Zero Knowledge with Rubik's Cubes and Non-abelian Groups

Emmanuel Volte[1], Jacques Patarin[2], and Valérie Nachef[1]

[1] Department of Mathematics, University of Cergy-Pontoise, CNRS UMR 8088
2 Avenue Adolphe Chauvin, 95011 Cergy-Pontoise Cedex, France
[2] PRISM, University of Versailles
45 Avenue des Etats-Unis, 78035 Versailles Cedex, France
emmanuel.volte@u-cergy.fr

Abstract. The factorization problem in non-abelian groups is still an open and a difficult problem [12]. The hardness of the problem is illustrated by the moves of the Rubik's cube. We will define a public key identification scheme based on this problem, in the case of the Rubik's cube, when the number of moves is fixed to a given value. Our scheme consists of an interactive protocol which is zero-knowledge argument of knowledge under the assumption of the existence of a commitment scheme. We will see that our scheme works with any non-abelian groups with a set of authorized moves that has a specific property. Then we will generalize the scheme for larger Rubik's cubes and for any groups.

Keywords: zero-knowledge, Rubik's cube, authentication, symmetric group, cryptographic protocol, factorization.

1 Introduction

The puzzles based on the Rubik's cube meet a great success. Generally speaking, Rubik's cube's owners try to solve the following problem: how to recover the initial position of the cube from a random position. At first sight, this problem seems very difficult, but there exist efficient algorithms to solve it [2]. Nevertheless, several other problems with the cube and its neighboring puzzles seem to be really difficult from a computing point of view. For example if we impose that the number of moves is equal (or inferior) to a fixed value d that makes **unique** or **almost unique** the moves that must be done to recover the cube, then we obtain a difficult problem. In [2] it is showed that finding an optimal solution (i.e. the minimum factorization) is NP-hard if we ignore some of the facets of the cube $n \times n \times n$. Moreover the size of the Rubik's group grows exponentially with the number of facets. In appendix A, we will also discuss some connections between these problems and NP-complete or NP space problems.

Consequently, we can try to build some public key zero knowledge argument of knowledge protocols with a proven security linked to these difficult problems (and also on the existence of a commitment scheme). Then we can use this protocol to do identification. It is well known that there exist cryptographic algorithms

M. Abdalla, C. Nita-Rotaru, and R. Dahab (Eds.): CANS 2013, LNCS 8257, pp. 74–91, 2013.

transforming every NP problem into a zero knowledge authentication protocol [5]. The theoretical way to do this is polynomial but nevertheless generally not efficient at all. This is why we will present and study some specific algorithms in this article, which can be used for practical cryptography and with a proven security based on some difficult well-known problems of the Rubik's cube.

Our algorithm is the first serious attempt to make zero knowledge argument of knowledge with the Rubik's cube. There were obvious ways to do zero-knowledge with this toy. For example, we can scramble the cube and memorize all the moves, then we can prove that we can recover the initial position under a scarf. Nevertheless, since some people can recover the cube even without seeing it, this is not a sure way to authenticate oneself. As Colmez says in [1], the Rubik's cube is one of the rare groups we can walk with in the street.

Organization of the paper. In Section 1 we introduce all the notations and the definition of the repositioning group that is crucial to write all our schemes. In Section 2 we define the problem we will use for our zero knowledge argument of knowledge, this problem is equivalent to the factorization with a fixed number of elements from a given set. We also see the generic attack for this problem. In Section 3, we show how to construct a scheme that is zero knowledge argument of knowledge, in the case of the Rubik's cube $3\times3\times3$, and we prove that this still works for any group and any set of generators that has a repositioning group. The scheme we will propose is an interactive one with 3 pass. We use a standard cut-and-choose technique.

- First, the Prover hides each move of the solution thanks to a rotation of the cube. By doing this, we still can see that she makes a basic move but without knowing which one.
  Then she masks all the turned moves with a unique random permutation that preserves the composition. Finally, the Prover only sends commitments of the rotation, of the random permutation used for masking and of all the masked permutations.
- The verifier asks for some verification. She has the choice of verifying the entire composition or only one of the turned moves. She can not check 2 moves simultaneously because she will have the information of the equality or not of the two initial moves.
- The prover reveals some of the permutations and the Verifier checks the answer, then accepts or not.

In Section 4, we try to do this with the Rubik's cube $5\times5\times5$. The difficulty is that the set of generators has no repositioning group. By working in larger groups, we manage to construct a scheme that is suitable for cryptographic applications, and that is quite efficient. In Section 5, we first generalize the scheme for any group and any set of generators, and then for a number of moves that is not constant but inferior to a given value, for example the diameter of a group. There are recent papers [14] that help us give an approximation of this value for some groups and for some set of generators. These works try to answer Babai's conjecture on the diameter of simple groups. In the case of the Rubik's cube, in [2] it is shown that "God's number", i.e. the minimal number of moves to solve a Rubik's cube $n \times n \times n$ is $\Theta(n^2/log(n))$. At last, in Section 7, we will briefly discuss the efficiency of our schemes.

2 Notations and Definitions

2.1 Mathematical Standard Notations and Definitions

Most of the following notations can be found in [8], which is an original way to learn algebra with toys such as the Rubik's cube and the Merlin's machine.

For a finite set X, S_X is the symmetric group of X. In the particular case $X = \{1; 2; \ldots; n\}$ where $n \in \mathbb{N}^*$, we call this group S_n. For $\sigma, \sigma' \in S_X$, we use the classic notation $\sigma\sigma'$ to design the composition $\sigma' \circ \sigma$.

When G is a group, and $(g_1, g_2, \ldots, g_\alpha) \in G^\alpha$, then $\langle g_1, g_2, \ldots, g_\alpha \rangle$ is the subgroup generated by $g_1, g_2, \cdots g_\alpha$.

We say that $\mathcal{F} = \{g_1, \ldots, g_\alpha\}$ is a **set of generators** of G when $\langle g_1, g_2, \ldots, g_\alpha \rangle = G$. This set is **symmetric** when for all $\sigma \in \mathcal{F}$ we have $\sigma^{-1} \in \mathcal{F}$.

When we have a symmetric set of generators $\mathcal{F}$ of a group G, we set that two elements g and g' are in relation if and only if $g^{-1}g' \in \mathcal{F}$. The corresponding graph is called the **Cayley graph** of the group.

Let G be a group, the **conjugation** on G is defined by

$$\forall(\sigma, \tau) \in G^2, \quad \sigma^\tau = \tau^{-1}\sigma\tau$$

Moreover we have:

$$\forall(\sigma, \sigma', \tau, \tau') \in G^4, \quad (\sigma^\tau)^{\tau'} = \sigma^{\tau\tau'}, \quad \sigma^\tau\sigma'^\tau = (\sigma\sigma')^\tau$$

We can also write $\boxed{\sigma^G = \{\sigma^g | g \in G\}}$.

2.2 Mathematical Representation of the Rubik's Cube

For the Rubik's cube, we can write a number on each facet except the centers. In this paper we consider that all the centers are white or void (there exists in fact a physical cube that has no centers). Not taking in consideration the centers will not really change the complexity of all the problems

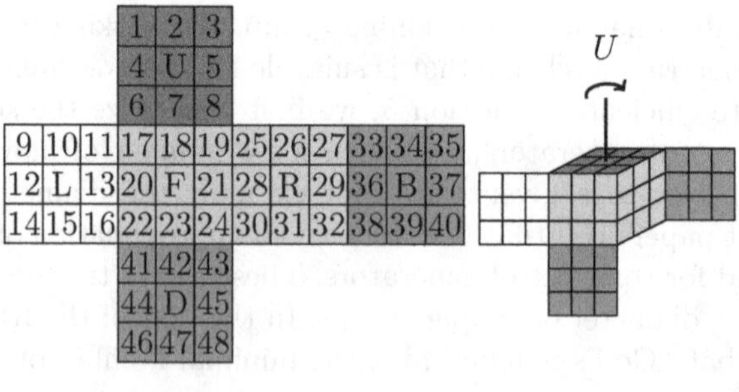

then we define 6 permutations of $G = S_{48}$ which are the basic clockwise quarter turns of the faces:

$$F = (17,19,24,22)(18,21,23,20)(6,25,43,16)(7,28,42,13)(8,30,41,11)$$
$$B = (33,35,40,38)(34,37,39,36)(3,9,46,32)(2,12,47,29)(1,14,48,27)$$
$$L = (9,11,16,14)(10,13,15,12)(1,17,41,40)(4,20,44,37)(6,22,46,35)$$
$$R = (25,27,32,30)(26,29,31,28)(3,38,43,19)(5,36,45,21)(8,33,48,24)$$
$$U = (1,3,8,6)(2,5,7,4)(9,33,25,17)(10,34,26,18)(11,35,27,19)$$
$$D = (41,43,48,46)(42,45,47,44)(14,22,30,38)(15,23,31,39)(16,24,32,40)$$

after the move σ, the facet $i \in \{1, 2, \ldots, 48\}$ is at the $\sigma(i)$ position.

The Rubik's cube group is $G_R = \langle F, B, L, R, U, D \rangle \subset S_{48}$. If you want to simulate the Rubik's cube, this can be done by using SAGE [16].

2.3 Cryptographic Notations

When X is a finite set, $\boxed{x \in_R X}$ means that we take a random element in X with a uniform probability.

In an interactive Protocol, there are two entities: the prover and the verifier. The Prover wants to convince the verifier that she knows a secret. Both interact and at the end, the verifier accepts or refuses. In Zero-Knowledge Protocols there is a possibility of fraud. A cheater will be able to answer some of the questions (but not all of them). The protocol must be designed such that an answer to one of the questions does not give any indication on the secret but if someone is able to answer all the questions then this will reveal the Prover's secret. We will use the following definitions in order to describe the properties that we want to be satisfied by our protocols:

1. The protocol has **perfect correctness** if a legitimate prover is always accepted.
2. The protocol is **statistically zero knowledge** if there exists an efficient simulating algorithm U such that for every feasible Verifier strategy V, the distributions produced by the simulator and the proof protocol are statistically indistinguishable.
3. The protocol is **proof of zero knowledge with error knowledge** α if there is a knowledge extractor K and a polynomial Q such that if p denotes the probability that K finds a valid witness for x using its access to a prover P^* and p_x denotes the probability that P^* convinces the honest verifier on x, and $p_x > \alpha$, then we have $p \geq Q(p_x - \alpha)$.

In our protocols, we will need string commitment schemes. A string commitment function is denoted by Com. The commitment scheme runs in two phases. In the first phase, the sender computes a commitment value $c = Com(s; \rho)$ and sends c to the receiver, where s is the committed string and ρ is a random string. In the second phase, the sender gives (s, ρ) and the receiver verifies if $c = Com(s; \rho)$. we require the two following properties of Com.

1. The commitment scheme is **statistically hiding** if for uniform (x, ρ) and (x', ρ') the distributions $Com(x, \rho)$ and $Com(x', \rho')$ are statistically indistinguishable. This means that the commitment to x reveals (almost) no information on x even to an infinitely powerful Verifier.
2. The commitment scheme is **computationally binding** if the probability to that two different values (x, ρ) and (x', ρ') produce the same $c = Com(x, \rho) = Com(x', \rho')$ is negligible in polynomial time, i.e. the chances to change the committed value after the first phase are very small.

A practical construction of such a commitment is given in [7].

For all of our schemes we will use an interactive commitment, it means that we have to send a key to unlock the commitment. We use the notation $Com_k(x)$ to design such a commitment of x with the key k where k is a 80-bit random word.

2.4 The Repositioning Group

In this Section, we will define precisely the repositioning group for a given set of elements $\mathcal{F}$. We will see in the next Sections that the existence of this group is the keystone of our schemes.

Definition 1. *Let $\mathcal{F} = \{f_1, \ldots, f_\alpha\} \subset G$, where G is a group. If there exists a subgroup $H \subset G$ such that ${f_1}^H = \{h^{-1} f_1 h \mid h \in H\} = \mathcal{F}$ then H is called a* ***repositioning*** *group of $\mathcal{F}$.*

Remark. In the case of the Rubik's cube, with $\mathcal{F} = \{F, B, L, R, U, D\}$, it is easy to see that we can go from one move to another by rolling the cube like a dice.

Proposition 1. *We suppose $\mathcal{F}$ has a repositioning group H. If we choose $\tau \in_R H$, $P({f_i}^\tau = f_j) = \frac{1}{\alpha}$ for all $(i, j) \in \{1; \ldots; \alpha\}^2$.*

Proof. Since ${f_1}^H = \mathcal{F}$, for all $i \in \{1, \ldots; \alpha\}$ there exists $\tau_i \in H$ such that ${f_1}^{\tau_i} = f_i$. Then, for all $j \in \{1; \ldots; \alpha\}$, ${f_i}^{{\tau_i}^{-1}\tau_j} = f_j$. We denote by $\tau_{ij} = {\tau_i}^{-1}\tau_j$. Now we have the equivalence:

$$f_i^{\tau} = f_j \iff {f_k}^{\tau_{ki}\tau\tau_{j\ell}} = f_\ell$$

for all $k, \ell \in \{1; \ldots; \alpha\}$. So $\{\tau \in H \mid {f_i}^\tau = f_j\}$ and $\{\tau \in H \mid {f_k}^\tau = f_\ell\}$ are in bijection and have the same cardinality.

Remark. It is not easy to find a repositioning group in the general case. When the group elements in $\mathcal{F}$ are not conjugate of each other, it is even impossible. We will still see a way to do this for the general case (i.e. for any set of generators $\mathcal{F}$), with the help of an extended set. Nevertheless the general construction is often not the optimal solution. For example, in the case of the Rubik $5 \times 5 \times 5$ the orientation preserving group of the cube enables us to work on ${S_{144}}^2$ instead of ${S_{144}}^{12}$.

3 Various Factorization Problems

For all the following problems, we have a finite group G with a set of α generators $\mathcal{F} = \{f_1; f_2; \ldots; f_\alpha\}$, containing all authorized permutations. Of course we have $f_i \neq f_j$, if $i \neq j$.
$id \in G$ is the neutral element of G.

Problem 1: *Solving the puzzle.*
Given $x_0 \in G$, find $d \in \mathbb{N}$ and $i_1, i_2, \ldots, i_d \in \{1; 2; \ldots; \alpha\}$ such that

$$x_0 f_{i_1} f_{i_2} \ldots f_{i_d} = id$$

Remark. This problem is equivalent to the factorization problem in G with elements of $\mathcal{F}$ because:

$$x_0 f_{i_1} f_{i_2} \cdots f_{i_d} = id \quad \Longleftrightarrow \quad x_0^{-1} = f_{i_1} f_{i_2} \cdots f_{i_d}$$

Problem 2: *Solving the puzzle in a given number of moves.*
Given $x_0 \in G$ and $d \in \mathbb{N}^*$, find $i_1, i_2, \ldots, i_d \in \{1; 2; \ldots; \alpha\}$ such that

$$x_0 f_{i_1} f_{i_2} \cdots f_{i_d} = id$$

Proposition 2. *We can find a solution of problem 2 with $O(d\alpha^{d/2})$ computations if d is even.*

Proof. This is a meet-in-the-middle attack. We notice that $f_{i_1} f_{i_2} \ldots f_{i_d} = x_0$ is equivalent to $x_0 f_{i_1} \ldots f_{i_{d/2}} = (f_{i_d})^{-1} \ldots (f_{i_{d/2+1}})^{-1}$.
So, for each $i_1, i_2, \ldots, i_{d/2} \in \{1, \ldots, \alpha\}$ we compute

$$Y_{i_1 i_2 \ldots i_{d/2}} = x_0 f_{i_1} f_{i_2} \cdots f_{i_{d/2}}$$
$$\text{and} \quad Z_{i_1 i_2 \ldots i_{d/2}} = (f_{i_1})^{-1} (f_{i_2})^{-1} \cdots (f_{i_{d/2}})^{-1}$$

Then we look for a collision between Y and Z.

Remark. There are other techniques of factorization [12] that are using a tower of groups. Nevertheless these techniques do not lead us to the minimal solution.

In this paper we will study how to transform these difficult problems into a zero-knowledge argument of knowledge identification scheme. In other words: we will study how to prove that we have a solution of one of these problems without revealing anything of the solution.

4 With Rubik's Cube 3 × 3 × 3

4.1 Introduction

We will first describe a zero-knowledge authentication scheme based on Rubik's classical cube $3 \times 3 \times 3$. We do this in order to introduce the main ideas with this relatively simple example. However with Rubik's cube $3 \times 3 \times 3$ the complexity of problem 2 is much smaller than 2^{80} and therefore we cannot use it for cryptographic security (for cryptographic applications we will use the Cube $5 \times 5 \times 5$ as we will see below).

We have in fact about 43.2×10^{18} different positions for this Rubik's cube, so about 2^{61} or 6^{25}. If we consider that half a turn counts as one move, we know that God's number (i.e. the minimal number of moves necessary to unscramble any position of the Rubik's cube) is 20 [15]. Nevertheless in our case we do not authorize un-clockwise quarter turns and half turns. So it seems reasonable to choose for problem 2 the value $d = 24$, and the security will be about $6^{24/2} = 6^{12} \approx 2^{30}$ computations.

4.2 Hiding the Secret

First we have to hide the permutation we make to go from a position to another, without hiding that we make one authorized permutation, i.e. one element of $\mathcal{F}$. An easy way to do this with the cube $3 \times 3 \times 3$ is to roll the cube like a dice (we always consider that the centers of the faces do not move or do not exist).

Let H be the group of the orientation-preserving symmetry of the cube. We have $H = \langle h_1, h_2 \rangle$ where h_1 is the cube rolling on its back , and h_2 the cube laying on the table but turning as a whole one clockwise quarter of a turn. To be more precise we have:

$$h_1 = RL^{-1}(2,39,42,18)(7,34,47,23)$$
$$h_2 = UD^{-1}(13,37,29,21)(12,36,28,20)$$

It is easy to check that $|H| = 24$, because for each face up, we have 4 choices for the face in front. Moreover we have $U^H = \mathcal{F}$.

Proposition 3. *If $f \in_R \mathcal{F}$ and $\tau \in_R H$, then f^τ is a random variable with a uniform law on $\mathcal{F}$.*

Proof. This is a direct consequence of Proposition 1.

Illustration. Let $x_0 \in G_R = \langle \mathcal{F} \rangle$ be one position of the cube and $x_1 = x_0 f$, the following diagram is commutative (i.e. $f\tau = \tau f^\tau$):

$$\begin{array}{ccc} x_0 & \xrightarrow{f} & x_1 \\ \tau \downarrow & & \tau \downarrow \\ x_0\tau & \xrightarrow{f^\tau} & x_1\tau \end{array}$$

Secondly, we want to hide each of the conjugate authorized moves, at each step of the resolution. For this we use a mask, a random permutation of G called σ_0. If $f_{i_1}, f_{i_2}, \dots f_{i_d}$ are the secret moves, we hide their conjugate moves this way (by defining σ_j for all $j \in \{1; 2; \dots; d\}$): ${f_{i_1}}^\tau = \sigma_0 \sigma_1^{-1}$, then ${f_{i_2}}^\tau = \sigma_1 \sigma_2^{-1}, \dots,$ and ${f_{i_d}}^\tau = \sigma_{d-1}\sigma_d^{-1}$. So we have $f_{i_1} \dots f_{i_d} = \sigma_0 {\sigma_d}^{-1}$.

4.3 ZK Protocol

In this subsection,we will give the general protocol for any group G, any set of generators $\mathcal{F}$ of a large subgroup G_R of G, and we suppose that this set has a repositioning group $H \subset G$. We will prove in the next subsection that it is a zero knowledge argument of knowledge scheme.

We can also use this protocol for the puzzle called $S41$ described in appendix C.

Public:

- A group G.
- A set $\mathcal{F} = \{f_1, \dots, f_\alpha\} \subset G$ of generators of G_R
- A repositioning group $H \subset G$ such that ${f_1}^H = \mathcal{F}$.
- $d \in \mathbb{N}$, $d \geq 3$
- G' subgroup of G generated by $\mathcal{F}$ and H. $G' = \langle \mathcal{F}, H \rangle$.
- K a set of keys, $|K| \geq 2^{80}$.

Secret key: $i_1, i_2, \dots, i_d \in \{1, 2, \dots, \alpha\}$.

Public key: $x_0 = (f_{i_1} f_{i_2} \dots f_{i_d})^{-1}$

Scheme (one round):

Prover		**Verifier**
Picks $\tau \in_R H$, $\sigma_0 \in_R G'$, $k_*, k_0, k_1, \dots, k_d \in_R K$ **Computes** $\forall j \in \{1, \dots, d\}$, $\sigma_j = ({f_{i_j}}^{\tau})^{-1} \sigma_{j-1}$ $c_0 = Com_{k_*}(\tau)$ $\forall i \in \{0, \dots d\}$, $s_i = Com_{k_i}(\sigma_i)$	$c_0, s_0, \dots, s_d$ $\longrightarrow$	
	q $\longleftarrow$	**Picks** $q \in_R \{0, \dots d\}$
Case $q = 0$	τ, σ_0 $\longrightarrow$ k_*, k_0, k_d	**Computes** $\sigma_d = \tau^{-1} x_0 \tau \sigma_0$ **Checks** $\tau \in H$, $Com_{k_*}(\tau) = c_0$, $Com_{k_0}(\sigma_0) = s_0$, $Com_{k_d}(\sigma_d) = s_d$ **If** all tests ok **then accepts else rejects.**
Case $q \neq 0$	${f_{i_q}}^{\tau}$, σ_q $\longrightarrow$ k_{q-1}, k_q	**Computes** $\sigma_{q-1} = {f_{i_q}}^{\tau} \sigma_q$ **Checks** ${f_{i_q}}^{\tau} \in \mathcal{F}$, $s_{q-1} = Com_{k_{q-1}}(\sigma_{q-1})$ $s_q = Com_{k_q}(\sigma_q)$ **If** all tests ok **then accepts else rejects.**

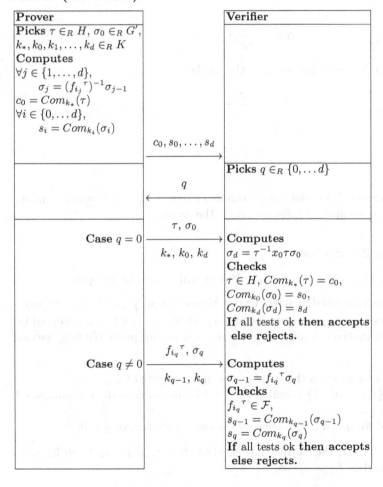

Remark. Since H is a small group, we can change a little the protocol by not sending c_0 in the first phase, and only sending σ_0 in the first case of the third phase. Then the Verifier will try all the possible values for τ. So it is quite obvious that it is not the size of H that secures the scheme.
Illustration. If we define for all $k \in \{1;\ldots;d\}$, $x_k = x_{k-1}f_{i_k}$, we have the following commutative diagram:

$$\begin{array}{ccccccc}
x_0 & \xrightarrow{f_{i_1}} & x_1 & \xrightarrow{f_{i_2}} & \ldots \quad x_{d-1} & \xrightarrow{f_{i_d}} & x_d = id \\
\tau\downarrow & & \tau\downarrow & & \tau\downarrow & & \tau\downarrow \\
x_0\tau & \xrightarrow[\sigma_0{\sigma_1}^{-1}]{{f_{i_1}}^{\tau}} & x_1\tau & \xrightarrow[\sigma_1{\sigma_2}^{-1}]{{f_{i_2}}^{\tau}} & \ldots \quad x_{d-1}\tau & \xrightarrow[\sigma_{d-1}{\sigma_d}^{-1}]{{f_{i_d}}^{\tau}} & \tau
\end{array}$$

With $q = 0$, the Verifier will check that the exterior composition way is correct:

$$\begin{array}{ccc}
x_0 & & x_d = id \\
\tau\downarrow & & \tau^{-1}\uparrow \\
x_0\tau & \xrightarrow[\sigma_0{\sigma_d}^{-1}]{} & \tau
\end{array}$$

With $q \neq 0$, the Verifier checks one of the meshes:

$$\begin{array}{ccc}
 & \xrightarrow{f_{i_q}} & \\
\tau\downarrow & & \tau\downarrow \\
 & \xrightarrow[\sigma_{q-1}{\sigma_q}^{-1}]{{f_{i_q}}^{\tau}} &
\end{array}$$

Here τ is not revealed, we just have a random element σ_{q-1} of G and a random element of $\mathcal{F}$, so we give no information on the secret.

4.4 Proof of ZK Protocol

Correctness. Obviously, a legitimate Prover will always be accepted.

Proof of Zero Knowledge with Error Knowledge $\frac{d}{d+1}$. We first suppose that a Prover can answer correctly for all possible values of q (i.e. is accepted by the Verifier). Since the commitment scheme is computationally binding, we can state that:

- σ_0 revealed for $q = 0$ is the same as the one computed for $q = 1$.
- σ_i for $i \in \{1;\ldots;d-1\}$ revealed for $q = i$ is the same as the one computed for $q = i + 1$.
- σ_d revealed for $q = d$ is the same as the one computed for $q = 0$.

For all $i \in \{1;\ldots;d\}$, the Verifier has checked that $\sigma_{i-1}{\sigma_i}^{-1} \in \mathcal{F}$, so let $u_i \in \{1;\ldots;\alpha\}$ such that $f_{u_i} = \sigma_{i-1}{\sigma_i}^{-1}$.

With $q = 0$, the Verifier established $id = x_0\tau\sigma_0\sigma_d{}^{-1}\tau^{-1}$, so

$$\begin{aligned} id &= x_0\tau(\sigma_0\sigma_1{}^{-1})(\sigma_1\sigma_2{}^{-1})\dots(\sigma_{d-1}\sigma_d{}^{-1})\tau^{-1} \\ &= x_0\tau f_{u_1}f_{u_2}\cdots f_{u_d}\tau^{-1} = \tau f_{u_1}\tau^{-1}\tau f_{u_2}\tau^{-1}\dots\tau f_{u_d}\tau^{-1} \\ &= x_0 f_{u_1}{}^{\tau^{-1}} f_{u_2}{}^{\tau^{-1}}\cdots f_{u_d}{}^{\tau^{-1}} \end{aligned}$$

Hence we have a solution of the initial problem.

Therefore, if we consider a Cheat Prover i.e. a person who does not have a solution to the initial problem, there is at least one of the Verifier's request (one of the q value) that will lead to a rejection. So the probability that the Cheat Prover can convince a Honest Verifier is less than $\frac{d}{d+1}$.

Statistically Zero Knowledge. Firstly we show that for a legitimate prover, each answer has a uniform probability over the corresponding set.

- $q = 0$.
  The Prover gives $(\tau, \sigma_0, k_*, k_0, k_d) \in H \times G' \times K^3$ which are all independent random values over the concerning set.
- $1 \leq q \leq d$.
  The Prover gives $(f_{i_q}{}^{\tau}, \sigma_q, k_{q-1}, k_q) \in F \times G' \times K^2$. Since we have $f_{i_1}\dots f_{i_q} = \tau\sigma_0\sigma_q^{-1}\tau^{-1}$, if we define $h = \tau^{-1}f_{i_q}{}^{-1}\dots f_{i_1}{}^{-1}\tau$, then we have $\sigma_q = h\sigma_0$ with σ_0 picked at random in G', so σ_q is a random permutation independent from $f_{i_q}{}^{\tau}$. Moreover, since $\tau \in_R H$, $f_{i_q}{}^{\tau}$ is uniformly chosen in F (see section 4.2, or below Proposition 1 for the generalization). So we have again a uniform probability over $F \times G' \times K^2$.

Secondly, we construct a black-box simulator which takes x_0 without knowing the secret, and interacts with a Cheating Verifier **CV**. We show that the simulator can impersonate the honest prover with probability $\frac{1}{d+1}$. The simulator randomly chooses a value $q^* \in_R \{0; 1; \dots; d\}$, this is a prediction what value **CV** will not choose. We consider two cases:

- $q^* = 0$
  The simulator picks $\tau \in_R H$, $f'_1, \dots, f'_d \in_R F$ and $\sigma_0 \in_R G'$. Then it computes for all $k \in \{1; \dots; d\}$ $\sigma_k = f_k'^{-1}\sigma_{k-1}$.
- $1 \leq q^* \leq d$
  It picks $f'_1, f'_2, \dots, f'_{q^*-1}, f'_{q^*+1}, \dots f'_d \in_R \mathcal{F}$. Then it picks $\tau \in_R H$ and $\sigma_0 \in_R G'$. It computes $f'_{q^*} \in G'$ (not necessary in $\mathcal{F}$) such that $x_0 f'_1 \dots f'_d = id$, and for all $k \in \{1; \dots; d\}$ $\sigma_k = f_k'^{\tau^{-1}}\sigma_{k-1}$

It is easy to check that, except for $q = q^*$, every request of **CV** will have a satisfying answer. So the probability that it fails is $\frac{1}{d+1}$. Moreover, when only the successful interactions are recorded, the communication tape is indistinguishable from what would have been obtained from an execution performed by the real Prover.

4.5 Number of Rounds for the Cube $3 \times 3 \times 3$

We quit the general case to consider our classical cube $3 \times 3 \times 3$. Here we will discuss of the number of times (r) the prover will do the protocol (one protocol is considered as one round), in order to prove with a good probability that she knows the secret. If we set this probability to $1 - 2^{-m}$, we must have $\left(\frac{d}{d+1}\right)^r \leq 2^{-m}$, so it gives $r \approx md\ln(2)$. For example, with $m = 30$ and $d = 24$, only 500 rounds are necessary. We simulate this scheme with a 3GHz computer, and a non-optimized algorithm (we used a rather slow hash function for the commitment), and it has token less than 1 second to simulate 100 times all the protocol.

5 Rubik's Cube $5 \times 5 \times 5$

For practical authentication we need a puzzle with at least 2^{160} different states. The Rubik's cube $4 \times 4 \times 4$ has (only) about 2^{152} positions. Thus, we choose the next cube, i.e. the cube $5 \times 5 \times 5$ which has about 2^{247} different positions (computation with Sage).

5.1 Mathematical Representation

We write numbers on each facet, except the centers. For the manipulation of the cube, we consider only 12 basic permutations. We will choose here the 6 clockwise quarter turns of the upper crown of each face (U, D, F, B, R, L), and the 6 clockwise quarter turns of the first intermediary crown of each face $(U_1, D_1, F_1, B_1, R_1, L_1)$. Nevertheless other choices are possible. We have:

$$G_R = \langle U, D, \ldots, L, U_1, D_1, \ldots, L_1 \rangle \subset S_{144}$$

5.2 Hiding the Secret

Just rolling the cube is not enough to hide an authorized move. This will only shuffle independently (U, D, F, B, R, L) and $(U_1, D_1, F_1, B_1, R_1, L_1)$. We need a

Fig. 1. Twin cubes, move (R_1, R)

new idea. A way to do this is to duplicate the cube, and so we will consider the group $G_R \times G_R$. Then, each time we use R_1 on the first cube, we will use R on the second cube (see figure 1), each time we use R on the first cube, we will use R_1 on the second cube, each time we use L_1 on the first cube, we use L on the second cube and so on.

We will call $\boldsymbol{e}$ the exchange of the two cubes, $\boldsymbol{e}$ is an extra element that exchanges the coordinates:

$$e^2 = id \quad \text{and} \quad \forall (a,b) \in G_R \times G_R, \quad \boldsymbol{e}(a,b)\boldsymbol{e} = (b,a).$$

To prove the existence of such an element, we can use an injective group morphism from G^2 to S_{288}, because we can decide that the facets of the second cube are numbered from 145 to 288.

Then $e = (1,145)(2,146)\dots(144,188)$ satisfies the requested properties. For convenience of notations we will still use the notation in G^2.

We set $\boldsymbol{F} = \{(U,U_1),\dots,(L,L_1),(U_1,U),\dots,(L_1,L)\}$ and $\boldsymbol{G_R} = \langle \boldsymbol{F} \rangle \subset G_R \times G_R$. The size of $\boldsymbol{G_R}$ is about the same as G_R. A computation with Sage gives $|G_R| \approx 2^{300}$ and $|\boldsymbol{G_R}| \approx 2^{364}$. We will hide the move by rolling in the same way the two cubes, and exchanging (or not) the two cubes. So we set $\boldsymbol{H} = \langle (h_1,h_1),(h_2,h_2),\boldsymbol{e} \rangle$. This time our repositioning group $\boldsymbol{H}$ has 48 elements: the 24 previous repositioning moves, and all these elements combined with the exchange of the cube (before or after, it has no importance).

5.3 ZK Protocol

The protocol in the previous section works for every set of generators with a repositioning group. In this case, we manage to construct a repositioning group by considering the group G^2 (or G^3 for the cubes $6 \times 6 \times 6$ and $7 \times 7 \times 7$, G^n for the cubes $(2n)^3$ and $(2n+1)^3$). We will see in the next section that we can construct in all the cases, a repositioning group by considering the group G^α. For the cube $5 \times 5 \times 5$, we manage to diminish the size of the group because the authorized moves already have some symmetry (rolling the cube shuffles some of the moves).

Then we need to adapt our scheme to the new problem: we will only care to rearrange the first cube, in other words, when we check for $q = 0$ the external way, we just look at the first coordinate in the set G^n ($n = 2$ for the cube $5 \times 5 \times 5$). See appendix B for the details of the scheme. The proof of the zero knowledge argument of knowledge is almost the same as the previous one.

5.4 Choice of *d* and the Number of Rounds for the Cube $5 \times 5 \times 5$

If we follow the generic attacks in Proposition 2, we see that we can choose $d = 42$. We have in fact $12^{42} \approx 2^{150}$ which is much smaller than the cardinality of the total number of positions. Nevertheless most of the times when we choose i_1, i_2 ..., i_d the solution is not unique because we can invert the permutations that commute. Then we can impose for the secret that two consecutive chosen permutations of $\mathcal{F}$ must be equal or do not commute. Then there are only $12 \times 9^{d-1}$ possible combinations. With $\boxed{d = 48}$ we have $12 \times 9^{47} \approx 2^{152}$, and $d \times 9^{d/2} > 2^{80}$.

The **number of necessary rounds** is $\boxed{988}$, since $\left(\frac{47}{48}\right)^{988} \leq 2^{-30}$.

6 Generalization with Any Group

6.1 General Method for Any Set of Generators

Let G be a group, $\alpha \in \mathbb{N}$ $(\alpha \geq 2)$, $\mathcal{F} = \{f_1, \ldots, f_\alpha\}$ such that $\langle \mathcal{F} \rangle = G$. We work with the group G^α and define for all $i \in \{1; \ldots; \alpha\}$

$$\boldsymbol{f}^i = (f_i, f_{i+1}, \ldots, f_\alpha, f_1, \ldots f_{i-1})$$

and we define an extra element $\boldsymbol{h}$ of G^α that verifies:

$$\boldsymbol{h}^\alpha = id \quad \text{and} \quad \forall (a_1, \ldots a_\alpha) \in G^\alpha, \quad \boldsymbol{h}^{-1}(a_1, \ldots, a_\alpha)\boldsymbol{h} = (a_2, \ldots, a_\alpha, a_1)$$

Again, we can prove the existence of such an element thanks to an injective group morphism from G^α to $S_{\alpha n}$, constructed with an injective morphism from G to S_n, because we know from the well-known theorem of Cayley that every finite group can be considered as a subgroup of a symmetric group [11]. Then h is defined in $S_{\alpha n}$ by:

$$\forall i \in \{1; \ldots; \alpha n\}, \quad h(i) = \begin{cases} i + n & \text{if } i \leq (\alpha - 1)n \\ i - (\alpha - 1)n & \text{if } i > (\alpha - 1)n \end{cases}$$

Then $\boldsymbol{H} = \langle \boldsymbol{h} \rangle$ is a repositioning group of $\boldsymbol{F} = \{\boldsymbol{f}^1; \ldots; \boldsymbol{f}^\alpha\}$.
We can use appendix B to construct our scheme.

6.2 ZK with Finite Factorization in Symmetric Groups

Here we consider the case where we do not fix the number of factors, we just give an upper bound of it. This case may seem more difficult than the previous ones, it is in fact a particular case of the previous subsection. We just have to add $f_0 = Id$ to the set of authorized functions, and fix the value d at the diameter of the group, i.e. the maximum distance between two vertices of the Cayley graph of the group. Then we use the same techniques as in previous subsection, it means that we work in $G^{\alpha+1}$ with some extra elements. We will give details of this technique in an extended version of the paper.

7 Efficiency

We suppose we have a symmetric group G whose cardinal is superior to 2^{160} and with a system of generators $\mathcal{F} = \{f_1; f_2; \ldots; f_\alpha\}$ so that there exists a permutation h of order α with $f_i = f_1^{h^{i-1}}$ for all $i \in \{1; \ldots; \alpha\}$. We denote $H = \langle h \rangle$ and H is a repositioning group of $\mathcal{F}$. The system parameters can be built from only h and f_1, so it can take only 320 bits, but in this case we have to compute at each round ${f_1}^{h^j}$ and it will cost about $\lceil \frac{3}{2} \ln_2 \alpha \rceil$ products of permutations (22 if $\alpha = 9240$).

The secret key is an element $(i_1, i_2, \ldots, i_d)$ of $\{1; \ldots; \alpha\}^d$, so we need $\lceil d \log_2(\alpha) \rceil$ bits.

The public key is $x_0 = f_{i_d}^{-1} \ldots f_{i_1}^{-1} \in G$, it takes about 160 bits if the cardinal of G is close to 2^{160}.

In order to compare with existing schemes, we will compute these values for the puzzle $S41$ (see appendix C). We mention in the following table the two different ways to implement $S41$, the first one with all the group H in memory, and the second one with only one generator of H and one element of $\mathcal{F}$. We will denote this last one by $S41'$. We can see in the following table that in terms of performance, our scheme is not so different from the other ones. Moreover, $S41'$ is the most compact of all the schemes, in terms of system parameters. And in both cases, no arithmetic operations are needed.

Table 1. Comparison of 3-pass schemes on 80-bit security against key-recovery attack when the impersonation probability is less than 2^{-30}

	SD [17]	CLE [18]	PP [13]	$S41$	$S41'$
round	52	52	73	260	260
system parameter (bit)	122,500	4,608	28,497	1,478,560	320
public key (bit)	350	288	245	165	165
secret key (bit)	700	192	177	165	165
communication (bit)	59,800	45,517	100,925	673,180	673,180
arithmetic op. (times/field)	$2/S_{700}$	$4/S_{24}$	$2/S_{161},S_{177}$	0	0
permutations (times/size)	$2/S_{700}$	$4/S_{24}$	$2/S_{161},S_{177}$	$3/S_{41}$	$23/S_{41}$ (***)
hash function (times)	4	4	8	14 (*) 2.08 (**)	14 (*) 2.08 (**)
best known recovery attack	2^{87}	2^{84}	$> 2^{74}$	2^{82}	2^{82}

(*) Prover (**) Verifier (***) mean value

8 Conclusion

In this paper, we have studied several authentication schemes built on various factorization problems in non abelian groups. Firstly we proposed zero-knowledge protocols based on different problems with the Rubik's cube and several other generalized cubes. Then we led the generalization for any non abelian group.

The keystone to our constructions relies on the existence of a repositioning group. Whereas the construction of such a group is quite natural for the Rubik's cube 3×3×3, the existence of the repositioning group needs a special construction for generalized Rubik's cubes. We also explained how to proceed in the general case. Besides, we showed how to construct a random puzzle over a small set that is suitable for the general scheme and can be used for a security in 2^{80}.

Moreover, it is also possible to transform these authentication schemes into signature schemes with the standard transformation used in the "Fiat-Shamir" protocol with a hash function [3].

Our constructions are much more efficient than those obtained with general process [5]. Other puzzles, not mentioned here, can be used in the same way for authentication, but there exist puzzles based on some PSpace complete problems or too dissymmetric puzzles that would be worth having specific analysis.

References

1. Colmez, P.: Le Rubik's cube, groupe de poche. ENS Ulm (May 2010)
2. Demaine, E.D., Demaine, M.L., Eisenstat, S., Lubiw, A., Winslow, A.: Algorithms for Solving Rubik's Cubes. In: Demetrescu, C., Halldórsson, M.M. (eds.) ESA 2011. LNCS, vol. 6942, pp. 689–700. Springer, Heidelberg (2011)
3. Fiat, A., Shamir, A.: How to prove yourself: Practical solutions to identification and signature problems. In: Odlyzko, A.M. (ed.) CRYPTO 1986. LNCS, vol. 263, pp. 186–194. Springer, Heidelberg (1987)
4. Garey, M.R., Johnson, D.S.: Computers and Intractability. A Guide to the Theory of NP-Completness, 2nd edn. W.H Freeman and Co. (1991, 1979)
5. Goldreich, O., Micali, S., Wigderson, A.: Proofs that yield nothing but their validity or all languages in NP have zero-knowledge proof systems. J. ACM 38, 690–728 (1991)
6. Goldreich, O., Oren, Y.: Definitions and properties of Zero-knowledge proof systems. Journal of Cryptology 7(1), 1–32 (1994)
7. Halevi, S., Micali, S.: Practical and Provably-Secure Commitment Schemes from Collision-Free Hashing. In: Koblitz, N. (ed.) CRYPTO 1996. LNCS, vol. 1109, pp. 201–215. Springer, Heidelberg (1996)
8. Joyner, D.: Adventures with Group Theory: Rubik's Cube, Merlin's Machine, and Other Mathematical Toys, 2nd edn. The Johns Hopkins University Press (2008)
9. Kendall, G., Parkes, A.J., Spoerer, K.: A Survey of NP-Complete Puzzles. ICGA Journal 31(1), 13–34 (2008)
10. Kozen, D.: Lower bounds for natural proof systems. In: FOCS, pp. 254–266 (1977)
11. Lang, S.: Algebra Revised. 3rd edn. Addison-Wesley (2002)
12. Petit, C., Quisquater, J.-J.: Rubik's for cryptographers. IACR Cryptology ePrint Archive, 2011:638 (2011)
13. Pointcheval, D.: A New Identification Scheme based on the Perceptrons Problem. In: Guillou, L.C., Quisquater, J.-J. (eds.) EUROCRYPT 1995. LNCS, vol. 921, pp. 319–328. Springer, Heidelberg (1995)
14. Pyber, L., Szabó, E.: Growth in finite simple groups of Lie type of bounded rank. ArXiv e-prints (May 2010)
15. Rokicki, T., Kociemba, H., Davidson, M., Dethrige, J.: God's number is 20, `http://cube20.org`
16. Stein, W.A., et al.: Sage Mathematics Software (Version 4.7-OSX-32bit-10.5). The Sage Development Team (2011), `http://www.sagemath.org`
17. Stern, J.: A New Identification Scheme Based on Syndrome Decoding. In: Stinson, D.R. (ed.) CRYPTO 1993. LNCS, vol. 773, pp. 13–21. Springer, Heidelberg (1994)
18. Stern, J.: Designing Identification Schemes with Keys of Short Size. In: Desmedt, Y.G. (ed.) CRYPTO 1994. LNCS, vol. 839, pp. 164–173. Springer, Heidelberg (1994)

A Possible Connections between NP Complete, NP Space and Rubik Problems

In section 3 we have seen several problems based on the Rubik's cube or on generalized Rubik's cubes. When one of the parameters of these puzzles (for example the size n of the cube) becomes large, we wonder how will grow the complexity, asymptotically speaking. We notice that we do not know if some of these problems are NP-complete yet (cf [9] p. 27). Moreover, it is plausible that they are not NP-complete because they have a power of description too limited to describe all the problems of the NP class.

Nevertheless, as we will explain further, some of NP-complete problems have a real similarity with the Rubik's cubes puzzles. So we can consider that these problems, used in this article for authentication, are part of a neighboring class, or a larger class, which is proved NP-complete or NP-space. This is not a proof of the difficulty of Rubik's cube related problems, but it is an indirect argument suggesting it could be true.

Example 1 From [4] p. 280 and [10] we know that the problem "Finite Function Generation" is P-space complete.

Finite Function Generation

INSTANCE: Finite set A, a collection F of functions $f\colon A \to A$ and a specified function $h\colon A \to A$.

QUESTION: Can h be generated from the functions in F by composition ?

Remark. We can notice that here the number of composition functions to be found is not considered, unlike for the Rubik's cube problems where this value d seems to be critical for the complexity.

Example 2 From [4] p. 213, we know that the problem "Longest path" is NP complete.

LONGEST PATH

INSTANCE: Graph $G = (V, E)$, length $l(e) \in \mathbb{Z}^+$ for each $e \in E$, positive integer K, specified vertices $s, t \in V$

QUESTION: Is there a simple path in G from s to t of length K or more, i.e. whose edge lengths sum to at least K ?

Remark. This problem remains NP complete if $l(e) = 1$ for all $e \in E$. Therefore this problem has some similarities with our Rubik problems for going from one position to another. However, as noticed in [4] p. 79 this problem becomes polynomial when we change "of length K or more" by "of length K or less". Nevertheless if we model our graph G such that each vertex is a position of a Rubik's cube $n \times n \times n$, the number of vertices (i.e. possible Cubes) will grow exponentially in n.

B Protocol When the Set of Generators Has No Obvious Repositioning Group

Public:

- A group G^n.
- A set $\mathcal{F} = \{f_1, \ldots, f_\alpha\}$ of generators of $G_R \subset G$

- A set $\boldsymbol{F} = \{\boldsymbol{f}^1, \dots, \boldsymbol{f}^\alpha\} \subset G^n$ with $\boldsymbol{f}^i = (f_1^i = f_i, f_2^i, \dots f_n^i)$ for all $i \in \{1, \dots \alpha\}$.
- A repositioning group $\boldsymbol{H}$ such that ${\boldsymbol{f}^1}^{\boldsymbol{H}} = \boldsymbol{F}$.
- $d \in \mathbb{N}, d \geq 3$
- A group $\boldsymbol{G_R}$ generated by $\boldsymbol{F}$ and $\boldsymbol{H}$. $\boldsymbol{G_R} = \langle \boldsymbol{F}, \boldsymbol{H} \rangle$.
- K a set of keys, $|K| \geq 2^{80}$.

Secret key: $i_1, i_2, \dots, i_d \in \{1, 2, \dots, \alpha\}$.
Public key: $x_0 = (f_{i_1} f_{i_2} \dots f_{i_d})^{-1}$ (or $\boldsymbol{X}^0 = (x_0, id, \dots, id)$)
Scheme (one round):

Prover		**Verifier**
Picks $\boldsymbol{\tau} \in_R \boldsymbol{H}$, $\boldsymbol{\sigma}_0 \in_R \boldsymbol{G_R}$, $k_*, k_0, k_1, \dots, k_d \in_R K$ **Computes** $\forall j \in \{1, \dots, d\}$, $\boldsymbol{\sigma}_j = ({\boldsymbol{f}^{i_j}}^{\boldsymbol{\tau}})^{-1} \boldsymbol{\sigma}_{j-1}$ $c_0 = Com_{k_*}(\boldsymbol{\tau})$ $\forall i \in \{0, \dots, d\}$, $s_i = Com_{k_i}(\boldsymbol{\sigma}_i)$	$c_0, s_0, \dots, s_d$ $\longrightarrow$	
	q $\longleftarrow$	**Picks** $q \in_R \{0, \dots d\}$
Case $q = 0$	$\boldsymbol{\tau}$, $\boldsymbol{\sigma}_0$, $\boldsymbol{\sigma}_d$ $\longrightarrow$ k_*, k_0, k_d	**Computes** $\boldsymbol{X}^d = \boldsymbol{X}^0 \boldsymbol{\tau} \boldsymbol{\sigma}_0 \boldsymbol{\sigma}_{\boldsymbol{d}}^{-1} \boldsymbol{\tau}^{-1}$ **Checks** $\boldsymbol{X}_1^d = id$ $\boldsymbol{\tau} \in \boldsymbol{H}$, $Com_{k_*}(\boldsymbol{\tau}) = c_0$, $Com_{k_0}(\boldsymbol{\sigma}_0) = s_0$, $Com_{k_d}(\boldsymbol{\sigma}_d) = s_d$ **If** all tests ok **then accepts else rejects.**
Case $q \neq 0$	${\boldsymbol{f}_{i_q}}^{\boldsymbol{\tau}}$, $\boldsymbol{\sigma}_q$ $\longrightarrow$ k_{q-1}, k_q	**Computes** $\boldsymbol{\sigma}_{q-1} = {\boldsymbol{f}_{i_q}}^{\boldsymbol{\tau}} \boldsymbol{\sigma}_q$ **Checks** ${\boldsymbol{f}_{i_q}}^{\boldsymbol{\tau}} \in \boldsymbol{F}$, $s_{q-1} = Com_{k_{q-1}}(\boldsymbol{\sigma}_{q-1})$ $s_q = Com_{k_q}(\boldsymbol{\sigma}_q)$ **If** all tests ok **then accepts else rejects.**

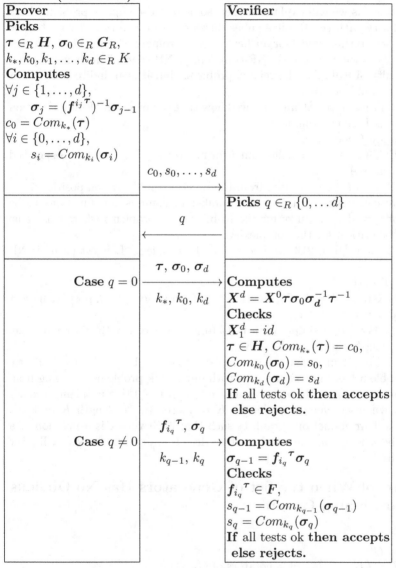

C A New Puzzle Called $S41$

We will present here a new puzzle whose performances seem interesting. We call it $S41$ because we work in the group $G = S_{41}$, which is is the first symmetric group whose cardinal is superior to 2^{160}. We have in fact $|G| \approx 2^{165}$.

With SAGE, we take two random elements h and f_1 in S_{41} until they generate all the group. In the following chart, we can see horizontally the order of $f_1^{\langle h \rangle}$ (α), and vertically the number of solutions for 1000 tries.

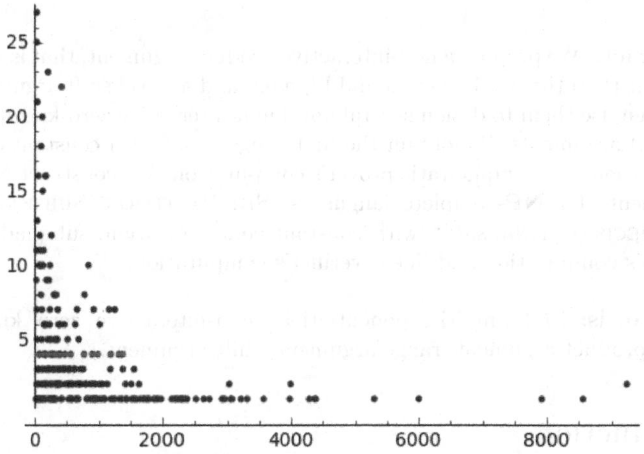

Then, we choose the instance with the biggest α, in order to have a smallest value for d, and in consequence, the smallest value for the number of rounds of the scheme. Here is the instance:

$$\begin{aligned} h = {} & (1,14,39,19,31,18,37)(3,36,4,23,20,34,16,25,17,26,35) \\ & (5,13,30,33)(6,7,10)(8,24,15,38,41,27,11,9) \\ & (12,40,32,21,28)(22,29), \end{aligned}$$

and

$$\begin{aligned} f_1 = {} & (1,11,31,6,17,34,25,24,22,12,4,28,3,14,5,27,32,13,26,8,23,2, \\ & 20,41,19,10,40,15,38,16,37,39,35,21,18)(7,29,36)(9,30). \end{aligned}$$

We set $H = \langle h \rangle$ and $\mathcal{F} = {f_1}^H$. With SAGE we have checked that $\mathcal{F}$ is a set of generators of G and $|H| = |\mathcal{F}| = \alpha = 9240$. We can fix $d = 12$ for a security in 82 bits. And for an impersonation probability less than 2^{-30} only $r = 260$ rounds are needed.

Efficient Modular NIZK Arguments from Shift and Product

Prastudy Fauzi[1], Helger Lipmaa[1], and Bingsheng Zhang[2]

[1] University of Tartu, Estonia
[2] National and Kapodistrian University of Athens, Greece

Abstract. We propose a non-interactive product argument, that is more efficient than the one by Groth and Lipmaa, and a novel shift argument. We then use them to design several novel non-interactive zero-knowledge (NIZK) arguments. We obtain the first range proof with constant communication and subquadratic prover's computation. We construct NIZK arguments for **NP**-complete languages, Set-Partition, Subset-Sum and Decision-Knapsack, with constant communication, subquadratic prover's computation and linear verifier's computation.

Keywords: FFT, multi-exponentiation, non-interactive zero knowledge, product argument, range argument, shift argument.

1 Introduction

By using a zero knowledge proof [20], a prover can prove the correctness of a statement without leaking any side information. Efficient non-interactive zero knowledge (NIZK, [4]) proofs are crucial in the design of cryptographic protocols. A typical application is e-voting, where the voters must prove the correctness of encrypted ballots and the servers must prove the correctness of the tallying process. Since the voters may not be available every time when one verifies the ballots, one cannot rely on interactive zero knowledge. Moreover, it is important to have succinct (e.g., logarithmic in input size) NIZK proofs with efficient verification. For example, in e-voting, correctness proofs are collected and stored, and then verified by many independent observers.

It is well-known that NIZK proofs are impossible in the standard model without any trust assumptions. One usually constructs NIZK proofs in the common reference string (CRS, [4]) model, where all parties have access to a CRS generated by a trusted third party. (We do not consider the random oracle model, since random oracles cannot always be instantiated [9,19].) Moreover, one can only construct succinct *computationally* sound proofs, also known as arguments [7].

Only a few generic techniques of constructing succinct NIZK arguments for non-trivial languages are known, unless **P** = **NP**. In [21], Groth constructed non-interactive witness-indistinguishable (and weakly sound, see [21]) product and permutation arguments. He used them, together with some other arguments, to construct the first succinct NIZK argument for an **NP**-complete language, Circuit-SAT. The latter argument is modular, i.e., it is in a black-box

M. Abdalla, C. Nita-Rotaru, and R. Dahab (Eds.): CANS 2013, LNCS 8257, pp. 92–121, 2013.

way based on a small number of basic arguments. Let $n = |C|$ be the circuit size. Groth's product and permutation arguments have CRS length and prover's computation $\Theta(n^2)$, while the communication and verifier's computation are constant. (The communication is given in group elements, and the computation is in group operations.) His CIRCUIT-SAT argument has the same complexity parameters, except that the verifier's computation is $\Theta(n)$, see Table 1. (The verifier's computation in Lipmaa's argument in Table 1 differs from what was claimed in [27]. The slightly incorrect claim from [27] was also replicated in [11]. See Remark 1 on page 108.)

Lipmaa [27] improved Groth's basic arguments. Let $r_3(N) = N^{1-o(1)}$ be the size of the largest known progression-free subset [14] of $[N] = \{1, \ldots, N\}$. (See Sect. 2.) Lipmaa's basic arguments have CRS length $\Theta(r_3^{-1}(n)) = n^{1+o(1)}$, and slightly better prover's computation. This results straightforwardly in a more efficient modular CIRCUIT-SAT argument. Another important property of Lipmaa's arguments is the flexibility in choosing the progression-free set. For small values of N the value $r_3(N)$ is much smaller than predicted by Elkin, [13,15]. For practically all interesting values of n, one should choose the Erdős-Turán progression-free set [15], which results in the CRS length $\Theta(n^{\log_2 3})$, with a very small constant. Given any progress in the theory of progression-free sets, Lipmaa's arguments can become even more efficient. Thus, Groth's and Lipmaa's basic arguments offer essentially optimal communication and verifier's computation, but they are quite inefficient in other parameters. We estimate that due to quadratic prover's computation, they can only handle circuits of size $\leq 2^{10}$.

The basic arguments of [21,27] can be used to construct other modular arguments. E.g., a modular range argument was constructed in [11]. As shown in [30], following the same framework, one can construct other basic arguments — for example, 1-sparsity in [30] — and use them to construct efficient modular arguments (shuffle in [30]). It is an important open problem to increase the library of basic arguments even further, and to investigate for which (complex) languages one can construct efficient arguments by using the basic arguments in a modular manner. Moreover, the basic arguments of Groth and Lipmaa are computationally intensive for the prover. It is desirable that the new basic arguments (that at the same time have meaningful applications) were more efficient.

We construct a more efficient variant of Lipmaa's product argument, and we propose a new efficient shift-by-ξ argument. We then demonstrate the power of the modular approach, by using the product argument and the shift argument — together with some other, even simpler, arguments — to make the modular range argument of [11] more efficient, and then to construct efficient modular arguments for SET-PARTITION, SUBSET-SUM and DECISION-KNAPSACK (all **NP**-complete languages). All new arguments have constant communication, and significantly improved prover's computation ($\Theta(r_3^{-1}(n) \log n)$ versus $\Theta(n^2)$ in previous work). By using the same basic arguments, one can clearly construct modular NIZK arguments for other languages.

More precisely, we first modify the commitment scheme from [27]. In that commitment scheme (and thus also in all related NIZK arguments), one uses a progression-free set Λ of odd positive integers. When the new commitment scheme is used, Λ can be an arbitrary progression-free set. This is important conceptually, making it clear that one requires progression-freeness of Λ (and nothing else) in similar arguments.

We then construct a more efficient product argument by applying two unrelated algorithmic techniques to the product argument of [27]. While not new, these techniques help us to significantly speed up the product argument, and thus also other arguments that we build on top of it. First, we use Fast Fourier Transform (FFT, [12]) based polynomial multiplication [17] to reduce the prover's computation from $\Theta(n^2)$ to $n^{1+o(1)}$ $\mathbb{Z}_p$-multiplications. In addition, one has to evaluate two $\Theta(n)$-wide and two $\Theta(r_3^{-1}(n))$-wide bilinear-group multi-exponentiations. Due to this, the new product argument has prover's computation and CRS length $n^{1+o(1)}$. We note that FFT-based techniques are not applicable to optimize the arguments of Groth [21], since there the largest element of Λ is $\Theta(n^2)$.

Second, we use Pippenger's [31] algorithm to speed up multi-exponentiations. More precisely, the prover must perform $\Theta(r_3^{-1}(n))$ bilinear-group multiplications to evaluate two $\Theta(r_3^{-1}(n))$-wide bilinear-group multi-exponentiations needed in Lipmaa's product argument. This is smaller than the number of $\mathbb{Z}_p$-multiplications but since bilinear-group multiplications are more expensive, we will count them separately.

We were unable to apply FFT to the permutation argument from [27]; this is since Lipmaa's product argument has an FFT-friendly construction while the permutation argument has a more complex structure. (Thus, the idea of using FFT is not as straightforward as it may seem initially.) Instead, we propose shift-by-ξ and rotation-by-ξ arguments that have constant communication and verifier's computation, and linear prover's computation and CRS length. None of these complexities depends on ξ. Thus, the new shift and rotation arguments are (in some parameters) $\Theta(n)$ times more efficient than Groth's permutation argument. As a drawback, we prove their security only by reduction to the Φ-PSDL assumption [11] (see Sect. 3), which is a generalization of the Λ-PSDL assumption from [27]. To show that the Φ-PSDL assumption is reasonable, we prove that the Φ-PSDL assumption is secure in the generic group model.

We show that based on the product and shift arguments, one can build efficient modular arguments for several important languages. All our applications use an intermediate scan argument that verifies that one vector is the scan [3] (or sum-of-all-prefixes) of another vector. While the scan argument can be straightforwardly constructed from the shift argument, it serves as a very useful intermediate building block.

In a range argument (or a range proof, see [6,29,26,8,10]), the prover aims to convince the verifier that the committed value belongs to an integer range $[L, H]$. Range arguments are needed in many cryptographic applications, typically in cases where for the security of the master protocol (e.g., e-voting or e-auctions) it is necessary to show that the encrypted or committed values come from a correct range. Construction of non-interactive range arguments has only taken off

Table 1. Comparison of modular NIZK arguments for **NP**-complete languages with (worst-case) sublinear argument size. Here, n is the size of circuit, $N = r_3^{-1}(n)$, and $N^* = r_3^{-1}(\sqrt{n})$, and m is the balancing parameter. Moreover, $\mathfrak{g}$ corresponds to 1 group element and $\mathfrak{a}/\mathfrak{m}/\mathfrak{m}_b/\mathfrak{e}/\mathfrak{p}$ correspond to 1 addition/$\mathbb{Z}_p$-multiplication/bilinear-group multiplication/exponentiation/pairing.

m	$\lvert\mathrm{CRS}\rvert$	$\lvert\mathrm{Argument}\rvert$	Prover comp.	Verifier comp.
		CIRCUIT-SAT arguments from [21]		
1	$\Theta(n^2)\mathfrak{g}$	$\Theta(1)\mathfrak{g}$	$\Theta(n^2)\mathfrak{e}$	$\Theta(n)\mathfrak{m}_b + \Theta(1)\mathfrak{p}$
$n^{1/3}$	$\Theta(n^{\frac{2}{3}})\mathfrak{g}$	$\Theta(n^{\frac{2}{3}})\mathfrak{g}$	$\Theta(n^{4/3})\mathfrak{e}$	$\Theta(n)\mathfrak{m}_b + \Theta(n^{\frac{2}{3}})\mathfrak{p}$
		CIRCUIT-SAT arguments from [27]		
1	$\Theta(N)\mathfrak{g}$	$\Theta(1)\mathfrak{g}$	$\Theta(n^2)\mathfrak{a} + \Theta(N)\mathfrak{e}$	$\Theta(n)\mathfrak{e} + 62\mathfrak{p}$
$\sqrt{n}$	$\Theta(N^*)\mathfrak{g}$	$\Theta(\sqrt{n})\mathfrak{g}$	$\Theta(n^{3/2})\mathfrak{a} + \Theta(\sqrt{n} \cdot N^*)\mathfrak{e}$	$\Theta(n)\mathfrak{e} + \Theta(\sqrt{n})\mathfrak{p}$
SET-PARTITION, SUBSET-SUM and DECISION-KNAPSACK arguments from the current paper				
1	$\Theta(N)\mathfrak{g}$	$\Theta(1)\mathfrak{g}$	$\Theta(N \log n)\mathfrak{m} + \Theta(N)\mathfrak{m}_b$	$\Theta(n)\mathfrak{m}_b + \Theta(1)\mathfrak{p}$
$\sqrt{n}$	$\Theta(N^*)\mathfrak{g}$	$\Theta(\sqrt{n})\mathfrak{g}$	$\Theta(\sqrt{n} \cdot N^* \log n)\mathfrak{m} + \Theta(\sqrt{n} \cdot N^*)\mathfrak{m}_b$	$\Theta(n)\mathfrak{m}_b + \Theta(\sqrt{n})\mathfrak{p}$

during the last few years [32,11]. In [11], Chaabouni, Lipmaa and Zhang used the product and permutation arguments of [27] to construct the first known constant-communication (interactive or non-interactive) range argument over prime-order groups. They achieved this by combining the basic arguments of [21,27] with several different (and unrelated) techniques that were developed specifically for range arguments in [29,10].

We use the new basic arguments to optimize the range argument from [11], reducing the prover's computation from $\Theta(h^2)$ to $\Theta(r_3^{-1}(h) \cdot \log r_3^{-1}(h))$ multiplications in $\mathbb{Z}_p$, and from $\Theta(r_3^{-1}(h))$ bilinear-group exponentiations to $\Theta(r_3^{-1}(h))$ bilinear-group multiplications. Here, $h = \log_2(H - L)$. The new argument is the first range argument at all (i.e., not only in prime-order groups) that has constant-length arguments and subquadratic-in-h prover's computation. See Sect. 6. We also note that [11] replicated the small mistake of [27] (see Remark 1) and thus the computational complexity of the argument of [11] is larger than claimed in [11]. We propose another modification of the range argument of [11] to make it even more efficient. We also discuss balanced versions of the new range argument with better prover's computation but larger communication.

We then proceed to demonstrate the power of the "shift-and-multiply" modular approach. We also construct an efficient NIZK argument for the **NP**-complete language SET-PARTITION (the prover knows a partition of the given set of integers to two sets that have the same sum), where the communication and computation are dominated by two product arguments and one shift argument. The new argument has parameters outlined in Table 1. In this case, n denotes the cardinality of the public set. We also construct an NIZK argument for the **NP**-complete language SUBSET-SUM (the prover knows a non-zero subset of the given set of integers that sums to 0), with parameters outlined in Table 1. In this case, n denotes the size of the input domain, that is, the public set S is known to belong to $[n]$. As the final example, we show that one can combine SUBSET-SUM and range arguments to construct an argument for DECISION-KNAPSACK, another **NP**-complete language.

When using the balancing techniques of [21,27] (briefly, instead of applying the basic arguments to length n-vectors, apply them in parallel to m length-(n/m) vectors), if $m = \sqrt{n}$, we obtain balanced NIZK arguments with the parameters, given in the last row of Table 1. (This means that by using the techniques of [21], one can construct a perfect zap with the same complexity.)

Gennaro et al [16] recently proposed an efficient CIRCUIT-SAT argument based either on quadratic span programs or quadratic arithmetic programs. Their argument has prover's computation $\Theta(n \log^3 n)$, which is larger than $\Theta(n^{\log_2 3} \log n)$ for all practical values of n. Subsequently, Lipmaa [28] improved the prover's computation to $\Theta(n \log^2 n)$. See also [2,1]. Since these arguments explicitly rely on the efficient arithmetic-circuit representation of the underlying language, it is unclear if they can be used to construct arguments with subquadratic prover's computation for other **NP**-complete languages. (Using polynomial-time reductions between **NP**-complete languages is usually not an option since we are interested in subquadratic complexity.) Since we are considering different **NP**-complete languages, direct efficiency comparison between [16,28] and the current work is not possible. Moreover, our approach seems to be more flexible, enabling one to construct direct NIZK arguments without a reduction to CIRCUIT-SAT.

2 Preliminaries

Let $[L, H] = \{L, L+1, \dots, H\}$ and $[H] = [1, H]$. By $\boldsymbol{a}$, we denote the vector $\boldsymbol{a} = (a_1, \dots, a_n)$. Since for groups G and H, their direct product $G \times H$ is also a group, we use freely notation like $(g, h)^a = (g^a, h^a)$. If $y = h^x$, then $\log_h y := x$. Let κ be the security parameter. We abbreviate probabilistic polynomial-time as PPT, non-uniform PPT by NUPPT. Let $\mathrm{poly}(\kappa)/\mathrm{negl}(\kappa)$ be an arbitrary polynomial/negligible function.

If Λ_1 and Λ_2 are subsets of some additive group ($\mathbb{Z}$ or $\mathbb{Z}_p$ in this paper), then $\Lambda_1 + \Lambda_2 = \{\lambda_1 + \lambda_2 : \lambda_1 \in \Lambda_1 \wedge \lambda_2 \in \Lambda_2\}$ is their *sum set* and $\Lambda_1 - \Lambda_2 = \{\lambda_1 - \lambda_2 : \lambda_1 \in \Lambda_1 \wedge \lambda_2 \in \Lambda_2\}$ is their *difference set*. If Λ is a set, then $k\Lambda = \{\lambda_1 + \dots + \lambda_k : \lambda_i \in \Lambda\}$ is an *iterated sumset*, $k \cdot \Lambda = \{k\lambda : \lambda \in \Lambda\}$ is a *dilation* of Λ, and $2^\frown \Lambda = \{\lambda_1 + \lambda_2 : \lambda_1 \in \Lambda \wedge \lambda_2 \in \Lambda \wedge \lambda_1 \neq \lambda_2\} \subseteq \Lambda + \Lambda$ is a *restricted sumset*. See [35].

A set $\Lambda = \{\lambda_1, \dots, \lambda_n\}$ is *progression-free* (or non-averaging, [15,35]), if no three elements of Λ are in arithmetic progression, that is, $\lambda_i + \lambda_j = 2\lambda_k$ only if $i = j = k$. That is, $2^\frown \Lambda \cap 2 \cdot \Lambda = \emptyset$. Let $r_3(N)$ be the cardinality of the largest progression-free set $\Lambda \subseteq [N]$. Recently, Elkin [14] proved that

$$r_3(N) = \Omega((N \cdot \log^{1/4} N)/2^{2\sqrt{2\log_2 N}}) .$$

Thus, for any $n > 0$, there exists $N = o(n 2^{2\sqrt{2\log_2 n}})$, such that $[N]$ contains an n-element progression-free subset. However, for say $N \leq 2^{25}$, the Erdős-Turán progression-free subset [15], of size $\approx N^{\log_3 2}$, is larger. For $N \leq 123$, the optimal values of $r_3(N)$ were recently computed in [13]. For any N, the currently best upper bound was proven by Sanders [34].

Polynomial factorization in $\mathbb{Z}_p[X]$ can be done in polynomial time [25,23]. Let $\mathsf{PolyFact}$ be an efficient polynomial factorization algorithm that on input a degree-d polynomial f outputs all $d+1$ roots of f.

Let $y_1, \ldots, y_M$ be monomials over the indeterminates $x_1, \ldots, x_N$. For every $y = (y_1, \ldots, y_M)$, let $L(y)$ be the minimum number of multiplications sufficient to compute $y_1, \ldots, y_M$ from $x_1, \ldots, x_N$ and the identity 1. Let $L(M, N, B)$ denote the maximum of $L(y)$ over all y for which the exponent of any indeterminate in any monomial is at most B. In [31], Pippenger proved that

Fact 1. *Assume that* $h = MN \cdot \log(B+1) \to \infty$. *Then* $L(M, N, B) = \min\{M, N\} \log B + h/\log h \cdot (1 + O((\log\log h/\log h)^{1/2})) + O(\max\{M, N\})$.

A bilinear group generator $\mathcal{G}_{\mathsf{bp}}$ outputs a description of a bilinear group [33,24,5] $\mathsf{gk} := (p, \mathbb{G}_1, \mathbb{G}_2, \mathbb{G}_T, \hat{e}) \leftarrow \mathcal{G}_{\mathsf{bp}}(1^\kappa)$, s.t. p is a κ-bit prime, $\mathbb{G}_1$, $\mathbb{G}_2$ and $\mathbb{G}_T$ are multiplicative cyclic groups of order p (with identity elements denoted by 1), $\hat{e} : \mathbb{G}_1 \times \mathbb{G}_2 \to \mathbb{G}_T$ is a bilinear pairing such that $\forall a, b \in \mathbb{Z}$, $g_1 \in \mathbb{G}_1$ and $g_2 \in \mathbb{G}_2$, $\hat{e}(g_1^a, g_2^b) = \hat{e}(g_1, g_2)^{ab}$. If g_z generates $\mathbb{G}_z$ for $z \in \{1, 2\}$, then $\hat{e}(g_1, g_2)$ generates $\mathbb{G}_T$. Also, it is efficient to decide membership in $\mathbb{G}_1$, $\mathbb{G}_2$ and $\mathbb{G}_T$, group operations and the pairing are efficiently computable, generators are efficiently sampleable, and the descriptions of the groups and group elements each are $O(\kappa)$ bits long. An optimal Ate pairing [22] over a subclass of Barreto-Naehrig curves can be implemented efficiently. Then, at security level of 128 bits, an element of $\mathbb{G}_1/\mathbb{G}_2/\mathbb{G}_T$ can be represented in respectively 256/512/3072 bits.

A trapdoor commitment scheme [7] Γ consists of five PPT algorithms: a randomized common reference string (CRS) generation algorithm $\mathcal{G}_{\mathsf{com}}$, a randomized commitment algorithm $\mathcal{C}om$, a randomized trapdoor CRS generation algorithm $\mathcal{G}com_{td}$, a randomized trapdoor commitment algorithm $\mathcal{C}om_{td}$, and a trapdoor opening algorithm $\mathcal{O}pen_{td}$. Here, (1) the CRS generation algorithm $\mathcal{G}_{\mathsf{com}}(1^\kappa)$ produces a CRS ck, (2) the commitment algorithm $\mathcal{C}om(\mathsf{ck}; \boldsymbol{a}; r)$, with a new randomizer r, outputs a commitment value A. A commitment $\mathcal{C}om(\mathsf{ck}; \boldsymbol{a}; r)$ is opened by revealing $(\boldsymbol{a}, r)$, (3) the trapdoor CRS generation algorithm $\mathcal{G}com_{td}(1^\kappa)$ outputs a CRS ck_{td}, which has the same distribution as $\mathcal{G}_{\mathsf{com}}(1^\kappa)$, and a trapdoor td, (4) the randomized trapdoor commitment algorithm $\mathcal{C}om_{td}(\mathsf{ck}_{td}; r)$ takes ck_{td} and a randomizer r as inputs, and outputs $\mathcal{C}om(\mathsf{ck}_{td}; \boldsymbol{0}; r)$, and (5) the trapdoor opening algorithm $\mathcal{O}pen_{td}(\mathsf{ck}_{td}, \mathsf{td}; \boldsymbol{a}; r)$ outputs an r_{td}, such that $\mathcal{C}om(\mathsf{ck}_{td}; \boldsymbol{0}; r) = \mathcal{C}om(\mathsf{ck}_{td}; \boldsymbol{a}; r_{td})$.

Γ is *computationally binding*, if no NUPPT adversary can open a commitment to two different values. That is, for every NUPPT $\mathcal{A}$,

$$\Pr\left[\begin{array}{l}\mathsf{ck} \leftarrow \mathcal{G}_{\mathsf{com}}(1^\kappa), (\boldsymbol{a}_1, r_1, \boldsymbol{a}_2, r_2) \leftarrow \mathcal{A}(\mathsf{ck}) : \\ (\boldsymbol{a}_1, r_1) \neq (\boldsymbol{a}_2, r_2) \wedge \mathcal{C}om(\mathsf{ck}; \boldsymbol{a}_1; r_1) = \mathcal{C}om(\mathsf{ck}; \boldsymbol{a}_2; r_2)\end{array}\right]$$

is negligible in κ. Γ is *perfectly hiding*, if the commitments of any two messages have the same distribution. That is, for any $\mathsf{ck} \in \mathcal{G}_{\mathsf{com}}(1^\kappa)$ and any $\boldsymbol{a}_1, \boldsymbol{a}_2$, the distributions $\mathcal{C}om(\mathsf{ck}; \boldsymbol{a}_1; \cdot)$ and $\mathcal{C}om(\mathsf{ck}; \boldsymbol{a}_2; \cdot)$ are equal.

The new commitment scheme allows committing to vectors of predetermined length n. Thus, one must input n (or a reasonable upper bound on n) as an additional parameter for the (trapdoor) CRS generation algorithms. We assume that the value of n is implicitly obvious while committing and trapdoor opening.

Let $\mathcal{R} = \{(C, w)\}$ be an efficiently computable binary relation with $|w| = \text{poly}(|C|)$. Here, C is a statement, and w is a witness. Let $\mathcal{L} = \{C : \exists w, (C, w) \in \mathcal{R}\}$ be an **NP**-language. Let $n = |C|$ be the input length. For fixed n, we have a relation $\mathcal{R}_n$ and a language $\mathcal{L}_n$. A *non-interactive argument* for $\mathcal{R}$ consists of three PPT algorithms: a common reference string (CRS) generator $\mathcal{G}_{\mathsf{crs}}$, a prover $\mathcal{P}$, and a verifier $\mathcal{V}$. For $\mathsf{crs} \leftarrow \mathcal{G}_{\mathsf{crs}}(1^\kappa, n)$, $\mathcal{P}(\mathsf{crs}; C, w)$ produces an argument π, and $\mathcal{V}(\mathsf{crs}; C, \pi)$ outputs either 1 (accept) or 0 (reject).

Π is *perfectly complete*, if for all $n = \text{poly}(\kappa)$,

$$\Pr[\mathsf{crs} \leftarrow \mathcal{G}_{\mathsf{crs}}(1^\kappa, n), (C, w) \leftarrow \mathcal{R}_n : \mathcal{V}(\mathsf{crs}; C, \mathcal{P}(\mathsf{crs}; C, w)) = 1] = 1 \ .$$

Π is *computationally sound*, if for all $n = \text{poly}(\kappa)$ and NUPPT $\mathcal{A}$,

$$\Pr[\mathsf{crs} \leftarrow \mathcal{G}_{\mathsf{crs}}(1^\kappa, n), (C, \pi) \leftarrow \mathcal{A}(\mathsf{crs}) : C \notin \mathcal{L} \wedge \mathcal{V}(\mathsf{crs}; C, \pi) = 1] = \text{negl}(\kappa) \ .$$

Π is *perfectly witness-indistinguishable*, if for all $n = \text{poly}(\kappa)$, if $\mathsf{crs} \in \mathcal{G}_{\mathsf{crs}}(1^\kappa, n)$ and $((C, w_0), (C, w_1)) \in \mathcal{R}_n^2$, then the distributions $\mathcal{P}(\mathsf{crs}; C, w_0)$ and $\mathcal{P}(\mathsf{crs}; C, w_1)$ are equal. Π is *perfectly zero-knowledge*, if there exists a PPT simulator $\mathcal{S} = (\mathcal{S}_1, \mathcal{S}_2)$, such that for all stateful NUPPT adversaries $\mathcal{A}$ and $n = \text{poly}(\kappa)$ (with td_π being the *simulation trapdoor*),

$$\Pr\begin{bmatrix} \mathsf{crs} \leftarrow \mathcal{G}_{\mathsf{crs}}(1^\kappa, n), \\ (C, w) \leftarrow \mathcal{A}(\mathsf{crs}), \\ \pi \leftarrow \mathcal{P}(\mathsf{crs}; C, w) : \\ (C, w) \in \mathcal{R}_n \wedge \mathcal{A}(\pi) = 1 \end{bmatrix} = \Pr\begin{bmatrix} (\mathsf{crs}; \mathsf{td}_\pi) \leftarrow \mathcal{S}_1(1^\kappa, n), \\ (C, w) \leftarrow \mathcal{A}(\mathsf{crs}), \\ \pi \leftarrow \mathcal{S}_2(\mathsf{crs}; C, \mathsf{td}_\pi) : \\ (C, w) \in \mathcal{R}_n \wedge \mathcal{A}(\pi) = 1 \end{bmatrix} .$$

3 New Commitment Scheme

Let $\Lambda = (\lambda_1, \dots, \lambda_n) \in \mathbb{Z}^n$ and $\upsilon \in \mathbb{Z}$. Next, we define the (Λ, υ) *trapdoor commitment scheme* in group $\mathbb{G}_z$, $z \in \{1, 2\}$. See Prot. 1. Intuitively, $\boldsymbol{a} = (a_1, \dots, a_n)$ is committed to as $g_z^{r\sigma^\upsilon + \sum a_i \sigma^{\lambda_i}}$, where r is the randomness, g_z is a generator of $\mathbb{G}_z$, and σ is the secret key. Groth [21] proposed a variant of this commitment scheme with $\Lambda = [n]$ and $\upsilon = 0$, while Lipmaa [27] generalized Λ to any set Λ with $0 < \lambda_i < \lambda_{i+1}$ and $\lambda_n = \text{poly}(\kappa)$ (while still letting $\upsilon = 0$).

We use the following security assumptions from [11]. Let p be as output by $\mathcal{G}_{\mathsf{bp}}$. Let $\Phi \subset \mathbb{Z}_p[X]$, with $d := \max_{\varphi \in \Phi} \deg \varphi$, be a set of linearly independent polynomials, such that $|\Phi|$, all coefficients of all $\varphi \in \Phi$, and d are polynomial in κ. Let 1 be the polynomial with $1(x) = 1$ for all $x \in \mathbb{Z}_p$.

Definition 1. $\mathcal{G}_{\mathsf{bp}}$ *is* Φ-PDL secure in $\mathbb{G}_z$, *if for any NUPPT* $\mathcal{A}$,

$$\Pr\begin{bmatrix} \mathsf{gk} := (p, \mathbb{G}_1, \mathbb{G}_2, \mathbb{G}_T, \hat{e}) \leftarrow \mathcal{G}_{\mathsf{bp}}(1^\kappa), g_z \leftarrow \mathbb{G}_z \setminus \{1\}, \sigma \leftarrow \mathbb{Z}_p : \\ \mathcal{A}(\mathsf{gk}; (g_z^{\varphi(\sigma)})_{\varphi \in \{1\} \cup \Phi}) = \sigma \end{bmatrix} = \text{negl}(\kappa) \ .$$

$\mathcal{G}_{\mathsf{bp}}$ *is* Φ-PSDL secure, *if for any NUPPT* $\mathcal{A}$,

$$\Pr\left[\begin{matrix}\mathsf{gk} := (p, \mathbb{G}_1, \mathbb{G}_2, \mathbb{G}_T, \hat{e}) \leftarrow \mathcal{G}_{\mathsf{bp}}(1^\kappa), g_1 \leftarrow \mathbb{G}_1 \setminus \{1\}, \\ g_2 \leftarrow \mathbb{G}_2 \setminus \{1\}, \sigma \leftarrow \mathbb{Z}_p : \mathcal{A}(\mathsf{gk}; (g_1^{\varphi(\sigma)}, g_2^{\varphi(\sigma)})_{\varphi \in \{1\} \cup \Phi}) = \sigma\end{matrix}\right] = \mathrm{negl}(\kappa) .$$

A much stronger version of the P(S)DL assumption was recently used in [2].

Theorem 1. *Let* Φ *and* d *be as in above.* Φ*-PSDL holds in the generic group model. Any successful generic adversary for* Φ*-PSDL requires time* $\Omega(\sqrt{p/d})$.

(See App. A for a proof.) As shown in [18], sublinear NIZK proofs are only possible under non-standard (e.g., knowledge) assumptions. We use the following knowledge assumption from [11]. For algorithms $\mathcal{A}$ and $X_\mathcal{A}$, we write $(y; y_X) \leftarrow (\mathcal{A}||X_\mathcal{A})(\sigma)$ if $\mathcal{A}$ on input σ outputs y, and $X_\mathcal{A}$ on the same input (including the random tape of $\mathcal{A}$) outputs y_X.

Definition 2. *Let* $z \in \{1, 2\}$. $\mathcal{G}_{\mathsf{bp}}$ *is* Φ-PKE secure in $\mathbb{G}_z$ *if for any NUPPT* $\mathcal{A}$ *there exists an NUPPT extractor* $X_\mathcal{A}$*, s.t. the following probability is negligible:*

$$\Pr\left[\begin{matrix}\mathsf{gk} := (p, \mathbb{G}_1, \mathbb{G}_2, \mathbb{G}_T, \hat{e}) \leftarrow \mathcal{G}_{\mathsf{bp}}(1^\kappa), g_z \leftarrow \mathbb{G}_z \setminus \{1\}, (\alpha, \sigma) \leftarrow \mathbb{Z}_p^2, \\ \mathsf{crs} \leftarrow (\mathsf{gk}; ((g_z, g_z^\alpha)^{\phi(\sigma)})_{\phi \in \Phi}), (c, \hat{c}; r, (a_\phi)_{\phi \in \Phi}) \leftarrow (\mathcal{A}||X_\mathcal{A})(\mathsf{crs}) : \\ \hat{c} = c^\alpha \wedge c \neq g_z^r \cdot \prod_{\phi \in \Phi} g_z^{a_\ell \phi(\sigma)}\end{matrix}\right] .$$

One can generalize the proof from [21] to show that Φ-PKE holds in the generic group model. Let $z = 1$. Consider a CRS ck that in particular specifies $g_2, \hat{g}_2 \in \mathbb{G}_2$. A commitment $(A, \hat{A}) \in \mathbb{G}_1^2$ is *valid*, if $\hat{e}(A, \hat{g}_2) = \hat{e}(\hat{A}, g_2)$. The case $z = 2$ is dual. The following theorem generalizes the corresponding results from [21,27].

Theorem 2. *Let* $z \in \{1, 2\}$. *Let* $\Lambda = (\lambda_1, \dots, \lambda_n)$ *with* $\lambda_i < \lambda_{i+1}$ *and* $\lambda_i = \mathrm{poly}(\kappa)$. *Let* $v > \lambda_n$ *be linear in* $\lambda_n - \lambda_1$. *Let* Γ *be the* (Λ, v) *knowledge commitment scheme in* $\mathbb{G}_z$ *of Prot. 1. Let*

$$\Phi_\Gamma := \{X^v\} \cup \{X^\ell\}_{\ell \in \Lambda} .$$

Then

System parameters: $\mathcal{G}_{\mathsf{bp}}$, $n = \mathrm{poly}(\kappa)$, $\Lambda = \{\lambda_1, \dots, \lambda_n\}$ with $\lambda_i < \lambda_{i+1}$, $\lambda_i = \mathrm{poly}(\kappa)$, and $v > \max_i \lambda_i$;
$\mathcal{G}\mathbf{com}_{td}(1^\kappa, n)$: Set $\mathsf{gk} := (p, \mathbb{G}_1, \mathbb{G}_2, \mathbb{G}_T, \hat{e}) \leftarrow \mathcal{G}_{\mathsf{bp}}(1^\kappa)$, $g_z \leftarrow \mathbb{G}_z \setminus \{1\}$, $(\sigma, \hat{\alpha}) \leftarrow \mathbb{Z}_p^2$;
For $i \in [n]$ do: $(g_{z,\lambda_i}, \hat{g}_{z,\lambda_i}) \leftarrow (g_z, g_z^{\hat{\alpha}})^{\sigma^{\lambda_i}}$; Set $(h_z, \hat{h}_z) \leftarrow (g_z, g_z^{\hat{\alpha}})^{\sigma^v}$; Let $\mathsf{ck} \leftarrow (\mathsf{gk}; (g_{z,\lambda_i} \hat{g}_{z,\lambda_i})_{i \in [n]}, h_z, \hat{h}_z)$; Return $(\mathsf{ck}; \mathsf{td} \leftarrow \sigma)$;
$\mathcal{G}_{\mathsf{com}}(1^\kappa, n)$: $(\mathsf{ck}; \mathsf{td}) \leftarrow \mathcal{G}_{\mathsf{com}}(1^\kappa)$; return ck;
$\mathcal{C}\mathbf{om}(\mathsf{ck}; \boldsymbol{a}; \cdot)$, $\boldsymbol{a} = (a_1, \dots, a_n) \in \mathbb{Z}_p^n$: $r \leftarrow \mathbb{Z}_p$; return $(h_z, \hat{h}_z)^r \cdot \prod_{i=1}^n (g_{z,\lambda_i}, \hat{g}_{z,\lambda_i})^{a_i}$;
$\mathcal{C}\mathbf{om}_{td}(\mathsf{ck}_{td}; \cdot)$: $r \leftarrow \mathbb{Z}_p$; return $(h_z, \hat{h}_z)^r$;
$\mathcal{O}\mathbf{pen}_{td}(\mathsf{ck}_{td}, \mathsf{td}; \boldsymbol{a}, r)$: return $r_{td} \leftarrow r - \sum_{i=1}^n a_i \sigma^{\lambda_i - v}$;

Protocol 1: The (Λ, v) trapdoor commitment scheme in $\mathbb{G}_z$ for $z \in \{1, 2\}$

(a) *Γ is perfectly hiding, and computationally binding under the Φ_Γ-PDL assumption in $\mathbb{G}_z$. The reduction overhead is dominated by the time to factor a degree-$(\upsilon - \lambda_1)$ polynomial in $\mathbb{Z}_p[X]$.*

(b) *If Φ_Γ-PKE holds in $\mathbb{G}_z$, then for any NUPPT $\mathcal{A}$ that outputs a valid commitment C, there exists an NUPPT extractor $X_\mathcal{A}$ that, given the input of $\mathcal{A}$ together with $\mathcal{A}$'s random coins, extracts the contents of C.*

Proof. PERFECT HIDING: follows since the output of $\mathcal{C}om$ is a random element of $\mathbb{G}_1$. COMPUTATIONAL BINDING: Assume $\mathcal{A}_{com}$ is an adversary that can break the binding property with non-negligible probability. We construct the following adversary $\mathcal{A}_{pdl}$, see Prot. 1, against the Φ_Γ-PDL assumption in $\mathbb{G}_1$ that works with the same probability. Here, $\mathcal{C}$ is the challenger of the PDL game.

$\mathcal{C}$ sets $\mathsf{gk} \leftarrow \mathcal{G}_{\mathsf{bp}}(1^\kappa)$, $g_z \leftarrow \mathbb{G}_z \setminus \{1\}$, and $\sigma \leftarrow \mathbb{Z}_p$;
$\mathcal{C}$ sends $(\mathsf{gk}; (g_z^{\sigma^\ell})_{\ell \in \{\upsilon\} \cup \Lambda})$ to $\mathcal{A}_{pdl}$;
$\mathcal{A}_{pdl}$ sets $\hat{\alpha}^* \leftarrow \mathbb{Z}_p$;
$\mathcal{A}_{pdl}$ sets $\mathsf{ck} \leftarrow (\mathsf{gk}; ((g_z, g_z^{\hat{\alpha}^*})^{\sigma^\ell})_{\ell \in \Lambda}, (g_z, g_z^{\hat{\alpha}^*})^{\sigma^\upsilon})$;
1 $\mathcal{A}_{pdl}$ obtains $(\boldsymbol{a}, r_a, \boldsymbol{b}, r_b) \leftarrow \mathcal{A}_{com}(\mathsf{ck})$;
if $\boldsymbol{a} \notin \mathbb{Z}_p^n \vee \boldsymbol{b} \notin \mathbb{Z}_p^n \vee r_a \notin \mathbb{Z}_p \vee r_b \notin \mathbb{Z}_p \vee (\boldsymbol{a}, r_a) = (\boldsymbol{b}, r_b) \vee \mathcal{C}om(\mathsf{ck}; \boldsymbol{a}, r_a) \neq \mathcal{C}om(\mathsf{ck}; \boldsymbol{b}, r_b)$ **then** $\mathcal{A}_{pdl}$ aborts **else**
2 $\mathcal{A}_{pdl}$ sets $\delta(X) \leftarrow (r_a - r_b) X^{\upsilon - \lambda_1} + \sum_{i=1}^n (a_i - b_i) X^{\lambda_i - \lambda_1}$.
$\mathcal{A}_{pdl}$ sets $(t_1, \dots, t_{\upsilon - \lambda_1 + 1}) \leftarrow \mathsf{PolyFact}(\delta)$;
3 $\mathcal{A}_{pdl}$ finds by an exhaustive search a root $\sigma_0 \in \{t_i\}_{i=1}^{\upsilon - \lambda_1 + 1}$, s.t. $g_z^{\sigma^{\lambda_1}} = g_z^{\sigma_0^{\lambda_1}}$;
$\mathcal{A}_{pdl}$ returns $\sigma \leftarrow \sigma_0$ to the challenger;
end

Algorithm 1. Adversary in Thm. 2

Assume that on step 1, $\mathcal{A}_{com}$ is successful with some probability ε_c. Thus, with probability ε_c, $(\boldsymbol{a}, r_a) \neq (\boldsymbol{b}, r_b)$ and

$$g_z^{r_a \sigma^\upsilon} \cdot \prod_{i \in [n]} g_z^{a_i \sigma^{\lambda_i}} = g_z^{r_b \sigma^\upsilon} \cdot \prod_{i \in [n]} g_z^{b_i \sigma^{\lambda_i}} .$$

But then

$$g_z^{(r_a - r_b)\sigma^\upsilon + \sum_{i=1}^n (a_i - b_i)\sigma^{\lambda_i}} = 1 ,$$

and thus

$$(r_a - r_b)\sigma^\upsilon + \sum_{i=1}^n (a_i - b_i)\sigma^{\lambda_i} \equiv 0 \pmod p ,$$

or equivalently,

$$(r_a - r_b)\sigma^{\upsilon - \lambda_1} + \sum_{i=1}^n (a_i - b_i)\sigma^{\lambda_i - \lambda_1} \equiv 0 \pmod p .$$

Since $\upsilon > \lambda_n$, $\delta(X)$, as defined on step 2 is a degree-$(\upsilon - \lambda_1)$ non-zero polynomial.

Thus, the adversary has generated a non-trivial degree-$(\upsilon - \lambda_1)$ polynomial $f(X)$ such that $f(\sigma) \equiv 0 \pmod{p}$. Hence, $\mathcal{A}_{pdl}$ can use polynomial factorization to find all roots of δ, and one of those roots must be equal to σ. On step 3, $\mathcal{A}_{pdl}$ finds the correct root by an exhaustive search among all roots returned in the previous step. Thus, clearly $\mathcal{A}_{pdl}$ returns the correct value of sk (and thus violates the Φ_Γ-PDL assumption) with probability ε_c. Finally, the time of $\mathcal{A}_{pdl}$ is clearly dominated by the execution time of $\mathcal{A}_{\mathcal{C}om}$ and the time to factor δ.

EXTRACTABILITY: By the Φ_Γ-PKE assumption in group $\mathbb{G}_z$, for every committer $\mathcal{A}$ there exists an extractor $X_\mathcal{A}$ that can open the commitment in group $\mathbb{G}_z$, given access to $\mathcal{A}$'s inputs and random tape. Since Γ is computationally binding, then the extracted opening has to be the same that $\mathcal{A}$ used. □

Sometimes, we use the same commitment scheme in both $\mathbb{G}_1$ and $\mathbb{G}_2$. In such cases, we will emphasize the underlying group by having a different CRS, but we will not change the name of the commitment scheme.

Let $\alpha = ||\boldsymbol{a}||_\infty = \max_i a_i$, and $n \geq 2$. When using Pippenger's algorithm, the computation of $\mathcal{C}om(\mathsf{ck}; \boldsymbol{a}; r)$ is dominated by $L(2, n, \alpha) = 2\log_2 \alpha + (2 + o(1)) \cdot n \log_2 \alpha / \log_2(n \log_2 \alpha) + O(n)$ $\mathbb{G}_z$-multiplications. In our applications, $n \gg \log_2 \alpha$ (e.g., $\alpha = 2$, $\alpha = n$, or even $\alpha = p$ given that n is reasonably large), and thus we get a simpler bound of $(2 + o(1)) \log_2 \alpha \cdot n / \log_2 n + O(n)$ multiplications. This can be compared to $3n \log_2 \alpha$ multiplications on average when using the square-and-multiply exponentiation algorithm.

4 Improved Hadamard Product Argument

Next, we propose a version of the product argument of [27] with respect to the (Λ, υ) commitment scheme of Sect. 3. As we will see (both in this section and in Sect. 5), the value of υ depends on the construction of the argument. E.g., while the commitment scheme is binding for $\upsilon > \lambda_n$, for the product argument to be (weakly[1]) sound we need $\upsilon > 2\lambda_n - \lambda_1$. If one uses several such arguments together (e.g., to construct a range argument or a SUBSET-SUM argument), one has to choose a value of υ that is secure for all basic arguments. We also show that one can use FFT and Pippenger's multi-exponentiation algorithm to make the product argument more efficient.

Assume that Γ is a trapdoor commitment scheme that commits to $\boldsymbol{a} = (a_1, \dots, a_n) \in \mathbb{Z}_p^n$ for $n \geq 1$. In an *Hadamard product argument*, the prover aims to convince the verifier that given commitments A, B and C, he can open them as $A = \mathcal{C}om(\mathsf{ck}; \boldsymbol{a}; r_a)$, $B = \mathcal{C}om(\mathsf{ck}; \boldsymbol{b}; r_b)$, and $C = \mathcal{C}om(\mathsf{ck}; \boldsymbol{c}; r_c)$, s.t. $c_i = a_i b_i$ for $i \in [n]$. A product argument has n constraints $c_i = a_i b_i$ for $i \in [n]$.

Lipmaa [27] constructed a product argument for the $(\Lambda, 0)$ commitment scheme with communication of 5 group elements, verifier's computation $\Theta(n)$, prover's computation of $\Theta(n^2)$ multiplications in $\mathbb{Z}_p$, and the CRS of $\Theta(r_3^{-1}(n))$ group elements. Prot. 2 presents a more efficient variant of this argument for

[1] For an explanation and motivation of weak soundness, we refer the reader to [21,27].

the (Λ, υ) commitment scheme Γ. Similarly to [27], we use Γ in both $\mathbb{G}_1$ (to commit to $\boldsymbol{a}$, $\boldsymbol{b}$, and $\boldsymbol{c}$) and $\mathbb{G}_2$ (to commit to $\boldsymbol{b}$ and $\mathbf{1}$). Let $\widehat{\mathsf{ck}}$ be the CRS in group $\mathbb{G}_1$, and $\widehat{\mathsf{ck}}^*$ be the dual CRS in group $\mathbb{G}_2$ (i.e., $\widehat{\mathsf{ck}}^*$ is defined as $\widehat{\mathsf{ck}}$, but with g_1 replaced by g_2). Thus, e.g., $(B, \hat{B}) = \mathcal{C}om(\widehat{\mathsf{ck}}; \boldsymbol{b}; r_b)$. Then, $\log_{g_1} A = r_a\sigma^\upsilon + \sum_{i=1}^n a_i\sigma^{\lambda_i}$, $\log_{g_1} B = r_b\sigma^\upsilon + \sum_{i=1}^n b_i\sigma^{\lambda_i}$, and $\log_{g_1} C = c_i\sigma^\upsilon + \sum_{i=1}^n r_c\sigma^{\lambda_i}$. The prover also computes an element B_2, s.t. $\hat{e}(g_1, B_2) = \hat{e}(B, g_2)$. Thus, for $(D, \hat{D}) = \mathcal{C}om(\widehat{\mathsf{ck}}^*; \mathbf{1}; 0)$ (in $\mathbb{G}_2$), $\log_{\hat{e}(g_1,g_2)}(\hat{e}(A, B_2)/\hat{e}(C, D)) = (r_a\sigma^\upsilon + \sum_{i=1}^n a_i\sigma^{\lambda_i})(r_b\sigma^\upsilon + \sum_{i=1}^n b_i\sigma^{\lambda_i}) - (r_c\sigma^\upsilon + \sum_{i=1}^n c_i\sigma^{\lambda_i})(\sum_{i=1}^n \sigma^{\lambda_i})$ can be written — after substituting σ with a formal variable X — as a sum of two formal polynomials $F_{con}(X)$ and $F_\pi(X)$, s.t. $F_{con}(X)$ (the constraint polynomial) has one monomial per constraint ($a_ib_i = c_i$) and is 0 if the prover is honest, while $F_\pi(X)$ has many more monomials. More precisely, F_π has $\Theta(r_3^{-1}(n))$ monomials, and the CRS has length $\Theta(r_3^{-1}(n))$. The honest prover has to compute $(\pi, \hat{\pi}) \leftarrow (g_2^{F_\pi(\sigma)}, \hat{g}_2^{F_\pi(\sigma)})$. The PSDL and the PKE assumptions guarantee that he cannot do it if at least one of the n constraints is not satisfied.

In [27], for soundness, one had to assume that the used set Λ is a progression-free set of odd positive integers. By using such Λ, [27] proved that the polynomials $F_{con}(X)$ and $F_\pi(X)$ were spanned by two non-intersecting sets of powers of X. From this, [27] then deduced (weak) soundness.

We will show that by using the (Λ, υ) commitment scheme (for a well-chosen value of υ), one can without any loss in efficiency assume that Λ is just a progression-free set. This makes the product argument slightly more efficient. More importantly, it makes it clear that the property that Λ has to satisfy is really progression-freeness, and not say having only odd integers as its members.

For a set Λ and an integer υ, define

$$\hat{\Lambda} := \{2\upsilon\} \cup (\upsilon + \Lambda) \cup 2\hat{\ }\Lambda \ . \tag{1}$$

(In [27], this definition was only given for $\upsilon = 0$. Then, $\hat{\Lambda} = \{0\} \cup \Lambda \cup 2\hat{\ }\Lambda$.)

Lemma 1. *Assume that $\Lambda = (\lambda_1, \dots, \lambda_n)$ with $\lambda_{i+1} > \lambda_i$, and $\upsilon > 2\lambda_n - \lambda_1$. Λ is a progression-free set if and only if $2 \cdot \Lambda \cap \hat{\Lambda} = \emptyset$.*

Proof. Assume Λ is progression-free. Then $2\hat{\ }\Lambda \cap 2 \cdot \Lambda = \emptyset$. Since $\upsilon > 2\lambda_n - \lambda_1$, $(\{2\upsilon\} \cup (\upsilon + \Lambda)) \cap 2 \cdot \Lambda = \emptyset$. (In [27], $\upsilon = 0$, and $(\{0\} \cup \Lambda) \cap 2 \cdot \Lambda = \emptyset$ was guaranteed by assuming that every integer in Λ is odd and non-zero.) Assume now that $2 \cdot \Lambda \cap \hat{\Lambda} = \emptyset$. Thus, $2 \cdot \Lambda \cap 2\hat{\ }\Lambda = \emptyset$, and Λ is a progression-free set. □

Lemma 2. *For any $n > 0$, there exists a progression-free set $\Lambda = \{\lambda_1, \dots, \lambda_n\}$, with $\lambda_i < \lambda_{i+1}$ and $\lambda_n = \mathrm{poly}(\kappa)$, and an integer $\upsilon > 2\lambda_n - \lambda_1$, υ linear in $\lambda_n - \lambda_1$, such that $|\hat{\Lambda}| = \Theta(r_3^{-1}(n))$.*

Proof. Let Λ be the progression-free set from [14], seen as a subset of $[\lambda_1, \lambda_n]$ (with λ_1 possibly being negative), with $\lambda_n - \lambda_1 \approx r_3^{-1}(n)$. Since $\upsilon > 2\lambda_n - \lambda_1$ is linear in $\lambda_n - \lambda_1$, $\hat{\Lambda} \subset [2\lambda_1, 2\upsilon]$ and $|\hat{\Lambda}| = \Theta(r_3^{-1}(n))$. □

CRS generation $\mathcal{G}_{crs}(1^\kappa, n)$:
Set $\mathsf{gk} := (p, \mathbb{G}_1, \mathbb{G}_2, \mathbb{G}_T, \hat{e}) \leftarrow \mathcal{G}_{bp}(1^\kappa)$, $(g_1, g_2) \leftarrow (\mathbb{G}_1 \setminus \{1\}, \mathbb{G}_2 \setminus \{1\})$;
Set $\sigma, \hat{\alpha} \leftarrow \mathbb{Z}_p$, $\hat{g}_1 \leftarrow g_1^{\hat{\alpha}}$;
For each $\ell \in \{v\} \cup \Lambda$ do: $(g_{1,\ell}, \hat{g}_{1,\ell}) \leftarrow (g_1, \hat{g}_1)^{\sigma^\ell}$;
For each $\ell \in \{v\} \cup \hat{\Lambda}$ do: $(g_{2,\ell}, \hat{g}_{2,\ell}) \leftarrow (g_2, g_2^{\hat{\alpha}})^{\sigma^\ell}$;
Set $D \leftarrow \prod_{i=1}^n g_{2,\lambda_i}$, $\widehat{\mathsf{ck}} \leftarrow (\mathsf{gk}; (g_{1,\ell}, \hat{g}_{1,\ell})_{\ell \in \{v\} \cup \Lambda})$;
Return $\mathsf{crs} \leftarrow (\widehat{\mathsf{ck}}, g_1, \hat{g}_1, (g_{2,\ell}, \hat{g}_{2,\ell})_{\ell \in \hat{\Lambda}}, D)$;
Argument generation $\mathcal{P}_\times(\mathsf{crs}; (A, \hat{A}, B, \hat{B}, B_2, C, \hat{C}), (\boldsymbol{a}, r_a, \boldsymbol{b}, r_b, \boldsymbol{c}, r_c))$:
Define $\mathfrak{I}_1(\ell) := \{(i,j) : i,j \in [n] \wedge i \neq j \wedge \lambda_i + \lambda_j = \ell\}$;
For each $\ell \in 2\hat{}\Lambda$ do: $\mu_\ell \leftarrow \sum_{(i,j) \in \mathfrak{I}_1(\ell)} (a_i b_j - c_i)$;
$(\pi, \hat{\pi}) \leftarrow (g_{2,2v}, \hat{g}_{2,2v})^{r_a r_b} \cdot \prod_{i=1}^n (g_{2,v+\lambda_i}, \hat{g}_{2,v+\lambda_i})^{r_a b_i + r_b a_i - r_c} \cdot \prod_{\ell \in 2\hat{}\Lambda} (g_{2,\ell}, \hat{g}_{2,\ell})^{\mu_\ell}$;
Return $\pi^\times \leftarrow (\pi, \hat{\pi}) \in \mathbb{G}_2^2$;
Verification $\mathcal{V}_\times(\mathsf{crs}; (A, \hat{A}, B, \hat{B}, B_2, C, \hat{C}), \pi^\times)$:
If $\hat{e}(A, B_2)/\hat{e}(C, D) = \hat{e}(g_1, \pi)$ and $\hat{e}(g_1, \hat{\pi}) = \hat{e}(\hat{g}_1, \pi)$ then accept, else reject.

Protocol 2: New product argument $[\![(A, \hat{A})]\!] \circ [\![(B, \hat{B}, B_2)]\!] = [\![(C, \hat{C})]\!]$

One can add any constant to all members of Λ and v, so that the previous results still hold. In particular, according to the previous two lemmas, the best value (in the sense of efficiency) of λ_n might be 0.

We state and prove the security of the new product argument when using the (Λ, v) knowledge commitment scheme by closely following the claim and the proof from [27]. The (knowledge) commitments are $(A, \hat{A})$, $(B, \hat{B})$ and $(C, \hat{C})$. For efficiency (and backwards compatibility) reasons, following [27], we include another element B_2 to the statement of the Hadamard product language.

Since for any $\boldsymbol{a}$ and $\boldsymbol{b}$, $(C, \hat{C})$ is a commitment of $(a_1 b_1, \ldots, a_n b_n)$ for *some* value of r_c, Prot. 2 cannot be computationally sound (even under a knowledge assumption). Instead, as in [21,27], we prove a weaker version of soundness that is sufficient to achieve soundness of the more complex arguments. The last statement of Thm. 3 basically says that no efficient adversary can output an input to the product argument together with an accepting argument and openings to all commitments and all other pairs of type $(y, \hat{y})$ that are present in the argument, s.t. $a_i b_i \neq c_i$ for some $i \in [n]$. See App:prodsec for the proof.

Theorem 3. *Let* $n = \mathrm{poly}(\kappa)$. *Let* $\Lambda = (\lambda_1, \ldots, \lambda_n)$ *be a progression-free set with* $\lambda_{i+1} > \lambda_i$, $\lambda_i = \mathrm{poly}(\kappa)$, $v > 2\lambda_n - \lambda_1$, *and* $v = \mathrm{poly}(\kappa)$. *Let* Γ *be the* (Λ, v) *commitment scheme in* $\mathbb{G}_1$. *Let* $\Phi_\times := \{X^v\} \cup \{X^\ell\}_{\ell \in \hat{\Lambda}}$.

1. *Prot. 2 is perfectly complete and perfectly witness-indistinguishable.*
2. *If* $\mathcal{G}_{bp}$ *is* $\Phi_\times$*-PSDL secure, then an NUPPT adversary against Prot. 2 has negligible chance, given* $\mathsf{crs} \leftarrow \mathcal{G}_{crs}(1^\kappa, n)$ *as an input, of outputting* $inp^\times \leftarrow (A, \hat{A}, B, \hat{B}, B_2, C, \hat{C})$ *and an accepting argument* $\pi^\times \leftarrow (\pi, \hat{\pi})$ *together with a witness* $w^\times \leftarrow (\boldsymbol{a}, r_a, \boldsymbol{b}, r_b, \boldsymbol{c}, r_c, (f_\ell^*)_{\ell \in \hat{\Lambda}})$, *such that*
   (a) $\boldsymbol{a}, \boldsymbol{b}, \boldsymbol{c} \in \mathbb{Z}_p^n$, $r_a, r_b, r_c \in \mathbb{Z}_p$, *and* $f_\ell^* \in \mathbb{Z}_p$ *for* $\ell \in \hat{\Lambda}$,
   (b) $(A, \hat{A}) = \mathcal{C}om(\widehat{\mathsf{ck}}; \boldsymbol{a}; r_a)$, $(B, \hat{B}) = \mathcal{C}om(\widehat{\mathsf{ck}}; \boldsymbol{b}; r_b)$, $B_2 = g_{2,v}^{r_b} \cdot \prod_{i=1}^n g_{2,\lambda_i}^{b_i}$, *and* $(C, \hat{C}) = \mathcal{C}om(\widehat{\mathsf{ck}}; \boldsymbol{c}; r_c)$,

(c) $\log_{g_2} \pi = \log_{\hat{g}_2} \hat{\pi} = \sum_{\ell \in \hat{\Lambda}} f_\ell^* \sigma^\ell$, *where* $\hat{g}_2 = g_2^{\hat{\alpha}}$, *and*
(d) for some $i \in [n]$, $a_i b_i \neq c_i$.
The reduction overhead is dominated by the time to factor a degree-$(2\upsilon - 2\lambda_1)$ *polynomial in* $\mathbb{Z}_p[X]$.

Next, we will show that the product argument of this section (and also the product argument of [27]) is computationally much more efficient than it was claimed in [27]. In [27], the prover was said to require computing $\Theta(n^2)$ multiplications in $\mathbb{Z}_p$ and $\Theta(r_3^{-1}(n))$ exponentiations in $\mathbb{G}_2$. We optimize the prover's computation so that it will require a significantly smaller number of multiplications and no exponentiations at all.

Theorem 4. *The communication (argument size) of Prot. 2 is* 2 *elements from* $\mathbb{G}_2$. *The prover's computation is dominated by* $\Theta(r_3^{-1}(n) \cdot \log r_3^{-1}(n))$ *multiplications in* $\mathbb{Z}_p$ *and two* $\Theta(r_3^{-1}(n))$*-wide multi-exponentiations in* $\mathbb{G}_2$. *The verifier's computation is dominated by* 5 *bilinear pairings and* 1 *bilinear-group multiplication. The CRS consists of* $\Theta(r_3^{-1}(n))$ *group elements.*

Proof. By Lem. 2, the size of the CRS is $\Theta(|\hat{\Lambda}|) = \Theta(r_3^{-1}(n))$. From the CRS, the verifier only needs to access g_1, $\hat{g}_1$, and D. Since $2 \frown \Lambda \subseteq \hat{\Lambda}$, the statement about the prover's computation follows from Fast Fourier Transform [12] based polynomial multiplication [17] techniques. To compute all the coefficients of the polynomial $\mu(X) := \sum_{i=1}^n \sum_{j=1:j\neq i}^n (a_i b_j - c_i) X^{\lambda_i + \lambda_j}$, the prover executes Alg. 2. Here, FFTMult denotes an FFT-based polynomial multiplication algorithm.

For $i \leftarrow 0$ to λ_n do: $a_i^\dagger \leftarrow 0$, $b_i^\dagger \leftarrow 0$, $c_i^\dagger \leftarrow 0$, $d_i^\dagger \leftarrow 0$;
For $i \leftarrow 1$ to n do: $a_{\lambda_i}^\dagger \leftarrow a_i$, $b_{\lambda_i}^\dagger \leftarrow b_i$, $c_{\lambda_i}^\dagger \leftarrow c_i$, $d_{\lambda_i}^\dagger \leftarrow 0$;
Denote $a^\dagger(X) := \sum_{i=0}^{\lambda_n} a_i^\dagger X^i$ and $b^\dagger(X) := \sum_{i=0}^{\lambda_n} b_i^\dagger X^i$;
Denote $c^\dagger(X) := \sum_{i=0}^{\lambda_n} c_i^\dagger X^i$ and $d^\dagger(X) := \sum_{i=0}^{\lambda_n} d_i^\dagger X^i$;
Let $\mu(X) \leftarrow \mathsf{FFTMult}(a^\dagger(X), b^\dagger(X))$; Let $\nu(X) \leftarrow \mathsf{FFTMult}(c^\dagger(X), d^\dagger(X))$;
For $i \leftarrow 1$ to n do: $\mu_{2\lambda_i} \leftarrow \mu_{2\lambda_i} - a_i b_i$;
Let $\mu(X) \leftarrow \mu(X) - \nu(X)$;

Algorithm 2. FFT-based prover's computation of $\{\mu_\ell\}$

After using FFTMult to compute the initial version of $\mu(X)$ and $\nu(X)$, $\mu_\ell = \sum_{(i,j)\in[n]^2:\lambda_i+\lambda_j=\ell} a_i b_j$ and $\nu_\ell = \sum_{(i,j)\in[n]^2:\lambda_i+\lambda_j=\ell} c_i$. Thus, after the penultimate step of Alg. 2, $\mu_\ell = \sum_{(i,j)\in\mathfrak{I}_1(\ell)} a_i b_j$, and after the last step, $\mu_\ell = \sum_{(i,j)\in\mathfrak{I}_1(\ell)} a_i b_j - c_i$, as required by Prot. 2. Since FFT takes time $\Theta(N \log N)$, where $N = r_3^{-1}(n)$ is the input size, we have shown the part about the prover's computational complexity. The verifier's computational complexity follows from the description of the argument. □

FFT does not help to speed up Groth's product argument [21], since there $\lambda_n = \Theta(n^2)$. FFT does also not seem to be useful in the case of the permutation argument from [27]. Finally, it may be possible to speed up Alg. 2, by taking into account the fact that all $a^\dagger$, $b^\dagger$, $c^\dagger$ and $d^\dagger$ have only n non-zero monomials.

Next, we use efficient multi-exponentiation for additional speed-up. Let $\alpha := \max(||a||_\infty, ||b||_\infty, ||c||_\infty)$, where the prover has committed to $\boldsymbol{a}$ and $\boldsymbol{b}$. (See Sect. 6 for the concrete values of α.) The number of bilinear-group operations the prover has to perform (on top of computing the exponents by using the FFT-based polynomial multiplication) to compute π is dominated by $L(2, n, p) + L(2, r_3^{-1}(n), \Theta((\alpha n)^2))$. The very conservative value $\Theta((\alpha n)^2)$ follows from $|\mu_\ell| = |\sum_{(i,j)\in\mathfrak{I}_1(\ell)}(a_i b_j - c_i)| \le \sum_{(i,j)\in\mathfrak{I}_1(\ell)} |a_i b_j - c_i| \le \sum_{(i,j)\in\mathfrak{I}_1(\ell)}(\alpha^2 + \alpha) < (n^2 - n)(\alpha^2 + \alpha) = \Theta((\alpha n)^2)$.

Due to Fact 1, for $n = \Omega(\log p)$, $L(2, n, p) = 2\log_2 p + (2 + o(1)) \cdot n \log_2(p+1)/(\log_2(2n\log_2(p+1))) + O(n) = (2 + o(1)) \cdot \log_2 p \cdot n/\log_2 n$, and, since in our applications, $n \gg \log_2 \Theta((\alpha n)^2)$, $L(2, r_3^{-1}(n), \Theta((\alpha n)^2)) = 2\log_2(\alpha n^2) + \frac{(2+o(1))r_3^{-1}(n)\log_2\Theta((\alpha n)^2)}{(\log_2(2r_3^{-1}(n)\log_2\Theta((\alpha n)^2)))} + O(r_3^{-1}(n)) = \frac{(2+o(1))r_3^{-1}(n)}{(\log_2 r_3^{-1}(n))} \cdot 2\log_2(\alpha n)$. Thus, the prover has to compute $(2 + o(1)) \cdot (\frac{n}{\log_2 n} \cdot \log_2 p + \frac{r_3^{-1}(n)}{\log_2 r_3^{-1}(n)} \cdot 2\log_2(\alpha n))$ bilinear-group multiplications. We will instantiate α and other values in Sect. 6.

5 Shift and Rotation Arguments

In a *right shift-by-ξ argument* (resp., right rotation-by-ξ argument), the prover aims to convince the verifier that for two commitments A and B, he knows how to open them as $A = \mathcal{C}om(\mathsf{ck}; \boldsymbol{a}; r_a)$ and $B = \mathcal{C}om(\mathsf{ck}; \boldsymbol{b}; r_b)$, such that $a_i = b_{i+\xi}$ for $i \in [n - \xi]$ and $a_{n-\xi+1} = \cdots = a_n = 0$ (resp., $a_{n-\xi+1} = b_1$, $\dots a_n = b_\xi$). That is, $(a_n, \dots, a_1) = (0, \dots, 0, b_n, \dots, b_{\xi+1})$ (resp., $(a_n, \dots, a_1) = (b_\xi, \dots, b_1, b_n, \dots, b_{\xi+1})$). Left shift and left rotation arguments are defined dually, we omit their descriptions.

Groth [21] and Lipmaa [27] defined NIZK arguments for arbitrary permutation ϱ (i.e., $a_{\varrho(i)} = b_i$ for public ϱ). However, their permutation arguments are quite complex and computationally intensive. Moreover, many applications do not require arbitrary permutations. We give examples of the latter in Sect. 6.

We now describe the new right shift-by-ξ argument $\mathsf{rsft}_\xi(\llbracket(A, \tilde{A})\rrbracket) = \llbracket(B, \tilde{B})\rrbracket$, that is much simpler and significantly more computation-efficient than the generic permutation arguments of Groth and Lipmaa. One can design a very similar rotation argument, see App. D. Let $\log_{g_1} A = r_a\sigma^v + \sum_{i=1}^n a_i\sigma^{\lambda_i}$ and $\log_{g_1} B = r_b\sigma^v + \sum_{i=1}^n b_i\sigma^{\lambda_i}$. We replace σ with a formal variable X. If the prover is honest (full derivation of this is given in the proof of Thm. 5), then $F(X) := X^\xi \cdot \log_{g_1} A - \log_{g_1} B = -\sum_{i=1}^\xi b_i X^{\lambda_i} + \sum_{i=\xi+1}^n b_i(X^{\lambda_{i-\xi}+\xi} - X^{\lambda_i}) + r_a X^{v+\xi} - r_b X^v$. Thus, one can verify that A is a right shift-by-ξ of B by checking that $\hat{e}(A, g_2^{\sigma^\xi})/\hat{e}(B, g_2) = \hat{e}(g_1, \pi)$, where $\pi = g_2^{F(\sigma)}$ is defined as in Prot. 3. As seen from the proof of the following theorem, the actual security proof, especially for the (weaker version of) soundness, is more complicated. Complications arise from the use of polynomials of type $X^i - X^j$ in the verification equation; because of this we must rely on a less straightforward variant of the PSDL assumption than before. One has also to be careful in the choice of the set Λ: if say $\lambda_{n-\xi} + \xi = \lambda_n$, then some of the monomials of $F(X)$ will collapse, and the security proof will not go through.

CRS generation $\mathcal{G}_{\mathsf{crs}}(1^\kappa, n)$:
Set $\mathsf{gk} := (p, \mathbb{G}_1, \mathbb{G}_2, \mathbb{G}_T, \hat{e}) \leftarrow \mathcal{G}_{\mathsf{bp}}(1^\kappa)$, $g_1 \leftarrow \mathbb{G}_1 \setminus \{1\}$, $g_2 \leftarrow \mathbb{G}_2 \setminus \{1\}$, $\sigma, \tilde{\alpha} \leftarrow \mathbb{Z}_p$;
For each $z \in \{1, 2\}$ do: $\tilde{g}_z \leftarrow g_z^{\tilde{\alpha}}$;
For each $\ell \in \{\upsilon\} \cup \Lambda$ do: $(g_{1,\ell}, \tilde{g}_{1,\ell}) \leftarrow (g_1, \tilde{g}_1)^{\sigma^\ell}$;
Set $g_{2,\xi} \leftarrow g_2^{\sigma^\xi}$;
For each $i \in \{\lambda_1, , \dots, \lambda_\xi, \upsilon, \upsilon + \xi\}$ do: $(g_{2,i}, \tilde{g}_{2,i}) \leftarrow (g_2, \tilde{g}_2)^{\sigma^i}$;
For each $i \in [1, n - \xi]$ do: $(h_{2,i}, \tilde{h}_{2,i}) \leftarrow (g_2, \tilde{g}_2)^{\sigma^{\lambda_i + \xi} - \sigma^{\lambda_{i+\xi}}}$;
Set $\widetilde{\mathsf{ck}} \leftarrow (\mathsf{gk}; (g_{1,\ell}, \tilde{g}_{1,\ell})_{\ell \in \{\upsilon\} \cup \Lambda})$;
Return $\mathsf{crs} \leftarrow (\widetilde{\mathsf{ck}}, g_1, \tilde{g}_1, g_2, g_{2,\xi}, (g_{2,i}, \tilde{g}_{2,i})_{i \in \{\lambda_1, \dots, \lambda_\xi, \upsilon, \upsilon+\xi\}}, (h_{2,i}, \tilde{h}_{2,i})_{i \in [1, n-\xi]})$;
Argument generation $\mathcal{P}_{\mathsf{rsft}}(\mathsf{crs}; (A, \tilde{A}, B, \hat{B}, \tilde{B}), (\boldsymbol{a}, r_a, \boldsymbol{b}, r_b))$:
$(\pi, \tilde{\pi}) \leftarrow \prod_{i=1}^{n-\xi} (h_{2,i}, \tilde{h}_{2,i})^{b_{i+\xi}} \prod_{i=1}^{\xi} (g_{2,\lambda_i}, \tilde{g}_{2,\lambda_i})^{-b_i} (g_{2,\upsilon+\xi}, \tilde{g}_{2,\upsilon+\xi})^{r_a} \cdot (g_{2,\upsilon}, \tilde{g}_{2,\upsilon})^{-r_b}$;
Return $\pi^{\mathsf{rsft}} \leftarrow (\pi, \tilde{\pi}) \in \mathbb{G}_2^2$;
Verification $\mathcal{V}_{\mathsf{rsft}}(\mathsf{crs}; (A, \tilde{A}, B, \hat{B}, \tilde{B}), \pi^{\mathsf{rsft}})$:
If $\hat{e}(A, g_{2,\xi}) / \hat{e}(B, g_2) = \hat{e}(g_1, \pi)$ and $\hat{e}(g_1, \tilde{\pi}) = \hat{e}(\tilde{g}_1, \pi)$ then accept, else reject;

Protocol 3: New right shift-by-ξ argument $\mathsf{rsft}_\xi([\![(A, \tilde{A})]\!]) = [\![(B, \tilde{B})]\!]$

Theorem 5. *Let* $n = \text{poly}(\kappa)$. *Let* $\Lambda = (\lambda_1, \dots, \lambda_n) \subset \mathbb{Z}$, *s.t.* $\lambda_{i+1} > \lambda_i$, $\lambda_i \neq \lambda_j + \xi$ *for* $i \neq j$, *and* $\lambda_i = \text{poly}(\kappa)$. *Let* $\upsilon > \lambda_n + \xi$ *be an integer, s.t.* $\upsilon = \text{poly}(\kappa)$. *Let* Γ *be the* (Λ, υ) *commitment scheme in* $\mathbb{G}_1$.
(1) Prot. 3 is perfectly complete and perfectly witness-indistinguishable.
(2) Let

$$\Phi_{\mathsf{rsft}}^\xi := \{X^\upsilon, X^{\upsilon+\xi}\} \cup \{X^{\lambda_i}\}_{i=1}^{\xi} \cup \{X^{\lambda_i + \xi} - X^{\lambda_{i+\xi}}\}_{i=1}^{n-\xi} .$$

If $\mathcal{G}_{\mathsf{bp}}$ *is* Φ_{rsft}^ξ*-PSDL secure, then an NUPPT adversary against Prot. 3 has negligible chance, given* $\mathsf{crs} \leftarrow \mathcal{G}_{\mathsf{crs}}(1^\kappa, n)$ *as an input, of outputting* $inp^{\mathsf{rsft}} \leftarrow (A, \tilde{A}, B, \tilde{B})$ *and an accepting argument* $\pi^{\mathsf{rsft}} \leftarrow (\pi, \tilde{\pi})$ *together with a witness* $w^{\mathsf{rsft}} \leftarrow (\boldsymbol{a}, r_a, \boldsymbol{b}, r_b, (f_\phi^*)_{\phi \in \Phi_{\mathsf{rsft}}^\xi})$, *such that*
(a) $\boldsymbol{a}, \boldsymbol{b} \in \mathbb{Z}_p^n$, $r_a, r_b \in \mathbb{Z}_p$, *and* $f_\phi^* \in \mathbb{Z}_p$ *for* $\phi \in \Phi_{\mathsf{rsft}}^\xi$,
(b) $(A, \tilde{A}) = \mathcal{C}om(\widetilde{\mathsf{ck}}; \boldsymbol{a}; r_a)$, $(B, \tilde{B}) = \mathcal{C}om(\widetilde{\mathsf{ck}}; \boldsymbol{b}; r_b)$,
(c) $\log_{g_2} \pi = \log_{\tilde{g}_2} \tilde{\pi} = \sum_{\phi \in \Phi_{\mathsf{rsft}}^\xi} f_\phi^* \cdot \phi(\sigma)$, *and*
(d) $(a_n, a_{n-1}, \dots, a_1) \neq (0, \dots, 0, b_n, \dots, b_{\xi+1})$.
The reduction time is dominated by the time it takes to factor a degree-$(\upsilon+1)$ *polynomial in* $\mathbb{Z}_p[X]$.

(See App. C for a proof.) In an upper level argument, the verifier must check that $\hat{e}(A, \tilde{g}_2) = \hat{e}(\tilde{A}, g_2)$, and $\hat{e}(B, \tilde{g}_2) = \hat{e}(\tilde{B}, g_2)$. A simple valid choice of Λ is the initial segment of $\mathbb{Z}_\xi \cup (\mathbb{Z}_\xi + 2\xi) \cup (\mathbb{Z}_\xi + 4\xi) \cup \cdots$.

Theorem 6. *Let* Λ *and* υ *be as defined in Thm. 5. Let* $\beta \leftarrow ||\boldsymbol{b}||_\infty$, $\beta < p$. *Assume* $n > \log_2 \beta$. *The argument size of Prot. 3 is* 2 *elements from* $\mathbb{G}_2$. *The prover's computation is dominated by* $\Theta(n)$ $\mathbb{Z}_p$*-multiplications and* $(2 + o(1)) \cdot \log_2 \beta \cdot n / \log_2 n + O(n)$ *bilinear-group multiplications. The verifier's computation is dominated by* 5 *bilinear pairings. The CRS consists of* $\Theta(n)$ *group elements.*

Proof. The prover computes two multi-exponentiations in $L(2,n,\beta) = 2\log_2\beta + (1+o(1))\cdot\frac{2n\log_2(\beta+1)}{(\log_2(2n\log_2(\beta+1)))} + O(n) = (2+o(1))\cdot\frac{n\log_2\beta}{\log_2 n} + O(n)$ bilinear-group multiplications. Other claims are straightforward. □

6 Applications

We will now describe how to use the new product and shift arguments to improve on the range argument of [11], and to construct new SET-PARTITION and SUBSET-SUM arguments. Then, we combine the SUBSET-SUM and range arguments to construct a DECISION-KNAPSACK argument. In all three cases, the shift argument is mainly used to construct an intermediate scan argument. Recall that vector $\boldsymbol{b}$ is a *scan* [3] of vector a, if $b_i = \sum_{j>i} a_j$. As abundantly demonstrated in [3], vector scan (also known as all-prefix-sums) is a powerful operator that can be used to solve many important computational problems. In the context of zero knowledge, we will only need to be able to *verify* that one vector is a scan of the second vector.

In a *scan argument*, the prover aims to convince the verifier that given two commitments A and B, he knows how to open them as $A = \mathcal{C}om(\mathsf{ck}; \boldsymbol{a}; r_a)$ and $B = \mathcal{C}om(\mathsf{ck}; \boldsymbol{b}; r_b)$, s.t. $b_i = \sum_{j>i} a_j$. A scan argument is just equal to a right shift-by-1 argument $\mathsf{rsft}_1([\![B]\!]) = [\![A+B]\!]$, that proves that $b_i = a_{i+1} + b_{i+1}$, for $i < n$, and $b_n = 0$. Thus, $b_n = 0$, $b_{n-1} = a_n$, $b_{n-2} = a_{n-1} + b_{n-1} = a_{n-1} + a_n$, and in general, $b_i = \sum_{j>i} a_j$.

6.1 Improved Range Argument

Since the used commitment scheme is homomorphic, the generic range argument (prove that the committed value x belongs to the interval $[L, H]$ for $L < H$) is equivalent to proving that the committed value $y = x - L$ belongs to the interval $[0, H - L]$. In what follows, we will therefore concentrate on this simpler case.

In [11], the authors proposed a range argument that is based on the product and permutation arguments from [27]. Interestingly, [11] makes use of the permutation argument only to show that a vector is a scan of another vector. More precisely, they first apply a permutation argument, followed by a product argument (meant to modify a rotation to a right shift-by-1 by clearing out one of the elements). Hence, we can replace the permutation and product arguments from [27] with the right shift-by-1 (or scan) and product arguments from the current paper. Thus, it suffices for Λ to be an arbitrary progression-free set. The resulting range argument is also shorter by one product argument. The security proof does not change significantly. To show that the range argument is computationally sound, one has to assume that the product argument and the right shift-by-1 argument are weakly sound (and that the PKE assumption holds).

The use of the new basic arguments will decrease the number of $\mathbb{Z}_p$-multiplications — except when computing the multi-exponentiations — in the main range argument from $\Theta(n^2 n_v)$, where $n_v \approx \log_2 u$, to $\Theta(r_3^{-1}(n)\cdot\log r_3^{-1}(n)\cdot n_v) = o(\log H \cdot 2^{2\sqrt{2\log_2\log_u H}}\cdot\log\log_u H)$. By using Pippenger's algorithm [31], the cost of the multi-exponentiation decreases to $(2 + o(1)) \cdot 2r_3^{-1}(n) \log_2(un)/\log_2 r_3^{-1}(n)$ bilinear-group multiplications. The communication decreases by $4 + 2 + 3 = 9$ group elements, due to the replacement of the permutation argument with the right shift-by-1 argument (minus 4), having one less product argument (minus 2), and also because one needs to commit to one less element $((C_{\mathsf{rrot}}, \hat{C}_{\mathsf{rrot}}, \tilde{C}_{\mathsf{rrot}})$ in [11], minus 3). The verifier also has to perform $7+5+4 = 16$ less pairings, due to the replacement of the permutation argument with the right shift-by-1 argument (minus 7) and one less product argument (minus 5). Also, it is not necessary to verify the correctness of $(C_{\mathsf{rrot}}, \hat{C}_{\mathsf{rrot}}, \tilde{C}_{\mathsf{rrot}})$ (minus 4). One can analogously compute the verifier's computation, see Table 2.

Remark 1. In the permutation argument of [27], the verifier also has to compute a certain triple $(T^*, \hat{T}^*, T_2^*)$ by using 3 multi-exponentiations. This is not included in the comparison table (or the claims) in [27], and the same mistake was replicated in [11]. Table 1 and Table 2 correct this mistake, by giving the correct complexity estimation of the arguments from [27,11]. The range argument from [11] only uses the permutation argument with one fixed permutation (rotation), and thus the value $(T^*, \hat{T}^*, T_2^*)$, that corresponds to this concrete permutation, can be put to the CRS. After this modification, the verifier's computational complexity actually does not increase compared to what was claimed in [11]. Since [11] itself did not mention this, we consider it to be an additional small contribution.

Since the non-balanced range argument only uses one permutation argument, the corrected permutation argument of this paper makes the argument shorter by 4 group elements, and decreases the verifier's workload by 7 pairings.

One can consider now several settings. The setting $u = 2$ minimizes the communication and the verifier's computational complexity. The setting $u = 2^{\sqrt{\log_2 H}}$ minimizes the total length of the CRS and the argument. The setting $u = H$ minimizes the prover's computational complexity. See Table 2. Here, $n \approx \log_u H$, $n_v = \lfloor \log_2(u-1) \rfloor$, $h = \log_2 H$, $N = r_3^{-1}(h) = o(h 2^{2\sqrt{2 \log_2 h}})$, and $N^* = r_3^{-1}(\sqrt{h}) = o(\sqrt{h} \cdot 2^{2\sqrt{\log_2 h}})$. The rest of the notation is as in Table 1.

Theorem 7. *Let Γ be the (Λ, v) commitment scheme in group $\mathbb{G}_1$. Let $\Lambda = (\lambda_1, \dots, \lambda_n) \in \mathbb{Z}^n$ be progression-free, s.t. $\lambda_{i+1} > \lambda_i + 1$ and $\lambda_i = \mathrm{poly}(\kappa)$. Let*

$$\Phi := \Phi_\times \cup \Phi_{\mathsf{rsft}}^1 = \{X^v, X^{v+1}, X^{\lambda_1}\} \cup \{X^{\lambda_{i-1}+1} - X^{\lambda_i}\}_{i=2}^n \cup \{X^\ell\}_{\ell \in \hat{\Lambda}} \ . \quad (2)$$

Let $v > \max(2\lambda_n - \lambda_1, \lambda_n + 1)$ be linear in $\lambda_n - \lambda_1$. The modified range argument is complete and computationally zero knowledge. Also, if $\mathcal{G}_{\mathsf{bp}}$ is Φ-PSDL secure and the Φ-PKE assumption holds in $\mathbb{G}_1$ and the Φ-PKE assumption holds in $\mathbb{G}_2$, then the range argument is computationally sound.

The proof is similar to [11]. Note that $\lambda_{i+1} > \lambda_i + 1$ guarantees that both $\lambda_{i+1} > \lambda_i$ and $\lambda_j \neq \lambda_i + 1$ for $i \neq j$.

Table 2. Comparison of NIZK range arguments

	$\|CRS\|$	$\|Argument\|$	Prover comp.	Verifier comp.
[32]	$\Theta(1)\mathfrak{g}$	$\Theta(h)\mathfrak{g}$	$\Theta(h)$	$\Theta(h)$
[32]	$\Theta(h/\log h)\mathfrak{g}$	$\Theta(h/\log h)\mathfrak{g}$	$\Theta(h/\log h)$	$\Theta(h/\log h)$
Chaabouni, Lipmaa, and Zhang [11]				
General	$\Theta(r_3^{-1}(n))\mathfrak{g}$	$(5n_v + 40)\mathfrak{g}$	$\Theta(n^2 n_v)\mathfrak{m} + \Theta(r_3^{-1}(n) n_v)\mathfrak{e}$	$\Theta(n)\mathfrak{e} + (9n_v + 81)\mathfrak{p}$
$u = 2$	$\Theta(N)\mathfrak{g}$	$40\mathfrak{g}$	$\Theta(h^2)\mathfrak{m} + \Theta(N)\mathfrak{e}$	$\Theta(h)\mathfrak{e} + 81\mathfrak{p}$
$u = 2^{\sqrt{h}}$	$\Theta(N^*)\mathfrak{g}$	$\approx (5\sqrt{h} + 40)\mathfrak{g}$	$\Theta(h^{3/2})\mathfrak{m} + \Theta(\sqrt{h} \cdot N^*)\mathfrak{e}$	$\Theta(\sqrt{h})\mathfrak{e} + (9\sqrt{h} + 81)\mathfrak{p}$
$u = H$	$\Theta(1)\mathfrak{g}$	$\approx (5h + 40)\mathfrak{g}$	$\Theta(h)\mathfrak{m} + \Theta(h)\mathfrak{e}$	$\Theta(1)\mathfrak{e} + (9h + 81)\mathfrak{p}$
The current paper				
General	$\Theta(r_3^{-1}(n))\mathfrak{g}$	$(5n_v + 31)\mathfrak{g}$	$\Theta(r_3^{-1}(n) \log r_3^{-1}(n) \cdot n_v)\mathfrak{m} + \Theta(r_3^{-1}(n) n_v)\mathfrak{m}_b$	$(9n_v + 65)\mathfrak{p}$
$u = 2$	$\Theta(N)\mathfrak{g}$	$31\mathfrak{g}$	$\Theta(N \cdot \log N)\mathfrak{m} + \Theta(N)\mathfrak{m}_b$	$65\mathfrak{p}$
$u = 2^{\sqrt{h}}$	$\Theta(N^*)\mathfrak{g}$	$\approx (5\sqrt{h} + 31)\mathfrak{g}$	$\Theta(\sqrt{h} \cdot N^* \cdot \log N^*)\mathfrak{m} + \Theta(\sqrt{h} \cdot N^*)\mathfrak{m}_b$	$\approx (9\sqrt{h} + 65)\mathfrak{p}$
$u = H$	$\Theta(1)\mathfrak{g}$	$(\approx 5h + 31)\mathfrak{g}$	$\Theta(h)\mathfrak{m} + \Theta(h)\mathfrak{m}_b$	$\approx (9h + 65)\mathfrak{p}$

6.2 Arguments for NP-Complete Languages

Finally, we construct efficient modular arguments, that only use product and shift arguments, for some **NP**-complete languages. CIRCUIT-SAT seems to require the use of permutation arguments [21,27], so we will find other problems.

Set-Partition. Let $n \ll p$. Given a multiset $\mathcal{S} = (s_1, \ldots, s_n)$, with $s_i \in \mathbb{Z}_p$, and a commitment B, in the SET-PARTITION *argument*, the prover has to convince the verifier that he knows how to open the commitment as $B = \mathcal{C}om(\mathsf{ck}; \boldsymbol{b}; r_b)$, such that $b_i \in \{-1, 1\}$, and $\sum_{i=1}^{n} b_i s_i = 0$. If we define $\mathcal{V} = \{i : b_i = 1\}$, then $\sum_{i=1}^{n} b_i s_i = 0$ is equivalent to $\sum_{i \in \mathcal{V}} s_i = \sum_{i \in \mathcal{S} \setminus \mathcal{V}} s_i$. The prover computes the SET-PARTITION argument as follows.

Compute a product argument π_1 for $b_i \cdot b_i = 1$, showing that $b_i \in \{-1, 1\}$;
Compute a product argument π_2 for $c_i = b_i \cdot s_i$;
Compute a scan argument π_3 showing that $\boldsymbol{d}$ is the scan of $\boldsymbol{c}$;
Compute a restriction argument π_4 showing the first coordinate of $\boldsymbol{c} + \boldsymbol{d}$ is 0;
The SET-PARTITION argument is equal to $(B, C, D, \pi_1, \ldots, \pi_4)$;

Here, C commits to $\boldsymbol{c} = (b_1 s_1, \ldots, b_n s_n)$, S commits to $\boldsymbol{s}$, and D commits to $\boldsymbol{d}$, the scan of $\boldsymbol{c}$. That is, $d_i = \sum_{j>i} c_j$, and in particular, $d_1 = \sum_{j>1} c_i$ and $c_1 + d_1 = \sum_{j \geq 1} c_j$. We omit the security proof of this argument since it is similar to the proof of the SUBSET-SUM argument.

Subset-Sum. Another example is SUBSET-SUM, where the prover aims to prove that he knows a non-zero subset of the input set S that sums to 0. In a SUBSET-SUM *argument*, the prover aims to convince the verifier that given $\mathcal{S} = (s_1, \ldots, s_n) \subseteq \mathbb{Z}_p$, $n \ll p$, and a commitment B, he knows how to open it as $B = \mathcal{C}om(\mathsf{ck}; \boldsymbol{b}; r_b)$, s.t. $\boldsymbol{b}$ is non-zero and Boolean, and $\sum_{i=1}^{n} b_i s_i = 0$. That is, $b_i = 1$ iff s_i belongs to the subset of S that sums to 0. (As always, the committed elements belong to $\mathbb{Z}_p$. Thus, $\sum_{i=1}^{n} b_i s_i = 0$ holds modulo p.)

In the new SUBSET-SUM argument, both parties compute a commitment S to $\boldsymbol{s}$. The prover commits to a Boolean vector $\boldsymbol{b}$ and to a vector $\boldsymbol{c}$, s.t. $c_i = b_i s_i$.

He computes a commitment D to the *scan* $\boldsymbol{d}$ of vector $\boldsymbol{c}$. I.e., $d_i = \sum_{j>i} c_j$, and in particular, $d_1 = \sum_{j>1} c_i$ and $c_1 + d_1 = \sum_{j\geq 1} c_j$. The resulting SUBSET-SUM argument can be seen as a slight modification of the SET-PARTITION argument. The main conceptual difference is that we also need to prove $\boldsymbol{b} \neq \boldsymbol{0}$ (not necessary in the SET-PARTITION argument).

> Compute a product argument π_1 for $b_i^2 = b_i$, showing that $\boldsymbol{b}$ is Boolean;
> Compute an argument π_2 showing that $\boldsymbol{b} \neq \boldsymbol{0}$;
> Compute a product argument π_3 showing that $c_i = b_i \cdot s_i$ for $i \in [n]$;
> Compute a scan argument π_4 showing that $\boldsymbol{d}$ is the scan of $\boldsymbol{c}$;
> Compute a restriction argument π_5 showing the first coordinate of $\boldsymbol{c} + \boldsymbol{d}$ is 0;
> The SUBSET-SUM argument is equal to $(B, C, D, \pi_1, \dots, \pi_5)$;

Here, π_5 is computed by using the restriction argument from [21], which adds linear number of elements to the CRS, but has a constant complexity otherwise. The subargument π_2 is computed as in Alg. 3.

Note that the verifier can check that $\mathring{B}$ is correct by checking that $\hat{e}(\mathring{B}, g_2) = \hat{e}(B, \mathring{g}_2)$. It is straightforward to prove that the new SUBSET-SUM argument is complete and perfectly zero-knowledge. It is also computationally sound under appropriate assumptions. See App. E for a proof.

The resulting SUBSET-SUM argument is simpler than the CIRCUIT-SAT arguments of [21,27] that consist of ≥ 7 product and permutation arguments. Moreover, instead of the product and permutation arguments it only uses product and a more efficient right shift-by-1 argument (zero argument is trivial).

> Assume $B = g_{1,\varrho}^{r_b} \prod g_{1,\lambda_i}^{b_i}$; `/* we want to show that` $\boldsymbol{b} \neq \boldsymbol{0}$ `*/`
> Assume that $\mathring{g}_{1,i} = g_{1i}^{\mathring{\alpha}}$ and $\mathring{g}_2 = g_2^{\mathring{\alpha}}$ for a secret $\mathring{\alpha}$;
> Create $\mathring{B} \leftarrow \mathring{g}_{1,\varrho}^{r_b} \cdot \prod_{i=1}^{n} \mathring{g}_{1,\lambda_i}^{b_i}$ and a hybrid $B^* \leftarrow g_{1,\varrho}^{r_b} \cdot \prod \mathring{g}_{1,\lambda_i}^{b_i}$;
> Show $\mathring{B}/B^* = (\mathring{g}_{1,\varrho}/g_{1,\varrho})^{r_b}$ commits to $\boldsymbol{0}$ by using the zero argument [30];
> Verifier checks that $\hat{e}(B, \mathring{g}_2) \neq \hat{e}(B^*, g_2)$;

Algorithm 3. Argument π_2

Decision-Knapsack. In the **NP**-complete DECISION-KNAPSACK *problem* one has to decide, given a set $\mathcal{S}$, integers W and B, and a benefit value b_i and weight w_i of every item of $\mathcal{S}$, whether there exists a subset $\mathcal{T} \subseteq \mathcal{S}$, such that $\sum_{i\in\mathcal{T}} w_i \leq W$ and $\sum_{i\in\mathcal{T}} b_i \geq B$. One can combine a version of the SUBSET-SUM argument of the current section with the range argument of Sect. 6.1 to construct a DECISION-KNAPSACK argument, where the prover convinces the verifier that he knows such a subset $\mathcal{T}$. See Alg. 6 in App. F.

Acknowledgments. The first two authors were supported from research theme IUT2-1 and European Regional Development Fund through the Estonian Center of Excellence in Computer Science, EXCS. The third author is supported by Project FINER, Greek Secretariat of Research and Technology. The work was partially done while the third author was working in University of Tartu.

References

1. Ben-Sasson, E., Chiesa, A., Genkin, D., Tromer, E., Virza, M.: SNARKs for C: Verifying Program Executions Succinctly and in Zero Knowledge. In: Canetti, R., Garay, J.A. (eds.) CRYPTO 2013, Part II. LNCS, vol. 8043, pp. 90–108. Springer, Heidelberg (2013)
2. Bitansky, N., Chiesa, A., Ishai, Y., Paneth, O., Ostrovsky, R.: Succinct Non-interactive Arguments via Linear Interactive Proofs. In: Sahai, A. (ed.) TCC 2013. LNCS, vol. 7785, pp. 315–333. Springer, Heidelberg (2013)
3. Blelloch, G.: Vector Models for Data-Parallel Computing. MIT Press (1990)
4. Blum, M., Feldman, P., Micali, S.: Non-Interactive Zero-Knowledge and Its Applications. In: STOC 1988, May 2-4, pp. 103–112. ACM Press, Chicago (1988)
5. Boneh, D., Franklin, M.: Identity-Based Encryption from the Weil Pairing. In: Kilian, J. (ed.) CRYPTO 2001. LNCS, vol. 2139, pp. 213–229. Springer, Heidelberg (2001)
6. Boudot, F.: Efficient Proofs That a Committed Number Lies in an Interval. In: Preneel, B. (ed.) EUROCRYPT 2000. LNCS, vol. 1807, pp. 431–444. Springer, Heidelberg (2000)
7. Brassard, G., Chaum, D., Crépeau, C.: Minimum Disclosure Proofs of Knowledge. Journal of Computer and System Sciences 37(2), 156–189 (1988)
8. Camenisch, J.L., Chaabouni, R., Shelat, A.: Efficient Protocols for Set Membership and Range Proofs. In: Pieprzyk, J. (ed.) ASIACRYPT 2008. LNCS, vol. 5350, pp. 234–252. Springer, Heidelberg (2008)
9. Canetti, R., Goldreich, O., Halevi, S.: The Random Oracle Methodology, Revisited. In: Vitter, J.S. (ed.) STOC 1998, Dallas, Texas, USA, May 23-26, pp. 209–218 (1998)
10. Chaabouni, R., Lipmaa, H., Shelat, A.: Additive Combinatorics and Discrete Logarithm Based Range Protocols. In: Steinfeld, R., Hawkes, P. (eds.) ACISP 2010. LNCS, vol. 6168, pp. 336–351. Springer, Heidelberg (2010)
11. Chaabouni, R., Lipmaa, H., Zhang, B.: A Non-interactive Range Proof with Constant Communication. In: Keromytis, A.D. (ed.) FC 2012. LNCS, vol. 7397, pp. 179–199. Springer, Heidelberg (2012)
12. Cooley, J.W., Tukey, J.W.: An Algorithm for the Machine Calculation of Complex Fourier Series. Mathematics of Computation 19, 297–301 (1965)
13. Dybizbański, J.: Sequences Containing No 3-Term Arithmetic Progressions. Electron. J. of Combin. 19(2), P15 (2012)
14. Elkin, M.: An Improved Construction of Progression-Free Sets. Israel J. of Math. 184, 93–128 (2011)
15. Erdős, P., Turán, P.: On Some Sequences of Integers. J. London Math. Soc. 11(4), 261–263 (1936)
16. Gennaro, R., Gentry, C., Parno, B., Raykova, M.: Quadratic Span Programs and NIZKs without PCPs. In: Johansson, T., Nguyen, P.Q. (eds.) EUROCRYPT 2013. LNCS, vol. 7881, pp. 626–645. Springer, Heidelberg (2013)
17. Gentleman, W.M., Sande, G.: Fast Fourier Transforms — For Fun and Profit. In: Fall Joint Computer Conf. AFIPS Proc., vol. 29, pp. 563–578. ACM, Washington, DC (1966)

18. Gentry, C., Wichs, D.: Separating Succinct Non-Interactive Arguments from All Falsifiable Assumptions. In: Vadhan, S. (ed.) STOC 2011, June 6-8, pp. 99–108. ACM Press, San Jose (2011)
19. Goldwasser, S., Kalai, Y.T.: On the (In)security of the Fiat-Shamir Paradigm. In: FOCS 2003, October 11–14, pp. 102–113. IEEE (2003)
20. Goldwasser, S., Micali, S., Rackoff, C.: The Knowledge Complexity of Interactive Proof-Systems. In: Sedgewick, R. (ed.) STOC 1985, May 6-8, pp. 291–304. ACM Press, Providence (1985)
21. Groth, J.: Short Pairing-Based Non-interactive Zero-Knowledge Arguments. In: Abe, M. (ed.) ASIACRYPT 2010. LNCS, vol. 6477, pp. 321–340. Springer, Heidelberg (2010)
22. Hess, F., Smart, N.P., Vercauteren, F.: The Eta Pairing Revisited. IEEE Transactions on Information Theory 52(10), 4595–4602 (2006)
23. van Hoeij, M., Novocin, A.: Gradual Sub-lattice Reduction and a New Complexity for Factoring Polynomials. In: López-Ortiz, A. (ed.) LATIN 2010. LNCS, vol. 6034, pp. 539–553. Springer, Heidelberg (2010)
24. Joux, A.: A One-Round Protocol for Tripartite Diffie-Hellman. In: Bosma, W. (ed.) ANTS 2000. LNCS, vol. 1838, pp. 385–393. Springer, Heidelberg (2000)
25. Lenstra, A.K., Lenstra Jr., H.W., Lovász, L.: Factoring Polynomials with Rational Coefficients. Mathematische Annalen 261, 513–534 (1982)
26. Lipmaa, H.: On Diophantine Complexity and Statistical Zero-Knowledge Arguments. In: Laih, C.-S. (ed.) ASIACRYPT 2003. LNCS, vol. 2894, pp. 398–415. Springer, Heidelberg (2003)
27. Lipmaa, H.: Progression-Free Sets and Sublinear Pairing-Based Non-Interactive Zero-Knowledge Arguments. In: Cramer, R. (ed.) TCC 2012. LNCS, vol. 7194, pp. 169–189. Springer, Heidelberg (2012)
28. Lipmaa, H.: Succinct Non-Interactive Zero Knowledge Arguments from Span Programs and Linear Error-Correcting Codes. In: Sako, K., Sarkar, P. (eds.) ASIACRYPT 2013 Part I. LNCS, vol. 8269, pp. 41–60. Springer, Heidelberg (2013)
29. Lipmaa, H., Asokan, N., Niemi, V.: Secure Vickrey Auctions without Threshold Trust. In: Blaze, M. (ed.) FC 2002. LNCS, vol. 2357, pp. 87–101. Springer, Heidelberg (2003)
30. Lipmaa, H., Zhang, B.: A More Efficient Computationally Sound Non-Interactive Zero-Knowledge Shuffle Argument. In: Visconti, I., De Prisco, R. (eds.) SCN 2012. LNCS, vol. 7485, pp. 477–502. Springer, Heidelberg (2012)
31. Pippenger, N.: On the Evaluation of Powers and Monomials. SIAM J. Comput. 9(2), 230–250 (1980)
32. Rial, A., Kohlweiss, M., Preneel, B.: Universally Composable Adaptive Priced Oblivious Transfer. In: Shacham, H., Waters, B. (eds.) Pairing 2009. LNCS, vol. 5671, pp. 231–247. Springer, Heidelberg (2009)
33. Sakai, R., Ohgishi, K., Kasahara, M.: Cryptosystems Based on Pairing. In: SCIS 2000, Okinawa, Japan (2000)
34. Sanders, T.: On Roth's Theorem on Progressions. Ann. of Math. 174(1), 619–636 (2011)
35. Tao, T., Vu, V.: Additive Combinatorics. Cambridge Studies in Advanced Mathematics. Cambridge University Press (2006)

A Proof of Thm. 1

Proof. In the generic group model, an adversary $\mathcal{A}$ only performs generic group operations (multiplications in $\mathbb{G}_1$, $\mathbb{G}_2$ and $\mathbb{G}_T$, bilinear pairings, and equality tests). A generic adversary produces an element of $\mathbb{Z}_p$, which depends only on gk and $((g_1, g_2)^{\phi(\sigma)})_{\phi \in \{1\} \cup \Phi}$. The only time $\mathcal{A}$ gets any information is when an equality (collision) between two previously computed elements of either $\mathbb{G}_1$, $\mathbb{G}_2$ or $\mathbb{G}_T$ occurs. We prove that finding even a single collision is difficult even if $\mathcal{A}$ can compute an arbitrary group element in unit time.

Assume that $\mathcal{A}$ can find a collision $y = y^*$ in group $\mathbb{G}_1$. Then it must be the case that

$$y = \prod_{\phi_\ell \in \{1\} \cup \Phi} g_1^{a_\ell \phi_\ell(\sigma)}$$

and

$$y^* = \prod_{\ell \in \{0\} \cup \Lambda} g_1^{a_\ell^* \phi_\ell(\sigma)}$$

for some known values of a_ℓ and a_ℓ^*. But then also

$$\sum_{\ell \in \{0\} \cup \Lambda} (a_\ell - a_\ell^*) \phi_\ell(\sigma) \equiv 0 \pmod{p} \ .$$

Since $\mathcal{A}$ does not know the actual representations of the group elements, it will perform the same group operations independently of σ. Thus a_ℓ and a_ℓ^* are independent of σ. By the Schwartz-Zippel lemma modulo p, the probability that

$$\sum_{\ell \in \{0\} \cup \Lambda} (a_\ell - a_\ell^*) \phi_\ell(\sigma) \equiv 0 \pmod{p}$$

is equal to d/p for randomly chosen a_ℓ and a_ℓ^*. If $\mathcal{A}$ works in polynomial time $\tau = \mathrm{poly}(\kappa)$, it can generate at most τ such group elements. The total probability that there exists a collision between any two generated group elements is thus upper bounded by $\binom{\tau}{2} \cdot d/p$, and thus a successful $\mathcal{A}$ requires time $\Omega(\sqrt{p/d})$ to produce one collision.

A similar bound $\binom{\tau}{2} \cdot d/p$ holds for collisions in $\mathbb{G}_2$. In the case of $\mathbb{G}_T$, the pairing enables $\mathcal{A}$ to compute up to τ different values

$$y = \hat{e}(g_1, g_2)^{\sum_{\phi_{1i} \in \{1\} \cup \Phi} \sum_{\phi_{2j} \in \{1\} \cup \Phi} a_{ij} \phi_{1i}(\sigma_1) \phi_{2j}(\sigma)} \ ,$$

and thus we get an upper bound $\binom{\tau}{2} \cdot 2d/p$, and thus a successful $\mathcal{A}$ requires time $\Omega(\sqrt{p/d})$ to produce one collision. □

B Proof of Thm. 3 (Product Argument Security)

Proof. Let $h \leftarrow \hat{e}(g_1, g_2)$ and $F(\sigma) \leftarrow \log_h(\hat{e}(A, B_2)/\hat{e}(C, D))$. Witness-Indistinguishability: since the argument $\pi^\times = (\pi, \hat{\pi})$ that satisfies the verification equations is unique, all witnesses result in the same argument, and therefore the Hadamard product argument is witness-indistinguishable.

Perfect completeness. Assume that the prover is honest. The second verification is straightforward. For the first one, note that (after replacing σ with a formal variable X)

$$\begin{aligned}F(X) =&(r_a X^{\upsilon} + \sum_{i=1}^{n} a_i X^{\lambda_i})(r_b X^{\upsilon} + \sum_{i=1}^{n} b_i X^{\lambda_i}) - (r_c X^{\upsilon} + \sum_{i=1}^{n} c_i X^{\lambda_i})(\sum_{i=1}^{n} X^{\lambda_i}) \\ =&r_a r_b X^{2\upsilon} + \sum_{i=1}^{n}(r_a b_i + r_b a_i - r_c) X^{\upsilon+\lambda_i} + \sum_{i=1}^{n}\sum_{j=1}^{n}(a_i b_j - c_i) X^{\lambda_i+\lambda_j} \enspace .\end{aligned}$$

Thus, $F(X) = F_{con}(X) + F_{\pi}(X)$, where

$$F_{con}(X) = \sum_{i=1}^{n}(a_i b_i - c_i) X^{2\lambda_i}$$

and

$$F_{\pi}(X) = r_a r_b X^{2\upsilon} + \sum_{i=1}^{n}(r_a b_i + r_b a_i - r_c) X^{\upsilon+\lambda_i} + \sum_{i=1}^{n}\sum_{j=1:j\neq i}^{n}(a_i b_j - c_i) X^{\lambda_i+\lambda_j} \enspace .$$

Here, $F(X)$, $F_{con}(X)$ and $F_{\pi}(X)$ are formal polynomials of X, and $F(X)$ is spanned by $\{X^{\ell}\}_{\ell \in 2 \cdot \Lambda \cup \hat{\Lambda}}$. More precisely, $F_{con}(X)$ is the constraint polynomial that has one monomial per constraint $c_i = a_i b_i$.

If the prover is honest, then $c_i = a_i b_i$ for $i \in [n]$, and $F(X) = F_{\pi}(X)$ is spanned by $\{X^{\ell}\}_{\ell \in \hat{\Lambda}}$. Denoting

$$\begin{aligned}\pi \leftarrow& g_{2,\upsilon}^{r_a r_b} \cdot \prod_{i=1}^{n} g_{2,\upsilon+\lambda_i}^{r_a b_i + r_b a_i - r_c} \cdot \prod_{i=1}^{n}\prod_{j=1:j\neq i}^{n} g_{2,\lambda_i+\lambda_j}^{a_i b_j - c_i} \\ =& g_{2,\upsilon}^{r_a r_b} \cdot \prod_{i=1}^{n} g_{2,\upsilon+\lambda_i}^{r_a b_i + r_b a_i - r_c} \cdot \prod_{\ell \in 2^{\frown}\Lambda} g_{2,\ell}^{\mu_\ell} \enspace ,\end{aligned}$$

where μ_ℓ is as in Prot. 2, we have $\hat{e}(g_1, \pi) = \hat{e}(g_1, g_2^{F(\sigma)}) = h^{F(\sigma)} = \hat{e}(A, B_2)/\hat{e}(C, D)$. Thus, the verification succeeds.

Weaker version of soundness. Assume that $\mathcal{A}_{\times}$ is an adversary that can break the last statement of the theorem. We construct the following adversary $\hat{\mathcal{A}}$ against the $\Phi_{\times}$-PSDL assumption, see Prot. 4.

Here, $\mathcal{C}$ is the challenger of the PSDL game. Let us analyse the advantage of $\hat{\mathcal{A}}$. First, clearly crs_{td} has the same distribution as $\mathcal{G}_{\mathsf{crs}}(1^{\kappa})$. Thus, $\mathcal{A}_{\times}$ gets a correct input. She aborts with some probability $1-\varepsilon$. Otherwise, with probability ε, $inp^{\times} = (A, \hat{A}, B, \hat{B}, B_2, C, \hat{C})$ and $w^{\times} = (\boldsymbol{a}, r_a, \boldsymbol{b}, r_b, \boldsymbol{c}, r_c, (f_{\ell}^{*})_{\ell \in \hat{\Lambda}})$, such that the conditions (2a–2d) hold.

The steps from step 1 onwards are executed with probability ε. Since $\mathcal{A}_{\times}$ succeeds and $2 \cdot \Lambda \cap \hat{\Lambda} = \emptyset$, at least for one $\ell \in 2 \cdot \Lambda$, $f(X)$ has a non-zero coefficient $a_\ell b_\ell - c_\ell$. $\hat{\mathcal{A}}$ succeeds on step 2, since $\log_{g_2} \pi = \sum_{\ell \in \hat{\Lambda}} f_{\ell}^{*} \sigma^{\ell}$. All non-zero coefficients of X^{ℓ} in $f^{*}(X)$ correspond to $\ell \in \hat{\Lambda}$. Since Λ is progression-free,

$\mathcal{C}$ forms crs as in Prot. 2; $\mathcal{C}$ sends crs to $\hat{\mathcal{A}}$; $\hat{\mathcal{A}}$ obtains $(inp^{\times}, w^{\times}, \pi^{\times}) \leftarrow \mathcal{A}_{\times}(\mathsf{crs})$;
if *the conditions (2a–2d) in Thm. 3 do not hold* **then** $\hat{\mathcal{A}}$ aborts **else**
1 $\hat{\mathcal{A}}$ expresses $F(X)$ as a polynomial $f(X) \leftarrow \sum_{\ell \in \hat{\Lambda} \cup 2 \cdot \Lambda} f_\ell X^\ell$;
2 $\hat{\mathcal{A}}$ computes a polynomial $f^*(X) \leftarrow \sum_{\ell \in \hat{\Lambda}} f^*_\ell X^\ell$;
$\hat{\mathcal{A}}$ lets $\delta(X) \leftarrow (f(X) - f^*(X)) \cdot X^{-2\lambda_1}$;
$\hat{\mathcal{A}}$ sets $(t_1, \dots, t_{2(\upsilon - \lambda_1)}) \leftarrow \mathsf{PolyFact}(\delta)$;
3 $\hat{\mathcal{A}}$ finds by an exhaustive search a root $\sigma_0 \in (t_1, \dots, t_{2(\upsilon-\lambda_1)})$, s.t. $g_2^{\sigma^\upsilon} = g_2^{\sigma_0^\upsilon}$;
$\hat{\mathcal{A}}$ returns $\sigma \leftarrow \sigma_0$ to the challenger;
end

Algorithm 4. Construction of $\hat{\mathcal{A}}$ in the security reduction of Thm. 3

$\upsilon > 2\lambda_n - \lambda_1$, and all elements of $2 \cdot \Lambda$ are distinct, then by Lem. 1, $\ell \notin 2 \cdot \Lambda$. Thus, all coefficients of $f^*(X)$ corresponding to any X^ℓ, $\ell \in 2 \cdot \Lambda$, are 0. Thus,

$$f(X) = \sum_{\ell \in \hat{\Lambda} \cup (2 \cdot \Lambda)} f_\ell X^\ell$$

and

$$f^*(X) = \sum_{\ell \in \hat{\Lambda}} f^*_\ell X^\ell$$

are different polynomials with $f(\sigma) = f^*(\sigma) = F(\sigma)$. All coefficients of X^ℓ, for $\ell < 2\lambda_1$, of both $f(X)$ and $f^*(X)$ are equal to 0.

Therefore, $\delta(X)$ is a non-zero degree-$(2\upsilon - 2\lambda_1)$ polynomial, such that

$$\delta(\sigma) = \sum_{\ell \in (\hat{\Lambda} \cup (2 \cdot \Lambda)) - 2\lambda_1} \delta_\ell \sigma^\ell = 0 \ .$$

$\hat{\mathcal{A}}$ uses polynomial factorization to find all $\leq 2(\upsilon - \lambda_1)$ roots of δ. One of the roots must be equal to σ. On step 3, $\hat{\mathcal{A}}$ finds which root is equal to σ by an exhaustive search among all roots returned in the previous step. Clearly $\hat{\mathcal{A}}$ returns the correct value of σ (and thus violates the $\Phi_\times$-PSDL assumption) with probability ε. The execution time of $\hat{\mathcal{A}}$ is clearly dominated by the execution time of $\mathcal{A}_\times$ and the time to factor δ. □

C Proof of Thm. 5 (Shift Argument Security)

Proof. Denote $h \leftarrow \hat{e}(g_1, g_2)$ and

$$F(\sigma) := \log_h(\hat{e}(A, g_{2,\xi}) / \hat{e}(B, g_2)) \ .$$

WITNESS-INDISTINGUISHABILITY: since argument π^{rsft} that satisfies the verification equations is unique, all witnesses result in the same argument, and therefore the permutation argument is witness-indistinguishable.

$\mathcal{C}$ forms crs as in Prot. 3;
$\mathcal{C}$ sends crs to $\tilde{\mathcal{A}}$;
$\tilde{\mathcal{A}}$ obtains $(inp^{\mathsf{rsft}}, w^{\mathsf{rsft}}, \pi^{\mathsf{rsft}}) \leftarrow \mathcal{A}_{\mathsf{rsft}}(\mathsf{crs})$;
if *the conditions (2a–2d) in the statement of Thm. 5 do not hold* **then** $\tilde{\mathcal{A}}$ aborts **else**
1 $\tilde{\mathcal{A}}$ expresses $F(X)$ as a polynomial $f(X) = \sum_{\phi \in \Phi^{\pi}} f_\phi \cdot \phi(X)$;
2 $\tilde{\mathcal{A}}$ computes a polynomial $f^*(X) := \sum_{\phi \in \Phi^{\xi}_{\mathsf{rsft}}} f^*_\phi \cdot \phi(X)$;
$\tilde{\mathcal{A}}$ lets $\delta(X) \leftarrow f(X) - f^*(X)$;
$\tilde{\mathcal{A}}$ uses a polynomial factorization algorithm in $\mathbb{Z}_p[X]$ to compute all $\leq (\upsilon + 2)$ roots of $\delta(X)$;
3 $\tilde{\mathcal{A}}$ finds by an exhaustive search a root σ_0, such that $g_1^{\sigma^\ell} = g_1^{\sigma_0^\ell}$;
$\tilde{\mathcal{A}}$ returns $\sigma \leftarrow \sigma_0$;
end

Algorithm 5. Construction of $\tilde{\mathcal{A}}$ in the security reduction of Thm. 5

PERFECT COMPLETENESS. The second verification is straightforward. For the first verification $\hat{e}(A, g_{2,\xi}) / \hat{e}(B, g_2) = \hat{e}(g_1, \pi)$, consider

$$F(X) := X^\xi \cdot \log_{g_1} A - \log_{g_1} B \enspace ,$$

where we have replaced σ with a formal variable X. Clearly,

$$\begin{aligned}
F(X) =& \sum_{i=1}^{n} a_i X^{\lambda_i + \xi} - \sum_{i=1}^{n} b_i X^{\lambda_i} + r_a X^{\upsilon+\xi} - r_b X^{\upsilon} \\
=& \sum_{i=n-\xi+1}^{n} a_i X^{\lambda_i+\xi} + \sum_{i=1}^{n-\xi} a_i X^{\lambda_i+\xi} - \sum_{i=1}^{\xi} b_i X^{\lambda_i} - \sum_{i=\xi+1}^{n} b_i X^{\lambda_i} + \\
& r_a X^{\upsilon+\xi} - r_b X^{\upsilon} \\
=& \sum_{i=1}^{\xi} a_{n-\xi+i} X^{\lambda_{n-\xi+i}+\xi} + \sum_{i=1}^{n-\xi} a_i X^{\lambda_i+\xi} - \sum_{i=1}^{\xi} b_i X^{\lambda_i} - \sum_{i=1}^{n-\xi} b_{i+\xi} X^{\lambda_{i+\xi}} + \\
& r_a X^{\upsilon+\xi} - r_b X^{\upsilon} \\
=& \underbrace{\sum_{i=1}^{n-\xi} (a_i - b_{i+\xi}) X^{\lambda_i+\xi} + \sum_{i=1}^{\xi} a_{n-\xi+i} X^{\lambda_{n-\xi+i}+\xi}}_{=:F_{con}(X)} + \\
& \underbrace{\sum_{i=1}^{n-\xi} b_{i+\xi} (X^{\lambda_i+\xi} - X^{\lambda_{i+\xi}}) - \sum_{i=1}^{\xi} b_i X^{\lambda_i} + r_a X^{\upsilon+\xi} - r_b X^{\upsilon}}_{=:F_\pi(X)} \enspace .
\end{aligned} \tag{3}$$

If the prover is honest, then $a_i = b_{i+\xi}$ for $i \in [n-\xi]$ and $a_i = 0$ for $i \in [n-\xi+1, n]$, and thus $F(X) = F_\pi(X)$ is spanned by $\{\phi(X)\}_{\phi \in \Phi^\xi_{\mathsf{rsft}}}$. With π as defined in Prot. 3, the second verification holds as

$$\hat{e}(g_1, \pi) = \hat{e}(g_1, \pi^{F(\sigma)}) = h^{F(\sigma)} = \hat{e}(A, g_{2,1})/\hat{e}(B, g_2) \ .$$

WEAKER VERSION OF SOUNDNESS. Assume that $\mathcal{A}_{\mathsf{rsft}}$ is an adversary that can break the last statement of the theorem. We construct an adversary $\tilde{\mathcal{A}}$ against the Φ^ξ_{rsft}-PSDL assumption, see Prot. 5. Here, $\mathcal{C}$ is the challenger of the PSDL game, and

$$\Phi^\pi := \{X^{\lambda_i+\xi}, X^{\lambda_i}\}_{i=1}^n \cup \{X^{v+\xi}, X^v\}$$

is defined by following the first line of Eq. (3). Let us analyse the advantage of $\tilde{\mathcal{A}}$. First, clearly crs_{td} has the same distribution as $\mathcal{G}_{\mathsf{crs}}(1^\kappa)$. Thus, $\mathcal{A}_{\mathsf{rsft}}$ gets a correct input, and succeeds with some probability $\mathsf{Succ}^{\mathsf{sound}}_{\mathcal{A}_{\mathsf{rsft}}}(\Pi_{\mathsf{rsft}})$. Clearly, $\tilde{\mathcal{A}}$ aborts with probability $1 - \mathsf{Succ}^{\mathsf{sound}}_{\mathcal{A}_{\mathsf{rsft}}}(\Pi_{\mathsf{rsft}})$.

Otherwise, with probability $\mathsf{Succ}^{\mathsf{sound}}_{\mathcal{A}_{\mathsf{rsft}}}(\Pi_{\mathsf{rsft}})$, $inp^{\mathsf{rsft}} = (A, \tilde{A}, B, \tilde{B})$ and $w^{\mathsf{rsft}} = (\boldsymbol{a}, r_a, \boldsymbol{b}, r_b, (f^*_\phi)_{\phi \in \Phi^\xi_{\mathsf{rsft}}})$, such that the conditions (2a–2d) hold. In particular, $f(X) = F(X)$ in Eq. (3), and

$$\begin{aligned} f^*(X) = &\sum_{i=1}^{\xi} f^*_{X^{\lambda_i}} \cdot X^{\lambda_i} + \sum_{i=\xi+1}^{n} f_{X^{\lambda_{i-\xi}+\xi} - X^{\lambda_i}} (X^{\lambda_{i-\xi}+\xi} - X^{\lambda_i}) + \\ &f^*_{X^{v+\xi}} X^{v+\xi} + f^*_{X^v} X^v \ . \end{aligned}$$

For the rest of the proof to go through, we need that all polynomials that are present in monomials $F_{con}(X)$ ($\Phi^* := \{X^{\lambda_i+\xi} : i \in [n-\xi]\} \cup \{X^{\lambda_{n-\xi+i}+\xi} : i \in [\xi]\} = \{X^{\lambda_i+\xi} : i \in [1, n-\xi]\} \cup \{X^{\lambda_i+\xi} : i \in [n-\xi+1, n]\} = \{X^{\lambda_i+\xi} : i \in [n]\}$) are different from each other and from all polynomials in Φ^ξ_{rsft}. This follows from the conditions (i) $\lambda_j \neq \lambda_i$, (ii) $\lambda_j + \xi \neq \lambda_i$, (iii) $\lambda_i \neq v$, and (iv) $\lambda_i + \xi \neq v$, for $i, j \in [n]$, $i \neq j$.

Since $(a_n, a_{n-1}, \ldots, a_1) \neq (0, \ldots, 0, b_n, \ldots, b_{\xi+1})$, $f(X)$ has at least one more non-zero monomial, either of type $a_i X^{\lambda_i+\xi}$ or of type $(a_{i-\xi} - b_i) X^{\lambda_{i-\xi}+\xi}$, than $f^*(X)$. Since $X^{\lambda_{i-\xi}+\xi}$ cannot be represented as a linear combination of polynomials from Φ^ξ_{rsft}, $f(X)$ and $f^*(X)$ are different polynomials with $f(\sigma) = f^*(\sigma) = F(\sigma)$.

Thus, $\delta(X)$ is a non-zero degree-$(v+1)$ polynomial, such that $\delta(\sigma) = 0$. Therefore, $\tilde{\mathcal{A}}$ can use an efficient polynomial factorization algorithm to find all roots of δ, and one of those roots must be equal to σ. On step 3, $\tilde{\mathcal{A}}$ finds which root is equal to σ by an exhaustive search among all roots returned in the previous step. Thus, clearly $\tilde{\mathcal{A}}$ returns the correct value of σ (and thus violates the Φ^ξ_{rsft}-PSDL assumption) with probability $\mathsf{Succ}^{\mathsf{sound}}_{\mathcal{A}_{\mathsf{rsft}}}(\Pi_{\mathsf{rsft}})$. Finally, the execution time of $\tilde{\mathcal{A}}$ is clearly dominated by the execution time of $\mathcal{A}_{\mathsf{rsft}}$ and the time to factor δ. □

D Rotation Argument

Since the rotation argument uses basically the same underlying ideas as the shift argument of Sect. 5, we will only comment on the differences between the new shift argument and the corresponding rotation argument.

In the right rotation-by-ξ argument,

$$\begin{aligned}
F(X) =& \sum_{i=1}^{n} a_i X^{\lambda_i+\xi} - \sum_{i=1}^{n} b_i X^{\lambda_i} + r_a X^{\upsilon+\xi} - r_b X^{\upsilon} \\
=& \sum_{i=n-\xi+1}^{n} a_i X^{\lambda_i+\xi} + \sum_{i=1}^{n-\xi} a_i X^{\lambda_i+\xi} - \sum_{i=\xi+1}^{n} b_i X^{\lambda_i} - \sum_{i=1}^{\xi} b_i X^{\lambda_i} + \\
& r_a X^{\upsilon+\xi} - r_b X^{\upsilon} \\
=& \sum_{i=1}^{\xi} a_{n-\xi+i} X^{\lambda_{n-\xi+i}+\xi} + \sum_{i=1}^{n-\xi} a_i X^{\lambda_i+\xi} - \sum_{i=1}^{n-\xi} b_{\xi+i} X^{\lambda_{\xi+i}} - \sum_{i=1}^{\xi} b_i X^{\lambda_i} + \\
& r_a X^{\upsilon+\xi} - r_b X^{\upsilon} \\
=& \underbrace{\sum_{i=1}^{\xi} (a_{n-\xi+i} - b_i) X^{\lambda_{n-\xi+i}+\xi} + \sum_{i=1}^{n-\xi} (a_i - b_{\xi+i}) X^{\lambda_i+\xi} +}_{=:F_{con}(X)} \\
& \underbrace{\sum_{i=1}^{\xi} b_i (X^{\lambda_{n-\xi+i}+\xi} - X^{\lambda_i}) + \sum_{i=1}^{n-\xi} b_{\xi+i} (X^{\lambda_i+\xi} - X^{\lambda_{\xi+i}}) + r_a X^{\upsilon+\xi} - r_b X^{\upsilon}}_{F_\pi(X)}
\end{aligned}$$

Thus, if the prover is honest then $F(X) = F_\pi(X)$.

Here, Φ is different,

$$\Phi_{\mathsf{rot}}^{\xi} = \{X^{\upsilon}, X^{\upsilon+\xi}\} \cup \{X^{\lambda_{n-\xi+1}+\xi} - X^{\lambda_i}\}_{i=1}^{\xi} \cup \{X^{\lambda_i+\xi} - X^{\lambda_{i+\xi}}\}_{i=1}^{n-\xi} .$$

Moreover, for the proof of soundness to go through, it is necessary that all polynomials that are present in $F_{con}(X)$ (i.e., from the set $\Phi^* := \{X^{\lambda_{n-\xi+i}+\xi} : i \in [\xi]\} \cup \{X^{\lambda_i+\xi} : i \in [n-\xi]\} = \{X^{\lambda_i+\xi} : i \in [n]\}$), are mutually different and also different from every polynomial in $\Phi_{\mathsf{rot}}^{\xi}$. For this it is sufficient that exactly the same conditions hold as in the case of the right shift-by-ξ argument, i.e., $\lambda_{i+1} > \lambda_i$, $\lambda_j \neq \lambda_i + \xi$ for $i \neq j$, and $\upsilon > \lambda_n + \xi$.

With this modification, one can construct a rotation argument that is very similar to Prot. 3.

E Subset-Sum

Recall $\Phi_\Gamma = (\{X^{\upsilon}\} \cup (X^{\lambda_i})_{i=1}^{n})$. We will need Φ_{res}-PKE assumptions to guarantee soundness of the restriction argument from [21], where Φ_{res} depends concretely on the restricted coordinates. Since $\Phi_{res} \subseteq \Phi_\Gamma$ (for example, in the following theorem, $\Phi_{res} := \{X^{\upsilon}\} \cup \{X^{\lambda_i}\}_{i=2}^{n}$), we will not have to explicitly mention it.

Theorem 8. *Let $\Gamma = (\mathcal{G}_{\mathsf{com}}, \mathcal{C}om, \mathcal{G}com_{td}, \mathcal{C}om_{td}, \mathcal{O}pen_{td})$ be the be the (Λ, υ) commitment scheme in group $\mathbb{G}_1$. Let $\Lambda = (\lambda_1, \dots, \lambda_n)$ be a progression-free tuple of integers, such that $\lambda_{i+1} > \lambda_i + 1$ and $\lambda_i = \mathrm{poly}(\kappa)$. Let Φ be as in Eq. (2). Let $\upsilon > \max(2\lambda_n - \lambda_1, \lambda_n + 1)$ be linear in $\lambda_n - \lambda_1$. The new* Subset-Sum *argument is perfectly complete and perfectly zero-knowledge. Also, $\mathcal{G}_{\mathsf{bp}}$ is Φ-PSDL secure and the Φ_Γ-PKE assumption holds in $\mathbb{G}_1$ and the Φ-PKE assumption holds in $\mathbb{G}_2$, then the* Subset-Sum *argument is computationally sound.*

Proof. Perfect completeness: Assume the prover is honest. The product arguments π_1 and π_3 will correctly verify due to Theorem 3 and replacing (A, B, C) in the theorem respectively to (B, B, B) and (B, S, C) in the Subset-Sum protocol. The correctness of the non-zero argument π_2 can be seen as follows: π_2 shows that $\mathring{B}$ commits to the same value (and uses the same randomizer) as B. It also shows that B^* commits to the same value as both B and $\mathring{B}$. More precisely, the zero argument convinces the verifier that B^* is correctly computed from $\mathring{B}$. Therefore the last check shows that B does not commit to 0, since otherwise $\hat{e}(B, \mathring{g}_2) = \hat{e}(B^*, g_2)$. The right shift-by-1 argument π_4 will also be correctly verified due to Theorem 5. Finally, π_5 correctly verifies that the first element of $\boldsymbol{c} + \boldsymbol{d}$ is 0 due to the completeness of the restriction argument [Gro10].

Adaptive computational soundness: Let A be an NUPPT adversary that produces commitments B, C, D and an accepting argument $(B, C, D, \pi_1, \dots, \pi_5)$. By the Φ-PKE assumption in $\mathbb{G}_2$ and by Thm. 3 and Thm. 5, the product and shift arguments are weakly sound according to the statements of corresponding theorems. (I.e., the extractor can open the inputs to the arguments to values that satisfy required restrictions.)

By the Φ_Γ-PKE assumption in $\mathbb{G}_1$, there exists a non-uniform PPT extractor X_A that, given A's input and access to A's random coins, extracts all openings of B, C, and D. From the weaker version of soundness of the product and shift arguments (Theorem 3 and Theorem 5), and the soundness of the non-zero argument, we have that if $\mathcal{G}_{\mathsf{bp}}$ is Φ-PSDL secure then the following relations hold:

1. B commits to $\boldsymbol{b}$ such that $b_i^2 = b_i \iff b_i \in \{0, 1\}$
2. $\boldsymbol{b} \neq 0$, so at least one of the b_i's is 1.
3. C commits to $\mathbf{c}$ such that $c_i = b_i s_i$.
4. D commits to $\boldsymbol{d}$ such that $d_i = \sum_{j>i} c_j$.

Up to this point, it has been verified that B is a commitment of a non-zero vector of boolean elements, and hence C is a commitment of $\boldsymbol{c} = (b_i s_i)$ where each element is either 0 or s_i, and at least one of the elements is $c_i = s_i$. Now since D is verified to be the scan of c, we have that the first element of $\boldsymbol{c} + \boldsymbol{d}$ is a sum $\sum_{i \geq 1} b_i s_i$. From the Φ_{res}-PKE assumption that guarantees the soundness of the restriction argument (Theorem 1 and Theorem 2 of [21]), we have that a correct verification implies that $(\boldsymbol{c} + \boldsymbol{d})_1 = 0$, so A has indeed committed to a correct solution of Subset-Sum.

PERFECT ZERO KNOWLEDGE: We construct a simulator $\mathcal{S} = (\mathcal{S}_1, \mathcal{S}_2)$. $\mathcal{S}_1$ will create a correctly formed CRS together with a simulation trapdoor $td = \sigma$. The adversary then outputs a correct statement C_S together with a witness w_S. The simulator $\mathcal{S}_2$ creates a commitment to $\boldsymbol{b} = (1, 1, \ldots, 1)$ and commitments to the corresponding vectors $\boldsymbol{c}, \boldsymbol{d}$. Due to the knowledge of trapdoor td and the commitment scheme being computationally (not perfect) binding, all the product, scan, non-zero and restriction arguments can be simulated correctly. This simulated NIZK argument ψ' is perfectly indistinguishable from the real argument ψ. □

F Decision-Knapsack

It is clear from the description of this argument that it works correctly. The DECISION-KNAPSACK argument is clearly perfectly zero knowledge and computationally sound under appropriate assumptions, see App. F. The concrete complexity of the DECISION-KNAPSACK argument depends on both how one defines m in Groth's balancing technique and u in the range argument.

Theorem 9. *Let $\Gamma = (\mathcal{G}_{\mathsf{com}}, \mathcal{C}om, \mathcal{G}com_{td}, \mathcal{C}om_{td}, \mathcal{O}pen_{td})$ be the be the (Λ, υ) commitment scheme in group $\mathbb{G}_1$. Let $\Lambda = (\lambda_1, \ldots, \lambda_n)$ be a progression-free tuple of integers, such that $\lambda_{i+1} > \lambda_i + 1$ and $\lambda_i = \mathrm{poly}(\kappa)$. Let Φ be as in Eq. (2). Let $\upsilon > \max(2\lambda_n - \lambda_1, \lambda_n + 1)$ be linear in $\lambda_n - \lambda_1$. The* DECISION-KNAPSACK *protocol described by Alg. 6 is perfectly complete and perfectly zero-knowledge. Also, if $\mathcal{G}_{\mathsf{bp}}$ is Φ-PSDL secure and the Φ_Γ-PKE assumption holds in $\mathbb{G}_1$ and the Φ-PKE assumption holds in $\mathbb{G}_2$, then the* DECISION-KNAPSACK *protocol is computationally sound.*

Proof. PERFECT COMPLETENESS: Assume the prover is honest. The product arguments $\pi_1, \pi_2, \pi_4, \pi_5, \pi_7$ will correctly verify due to Theorem 3 and replacing (A, B, C) in the theorem respectively to (T, T, T), $(T, \boldsymbol{W}, W_T)$, (A, F, C), $(T, \boldsymbol{B}, B_T)$ and (D, F, E) in the DECISION-KNAPSACK protocol. Here, $F = \{1, 0, \cdots, 0\}$. The right shift-by-1 arguments π_3, π_6 will also be correctly verified due to Theorem 5. Finally, π_8 and π_9 correctly verifies from the completeness of the range argument.

ADAPTIVE COMPUTATIONAL SOUNDNESS: Let A be a non-uniform PPT adversary that produces commitments B, C, D and an accepting NIZK argument $(T, W_T, A, C, B_T, D, E, \pi_1, \cdots, \pi_9)$. By the Φ-PKE assumption in $\mathbb{G}_2$ and by Thm. 3 and Thm. 5, the product and shift arguments are weakly sound according to the statements of corresponding theorems. (That is, the extractor can open the inputs to the arguments to values that satisfy required restrictions.) By Thm. 7, the range argument is computationally sound.

By the Φ_Γ-PKE assumption in $\mathbb{G}_1$, there exists a non-uniform PPT extractor X_A that, given A's input and access to A's random coins, extracts all openings of T, W_T, A, C, B_T, D, E, and F. From the weaker version of soundness of the product and shift arguments (Thm. 3 and Thm. 5), and the soundness of the non-zero argument (Thm. 7), we have that the following relations hold:

Let F be a commitment of $\boldsymbol{f} = (1, 0, \ldots, 0, 0)$ with randomness 0;
Let $t_i = 1$ iff $i \in \mathcal{T}$;
Generate a commitment T of $\boldsymbol{t}$;
Prove that T is Boolean by using a product argument π_1;
Generate a commitment W_T of $\boldsymbol{w_T} = (w_1 t_1, \ldots, w_n t_n)$;
Prove that W_T was computed correctly by using a product argument π_2;
Generate a scan A of W_T, $a_i = \sum_{j>i} w_j t_j$;
Prove that A was computed correctly by using a scan argument π_3;
Generate a commitment C of $(\sum_{i=1}^{n} w_i t_i, 0, \ldots, 0)$;
Prove that C was created correctly ($\boldsymbol{c}$ is a Hadamard product of $\boldsymbol{f}$ and $\boldsymbol{w_T} + \boldsymbol{a}$) by using a product argument π_4;
Generate a commitment B_T of $\boldsymbol{b_T} = (b_1 t_1, \ldots, b_n t_n)$;
Prove that B_T was computed correctly by using a product argument π_5;
Generate a scan D of B_T, $d_i = \sum_{j>i} b_j t_j$;
Prove that D was computed correctly by using a scan argument π_6;
Generate a commitment E of $(\sum_{i=1}^{n} b_i t_i, 0, \ldots, 0)$;
Prove that E was created correctly ($\boldsymbol{e}$ is a Hadamard product of $\boldsymbol{f}$ and $\boldsymbol{b_T} + \boldsymbol{d}$) by using a product argument π_7;
Prove that the first element of C is $\leq W$ by using a range argument π_8;
Prove that the first element of E is $\geq B$ by using a range argument π_9;
The whole argument is $(T, W_T, A, C, B_T, D, E, \pi_1, \ldots, \pi_9)$;

Algorithm 6. The DECISION-KNAPSACK argument

1. T commits to $\boldsymbol{t}$ such that $t_i^2 = t_i \iff t_i \in \{0, 1\}$,
2. W_T commits to $\boldsymbol{w_T}$ such that $(w_T)_i = w_i t_i$,
3. A commits to $\boldsymbol{a}$ such that $a_i = \sum_{j>i} w_j t_j$,
4. C commits to the Hadamard product $\boldsymbol{c}$ of $\boldsymbol{f}$ and $\boldsymbol{w_T} + \boldsymbol{a}$, so $\boldsymbol{c} = (1 \cdot (\boldsymbol{w_T} + \boldsymbol{a})_1, 0 \cdot (\boldsymbol{w_T} + \boldsymbol{a})_2, \ldots, 0 \cdot (\boldsymbol{w_T} + \boldsymbol{a})_n) = (\sum_{i=1}^{n} w_i t_i, 0, \cdots, 0)$,
5. B_T commits to $\boldsymbol{b_T}$ such that $(b_T)_i = b_i t_i$,
6. D commits to $\boldsymbol{d}$ such that $d_i = \sum_{j>i} b_j t_j$,
7. E commits to the Hadamard product $\boldsymbol{e}$ of $\boldsymbol{f}$ and $\boldsymbol{b_T} + \boldsymbol{d}$, so $\boldsymbol{e} = (1 \cdot (\boldsymbol{b_T} + \boldsymbol{d})_1, 0 \cdot (\boldsymbol{b_T} + \boldsymbol{d})_2, \cdots, 0 \cdot (\boldsymbol{b_T} + \boldsymbol{d})_n) = (\sum_{i=1}^{n} b_i t_i, 0, \cdots, 0)$.

From the soundness of the range argument, a correct verification of π_8 will imply that $\boldsymbol{c}_1 \in [0, B]$ while a correct verification of π_9 will imply that $\boldsymbol{e}_1 \in [E, 2^{\kappa}]$ for some κ.

PERFECT ZERO KNOWLEDGE: We can construct a simulator $\mathcal{S} = (\mathcal{S}_1, \mathcal{S}_2)$ analogous to the simulator for SUBSET-SUM. □

Strongly Secure One-Round Group Authenticated Key Exchange in the Standard Model

Yong Li* and Zheng Yang**

Horst Görtz Institute for IT Security
Ruhr-University Bochum, Germany
{yong.li,zheng.yang}@rub.de

Abstract. One-round group authenticated key exchange (GAKE) protocols typically provide implicit authentication and appealing bandwidth efficiency. As a special case of GAKE – the pairing-based one-round tripartite authenticated key exchange (3AKE), recently gains much attention of research community due to its strong security. Several pairing-based one-round 3AKE protocols have recently been proposed to achieve provable security in the g-eCK model. In contrast to earlier GAKE models, the g-eCK model particularly formulates the security properties regarding resilience to the leakage of various combinations of long-term key and ephemeral session state, and provision of weak perfect forward secrecy in a single model. However, the g-eCK security proofs of previous protocols are only given under the random oracle model. In this work, we give a new construction for pairing-based one-round 3AKE protocol which is provably secure in the g-eCK model without random oracles. Security of proposed protocol is reduced to the hardness of Cube Bilinear Decisional Diffie-Hellman (CBDDH) problem for symmetric pairing. We also extend the proposed 3AKE scheme to a GAKE scheme with more than three group members, based on multilinear maps. We prove g-eCK security of our GAKE scheme in the standard model under the natural multilinear generalization of the CBDDH assumption.

Keywords: one-round, group key exchange, bilinear maps, multilinear maps.

1 Introduction

The situation where three or more parties share a secret key is often called group (conference) keying. A group authenticated key exchange protocol (GAKE) allows a set of parties communicating over public network to create a common shared key that is ensured to be known only to those entities. In a public key infrastructure (PKI) based GAKE protocol, each party typically possesses a pair

* Supported by Secure eMobility grant number 01ME12025.
** Corresponding Author Supported by CSC China. The author names are sorted lexicographically.

M. Abdalla, C. Nita-Rotaru, and R. Dahab (Eds.): CANS 2013, LNCS 8257, pp. 122–138, 2013.

of long-term public/private key. The public key is expected to be certified with a party's identity and corresponding private key is kept secretly for authentication. GAKE protocols are essentially generalized from two party authenticated key exchange (2AKE) protocols to the case of multiple parties. However, this brings new challenges not only in the design but also in the analysis of the GAKE protocols. The formal security model for GAKE was first studied by Bresson et al. [8], where the secrecy (indistinguishability) of the established group key and mutual authentication are modelled following the seminal work of the 2AKE model by Bellare and Rogaway [5]. Since then, figuring out new useful security properties for certain class of GAKE and modelling them become continuing trends.

One-Round GAKE. One import research direction in the research field of GAKE is to construct secure one-round protocol due to its appealing bandwidth-efficiency (in contrast to other multiple-round GAKE). A prominent example is the pairing-based tripartite protocol introduced by Joux [14] which extends the classical two-party Diffie-Hellman KE protocol to the three party case. However Joux's protocol is unauthenticated and subject to well known man-in-the-middle attacks. Hence how to transform Joux's protocol to a secure one-round protocol in presence of active adversaries turns out to be an interesting topic. Several attempts, e.g. [1,17,18,10], have been made to improve the original Joux's protocol. This has also pushed forward the development of security model for GAKE. Meanwhile, the most recently proposed one is the g-eCK model by Fujioka et al. [10]. The g-eCK model basically can be seen as a generalization from the two party eCK model [15]. In contrast to earlier GAKE models, e.g. [8,7,12], the peculiarity of g-eCK model is that it captures lots of desirable security properties regarding resilience to the leakage of various combinations of long-term key and ephemeral session state from target sessions (i.e. the test session and its partner session in the security game), and provision of weak perfect forward secrecy (wPFS) in a single model. So far the g-eCK model is known as one of the strongest security model for one-round GAKE[10]. Therefore proving security for one-round GAKE in the g-eCK model may provide more guarantees.

Motivations. In 2012, Fujioka et al. (FMSU) [10] generalized previous 3AKE protocols into one framework based on admissible polynomials which yields many further one-round 3AKE protocols. The generic FMSU protocol [10] was shown to satisfy g-eCK security. However its security proof is given in the random oracle model (ROM) [4] under a specific strong assumption, i.e. gap Bilinear Diffie-Hellman (GBDH) assumption [2]. It is well-known that the security proof in the random oracle model may not imply that corresponding protocol is secure in the real world. Several results, e.g., [9,3], have demonstrated that there exist schemes which are provably secure in the random oracle model, but are insecure as soon as one replaces the random oracle by any concrete hash functions. This also makes the schemes secure in the standard model to be more appealing than that in the random oracle model. So far we are not aware of previous GAKE protocols being able to achieve g-eCK security in the standard model. Hence, one of the open problems in research on GAKE is to construct a secure scheme in the g-eCK model under standard assumptions without resorting to random oracles. Another important motivation of this paper is try to simplify the security proof for GAKE protocols under the g-eCK model from the perspective of reducing the freshness ceases that require to prove. Since under the g-eCK model, the freshness cases are related to the group size which are not a small amount. Taking the 3AKE as example, there might be fourteen freshness cases at all that may lead proof to be very tiresome. When the group size is very large, the situation might be worse because the possible freshness cases are exponential in the number of group members. Those facts make us necessary to somehow reduce the upper bound of the freshness cases that require to do proof simulation.

Contributions. We solve the above open problems by starting from 3AKE. We firstly give a concrete construction in Section 5 for one-round 3AKE protocol that is g-eCK secure in the standard model under standard assumptions. The proposed protocol is based on bilinear groups, target collision resistant hash function family, and pseudo-random function family. In order to withstand active attackers, each (either long-term or ephemeral) public key is required to be associated with some kind of 'tag' which is used to verify the consistency of corresponding public key. Those tags are particularly customized using specific weak Programmable Hash Functions (PHF) [13] for ephemeral key and long-term key respectively, whose output lies in a pairing group. Interestingly the proposed protocol is built to be able to run without knowing any priori information about its partners' long-term public key. Intuitively, these *tags* are what give us the necessary leverage to deal with the non-trivial g-eCK security. In order to facilitate the security analysis of 3AKE protocols in the g-eCK model, we introduce propositions to formally reduce fourteen freshness cases (which cover all freshness cases for 3AKE protocols) to four freshness cases. Then it is only necessary to prove the security of considered protocol under the reduced four freshness cases. It is not hard to check the validity of these reductions to all one-round 3AKE protocols in which the message sent by a party is independent of the messages sent by the other parties. Any g-eCK security analyzers for one-round 3AKE protocols might benefit from these results. We then provide a succinct and rigorous game-based security proof by reducing the g-eCK security of proposed 3AKE protocol in the standard model to breaking the cubic Bilinear Decisional Diffie-Hellman (CBDDH) assumption which is slightly modified from the Bilinear Decisional Diffie-Hellman (BDDH) assumption [14].

In the latter we present a GAKE scheme with constant maximum group size in Section 6 following the construction idea of 3AKE. Nevertheless the proposed GAKE scheme is based on the symmetric multilinear map which is first postulated by Boneh and Silverberg [6]. We prove g-eCK security of our scheme in the standard model under a natural multilinear generalization of the CBDDH assumption which is called n-Multiliear Decisional Diffie-Hellman Assumption (nMDDH). In particular we give a general game-based security proof for our proposed GAKE scheme which is given under any polynomial number of freshness cases.

2 Preliminaries

Notations. We let $\kappa \in \mathbb{N}$ denote the security parameter and 1^κ the string that consists of κ ones. Let a capital letter with a 'hat' denote an identity; without the hat the letter denotes the public key of that party. Let $[n] = \{1, \ldots, n\} \subset \mathbb{N}$ be the set of integers between 1 and n. If S is a set, then $a \xleftarrow{\$} S$ denotes the action of sampling a uniformly random element from S. Let '$||$' denote the operation concatenating two binary strings. In the sequel, we briefly describe the complexity assumptions which lay the foundation of our constructions. Besides we will also make use of target collision resistant hash function family and pseudo-random function family. The corresponding definitions can be found in [16].

Bilinear Groups. In the following, we briefly recall some of the basic properties of bilinear groups. Our AKE solution mainly consists of elements from a single group $\mathbb{G}$. We therefore concentrate on symmetric bilinear maps. Our pairing based scheme will be parameterized by a symmetric pairing parameter generator, denoted by $\mathsf{PG.Gen}$. This is a polynomial time algorithm that on input a security parameter 1^κ, returns the description of two multiplicative cyclic groups $\mathbb{G}$ and $\mathbb{G}_T$ of the same prime order p, generator g for $\mathbb{G}$, and a bilinear computable pairing $e : \mathbb{G} \times \mathbb{G} \to \mathbb{G}_T$.

Definition 1 (Symmetric Bilinear groups). *We call* $\mathcal{PG} = (\mathbb{G}, g, \mathbb{G}_T, p, e) \xleftarrow{\$} \mathsf{PG.Gen}(1^\kappa)$ *be a set of symmetric bilinear groups, if the function e is an (admissible) bilinear map and it holds that:*

1. ***Bilinear:*** $\forall(a, b) \in \mathbb{G}$ *and* $\forall(x, y) \in \mathbb{Z}_p$, *we have* $e(a^x, b^y) = e(a, b)^{xy}$.
2. ***Non-degenerate:*** $e(g, g) \neq 1_{\mathbb{G}_T}$, *is a generator of group* $\mathbb{G}_T$.
3. ***Efficiency:*** $\forall(a, b) \in \mathbb{G}$, *e is efficiently computable.*

Multilinear Groups. In the following, we recall the definition of symmetric multilinear groups introduced in [6]. We assume that a party can call a group generator $\mathsf{MLG.Gen}(1^\kappa, n)$ to obtain a set of multilinear groups. On input a security parameter κ and a positive integer $2 < n \in \mathbb{N}$, the polynomial time group generator $\mathsf{MLG.Gen}(1^\kappa, n)$ outputs two multiplicative cyclic groups $\mathbb{G}$ and $\mathbb{G}_T$ of the same prime order p, generator g for $\mathbb{G}$, and a n-multilinear map $me : \mathbb{G}^n \times \mathbb{G} \to \mathbb{G}_T$.

We summarize the properties of n-multilinear groups in the following definition.

Definition 2 (Symmetric Multilinear groups). *We call* $\mathcal{MLG} = (\mathbb{G}, \mathbb{G}_T, p, me) \xleftarrow{\$} \mathsf{MLG.Gen}(\kappa, n)$ *be a set of symmetric multilinear groups, if the n-multilinear map me holds that:*

1. ***n-multilinear:*** $\forall(c_1, \ldots, c_n) \in \mathbb{G}$ *and* $\forall(y_1, \ldots, y_n) \in \mathbb{Z}_p$, *we have* $me(c_1^{y_1}, \ldots, c_n^{y_n}) = me(c_1, \ldots, c_n)^{y_1 \cdots y_n}$.
2. ***Non-degenerate:*** $me(g, \ldots, g) \neq 1_{\mathbb{G}_T}$, *is a generator of group* $\mathbb{G}_T$.
3. ***Efficiency:*** $\forall(c_1, \ldots, c_n) \in \mathbb{G}$, *the operation* $me(c_1, \ldots, c_n)$ *is efficiently computable.*

Concrete multilinear maps can be found in [11] by Garg, Gentry, and Halvei. We here just focus on a general definition of symmetric n-multilinear groups without loss of generality.

CUBE BILINEAR DECISIONAL DIFFIE-HELLMAN ASSUMPTION. With respect to our construction for one-round tripartite AKE, we need a new complexity assumption defined as follows.

Definition 3. *We say that the* CBDDH *problem relative to generator* PG.Gen *is* $(t, \epsilon_{\mathsf{CBDDH}})$*-hard, if the probability bound* $|\Pr[\mathsf{EXP}^{cbddh}_{\mathsf{PG.Gen},\mathcal{A}}(\kappa, n) = 1] - 1/2| \leq \epsilon_{\mathsf{CBDDH}}$ *holds for all adversaries* $\mathcal{A}$ *running in probabilistic polynomial time t in the following experiment:*

$\mathsf{EXP}^{cbddh}_{\mathsf{PG.Gen},\mathcal{A}}(\kappa, n)$
$\mathcal{PG} = (\mathbb{G}, g, \mathbb{G}_T, p, e) \stackrel{\$}{\leftarrow} \mathsf{PG.Gen}(1^\kappa)$;
$a, \gamma \stackrel{\$}{\leftarrow} \mathbb{Z}_p^*$;
$b \stackrel{\$}{\leftarrow} \{0, 1\}$, *if* $b = 1$ $\Gamma \leftarrow e(g, g)^{a^3}$, *otherwise* $\Gamma \leftarrow e(g, g)^\gamma$;
$b' \leftarrow \mathcal{A}(1^\kappa, \mathcal{PG}, g^a, \Gamma)$;
if $b = b'$ *then return 1, otherwise return 0;*

where $\epsilon_{\mathsf{CBDDH}} = \epsilon_{\mathsf{CBDDH}}(\kappa)$ *is a negligible function in* κ.

The proof for the security of CBDDH assumption in the generic group model [19] is presented in the full version of this paper [16].

N-MULTILINEAR DECISIONAL DIFFIE-HELLMAN ASSUMPTION. We present a generalization of the CBDDH assumption in n-multilinear groups that we call the n-Multilinear Decisional Diffie-Hellman (nMDDH) assumption.

Definition 4. *We say that the* nMDDH *problem relative to generator* MLG.Gen *is* $(t, \epsilon_{\mathsf{nMDDH}})$*-hard, if the probability bound* $|\Pr[\mathsf{EXP}^{nmddh}_{\mathsf{PG.Gen},\mathcal{A}}(\kappa, n) = 1] - 1/2| \leq \epsilon_{\mathsf{nMDDH}}$ *holds for all adversaries* $\mathcal{A}$ *running in probabilistic polynomial time t in the following experiment:*

$\mathsf{EXP}^{nmddh}_{\mathsf{PG.Gen},\mathcal{A}}(\kappa)$
$\mathcal{MLG} = (\mathbb{G}, \mathbb{G}_T, g, p, me) \stackrel{\$}{\leftarrow} \mathsf{MLG.Gen}(\kappa, n)$;
$a, \gamma \stackrel{\$}{\leftarrow} \mathbb{Z}_p^*$, $b \stackrel{\$}{\leftarrow} \{0, 1\}$;
$\Gamma \leftarrow me(g, \ldots, g)^{a^{n+1}}$ *if* $b = 1$, *otherwise* $\Gamma \leftarrow me(g, \ldots, g)^\gamma$;
$b' \leftarrow \mathcal{A}(1^\kappa, \mathcal{MLG}, g^a, \Gamma)$;
if $b = b'$ *then return 1, otherwise return 0;*

where $\epsilon_{\mathsf{nMDDH}} = \epsilon_{\mathsf{nMDDH}}(\kappa)$ *is a negligible function in* κ.

3 Security Model for Group Authenticated Key Exchange

In this section we present the formal security model for PKI-based group authenticated key-exchange (GAKE) protocols. In this model, while emulating the real-world capabilities of an active adversary, we provide an 'execution environment' for adversaries following an important line of research [15,18,10] which is initiated by Bellare and Rogaway [5]. We formalize the capabilities of an adversary in a strong sense who is provided enormous power to take full control over the communication network (e.g., alter or inject messages as she wishes), in particular she may compromise long-term keys of parties or secret states of protocol instances at any time. Let $\mathcal{K}_{\mathsf{AKE}}$ be the key space of session key, and $\{\mathcal{PK}, \mathcal{SK}\}$ be key spaces for long-term public/private key respectively. Those spaces are associated with security parameter κ of considered protocol.

Execution Environment. In the execution environment, we fix a set of honest parties $\{\mathsf{ID}_1, \ldots, \mathsf{ID}_\ell\}$ for $\ell \in \mathbb{N}$, where ID is identity of a party which is chosen uniquely from space $\mathcal{IDS}$. Each identity is associated with a long-term key pair $(sk_{\mathsf{ID}_i}, pk_{\mathsf{ID}_i}) \in (\mathcal{SK}, \mathcal{PK})$ for entity authentication, and is indexed via integer $i \in [\ell]$ in the model. Note that those identities are also lexicographically indexed via variable $i \in [\ell]$. For public key registration, each party ID_i might be required to provide extra information (denoted by proof) to prove either the knowledge of the secret key or correctness of registered public key (via e.g. non-interactive proof of knowledge schemes). Each honest party ID_i can sequentially and concurrently execute the protocol multiple times with different indented partners, this is characterized by a collection of oracles $\{\pi_i^s : i \in [\ell], s \in [\rho]\}$ for $\rho \in \mathbb{N}$. Oracle π_i^s behaves as party ID_i carrying out a process to execute the s-th protocol instance, which has access to the long-term key pair $(sk_{\mathsf{ID}_i}, pk_{\mathsf{ID}_i})$ of ID_i and to all other public keys. Moreover, we assume each oracle π_i^s maintains a list of independent internal state variables with following semantics: (i) pid_i^s – storing a set of partner identities in the group with whom π_i^s intends to establish a session key (including ID_i itself), where the identities are ordered lexicographically; (ii) Φ_i^s – storing the oracle decision $\Phi_i^s \in \{\mathtt{accept}, \mathtt{reject}\}$; (iii) K_i^s – recording the session key $K_i^s \in \mathcal{K}_{\mathsf{KE}}$ for symmetric encryption; (iv) st_i^s – storing the maximum secret session states that are allowed to be leaked (e.g., the exponent of exchanged ephemeral public key); (v) T_i^s – storing the transcript of all messages sent and received by π_i^s during its execution, where the messages are ordered by round and within each round lexicographically by the identities of the purported senders.

All those variables of each oracle are initialized with empty string denoted by symbol $\emptyset$ in the following. At some point, each oracle π_i^s may complete the execution always with a decision state Φ_i^s. Furthermore, we assume that the session key is assigned to the variable K_i^s (such that $K_i^s \neq \emptyset$) iff oracle π_i^s has reached an internal state $\Phi_i^s = \mathtt{accept}$.

Adversarial Model. An adversary $\mathcal{A}$ in our model is a PPT Turing Machine taking as input the security parameter 1^κ and the public information (e.g. generic description of above environment), which may interact with these oracles by issuing the following queries.

- $\mathsf{Send}(\pi_i^s, m)$: The adversary can use this query to send any message m of his own choice to oracle π_i^s. The oracle will respond the next message m^* (if any) to be sent according to the protocol specification and its internal states. Oracle π_i^s would be initiated via sending the oracle the first message $m = (\top, \mathsf{pid}_i^s)$ consisting of a special initialization symbol $\top$ and a variable storing partner identities. After answering a Send query, the variables $(\mathsf{pid}_i^s, \Phi_i^s, K_i^s, st_i^s, T_i^s)$ might be updated depending on the specific protocol.
- $\mathsf{RevealKey}(\pi_i^s)$: Oracle π_i^s responds with the contents of variable K_i^s.
- $\mathsf{StateReveal}(\pi_i^s)$: Oracle π_i^s responds with the secret state stored in variable st_i^s, e.g. the random coins used to generate the session key.
- $\mathsf{Corrupt}(\mathsf{ID}_i)$: Oracle π_i^1 responds with the long-term secret key sk_{ID_i} of party ID_i if $i \in [\ell]$. After this query, oracles $\pi_i^s (s > 1)$ can still answer other queries.
- $\mathsf{RegisterCorrupt}(\mathsf{ID}_\tau, pk_{\mathsf{ID}_\tau}, \mathsf{proof}_{\mathsf{ID}_\tau})$: This query allows the adversary to register an identity ID_τ ($\ell < \tau$ and $\tau \in \mathbb{N}$) and a static public key pk_{ID_τ} on behalf of a party ID_τ, if ID_τ is unique and pk_{ID_τ} is ensured to be sound by evaluating the non-interactive proof $\mathsf{proof}_{\mathsf{ID}_\tau}$. We only require that the proof is non-interactive in order to keep the model simple. Parties established by this query are called dishonest.
- $\mathsf{Test}(\pi_i^s)$: This query may only be asked once throughout the experiment. Oracle π_i^s handles this query as follows: If the oracle has state $\Omega = \texttt{reject}$ or $K_i^s = \emptyset$, then it returns some failure symbol $\bot$. Otherwise it flips a fair coin b, samples a random element K_0 from key space $\mathcal{K}_{\mathsf{KE}}$, sets $K_1 = K_i^s$ to the real session key, and returns K_b.

We stress that the exact meaning of the StateReveal must be defined by each protocol separately, and each protocol should be proven secure to resist with such kind of state leakage as claimed. Namely a protocol should specify the content stored in the variable st during protocol execution. In order to protect those critical session states of AKE protocols, utilizing secure (e.g. tamper-proof) device might be a natural solution, namely at each party an untrusted host machine is used together with a secure hardware. In this way it is possible to adopt a 'All-and-Nothing' strategy to define the session states — namely we can assume that *all states* stored on untrusted host machine can be revealed via StateReveal query and *no state* would be exposed at secure device without loss of generality. The RegisterCorrupt query is used to model the chosen identity and public key attacks. In this query, the detail form of proof_τ (i.e. how to register an identity and corresponding public key) should be specified by each protocol. Please note that if the protocol allows for arbitrary key registration then one could set the parameter $\mathsf{proof} = \emptyset$. Basically, our execution environment is consistent to the g-eCK model [10] except for the RegisterCorrupt query. In the original g-eCK model, the adversary is allowed to register a public key (via AddUser query) by checking whether corresponding register key comes from the key space for public key. However in our model, we model the requirement of the key registration in a more general way via parameter proof.

Secure AKE Protocols. To formalize the notion that two oracles are engaged in an on-line communication, we define the partnership via *matching sessions.* We assume that messages in a transcript T_i^s are represented as binary strings.

Definition 5. *We say that an oracle* π_i^s *has a* matching session *to oracle* π_j^t, *if* $\mathsf{pid}_i^s = \mathsf{pid}_j^t$ *and* π_i^s *has sent all protocol messages and* $T_i^s = T_j^t$.

Definition 6 (Correctness). *Let* π_i^s *and* π_j^t *be two oracles. We say a GAKE protocol* Σ *is* correct, *if both oracles* π_i^s *and* π_j^t *accept such that* π_i^s *and* π_j^t *have matching sessions, then it holds that* $K_i^s = K_j^t$.

Security Game. The security game is played between a challenger $\mathcal{C}$ and an adversary $\mathcal{A}$, where the following steps are performed:

1. At the beginning of the game, the challenger $\mathcal{C}$ implements the collection of oracles $\{\pi_i^s : i \in [\ell], s \in [\rho]\}$, and generates ℓ long-term key pairs $(pk_{\mathsf{ID}_i}, sk_{\mathsf{ID}_i})$ and corresponding proof proof_i for all honest parties ID_i where the identity $\mathsf{ID}_i \in \mathcal{IDS}$ of each party is chosen uniquely. $\mathcal{C}$ gives adversary $\mathcal{A}$ $\{(\mathsf{ID}_1, pk_{\mathsf{ID}_1}, \mathsf{proof}_{\mathsf{ID}_1}), \ldots, (\mathsf{ID}_\ell, pk_{\mathsf{ID}_\ell}, \mathsf{proof}_{\mathsf{ID}_\ell})\}$ as input.
2. $\mathcal{A}$ may issue polynomial number of queries: Send, StateReveal, Corrupt, RegisterCorrupt and RevealKey.
3. At some point, $\mathcal{A}$ may issue a $\mathsf{Test}(\pi_i^s)$ query on an oracle π_i^s during the experiment but only once.
4. At the end of game, the $\mathcal{A}$ may terminate with outputting a bit b' as its guess for b of Test query.

For the security definition, we need the notion about the freshness of oracles which formulates the restrictions on the adversary with respect to performing these above queries.

Definition 7 (Freshness). *Let* π_i^s *be an accepted oracle.*
Let $\pi_S = \{\pi_j^t\}_{\mathsf{ID}_j \in \mathsf{pid}_i^s, j \neq i}$ *be a set of oracles (if they exist), such that* π_i^s *has a matching session to* π_j^t. *Then the oracle* π_i^s *is said to be fresh if none of the following conditions holds:*
(i) $\mathcal{A}$ *queried* $\mathsf{RegisterCorrupt}(\mathsf{ID}_j, pk_{\mathsf{ID}_j}, \mathsf{proof}_{\mathsf{ID}_j})$ *with some* $\mathsf{ID}_j \in \mathsf{pid}_i^s$; *(ii)* $\mathcal{A}$ *queried either* $\mathsf{RevealKey}(\pi_i^s)$ *or* $\mathsf{RevealKey}(\pi_j^t)$ *for some oracle* $\pi_j^t \in \pi_S$; *(iii)* $\mathcal{A}$ *queried both* $\mathsf{Corrupt}(\mathsf{ID}_i)$ *and* $\mathsf{StateReveal}(\pi_i^s)$; *(iv) For some oracle* $\pi_j^t \in \pi_S$, $\mathcal{A}$ *queried both* $\mathsf{Corrupt}(\mathsf{ID}_j)$ *and* $\mathsf{StateReveal}(\pi_j^t)$; *(v) If* $\mathsf{ID}_j \in \mathsf{pid}_i^s$ $(j \neq i)$ *and there is no oracle* π_j^t *such that* π_i^s *has a matching session to* π_j^t, $\mathcal{A}$ *queried* $\mathsf{Corrupt}(\mathsf{ID}_j)$.

Definition 8 (g-eCK Security). *We say that an adversary* $\mathcal{A}$ (t, ϵ)*-breaks the g-eCK security of a correct group AKE protocol* Σ, *if* $\mathcal{A}$ *runs the AKE security game within time* t, *and the following condition holds:*

– *If a* Test *query has been issued to a fresh oracle* π_i^s, *then the probability that the bit* b' *returned by* $\mathcal{A}$ *equals to the bit* b *chosen by the* Test *query is bounded by*

$$|\Pr[b = b'] - 1/2| > \epsilon,$$

We say that a correct group AKE protocol Σ *is* (t, ϵ)*-g-eCK-secure, if there exists no adversary that* (t, ϵ)*-breaks the g-eCK security of* Σ.

4 Simplify the Security Proof for One-Round GAKE in the g-eCK Model

We first present a generic definition of one-round group authenticated key exchange (ORGAKE) to allow us to describe our generic result for this class of protocols. In a ORGAKE protocol, each party may send a single 'message' and this message is always assumed to be independent of the message sent by the other party without loss of generality. The independence property of sent messages is required since the session participants can't achieve mutual authentication in one-round and it enables parties to run protocol instances simultaneously (which is a key feature of one-round protocol). The key exchange procedure is done within two pass and a common shared session key is generated to be known only by session participants.

Let $\mathsf{GD} := ((\mathsf{ID}_1, pk_{\mathsf{ID}_1}), \ldots, (\mathsf{ID}_n, pk_{\mathsf{ID}_n}))$ be a list which is used to store the public information of a group of parties formed as tuple $(\mathsf{ID}_i, pk_{\mathsf{ID}_i})$, where n is the size of the group members which intend to share a key and pk_{ID_i} is the public key of party $\mathsf{ID}_i \in \mathcal{IDS}$ $(i \in [n])$. Let T denote the transcript storing the messages sent and received by a protocol instance at a party which are sorted orderly. A general PKI-based ORGAKE protocol may consist of four polynomial time algorithms (ORGAKE.Setup, ORGAKE.KGen, ORGAKE.MF, ORGAKE.SKG) with following semantics:

- $pms \leftarrow \mathsf{Setup}(1^\kappa)$: This algorithm takes as input a security parameter κ and outputs a set of system parameters storing in a variable pms.
- $(sk_{\mathsf{ID}}, pk_{\mathsf{ID}}, \mathsf{proof}_{\mathsf{ID}}) \xleftarrow{\$} \mathsf{ORGAKE.KGen}(pms, \mathsf{ID})$: This algorithm takes as input system parameters pms and a party's identity ID, and outputs a pair of long-term private/public key $(sk_{\mathsf{ID}}, pk_{\mathsf{ID}}) \in (\mathcal{PK}, \mathcal{SK})$ for party ID and a non-interactive proof for pk_{ID} (which is required during key registration.).
- $m_{\mathsf{ID}_1} \xleftarrow{\$} \mathsf{ORGAKE.MF}(pms, sk_{\mathsf{ID}_1}, r_{\mathsf{ID}_1}, \mathsf{GD})$: This algorithm takes as input system parameters pms and the sender ID_1's secret key sk_{ID_1}, a randomness $r_{\mathsf{ID}_1} \xleftarrow{\$} \mathcal{R}_{\mathsf{ORGAKE}}$ and the group information variable GD, and outputs a message to be sent in a protocol pass, where $\mathcal{R}_{\mathsf{ORGAKE}}$ is the randomness space.[1]
- $K \leftarrow \mathsf{ORGAKE.SKG}(pms, sk_{\mathsf{ID}_1}, r_{\mathsf{ID}_1}, \mathsf{GD}, \mathsf{T})$: This algorithm take as the input system parameters pms and ID_1's secret key sk_{ID_1}, a randomness $r_{\mathsf{ID}_1} \xleftarrow{\$} \mathcal{R}_{\mathsf{ORGAKE}}$ and the group information GD and a transcript T orderly recorded all protocol messages exchanged[2], and outputs session key $K \in \mathcal{K}_{\mathsf{ORGAKE}}$.

[1] We remark that the parameter GD of algorithm ORGAKE.MF is only optional, which can be any empty string if specific protocol compute the message without knowing any information about its indented partners.

[2] The detail order needs to be specified by each protocol.

For correctness, we require that, on input the same group description $\mathsf{GD} = ((\mathsf{ID}_1, pk_1), \ldots, (\mathsf{ID}_n, pk_n))$ and transcript T, algorithm $\mathsf{ORGAKE.SKG}$ satisfies the constraint: $\mathsf{ORGAKE.SKG}(pms, sk_{\mathsf{ID}_1}, r_{\mathsf{ID}_1}, \mathsf{GD}, \mathsf{T}) = \mathsf{ORGAKE.SKG}(pms, sk_{\mathsf{ID}_i}, r_{\mathsf{ID}_i}, \mathsf{GD}, \mathsf{T})$, where sk_{ID_i} is the secret key of a party $\mathsf{ID}_i \in \mathsf{GD}$ who generates randomness $r_{\mathsf{ID}_i} \in \mathcal{R}_{\mathsf{ORGAKE}}$ for $i \in [n]$.

Besides these algorithms, each protocol might consist of other steps such as long-term key registration and message exchange, which should be described by each protocol independently.

Simplify the Security Proof for One-round Tripartite AKE in the g-eCK model. We show how to reduce the complexity of the security proof of any one-round 3AKE protocol with the above form in the g-eCK model. To prove the security of a protocol in the g-eCK model, it is necessary to show the proof under all possible freshness cases formulated by Definition 7. Let oracle $\pi^{s^*}_{\hat{A}}$ be the test oracle with intended partner $\hat{B}$ and $\hat{C}$ for instance. If any adversary breaks the indistinguishability security property of am OR3AKE protocol, then at least one of the following fresh events must occur:

- **Event 0**: There are oracles $\pi^{t^*}_{\hat{B}}$ and $\pi^{l^*}_{\hat{C}}$, such that $\pi^{s^*}_{\hat{A}}$ has matching session to $\pi^{t^*}_{\hat{B}}$ and to $\pi^{l^*}_{\hat{C}}$ respectively.
- **Event 1**: There is an oracle $\pi^{t^*}_{\hat{F}}$ such that $\pi^{s^*}_{\hat{A}}$ and $\pi^{t^*}_{\hat{F}}$ have matching sessions but there is no oracle of $\hat{D}$ having matching session to $\pi^{s^*}_{\hat{A}}$, where $\hat{F}$ and $\hat{D}$ are parties such that $\hat{F}, \hat{D} \in \{\hat{B}, \hat{C}\}$ and $\hat{D} \neq \hat{F}$.
- **Event 2**: $\pi^{s^*}_{\hat{A}}$ has no matching session.

In the Table 1, we show the freshness cases regarding to $\mathsf{StateReveal}$ and $\mathsf{Corrupt}$ query which might be occurred in each event. Let 'nRS' denote the situation that the adversary did not issue $\mathsf{StateReveal}$ query to specific oracle, and 'nC' denote the situation adversary did not issue $\mathsf{Corrupt}$ query to corresponding party (e.g. the owner of certain oracle).

Table 1. Freshness Cases in Each Event

Event 0	$\pi^{s^*}_{\hat{A}}$	$\pi^{t^*}_{\hat{B}}$	$\pi^{l^*}_{\hat{C}}$	Event 1	$\pi^{s^*}_{\hat{A}}$	$\pi^{t^*}_{\hat{F}}$	$\hat{D}$	Event 2	$\pi^{s^*}_{\hat{A}}$	$\hat{B}$	$\hat{C}$
Case 1 (C1)	nRS	nRS	nRS	Case 9 (C9)	nRS	nRS	nC	Case 13 (C13)	nC	nC	nC
Case 2 (C2)	nC	nRS	nRS	Case 10 (C10)	nC	nRS	nC	Case 14 (C14)	nRS	nC	nC
Case 3 (C3)	nRS	nRS	nC	Case 11 (C11)	nC	nC	nC				
Case 4 (C4)	nC	nRS	nC	Case 12 (C12)	nRS	nC	nC				
Case 5 (C5)	nRS	nC	nRS								
Case 6 (C6)	nC	nC	nRS								
Case 7 (C7)	nC	nC	nC								
Case 8 (C8)	nRS	nC	nC								

In order to complete the proof, we must provide the security proofs under all fourteen cases that might be tiresome. However we introduce the following general propositions to facilitate the proof of any OR3AKE protocols in the form of the above description. Our goal is to reduce the freshness cases which have the similar restrictions on adversary's queries.

Proposition 1. *If adversary $\mathcal{A}_1$ $(t_1, \epsilon_{\mathcal{A}_1})$-breaks the g-eCK security of a OR3AKE protocol Σ in case $C2$, then there exists an adversary $\mathcal{A}_2$ who can $(t_2, \epsilon_{\mathcal{A}_2})$-breaks the g-eCK security of Σ in case $C5$, such that $t_1 \approx t_2$ and $\epsilon_{\mathcal{A}_1} = \epsilon_{\mathcal{A}_2}$.*

Proposition 2. *If adversary $\mathcal{A}_1$ $(t_1, \epsilon_{\mathcal{A}_1})$-breaks the g-eCK security of a OR3AKE protocol Σ in case $C3$ $(C5)$, then there exists an adversary $\mathcal{A}_2$ who can $(t_2, \epsilon_{\mathcal{A}_2})$-breaks the g-eCK security of Σ in case $C9$, such that $t_1 \approx t_2$ and $\epsilon_{\mathcal{A}_1} = \epsilon_{\mathcal{A}_2}$.*

Proposition 3. *If adversary $\mathcal{A}_1$ $(t_1, \epsilon_{\mathcal{A}_1})$-breaks the g-eCK security of a OR3AKE protocol Σ in case $C7$, then there exists an adversary $\mathcal{A}_2$ who can $(t_2, \epsilon_{\mathcal{A}_2})$-breaks the g-eCK security of Σ in case $C11$. If such adversary $\mathcal{A}_2$ exists, then there exists an adversary $\mathcal{A}_3$ who can $(t_3, \epsilon_{\mathcal{A}_3})$-breaks the g-eCK security of Σ in case $C13$. We have that $t_1 \approx t_2 \approx t_3$ and $\epsilon_{\mathcal{A}_1} = \epsilon_{\mathcal{A}_2} = \epsilon_{\mathcal{A}_3}$.*

Proposition 4. *If adversary $\mathcal{A}_1$ $(t_1, \epsilon_{\mathcal{A}_1})$-breaks the g-eCK security of a OR3AKE protocol Σ in case $C4$, then there exists an adversary $\mathcal{A}_2$ who can $(t_2, \epsilon_{\mathcal{A}_2})$-breaks the g-eCK security of Σ in case $C10$. If such adversary $\mathcal{A}_2$ exists, then there exists an adversary $\mathcal{A}_3$ who can $(t_3, \epsilon_{\mathcal{A}_3})$-breaks the g-eCK security of Σ in case $C12$. If such adversary $\mathcal{A}_3$ exists, then there exists adversary $\mathcal{A}_4$ who can $(t_4, \epsilon_{\mathcal{A}_4})$-breaks the g-eCK security of Σ in case $C14$. We have that $t_1 \approx t_2 \approx t_3 \approx t_4$ and $\epsilon_{\mathcal{A}_1} = \epsilon_{\mathcal{A}_2} = \epsilon_{\mathcal{A}_3} = \epsilon_{\mathcal{A}_4}$.*

Proposition 5. *If adversary $\mathcal{A}_1$ $(t_1, \epsilon_{\mathcal{A}_1})$-breaks the g-eCK security of a OR3AKE protocol Σ in case $C6$, then there exists an adversary $\mathcal{A}_2$ who can $(t_2, \epsilon_{\mathcal{A}_2})$-breaks the g-eCK security of Σ in case $C8$. If such adversary $\mathcal{A}_2$ exists, then there exists an adversary $\mathcal{A}_3$ who can $(t_3, \epsilon_{\mathcal{A}_3})$-breaks the g-eCK security of Σ in case $C12$. We have that $t_1 \approx t_2 \approx t_3$ and $\epsilon_{\mathcal{A}_1} = \epsilon_{\mathcal{A}_2} = \epsilon_{\mathcal{A}_3}$.*

The proofs of above propositions can be found in the full version of this paper [16]. Due to the above reductions, one could prove the security of any one-round 3AKE protocol in the g-eCK model only under freshness cases $C1$, $C9$, $C13$ and $C14$. This would be dramatically simplify the security proof. In the sequel, we call these freshness cases require to write proof as target freshness cease.

Towards Lower Bound of Target Freshness Cases for the Proof of One-round GAKE with Arbitrary Group Size in the g-eCK Model. In order to make the proof for one-round GAKE protocol in the g-eCK model to be more tight, we might also need to do the analogous reductions about the freshness cases as it is done for OR3AKE. So that we make a conjecture for the lower bound of target freshness cases for the proof of AKE protocol with arbitrary group size n in the g-eCK Model.

Conjecture 1. For any one-round group AKE protocol with members $n + 1$, we have $n + 2$ freshness cases that require proof simulations.

The proof idea of this conjecture is presented in [16].

5 A Tripartite AKE Protocol from Bilinear Maps

In this section we present a three party one-round AKE protocol based on symmetric bilinear groups, a target collision resistant hash function and a pseudo-random function family. The requirements for underlying building blocks are standard, the proposed protocol provides g-eCK security without random oracles.

5.1 Protocol Description

Setup: The proposed protocol takes as input the following building blocks which are initialized respectively in terms of the security parameter $\kappa \in \mathbb{N}$: (i) Symmetric bilinear groups $\mathcal{PG} = (\mathbb{G}, g, \mathbb{G}_T, p, e) \stackrel{\$}{\leftarrow} \mathsf{PG.Gen}(1^\kappa)$ and a set of random values $\{u_i\}_{0 \le i \le 3} \stackrel{\$}{\leftarrow} \mathbb{G}$; (ii) a target collision resistant hash function $\mathsf{TCRHF}(hk_{\mathsf{TCRHF}}, \cdot) : \mathcal{K}_{\mathsf{TCRHF}} \times \mathbb{G} \to \mathbb{Z}_p$, where $\mathcal{K}_{\mathsf{TCRHF}}$ is the key space of TCRHF and $hk_{\mathsf{TCRHF}} \stackrel{\$}{\leftarrow} \mathsf{TCRHF.KG}(1^\kappa)$; and (iii) a pseudo-random function family $\mathsf{PRF}(\cdot,\cdot) : \mathbb{G}_T \times \{0,1\}^* \to \mathcal{K}_{\mathsf{AKE}}$. The system parameters encompass $pms := (\mathcal{PG}, \{u_i\}_{0 \le i \le 3}, hk_{\mathsf{TCRHF}})$.

$\hat{A}$	$\hat{B}$	$\hat{C}$
$x \stackrel{\$}{\leftarrow} \mathbb{Z}_p^*, X := g^x$	$y \stackrel{\$}{\leftarrow} \mathbb{Z}_p^*, Y := g^y$	$z \stackrel{\$}{\leftarrow} \mathbb{Z}_p^*, Z := g^z$
$h_X := \mathsf{TCRHF}(X)$	$h_Y := \mathsf{TCRHF}(Y)$	$h_Z := \mathsf{TCRHF}(Z)$
$t_X := (u_0 u_1^{h_X} u_2^{h_X^2} u_3^{h_X^3})^x$	$t_Y := (u_0 u_1^{h_Y} u_2^{h_Y^2} u_3^{h_Y^3})^y$	$t_Z := (u_0 u_1^{h_Z} u_2^{h_Z^2} u_3^{h_Z^3})^z$
broadcast $(\hat{A}, A, t_A, X, t_X)$	*broadcast* $(\hat{B}, B, t_B, Y, t_Y)$	*broadcast* $(\hat{C}, C, t_C, Z, t_Z)$
$h_B := \mathsf{TCRHF}(B)$	$h_A := \mathsf{TCRHF}(A)$	$h_A := \mathsf{TCRHF}(A)$
$h_C := \mathsf{TCRHF}(C)$	$h_C := \mathsf{TCRHF}(C)$	$h_B := \mathsf{TCRHF}(B)$
$h_Y := \mathsf{TCRHF}(Y)$	$h_X := \mathsf{TCRHF}(X)$	$h_X := \mathsf{TCRHF}(X)$
$h_Z := \mathsf{TCRHF}(Z)$	$h_Z := \mathsf{TCRHF}(Z)$	$h_Y := \mathsf{TCRHF}(Y)$
$U_B := u_0 u_1^{h_B} u_2^{h_B^2} u_3^{h_B^3}$	$U_A := u_0 u_1^{h_A} u_2^{h_A^2} u_3^{h_A^3}$	$U_A := u_0 u_1^{h_A} u_2^{h_A^2} u_3^{h_A^3}$
$U_C := u_0 u_1^{h_C} u_2^{h_C^2} u_3^{h_C^3}$	$U_C := u_0 u_1^{h_C} u_2^{h_C^2} u_3^{h_C^3}$	$U_B := u_0 u_1^{h_B} u_2^{h_B^2} u_3^{h_B^3}$
$U_Y := u_0 u_1^{h_Y} u_2^{h_Y^2} u_3^{h_Y^3}$	$U_X := u_0 u_1^{h_X} u_2^{h_X^2} u_3^{h_X^3}$	$U_X := u_0 u_1^{h_X} u_2^{h_X^2} u_3^{h_X^3}$
$U_Z := u_0 u_1^{h_Z} u_2^{h_Z^2} u_3^{h_Z^3}$	$U_Z := u_0 u_1^{h_Z} u_2^{h_Z^2} u_3^{h_Z^3}$	$U_Y := u_0 u_1^{h_Y} u_2^{h_Y^2} u_3^{h_Y^3}$
reject if either	reject if either	reject if either
$e(t_B, g) \neq e(U_B, B)$ *or*	$e(t_A, g) \neq e(U_A, A)$ *or*	$e(t_A, g) \neq e(U_A, A)$ *or*
$e(t_C, g) \neq e(U_C, C)$ *or*	$e(t_C, g) \neq e(U_C, C)$ *or*	$e(t_B, g) \neq e(U_B, B)$ *or*
$e(t_Y, g) \neq e(U_Y, Y)$ *or*	$e(t_X, g) \neq e(U_X, X)$ *or*	$e(t_X, g) \neq e(U_X, X)$ *or*
$e(t_Z, g) \neq e(U_Z, Z)$	$e(t_Z, g) \neq e(U_Z, Z)$	$e(t_Y, g) \neq e(U_Y, Y)$
Each party has $\mathsf{sid} := \hat{A} \| A \| t_A \| X \| t_X \| \hat{B} \| B \| t_B \| Y \| t_Y \| \hat{C} \| C \| t_C \| Z \| t_Z$		
Each party rejects if some values recorded in sid are identical		
$k := e(BY, CZ)^{a+x}$	$k := e(AX, CZ)^{b+y}$	$k := e(AX, BY)^{c+z}$
$k_e := \mathsf{PRF}(k, sid)$	$k_e := \mathsf{PRF}(k, sid)$	$k_e := \mathsf{PRF}(k, sid)$

Fig. 1. One-round Tripartite AKE Protocol

Long-term Key Generation and Registration: On input pms, a party $\hat{A}$ may run an efficient algorithm $(sk_{\hat{A}}, pk_{\hat{A}}, \emptyset) \stackrel{\$}{\leftarrow} \mathsf{ORGAKE.KGen}(pms, \hat{A})$ to generate the long-term key pair as: $sk_{\hat{A}} = a \stackrel{\$}{\leftarrow} \mathbb{Z}_p^*, pk_{\hat{A}} = (A, t_A)$ where $A = g^a$, $t_A := (u_0 u_1^{h_A} u_2^{h_A^2} u_3^{h_A^3})^a$ and $h_A = \mathsf{TCRHF}(A)$. Please note that we allow arbitrary key registration, i.e. the adversary is able to query $\mathsf{RegisterCorrupt}(\hat{A}, pk_{\hat{A}}, \emptyset)$ with $\mathsf{proof}_{\hat{A}} = \emptyset$.

Protocol Execution: On input pms, the protocol among parties $\hat{A}$, $\hat{B}$ and $\hat{C}$ is depicted in the Figure 1.

Implementation and Session States: We assume that the maximum states of party $\hat{A}$ allowing for leakage consist of ephemeral private key x (resp. y and z for parties $\hat{B}$ and $\hat{C}$) – namely those values would be stored in the state variable st of each oracle at any time. For example this can be guaranteed by performing the computations for k and k_e on secure device. Note that the all pairing operations including $e(BY, CZ)$ can be done on host machine.

We notice that a party $\hat{A}$ has to do consistency check on long-term key in every sessions that might be wasteful. An alternative solution could make the Certificate Authority to check the consistency of long-term public key during key registration procedure. In this way, it might reduce two pairing operations for protocol execution and also the number of public key. To register a public key $pk_{\hat{A}} = A$, each party $\hat{A}$ should at least prove the consistency via tag t_A. Then the public key A is registered if $e(t_A, g) = e(A, u_0 u_1^{h_A} u_2^{h_A^2} u_3^{h_A^3})$. Thus this check would be done only once at CA. The downside of this approach is that it might increase the burden of CA. In particular, the tag t_A is required while querying the $\mathsf{RegisterCorrupt}(\hat{A}, pk_{\hat{A}}, \mathsf{proof}_{\hat{A}})$ in the security game, i.e. $\mathsf{proof}_{\hat{A}} = t_A$.

5.2 Security Analysis

We show the security of proposed protocol in the g-eCK model.

Theorem 1. *Assume each ephemeral key chosen during key exchange has bit-size $\lambda \in \mathbb{N}$. Suppose that the* CBDDH *problem is $(t, \epsilon_{\mathsf{CBDDH}})$-hard in the symmetric bilinear groups $\mathcal{PG}$, the* TCRHF *is $(t, \epsilon_{\mathsf{TCRHF}})$-secure target collision resistant hash function family, and the* PRF *is $(q, t, \epsilon_{\mathsf{PRF}})$-secure pseudo-random function family. Then the proposed protocol is (t', ϵ)-session-key-secure in the sense of Definition 8 with $t' \approx t$, $q \geq 3$ and $\epsilon \leq \frac{(\rho\ell)^2}{2^\lambda} + \epsilon_{\mathsf{TCRHF}} + 4(\rho\ell)^3 \cdot (\epsilon_{\mathsf{CBDDH}} + \epsilon_{\mathsf{PRF}})$.*

Proof sketch. We give a brief sketch of the proof of Theorem 1 (more details can be found in [16]). It is straightforward to see that two oracles accept with matching sessions would compute the same session key. Namely the proposed protocol is correct. In the sequel, we wish to show that the adversary is unable to distinguish random value from the session key of any fresh oracle.

To complete the proof of Theorem 1, we only need to prove the advantage of the adversary is negligible under target freshness cases $C1$, $C9$, $C13$ and $C14$, due to the reductions in Section 4. The proof proceeds in a sequence of games, following [20]. Let S_δ be the event that the adversary wins the security experiment in Game G_δ under freshness cases in $\{C1, C9, C13, C14\}$. Let $\mathsf{Adv}_\delta := \Pr[\mathsf{S}_\delta] - 1/2$ denote the advantage of $\mathcal{A}$ in Game G_δ.

Game G_0. This is the original game with adversary $\mathcal{A}$. The system parameters are chosen honestly by challenger as protocol specification. Thus we have that $\Pr[\mathsf{S}_0] = 1/2 + \epsilon = 1/2 + \mathsf{Adv}_0$.

Game G_1. In this game, the challenger aborts, if during the simulation an ephemeral key replied by an oracle π_i^s but it has been sample by another oracle or sent by adversary before. We have that $\mathsf{Adv}_0 \leq \mathsf{Adv}_1 + \frac{(\rho\ell)^2}{2^\lambda}$.

Game G_2. In this game, the challenger aborts if two oracles output the same hash value of TCRHF. Thus we have $\mathsf{Adv}_1 \leq \mathsf{Adv}_2 + \epsilon_{\mathsf{TCRHF}}$.

Game G_3. This game proceeds as previous game, but $\mathcal{C}$ aborts if one of the following guesses fails: (i) the freshness case occurred to test oracle from the set $\{C1, C9, C13, C14\}$, (ii) the test oracle, (iii) its partner parties, and (iv) corresponding oracles (if any) each of which has a matching session to test oracle, in terms of specific guessed freshness case. Since there are four considered fresh cases, ℓ parties and at most ρ oracles for each party, then the probability that all above guesses of $\mathcal{C}$ are correct is at least $1/4(\rho\ell)^3$. Thus we have that $\mathsf{Adv}_2 \leq 4(\rho\ell)^3 \cdot \mathsf{Adv}_3$. Please note that there are at least three uncompromised (either long-term and ephemeral) Diffie-Hellman keys which are used by test oracle to generate its key material k^*, as otherwise the test oracle is not g-eCK-fresh any more. We call such guessed three uncompromised DH keys as *target DH keys*.

Game G_4. Technically, this game is proceeded as previous game, but the challenger $\mathcal{C}$ replaces the key material k_i^s with random value $\widetilde{k_i^s}$ for oracles $\{\pi_i^s : i \in [\ell], s \in [\rho]\}$ which satisfy the following conditions: (i) The k_i^s is computed involving the three *target DH keys*, and (ii) Those *target DH keys* used by π_i^s are from three distinct parties. If there exists an adversary $\mathcal{A}$ can distinguish the Game G_4 from Game G_3 then we can make use of it to solve the CBDDH problem. We therefore obtain that $\mathsf{Adv}_3 \leq \mathsf{Adv}_4 + \epsilon_{\mathsf{CBDDH}}$.

Game G_5. In this game, we change function $\mathsf{PRF}(\widetilde{k^*}, \cdot)$ to a truly random function for test oracle and its partner oracles (if they exist). Thus we have that $\mathsf{Adv}_4 \leq \mathsf{Adv}_5 + \epsilon_{\mathsf{PRF}}$ due to the security of PRF. Note that in this game the session key returned by Test-query is totally a truly random value which is independent to the bit b and any messages. Thus the advantage that the adversary wins this game is $\mathsf{Adv}_5 = 0$. Sum up the probabilities from Game G_0 to Game G_5, we proved this theorem.

6 A GAKE Construction from Multilinear Maps

An interesting work is to extend the proposed 3AKE scheme to GAKE scheme with more than three group members. Based on bilinear groups might be impossible to achieve so. Since we can not get an aggregate long-term shared key for a group of members from bilinear map. However, Boneh and Silverberg [6] have given us inspiration on how to generalize the 3AKE to GAKE by exploiting multilinear maps.

6.1 Protocol Description

Setup: The proposed GAKE protocol takes as input the following building blocks which are initialized respectively in terms of the security parameter $\kappa \in \mathbb{N}$ and upper-bound of number of users $n+1$: (i) n-mulitilinear groups $\mathcal{MLG} = (\mathbb{G}, \mathbb{G}_T, g, p, me) \stackrel{\$}{\leftarrow} \mathsf{MLG.Gen}(\kappa, n)$ and a set of random values $\{u_j\}_{0 \le j \le n+1} \stackrel{\$}{\leftarrow} \mathbb{G}$; (ii) a target collision resistant hash function $\mathsf{TCRHF}(hk_{\mathsf{TCRHF}}, \cdot) : \mathcal{K}_{\mathsf{TCRHF}} \times \mathbb{G} \to \mathbb{Z}_p$, where $hk_{\mathsf{TCRHF}} \stackrel{\$}{\leftarrow}$
$\mathsf{TCRHF.KG}(1^\kappa)$; and (iii) a pseudo-random function family $\mathsf{PRF}(\cdot,\cdot) : \mathbb{G}_T \times \{0,1\}^* \to \mathcal{K}_{\mathsf{AKE}}$. Let $pms := (\mathcal{MLG}, \{u_j\}_{0 \le j \le n+1}, hk_{\mathsf{TCRHF}})$ be the variable used to store the public system parameters.
Long-term Key Generation and Registration: On input pms, a party $\hat{A}$ may run an efficient algorithm $(sk_{\hat{D}}, pk_{\hat{D}}, \emptyset) \stackrel{\$}{\leftarrow} \mathsf{ORGAKE.KGen}(pms, \hat{D})$ to generate the long-term key pair for a party $\hat{D}$ as: $sk_{\hat{D}} = d \stackrel{\$}{\leftarrow} \mathbb{Z}_p^*, pk_{\hat{D}} = (D, t_D)$, where $D = g^a$, $t_D := \prod_{j=0}^{n+1} u_j^{h_D^j}$ and $h_A = \mathsf{TCRHF}(A)$. Please note that we allow arbitrary key registration.

Let ω denote the size of group for a protocol instance such that $2 \le \omega \le n+1$. An important attribute for a GAKE protocol is the scalable group size. In the following we show our construction for protocol execution phase which is scalable with range between 2 and $n+1$.
Protocol Execution: We consider the protocol execution for a protocol instance with ω group members denoted by $(\hat{D}_1, \hat{D}_2, \ldots, \hat{D}_\omega)$, where each party $\hat{D}_i$ $(1 \le i \le \omega)$ has long-term key D_i. In the key exchange phase, each party $\hat{D}_i$ generates an ephemeral key $X_i = g^{x_i}$, computes tag $t_{X_i} := \prod_{j=0}^{n+1} u_j^{h_{X_i}^j}$ and broadcasts $(\hat{D}_i, D_i, t_{D_i}, X_i, t_{X_i})$ to its intended communication partners, where $x_i \stackrel{\$}{\leftarrow} \mathbb{Z}_p^*$ and $h_{X_i} := \mathsf{TCRHF}(X_i)$. Upon receiving all messages $\{\hat{D}_l, D_l, t_{D_l}, X_l, t_{X_l}\}_{1 \le l \le \omega, l \ne i}$ from each session participant, the party $\hat{D}_i$ rejects the session if the consistency check on one of the received either long-term or ephemeral keys fails, i.e. $me(t_{W_l}, g, \ldots, g) \ne me(\prod_{j=0}^{n+1} u_j^{h_{W_l}^j}, W_l, g, \ldots, g)$ where $W_l \in \{D_l, X_l\}$ for $1 \le l \le \omega, l \ne i$ and $h_{W_l} = \mathsf{TCRHF}(W_l)$. The party $\hat{D}_i$ sets $\mathsf{sid} := \hat{D}_1 || D_1 || t_{D_1} || X_1 || t_{X_1} || \ldots || \hat{D}_\omega || D_\omega || t_{D_\omega} || X_\omega || t_{X_\omega}$, and rejects the session if some values recorded in sid are identical. To this end, the party $\hat{D}_i$ generates the key material $k := me(D_1X_1, \ldots, D_{i-1}X_{i-1}, D_{i+1}X_{i+1}, \ldots, D_\omega X_\omega, \ldots, D_\omega X_\omega)^{d_i + x_i}$ and session key $k_e := \mathsf{PRF}(k, \mathsf{sid})$, where the values $D_0, X_0, D_{\omega+1}, X_{\omega+1}$ are 'empty' which should be omitted. Other parties in this group will do the similar procedures to generate the session key.

Please note that the scalability is achieved generally by setting all Diffie-Hellman keys after the position ω in n-multilinear map me to be $D_\omega X_\omega$. This is possible since at least one DH key in (D_ω, X_ω) is not compromised by adversary

in the security game. As otherwise such session is no longer fresh in terms of Definition 7.
Implementation and Session States: We assume that the maximum states of party $\hat{D}_i$ allowing for leakage from a session consist of ephemeral private key x_i – namely those values would be stored in the variable in the state variable st of each oracle at any time. The implementation scenario is similar to the three party case presented in Section 5.

6.2 Security Analysis

We show the security of above group AKE protocol in the g-eCK model.

Theorem 2. *Assume each ephemeral key chosen during key exchange has bit-size* $\lambda \in \mathbb{N}$. *Suppose that the* nMDDH *problem is* $(t, \epsilon_{\mathsf{nMDDH}})$*-hard in the symmetric multilinear groups* $\mathcal{MLG}$, *the* TCRHF *is* $(t, \epsilon_{\mathsf{TCRHF}})$*-secure target collision resistant hash function family, and the* PRF *is* $(q, t, \epsilon_{\mathsf{PRF}})$*-secure pseudo-random function family. Then the proposed protocol of size* $2 \leq \omega \leq n+1 \leq \ell$ *is* (t', ϵ)*-g-eCK-secure in the sense of Definition 8 with* $t' \approx t$, $q \geq n+1$ *and* $\epsilon \leq \frac{(\rho\ell)^2}{2^\lambda} + \epsilon_{\mathsf{TCRHF}} + (n+2)(\rho)^{n+1}\binom{\ell}{n+1} \cdot (\epsilon_{\mathsf{nMDDH}} + \epsilon_{\mathsf{PRF}})$.

The proof of theorem 2 is presented in the full version of this paper [16]. We lose a factor $(n+2)(\rho)^{n+1}\binom{\ell}{n+1}$ here which is exponential in group size n. Hence, in order to make the overall advantage of adversary to be negligible, one may need to use a larger security parameter or to limit the maximum group members.

Acknowledgments. We would like to thank the anonymous reviewers of CANS 2013 for their helpful comments.

References

1. Al-Riyami, S.S., Paterson, K.G.: Tripartite authenticated key agreement protocols from pairings. In: Paterson, K.G. (ed.) Cryptography and Coding 2003. LNCS, vol. 2898, pp. 332–359. Springer, Heidelberg (2003)
2. Baek, J., Safavi-Naini, R., Susilo, W.: Efficient multi-receiver identity-based encryption and its application to broadcast encryption. In: Vaudenay, S. (ed.) PKC 2005. LNCS, vol. 3386, pp. 380–397. Springer, Heidelberg (2005)
3. Bellare, M., Boldyreva, A., Palacio, A.: An uninstantiable random-oracle-model scheme for a hybrid-encryption problem. In: Cachin, C., Camenisch, J. (eds.) EUROCRYPT 2004. LNCS, vol. 3027, pp. 171–188. Springer, Heidelberg (2004)
4. Bellare, M., Rogaway, P.: Random oracles are practical: A paradigm for designing efficient protocols. In: Ashby, V. (ed.) ACM CCS 1993: 1st Conference on Computer and Communications Security, pp. 62–73. ACM Press (November 1993)
5. Bellare, M., Rogaway, P.: Entity authentication and key distribution. In: Stinson, D.R. (ed.) CRYPTO 1993. LNCS, vol. 773, pp. 232–249. Springer, Heidelberg (1994)
6. Boneh, D., Silverberg, A.: Applications of multilinear forms to cryptography. IACR Cryptology ePrint Archive, Report 2002/80 (2002), `http://eprint.iacr.org/`

7. Bresson, E., Chevassut, O., Pointcheval, D.: Dynamic group Diffie-Hellman key exchange under standard assumptions. In: Knudsen, L.R. (ed.) EUROCRYPT 2002. LNCS, vol. 2332, pp. 321–336. Springer, Heidelberg (2002)
8. Bresson, E., Chevassut, O., Pointcheval, D., Quisquater, J.-J.: Provably authenticated group Diffie-Hellman key exchange. In: ACM CCS 2001: Conference on Computer and Communications Security, pp. 255–264. ACM Press (November 2001)
9. Canetti, R., Goldreich, O., Halevi, S.: The random oracle methodology, revisited (preliminary version). In: 30th Annual ACM Symposium on Theory of Computing, pp. 209–218. ACM Press (May 1998)
10. Fujioka, A., Manulis, M., Suzuki, K., Ustaoğlu, B.: Sufficient condition for ephemeral key-leakage resilient tripartite key exchange. In: Susilo, W., Mu, Y., Seberry, J. (eds.) ACISP 2012. LNCS, vol. 7372, pp. 15–28. Springer, Heidelberg (2012)
11. Garg, S., Gentry, C., Halevi, S.: Candidate multilinear maps from ideal lattices. In: Johansson, T., Nguyen, P.Q. (eds.) EUROCRYPT 2013. LNCS, vol. 7881, pp. 1–17. Springer, Heidelberg (2013)
12. Gorantla, M.C., Boyd, C., González Nieto, J.M.: Modeling key compromise impersonation attacks on group key exchange protocols. In: Jarecki, S., Tsudik, G. (eds.) PKC 2009. LNCS, vol. 5443, pp. 105–123. Springer, Heidelberg (2009)
13. Hofheinz, D., Jager, T., Kiltz, E.: Short signatures from weaker assumptions. In: Lee, D.H., Wang, X. (eds.) ASIACRYPT 2011. LNCS, vol. 7073, pp. 647–666. Springer, Heidelberg (2011)
14. Joux, A.: A one round protocol for tripartite diffie-hellman. In: Bosma, W. (ed.) ANTS-IV 2000. LNCS, vol. 1838, pp. 385–394. Springer, Heidelberg (2000)
15. LaMacchia, B.A., Lauter, K., Mityagin, A.: Stronger security of authenticated key exchange. In: Susilo, W., Liu, J.K., Mu, Y. (eds.) ProvSec 2007. LNCS, vol. 4784, pp. 1–16. Springer, Heidelberg (2007)
16. Li, Y., Yang, Z.: Strongly secure one-round group authenticated key exchange in the standard model. In: Abdalla, M., Nita-Rotaru, C., Dahab, R. (eds.) CANS 2013. LNCS, vol. 8257, pp. 123–142. Springer, Heidelberg (2013)
17. Lim, M.-H., Lee, S., Park, Y., Lee, H.: An enhanced one-round pairing-based tripartite authenticated key agreement protocol. In: Gervasi, O., Gavrilova, M.L. (eds.) ICCSA 2007, Part II. LNCS, vol. 4706, pp. 503–513. Springer, Heidelberg (2007)
18. Manulis, M., Suzuki, K., Ustaoglu, B.: Modeling leakage of ephemeral secrets in tripartite/group key exchange. In: Lee, D., Hong, S. (eds.) ICISC 2009. LNCS, vol. 5984, pp. 16–33. Springer, Heidelberg (2010)
19. Shoup, V.: Lower bounds for discrete logarithms and related problems. In: Fumy, W. (ed.) EUROCRYPT 1997. LNCS, vol. 1233, pp. 256–266. Springer, Heidelberg (1997)
20. Shoup, V.: Sequences of games: a tool for taming complexity in security proofs. Cryptology ePrint Archive, Report 2004/332 (2004), `http://eprint.iacr.org/`

Achieving Correctness in Fair Rational Secret Sharing

Sourya Joyee De and Asim K. Pal

Management Information Systems Group,
Indian Institute of Management Calcutta, India

Abstract. In rational secret sharing, parties may prefer to mislead others in believing a wrong secret as the correct one over everybody obtaining the secret (i.e. a fair outcome). Prior rational secret reconstruction protocols for non-simultaneous channel only address the case where a fair outcome is preferred over misleading and hence are fair but not correct. Asharov and Lindell (2010) proposed the first and the only protocol that takes care of both the preferences. In this paper, we propose a new rational secret sharing protocol that addresses both the preferences and is fair and correct in the non-simultaneous channel model. Additionally, it is independent of the utility of misleading. Each rational party is given a list of sub-shares of shares of the actual secret and fake shares. In each round of the protocol each party sends the current element in its list to the other party and then reconstructs a share from the sub-shares obtained. The main idea is to use a checking share which is a share of the original secret as a protocol–induced membership auxiliary information to check whether the shares obtained till a certain round can be used to reconstruct the correct secret. We overcome the disadvantages of the presence of auxiliary information by using the time-delayed encryption scheme used by the protocol of Lysyanskaya and Segal (2010) that tolerates players with arbitrary side information. In our case, the side information used is not arbitrary but introduced by the mechanism/protocol designer to put all players on equal footing. We show that our protocol is in computational strict Nash equilibrium in the presence of protocol-induced auxiliary information.

1 Introduction

Since the introduction of the concept of rational players in (t, n) threshold secret sharing by [6], the area which henceforth came to be known as rational secret sharing (RSS) and its application in secure multiparty computation (known as rational multi-party computation or RMPC) has attracted a lot of fruitful research [1, 2, 5, 7–9, 13, 15–17, 19–21]. Briefly, the RSS problem is as follows. Each of n players $P_1, P_2, \ldots, P_n$ is given a share of a secret s by a dealer. The secret can be reconstructed if at least any t of them cooperate. However, the point of contention is that each player wishes to learn the secret himself while allowing as few others as possible to learn the correct value. What strategy will each player need to adopt so that each player comes to know the secret?

M. Abdalla, C. Nita-Rotaru, and R. Dahab (Eds.): CANS 2013, LNCS 8257, pp. 139–161, 2013.

Inherent to the RSS problem is the problem of achieving fairness. Each player wants to obtain the secret alone and is unfair to others i.e. for each player, the utility of obtaining the secret alone (U^{TN}) is the maximum. The other utilities of a rational party are that of everybody obtaining the secret (U^{TT}), that of nobody obtaining the secret (U^{NN}) and that of everybody else obtaining the secret (U^{NT}). So each player has a preference of $U^{TN} > U^{TT} > U^{NN} > U^{NT}$. The desirable outcome of the secret reconstruction game is the fair one in which everybody obtains the secret. A rational secret reconstruction scheme or protocol is a strategy for each player suggested by the protocol designer such that this fair outcome can be obtained and there is no incentive for any player to deviate from this strategy. Nash equilibrium and its variants (computational Nash, strict Nash etc) are the most used equilibrium concepts in this context. Much of the RSS literature [2, 6, 15, 21] focusses on obtaining fair rational secret reconstruction mechanisms under different assumptions such as the type of communication channel present (simultaneous/ non-simultaneous) or the nature of the dealer (online/offline). We present a brief comparative summary of such protocols in Table 1. The basic assumption about the preference $U^{TN} > U^{TT} > U^{NN} > U^{NT}$ of rational players is common to all the RSS protocols proposed so far (hence, we do not mention this separately in Table 1). In some cases, there are some special assumptions (which we mention in Table 1, under 'Special Preferences ') about the nature of players (for eg., [16] assumes a rational majority along with a minority of honest players) and their preferences. These special preferences are related to the correctness of the secret obtained ([2]).

Parties in a rational secret reconstruction mechanism may often be considered to derive some positive utility from misleading other players into believing a wrong value to be the correct secret when it itself obtains nothing (U^{NF}). A fair reconstruction protocol gives the utility of U^{TT} to each player. Therefore it is also correct as long as $U^{NF} < U^{TT}$. However, when parties prefer misleading others over everybody obtaining the correct secret (i.e. $U^{NF} \geq U^{TT}$), a fair rational secret reconstruction protocol for the non-simultaneous channel model does not remain correct (we shall soon discuss why this is so). Unfortunately, this problem has received very little attention from researchers and this can be easily identified from Table 1. [2] proposed the first and the only correct and fair rational secret reconstruction protocol for the case when both scenarios may hold in the $(2, 2)$ setting. Prior to their work, all works on rational secret sharing either assumed the existence of simultaneous broadcast channel [5, 6] (where this problem does not exist) or assumed that rational parties prefer everybody to obtain the output of the protocol than misleading others [9, 15, 21]. We therefore aim to design a correct and fair rational secret reconstruction protcol in the non-simultaneous channel.

A desirable property of any rational secret reconstruction scheme is utility-independence. If a particular RSS scheme is dependent on utility values of players then it requires the protocol designer to be able to accurately estimate the utility values or at least the range of these values in order to set the appropriate parameters during the execution of that RSS scheme. The work of [2] has extensively dealt with the property of utility-independence. It proposes a (t, n) (where $n \geq 3$,

$2 < t \leq n$) rational secret reconstruction protocol which is completely utility-independent (i.e. the protocol designer is not required to know any utility value) in the simultaneous channel model. However, [2] also showed that, in the non-simultaneous channel model, there does not exist any $(2, 2)$ fair rational secret reconstruction protocol that is independent of the utility value U^{NF}. Consequently, the $(2, 2)$ correct and fair rational secret reconstruction protocol they suggest in the non-simultaneous channel, although correct even when $U^{NF} \geq U^{TT}$, is U^{NF} utility–dependent. In this paper we remove this utility dependency. So the basic question that we address here is whether it is possible to have a rational secret reconstruction protocol that is both correct and fair even when $U^{NF} \geq U^{TT}$ and given that, whether it is possible to achieve U^{NF}–independence for such a protocol. We propose a $(2, 2)$ fair rational secret reconstruction mechanism in the non-simultaneous channel that is 1) correct even if rational parties prefer to mislead others i.e. $U^{NF} \geq U^{TT}$ and 2) U^{NF}–independent. We also suggest its extension to the (t, n) setting. However, like the protocol of [2], our protocol is dependent on other utility values such as U^{TN}, U^{TT} and U^{NN}. In many scenarios, the act of misleading can be potentially more harmful than the act of selfishness. If a protocol designer wrongly estimates the U^{NF} utility values, the execution of a correct and fair RSS protocol may still result in some of the parties being misled due to the wrongly estimated parameter. Moreover, we believe that estimation of U^{NF} is more difficult than that of U^{TN}, U^{TT} or U^{NN}. The impact of knowing the correct value of a secret is more well–understood than that of believing in a wrong value as the correct one. The existence of a U^{NF}–independent correct and fair rational secret reconstruction protocol is therefore advantageous even if it is dependent on other utility values.

Until now, a general pattern for a rational secret sharing scheme has been the following. Each party gets from the dealer a list of shares, one of which is that of the actual secret and the remaining of fake secrets. The position of this actual share is not known to the players beforehand. This position is chosen according to a geometric distribution $\mathcal{G}(\beta)$, where the parameter β in turn depends on the utility values. In each round of communication, players (either simultaneously or non-simultaneously) broadcast or send individually to each of the other players (in absence of broadcast channel) the current share in its list. The shares are signed by the honest dealer, so no player can give out false shares undetected and the only possible actions in a round are to 1) send the message or 2) remain silent. The round in which the shares of the actual secret are revealed and hence the secret is reconstructed is called the revelation/definitive round. The players are made aware that they have crossed the revelation round by the reconstruction/exchange of an indicator (a bit in [9], a signal in [15]) in the subsequent round. In case of non-simultaneous channels, the indicator cannot be reconstructed/interpreted, as the player who is to communicate last in this round already knows that the round before was the revelation round (because he has the indicator) and quits the protocol immediately without sending messages (shares/signals as the case may be) further. When the deviating player quits, other players also conclude that the secret has been reconstructed in the last round.

Basically, when a party quits in any round, there can be two scenarios: 1) the party quits because it has already obtained the secret and 2) the party quits because it wants others to believe that the secret has been obtained when in reality it is not so. In secret reconstruction protocols for non-simultaneous channels, we see that, whenever a party aborts, the other party assumes that this abortion signifies that the former has obtained its output and hence it also outputs the value obtained in the last round[1]. There is no way for the non-deviating party to verify whether this is actually the revelation round i.e. to find out whether scenario (1) holds or scenario (2). This gives rise to the outcome where one party is misled to believe in a false secret as the actual secret whereas the other party gets nothing. Herein arises the question of correctness of protocol output for fair rational secret reconstruction. The means to restore fairness described so far is fine if it is known that parties have the preference $U^{NF} < U^{TT}$. On the other hand if parties have the preference $U^{NF} \geq U^{TT}$, this way of achieving fairness jeopardizes correctness. [2] achieves the solution to this problem by introducing special fake rounds called completely fake rounds (apart from the normal fake rounds that enable fair secret reconstruction) such that the first player to send a share knows which rounds are the special fake rounds and if the second player, who is unaware of this information, halts to pretend that the end of the list has been reached in any of the completely fake rounds then the first player knows that the other party has cheated. However, this protocol is dependent on the value of U^{NF}. Specifically, with probability α a particular round is a completely fake round and with probability $(1 - \alpha)$ it is not. Then for a player to follow the suggested strategy, it can be easily shown that $\alpha < (U^{TT} - U^{NN})/(U^{NF} - U^{NN})$. The dependence of the correctness of their protocol on the value of α introduces utility-dependence. In comparison, we do not use any such parameter. For our protocol to be correct, we take help of auxiliary information introduced by the protocol designer to allow players to check whether the secret reconstructed by them is correct or not. Since the auxiliary information does not depend on any utility values our protocol is U^{NF}–independent [2].

[1] In fact, this seems to be a widely used concept for restoring fairness when another party aborts prematurely. In his work on Oblivious Transfer, one of the most important cryptographic primitives used in secure computation, Rabin [23] had implicitly suggested this general notion of achieving fairness: the design of a protocol to ensure fairness is such that the very act of aborting by one party should reveal crucial information to the other party which helps it to restore fairness. Gordon who observed this in [24] says that this concept turns out to be very similar to the one they use in their work on complete fairness in secure computation with malicious adversary. Specifically, in their protocol for complete fairness in two-party computation of functions over polynomial-sized domains and without an embedded XOR, if the malicious adversary aborts in any round, then the honest party gets information about the adversary's input in the computation and can compute the value of the function itself, restoring fairness.

[2] Our protocol is only U^{NF}–independent because for maintaining fairness we still use a geometric distribution $\mathcal{G}(\beta)$ where β depends on U^{TN}, U^{TT} and U^{NN}.

Table 1. A Comparison of the Characteristics of Rational Secret Reconstruction Mechanisms

RSS Protocols	Special Preferences	Channel/Dealer Charateristics	Properties
Halpern & Teague (2004) [6]		Simultaneous Broadcast; Online Dealer	Valid for $n \geq 3$; Unconditional
Gordon & Katz (2006) [5]		Simultaneous Broadcast; Online Dealer	Valid for $n \geq 2$; Unconditional
Kol & Naor (two protocols) (2008) [9]	$U^{TT} > U^{NF}$	1)Simultaneous broadcast; 2) Non-Simultaneous Broadcast; Offline Dealer	Fair but not correct for $U^{NF} \geq U^{TT}$ in non-simultaneous case; Unconditional; $(2,2)$, t-out-of-n
Ong et al. (2009) [16]	Majority: Rational; Minority: Honest	Non-Simultaneous Broadcast; Offline Dealer	Unconditional; only 2 rounds of communication
Asharov & Lindell (2010) [2]; two protocols	2) $U^{TT} > U^{NF}$ & $U^{NF} \geq U^{TT}$	1) Simultaneous Broadcast; Online Dealer; 2) Non-simultaneous; Offline Dealer	Complete utility independence for $n \geq 3$; Unconditional; First to achieve both correctness and fairness in non-simultaneous channel (with U^{NF} dependence). Also proved impossibility of fair reconstruction protocol in presence of side information. Proved impossibility of U^{NF} independence in non-simultaneous channel for $(2,2)$ case.
Fuchsbauer et al. (2010) [15]; three protocols	$U^{TT} > U^{NF}$	1) Non-simultaneous, 2) point-to-point, Synchronous 3) Asynchronous; Offline Dealer	$(2,2)$; exactly t-out-of-n; Verifiable Random Function (VRF)
Lysyanskaya & Segal (2010) [21]	$U^{TT} > U^{NF}$	Non-simultaneous, point-to-point, synchronous; Offline Dealer	First fair reconstruction protocol in presence of arbitrary side information; (n,n) case; Use of Time Delayed Encryption (TDE) and VRF
Proposed protocol	$U^{TT} > U^{NF}$ & $U^{NF} \geq U^{TT}$	Non-Simultaneous Broadcast; Offline Dealer	U^{NF} independence; $(2,2)$. (t,n) cases; Use of TDE; Uses protocol generated side information.

Our Contributions. Rational parties preferring to mislead others over everybody knowing the correct output may be quite common. When a piece of secret information is to be revealed, then a rational player who believes that others may have the ability to derive a greater benefit from the information than he can, may decide that it is better to mislead others with wrong information even if that means not getting the correct information himself rather than everyone getting the correct information. However, this scenario has received very little attention from researchers till now. In this work we propose a new (2, 2) correct and fair rational secret sharing protocol for non-simultaneous channels even if rational parties prefer to mislead and it is in computational strict Nash equilibrium in the presence of protocol-induced auxiliary information. The uniqueness of our protocol is that it is independent of a rational party's utility of misleading. The only other protocol suggested in this scenario [2] is dependent on this utility. We also suggest generalization of our protocol to the (t, n) settings. We allow each party to possess protocol-induced auxiliary information in the form of a checking share to be able to check whether the last round was indeed a revelation round. So even after one party aborts, the other party is armed to check whether he has been misled. This in turn causes no party to have any incentive to deviate from the protocol by aborting arbitrarily, before it has obtained the output. The introduction of auxiliary information has its problems which we combat using the time delayed encryption scheme based on cryptographic memory bound functions as proposed in [21].

Organization of the Paper. The paper is organized as follows: in section 2 we formally introduce the nature of parties and the concepts of fairness and correctness and the role of auxiliary information that we use for further discussions; in section 3 we provide an overview of our protocol, discuss about protocol-induced membership-auxiliary information, checking shares, time delayed encryption and the equilibrium concept used in our protocol and then formally present our protocol for rational secret sharing, followed by an analysis of the protocol. In section 4 we suggest extenstion to (t, n) setting and in section 5, we perform complexity analysis. Finally we conclude in section 6.

2 Preliminaries

2.1 Rational Secret Sharing and the Preference of Rational Players

Shamir's (t, n) secret sharing scheme [11] is used to distribute the shares of a secret among n players such that the secret can be reconstructed only when at least t of them cooperate. In the first phase of such a scheme, called the secret sharing phase, a dealer generates n shares $s_1, \ldots, s_n$ of the original secret s and distributes one share to each of the players. In the next phase, called the secret reconstruction phase, the players exchange their shares. If at least t players cooperate in this phase then the secret can be reconstructed. An adversary controlling less than t players cannot reconstruct the secret. In this scenario, the notion of rational players instead of honest players and players controlled by an adversary was introduced in [6]. They pointed out that if players are rational and have specific preferences such as getting the secret itself and allowing as few others possible know the secret, then no player will ever send his share during the reconstruction phase.

A (t, n) rational secret reconstruction protocol $(\Gamma, \overrightarrow{\sigma})_{t,n}$ (where $\overrightarrow{\sigma}=(\sigma_1, \ldots, \sigma_n)$ denotes the strategies followed by the players) may have different outcomes where an outcome is denoted by $\overrightarrow{o((\Gamma, \overrightarrow{\sigma})_{t,n})}=(o_1, \ldots, o_n)$. The utility function

u_i of each party P_i is defined over the set of possible outcomes of the game and are polynomial in the security parameter k. Thus $U_i^{TN} = u_i(1^k, (o_i = s, o_j = \perp))$, $U_i^{TT} = u_i(1^k, (o_i = s, o_j = s))$ (where $i \neq j$) and so on. Different outcomes of the game may result due to the different preferences of each party. Table 2 [3] describes the possible outcomes and corresponding utilities for t=n=2 and any arbitrary alternative strategy σ_i^{dev} and the suggested strategy σ_i corresponding to a party P_i, $(i = 1, 2)$.

Table 2. Outcomes and Utilities for $(2, 2)$ rational secret reconstruction

P_1's outcome (o_1)	P_2's outcome (o_2)	P_1's Utility $U_1(o_1, o_2)$	P_2's Utility $U_2(o_1, o_2)$
o_1=s	o_2=s	$U_1^{TT}(U_1)$	$U_2^{TT}(U_2)$
o_1=$\perp$	o_2=$\perp$	$U_1^{NN}(U_1^-)$	$U_2^{NN}(U_2^-)$
o_1=s	o_2=$\perp$	$U_1^{TN}(U_1^+)$	$U_2^{NT}(U_2^{--})$
o_1=$\perp$	o_2=s	$U_1^{NT}(U_1^{--})$	$U_2^{TN}(U_2^+)$
o_1=$\perp$	$o_2 \notin \{s, \perp\}$	$U_1^{NF}(U_1^f)$	U_2^{FN}
$o_1 \notin \{s, \perp\}$	o_2=$\perp$	U_1^{FN}	$U_2^{NF}(U_2^f)$

There can be other combinations of the outcomes mentioned in the table, other outcomes and corresponding utilities too but we shall consider only the above. Players have their preferences based on the different possible outcomes. We shall refer to the following preference relationships of a party P_i throughout our paper:

1. $\mathcal{R}_1 : U_i^{TN} > U_i^{TT} > U_i^{NN} > U_i^{FN}$ and $U_i^{NF} \geq U_i^{TT}$
2. $\mathcal{R}_2 : U_i^{TN} > U_i^{TT} > U_i^{NN} > U_i^{FN}$ and $U_i^{NF} < U_i^{TT}$

We call $\{U^{TN}, U^{TT}, U^{NN}, U^{NT}, U^{FN}, U^{NF}\}$ the set of utility types. Since both parties in a reconstruction protocol are considered to have the same preference relation, we can represent the above preference relations (by using utility types in place of particular utility values) respectively as follows:

1. $U^{TN} > U^{TT} > U^{NN} > U^{FN}$ and $U^{NF} \geq U^{TT}$
2. $U^{TN} > U^{TT} > U^{NN} > U^{FN}$ and $U^{NF} < U^{TT}$

2.2 Correctness and Fairness

Let $(\Gamma, \overrightarrow{\sigma})_{2,2}$ be a $(2, 2)$ rational secret reconstruction mechanism. Then, we follow the same definitions of complete fairness and correctness in [2] for the two party scenario:

[3] The notations (e.g., U_1 , U_1^- etc.) in brackets for the last two columns represent the corresponding notations used in [2] and [21].

Definition 1. *(Fairness) A rational secret reconstruction mechanism* $(\Gamma, \vec{\sigma})$ *is said to be completely fair if for every arbitrary alternative strategy* σ_i' *followed by party* P_i, $(i \in \{1,2\})$ *there exists a negligible function* μ *in the security parameter* k *such that the following holds:*

$$Pr[o_i(\Gamma, (\sigma_i', \sigma_{-i})) = s] \leq Pr[o_{-i}(\Gamma, (\sigma_i', \sigma_{-i})) = s] + \mu(k)$$

Definition 2. *(Correctness) A rational secret reconstruction mechanism* $(\Gamma, \vec{\sigma})$ *is said to be correct if for every arbitrary alternative strategy* σ_i' *followed by party* P_i, $(i \in \{1,2\})$ *there exists a negligible function* μ *in the security parameter* k *such that the following holds:*

$$Pr[o_{-i}(\Gamma, (\sigma_i', \sigma_{-i})) \notin \{s, \perp\}] \leq \mu(k)$$

2.3 Utility-Independence

A mechanism $(\Gamma, \vec{\sigma})$ is said to be independent of a given utility type if it achieves its desired set of properties for any value of that utility type [2]. We define utility-independence as in [2]. We have $U = \{U^{TN}, U^{TT}, U^{NN}, U^{NT}, U^{FN}, U^{NF}\}$.

Definition 3. *(utility independence, adapted from [2]) Let* $\tilde{U} \in U$ *be a particular utility type and* $U' = \{U_i^{TN}, U_i^{TT}, U_i^{NN}, U_i^{FN}, U_i^{NT}, U_i^{NF}\}_{i=1}^n \backslash \tilde{U}_{i=1}^n$ *be a set of polynomial utility functions excluding all* $\tilde{U}_i$ *values. A mechanism* $(\Gamma, \vec{\sigma})$ *is said to be* $\tilde{U}$*–utility independent if for all polynomial utility functions* $\tilde{U}_{i=1}^n$ *for which the elements in* $U = U' \cup \tilde{U}_{i=1}^n$ *satisfies a certain preference relationship* $\mathcal{R}$*, it holds that* $(\Gamma, \vec{\sigma})$ *is a fair reconstruction mechanism for that preference relationship* $\mathcal{R}$ *among the elements of* U.

2.4 The Role of Auxiliary Information

[2] discusses the effect of side information possessed by a rational party in a secret reconstruction mechanism. Referring to the secret reconstruction mechanism of [9] they argued that given any auxiliary information about the secret or the access to some membership oracle O that can be queried on whether the current secret s' in the list is the actual secret s, a party possessing a list of fake secrets and the real secret (the long party in the Kol-Naor mechanism) has no incentive to broadcast the secret during the definitive iteration causing the other party not to learn the secret. Prior protocols for secret reconstruction in the rational setting did not allow side information although possession of side information is natural in most practical scenarios. In [2], it has been shown that this limitation is inherent to the non-simultaneous channel assumption. However, recently, the authors in [21] have developed a time delayed encryption scheme based on cryptographic memory-bound functions and using the same have overcome this impossibility result. In this work, we use protocol-induced auxiliary information to allow parties to check whether the secret they reconstruct is a correct one. By 'protocol–induced'we mean that such auxiliary information is a choice of the

mechanism/protocol designer and participants of the protocol have no freedom to choose it.

We adapt the definition of a membership oracle and a fair reconstruction mechanism with membership-auxiliary information given by [2].

Definition 4. *(membership oracle [2]). Let s be the actual secret and one needs to check whether x is same as the actual secret or not. S is the set of all such x. Then, a membership oracle* $O : S \rightarrow \{0, 1\}$ *is defined as follows:*

$$O_S(x) = \begin{cases} 1 & \text{if } x = s \\ 0 & \text{otherwise} \end{cases} \quad (1)$$

In previous works with auxiliary information, a general case was considered where a party can possess any membership oracle or any side information that enabled it to recognize the secret once it was reconstructed. Our aim is different. When left to themselves, parties may not possess any side information at all or the nature of side information can vary from party to party (some parties may possess incorrect membership oracles). Therefore, the membership oracle that we use must be correct and provided by the protocol itself to the participants.

Definition 5. *(correct membership oracle) A correct membership oracle* O : $S \rightarrow 0, 1$ *is a membership oracle which has the following properties:*

1. $Pr[O_S(x) = 1] \leq \mu(k)$ *for any* $x \neq s$ *and*
2. $Pr[O_S(x) = 0] \leq \mu(k)$ *for* $x = s$.

where $\mu(k)$ *is a negligible function in the security parameter k.*

Definition 6. *(protocol-induced membership oracle) A correct membership oracle* $O^{\pi}_{q,i}$ *provided by the protocol* π *to its participant* P_i, $(i = 1, 2)$ *for the qth execution of* π *is called a protocol-induced membership oracle.*

3 Correct and Fair Reconstruction Mechanism in Non-simultaneous Channel Model

In this section, we first provide a brief sketch of our $(2, 2)$ rational secret sharing protocol. Next we discuss the role of checking share used in our protocol in more details as well as the time delayed encryption scheme and the equilibrium concepts used before the final formal representation of our protocol.

3.1 Sketch of Our Protocol

The main idea behind our protocol is to release the secret gradually, share by share. Each player is given a list of sub-shares, one for the share to be reconstructed in each round. The secret can be reconstructed after sufficient number of these shares have been reconstructed by each party.

The minimum number of rounds r required to generate enough shares so that the secret can be reconstructed is determined by the dealer randomly from a geometric distribution with parameter β. We want β such that

$$\beta < (U^{TT} - U^{NN})/(U^{TN} - U^{NN}).$$

We call this round the revelation round. The dealer therefore has to generate shares of the secret s according to $(r, r+1)$ Shamir's secret sharing scheme so that $r+1$ shares are obtained. If each party possesses r of these shares of the secret (called the reconstruction shares) then they can reconstruct the secret. None of the parties are aware of the value of r.

The dealer randomly chooses one of the $r+1$ shares as the checking share. For each of the remaining shares, sub-shares are generated for each party so that a list of sub-shares for each party is formed. The dealer also generates shares of d fake secrets where d is also chosen from a geometric distribution with parameter β. Therefore a list distributed to a player contains r sub-shares of the shares of the actual secret followed by shares of d fake secrets such that the total number of rounds is m=r+d, the rth round being the revelation round. The fake secrets are required because each party is given the list of shares beforehand to avoid repeated interaction with the dealer. The checking share is distributed separately. The dealer is assumed to be honest and sends the sub-shares digitally signed (information theoretically secure MACs are used).

In each round, players are required to send the sub-share corresponding to the current round in their lists one by one i.e. non-simultaneously. Players are capable of only two actions in a round: send the correct sub-share (if they send an incorrect sub-share then it can be detected and the protocol can be aborted) or remain silent. If in any round a player does not receive a sub-share from the other party then it aborts. We also require that the first round cannot be chosen to be the revelation round; the dealer may send a special abort message if he gets r=1 and selects r once again. Players are guaranteed to be able to reconstruct the secret if they cooperate and reconstruct all the shares from all the sub-shares available in their lists.

Given the reconstruction shares and the secret, the extra share called the checking share (which is the protocol induced auxiliary information in our case) can be used to determine correctly whether the secret is the correct one. Also, the checking share itself does not reveal any information about the secret. In addition, the checking share acts as an indicator of the revelation round. So, the purpose of the checking share is to achieve correctness. We provide a detailed discussion on protocol-induced auxiliary information and specifically, the checking share in section 3.2. Introduction of the checking share leads to the problem that the party communicating last in any round can use it to identify the actual secret and quit before the other party obtains the secret (this is discussed further in section 3.2). We solve this problem by encrypting each share with the time–delayed encryption scheme introduced in [21] and then generating sub-shares from the encrypted share. A detailed description of this encryption scheme together with how it solves the problem due to introduction of the checking share is given in section 3.3.

Now, the question is whether a rational player P_j will want to deviate in this situation. We shall show in section 3.6 that a player does not gain anything by deviating.

3.2 Protocol-Induced Membership-Auxiliary Information

As mentioned before, we introduce protocol-induced membership-auxiliary information in the form of an extra share of the secret, called the checking share, to check the correctness of the secret reconstructed. A protocol-induced membership oracle (see definition in section 2.3)should not reveal any information about the secret itself i.e. a party should not be able to conclude anything about the secret by simply observing the auxiliary information or by using arbitrary values as input to the oracle. Moreover, given the secret, the oracle must always (except with negligible probability) give the correct decision on whether this input is the actual secret or not. The approach used by us does not benefit a party considering deviation by giving it any additional power in discovering the secret. This is because the additional information is very specific to the particular execution of the secret sharing and reconstruction mechanism and does not impart any information about the secret when used without participating in the protocol.

Let $(\Gamma_f, \overrightarrow{\sigma_f})$ be a fair secret reconstruction mechanism that assumes only $U^{NF} < U^{TT}$. Suppose that in each round r of the secret reconstruction mechanism, P_1 communicates first and P_2 communicates second. At the end of each such round, a value of the form s_r is reconstructed. If one of the parties quit at any round j then the other party is supposed to output the value reconstructed in the previous round i.e. s_{j-1}. Now, let $(\Gamma_{fc}, \overrightarrow{\sigma_{fc}})$ be a fair secret reconstruction mechanism with a protocol-induced membership oracle O_q^π. $\overrightarrow{\sigma_{fc}} = (\sigma_{fc,1}, \sigma_{fc,2})$ is a slight modification of $\overrightarrow{\sigma_f} = (\sigma_{f,1}, \sigma_{f,2})$. $\sigma_{fc,i}$ tells party P_i to follow $\sigma_{f,i}$ till an output as defined by $\sigma_{f,i}$ is obtained and then instructs it to query O_q^π with the value received in that step to check whether it is the correct one.

Theorem 1. *Let $(\Gamma_{fc}, \overrightarrow{\sigma_{fc}})$ be a $(2, 2)$ fair secret reconstruction mechanism with a protocol-induced membership oracle O_q^π.Then $(\Gamma_{fc}, \overrightarrow{\sigma_{fc}})$ is also a correct secret reconstruction mechanism.*

Proof. We delay the proof to Appendix A.

For our protocol, we shall consider that each party P_i is given the protocol-induced auxiliary information $aux_q^{\pi,s}$ and the protocol–induced membership oracle $O_q^{\pi,s}$. We note here that because of the presence of our protocol-induced membership-auxiliary information, our protocol cannot tolerate any other auxiliary information that parties may possess themselves (See Appendix D).

Shamir's (1979) (t, n) threshold secret sharing scheme [11] is inherently linked with the protocol–induced membership oracle we use. Shamir's scheme enables one to generate n shares of a secret s such that any t out of these n shares can be used to reconstruct the secret. The dealer chooses a random $t-1$ degree polynomial $f(x) = a_0 + a_1 x + a_2 x^2 + \ldots + a_{t-1} x^{t-1}$ where a_0 is set to be equal to the secret s and the remaining coefficients $a_1, \ldots, a_{t-1}$ are randomly chosen from a uniform distribution over the integers in $[0, p)$ where p is a prime greater than both s and n. The shares are computed as $s_i = f(y_i) mod p$, where $0 < y_i < p$ and $i = 1 \ldots n$.

Now let us consider that the value of t is unknown to Bob who wants to reconstruct a secret from r shares ($r < n$) he has gathered. Therefore, it is completely unknown to him whether he has sufficient shares (i.e. if $r > t$) to reconstruct the secret. Even if he is told that he has sufficient shares, then also he does not know exactly how many of these shares should be used to reconstruct the correct secret. We use this fact to our benefit.

Bob can hold in reserve one of the shares he has and try to reconstruct the secret using different numbers of shares from the remaining shares. After each reconstruction he can use the reserved share to check whether the reconstructed value is the correct secret or not. Specifically on reconstructing a secret $s_{r}^{'}$ from $r^{'} < r$ shares, he can write the following:

$$f_{r'}(x) = s_{r'} + a_1^{'}x + a_2^{'}x^2 + \ldots + a_{r'-1}^{'}x^{r^{'}-1}$$

Now let us assume that the reserved share s_q is represented as $(y_q, f(y_q) mod p)$.

Claim 1. *If $f_{r'}(y_q) = f(y_q)$, then a player can definitely conclude that $s_{r'} = s$; otherwise it concludes that $s_{r'} \neq s$.*

Proof. For the claim to be true the following two conditions should be fulfilled [by definition of correct membership oracle]:

1. $Pr[f_{r'}(y_q) = f(y_q)] \leq \mu(p)$ for any $s_{r'} \neq s$.
2. $Pr[f_{r'}(y_q) \neq f(y_q)] \leq \mu(p)$ for $s_{r'} = s$.

The second condition always holds by the property of polynomial interpolation. Now, is it possible that even if $s_{r'} \neq s$, $f_{r'}(y_q) = f(y_q)$ holds true? Since $f(x)$ is a randomly chosen polynomial in $[0, p)$, the probability of the point represented by the reserved share lying on both $f(x)$ and $f_{r'}(x)$ where $r^{'} \neq t$ is negligible. So the first condition also holds. Therefore we can conclude that the reserved share (which we call checking share throughout the paper) can serve as a protocol-induced auxiliary information.

Checking Shares. Let us suppose that the player P_1 communicates first in each round whereas the player P_2 communicates last. When P_2 quits in any round then it can have two meanings for P_1: 1) P_2 has already obtained the secret in the last round (i.e. P_2 has the preference $U_2^{NF} < U_2^{TT}$) or 2) P_2 has not obtained the secret but is trying to mislead P_1 in believing that the secret has been obtained in the last round (i.e. P_2 has the preference $U_2^{NF} \geq U_2^{TT}$). By giving a checking share (a share of the actual secret) we enable P_1 to distinguish between scenarios (1) and (2). However, if the checking share is available only to P_1, then P_2 is dependent on the P_1 to know when the revelation round takes place and is thus vulnerable to deviations by P_1. If the checking share is available only to P_2 , then at the end of each round P_2 can check whether it has enough shares to be able to reconstruct the secret and hence comes to know the revelation round before both parties obtain the secret thereby resulting in an unfair outcome. Therefore the checking share needs to be given to both the parties in such a way that it cannot be used to check whether the current round is the revelation round but can be used to detect if the last round was a revelation round.

The advantage of such a checking share over indicators is that the checking share does not require reconstruction and is readily available to both players whereas indicators are only available to each player if both players send their message in that round. So even when one party aborts prematurely, the other party can check whether the secret reconstructed with the available shares is the correct one by using the checking share. This is not possible with an indicator bit which will not even be reconstructed in the event of one party deviating prematurely. However, the disadvantage is that the checking share acts as auxiliary information that enables to identify the correct secret whereas an indicator bit is in no way related to the correct secret itself. Before sending its share in each round, with the help of this checking share P_2 can check whether it has obtained the actual secret. If it has, then P_2 will quit before sending its message for that round to P_1. Therefore, P_1 will be unable to get the secret leading to an unfair outcome. Therefore it is important to use the checking share in such a manner that it cannot provide any undue advantage to any party in identifying the secret (for example P_2 cannot take the help of the checking share to identify the revelation round before P_1). In [21], the authors have proposed a secret reconstruction mechanism in the standard point-to-point network where parties have auxiliary information. Their protocol develops and uses the concept of Cryptographic Memory-bound Functions which is used in a time delayed encryption scheme to prevent a party from identifying the correct secret before others with the help of the auxiliary information it has. We use the same concept to prevent misuse of the checking share by any party.

We can show that the introduction of the checking share is done without relying on the actual value of U^{NF}.

3.3 Time Delayed Encryption

When players have auxiliary information, then in each round, a deviating player tries to decide whether the current round is the revelation round by checking the reconstructed secret with the auxiliary information. Once the auxiliary information tells this player that the secret has been reconstructed, the player immediately quits without sending its own share. This results in unfairness as the other player cannot reconstruct the secret. A time delayed encryption scheme becomes handy in this situation. A message that has been encrypted by this scheme can only be decrypted after a moderate amount of time has elapsed. Although there has been much work on this type of schemes in the field of time release cryptography, the construction of a time delayed encryption scheme where the time delay is introduced with the help of cryptographic memory bound functions (instead of Time Lock Puzzles [25] that require a huge computational overhead and hence is dependent on CPU speed) was proposed in [21].

A time delayed encryption scheme $(Gen, Enc_K, Dec_K, Unseal_F)$ consists of 1) the algorithm Gen that on input the security parameter 1^k and the hardness parameter h (such that 2^h is a large polynomial in k) outputs a key K, a sealed key K' and some additional information F used to find the key; 2) the encryption and decryption algorithms Enc_K and Dec_K respectively that use the key K and 3) the algorithm $Unseal_F$ such that $Unseal_F(K')=K$. The time delay is introduced by $Unseal_F$ because its running time is lower bounded by $\Omega(2^h)$ i.e. if the reconstructed message is each round is encrypted with this scheme then none of the parties can recover the message in less than $\Omega(2^h)$ steps. Because Cryptographic Memory-Bound Function is used for the construction, these steps are in fact memory accesses i.e. the evaluation of $Unseal_F(\tilde{K})$ requires at least $\Omega(2^h)$ memory accesses.

We use this time-delayed encryption scheme to encrypt the r shares of the secret generated by the dealer (i.e. all shares except the checking share) and then generate sub-shares from the encrypted shares for distribution to the players. This allows the players to reconstruct the encrypted share in each round but does not allow any of them to decrypt the share obtained in the current round till a certain time has elapsed. Each round has to be completed within a certain time limit. If a party does not receive any message for a particular round from the other party within this deadline then it assumes that the other party has quit. If a player wants to decrypt the encrypted share then it has to make a minimum number of memory accesses. The time delay in decryption is such that it causes the party to miss the deadline for sending the message in this round. Therefore a party cannot decide whether the actual secret has been obtained in the current round without missing the deadline which in turn informs the other party of the misbehavior.

We discuss the timing model necessary for fruitfully utilizing the time-delayed encryption scheme in Appendix B.

3.4 Equilibrium Concept

Due to lack of space we defer a discussion on the equilibrium concepts used in the literature of rational secret reconstruction mechanisms to Appendix C. For our protocol we use computational strict Nash Equilibrium in the presence of protocol-induced auxiliary information. We must note that in our case all the players have the same side information denoted by $(aux_q^{\pi,s}, O_q^{\pi,s})$ when induced by the suggested strategy i.e. protocol π.

Definition 7. *(Computational Nash Equilibrium with protocol-induced side information [21]) The suggested strategy σ in the mechanism (Γ, σ) is a computational Nash Equilibrium in the presence of protocol–induced auxiliary information $(aux_q^{\sigma,\pi,s}, O_q^{\sigma,\pi,s})$ if for every P_i any probabilistic polynomial time strategy $\sigma_i^{'}$, $u_i((\sigma_i^{'}, \sigma_{-i}), aux_q^{\sigma,\pi,s}, O_q^{\sigma,\pi,s}) \leq u_i(\sigma, aux_q^{\sigma,\pi,s}, O_q^{\sigma,\pi,s}) + \mu^{'}(k)$ for some negligible $\mu^{'}$.*

Let $\sigma_i^{'} \not\approx (aux_q^{\sigma,\pi,s}, O_q^{\sigma,\pi,s})\sigma$ denote equivalent play (originally defined in [15] and modified in [21] for the case of side information) in the presence of protocol-induced side information. We refer the reader to [21] for detailed discussion.

Definition 8. *(Computational strict Nash Equilibrium with protocol-induced side information [21]) The suggested strategy σ in the mechanism (Γ, σ) is a computational strict Nash Equilibrium in the presence of protocol-induced auxiliary information if it is a Nash Equilibrium with protocol-induced auxiliary information and for every $P_i$for any probabilistic polynomial time strategy $\sigma_i^{'} \not\approx (aux_q^{\sigma,\pi,s}, O_q^{\sigma,\pi,s})\sigma$, $u_i((\sigma_i^{'}, \sigma_{-i}), aux_q^{\sigma,\pi,s}, O_q^{\sigma,\pi,s}) < u_i(\sigma, aux_q^{\sigma,\pi,s}, O_q^{\sigma,\pi,s}) + \mu^{''}(k)$ for some negligible $\mu^{''}$.*

3.5 Our Protocol

In this section, we give the formal description of our protocol. Note that in the description below $(Gen, Enc_K, Dec_K, Unseal_F)$ is the time delayed encryption scheme described in section 4.3.

Protocol ShareGen : The Dealer's Protocol
Inputs. The secret s possessed by the dealer; β, the parameter for the geometric distribution $\mathcal{G}(\beta)$
Computation. The dealer does the following:

1. Generate $r \sim \mathcal{G}(\beta)$.
2. $K_i, K_i^{'}, F_i \leftarrow Gen(1^k), i = 1, \ldots, r$.
3. Use $(r, r+1)$ Shamir's Secret Sharing Scheme to generate r shares of s. Suppose the polynomial used is $f(x)$ where $f(0)$ is set to be equal to the secret s and the remaining coefficients $a_1, \ldots, a_{r-1}$ are randomly chosen from a uniform distribution over the integers in $[0, p)$ where p is a prime number greater than both s and $r+1$. Each share s_i can be represented as $(y_i, f(y_i))$[4] where $0 < y_i < p$ for each $i = 0, \ldots, r$, y_i is chosen randomly.
4. Choose s_{check} to be the 0th share among these $(r+1)$ shares such. Then, s_{check} is of the form $(y_0, f(y_0))$.
5. For each share s_i, $i = 1, \ldots, r$, compute $c_i \leftarrow Enc_{K_i}(s_i)$ and set $c_i^{'} \leftarrow (c_i, K_i^{'})$.
6. For each encrypted share $c_i^{'}$, $i = 1, \ldots, r$, generate sub-shares $c_{i,j}^{'}$ $(j = 1, 2)$ such that $c_i^{'} = c_{i,1}^{'} \oplus c_{i,2}^{'}$.
7. Generate random values $c_{i,j}^{'}$ (for $i = r+1, \ldots, r+d$ and $j = 1, 2$), d is chosen according to the geometric distribution $\mathcal{G}(\beta)$.
8. Construct list $list_j$, $(j = 1, 2)$ to contain $c_{1,j}^{'}, \ldots, c_{r+d,j}^{'}$ for player P_j $(j = 1, 2)$.

Output. Distribute to each player P_j a list $list_j$, $j = 1, 2$. Also distribute the checking share s_{check} to each player.

[4] The accurate way to write is $(y_i, f(y_i) mod p)$. We drop $mod p$ for simplicity of representation.

Protocol Reconstruct: The Players' Protocol
This protocol consists of two phases, the Communication Phase and the Processing Phase. In the Communication Phase players communicate to gather sub-shares, whereas in the Processing Phase players process these sub-shares obtained in the Communication Phase to get the shares of the secret. Thus the Processing Phase for one share works in parallel with the Communication Phase for a subsequent share. An 'abort' in any round of the Communication Phase implies quitting further communication with the other party; however, the aborting party still continues with the processing phase to see whether the secret can be reconstructed from the shares obtained till that round. A 'quit' in the Processing Phase means either the secret has been obtained and hence the next round in the Communication Phase is no longer required or the Communication Phase has been aborted and the shares obtained till the round of abort are not sufficient to reconstruct the secret.

Inputs. List of sub-shares $list_j$ received by each player P_j , $j = 1, 2$ from the dealer.

Communication Phase
In each round, P_1 communicates first.
P_1 communicates first as follows:

1. If in the last round (except if the current round is the first one) P_1 has not received a share within the specified deadline from P_2 or if the share received is not signed properly then abort; else continue till the Processing Phase outputs the secret.
2. Send the current share from $list_1$.
3. Check for shares sent by P_2 till the specified deadline.

P_2 communicates next as follows:

1. If in the current round P_2 has not received a share from P_1 within the specified deadline or if the share received is not signed properly then abort; else continue till the Processing Phase outputs the secret.
2. Send the current share in the list $list_2$.
3. Check for shares sent by P_1 till the specified deadline.

Processing Phase
This phase is carried out by each party on its own in parallel to the communication phase. It can start at least after one round of communication i.e. after the sub-shares of at least one encrypted share of the secret has been gathered by each party.

Until the sub-shares obtained from the Communication Phase is exhausted or until the secret is obtained, each P_j ($j = 1, 2$) does the following in the ith round of the Processing Phase:

1. Reconstruct $c_i^{'}$ from $c_{i,1}^{'}$ and $c_{i,2}^{'}$.
2. Interpret $c_i^{'}$ as $(c_i, K_i^{'})$.

3. Compute $K_i \leftarrow Unseal_{F_i}(K_i^{'})$ and find $share_i = Dec_{K_i}(c_i)$.
4. If $i > 1$, reconstruct a polynomial $f_i(x)$ of degree $(i-1)$ corresponding to the shares decrypted till the ith round; else move to the first step.
5. Now, s_{check} is $(y_0, f(y_0))$. If $f_i(y_0) = f(y_0)$ then output the constant term $f_i(0)$ of this polynomial as the desired secret and quit. Otherwise, continue. If all sub-shares obtained from the communication round are exhausted and $f_i(y_0) = f(y_0)$ does not hold then output $\perp$.

Output. Either each party outputs the secret s or each party outputs $\perp$.

3.6 Analysis

Theorem 2. *Let our rational secret reconstruction mechanism be denoted by $(\Gamma, \vec{\sigma})$. Then 1) the prescribed strategy $\vec{\sigma}$ of the game Γ is in computational strict Nash Equilibrium in presence of protocol-induced auxiliary information; 2) the output obtained by following $\vec{\sigma}$ is correct and 3) $(\Gamma, \vec{\sigma})$ is U_{NF} utility-independent.*

Proof. We consider that each share in the lists that the parties receive is signed by the dealer. Therefore neither party can undetectably send a wrong message to the other (since information theoretic MACs are used). In each round, each party either sends the message or chooses not to send it. The point of contention is that the protocol-induced auxiliary information may incentivize a party to deviate by allowing it to check whether the shares obtained till a certain round gives the correct secret or not thus helping in deciding whether to quit or send its share in that round to the other party. We argue that our protocol is a computational strict Nash equilibrium for a party P_i with $U^{TN} > U^{TT} > U^{NN}$ even in the presence of protocol-induced auxiliary information.

Case I. Suppose, P_1 follows the reconstruction protocol whereas P_2 uses an alternate strategy that instructs it to follow the protocol till the qth round. Now if P_2 decides to quit in round $(q+1)$, P_1 aborts and henceforth no exchange of shares takes place. Since P_2 communicates his share following P_1 in each round, P_2 receives the $(q+1)$th sub-share from P_1. However, by the deadline of round $(q+1)$, P_2 cannot decipher his $(q+1)$th share, by the property of time-delayed encryption. If $(q+1) < r$, then P_2 has not gathered enough shares to be able to reconstruct the secret. If $(q+1) > r$ then both parties obtain the secret. The share obtained in the $(q+1)$th round does not help P_2 in any way. Thus, P_2's expected utility of quitting at any round $(q+1)$ is $\delta U_2^{TN} + (1-\delta)U_2^{NN} \leq \beta U_2^{TN} + (1-\beta)U_2^{NN} < U_2^{TT}$ for $r \geq 1$ (where the probability that the secret is reconstructed with $q+1 = r$ shares is given by $\delta = \beta(1-\beta)^{r-1}$), by our choice of β. Note that if P_2 uses its checking share in place of the $(q+1)$th share for the secret reconstruction, then it loses the capability of making sure whether it has obtained the correct secret and hence loses the capability to decide definitely (instead of guessing) whether to quit or not.

Case II. If we assume that P_2 follows the reconstruction protocol whereas P_1 deviates by using a strategy that instructs it to follow the protocol till the qth round and quit immediately after that, then P_1 does not even get the share in the $(q+1)$th round and the same reasoning as Case I also applies here.

What remains to be shown is that the protocol is correct and U^{NF} independent. We first argue that our protocol is a computational strict Nash equilibrium with protocol-induced side information even when $U^{NF} \geq U^{TT}$. Suppose that P_2 quits in the $(q+1)$th round. Then, by the property of the checking share, P_1 instead of outputting a secret formed from all the shares till the qth round can use the checking share to find whether $q+1 > r$. If not, then P_1 outputs a default value. Therefore P_1 can now distinguish between a silent party P_2 with $U_2^{NF} \geq U_2^{TT}$ and a silent party P_2 with $U_2^{TT} > U_2^{NF}$. So a party with $U^{NF} \geq U^{TT}$ gains only U^{NN} due to its deviation whereas if it follows the protocol it gains U^{TT}. Since $U^{TT} > U^{NN}$, the protocol is a computational strict Nash Equilibrium with protocol–induced side information even for $U^{NF} \geq U^{TT}$. Thus we observe that the equilibrium condition is satisfied for any value of U^{NF} as long as $U^{TT} > U^{NN}$ holds. The value of U^{NF} has not been used to introduce the checking share which plays the crucial role in deciding whether the secret obtained till a particular round is correct or not. Therefore, our protocol is U^{NF} independent. Moreover, by the properties of protocol-induced auxiliary information/ membership oracle, the checking share always succeeds in identifying correctly whether a secret is correct or not. Hence our protocol is correct.

4 Generalization to (t, n) Setting

Assuming the presence of non-simultaneous broadcast channel, our protocol can be extended to the (t, n) setting with some modifications. The dealer would need to generate (t, n) sub-shares from each encrypted share (by using (t, n) Shamir's secret sharing) and distribute these sub-shares to the n players. Players would communicate one-by-one in each round. If within the deadline of any round a player obtains less than t shares, he quits. Obviously, we can consider a rushing adversary i.e. the deviating party is the last (i.e. the tth person) to communicate in any round. In that case, this party has to decide whether or not to quit in any round before he is able to decrypt the share he reconstructs from the sub-shares obtained in that round. If he tries to decrypt before taking the decision then, by the property of time-delayed encryption, the deadline for that round is over and all other players quit. So, the same logic as presented in section 3.6 applies here also.

However, if point-to-point network is considered for the (t, n) setting, then the generalization is not easy. In that case, instead of the most general (t, n) setting, we can first look at the (n, n) setting as in[21, 15] or exactly t-out-of-n setting as in [15].

5 Complexity Analysis

In our protocol, the communication phase and the processing phase run parallely. For each player and for each share i to be reconstructed, we need a round of communication phase i.e. CP_i and a round of processing phase PP_i. The processing phase PP_i will coincide in time with CP_{i+1} (since the processing phase must start after one round of communication phase) and overlap partially with CP_{i+2} in time. So the time required for one round of Processing Phase is $(1+\theta)$ times the time required for one round of Communication Phase where θ is chosen by protocol designer and the time delay for the time-delayed encryption scheme should be designed to accomodate θ. The number of rounds for both Communication Phase and Processing Phase is r. So the total elapsed time for Protocol Reconstruct is $(1 + r + \theta)T_{cp}$ where T_{cp} is the time required for one round of Communication Phase. Therefore we are interested on the upper-bound of r.

The size of each list of sub-shares distributed to each player will depend on $r + d$. So we also calculate the upper-bound on $r + d$.

Upper-Bound on *r*. We have assumed that r is chosen according to a geometric distribution $\mathcal{G}(\beta)$. Also, for a fair rational secret reconstruction protocol, the choice of β is such that

$$0 < \beta < \beta_0 = (U^{TT} - U^{NN})/(U^{TT} - U^{NN}) < 1.$$

Now, given any $\epsilon > 0$ error, we wish to have

$$Pr[r > R] < \epsilon$$
$$i.e. Pr[r > R] = (1-\beta)^R < \epsilon$$
$$i.e. R > \ln \epsilon / \ln(1-\beta)$$

Therefore, we have $Pr[r \leq \lceil \ln \epsilon / \ln(1-\beta) \rceil] > 1 - \epsilon$, where $0 < \epsilon < 1$.

Upper-Bound on *r* + *d*. We have $r, d \sim \mathcal{G}(\beta)$, r and d are i.i.d random variables, where $0 < \beta < \beta_0 = (U^{TT} - U^{NN})/(U^{TT} - U^{NN}) < 1$.

Given any error $\epsilon > 0$, to have $Pr[r > T/2] < \epsilon/2$, we need

$$T/2 > \ln(\epsilon/2)/\ln(1-\beta)$$

where T is a constant.

This also holds for d.

Now,

$$\begin{aligned} & Pr[r + d > T] \\ & \leq Pr[r > T/2 or d > T/2] \\ & \leq Pr[r > T/2] + Pr[d > T/2] \\ & = 2Pr[r > T/2] < \epsilon, \end{aligned}$$

if $T/2 > \ln(\epsilon/2)/\ln(1-\beta)$ or $T > 2\ln(\epsilon/2)/\ln(1-\beta)$.
Therefore,

$$Pr[r + d \leq \lceil 2\ln(\epsilon/2)/\ln(1-\beta)\rceil] > 1 - \epsilon$$

for $0 < \epsilon < 1$.

6 Conclusion

This paper deals with a problem in rational secret sharing that has received very little attention till now. We have proposed a $(2,2)$ rational secret sharing protocol that is fair and correct as well as independent of the U^{NF}–utility of a rational participant even when $U^{NF} \geq U^{TT}$ in the non-simultaneous channel model and show that it is in computational strict Nash equilibrium in the presence of protocol-induced auxiliary information. We have also given a generalization the protocol to the (t,n) settings.

Acknowledgement. We are indebted to the anonymous reviewers for their numerous useful comments and suggestions. We would like to thank them for their kind efforts to help us improve our work.

References

1. Abraham, I., Dolev, D., Gonen, R., Halpern, J.: Distributed computing meets game theory: robust mechanisms for rational secret sharing and multiparty computation. In: PODC 2006 Proceedings of the Twenty-fifth Annual ACM Symposium on Principles of Distributed Computing, pp. 53–62. ACM, New York (2006)
2. Asharov, G., Lindell, Y.: Utility Dependence in Correct and Fair Rational Secret Sharing. Journal of Cryptology 24(1), 157–202 (2010)
3. Dodis, Y., Rabin, T.: Cryptography and Game Theory. In: Nisan, N., Roughgarden, T., Tardos, E., Vazirani, V.V. (eds.) Algorithmic Game Theory, pp. 181–205. Cambridge University Press, New York (2007)
4. Goldreich, O.: Foundations of Cryptography Basic Applications, vol. II. Cambridge University Press, Cambridge (2004)
5. Gordon, S.D., Katz, J.: Rational Secret Sharing, Revisited. In: De Prisco, R., Yung, M. (eds.) SCN 2006. LNCS, vol. 4116, pp. 229–241. Springer, Heidelberg (2006)
6. Halpern, J., Teague, V.: Rational secret sharing and multiparty computation: extended abstract. In: STOC 2004 Proceedings of the Thirty-sixth Annual ACM Symposium on Theory of Computing, pp. 623–632. ACM, New York (2004)
7. Izmalkov, S., Micali, S., Lepinski, M.: Rational secure computation and ideal mechanism design. In: 46th Annual IEEE Symposium on Foundations of Computer Science, FOCS 2005, pp. 585–594 (2005)
8. Katz, J.: Bridging game theory and cryptography: Recent results and future directions. In: Canetti, R. (ed.) TCC 2008. LNCS, vol. 4948, pp. 251–272. Springer, Heidelberg (2008)
9. Kol, G., Naor, M.: Games for exchanging information. In: STOC 2008 Proceedings of the 40th Annual ACM Symposium on Theory of Computing, pp. 423–432. ACM, New York (2008)

10. McGrew, R., Porter, R., Shoham, Y.: Towards a general theory of non-cooperative computation. In: TARK 2003 Proceedings of the 9th Conference on Theoretical Aspects of Rationality and Knowledge, pp. 59–71. ACM, New York (2003)
11. Shamir, A.: How to share a secret. Communications of the ACM 22(11), 612–613 (1979)
12. Shoham, Y., Tenneholtz, M.: Non-cooperative computation: Boolean functions with correctness and exclusivity. Theoretical Computer Science 343(1-2), 97–113 (2005)
13. Lysyanskaya, A., Triandopoulos, N.: Rationality and Adversarial Behavior in Multi-party Computation. In: Dwork, C. (ed.) CRYPTO 2006. LNCS, vol. 4117, pp. 180–197. Springer, Heidelberg (2006)
14. Mas-Collel, A., Whinston, M.D., Green, J.R.: Microeconomic Theory. Oxford University Press, New York (1995)
15. Fuchsbauer, G., Katz, J., Naccache, D.: Efficient Rational Secret Sharing in Standard Communication Networks. In: Micciancio, D. (ed.) TCC 2010. LNCS, vol. 5978, pp. 419–436. Springer, Heidelberg (2010)
16. Ong, S.J., Parkes, D.C., Rosen, A., Vadhan, S.: Fairness with an Honest Minority and a Rational Majority. In: Reingold, O. (ed.) TCC 2009. LNCS, vol. 5444, pp. 36–53. Springer, Heidelberg (2009)
17. Kol, G., Naor, M.: Cryptography and Game Theory: Designing protocols for exchanging information. In: Canetti, R. (ed.) TCC 2008. LNCS, vol. 4948, pp. 320–339. Springer, Heidelberg (2008)
18. Osborne, M., Rubinstein, A.: A Course in Game Theory. MIT Press, Cambridge (2004)
19. Groce, A., Katz, J.: Fair Computation with Rational Players. Cryptology ePrint Archive: Report 2011/396 (2011)
20. Gordon, S.D., Hazay, C., Katz, J., Lindell, Y.: Complete Fairness in Secure Two-Party Computation. Journal of the ACM 58(6), Article No. 24 (2011)
21. Lysyanskaya, A., Segal, A.: Rational Secret Sharing with Side Information in Point-to-Point Networks via Time Delayed Encryption. IACR Cryptology ePrint Archive: Report 2010/540. IACR (2010)
22. Dwork, C., Goldberg, A.V., Naor, M.: On Memory-bound Functions for Fighting Spam. In: Boneh, D. (ed.) CRYPTO 2003. LNCS, vol. 2729, pp. 426–444. Springer, Heidelberg (2003)
23. Rabin, M.O.: How to Exchange Secrets with Oblivious Transfer. Technical Report TR-8, Aiken Computation Lab, Harvard University (1981), `http://eprint.iacr.org/2005/187`
24. Gordon, S.D.: On Fairness in Secure Computation. Ph. D. Thesis. University of Maryland, College Park, USA (2010)
25. Rivest, R.L., Shamir, A., Wagner, D.A.: Time-lock puzzles and timed-release crypto. Technical report. Cambridge, MA, USA (1996)

A Correctness in Presence of Protocol-Induced Auxiliary Information

Theorem. *Let* $(\Gamma_{fc}, \overrightarrow{\sigma_{fc}})$ *be a* $(2, 2)$ *fair secret reconstruction mechanism with a protocol-induced membership oracle* O_q^{π}*. Then* $(\Gamma_{fc}, \overrightarrow{\sigma_{fc}})$ *is also a correct secret reconstruction mechanism.*

Proof. By assumption, in spite of the presence of a membership oracle with each party, the reconstruction mechanism is fair i.e. none of the parties can identify the revelation round before the other. Now suppose party P_2 has a deviation strategy σ_{dev} that tells it to play according to σ_2 for the first r' rounds and then quit (i.e. remain silent in all rounds henceforth). By assumption, P_1 possesses $O^{\pi}_{q,1}$ and P_2 possesses $O^{\pi}_{q,2}$. Now, if P_2 quits in round $(r' + 1)$, then by the suggested strategy $_{fc,1}$, P_1 outputs $s_{r'}$ if $O^{\pi}_{q,1}(s_{r'}) = 1$ else it outputs $\perp$. The same argument also holds if P_1 is the deviating party and P_2 the non-deviating party. We have already seen that $u_2(\sigma_1, \sigma_{dev}) = U_2^{NF}$ whereas $u_2(\sigma_1, \sigma_2) = U_2^{TT}$. Since $U_2^{NF} \geq U_2^{TT}$, P_2's best strategy is to follow σ_{dev} rather than the suggested strategy σ_2. So (σ_1, σ_2) is no more an equilibrium strategy. On the other hand, $u_2(\sigma_{fc,1}, \sigma_{dev}) = U_2^{NN}$ while $u_2(\sigma_{fc,1}, \sigma_{fc,2}) = U_2^{TT}$. So $(\sigma_{fc,1}, \sigma_{fc,2})$ is a strictly better strategy profile than $(\sigma_{fc,1}, \sigma_{dev})$ and is an equilibrium strategy whenever there is a party with $U^{NF} \geq U^{TT}$.

B Timing Model

If the time delayed encryption scheme is to be used fruitfully to prevent the misuse of auxiliary information, then it is necessary for each party to know how to find out whether a certain message from another party was received within a given deadline. The timing model for this purpose is discussed in details in [21]. We describe it here very briefly. Both parties must agree on the maximum values for clock drift (τ), network latency (Δ) and speed ($speed_{max}$) of each party. If P_2 is supposed to send a message to P_1 at time t then P_1 must know that if P_2 is following the protocol, then his message must reach P_1 by the time his local clock shows $t + \Delta + \tau$. If any round requires l computation steps scheduled to begin at time t then both parties must have completed the computation by time $t + l/speed_{min}$ where $speed_{min}$ is the minimum of the speeds of both the parties. For our protocol we assume (as in [21]) that the first round of the protocol begins at the pre–decided time t_1. Henceforth, round $q > 1$ starts at $t_q = t_{q-1} + \Delta + \tau + m/speed_{min}$ where m is the maximum number of steps required for computations in each round. So at local time t_q, each party checks whether it can compute s or some party deviated in the last round (i.e. the message from that party for round $q-1$ did not reach till t_q). If the later is true then it quits and moves to the post-processing steps. Each party computes its own message and sends it to the other by time $t_q + m/speed_{min}$.

C Equilibrium Concepts Used in Rational Secret Reconstruction Mechanisms

A rational secret reconstruction protocol should be such that no player has any incentive to deviate from this protocol. Consequently, Nash equilibrium and its several variants have been used as equilibrium concept in the literature of rational secret sharing. A suggested strategy is in Nash equilibrium when given that everyone else is following the suggested strategy, there is no incentive for a player to deviate from this strategy. However it can be easily shown that even though Shamir's (1979) secret sharing protocol is a Nash equilibrium for $t < n$, there are still strategies that are weakly better than it. This suggests the need for stronger versions of Nash equilibrium to remove such unstable solutions. Again, in the setting of rational secret sharing, in most cases, players are assumed to be polynomial time which calls for a suitable modification in the notion of Nash equilibrium used. Taking such facts into consideration following variants of Nash equilibrium have been used: 1) Nash equilibrium that survives iterated deletion of weakly dominated strategies [6]; 2) strict Nash equilibrium which becomes useful when the payoffs from playing a good strategy and a bad strategy are so close that any minor changes in the beliefs of players about the strategy others are going to adopt may lead each of them to play the bad strategy [9]; 3) computational strict Nash equilibrium [15] where except for non-negligible probability a polynomial time player has a non-negligible loss from deviating; 4) computational Nash equilibrium that is stable with respect to trembles [15] where every other player follows the suggested strategy with high probability; 5) computational strict Nash equilibrium with side information and computational Nash equilibrium with respect to trembles [21] which take into account the fact that each player has access to auxiliary information and a side information oracle.

D Fairness in Presence of Auxiliary Information

The protocol of [21] is fair in spite of the presence of arbitrary auxiliary information. In contrast, our protocol cannot tolerate arbitrary auxiliary information that parties may possess themselves, other than the protocol-induced one. When a party possesses auxiliary information that enables it to identify the actual secret, then it will use the checking share to reconstruct the secret instead of using it for checking purpose. It will then use the auxiliary information it possesses to verify whether the actual secret is obtained. Once it knows this, it will abort early causing other parties to have one share less than required to reconstruct the secret. Thus the protocol will then become unfair.

BotSuer: Suing Stealthy P2P Bots in Network Traffic through Netflow Analysis

Nizar Kheir[1] and Chirine Wolley[2]

[1] Orange Labs, Issy-Les-Moulineaux, France
nizar.kheir@orange.com
[2] Aix-Marseille University, LSIS UMR 7296, Marseille, France
chirine.wolley@etu.univ-amu.fr

Abstract. A large proportion of modern botnets are currently shifting towards structured overlay topologies, using P2P protocols, for command and control. These topologies provide a better resilience against detection and takedown as they avoid single nodes of failure in the botnet architecture. Yet current state of the art techniques to detect P2P bots mostly rely on swarm effects. They detect bots only when there is multiple infected nodes belonging to the same botnet inside a network perimeter. Indeed, they cannot detect botnets that use public P2P networks such as the TDSS malware using Kad, let alone botnets that encapsulate P2P overlays within HTTP traffic, such as waledac, or even hide behind Tor networks.

In this paper, we propose a new and fully behavioral approach to detect P2P bots inside a network perimeter. Our approach observes only high-level malware traffic features with no need of deep packet inspection. We run samples of P2P malware inside a sandbox and we collect statistical features about malware traffic. We further use machine learning techniques in order to first clean the features set by discarding benign-like malware P2P behavior, and second to build an appropriate detection model. Our experimental results prove that we are able to accurately detect single infected P2P bots, while also satisfying a very low false positives rate.

Keywords: Botnet detection, P2P malware, machine learning, netflow.

1 Introduction

Malware has recently become the mainstream arsenal for cyber attackers, including thousands of malware samples being created every day [25]. It embeds zero-day exploits, self replication mechanisms, propagation capabilities, and more importantly it connects to a master server as to retrieve commands or to send stolen data. Arguably, botnets are the most common type of malware today. These are networks of infected nodes (bots) that are controlled by the same entity (botmaster) via shared Command and Control (C&C) channels. Early botnet C&C channels were mostly centralized, using protocols such as `IRC` and `HTTP` [19]. Although being easy to manage and highly responsive, centralized

M. Abdalla, C. Nita-Rotaru, and R. Dahab (Eds.): CANS 2013, LNCS 8257, pp. 162–178, 2013.

C&C channels are susceptible to detection and takedown because they include single nodes of failure in their botnet architecture. Therefore, botnet C&C channels started shifting towards decentralized architectures that use peer-to-peer protocols (P2P) [21,23]. P2P botnets are robust because they constitute overlay networks where bots can distribute commands without the need for a central C&C server [10].

Nowadays, botnets are no longer being used only to trigger massive distributed attacks such as spam and DDoS. They are becoming stealthier in the way they perform malicious activities, seeking financial benefits and sensitive user data [27]. Botnet herders also use code obfuscation in order to hide malware payloads within the large amount of network traffic [18], and so to evade IDS signatures. Network detection solutions are thus increasingly confronted to *stealthy bots*, along with *encrypted C&C communications* and *only few infections* inside a network perimeter. Yet the use of overlay networks makes detection more difficult due to the inability to build blacklists of URLs or malicious domain names, as for centralized botnet topologies [5]. We thus derive four main requirements for network-based systems in order to detect P2P bots. First, they should be able to detect bots even when no malicious activity is being observed. Besides, they should be able to detect even single infected bots inside a network perimeter. They should also detect P2P bots using only network layer features, without the need to access encrypted packet payloads. Last of all, they should detect P2P bots based on their overall network footprints, and not based on every single connection. While the first three requirements look straightforward, the fourth one stems from the fact that P2P bots locate and retrieve commands using the overlay network. Two infected bots are thus unlikely to connect to the same set of peers, even though some overlaps may occur. Therefore, the system should be able to detect P2P infected nodes based on the way these nodes interact with the overlay network, and not based on the single IP addresses being contacted.

This paper presents BotSuer, a system that detects P2P bots by monitoring traffic inside a network perimeter. BotSuer leverages the fact that malware belonging to the same family communicates with the overlay P2P botnet in a similar way. In fact, P2P control flows implement multiple functionalities such as keep-alive, route discovery and data queries. As shown in [14], flow size distributions exhibit discontinuities almost for all P2P protocols. Such discontinuities characterize clusters of flows that implement the same P2P functionality, and so they would have similar network behavior in terms of flow size, number of packets and flow duration. While certain clusters may be common for both malware and benign P2P communications (e.g. keep-alive messages), others clearly show differences that can be accounted for during detection. For instance, data search queries for the Zeus P2P botnet show periodicities that are unlikely to appear in other benign kademlia P2P traffic [12]. Yet we observed a significantly lower chunk rate for route discovery requests triggered by a Sality botnet, compared to other benign P2P applications.

BotSuer monitors network traffic triggered by P2P malware samples running in a controlled environment. It builds a training set of malware P2P traffic by first filtering non-P2P traffic, and then clustering malware P2P flows in order to group together those that implement the same P2P functionality (e.g. keep-alive, route discovery, data search and push requests). Some malware P2P clusters are likely to appear in benign P2P traffic and these should be discarded as they cannot be used during detection. For instance, keep-alive flows triggered by a TDSS malware that uses the kad network are similar to those triggered by benign P2P applications that implement the same kademlia protocol. BotSuer thus correlates cluster footprints for both malware and benign P2P applications in order to discard non-discriminatory P2P clusters. It uses remaining clusters as a training set in order to build a P2P botnet detection model.

We evaluated BotSuer against real-world P2P traffic, including both botnet and benign P2P applications. We obtained samples of P2P malware, all being active in the wild by the time they were collected, and that implement different P2P protocols. We also tested our system against traffic collected from a corporate network, as well as anonymized traffic collected from a large ISP network. Our experimental results prove the ability of BotSuer to accurately differentiate malware and benign P2P applications, with only few false positives.

This paper will be structured as follows. Section 2 summarizes related work. Section 3 provides an overview of our system. Section 4 describes the workflow and the different modules that constitute BotSuer. Section 5 presents our experiments and main results. Section 6 discusses the limitations and provides future work. Finally, section 7 concludes.

2 Related Work

Related work includes several approaches that detect P2P botnets by monitoring network traffic. First of all, solutions such as BotGrep [16], BotTrack [9] and BotMiner [11] correlate netflow data [6] and localize P2P bots based on their overlay C&C topologies. They cluster hosts in order to isolate groups of hosts that form P2P networks. Then they separate malicious and benign P2P groups using information about infected nodes collected from multiple sources such as honeypots and intrusion detection systems. However, botnet activity is becoming stealthier and cannot be easily detected by IDS signatures, thus limiting the coverage of these techniques.

Another trend of research aims at detecting infected P2P bots inside a given network perimeter [29,30]. In this category, Yen et al. [29] discard benign P2P applications based on features such as the volume of P2P traffic and the persistence of P2P applications. Unfortunately, these features do not reliably separate benign and botnet P2P flows. In fact, authors rule out the possibility that certain benign P2P applications such as skype may not implement P2P file sharing and so they would be difficult to separate from malicious P2P flows. On the other hand, Zhang et al. [30] propose an alternative approach using only P2P control flows. This approach is similar to ours by means of using only control flows for

P2P botnet detection. However, it detects P2P bots only when there is multiple infected nodes belonging to the same botnet. It computes distances between clusters of flows triggered by different nodes in the network. It also uses flow sizes and contacted IP addresses as a basis to compute distances between P2P nodes. Indeed we believe these metrics would generate false positives in case of popular P2P applications such as skype. For example, we observed strong overlap between the remote IP addresses contacted by two skype clients running on two different nodes in the same network. Hence, the approach presented in this paper provides a better alternative as it only relies on the way bots interact with their overlay C&C networks, and not on the single remote IP addresses being contacted.

Last of all, Bilge et al. propose an alternative approach to detect botnets through large scale netflow analysis [4]. This approach is similar to ours as it processes and correlates netflow records in order to detect infected bots. Yet it observes traffic at large ISP networks and detects only central C&C servers. Therefore, it is efficient only against centralized botnet architectures, but does not detect distributed P2P botnets.

3 System Overview

Our system operates in two phases, the training phase and the detection phase, as illustrated in Fig. 1. The training phase builds a behavioral model using a dataset of malware and benign P2P traffic. The detection phase applies the behavioral model on network traffic in order to detect P2P bots.

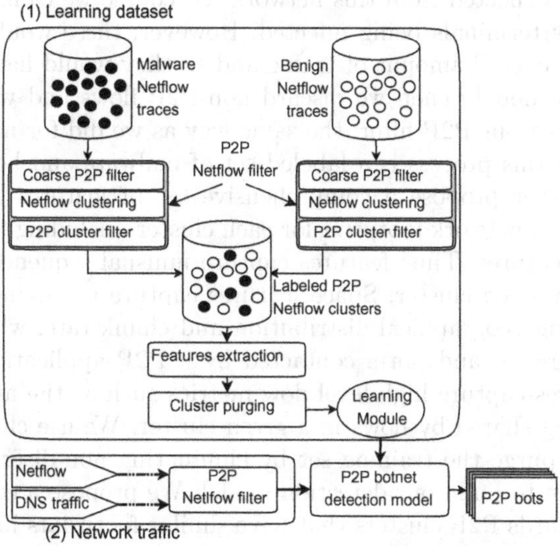

Fig. 1. Botnet Detection System

In the training phase, malicious traffic is obtained by executing malware in a controlled environment such as Anubis[2], CWSandbox[28] or Cuckoobox[1]. We pick-up P2P malware samples by checking antivirus (AV) signatures using the virusTotal API[1]. Such malware often triggers non-P2P traffic in addition to its C&C communications. We thus propose a filtering module that discards non-P2P traffic and keeps only P2P flows as input to the training phase. Our P2P filter implements two levels of filtering, including coarse and fine-grained filtering. Coarse filtering discards flows using high-level features such as DNS traffic and chunk rates. For example, overlay networks usually operate outside the DNS system, so we discard flows preceded with a successful DNS resolution as not being P2P flows. After the coarse filter, we cluster remaining flows for each malware sample in order to group together flows that are similar enough to be considered as part of the same application (e.g. spam campaign, scan, P2P keep alive, P2P search queries). We use statistical features such as flow size, number of packets, and the average bit rate. Control flows that implement the same P2P functionality for a given P2P protocol have similar network features and so they will be grouped within same clusters. The fine filter further eliminates clusters that do not implement P2P functionalities, and keeps only P2P clusters as input to train our detection module.

Benign P2P flows are more difficult to obtain as we lack the ground truth about the legitimate behavior of these applications. In this paper, we collected netflow packets from a well-protected corporate network. Terminals connected to this network abide to strict security policies, and they are all equiped with updated AV softwares. Access to this network is monitored using a proxy server with SSL inspection capability. Therefore, it is fairly reasonable to consider as benign all traffic collected from this network. Of course we cannot rule-out the possibility of few terminals being infected. However, these would be limited if compared to the overall amount of traffic and so they would have little impact on our detection model. Then we discard non-P2P flows and we build benign P2P clusters, using our P2P filter, the same way as we did for malware traffic.

The output of this process is a labeled set of malware and benign P2P flow clusters. We further propose a comprehensive set of features that we use in order to compute a network footprint for each cluster, including time, space and flow size-based features. Time features capture unusual sequences of flows and periodicities in a given cluster. Space features capture the dynamics of a P2P network, including geographical distribution and chunk rate, which is the rate of (new) IP addresses and ports contacted by a P2P application. Last of all, size-based features capture high-level flow metrics such as the amount of bytes and packets being shared by flows in a given cluster. We use cluster footprints in order to first purge the training set by eliminating non-discriminatory P2P clusters, and then to build our detection model. We propose a cross-correlation process that discards P2P clusters that have similar footprints in both malware and benign P2P applications. These are mostly keep-alive flow clusters that are likely to have similar implementations in both categories of P2P application. We

[1] `http://www.virustotal.com/`

further use remaining cluster footprints as input to train and build our detection model. In the detection phase, BotSuer applies this model on network traffic in order to detect P2P bots, without the need to inspect packet payloads. In the following section we describe our system and we build our detection model.

4 System Description

4.1 P2P Training Set

BotSuer processes P2P flows obtained during malware execution in a sandbox. During the buildup phase, we discard non P2P malware by checking AV signatures in virusTotal. Sure we may keep non P2P malware in our dataset due to misclassifications in virusTotal, but this malware will be dropped by our system as seen further in this section.

Coarse P2P filter applies to both malware and benign flows. It discards as many non-P2P flows prior to flow clustering and the fine P2P filter.

First, it discards flows preceded with a successful DNS resolution. P2P networks constitute environments of unpredictable IP addresses where nodes constantly join and leave the network. Peering nodes contact other peers using routing tables for the overlay network, with no prior DNS resolution. When access to a central server through DNS resolution is still possible at bootstrap, nodes further communicate using IP addresses in the overlay network [3].

Second, the churn effect is an inherent property of P2P systems and critical to their design and implementation [24]. It is a direct consequence of the independent arrival and departure by thousands of peers in the network, and results in a significant rate of failed connection attempts. We use this rate within malware and benign traffic in order to discard those that do not implement P2P applications. We set a threshold τ_{fc} for the ratio of failed flows with respect to the total number of flows triggered by a malware or a network terminal. We empirically set τ_{fc} to 0.15, based on P2P malware samples that we observed in our dataset. Our filter drops all malware and benign terminals whose rate of failed connection attempts does not exceed this threshold.

Netflow Clustering: The coarse filter significantly reduces the volume of input data by discarding flows that are unlikely to implement P2P applications. However, other non-P2P flows that have similar properties, such as spam and scan, may also match this filter. Indeed, we want to *cluster flows for a given malware or benign terminal* in order to put together flows that are likely to implement the same functionality, and then to discard non-P2P clusters. As in [14], control flows for a given P2P protocol usually implement preferred packet sizes, resulting in similar flows when observed at the network layer. These flows are grouped into categories where they implement the same P2P control activity. We propose a clustering process where flows that implement similar functionalities for a given malware or benign terminal are grouped within the same clusters. The fine filter further keeps only P2P clusters as input to our learning module. In fact we cluster flows using high level features, without access to packet payloads. We represent a flow f using the following features vector V_f:

$$V_f =< Pckt_s, Pckt_r, Byte_s, Byte_r, BRate_s, BRate_r >$$

$Pckt_s$ and $Pckt_r$ respectively represent the number of packets sent and received; $Byte_s$ and $Byte_r$ respectively represent the number of bytes sent and received; and $BRate_s$ and $BRate_r$ represent the byte rate sent and received. We define the distance between two flows as the Euclidian distance between their respective feature vectors. Then we apply the unsupervised, incremental k-means [20] to cluster flows $\mathcal{F}_\alpha$ triggered by malware M_α or a terminal T_α. Incremental k-means is a fast algorithm that requires no prior knowledge about the number of clusters, which is a key requirement to our approach. It provides a better alternative to the hierarchical clustering as we can set the threshold to create a new cluster based on our learning set of malware and benign P2P flows. In fact, incremental k-means creates a new cluster when the distance of an entry to all existing clusters exceeds a given threshold (τ_{cl}). We tested the incremental k-means algorithm against our set of malware P2P flows in order to find the optimal threshold τ_{cl}. We manually checked the outcome of the clustering process for different values of τ_{cl}. We thus empirically set τ_{cl} to the value 60, that we found to give the best output clusters (section 5.1 discusses more in details the impact of this threshold).

Fine P2P Filter implements two levels of filtering, using the distributions of autonomous systems and destination ports contacted by flows in each cluster.

Filtering by destination ports distribution: P2P applications usually hide while using nonstandard ports [13]. The use of multiple and oftentimes random destination ports is a distinctive P2P characteristic, as opposed to other activities such as spam or scan. For instance, a 10 minutes netflow trace includes at least 180 distinct destination port in case of skype, and almost 4690 distinct ports in case of bittorrent. We discard non-P2P clusters based on the distribution of new ports contacted. We compute the duration of each cluster, which is the lapse of time between the first and the last flow in the cluster. We split this interval into n sub-intervals of equal lengths. We compute, for each sub-interval, the number of new destination ports, that is the destination ports not appearing in previous sub-intervals. Then we compute the mean value for this distribution within each cluster, and we discard clusters where this value does not exceed a threshold τ_{np}. We conservatively set the value of τ_{np} using our dataset of malware P2P traffic, and that corresponds to the value $\tau_{np} = 0.6$.

Filtering by destination AS: Certain P2P malware, such as waledac, may bypass our port-based filter as it encapsulates its P2P activity within HTTP traffic, using the tcp port 80 [26]. However, the overlying P2P network still constitutes an overlay architecture that connects nodes distributed on multiple autonomous systems (AS). We thus use the number of contacted AS as another distinctive feature of P2P control clusters. Note that other clusters, mostly those containing malware scan flows, may also include a large number of destination AS. However, these clusters include a large number of flows, resulting in a low ratio of destination AS with respect to the number of flows in a cluster. We define the ratio of contacted AS in a cluster c as $\mathcal{R}_{AS_c} = \frac{\#AS_c}{\#Flw_c}$, where $\#AS_c$ is the number of destination AS and $\#Flw_c$ is the number of flows in c. Values of $\mathcal{R}_{AS_c}$ for P2P applications in our dataset were all found to fit in the interval $[0.3, 0.5]$, whereas values of $\mathcal{R}_{AS_c}$ for other malicious clusters such as scan activities were all found to be less than 0.05. We thus conservatively introduce a minimal threshold $\tau_{as} = 0.2$ for $\mathcal{R}_{AS_c}$, and we discard all netflow clusters c that match the condition $\mathcal{R}_{AS_c} < \tau_{as}$.

4.2 Features Extraction

The use of netflow data for machine learning and botnet detection is often criticized because it provides only generic information such as port numbers or contacted IPs [6]. The raw use of those features usually leads to overfitted models that only detect malware in the initial training set. This paper thus proposes a set of features that goes beyond the intrinsic characteristics of every single netflow record. It better describes the relationship and common trends among all netflow records within a single cluster. Such features capture invariants in C&C channels for P2P botnets. They cannot be easily evaded, yet they are generic enough to detect P2P botnets not initially represented in the training set. Our training features can be grouped into three categories, as follows.

Time-based features: Malware P2P control flows may be similar to benign flows when observed during short intervals of time. However, observing these flows at longer durations may reveal periodicities that are unlikely to exist in benign P2P flows. Table 1 illustrates the periods between communication rounds for P2P malware in our dataset. Time-based features capitalize on this observation in order to characterize the occurrence of control flows within a cluster as a function of time. We leverage periodicities in a cluster using the recurrence period density entropy (RPDE)[15]. RPDE is a normalized metric in time series analysis that determines the periodicity of a signal. It is equal to 0 in case of perfectly periodic signals and equal to 1 for white random noise signals. We compute the RPDE metric, the same as explained in [15], using a time series that represent the flow arrival times within a cluster. In addition to the RPDE, we also compute the mean and standard deviation (std) for inter-flow arrival times in each cluster. The sequence of inter-flow arrival times is derived from the time series by taking the difference between every couple of consecutive flows. However, the mean inter-flow arrival time is a linear metric, as opposed to the RPDE metric that rather applies in the phase space [15].

Space-based features characterize the way a P2P node contacts other peers in the network. P2P bots usually have a lower chunk rate compared to other benign peers [29]. During bootstrap, infected nodes often use hard-encoded lists of peers.

Such lists imply a lower chunk rate, which makes it a distinctive feature for P2P botnets. It is manifested through the number of IP addresses contacted and the port distribution. We characterize space features using the mean and std for the distributions of (new) IP addresses and destination ports contacted. We use the same distribution of destination ports as the one described for P2P filtering, and we add its mean and std to our features vector. Regarding IP addresses, we compute the distributions of both IP addresses and *new* IP addresses contacted. The former represents the distribution of the number of remote IP addresses within n sub-intervals of short duration, compared to the longer duration of a cluster. It characterizes the number of IP addresses concurrently contacted by a P2P node at a given time. The latter distribution, computed the same way as for destination ports, characterizes the chunk rate of a P2P application. We add the means and stds of both distributions to our features vector.

Flow size-based features characterize the number of bytes and packets transferred in P2P flows. They capture specific control operations for a given P2P application [14]. We extract both *unique* and *statistical* flow size features. The former represents the distribution of unique flow sizes against the number of flows that have a given size in a cluster. We compute the mean and std for this distribution and add these to our features vector. On the other hand, statistical flow sizes characterize the regularity of flow size behavior over time within a cluster. We group flows in a cluster into a time series according to their arrival times. We further split this interval into n sub-intervals of equal lengths. For each sub-interval, we compute the mean size for all flows in this interval, thus obtaining a time-based distribution of mean flow sizes in a cluster. We compute both mean and std of this new distribution and add these to our features vector.

4.3 P2P Botnet Detection Model

P2P clusters cannot be all used for training as some of these are likely to appear in both malware and benign P2P flows. In fact, while certain malware implements its own version of P2P protocols (e.g. waledac), others use existing overlay protocols like overnet (e.g. Storm) and kademlia (e.g. TDSS). Clusters provided by the second category of malware may share similar patterns with other benign P2P flow clusters for specific P2P control operations such as keep alive or route discovery, and so they would share similar network footprints. They should be thus discarded prior to building the detection model. In fact, we want to keep only clusters of P2P flows that implement P2P control operations that can be accounted for during detection, such as P2P communication rounds, chunk rates and IP distributions.

We discard non-discriminatory clusters by cross-correlating our combined set of malware and benign P2P clusters. Non-discriminatory clusters include flows triggered by malware and benign P2P applications that use the same P2P protocols (e.g. emule, overnet) and that implement the same P2P functionalities. We apply hierarchical clustering, using our features vector, in order to build a dendrogram where leaf nodes are P2P clusters and the root node is a set of all P2P clusters. Then we use the Davies-Bouldin index [8] to find the best cut in the dendrogram, and so we obtain meta-clusters of malware and benign P2P clusters. A meta-cluster corresponds to a node in the dendrogram, and that includes either or both malware and benign P2P clusters. Discriminatory meta-clusters include almost only malware or benign P2P clusters, and these are kept as input to the training phase. We thus discard as non-discriminatory meta-clusters all meta-clusters where the proportion of malware or benign P2P clusters does not exceed a threshold τ_d. We experimentally set the value of τ_d based on our P2P training set, as seen further in section 5.2.

We tested multiple learning algorithms in order to build our detection model, including SVM, J48 and C4.5 decision tree classifiers [7,22]. SVM provides an extension to nonlinear models that is based on the statistical learning theory. On the other hand, decision trees are a classic way to represent information from a machine learning algorithm, and offer a way to express structures in data. We evaluated the detection rates, including False Positives (FP) and False Negatives (FN), for these available learning algorithms using our labeled set of P2P clusters. We obtained higher detection accuracies using the SVM classifier, and therefore we use this algorithm to build our detection model.

5 Experimentation

This section describes the design of our experiments, as well as the dataset that we used in order to build and validate our approach. First, we build a P2P botnet detection model using a learning set of malware and benign P2P applications. Then we evaluate in this section three properties of our system. First, we use a cross-validation method in order to assess the accuracy of our P2P botnet detection model. Then, we evaluate the contribution for the different features of our model towards detection and we discuss results of these experiments using our initial P2P learning set. Last of all, we evaluate the coverage of our system through application to live netflow traffic.

5.1 Training Dataset

We obtained samples of malware traffic from a security company which collects binaries using its own honeypot platform. Traffic samples, provided as pcap files labeled with the malware md5, included 1 hour of malware network activity collected during execution in a sandbox. We use the virustotal API in order to identify P2P malware samples in our dataset using their md5 labels. We extracted all malware samples that were matching with more than 10 known P2P antivirus signatures in virustotal. In fact current antivirus scanners usually provide conflicting signatures for a same malware sample. Yet we need a valid ground truth of P2P malware samples in order to build and evaluate our system. Hence, we keep only malware samples that match with more than a single known P2P malware signature in virusTotal. We empirically set the number of matching P2P signatures to 10, which is almost the third of matching antivirus

Table 1. Malware samples by families of malware

Family	P2P functionality	Period	P2P Protocol
Sality (v3, v4)	Primary C&C	40 min	Custom protocol, encrypted-RC4 packets over UDP
Kelihos	Primary C&C	10 min	Custom protocol, P2P over HTTP traffic
Zeus v3	Primary C&C	30 min	Kademlia-like protocol transported over UDP
TDSS	Backup C&C	–	Public Kad network
Waledac	Primary C&C	30 sec	Custom protocol, P2P over HTTP traffic
ZeroAccess v1	Primary C&C	15 min	Custom protocol, transported over TCP and UDP
Storm	Primary C&C	10 min	Overnet protocol

scanners, and that we believe it provides enough confidence of a P2P malware sample. We obtained an overall number of 1,317 distinct malware samples. Note that malware uses P2P protocols for different purposes, including primary C&C, bootstrap, spreading and failover. Table 1 illustrates the most predominant malware families that we found in our dataset.

We process malware samples using our P2P filter in order to build clusters of P2P flows. We discard non-P2P flows using our coarse filter, then we create clusters of flows for each malware sample. We implement the incremental k-means algorithm, using different values for the threshold τ_{cl}. A low value of τ_{cl} causes the clustering process to create almost a new cluster for every new flow. Such clusters are usually discarded by the fine filter because of their relatively low AS and port distributions, thus leading to higher false negatives rates. On the other hand, a high value for τ_{cl} regroups flows that are not similar within the same clusters. These clusters would include flows that are not triggered by the same application, thus leading to more false positives. To find the best trade-off for τ_{cl}, we applied the clustering process to our training set of P2P malware. We tested several values for τ_{cl}, each time using the output clusters as input to our fine P2P filter. The optimal value for τ_{cl} is the highest value that still provides zero false negatives, assuming that there would be no false positives in case of only P2P traffic. In our case, we achieved a maximum detection accuracy for a value of $\tau_{cl} = 60$. We obtained around 10 thousand clusters, that is almost 10 netflow clusters for each malware sample. The fine P2P filter further provided around 3 thousand clusters, other clusters being dropped as non-P2P flows. In fact, we observed that almost 60% of discarded clusters include less than 40 flows. These clusters mostly implement network discovery protocols or activities related to the sandbox environment (e.g. SMB service). We also observed among discarded clusters a long tail of clusters that include a high number of flows. These are all scan clusters that were mostly discarded by the AS-based filter. The remaining clusters include mostly P2P flows and spam flows. The latter were discarded by the port-based filter, thus obtaining a total number of 2,975 malware P2P clusters.

On the other hand, we build benign P2P clusters using traffic that we collected from a well protected corporate network. It consists of netflow packets obtained during one month of activity for nearly 150 network terminals. Unfortunately certain P2P applications such as bittorrent were banned due to policy restrictions. We thus completed our training set by manually executing P2P applications in a controlled environment. Then we applied our filter in order to build clusters of benign P2P flows. We obtained a total number of 415 benign P2P clusters, associated with 53 distinct IP addresses. Almost half of our benign P2P clusters included skype flows (230), but we also obtained other clusters such as eMule (43), kademlia (37) and Gnutella (35). We mostly obtained skype flows mainly because the corporate network is aimed for professional usage, and other P2P applications were being occasionally used. On the other hand, we collected 379 benign P2P clusters from manually executed P2P applications, including bittorrent, eDonkey and Manolito. Our training set thus included 794 benign P2P clusters that we used as input to our detection model.

5.2 P2P Botnet Detection Model

The P2P filter provided a resulting set of 3,769 P2P clusters, including 2,975 of malware and 794 of benign P2P clusters. The purging process discards P2P clusters that are shared between both malware and benign P2P flows. Hence, we cross-correlated our set of 3,769 P2P clusters, using hiearchical clustering, and we obtained 53 meta-clusters, including 41 discriminatory meta-clusters. The latter include more than 93% of only benign or malware P2P flows, such as 7 meta-clusters which clearly included Sality flows, 4 meta-clusters included Waledac, and 9 meta-clusters included Skype flows. On the other hand, 12 meta-clusters included both malware and benign flows, and so they are discarded as non-discriminatory clusters. For instance, and regarding the kademlia protocol, 10 meta-clusters were found to include kademlia-like P2P clusters. In fact kademlia protocol includes 4 message types: `ping`, `store`, `find_node` and `find_value`. 7 meta-clusters included more than 93% of only malware or benign P2P flows. These meta-clusters included strictly `find_node` and `find_value` messages. Malware and benign P2P clusters were falling into different meta-clusters mostly because of their different chunk rates. The three remaining meta-clusters included between 60 and 70% of malware clusters. These clusters included mainly `ping` requests, which are dropped by the purging module as being non-discriminatory flows. We obtained as output to this process a training set of 2,647 P2P clusters, including 2,143 malware clusters and 504 benign P2P clusters.

Cross-Validation: We performed a cross validation experiment, using our labeled ground truth dataset, in order to evaluate the detection accuracy of BotSuer. We split our malware dataset into two subsets: 80% of malware samples that we use for training, and the remaining 20% that we use for evaluation. Yet for the 53 IP addresses that were using P2P protocols in the corporate network, we randomly extracted 10 IP addresses from our training set so we can use use them for evaluation. Then we merged traffic for our 20% malware evaluation set with random IP addresses that we extracted from the corporate network traffic. We further use our training set of malware and benign P2P traffic as input to our P2P filter, and then we applied our cluster purging module with different values of the threshold τ_d. We obtained for each value of τ_d a different number of labeled P2P clusters that we use to train our SVM classifier. We evaluated the

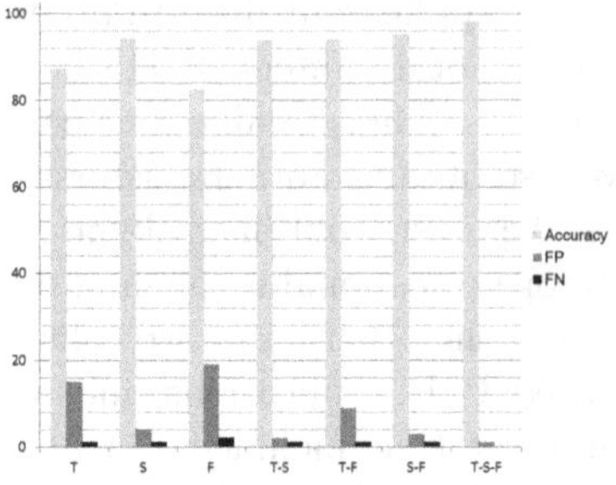

Fig. 2. Contribution of features towards detection

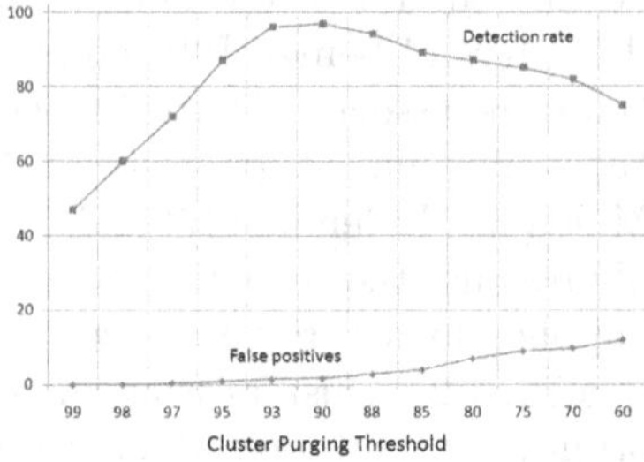

Fig. 3. Detection rate and false positives rate for BotSuer

detection models that we obtained using the validation dataset, including traffic from the corporate network merged with the traffic from the 20% remaining malware samples. We measured the detection rate and the false positives rate for each value of τ_d, and that we illustrate with the ROC curve in Fig. 3.

As in Fig. 3, a high value for τ_d - *i.e. closer to the y-axis* - leads to lower detection rates and less false positives. In fact, a high value for τ_d discards more clusters during the learning process, and so it reduces the coverage of BotSuer. On the other hand, lower values for τ_d allows less discriminatory clusters to go through the purging process. These would reduce the accuracy of BotSuer, leading to a higher false positives rate and a lower detection accuracy. We found a linear increase in the detection rates for values of τ_d lower than 93%. Yet we obtained the best detection rates for values of τ_d in the interval $[90 - 93\%]$, including 97% detection rate and 1.6% false positives.

Contribution of Features towards Detection: We used the cross-validation method to evaluate the contribution of our features towards detection. We built detection models by separately using each class or combinations of these classes, and then we evaluated the detection accuracy, including false positives and negatives, as illustrated in Fig. 2.

Our model achieves almost 97% detection accuracy when combining all classes of features. When evaluated separately, space-based features ($\mathcal{S}$) provided the best detection accuracy (93%). We believe this is due to the fact that our learning set includes netflow packets collected during only 1 hour of malware execution time. Hence, time-based features provided a lower accuracy because the execution time is not long enough to accurately characterize periodicities in P2P control flows. On the other hand, size-based features provided low detection accuracy when solely used to build the detection model, almost with 20% false positives rate. This was not surprising because malware may still bypass size-based features by adding noise or paddings to P2P control flows. Although only few malware currently uses such techniques, we observe that size-based features cannot be used as standalone features for P2P botnet detection. As opposed to time and space features, size-based features may still be bypassed without modifying the underlying overlay protocol.

Testing with ISP Flows: The test against ISP flows was indeed challenging because we lack the ground truth about the nature of detected infections. We trained our detection model with all P2P clusters at our disposal, and we used the value of τ_d that provided the best detection accuracy. The ISP flows included 3 hours of anonymized netflow for almost 4,347 distinct IP addresses, collected at a peek traffic rate. The DNS coarse filter was applied at the source, and so the netflow trace that we obtained included only flows not preceded with susccessful DNS resolutions. We split this traffic into one hour length intervals, which corresponds to the malware execution time in our dataset. Then we applied our P2P filter and botnet detection model on traffic in each time interval. Our filter extracted 793 P2P flow clusters, associated with 146 distinct IP addresses. In order to validate our P2P filter, we also obtained from the ISP a list of the anonymized IP addresses that were found to be implementing P2P applications in our netflow trace, and that were detected using proprietary P2P protocol signatures. We admit that these signatures cannot formally validate our approach, but they may still provide a ground truth to evaluate our results. P2P signatures detected 169 distinct IP addresses that implement P2P applications, including 23 IP addresses not detected by our filter. In fact 18 of these addresses triggered less than 10 P2P flows. They provided small P2P clusters that are discarded by our P2P filter. We asked the ISP to verify about the origin of these flows since the source IP addresses for the traffic at our disposal were all anonymized. We found that these were mostly signaling flows for external IP addresses being routed through the ISP network. Therefore, we would not consider them as false negatives. On the other hand, the 5 remaining IP addresses detected by the P2P signatures were indeed false negatives. They mostly included utorrent P2P over HTTP flows, and so they were discarded by our port-based filter. They were also discarded by the AS-based filter most likely because these P2P applications were dormant during the observation window. In fact we observed mostly incoming flows, but there were relatively little outgoing P2P flows for these IP addresses.

We used the 793 P2P clusters as input to our detection model. It identified 11 malicious flow clusters associated with 3 distinct IP addresses. Since traffic was all anonymized, we validated our approach using public IP blacklists[2]. In fact we consider a cluster to include malware P2P flows when at least 20% of remote IP addresses in this cluster appear in public backlists. Indeed we identified using these blacklists 4 netflow clusters as being malicious, *all associated with the same IP address*. We thus consider this as a strong evidence of a malware infection, and so it is a true positive. Yet the same infected IP address was appearing in the list of IP addresses that were found to be implementing P2P applications by the proprietary ISP signatures. This is another clear evidence of the ability of BotSuer to detect P2P bots that use known benign P2P protocols. Unfortunately we couldn't validate the 7 remaining clusters using the publicly available blacklists, and so they are likely to be misclassified by our system. We thus achieved 0.8% false positives, associated with two distinct IP addresses

[2] RBLS is a free API to check multiple public IP blacklists - `http://www.rbls.org/`

during 3 hours of traffic monitoring for 4,347 distinct IP addresses, which is a fairly reasonable number of alerts to be handled by the system administrator.

6 Discussion

BotSuer detects malware using statistical features such as chunk rates, periodicities and botnet distribution. It also classifies flows for a specific P2P application using high level features such as flow size and number of packets. It would be thus unable to accurately detect P2P bots if the attacker modifies P2P communication intervals, contacts a larger set of peers, or uses random paddings in its malware P2P traffic. Such maneuvers modify the statistical consistency in malware P2P flows and so it makes detection more difficult. However, these techniques require an attacker to rebuild its malware P2P toolkit. They also increase overhead and reduce botnet stability, which makes botnet management more difficult. Indeed botnets would no longer be able to dissimulate within benign P2P flows, and so they will be exposed to other detection techniques.

On the other hand, BotSuer differentiates malware and benign P2P control flows using only a binary classification. We aim to extend this study by proposing new techniques to identify specific botnet families during detection. We will explore unsupervised clustering algorithms that apply to our set of malicious P2P flows. These algorithms separate in different clusters P2P flows that are likely to be generated by common families of botnets (e.g. Sality, Storm, Nugache).

Certain malware uses P2P protocols only as a failover mechanism to replace its primary C&C channels, and so it would not contribute to building the detection model. In [17], authors propose an approach that detects primary C&C channels during malware execution in a sandbox. It dynamically intercepts primary C&C channels and forces malware to engage in a failover strategy. Using techniques such as [17] enables to trigger P2P failover strategies so we can take these into account in our detection model. These techniques usually apply during malware sandbox analysis and so they are out of scope in this study.

7 Conclusion

This paper presented BotSuer, a new approach to detect P2P bots inside a network perimeter. To the best of our knowledge, BotSuer is the first to detect even single infected P2P bots. BotSuer implements a fully behavioral approach to detect malware infected nodes in the network. Yet it does not use deep packet inspection nor intrusion detection alerts. It is thus resilient against malware obfuscation mechanisms and detects bots that use encrypted P2P communications for command and control. It also detects stealthy P2P bots, as well as targeted infections inside a network perimeter. We tested BotSuer against real world P2P traffic, including malware and benign P2P flows. Our experimental results validate our approach, which provides a high detection accuracy with a very low false positives rate.

References

1. Cuckoo: Automated malware analysis system (2010), http://www.cuckoobox.org/
2. Anubis: Analyzing unknown binaries (2011), http://anubis.iseclab.org
3. Aberer, K., Hauswirth, M.: An overview on peer-to-peer information systems. In: Proceedings of the 4th workshop on Distributed Data and Structures (2002)
4. Bilge, L., Balzarotti, D., Robertson, W., Kirda, E., Kruegel, C.: Disclosure: Detecting botnet command and control servers through large-scale netflow analysis. In: Proceedings of the 28th Annual Computer Security Applications Conference, ACSAC (2012)
5. Bilge, L., Kirda, E., Kruegel, C., Balduzzi, M.: Exposure: Finding malicious domains using passive dns analysis. In: Proceedings of the 18th Network and Distributed System Security Symposium, NDSS (2011)
6. Claise, B.: Cisco systems netflow services export version 9. RFC 3954 (October 2004)
7. Cristianini, N., Shawe-Taylor, J.: An Introduction to Support Vector Machines and Other Kernel-based Learning Methods. Cambridge University Press (2000)
8. Davies, D.I., Bouldin, D.W.: A cluster seperation measure. IEEE Transactions on Pattern Analysis and Machine Intelligence (1979)
9. François, J., Wang, S., State, R., Engel, T.: BotTrack: Tracking botnets using netFlow and pageRank. In: Domingo-Pascual, J., Manzoni, P., Palazzo, S., Pont, A., Scoglio, C. (eds.) NETWORKING 2011, Part I. LNCS, vol. 6640, pp. 1–14. Springer, Heidelberg (2011)
10. Grizzard, J.B., Sharma, V., Nunnery, C., Kang, B.B.: Peer-to-peer botnets: Overview and case study. In: Proceedings of USENIX HotBots (2007)
11. Gu, G., Perdisci, R., Zhang, J., Lee, W.: Botminer: Clustering analysis of network traffic for protocol and structure independent botnet detection. In: Proceedings of the IEEE Symposium on Security and Privacy, SSP (2008)
12. Kapoor, A., Mathur, R.: Predicting the future of stealth attacks. In: Virus Bulletin (2011)
13. Karagiannis, T., Broido, A., Brownlee, N., Claffy, K., Faloutsos, M.: Is p2p dying or just hiding? In: IEEE GLOBECOM, vol. 3, pp. 1532–1538 (2004)
14. Karagiannis, T., Broido, A., Brownlee, N., Claffy, K., Faloutsos, M.: File-sharing in the internet: A characterization of p2p traffic in the backbone. UC Riverside technical report (November 2003)
15. Little, M.A., McSharry, P.E., Roberts, S.J., Costello, D.A., Moroz, I.M.: Exploiting nonlinear recurrence and fractal scaling properties for voice disorder detection. Biomedical Engineering Online 6 (2007)
16. Nagaraja, S., Mittal, P., Hong, C.-Y., Caesar, M., Borisov, N.: Botgrep: Finding p2p bots with structured graph analysis. In: Proceedings of the 19th USENIX Security (2010)
17. Neugschwandtner, M., Comparetti, P.M., Platzer, C.: Detecting malware's failover c&c strategies with squeeze. In: Proceedings of the 27th Annual Computer Security Applications Conference, ACSAC (2011)
18. O'Kane, P., Sezer, S., McLaughlin, K.: Obfuscation: The hidden malware. In: IEEE Security & Privacy, pp. 41–47 (2011)
19. Ollmann, G.: Botnet communication topologies: Understanding the intricacies of botnet command-and-control. Damballa White Paper (2009)
20. Ordonez, C.: Clustering binary data streams with k-means. In: Proceedings of the 8th Workshop on Research Issues in Data Mining and Knowledge Discovery, pp. 12–19 (2003)

21. Porras, P., Saidi, H., Yegneswaran, V.: Conficker c p2p protocol and implementation. Technical report, Computer Science Laboratory, SRI International (2009)
22. Quinlan, J.R.: C4.5: Programs for Machine Learning. Morgan Kaufmann Publishers (1993)
23. Stover, S., Dittrich, D., Hernandez, J., Dietrich, S.: Analysis of the storm and nugache trojans: P2p is here. In: USENIX, vol. 32 (December 2007)
24. Stutzbach, D., Rejaie, R.: Understanding churn in peer-to-peer networks. In: Proc. ACM SigComm Internet Measurement Conference (2006)
25. Symantec. Internet security threat report. 2012 Trends 18 (April 2013)
26. Tenebro, G.: W32.waledac threat analysis. Symantec Technical Report (2009)
27. Trusteer. No silver bullet: 8 ways malware defeats strong security controls (2012), Whitepaper accessible on `http://www.trusteer.com/resources/white-papers`
28. Willems, C., Holz, T., Freiling, F.: Cwsandbox: Towards automated dynamic binary analysis. In: IEEE Security & Privacy (2007)
29. Yen, T.-F., Reiter, M.K.: Are your hosts trading or plotting? Telling p2p file-sharing and bots apart. In: 30th Conf. Distributed Computing Systems (2010)
30. Zhang, J., Perdisci, R., Lee, W., Sarfraz, U., Luo, X.: Detecting stealthy p2p botnet using statistical traffic fingerprints. In: Proc. 41st DSN (2011)

Resource Access Control in the Facebook Model

Konstantinos Chronopoulos[1,⋆], Maria Gouseti[1,⋆], and Aggelos Kiayias[2]

[1] University of Amsterdam, Amsterdam, Netherlands
[2] National and Kapodistrian University of Athens, Athens, Greece
{kon.chrono,mgouseti}@gmail.com, aggelos@di.uoa.gr

Abstract. We study the fundamental security properties of *resource access control* as suggested by the operation of current social networks including Facebook. The "facebook model", which treats the server as a trusted party, suggests two fundamental properties, "owner privacy" and "server consistency", and two different modes of revocation, implicit and explicit. Through black-box experimentation, we determine Facebook's implementation for resource access control and we analyze its security properties within our formal model. We demonstrate, by the construction of explicit attacks, that the current implementation is not secure: specifically, we attack privacy with implicit revocation and server consistency. We evaluate the implications of the attacks and we propose amendments that can align the current implementation with all its intended security properties. To the best of our knowledge this is the first time that a security analysis of the Facebook resource access control mechanism is performed within a proper security model.

Keywords: Access control, social networks, security analysis.

1 Introduction

Increasingly the basic mode of sharing resources between individuals over the Internet is over social networking sites, of which the most popular by far is Facebook [12]. A common characteristic of the majority of these systems is that they rely on a trusted server that is supposed to manage the access control of the submitted resources in a way that is consistent to the social graph that reflects the relationships between the users. More sophisticated sites as Facebook logically divide the entities of the system into resource owners and "resource consumers" that, without loss of generality, can be all thought of as applications that perform various functions over the resources of the social network that are available to them. In the above setting, the social networking server, acting as a trusted party, is supposed to maintain an access control matrix that pairs owners and applications. Each entry specifies a level of access that an owner permits to an application. A suite of protocols should be available to the entities of the system that enable the update of the matrix according to a set of well-defined

⋆ Work performed while at the National and Kapodistrian University of Athens. Research partly supported by ERC project CODAMODA.

M. Abdalla, C. Nita-Rotaru, and R. Dahab (Eds.): CANS 2013, LNCS 8257, pp. 179–198, 2013.

rules that are publicized by the server. In the case of Facebook the suite of protocols broadly follows the directives set out in the OAuth standard [13], and puts forth the following security rules regarding the management of resources.

- Each owner has a vector of resources so that each entry has at least two levels of access: public and protected. The first suggests that the resource is available to anyone, while the second suggests that its availability to other users (the owner's "friends") will be explicitly managed by the owner.
- Each application can selectively request access to an owner's resources including the resources of the owner's friends that are accessible to her, in exchange for a certain service.
- Access to the resources can be revoked by the owner in at least two different modes: (i) explicit, which takes place when the owner requests the server to revoke access, (ii) implicit, which takes place when the owner ceases to use the application for a certain specified period of time (this type of revocation concerns only applications and not the owner's friends).

Given the above rules, the suite of protocols that implements the access control system should meet the following intuitive objective: the access to resources gained by an adversary that controls a set of malicious owners and applications and is directing an orchestrated attack against the system should never exceed the union of resources that the adversarially controlled entities can access individually. Furthermore it is sensible that an additional property should also be satisfied: the server should be capable of *justifying* any action of resource access that takes place, by previous actions that have previously taken place. For example, when an application A accesses a resource R of an owner O, this can be justified by, e.g., the existence of a previous authorization action where O explicitly allowed A to have access to R.

These two properties can be termed respectively "Owner Privacy" and "Server Consistency." The proper modeling of these properties in the setting of social networks with a trusted server and the degree that the Facebook implementation for resource access control satisfies them is the focus of our work.

Contribution #1: Security Model. We put forth a formal model for the properties of owner privacy and server consistency. To this effect, we define a security protocol problem that we call "Resource Access Control in Social Networks" or RACS. The RACS problem calls for the design of a set of protocols that enable parties of three types, the server, the owners and the applications (or clients), to store and access resources.

An adversary attacking owner privacy against a RACS implementation, can be thought of as playing a game with a challenger that represents the part of the system that remains uncorrupted. The objective of the adversary is to distinguish the value that is found in a certain resource location of an honest owner out of two possible choices. The adversary in the course of the game can corrupt owners and applications and request access to resources. The access may include the target location provided the access is revoked (explicitly or implicitly) prior to the challenge value being placed in the location. A RACS implementation satisfies owner privacy if no matter the course of action the adversary takes, it gains no advantage in predicting the value of the target location.

An adversary attacking server consistency, aims to bring the server to a state where it cannot justify a certain resource access action by the previous actions. This attack can be also thought of as a game between the adversary and a challenger. In this case, the challenger simply records all actions taken by the adversary who as before controls a set of malicious owners and applications. The challenger checks the history of all actions to ensure that all resource accesses are justifiable. The adversary wins the game in case the challenger discovers an unjustifiable action. A RACS implementation satisfies server consistency if no adversary can win the above game with probability that is non-negligible.

Contribution #2: Experimenting with Facebook. From the perspective of the above model, Facebook implements a protocol suite solving the RACS problem. While the implementation is private and one cannot be certain of the actual source code, the implementation of the protocol suite can be relatively easily extracted at a sufficient level of detail to perform a security analysis. To achieve that, we created several applications that used the most representative ways of client authorization (server-side and client-side), either via custom code or via the SDK's provided by Facebook (specifically, the PHP SDK and the Javascript SDK). We also created a small number of Facebook users and connected them through "friend" relationships.

For each application we captured the transcripts that were generated during the protocol execution and collected all artifacts produced by the protocols such as access tokens and authorization codes. We attempted a variety of "improper" protocol executions, such as sharing tokens from one protocol execution instance to another and attempted to access resources with applications that were not properly authorized. All the above operations gave a relatively complete picture of the protocol implementation at least with respect to the security features that are of interest in this work. In a nutshell, Facebook appears to be using standard cryptographic primitives to generate tokens (such as pseudorandom functions and encryption) and performs access control at the logical level as expected of a system providing resource access control in the trusted server setting.

Contribution #3: Attacking the Facebook Implementation. We subjected the Facebook RACS implementation to a security analysis with respect to the properties of owner privacy and server consistency. Our findings are as follows.

First, we discover an attack against owner privacy in the case of implicit revocation. Recall that implicit revocation means that an application ceases to have access to the owner's data when the owner does not use it for a certain period of time. This is something that Facebook supports as evidenced by the following: *"... If you haven't used an app in a while, it won't be able to continue to update the additional information you've given them permission to access."* [1]. A simple description of our attack is as follows: an adversarial application is initially authorized by two users that are friends and has access to their resources.

Subsequently, the access to the first user's resources is implicitly revoked while the second user continues to use the application. We show how the malicious application can exploit an access token obtained via the second user to break the implicit revocation from the first user and gain access to the resources that should have been otherwise unavailable to it.

Second, we demonstrate that the Facebook implementation does not satisfy server consistency. Specifically, we show that an adversary controlling two applications is capable of transferring access tokens from one application to the other, thus generating access resource actions that cannot be justified by the server (we note that this problem was already hinted in [17] in work independent to our experiments that dealt with OAuth in general); still our work better exemplifies the ramifications of the issue by putting it in the context of an attack against the server consistency property. Note that the way access tokens are defined in Facebook have lead to problems before [24]; as our work exemplifies, even though they have been improved since then, they are still not entirely secure.

Third, we show that Facebook satisfies owner privacy when only explicit revocation is taken into account. This holds true under the assumption that the function that is used to implement the access tokens has the characteristics of a pseudorandom function (a plausible assumption).

Finally, we complete our exposition with a set of modifications that can be applied in order to enable Facebook to conform to the formal model and satisfy both owner privacy and server consistency.

We stress that all our attacks were experimentally verified with the Facebook API and that the Facebook security team was notified of our findings.

Related Work. Facebook follows the general OAuth standard. For OAuth, there exist recent works formally studying its security [5],[6] and a security analysis of OAuth implementations from the single-sign on perspective was performed in [17]. These analyses do not capture what we term the "Facebook model", where a trusted server manages resources within a social network and takes into account the fact that users can manage access to the resources of their friends as well; this is an essential feature that goes beyond OAuth and for the case of Facebook (and other social networking sites) security ought to be considered in this perspective; our properties (and in fact some of our attacks as well) rely critically on the social networking aspects.

Previous work for resource access control in the setting of social networks can be divided in two broad categories.

First, there is a substantial amount of work, e.g., [14],[15],[16] that considers the expression of access control directives in the setting of social networks. This enhances classical ideas in access control (e.g., [19],[20],[21]) with the notion of the social graph and the complexities that come with relationships between entities in this setting. Our work is orthogonal to this line of work: we consider the formal modeling of security properties and whether a certain protocol implementation conforms to the model *independently* of how the actual implementation of the access control system works.

Second, a sequence of works [7],[8],[9],[10],[11] considered the problem of privacy in the setting of an untrusted server. This work can be further divided in works that attempt to provide privacy within an existing system (including Facebook, e.g.,[7],[8],[9]), while others solved the problem following a "clean-slate" approach redesigning the whole system from scratch, e.g., [10],[11]. While considering privacy against an untrusted server is an important direction, our work demonstrates that the problem of formally modeling privacy and consistency in the trusted server model (for a sophisticated system such as Facebook) is already challenging and there are substantial benefits to be gained from the security analysis as the attacks we discovered exemplify.

2 The RACS Problem

The RACS problem refers to how owners, who have stored their protected resources in a server, can share them with clients (applications) using the help of the server. Since the RACS problem concerns social networks, owners are also able to make connections and share their resources with other owners. Every owner is entitled to share her resources as well as the resources that other owners share with her by authorizing clients and declaring to the server the scope of the clients' access.

We express the RACS functionality by describing the valid set of actions that captures all the possible interactions between the server and the client or the owner. We will use the notation O and O_i, and C and C_i where $i = 1, 2, ..$ to represent the unique id that identifies owners and clients respectively. We assume that these sets of clients' ids and owners' ids are disjoint.

Owner's actions:

- register(O): O registers with the server,
- authenticate(O): O authenticates herself to the server,
- update(O, $\langle resources \rangle$): O updates her protected resources,
- authorize_owner(O_1, O_2, f_o): O_1 makes a connection with O_2 and authorizes her to access the subset of her protected resources as expressed by the function f_o. The function f_o is a projection ($D^n \rightarrow D^k$) where $k \leq n$ and D is the space of the owner's resources. We will also use f to represent the set of indexes of the projection. Informally, this function defines the subset of the resources O_1 shares with O_2,
- authorize_client($O, C, f_\mathrm{s}, f_\mathrm{g}$): O authorizes C to access the subset of her protected resources as expressed by the function f_s, and the subset of the resources of the owners connected to her, as defined by the intersection of function f_g and the resources accessible by her,
- use(O, C): O uses C's service,
- revoke(O, C): O explicitly revokes C's access to her protected resources,
- logout(O): O ceases interacting with the server.

Client's actions:

- register(C): C registers with the server,
- authenticate(C): C authenticates itself to the server,
- access_resources(C, O, f): C makes a resource request to access the subset of O's protected resources defined by function f.

A solution to the RACS problem is a set of protocols that involve three parties, the owner O, the client C and the server S. The owner O is an entity capable of granting access to a protected resource, after registering and authenticating with the server. The client C is an application offering a service to the owner O. In order to do that it makes protected resource requests. The server S maintains a matrix $r()$ containing the protected resources of each owner; moreover, it has three access control matrices `oos_ac`(), `ocs_ac`(), `ocg_ac`(), containing the permissions owners have granted to: other owners (owner-to-owner for herself), clients about their own resources (owner-to-client for herself), and clients about the resources of their connections (owner-to-client according to social graph), respectively. Also it keeps an expiration time matrix `expt`() and a log file `log_file` with all the actions generated by the affiliated parties (owners and clients).

Registration & Authentication Protocols. Firstly, both owners and clients have to register to the server. When a party (owner or client) registers with the server, it acquires a unique identifier *id* and the server records the action register(*id*). Then, the server can identify a party as either an owner or a client with id *id* and the action authenticate(*id*) is recorded.

Client Authorization Protocol. O authorizes C to access the subset of her resources that is defined by the function f_{authS} and the subset of the resources of the owners connected to her defined by f_{authG}. This protocol ends successfully if the first function is stored in `ocs_ac`$[O, C]$, the second in `ocg_ac`$[O, C]$ and the action authorize_client($O, C, f_{\mathsf{authS}}, f_{\mathsf{authG}}$) is recorded in the server's `log_file`.

Owner Authorization Protocol. With this protocol O_1 can create a connection between herself and O_2. In this process O_1 also provides to the server the function f_{o} determining the resources she wishes to share with O_2. The server is responsible to store in the cell `oos_ac`$[O_1, O_2]$ the function f_{o}. After updating the matrix `oos_ac` the server records the action authorize_owner(O_1, O_2, f_{o}).

Client Access Resources Protocol. This protocol enables C to access O's resources from the server. It is divided into two cases depending on the party that initiates the protocol.

In the first case, O wants to use C's service. In return, C requests access to a subset of O's protected resources. To accomplish that, C, after being authenticated by the server, makes a request providing its desired function f. If C is not authorized, the "Client Authorization Protocol" is executed; else, the server responds according to the information saved in its access control matrices and the desired functions. Also the action use(O, C) will be recorded in `log_file`.

In the other case, C wishes to access a subset of O's protected resources on its own accord. To achieve that, after authenticating itself, it makes a protected resource request to the server providing O's id and its desired function f. Then, the server can verify that C is authorized, that its access has not expired, and responds accordingly to the information saved in its access control matrices and the desired functions.

In both cases, if the protocol ends with the client acquiring any subset f' of the requested resources, the action access_resources(C, O, f') should be recorded in the server's `log_file`.

Client Revocation Protocol. There are two cases in which C's access can be revoked. In the first case, C's access is revoked implicitly by the server (*Implicit Revocation*) after a certain period of time has passed since O used C's service for the last time. This period of time is set by the server. C's access is revoked until O uses its service again.

In the other case, C's access is revoked explicitly by O (*Explicit Revocation*), even if it has not expired. To accomplish that, the server, after authenticating O and if O requests it, it will set the functions $\texttt{ocs\_ac}[O, C]$ and $\texttt{ocg\_ac}[O, C]$ to be f^* (the default level of public access). After the revocation is complete the action revoke(O, C) is recorded in the server's `log_file`.

Owner Revocation Protocol. O_1 is able to break a connection with O_2 and revoke O_2's access to her resources (explicit revocation); $\texttt{oos\_ac}[O_1, O_2]$ is set to f^* and the action revoke(O_1, O_2) is recorded in the server's `log_file`.

2.1 Correctness and Security Properties

To argue about correctness and security we will introduce a security parameter λ which will capture the level of security associated with our proposed solutions.

Correctness. For all O, $O' \neq O$, C, $f : D^n \to D^k$ where $k \leq n$, if

$$\Big((f \subseteq \texttt{ocs\_ac}[O, C]) \wedge (server\_time < \texttt{expt}[O, C])\Big) \vee$$
$$\Big((f \subseteq (\texttt{ocg\_ac}[O', C] \cap \texttt{oos\_ac}[O, O'])) \wedge (server\_time < \texttt{expt}[O', C])\Big),$$

then C, by running the "Client Access Resources Protocol", will receive the resources $f(\texttt{r}[O])$ and the server will record the action access_resources(C, O, f).

Owner Privacy. In order to reason about the owner privacy property, we have to consider the two cases of revocation, explicit and implicit. In the case of owner privacy with explicit revocation, we consider attacks where a client gains access to an owner's protected resources while it is not authorized (either because its access was explicitly revoked by the owner or because it was never authorized). In case of owner privacy with implicit revocation, we also consider attacks where an authorized client accesses an owner's resources while its access has expired.

In both cases, we define an adversary A who has access to some owners' and clients' accounts. We express the security property as a game G^A between a challenger and the adversary A. The challenger operates the server and all the honest owners. The game allows the adversary to provide two values so that one of them at random is stored at an adversarially chosen resource location for an owner of the adversary's choice that is outside of its social network. The adversary, then, tries to find out which of the two values was used and if it succeeds in its guess it wins the game. For this game G^A, the suggested protocol solution satisfies the security property only if the adversary cannot win the game with significant advantage. Definition 1 in appendix formally describes this property. Note that this type of modeling is similar to the modeling of security of encryption in the IND-CPA sense [22].

In the other case, we have the adversary A, as we defined it in the previous section, but we change the behavior of the challenger. The security property related to implicit revocation is intended to capture the fact that a client C can access the owner's O resources even if the owner is not using the client's service in a period of time of dt units, however, after the end of this time period the C's access is revoked. The number dt is a system parameter that the server S is initialized with and expresses the maximum amount of time that should pass from the last use of the client by the owner within which the client is still allowed to access the owner's resources. Given that the security property is time sensitive we need to capture the passage of time in the server. The challenger increases by one the number of time units that have passed each time the adversary completes an action; moreover, in the course of the game we allow the adversary to advance the time of the server by issuing "advance clock" instructions if it wishes. Definition 2 in appendix formally describes this property.

Server Consistency. In addition to the owner privacy property, the server S should be able to justify, from its log file, every client's access to owners' resources. To accomplish that, it should not allow access to the owner's resources unless it authenticates the client and is certain that the client is authorized to access these resources.

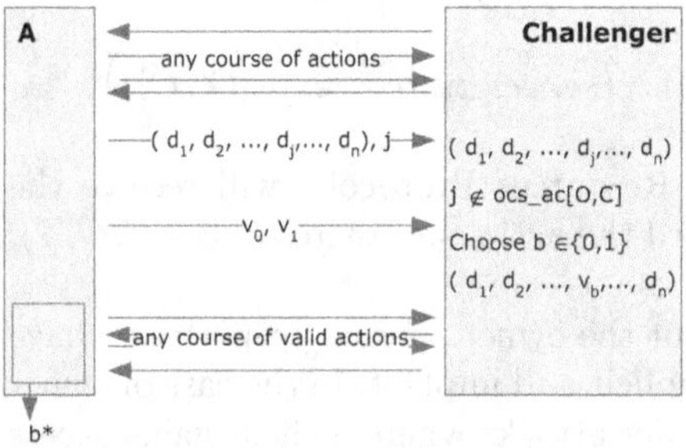

Fig. 1. The adversary A should not guess b with probability different than $\frac{1}{2}$ (Explicit revocation)

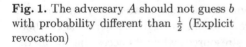

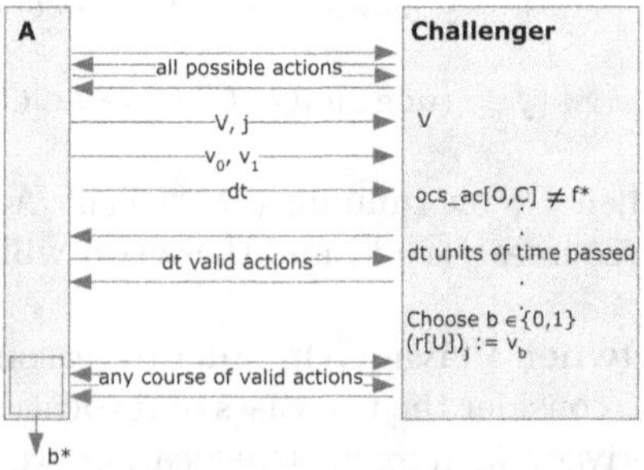

Fig. 2. The adversary A should not guess b with probability different than $\frac{1}{2}$ (Implicit revocation)

We define a predicate $P(\texttt{log\_file}, dt)$ as follows, P is true if and only if every record of the action access_resources(·) in the log file log_file follows one of the sequences of actions mentioned below, for any $O, C, t_0, t_1, t_2, t_3, t_4, t_5$:

1. $\langle \text{authenticate}(O), t_0 \rangle$
2. $\langle \text{authorize\_client}(O, C, f_s, f_g), t_1 \rangle$
3. any of $\langle \text{authenticate}(O), t_2 \rangle$ or $\langle \text{use}(O, C), t_3 \rangle$
4. $\langle \text{authenticate}(C), t_4 \rangle$
5. $\langle \text{access\_resources}(C, O, f_s'), t_5 \rangle$, where $(f_s' \subseteq f_s)$.

In addition, the following statements should be also true (i) $t_0 < t_1 < t_3 < t_5$, (ii) $t_4 < t_5$, (iii) if action use(·) exists then $t_5 - t_3 < dt$, else $t_5 - t_1 < dt$, (iv) between t_0 and t_1, or t_0 and t_3, or t_2 and t_3 the action logout(O) should not exist, (v) between t_1 and t_5 the action revoke(O, C) should not exist. As long as these statements are true all protocol actions are allowed.

This sequence of actions expresses that O has given access to C. However, C can gain access to O's resources through the owners connected to her, as a result the predicate will be true if an owner O' exists such that the owner O has shared her resources $\texttt{oos\_ac}[O, O']$ with O', and O' has authorized C to access the resources of the owners connected to her defined by a function $\texttt{ocg\_ac}[O', C]$. Consequently, the action access_resources(C, O, f'), where $f' \subseteq (\texttt{oos\_ac}[O, O'] \cap \texttt{ocg\_ac}[O', C])$, would be justified.

Finally, for all PPT adversaries A, the probability of the event P to be false should be negligible: $Pr[P(\texttt{log\_file}, dt) = 0] = negl(\lambda)$, where P is the predicate described before and log_file is a random variable that reflects the log file given the activity of A as described above.

3 Facebook's Implementation

In this section we will focus on the implementation of Facebook as we observed it works, based on its public documentation and our efforts to analyze it. The correspondence between the parties of the RACS problem and the parties that participate in the social network of Facebook is described as follows: Facebook is the server, the client or Facebook app is the client and the user is the owner. A connection between two users is called friendship and it requires authorization from both users to be considered valid. However, the functions that define the resources they share with each other do not have to be the same. The security properties that Facebook intends to provide include explicit revocation *as well as* implicit revocation.

As a solution to the RACS problem, Facebook implements a set of protocols which involve three parties, the user U, Facebook S and the client C. We assume, without loss of generality, that Facebook has the same matrices for access control and storing resources as the server in RACS with one small deviation: it appears that instead of the expiration time, it keeps the last time a user accessed a client service, as a result matrix expt corresponds to the last time of usage plus dt. We also assume that clients have a matrix c_at to store access tokens.

Registration & Authentication Protocols. Users register by providing an email and a password and obtain a user account with a unique id. On the other hand, clients register with Facebook and obtain a unique identifier "app_id" and an "app_secret." After the assignment of a unique identifier, the action register(·) is recorded. Then, both owners and clients are able to use their credentials to authenticate with Facebook. If Facebook identifies a user or a client with id *id*, the action authenticate(*id*) is recorded.

Client Authorization Protocol. U is redirected by Facebook to a pop up dialog that informs her about the *users permissions*, expressed by f_{authS}, and the *friends data permissions* (which are about her friends), expressed by f_{authG} she has to give to C in return for service. These functions are provided in every authorization request by C. If U accepts to share these resources, the functions are stored in ocs_ac$[U, C]$ and ocg_ac$[U, C]$. Additionally, the action authorize_client($U, C, f_{\mathsf{authS}}, f_{\mathsf{authG}}$) is recorded.

Friend Authorization Protocol. In Facebook, U_1 is able to make a *"friend request"* to U_2 who has the choice to accept or decline. Only when U_2 accepts the request, Facebook stores in cell oos_ac$[U_1, U_2]$ the function f_1 that defines the resources U_1 shares with U_2 and in oos_ac$[U_2, U_1]$ the function f_2 that expresses the resources U_2 shares with U_1. In addition, the actions authorize_owner(U_1, U_2, f_1) and authorize_owner(U_2, U_1, f_2) are recorded.

Client Access Resources Protocol. In order to gain access to U's resources, C has to use an access token that represents its access rights. This token is issued to C only when U initiates this protocol. U initiates the flow by requesting C's service from Facebook, (Fig. 3, step 1). Then, Facebook verifies that C is authorized by checking the function in ocs_ac$[U, C]$, (Fig. 3, step 2). If U has not authorized the client, Facebook initiates the "Client Authorization Protocol" (Fig. 3, step 3). Else, the user is redirected immediately to C's service providing the signed_request as shown in step 4 of Fig. 3.

The signed_request is a signed parameter, which contains a "short-lived" access token[1]. The signed_request is the concatenation of an HMAC SHA-256 signature, a period '.' and a base64url encoded JSON object. The signature potion is signed using the C's app_secret which is only known by it and Facebook. A short-lived access token and its expiration time along with other public information concerning U are included in the signed_request [23].

Then, C has the option to send the short-lived access token to Facebook, along with its app_id and its app_secret to get a "long-lived"[2] one, (see Fig. 3, step 5). Based on our experiments, in this step Facebook considers that U accessed

[1] This has duration 1 to 2 hours, it has the form $CAA\{(0-9) \cup (a-z) \cup (A-Z)\}^9 BA\{(0-9) \cup (a-z) \cup (A-Z)\}^l ZDZD$ and is only acceptable when the user is signed in.

[2] This has duration 60 days and is renewed each time the user accesses the service; it has the form $CAA\{(0-9) \cup (a-z) \cup (A-Z)\}^9 BA\{(0-9) \cup (a-z) \cup (A-Z)\}^l ZD$ and can be used even if the user is offline.

C's service, it stores the current server time (server time + dt in $\texttt{expt}[U, C]$) and the action use(U, C) is recorded. C can store the long-lived access token and make protected resource requests with either the short-lived access token or the long-lived one as it is described below.

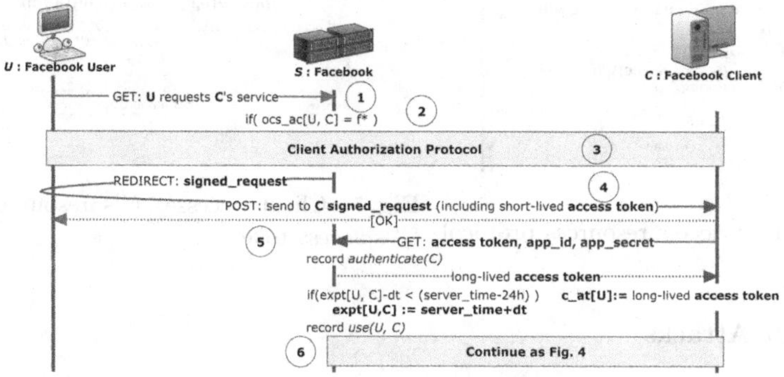

Fig. 3. Client access resources protocol (when initiated by user)

If C is not authorized it can access only a user's public resources (f^*). However, if it wishes to access more resources of U, C can make protected resource requests providing an access token from a user that it has stored in $\texttt{c\_at}$ and the function f which expresses the desirable resources. If the access token has expired or is invalid for any reason, C does not receive U's resources. On the other hand, if the access token is valid, then Facebook responds to C with f', the subset of resources defined by the intersection of f and the functions stored in $\texttt{ocs\_ac}$ and $\texttt{ocg\_ac}$(see Fig. 4 and Fig. 5). Additionally Facebook records the action access_resources(C, U, f'). In our experiments we observed that when a client makes a protected resource request and it is asking for resources that it cannot access, then an empty vector is returned to it, which is justified by our assumption that Facebook responds to a client's request with the intersection of the requested resources and the authorized ones.

Client Revocation Protocol

- *Implicit Revocation.* The access of C is implicitly revoked by Facebook if U does not access C's service for a certain period of time, currently set to 60 days [2]. If Facebook receives a protected resource request after $\texttt{expt}[U, C]$ has passed, it should not grant access to C until U visits C's service again.
- *Explicit Revocation.* If U wishes to revoke C's access, Facebook sets the functions $\texttt{ocs\_ac}[U, C]$ and $\texttt{ocg\_ac}[U, C]$ to f^* and the action revoke(U, C) is recorded.

Unfriend Protocol. U_1 can revoke U_2's access to her resources only by explicitly requesting Facebook. To accomplish that, U_1 can request to "unfriend" U_2. As a result, Facebook will change the functions $\texttt{oos\_ac}[U_1, U_2]$ and $\texttt{oos\_ac}[U_2, U_1]$ to f^* and the actions revoke(U_1, U_2) and revoke(U_2, U_1) are recorded.

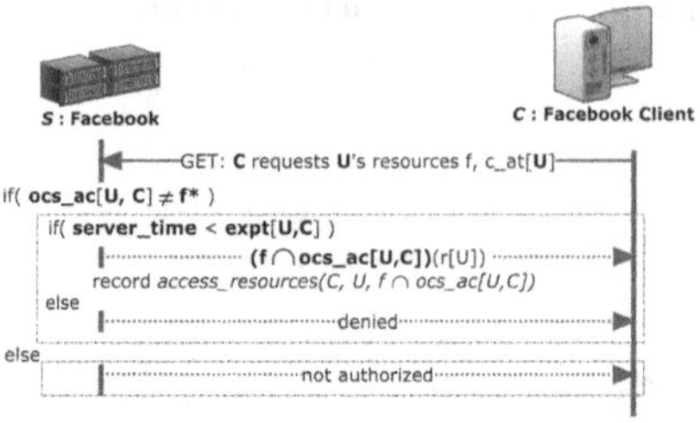

Fig. 4. Client access resources protocol

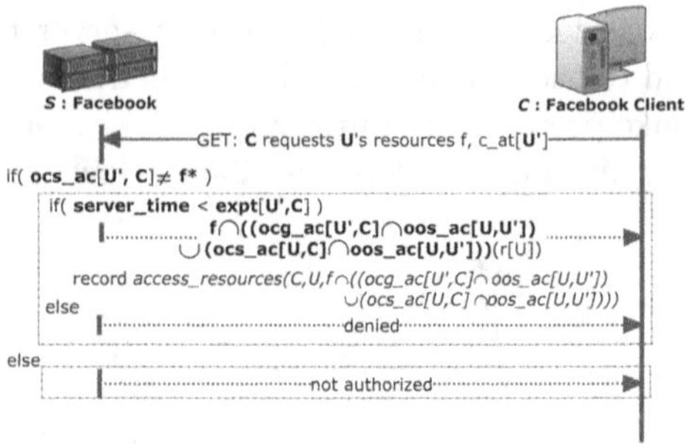

Fig. 5. Client accesses U's resources using U''s access token

3.1 Our Attacks

Owner Privacy with Implicit Revocation. We show how an attacker is able to access the user's resources even after its access has expired (implicitly). The attack relies on the fact that during the client access resources protocol (as described in Fig. 5), Facebook does not properly verify the permissions that U' has given to the client regarding her friends. Consequently a client can use a token issued by U' to access another user's U resources defined by $\texttt{ocs\_ac}[U, C] \cap \texttt{oos\_ac}[U, U']$ which may be a superset of $\texttt{ocg\_ac}[U', C] \cap \texttt{oos\_ac}[U, U']$; this will be in violation of access control rules in the case that U has not used client C for a period of time and thus access to resources $\texttt{ocs\_ac}[U, C]$ should be implicitly revoked.

For example in Fig. 7, we define two friends U and U' and a resource j that U shares with U'. Further we define a client C that is authorized by U' but is not given access to her friends' resources ($\texttt{ocg\_ac}[U', C] = f^*$). However, C is authorized by U to view resource j ($j \in \texttt{ocs\_ac}[U, C]$). Consider now that U does not use C's service for more than dt seconds, while U' continues using this service. It follows that C should have access only to U''s resources and not to the resource j of U. However, if C requests j using U''s access token, Facebook will respond with $(\texttt{oos\_ac}[U, U'] \cap \texttt{ocs\_ac}[U, C])(\texttt{r}[U])$ which contains $(\texttt{r}[U])_j$.

Attack Implementation. In this paragraph we will present an application that implements the attack we described in Sec. 3.1. The application records in a database every user that has used its service along with their access tokens. In this way the application is able to request the users' resources even if they are offline and present them in a table. If the access of the application to a user's resources has expired, it tries to obtain her resources first as public information, and then through her friends' access tokens. This is possible by asking Facebook for the user's friends cross-referencing the response with its database and then trying her friends' access tokens until it is successful.

For instance, consider an attacker that wants to access user P's activities. Suppose that user P has not used the application and its access has expired.

Further, no other user that accesses this application has access to P's activities which are private and hence the application cannot access the user's activities.

Now consider a friend of P, named K, who has access to P's activities and authorizes the application but without granting any *friends data permissions*, hence the application should not be allowed to view P's activities via K's authorization. However, the application, in violation of the implicit revocation, will be able to use the access token of K to obtain P's resources as we can see in Fig. 6.

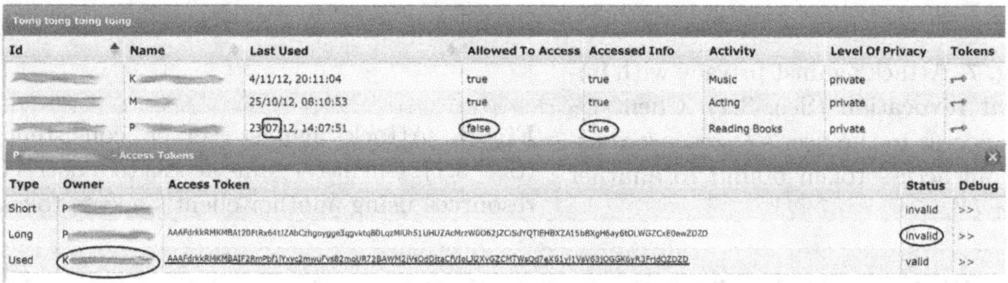

Fig. 6. Implementation of the attack against privacy with implicit revocation (Sec. 3.1). The application's access to P's resources has expired and her resources are private, however, because K is P's friend the application can use his valid token to access her resources even though K has not authorized it.

Server Consistency. We next show how an attacker can violate the server consistency property, i.e., bring the Facebook server to a state where a certain access resources action takes place by a client without being justifiable given Facebook's access control matrices. The attack relies on the fact that Facebook does not authenticate properly the client that transmits an access token[3]. For example in Fig. 8 we define a user U and two clients C_1, C_2 both controlled by the attacker. U revokes C_2's access while it authorizes C_1. The attacker transfers the access token to C_2 and initiates the "Client Resource Access Protocol." Facebook does not authenticate the client - it only verifies the token. This means that the predicate $P(\texttt{log\_file}, dt)$ is false since in the log file `log_file` the action $authenticate(C_1)$ does not precede the action $\text{access\_resources}(C_1, U, j)$.

We also prove positive results about the Facebook implementation (correctness and explicit revocation) that are presented in the appendix.

3.2 How to Fix It

As we have seen in Sec. 3.1 Facebook fails to satisfy the owner privacy property with implicit revocation and the server consistency property. Both problems can be easily fixed by changing the Facebook implementation.

Facebook does not satisfy the owner privacy property with implicit revocation because when it accepts a protected resource request in which the access token does not correspond to the user U, who owns the resources, but to another

[3] We note that a similar issue was pointed out in [17] however without a formal framework within which an attack can be described.

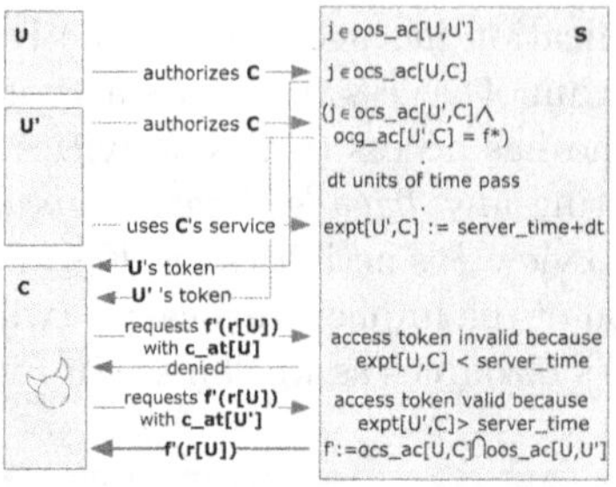

Fig. 7. Attack against privacy with implicit revocation (Sec. 3.1). Client C_2 has access to the user's U resources using an access token bound to another user U'.

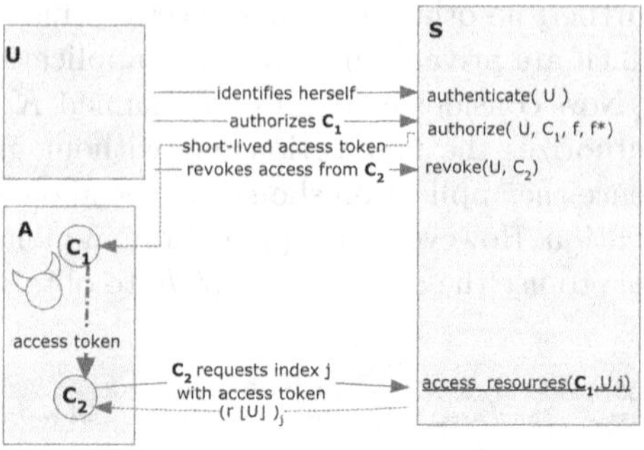

Fig. 8. Attack against server consistency (Sec. 3.1). Client C_2 gains access to a user's U resources using another client's access token.

user U', it grants the client C access to the intersection of the resources that were prior to revocation visible by the client and accessible to U' while it ignores U''s *friends data permissions*. This enables the application to access data that otherwise — per Facebook's public policy — should have been unavailable to it. In order to satisfy this property and continue to operate correctly, Facebook should respond with the intersection of the user's U resources that U' can access and the *friends data permissions* that U' has given to the client i.e., $(\mathsf{oos\_ac}[U, U'] \cap \mathsf{ocg\_ac}[U', C])$. In this way, the access token provides the access to friends' resources that the user it is bound to has authorized and it is consistent with the expiration time.

Facebook does not satisfy the server consistency property because the binding of access tokens to clients is not properly verified during the resource access protocol. In order to solve this problem Facebook should verify the identity of the client and compare it to the client id extracted from the token. There are various ways to achieve that, as we will discuss below.

Facebook may provide the opportunity to clients to sign in as users do. Facebook could verify that the client requesting access through an authenticated session matches the recipient of the access token. In this way, the action authenticate(·) with the proper client will be recorded in the server log.

Another way of identifying the client can be through its IP address. Clients are obliged to register their domain, so without adding any overhead to the clients, Facebook could check that the IP address, from which the request came, is registered by the client who is bound to the access token. In this case, if the IP address matches, the action authenticate(·) will be recorded to the log and hence server consistency will hold.

A more sound method would be to bind the resource request to the identity of the client cryptographically. This functionality is already used elsewhere in the Facebook implementation, since a message authentication code, signed_request, is used by the Facebook server to prove to a client that a short-lived access token came from it. In the same way a client can use its app_secret to sign the access token and a random value to ensure liveness (for instance current time) and then send it to Facebook. As a result, Facebook will be able to verify the identity of the client and in this way record the action authenticate(·) to its log.

The above description treats the client as an independent entity from the user. Facebook provides also a second way to execute client code, which is by a JavaScript SDK. In this way the client's service runs on the user's browser. This complicates matters further since it would be precarious to include the client's app_secret into the Javascript code (as this would reveal it to the user). In this case, Facebook may restrict the scope of the access token to be used within the session that was issued only. Note that this only partially solves the problem as the attack can still be mounted if the attacking clients are running concurrently by the same user, however it prohibits sharing tokens across sessions and hence restricts the inconsistency that can be introduced by the adversary.

4 Conclusion

In this work we presented a security model for the problem of resource access control in social networks. We focused on the setting of a trusted server and extracted the basic rules of access control as suggested by the operation of Facebook (hence the use of the term the "Facebook model"). We abstracted the problem of solving access control in this setting as the RACS problem. Via experimentation we extracted the RACS implementation of Facebook and we performed a security analysis of it with respect to our two security properties: owner privacy and server consistency. Our analysis revealed vulnerabilities of Facebook's implementation that we exploited. The resulting attacks we described rendered the implementation deficient in terms of owner privacy and consistency. We also suggested ways that these vulnerabilities can be (easily) patched.

To the best of our knowledge this is the first time that a security analysis of how Facebook manages resource access control is attempted within a proper security model. While the vulnerabilities of Facebook we discover can be easily fixed, our work shows the value of analysis within a security model and can enable future work in the security evaluation of other social networking sites with respect to the problem of sharing resources securely. Our security model can be extended easily to capture more complex access control relations as well as consider a partially malicious server. We leave these directions as future work.

References

1. Facebook: Data Use Policy | Facebook (October 15, 2012), `http://www.facebook.com/about/privacy/your-info-on-other`
2. Facebook: Removal of offline_access permission (October 16, 2012), `https://developers.facebook.com/roadmap/offline-access-removal`
3. Facebook: Access Tokens and Types (November 14, 2012), `http://developers.facebook.com/docs/concepts/login/access-tokens-and-types`

4. Facebook: New security restrictions for OAuth authorization codes (November 14, 2012), https://developers.facebook.com/roadmap
5. Chari, S., Jutla, C., Roy, A.: Universally composable security analysis of OAuth v2.0. Cryptology ePrint Archive, Report 2011/526 (2011)
6. Pai, S., Sharma, Y., Kumar, S., Pai, R.M., Ringh, S.: Formal verification of OAuth 2.0 using Alloy framework. In: Proceedings of the International Conference on Communication Systems and Network Technologies (CSNT), pp. 655–659 (2011)
7. Luo, W., Xie, Q., Hengartner, U.: FaceCloak: An architecture for user privacy on social networking sites. In: PASSAT (2009)
8. Lucas, M.M., Borisov, N.: flyByNight: Mitigating the privacy risks of social networking. In: WPES (2008)
9. Guha, S., Tang, K., Francis, P.: NOYB: Privacy in online social networks. In: WOSN (2008)
10. Baden, R., Bender, A., Spring, N., Bhattacharjee, B., Starin, D.: Persona: An online social network with user-defined privacy. In: SIGCOMM (2009)
11. Jahid, S., Mittal, P., Borisov, N.: EASiER: Encryption-based Access Control in Social Networks with Efficient Revocation. In: ASIACCS (2011)
12. Top 15 Most Popular Social Networking Sites (November 16, 2012), http://www.ebizmba.com/articles/social-networking-websites
13. Hardt, D. (ed.): The OAuth 2.0 Authorization Protocol (November 16, 2012), http://tools.ietf.org/html/draft-ietf-oauth-v2-31
14. Carminati, B., Ferrari, E., Heatherly, R., Kantarcioglu, M., Thuraisingham, B.M.: A semantic web based framework for network access control. In: SACMAT, pp. 177–186 (2009)
15. Sandhu, R., Coyne, E., Feinstein, H., Youman, C.: Role-Based Access Control Models. IEEE Computer 29(2) (1996)
16. Kruk, S.R., Grzonkowski, S., Gzella, A., Woroniecki, T., Choi, H.-C.: D-FOAF: Distributed identity management with access rights delegation. In: Mizoguchi, R., Shi, Z.-Z., Giunchiglia, F. (eds.) ASWC 2006. LNCS, vol. 4185, pp. 140–154. Springer, Heidelberg (2006)
17. Sun, S.-T., Beznosov, K.: The Devil is in the (Implementation) Details: An Empirical Analysis of OAuth SSO Systems. CCS (2012)
18. Lang, B.: Trust Degree Based Access Control for Social Networks. In: Proc. of the International Conference on Security and Cryptography (2010)
19. Ferraiolo, D., Kuhn, R.: Role-based access controls. In: 15th NIST-NCSC National Computer Security Conference, pp. 554–563 (October 1992)
20. Sandhu, R.S.: Lattice-based access control models. IEEE Computer 26(11), 9–19 (1993)
21. Sandhu, R.S., Samarati, P.: Access Control: Principles and Practice. In: IEEE Communications Magazine, pp. 40–48 (September 1994)
22. Bellare, M., Desai, A., Pointcheval, D., Rogaway, P.: Relations Among Notions of Security for Public-Key Encryption Schemes. In: Krawczyk, H. (ed.) CRYPTO 1998. LNCS, vol. 1462, pp. 26–45. Springer, Heidelberg (1998)
23. Facebook: Using the signed_request Parameter, http://developers.facebook.com/docs/howtos/login/signed-request/ (March 18, 2013)
24. Doshi, N.: Facebook Applications Accidentally Leaking Access to Third Parties - Updated (May 10, 2011), http://www.symantec.com/connect/blogs/facebook-applications-accidentally-leaking-access-third-parties (June 26, 2013)

A Definitions

A.1 Definitions of Privacy

Here we present the formal definition of owner privacy property with explicit revocation.

Definition 1. *Given a RACS implementation, consider an adversary A who controls a set of owners O^* and a set of clients C^* and performs the following actions:*

1. *follows an arbitrary course of actions using the sets of owners O^* and clients C^* and is able to request from the challenger to execute any action on behalf of honest owners and clients; these actions include all the actions of the protocol as described in Sec. 2.*
2. *chooses an owner $O \notin O^*$, $j \in \{1, ..., n\} \wedge (j \notin f^*)$ and provides data to fill the resource vector $\mathtt{r}[O]$,*
3. *then provides two values v_0 and v_1 so that the challenger can choose $b \in \{0,1\}$ at random and set $(\mathtt{r}[O])_j$ to be v_b. For the game to continue it should be that the adversary has neither direct access, authorized by the owner, to the resources stored in index j nor through other owners (but it may still have the ability to access the rest of the resources of the owner O). Formally: (i) $j \notin \mathsf{ocs\_ac}[O, C]$, where $C \in C^*$, (ii) $j \notin \mathsf{oos\_ac}[O, O']$, where $O' \in O^*$, (iii) $j \notin (\mathsf{ocg\_ac}[O'', C] \cap \mathsf{oos\_ac}[O, O''])$, for any owner O'',*
4. *continues playing the game by following an arbitrary course of actions in order to produce b^*; the challenger responds to all its requests except for those that trivialize its task, namely: (i) $\mathrm{authorize\_client}(O, C, f_s, f)$, $(C \in C^*) \wedge (j \in f_s)$, (ii) $\mathrm{authorize\_owner}(O, O', f_o)$, where $(O' \in O^*) \wedge (j \in f_o)$, (iii) $\mathrm{authorize\_client}(O'', C, f, f_g)$, $(j \in (f_g \cap \mathsf{oos\_ac}[O, O'']))$.*
5. *the output of the game G^A is 1 iff "$(b^* = b)$".*

The Explicit Revocation *property states that for all PPT adversaries A, A should not win the game G^A with probability different than $\frac{1}{2}$ plus something negligible. Formally, for all PPT A, $Pr[G^A(1^\lambda) = 1] = \frac{1}{2} + negl(\lambda)$.*

Definition 2. *Given a RACS implementation, consider an adversary A who controls a set of owners O^* and a set of clients C^* and performs the following actions:*

1. *follows an arbitrary course of actions using the sets of owners O^* and clients C^* and is able to request from the challenger to execute any action on behalf of honest owners and clients; these actions include all the actions of the protocol as described in Sec. 2.*
2. *chooses an owner $O \notin O^*$, $j \in \{1, ..., n\} \wedge j \notin f^*$ and provides data to fill the resource vector $\mathtt{r}[O]$,*
3. *provided that for all $O' \in O^*$, $j \notin \mathsf{oos\_ac}[O, O']$, it provides two values v_0 and v_1 after which point, when dt units of time after the last authorization of any adversarial client or the last use of client's services took place by O*

or any other owner connected to O with access to index j of O's resource vector, the challenger chooses $b \in \{0,1\}$ at random and sets $(\mathtt{r}[O])_j$ to be v_b. After this point, the actions:
- use(O, C), *where* $C \in C^*$,
- authorize_client$(O, C, f_\mathsf{s}, f_\mathsf{g})$, *where* $(C \in C^*) \wedge (j \in f_\mathsf{s})$,
- authorize_owner(O, O', f_o), *where* $(O' \in O^*) \wedge (j \in f_\mathsf{o})$,
- use(O'', C), *where* $(C \in C^*) \wedge (j \in (\mathtt{ocg\_ac}[O'', C] \cap \mathtt{oos\_ac}[O, O'']))$,
- authorize_client$(O'', C, f_\mathsf{s}, f_\mathsf{g})$, *where* $(C \in C^*) \wedge (j \in (f_\mathsf{g} \cap \mathtt{oos\_ac}[O, O'']))$,

are not allowed for the rest of the game.

4. *continues playing the game by following an arbitrary course of valid actions (all actions of the protocol except from the ones in the previous step) using the sets of owners O^* and clients C^*, in order to produce b^*, (Fig. 2)*
5. *the output of the game G^A is '1' when the event "$(b^* = b)$" happens,*

The Implicit Revocation *property states that for all PPT adversaries A, A should not win the game G^A with probability different than $\frac{1}{2}$ plus something negligible. Formally, for all PPT A, $Pr[G^A(1^\lambda) = 1] = \frac{1}{2} + negl(\lambda)$.*

A.2 Definition of Pseudorandom Functions

Definition 3. *A function, $F : X \rightarrow \{0,1\}^\lambda$ is called pseudorandom if for every probabilistic polynomial-time oracle machine M and for all sufficiently large λ*

$$|Pr[M^F(1^\lambda)] - Pr[M^H(1^\lambda)]| < \varepsilon_{\mathsf{PRF}} < negl(\lambda)$$

where function $H : X \rightarrow \{0,1\}^\lambda$ is a random function.

B The Security and Correctness Properties That Hold

Theorem 1. *Facebook's implementation is correct as it was defined in Sec. 2.1.*

Proof. We will prove that if the assumptions of the definition in Sec. 2.1 are true and a client runs the "Client Access Resources Protocol", then the client will receive the requested resources and Facebook will record the appropriate action. Suppose that f is the requested resources of U by client C and

$$\Big((f \subseteq \mathtt{ocs\_ac}[U, C]) \wedge (server\_time < \mathtt{expt}[U, C])\Big) \vee$$
$$\Big((f \subseteq (\mathtt{ocg\_ac}[U', C] \cap \mathtt{oos\_ac}[U, U'])) \wedge (server\_time < \mathtt{expt}[U', C])\Big)$$

where U' is any other user. We distinguish the following cases:
$f \subseteq f^*$ - In this case C asks for public information that can be recovered by anyone hence correctness holds.
$f \supset f^*$ *and* $f \subseteq \mathtt{ocs\_ac}[U, C]$ - In this case, C already possesses an access token from U by executing the protocol in Fig. 3. Thus, when C runs the "Client Access Resources Protocol" in Fig. 4 it will receive $f(\mathtt{r}[U])$ since $(server\_time < \mathtt{expt}[U, C])$ and the action access_resources(U, C, f) will be recorded.

$f \supset f^*$ *and* $f \subseteq \texttt{ocg\_ac}[U', C] \cap \texttt{oos\_ac}[U, U']$) - In this case, C already possesses an access token from U' authorizing to access the resources of U defined by f. Running the protocol in Fig. 5 it will receive $f(\texttt{r}[U])$ since $server\_time < \texttt{expt}[U', C]$ and the action access_resources(U, C, f) will be recorded. □

Owner Privacy with Explicit Revocation

Theorem 2. *Facebook satisfies the owner privacy property with explicit revocation (Sec. 2.1) under the access token pseudorandomness assumption and the assumption that the adversary cannot obtain an access token through any other means*[4] *(e.g., by hacking another client).*

Proof. Access Token Pseudorandomness Assumption. We will assume that the functions longTokenGenerator$(U, C, origin, session)$ and shortTokenGenerator$(U, C, u_session, exp, origin)$ are pseudorandom. Informally, a pseudorandom function is a function which cannot be distinguished from a truly random function by any efficient procedure which can get the value of the function at arguments of its choice. Hence, the distinguishing procedure may query the function being examined at various points, depending possibly on previous answers obtained, and yet cannot tell whether the answers were supplied by a pseudorandom function or by a random function (see Definition 3 in the appendix). We will assume that there is a PPT adversary A, as described in Sec. 2.1, and we define WIN^A the event "$(b = b^*)$". Let us first assume that the functions are random. Then we construct an algorithm B (Fig. 9) who will simulate the user U and Facebook in the game (as described in Sec. 2.1) to the adversary A. B answers all requests from A but it does not authorize it to gain access to index j of the user's resource vector. Additionally, if requested, B can authorize clients that are not controlled by A to access the target resource.

The event D, which represents that A found a token that grants access to the target resource, is defined in the environment created by B.

$$Pr[WIN^A] = Pr[WIN^A|D] * Pr[D] + Pr[WIN^A|\bar{D}] * Pr[\bar{D}]$$

The event $WIN^A|\bar{D}$ means that A did not find the user's access token (long-lived or short-lived), so it does not have access to the user's resources and the way it chooses between '0' and '1' is arbitrary. Due to the fact that algorithm B chooses b uniformly over $\{0, 1\}$ the probability is $\frac{1}{2}$. $Pr[WIN^A|D]$ is less or equal 1 from the definition of probability. So:

$$Pr[WIN^A] \leq Pr[D] + \frac{1}{2} * Pr[\bar{D}] \Rightarrow Pr[WIN^A] \leq \frac{1}{2} + \frac{Pr[D]}{2}$$

If A asks B to authorize q clients that are not controlled by it to access index j of U's protected resources, then B will have to generate q access tokens that

[4] In order to prove that the implementation satisfies the owner privacy property with explicit revocation we are going to assume that a PPT adversary A has negligible probability to find a long-lived or a short-lived access token that was produced by Facebook and was not given to it.

will grant access to the target resource. The probability of A to guess a specific token is $\frac{1}{2^\lambda}$, assuming that the count of all possible long-lived and short-lived access tokens is 2^λ. Consequently, $Pr[D]$ is $\frac{q}{2^\lambda}$ and the probability of A winning the game is: $Pr[WIN^A] \leq \frac{1}{2} + \frac{q}{2^{\lambda+1}}$. Finally, if we add the cost of the PRF to this probability, we have:

$$Pr[WIN^A] \leq \frac{1}{2} + \frac{q}{2^{\lambda+1}} + \varepsilon_{\mathsf{PRF}}$$

Since $\frac{q}{2^{\lambda+1}} + \varepsilon_{\mathsf{PRF}}$ is negligible, A cannot win the game with significant probability and owner privacy property with explicit revocation is proven under the access token pseudorandomness assumption. □

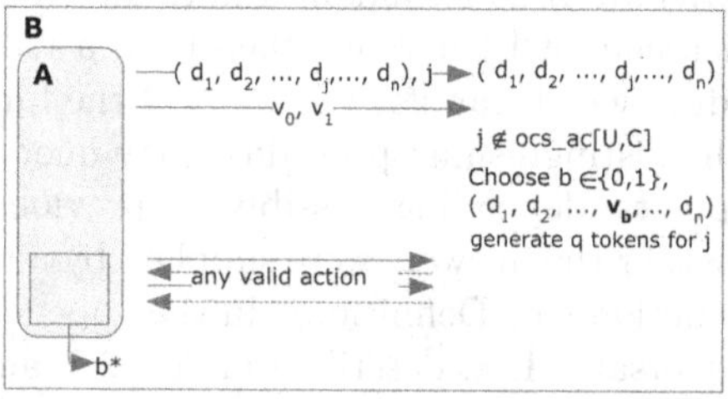

Fig. 9. Algorithm B simulates Facebook S and user U to the adversary A (part of proof of theorem 2)

Wave-to-Access: Protecting Sensitive Mobile Device Services via a Hand Waving Gesture

Babins Shrestha, Nitesh Saxena, and Justin Harrison

Computer and Information Sciences
University of Alabama at Birmingham
{babins,saxena,justinh}@uab.edu

Abstract. Mobile devices, such as smartphones and tablets, offer a wide variety of important services to everyday users. Many of these services (such as NFC payments) are highly sensitive and can be abused by malicious entities, without the knowledge of the device user, in the form of insider attacks (such as malware) and/or outsider attacks (such as unauthorized reading and relay attacks).

In this paper, we present a novel application permission granting approach that can be used to protect any sensitive mobile device service. It captures user's intent to access the service via a lightweight hand waving gesture. This gesture is very simple, quick and intuitive for the user, but would be very hard for the attacker to exhibit without user's knowledge. We present the design and implementation of a hand waving gesture recognition mechanism using an ambient light sensor, already available on most mobile devices. We integrate this gesture with the phone dialing service as a specific use case to address the problem of malware that makes premium rate phone calls. We also report on our experiments to analyze the performance of our approach both in benign and adversarial settings. Our results indicate the approach to be quite effective in preventing the misuse of sensitive resources while imposing only minimal user burden.

1 Introduction

The deployment and usage of mobile devices, such as smartphones and tablets, is continuously rising. These devices open up immense opportunities for everyday users offering valuable resources and services. In addition to traditional capabilities, such as voice calling, SMS and web browsing, many smartphones come equipped with the NFC (Near Field Communication) functionality, a form of RFID (Radio Frequency IDentification). An NFC phone can be used as a RFID contactless payment token, such as a credit or an ATM card. It can also be used as an RFID reader that can "read" other RFID cards or NFC phones in close physical proximity. NFC equipped devices, such as Samsung Galaxy Nexus and Nexus 7 are already in the US market. All these different features on modern mobile devices have attracted not only millions of consumers to smartphones and tablets but have also motivated the developers to write varieties of apps for these devices, such as the Google Wallet app for NFC-based payment using Android phones.

M. Abdalla, C. Nita-Rotaru, and R. Dahab (Eds.): CANS 2013, LNCS 8257, pp. 199–217, 2013.

1.1 Security and Privacy Threats

Due to the increasing popularity of mobile devices, they have become a prime target of malicious attackers and cyber criminals. In particular, such malicious entities attempt to misuse the sensitive services provided by these devices. For example, they might be interested in making free (premium rate) phone calls or sending free SMS using a legitimate user's phone, or want to make NFC payments which will be charged to the user's account. Specifically, two major threats exist that form the primary focus of this paper: (1) the insider attacks in the form of malware, and (2) the outsider attacks in the form of NFC unauthorized reading, as explained below.

Mobile Device Malware: There has been a rapid increase in mobile device malware targeting different smartphone platforms [15, 17, 16, 7, 33, 22, 28, 30]. This is made possible especially because users often download applications from untrusted sources, many of which may contain hidden malicious code. Such malware, once installed on the smartphone, can exploit the smartphones in many different ways. For example, the malware can use the resources/sensors of the phone to learn something sensitive about the user, such as it can use the camera and take the pictures of the user and surrounding, or it can make premium rate phone calls or send premium rate SMS messages without user's knowledge, or use NFC reader to skim for physical credit cards in close proximity. Indeed, a proof-of-concept Trojan Horse electronic pickpocket program under the cover of a tic-tac-toe game has already been developed by Identity Stronghold [2].

Unfortunately, current operating systems (e.g., Android and iOS) provide inadequate security against these malware attacks. For granting permission to an application requiring access to the resources, these operating systems either require out-of-context, uninformed decisions at the time of installation via manifest [3, 32] or prompt users to determine their interest via system prompt [29, 32]. This approach relies upon user diligence and awareness – it is well-known that most users do not pay attention to such "Yes/No" prompts and frequently just select "Yes" so as to proceed with the installation. Once granted the permission, applications have full authority over the resources and can access them without owner's consent. In addition to relying upon user permission, application review process is also undertaken. However, review process has failed in the past [40, 23], and users gaining the root permission/ jail-breaking the phone can easily install the third party applications which may not have been reviewed [40, 23].

NFC Unauthorized Reading and Relay Attacks: The NFC (tag) chip on a smartphone stores sensitive information. In particular, it stores the credit card number and other relevant information. Such an information can easily be subject to clandestine eavesdropping. For example, an adversary with an NFC reader can walk past a victim carrying an NFC phone, and can read the credit card information stored on the NFC chip. This clearly allows for fraud or illegitimate purchases for which the owner will be charged. It can also lead to owner tracking and privacy problems [1]. This information may also be used to impersonate an NFC device via cloning [1].

Furthermore, similar to RFID tags, NFC devices are susceptible to "ghost-and-leech" relay attacks [42]. Here an adversary, called a "ghost," relays the information surreptitiously read from a legitimate RFID device to another colluding adversary, called a "leech." The leech transmits this information to a legitimate reader and vice versa, and can thus impersonate the RFID tag. All cryptographic authentication protocols are vulnerable to this form of an attack [18].

1.2 Controlling Access via Intuitive Gestures

In this paper, we set out to defend against the aforementioned insider attacks (malware) and outsider attacks (unauthorized reading and relay attacks) against critical mobile device services. We observe that all these attacks, in order to remain stealthy, occur in scenarios where the device user has no intention to access the underlying services. Thus, if the user's intent to access the services can be captured in some way, these attacks could be prevented. We propose to elicit user's intent via simple gestures performed by the user prior to accessing the services. In other words, whenever the user wants to access the service, she will simply perform a particular gesture. On the other hand, if the attacker attempts to access the service, the gesture will be missing and the access request will be blocked. This general idea was first introduced in a recent (short) paper [27] limited to address the specific problem of NFC malware-based attacks. In the current paper, we extend the scope of the approach to cover NFC unauthorized reading and relay attacks as well as introduce novel gesture recognition schemes for malware-based attacks against any sensitive service.

Access control using a simple gesture has significant usability advantages when compared to typing in a complex password, which are often forgotten, and has significant security advantages over using nothing at all. The approach is also *more secure than using a "Yes/No" dialog box*, given that most users are already *habituated* to pressing "Yes" when prompted. Hand waving gesture is only one of the gestures for human-enabled authorization of actions, and there can be a number of gestures in the future, which when used carefully can overcome the problem of habituation of pressing "Yes." Moreover, a Yes/No dialog box will require the user to *explicitly press a button* when an application requires access to a resource while the user is performing another activity on the device. The gesture-based approach, on the other hand, would not require a user interface, but rather the user can just be prompted using a "Toast" mechanism, available for example in Android, or notified using a notification bar.

1.3 Our Contributions

We propose how a gesture-based mechanism can be used to elevate the permission for applications which require access to critical mobile device resources and services (see Figure 2). The main contributions of this paper are summarized as follows.

1. We propose a novel approach to malware defense for mobile devices based on intuitive gesture recognition. Specifically, we suggest a new lightweight hand waving gesture that utilizes the ambient light sensor and accelerometer, ubiquitously available on smartphones and tablets.
2. We also introduce the use of the waving gesture for the purpose of selective unlocking for NFC/RFID tag. Instead of promiscuously providing the information to any reader, we argue for a model which only approves the permission to read the tag's information once the gesture is detected.
3. We report on the implementation of our prototypes for the wave gesture recognition scheme on the Android platform. As a specific use case for defending against malware that makes *premium rate phone calls*, we integrate this gesture recognition scheme with the phone's voice dialing service. The resulting app requires the user to perform the wave gesture before making a phone call (or a phone call to a premium rate number) .
4. To evaluate our approach, we conduct many experiments simulating the behavior of malicious attacker and normal user usage activity. Our results demonstrate the waving gesture to be quite effective in protecting critical mobile device services without imposing much burden on the user.

2 Related Work

2.1 Malware Detection and Prevention

There is a plenty of prior work on defending against malware on traditional desktop computers. Static analysis[10, 38, 36], also known as signature-based detection, is based on source or binary code inspection to find suspicious patterns (malware) inside the code. However, malware authors can evade this analysis by simple obfuscation, polymorphism and packing techniques. Also it cannot detect zero day attacks. Dynamic analysis[14, 39, 5, 41], also known as behavior-based detection, monitors and compares the running behavior of an application (e.g., system calls, file accesses, API calls) against malicious and/or normal behavior profiles through the use of machine learning techniques. It is more resilient to polymorphic worms and code obfuscation and has the potential to defeat zero-day worms.

These techniques for desktop computers are still considered too time consuming for resource-constrained mobile devices operated on battery. Most existing research focuses on optimizing desktop solutions to fit on mobile devices. The work of [38] tries to speed up the signature lookup process in static analysis by using hashes. Several collaborative analysis techniques have been proposed to distribute the work of analysis by a network of devices [34, 37]. Remote server assisted analysis techniques have also been proposed to reduce the overhead of computation on individual devices [9, 6].

2.2 Gesture Recognition and Security

Gesture recognition has been extensively studied to support spontaneous interactions with consumer electronics and mobile devices in the context of pervasive computing [4, 8, 25]. Due to the uniqueness of gestures to different users, personalized gestures have been used for various security purposes.

Gesture recognition has been used for user authentication to address the problem of misuse of stolen devices [19, 11]. In [19], a mobile device gets unlocked for use when it detects the gait (walking pattern) of the legitimate owner. In [11], a smartphone gets locked when it does not detect the "picking-up phone" gesture which the owner naturally performs to answer a phone. Both works provide transparent user authentication and do not require explicit user involvement. [26] reports a series of user studies that evaluate the feasibility and usability of light-weight user authentication based on gesture recognition using a single tri-axis accelerometer.

Related to our work, gesture recognition has also been suggested to defend against unauthorized reading and ghost-and-leech relay attacks in RFID systems [12, 21]. The secret handshakes scheme proposed in [12] allows an RFID tag to respond to reader query selectively when the tag owner moves the tag in a certain pattern (i.e., secret handshake). In contrast to our hand waving gesture recognition, secret handshakes requires a pre-stored template, and the underlying gestures themselves may not be very intuitive for the user. The work of [21] uses posture as a valid context to unlock an implanted RFID device without changing the underlying user usage model. This approach, however, can have high false positive rate in practice and is not applicable in the context of mobile devices that are not implanted.

The use of unique key press gestures or secure attention sequences (SASs), such as CTRL-ALT-DEL, may also serve as a means to defend against malware and unauthorized reading attacks. However, we are not aware of SASs being currently used on mobile phones. SASs need to be unique and usually require multiple key presses simultaneously (e.g., CTRL-ALT-DEL). Such sequences will be very hard for the user to perform on phones. The hand waving gesture proposed in our paper can be viewed as a form of novel and user-friendly SAS suitable for phones.

Recently published paper [20] is also relevant to our work. Like ours, it focuses on the hand-wave gesture but utilizes reflected sound waves instead of light. Specifically, it applies "Doppler Effect" to sense hand waving gestures. It uses speaker to generate inaudible sound waves and microphone to receive the reflected frequency-shifted wave. The approach involves calculating the frequency of the received signal to infer various gestures such hand wave, double-tap, and two-handed seesaw movements. Based on these "in-air" gestures, the paper suggests different non-security use cases and applications. It might be possible to use this gesture recognition scheme for the purpose of protecting sensitive mobile device services. However, there are a few caveats. First, an adversary can send inaudible sound waves to a victim's smartphone with varying frequency so as to mimic one of the gestures. This will undermine the security of this scheme. Second, the sound wave generated by the speaker can be annoying for children and pets who can hear the high frequency sound waves. Furthermore, compared to our gesture recognition mechanism, this approach is computationally-intensive, and power-exhaustive, for mobile phones.

3 Threat Model and Design Goals

3.1 Threat Model

In our security model, we consider both insider attacks and outsider attacks against mobile devices. In the context of an insider attack, the attacker is assumed to be a malicious application or malware. We assume that attackers use malware to access sensitive services (such as phone call, SMS, NFC, or GPS) for various malicious intentions. The malware can be hidden in a normal application. Malware can spread through various paths to the phone via various communication channels such as Bluetooth, WiFi, and GSM. We assume that the malware has already been downloaded and installed on the phone without any user suspicion. This can happen, for instance, when a user downloads an application from an untrustworthy source that looks like a game but contains malicious code. How to prevent malware from being installed on the phone is beyond the scope of our model.

In the context of an outsider attack against the NFC service running on a mobile device, the attacker is a device that can read the contents stored on the NFC chip and can later use this information for illegitimate purposes. The attacker could also constitute two colluding entities who can launch a ghost-and-leech attack against NFC.

We assume the mobile device OS kernel itself is healthy and immune to malware infection; hardening the kernel is an orthogonal problem [35, 31]. So the malware is not able to maliciously alter the kernel control flow. The malware is not able to alter data values of on-board sensors too. Otherwise, the malware can supply fake sensor data to escape detection. However, the action from malware is neither human triggered nor can it maliciously alter the kernel control flow.

We assume the attacker may be physically near the user. The attacker is unable to persuade the user to perform the gesture to access a particular service. However, she may coerce/fool the user into moving a particular manner with a hope that such movement can generate similar motion as a valid gesture. We do not, however, allow this attacker to have physical access to the phone. That is, if the attacker has physical access to the phone, then he can lock/unlock a resource just like the phone's user. In other words, our mechanisms are not meant for user authentication and do not provide protection in the face of loss or theft of phone.

3.2 Design Goals

For our security approach to be useful in practice, it must satisfy the following properties:

- The approach should be *lightweight* in terms of the various resources available on the phone, such as memory, computation and battery power. A biometrics-based approach does not satisfy our goal as it is not lightweight and can be time-consuming [24].
- The approach should *incur little delay*. Otherwise, it can affect the overall usability of the system. We believe that no more than a few seconds should be spent executing the approach.
- The approach should be *tolerant to errors*. Both the False Negative Rate (FNR) and False Positive Rate (FPR) should be quite low. A low FNR means that a user would, with a high probability, be able to execute an application (which accesses some sensitive services) without being rejected. Low FNR also implies a better usability. On the other hand, low FPR means that there should be a little probability to grant access to a sensitive service when a user does not intend to do so. Low FPR clearly implies a little chance for malicious entity to evade detection.
- The solution should *require little changes to the usage model* of existing smartphone applications. An intuitive gesture should be required from the user that may involve simple hand movements defined by that gesture. In this case, only minor changes to the adopted usage model will be imposed.

4 Hand Wave Detection

The primary sensor that we use to detect the hand waving gesture is an ambient light sensor, commonly available on smartphones and tablets.[1] A light sensor measures the intensity of ambient light. The light intensity is measured in *lux* which defines how bright or dark the surrounding environment is. The primary reason the light sensors are deployed on smartphones, and tablets and laptops, is for prolonging battery life. The brightness of the screen display of the phone is adjusted according to the intensity of the surrounding light measured by the light sensor. For example, in a dark environment, the display is dimmed which helps reduce the battery consumption. This is the reason the light sensor is located in the front of the mobile phone at the top of its display (see Figure 1). This is true for most, if not all, smartphones and tablets, including the Androids and iPhones. We note that this is a property that we carefully leverage in developing our waving gesture mechanism aimed at improving the security of mobile phones. Specifically, our gesture interfaces with the light sensor, and due to the location of the light sensor, it does not interfere with the gestures made by the user while interacting with the device's (touch screen) display, thereby significantly reducing the False Positive Rate (FPR).

In order to utilize the light sensor for our purpose, we needed a human gesture that can "trigger" the sensor in some way and is not likely to be exhibited in daily activities. We chose waving (depicted in Figure 2) as a simple and a convenient gesture mechanism since it can be easily executed by a human user

[1] A proximity sensor may also be used to detect a hand wave as suggested in [27], but tablets do not commonly come equipped with this sensor.

Fig. 1. Location of the Light Sensor (Samsung Galaxy Nexus)

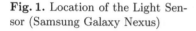

Fig. 2. Permission Granting via a Hand Waving Gesture. In order to access a sensitive service, the user is asked to simply wave her hand in front of the phone; this unlocks the service for use. A malicious application, in contrast, would fail to exhibit such a gesture and will not be able to access the service.

and easily detected by a smartphone. The algorithm to detect quick fluctuations in the reading of the light sensor is very simple and straightforward, and, unlike many other gesture recognition algorithms, do not even need any pre-established templates. This makes our approach extremely lightweight, satisfying one of our design goals (Section 3.2).

To detect the hand wave gesture, whenever there is a change in reading from the light sensors, we record the light sensor readings along with their respective timestamps. We then analyze this light data and time recorded to determine the fluctuation in the light intensity. If the light value fluctuates beyond a given threshold for certain number of times within an allocated time, then we consider such fluctuations in light values as being triggered by the hand wave gesture. The threshold to determine if the light has fluctuated depends upon the current ambient light intensity. When it is dark, i.e, the ambient light intensity is below 200 lux, then using a threshold of 20 lux is optimal to detect the fluctuation as per our measurements. However, when ambient light is around 60,000 lux, i.e, in the presence of bright sunlight, optimum value of threshold is around 15,000 lux.

We used eight different thresholds for eight different ranges of light intensity to accurately determine the wave gesture.[2] For the analysis of fluctuation, we used certain number of light readings $WINDOW\_SIZE\_FOR\_LIGHT$ (16). If we detect the change in light intensity beyond the $LIGHT\_THRESHOLD$ (20 – 15,000 lux), then we add up the light change count ($extremaCount$). After analysis of $WINDOW\_SIZE\_FOR\_LIGHT$ readings of data, if the light change count is greater than $CHANGE\_COUNT\_FOR\_LIGHT$ (6) and all the light under analysis is within $WAVE\_TIME\_LIMIT\_FOR\_LIGHT$ (2 seconds; the maximum duration for the hand wave gesture), then we determine it as a wave gesture. However, sometimes environmental effects may trigger the light sensors to

[2] All the thresholds and range buckets were determined through active experimentation.

Algorithm 1. Wave Detection using Light Sensor (and Accelerometer)

1: IF sensors are locked THEN wait for $MOVEMENT\_LOCK\_TIME$
ELSE get accelerometer sensor readings x, y and z.

2: IF

$$\sqrt{x^2 * y^2 * z^2} > ACC\_THRESHOLD$$

THEN lock the sensors for $MOVEMENT\_LOCK\_TIME$ and RETURN to step 1.

3: IF sensors are not locked THEN get light sensors reading to check if wave gesture is detected.

1. Analyze $WINDOW\_SIZE\_FOR\_LIGHT$ data to find out how many extremas (maximas and minimas) were there using $LIGHT\_THRESHOLD$.
2. IF *extremaCount* $> CHANGE\_COUNT\_FOR\_LIGHT$ AND All the light data are recorded within $WAVE\_TIME\_LIMIT\_FOR\_LIGHT$ THEN SET *unlockAttempted* = *true*,
RECORD first unlock attempted time
DISPLAY Message "Stop Waving" for $WAVE\_TIME\_LIMIT\_FOR\_LIGHT$.
3. IF *unlockAttempted* THEN
   (a) IF another unlockAttempt is obtained within less than $WAVE\_TIME\_LIMIT\_FOR\_LIGHT$ THEN Do not unlock, reset everything and start over, i.e., return to Step 2.
   (b) IF another *unlockattempt* is not obtained within $WAVE\_TIME\_LIMIT\_FOR\_LIGHT$ THEN *Unlock* the phone for $UNLOCK\_TIME\_FRAME$.

detect it as wave gestures. So instead of unlocking the phone straightaway (i.e., allowing access to the requested service), we delay the unlock for certain time $WAVE\_TIME\_LIMIT\_FOR\_LIGHT$. If no gesture is detected within this time-frame, then we unlock the phone for certain time $UNLOCK\_TIME\_FRAME$ (1 second).

In our scheme, the light sensor data is used in conjunction with the accelerometer data to detect the wave gesture. The accelerometer sensor is used for the purpose of reducing FPRs. Whenever the phone is moved, there will be a relative change in the position of the phone with respect to the light source triggering a change in light intensity. This will in turn be detected as a wave gesture, leading to a high FPR (since the user did not wave in front of the phone). In order to reduce this effect, if the phone detects movement, greater than a certain threshold ($ACC\_THRESHOLD$), as per the accelerometer data, it does not register it as a hand wave gesture; further it locks the light sensor as well. Thus, when an application requests for the permission to access the resource/service, the algorithm will first check if the sensors are locked. If the sensors are locked, then the algorithm will wait for certain time ($MOVEMENT\_LOCK\_TIME$) before it starts reading the light and accelerometer signal again. Note that when the algorithm is first executed, both sensors are active, and the corresponding data is read. A detailed pseudocode for this simple procedure is outlined as Algorithm 1.

5 Implementation and Evaluation

5.1 Test Prototype: Wave-to-Call

To evaluate the feasibility of the wave gesture detection mechanism, we developed our prototype in Android Operating System using Motorola Droid X2. The project build target was chosen for Android 2.3.3 platform or above using API level 10. A simple UI was created to emulate the unlocking of a service using the hand waving gesture. The goal of the prototype was to add a layer of security to Android permission model where user needs to provide a gesture to use a resource/service. In our prototype, we specifically asked user to wave their hand in front of the phone as a gesture to make an *outgoing call.* If the gesture is not received within 10 seconds, the application will not allow a call.

We created a service that intercepts all the outgoing calls and two activities, one for turning on/off the service and another for receiving the wave gesture. When the service is turned on, whenever there is an intent to make a phone call, our service will intercept that intent and start the activity to receive the gesture. This activity turns the sensors on and reads the sensor value to analyze it using our gesture recognition algorithm (Algorithm 1). If the readings from the sensor satisfy the algorithm, then it will return true and provides an approval token to make a call. If the sensor data does not satisfy the algorithm within certain time duration, then the service will shut down the activity waiting for gesture along with the sensors, i.e., sensors are only activated whenever there is an intent to use a service and not all the time. These steps while making a call are shown in Figure 3.

The service to intercept outgoing calls is turned on when user sets his preference via one of the activities mentioned above. However, the service must also be turned on when the device boots up from being shutdown. We utilized the BroadcastReceiver from Android SDK for this purpose. This is explained in Figure 4.

Our approach does not involve any modification to the Android OS, rather we created an application with about 500 lines of Java Code to turn on the service as well as intercept the intent and make a call. Adding another intent intercept will require few additional lines of code. Android OS provides limited number of intents that we can intercept. Available intents can be found in [13].

5.2 Hand Wave Detection Experiments and Results

In this section, we report on the evaluation of our hand wave gesture recognition scheme. This scheme is designed to protect against the malware and other malicious entities trying to access phone's resources or services without user awareness. We conducted several experiments to evaluate our prototype implementing

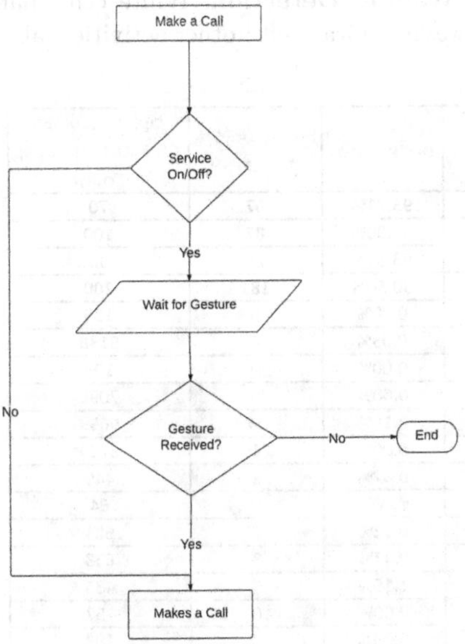

Fig. 3. Process while making a call

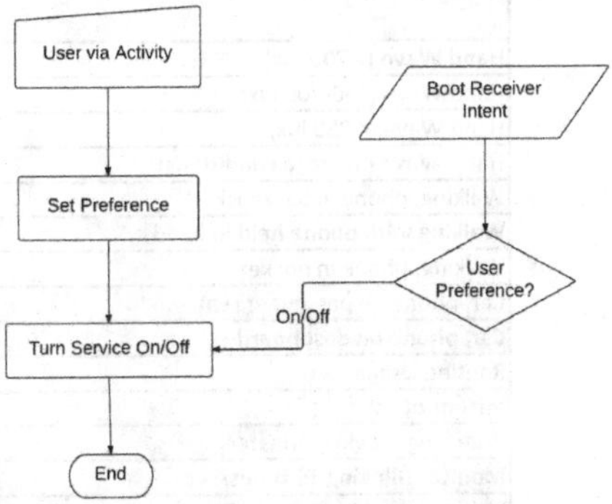

Fig. 4. Turning the service on/off. Service can either be turned on by user via setting up the preference or when the device boots up after checking the user preference

the hand-wave detection mechanism. The goal of our tests was to primarily estimate the error rates, i.e., FNR and FPR. A summary of our experimental results is depicted in Table 1, and the details are explained below.

FNR Experiments: In order to determine the FNR, one of the authors attempted to unlock the phone himself using the hand waving gesture. Out of forty trials performed, the user failed to unlock the device only 3 times. Most of these failures occurred when the user tried to wave the hand far away from the phone (farther than 30 cm), resulting in an average recognition rate of 92.5% (or FNR of 7.5%).

Since multiple trials may have trained this user significantly, likely leading to a bias, we further conducted our tests with multiple other users. These volunteers were drawn from our Department (Computer Science) and were mostly students at undergraduate and graduate levels. The users were first explained the purpose of the study and then demonstrated the gestures using which they were to unlock a service on the phone. The users were specified the location of the light sensor on the phone. Although in real life, users may not be aware of the location of the light sensor, they can be easily provided with this information using a simple interface. For example, an arrow pointer could be provided on the screen which points to the light sensor, and user could be asked to execute the wave gesture accordingly.

A total of 20 volunteers participated in our study. Each of them was requested to perform the hand waving based unlocking procedure 10 times and the results were recorded automatically by our program. The resulting average recognition rate observed was 90.5% (181/200; FNR of 9.5%). Most of these FNR occurred

Table 1. Recognition Rates for Hand Waving Detection. White cells: hand waving attempts correctly detected as hand waving; Gray cells: other activities falsely detected as hand waving

Activity	Hand Wave	Phone Unlock Count	Light Readings Change (Attempt) Count
Hand Wave (> 700 lux)	**95.71%**	**67**	**70**
Hand Wave (350-700 lux)	87.00%	87	100
Hand Wave (< 350 lux)	83.33%	25	30
Hand Wave (average conditions)	**90.50%**	**181**	**200**
Walking, phone in backpack	0.00%	0	155
Walking with phone held in hand	**0.08%**	**4**	**5138**
Walking, phone in pocket	0.00%	0	103
Car, phone on passenger seat	0.00%	0	7098
Car, phone on dashboard	**0.15%**	**14**	**9053**
Routine Usage	0.00%	1	8729
Infront of TV	**0.67%**	**3**	**449**
Watching movie in theater	0.00%	0	64
Monitor Blinking 10 times/sec	**0.32%**	**2**	**623**
Monitor Blinking 5 times/sec	**0.47%**	**3**	**633**
Monitor Blinking 3.3 time/sec	**1.15%**	**5**	**435**
Monitor Blinking 1.67 times/sec	0.00%	0	257
Monitor Blinking 1 times/sec	0.00%	0	183
Manually flickering the light 40 times/min	0.00%	0	176
Manually flickering the light 30 times/min	**0.49%**	**2**	**408**
Drop Test	0.00%	0	43
Game Playing Landscape 1	**0.44%**	**4**	**911**
Game Playing Landscape 2	**0.43%**	**4**	**925**
Game Playing O3 Portrait	**0.23%**	**2**	**871**

when there was less ambient light. When the light intensity was greater than 700 lux, recognition rate was observed to be 95.71% (67/70) whereas when it was between 350 lux and 700 lux, the rate was 87% (87/100), and when it was lower than 350 lux, it was observed to be 83.3% (35/40).

In general, these error rates can be deemed to be fairly low and are in line with prior research on gesture recognition (e.g., [12, 21]). We expect them to further reduce significantly as users become more and more familiar with the hand waving gesture.

FPR Experiments: Next, we set out to evaluate the likelihood of false unlocking under different activities. These activities might be just routine user activities, or activities coerced by a nearby attacker. The experimenter conducted several tests emulating different user activities that have the potential of triggering the light sensor fluctuations. The phone recorded the number of times it has been unlocked, i.e., when the activity is recognized as a wave gesture by our algorithm, out of a total number of registered light fluctuations.

First, to simulate a walking activity, the mobile phone was stowed in a backpack and the experimenter, carrying the backpack on the shoulders, walked around for 20 minutes. No unlocking events occurred in this case, although 155 light fluctuations were observed. This experiment was repeated at a later point of time, but the phone was held in hand emulating the reading of text messages while walking (for 20 minutes). This time, the phone was unlocked 4 times, out of 5138 light fluctuations, leading to an FPR of 0.08%. The phone was unlocked when sunlight was coming from behind and shadow from the moving shoulder was partially obstructing the phone. We further continued this walking experiment for a duration of another 20 minutes but this time the phone was kept in a pocket. No unlocking events occurred even in this case.

To verify if the phone will get unlocked when it is carried by its owner inside a car, the phone was first kept on the passenger seat of a car, while the car was driven. The phone did not get unlocked in this scenario. Next, the phone was placed on the dashboard of the car underneath the windshield and the car was driven around for one hour. In this case, we noticed that the phone got unlocked 14 times out of a total of 9053 light reading changes, which yields an FPR of 0.15%. Note that once the car moves at a constant speed, the accelerometer reading will not change significantly, allowing the light sensor to detect the wave gesture. Although not frequent, in general, we can see a potential for the phone to get unlocked when there is bright light from windshield coming onto the phone, while the car passes beneath a tree. The phone was further carried in the car in the same way as above in dark (i.e. light intensity below 300 lux) for 5 minutes, but, as expected, no unlocking was observed.

Next, the phone was treated as a user's own phone for about one day (20 hours). Different routine activities were performed during this experiment, such as walking with the phone in pocket, going upstairs/downstairs, and sending messages and making/taking calls. The phone was also placed on a desk alongside the user's laptop. Only 1 unlock was registered in this case, out of a total of 8729 changes in the light values. This suggests that normal usage of the phone will only have a little likelihood of unlocking.

Another experiment was conducted to see if a bright and dynamic light source, such as a Television, can trigger the phone's unlocking. Here, the phone was placed in front of a Television, 6ft away from it, while watching a program for 1 hour. In this case, we found that the phone got unlocked 3 times, out of a total of 449 light fluctuation events, equivalent to an FPR of 0.67%. Interestingly, we also noticed that such event occurs only if the surrounding is dark enough such that the threshold is low enough for the TV to fluctuate the light intensity. Also, to unlock, the TV screen must display a bright light and flicker quickly. Extending this general experiment further, the phone was also carried to a movie theater, where it was kept outside the user's pocket while the user watched a 2 hour long movie. In this case, interestingly, no unlocking was registered.

A similar experiment was conducted using a computer monitor. Here again, we held the phone in front of a flickering monitor. We flickered the monitor with different frequencies. The phone got unlocked twice, out of 623 light change events (FPR of 0.32%), when the monitor was flickering with a frequency of 10 times/second. It unlocked thrice when the frequency was 5 times/second (633 light changes; FPR 0.47%), and five times when time interval for flickering rate was 3.3 times/second (435 light changes; FPR 1.15%). When the frequency of flickering was reduced, it could not unlock the phone since time interval exceeded $WAVE\_TIME\_LIMIT\_FOR\_LIGHT$.

To trigger sudden fluctuations to the light sensor readings, we next conducted a "drop and fall" test. This mimicked a situation where the phone accidentally drops on, or is thrown at, a surface. Clearly, we could not just drop or throw our test device on the floor to avoid damaging it. To do this meaningfully, therefore, we first threw our test device on a bed from a height of around 1 meter. Number of trials of this test were performed for two minutes. Phone was thrown straight to the bed as well as rolled over so that there is change in the relative position of the light source. No unlocking events were recorded over this set of tests since the change in accelerometer readings was large enough to even trigger the light reading detection.

We also conducted tests to simulate a nearby adversary who may (deliberately) try to change the surrounding ambient light and unlock the phone. Although, this may create suspicion, we simulated such a scenario as the attacker would have a high incentive to exploit. For example, the attacker can flicker lights in a building which may enable all malware-infected mobile devices in that building to access the phone's resources. To do this, the light was turned on and off in the evening when the primary source of light was the fluorescent lamps. When the light was switched on/off slowly, i.e., 30 times per min, it did not unlock the phone. However, when the light was turned on/off 40 times per min, it unlocked the phone twice, out of a total of 408 light change events, leading to a FPR of 0.49%.

Finally, we analyzed a scenario where the user would be playing a game on her smartphone. We were interested in finding out the likelihood of unlocking the phone by hand movements which may trigger the light sensor fluctuation mimicking hand waving. We emulated the game play activity on the phone under portrait and landscape orientations. When the phone was held in portrait mode, fingers are far away from the light sensor and may not trigger the light sensor. However, when the phone is held in either of the landscape orientations using two hands, fingers plays a vital role in light sensor readings. The game playing activity was mimicked by our experimenter for two minutes. It unlocked the phone four times in each landscape orientation (out of 911 and 925 light changes; FPR of 0.44% and 0.45%), and twice in portrait (out of 871 light changes; FPR of 0.23%). Indeed, this confirmed our hypothesis that game play under portrait mode is less likely to unlock the phone than under landscape modes.

6 Discussion

Overall, our experiment results in previous section show that hand waving can be effectively used to infer the "right" human activity in order to unlock the use of sensitive services/resources on smartphones, thus preventing unauthorized and stealthy access by malicious entities. The low FNR (less than 10%) and short delay (up to 2 seconds) demonstrate the usability of our approach. Note that, in practice, the user will be given up to 3 attempts to perform the gesture correctly, which would mean that the effective FNR will be nearly 0%, and it will still take only a few seconds to perform the gestures. We believe that the FNR can be further reduced as users become more and more familiar with the underlying gesture. The low FPR (less than 1% in most cases), on the other hand, shows that our approach will provide a high degree of security in practice. Although there exists some potential for unlocking the phone (e.g., while the user is watching a TV or riding a car), the likelihood is extremely low. Moreover, it will be very hard for the malicious attacker to constantly wait for, and synchronize with, scenarios in which unlocking is possible, further confirming the robustness of our approach.

In the rest of this section, we further analyze and interpret the performance of our hand waving gesture recognition scheme, and discuss other relevant aspects.

Ease of Use and Convenience: Hand waving is a gesture that captures users' intent to access a mobile device service. It simply requires user to perform a simple hand movement to unlock a desired service/resource. This does require an extra user effort to access a service. However, hand wave gesture is quite intuitive and can be easily performed unlike traditional passwords and PINs which user has to memorize and input diligently, and add an extra burden when the user forgets them. Certainly, passwords and PINs are more secure compared to gestures, but we are, in this work, concerned about protection against the malware and unauthorized reading attacks rather than against theft and unauthorized usage by other person. The explicit gesture is a minimal cost required to add security against such attacks. We believe that the hand waving gesture is as easy as a "finger-swiping" gesture commonly deployed on many smartphones.

The hand wave gesture is user-independent as shown by our experiment results. That means, the service/phone can be shared by multiple users without registering his/her own template. In fact, there is no template employed in this scheme and there is no need to train the device. This scheme therefore offers a high level of convenience to the users, and might be easily adoptable. A mentioned above, it does not prevent unauthorized use of such service when the phone is stolen. However, allowing the user to change the threshold and wave time limit parameters are future modifications to personalize and detect the wave gesture accurately for a specific device owner.

Battery Consumption and Efficiency: Another important issue to cover in our work is the power consumed by the sensors while trying to capture the user gesture. Since the battery-life is one of the most important factors to be considered for user's day to day activity, our design needs to be battery-friendly.

The waving gesture proposed by our design is very short (up to 2 seconds). When there is a request for the sensitive service/resource which requires users gestures, only then the sensors will be turned on and the gesture detection algorithm will be executed. Once the kernel captures the required gesture, the permission will be granted to the active application and sensor will be turned off. If kernel fails to capture the gesture for certain duration, the sensor will be turned off and application will be denied to use the resources.

For the sake of our experiments, we have turned on the sensor all the time. This was done so as to determine the FPRs, i.e., to calculate the rate at which the algorithm will fail to provide security.

Effect of Light: Since we are using the light sensor, the ambient light plays a crucial role in the detection of hand wave gesture. We can see from our experiment that, as the surrounding light intensity decreased, the FNR increased. As soon as the light intensity drops below a certain level, the hand wave gesture will not be able to alter the light intensity even by a minimum threshold. Hence, when it is completely dark, our hand wave detection will not work. This situation can be remedied by resorting to a more complex touch screen gesture from the user, such as tapping on the screen a few times in succession, whenever the phone detects the surrounding to be dark enough.

Targeted Attacks: Our experiments demonstrate very low FPR, which means that there is little probability that an application will gain access to resources without the knowledge of its owner. This is based on an assumption that the attacker can not create the required gesture. However, a malware can fool a user by launching a social-engineering attack. For example, a malware developer can design a game such that user has to move his hand in certain ways mimicking the hand wave gesture. While such attacks are likely, they still require the malware program to constantly wait for, and synchronize with, the desired user gesture, which may make these programs easily detectable by the OS. Nevertheless, our approach still significantly raises the bar against many existing malware attacks, a prominent advancement in state-of-the-art in smartphone malware prevention.

Sensitivity of Sensors: We are using two sensors to detect the hand wave gesture, namely a light sensor and an accelerometer. There are different types of these sensors available on different devices. The frequency at which the sensor feeds the data to the kernel not only depends upon the kind of sensor but also on the processor speed, and number of application the phone is running, among other things. When we compared the sensor of our prototype device (Motorola Droid X2 running Android 2.3.3 on a Dual-core 1 GHz Cortex-A9 processor) with other devices (Samsung Galaxy Nexus (Android 4.0.3, Dual-core 1.2 GHz Cortex-A9), we found that light sensor reading on our device (Droid X2) changes quite frequently, i.e., the light sensor on this device is highly sensitive. On the other hand, the accelerometer readings changes more rapidly on the other device (Galaxy Nexus). For the hand wave gesture to be recognized accurately on a given device, the threshold and the wave time limit should be modified according to that device's configuration and the sensitivity of its sensors.

Extending to RFID Tags: Our scheme is also applicable for preventing unauthorized reading and relay attacks against standalone RFID tags (such as contactless credit cards or access cards). In this case, the RFID tag will need an on-board ambient light sensor and an accelerometer, and the user will simply need to wave in front of the tag to access it. Unlike prior security mechanisms that use sensor-equipped tags (e.g., [12, 21]), our approach is very simple and lightweight, and can be easily accommodated within the constraints of typical RFID tags.

7 Conclusion and Future Work

In this paper, we presented a novel approach to protecting sensitive mobile device services against many prominent attacks. The approach captures user's intent to access a given service via a lightweight hand waving gesture. This gesture is very simple, quick and intuitive for the user, but would be very hard for the attacker to exhibit without user's knowledge. We presented the design and implementation of the hand waving gesture using an ambient light sensor, already available on most smartphones and tablets. We also reported on our experiments to analyze the performance of our approach. Our results indicate the approach to be quite effective in preventing the misuse of sensitive resources with a very little user effort. Our future work constitutes further evaluating our approach on different devices and integrating it with services/resources beyond voice dialing, such as SMS and NFC.

Acknowledgments. The authors thank the CANS'13 anonymous reviewers for their feedback. This work was funded in part by the NSF CNS-1201927 grant.

References

[1] Juels, A.: RFID Security and Privacy: A Research Survey. In: Journal on Selected Areas in Communications (2006)
[2] Augustinowicz, W.: Trojan horse electronic pickpocket demo by identity stronghold (June 2011), http://www.youtube.com/watch?v=eEcz0XszEic
[3] Ballano, M.: Android threats getting steamy (2011), http://www.symantec.com/connect/blogs/android-threats-getting-steamy
[4] Baudel, T., Michel, B.-L.: Charade: remote control of objects using free-hand gestures. Communication of ACM 36, 28–35 (1993)
[5] Bose, A., Hu, X., Shin, K., Park, T.: Behavioral detection of malware on mobile handsets. In: MobiSys 2008 (2008)
[6] Burguera, I., Zurutuza, U., Nadjm-Tehrani, S.: Crowdroid: Behavior-based malware detection systems for Android. In: ACM CCSW Workshop (2011)
[7] Cai, L., Chen, H.: Touchlogger: inferring keystrokes on touch screen from smartphone motion. In: Proc. of USENIX HotSec (2011)
[8] Cao, X., Balakrishnan, R.: VisionWand: interaction techniques for large display using a passive wand tracked in 3D. In: ACM UIST 2003 (2003)
[9] Cheng, J., Wong, S., Yang, H., Lu, S.: Smartsiren: virus detection and alert for smartphones. In: 5th International Conference on Mobile Systems, Applications and Services, MobiSys 2007 (2007)
[10] Christodorescu, M., Jha, S.: Static analysis of executables to detect malicious patterns. In: 12th Conference on USENIX Security Symposium (2003)
[11] Conti, M., Zachia-Zlatea, I., Crispo, B.: Mind how you answer me!: transparently authenticating the user of a smartphone when answering or placing a call. In: Proceedings of the 6th ACM Symposium on Information, Computer and Communications Security, ASIACCS 2011 (2011)

[12] Czeskis, A., Koscher, K., Smith, J.R., Kohno, T.: Rfids and secret handshakes: defending against ghost-and-leech attacks and unauthorized reads with context-aware communications. In: Proceedings of the 15th ACM Conference on Computer and Communications Security, CCS 2008, pp. 479–490. ACM, New York (2008)
[13] Android Developers. Intent, http://developer.android.com/reference/android/content/Intent.html
[14] Ellis, D.R., Aiken, J.G., Attwood, K.S., Tenaglia, S.D.: A behavioral approach to worm detection. In: ACM Workshop on Rapid malcode, WORM (2004)
[15] F-Secure. Bluetooth-worm:symbos/cabir, http://www.f-secure.com/v-descs/cabir.shtml
[16] F-Secure. Trojan:symbos/viver.a, http://www.f-secure.com/v-descs/trojan_symbos_viver_a.shtml
[17] F-Secure. Worm:symbos/commwarrior, http://www.f-secure.com/v-descs/commwarrior.shtml
[18] Hancke, G.: Practical Attacks on Proximity Identification Systems. In: Symposium on Security and Privacy (2006)
[19] Gafurov, D., Helkala, K., Søndrol, T.: Biometric gait authentication using accelerometer sensor. Journal of Computers 1(7), 51–59 (2006)
[20] Gupta, S., Morris, D., Patel, S., Tan, D.: Soundwave: using the doppler effect to sense gestures. In: Proceedings of the 2012 ACM Annual Conference on Human Factors in Computing Systems, CHI 2012 (2012)
[21] Halevi, T., Lin, S., Ma, D., Prasad, A., Saxena, N., Voris, J., Xiang, T.: Sensing-enabled defenses to rfid unauthorized reading and relay attacks without changing the usage model. In: PerCom 2012 (2012)
[22] Han, J., Owusu, E., Nguyen, T.-L., Perrig, A., Zhang, J.: ACComplice: Location Inference using Accelerometers on Smartphones. In: Proc. of COMSNETS (January 2012)
[23] Kolesnikov-Jessop, S.: Hackers go after the smartphone (2011), http://www.nytimes.com/2011/02/14/technology/14iht-srprivacy14.html
[24] Li, H., Ma, D., Saxena, N., Shrestha, B., Zhu, Y.: Tap-wave-rub: Lightweight malware prevention for smartphones using intuitive human gestures. CoRR, abs/1302.4010 (2013)
[25] Liu, J., Wang, Z., Zhong, L., Wickramasuriya, J., Vasudevan, V.: uWave: Accelerometer-based personalized gesture recognition and its applications. Pervasive and Mobile Computing 5(6), 657–675 (2009)
[26] Liu, J., Zhong, L., Wickramasuriya, J., Vasudevan, V.: User evaluation of lightweight user authentication with a single tri-axis accelerometer. In: MobileHCI (2009)
[27] Ma, D., Saxena, N., Shrestha, B., Xiang, T., Zhu, Y.: Tap-wave-rub: Lightweight malware prevention for smartphones using intuitive human gestures (short paper). In: ACM Conference on Wireless Network Security, WiSec (2013)
[28] Marquardt, P., Verma, A., Carter, H., Traynor, P. (sp)iPhone: decoding vibrations from nearby keyboards using mobile phone accelerometers. In: Proc. of ACM CCS (2011)
[29] Microsoft. What is user account control? (2011), http://windows.microsoft.com/en-US/windows-vista/What-is-User-Account-Control
[30] Owusu, E., Han, J., Das, S., Perrig, A., Zhang, J.: ACCessory: Keystroke Inference using Accelerometers on Smartphones. In: Proc. of HotMobile (February 2012)
[31] Petroni Jr., N.L., Hicks, M.: Automated detection of persistent kernel control-flow attacks. In: CCS 2007: Proceedings of the 14th ACM Conference on Computer and Communications Security, pp. 103–115. ACM, New York (2007)

[32] Roesner, F., Kohno, T., Moshchuk, A., Parno, B., Wang, H.J., Cowan, C.: User-driven access control: Rethinking permission granting in modern operating systems. In: IEEE Symposium on Security and Privacy (2012)
[33] Schlegel, R., Zhang, K., Yong Zhou, X., Intwala, M., Kapadia, A., Wang, X.: Soundcomber: A stealthy and context-aware sound trojan for smartphones. In: Proc. of NDSS (2011)
[34] Schmidt, A.-D., Bye, R., Schmidt, H.-G., Clausen, J., Kiraz, O., Yksel, K., Camtepe, S., Sahin, A.: Static analysis of executables for collaborative malware detection on Android. In: ICC 2009 Communication and Information Systems Security Symposium (2009)
[35] Seshadri, A., Luk, M., Qu, N., Perrig, A.: Secvisor: a tiny hypervisor to provide lifetime kernel code integrity for commodity oses. In: Proceedings of Twenty-first ACM SIGOPS Symposium on Operating Systems Principles, SOSP 2007, pp. 335–350. ACM, New York (2007)
[36] Shabtai, A., Moskovitch, R., Elovici, Y., Glezer, C.: Detection of malicious code by applying machine learning classifiers on static features: A state-of-the-art survey. Inf. Secur. Tech. 14, 16–29 (2009)
[37] Shamili, A.S., Bauckhage, C., Alpcan, T.: Malware detection on mobile devices using distributed machine learning. In: 20th International Conference on Pattern Recognition, ICPR 2010 (2010)
[38] Venugopal, D.: An efficient signature representation and matching method for mobile devices. In: WICON 2006 (2006)
[39] Venugopal, D., Hu, G., Roman, N.: Intelligent virus detection on mobile devices. In: PST 2006 (2006)
[40] Ward, M.: Smartphone security put on test (2010), `http://www.bbc.com/news/technology-10912376`
[41] Liang, X., Zhang, X., Seifert, J.-P., Zhu, S.: pBMDS: A behavior-based malware detection system for cellphone devices. In: WiSec 2010 (2010)
[42] Kfir, Z., Wool, A.: Picking Virtual Pockets using Relay Attacks on Contactless Smartcard. In: Security and Privacy for Emerging Areas in Communications Networks (2005)

Semantically-Secure Functional Encryption: Possibility Results, Impossibility Results and the Quest for a General Definition

Mihir Bellare[1] and Adam O'Neill[2]

[1] Department of Computer Science & Engineering
University of California San Diego
9500 Gilman Drive, La Jolla, California 92093, USA
mihir@cs.ucsd.edu
http://www.cs.ucsd.edu/users/mihir
[2] Department of Computer Science
Georgetown University
3700 Reservoir Road NW, Washington, DC 20057, USA
adam@cs.georgetown.edu
http://www.cs.georgetown.edu/~adam

Abstract. This paper explains that SS1-secure functional encryption (FE) as defined by Boneh, Sahai and Waters implicitly incorporates security under key-revealing selective opening attacks (SOA-K). This connection helps intuitively explain their impossibility results and also allows us to prove stronger ones. To fill this gap and move us closer to the (laudable) goal of a general and achievable notion of FE security, we seek and provide two "sans SOA-K" definitions of FE security that we call SS2 and SS3. We prove various possibility results about these definitions. We view our work as a first step towards the challenging goal of a general, meaningful and achievable notion of FE security.

1 Introduction

BACKGROUND. Functional encryption (FE) was introduced by Boneh, Sahai and Waters (BSW) [14] and formalized independently by O'Neill [35]. A FE-scheme for a functionality $\mathcal{F}$: $\mathbb{N}\times\{0,1\}^*\times\{0,1\}^* \to \{0,1\}^*\cup\{\perp\}$ is a tuple of algorithms $\mathsf{FE} = (\mathsf{Setup}, \mathsf{KDer}, \mathsf{Enc}, \mathsf{Dec})$. An authority lets $(pk, sk) \leftarrow\!\!\$\ \mathsf{Setup}(\lambda)$, where λ is the security parameter, and publishes pk. Anyone may now encrypt an input x via $c \leftarrow\!\!\$\ \mathsf{Enc}(pk, x)$. A user may provide the authority with a *functionality index* a and receive a secret key $sk_a \leftarrow\!\!\$\ \mathsf{KDer}(sk, a)$. If the user now applies the decryption algorithm to sk_a and any encryption c of x, the result $\mathsf{Dec}(sk_a, c)$ will equal $\mathcal{F}(\lambda, a, x)$. Security requires that the user learns nothing more.

The intent was to generalize and unify many forms of encryption including IBE (Identity-based encryption) [38,13], ABE (Attribute-based encryption) [37,26] and PE (Predicate encryption) [28]. An existing form $\mathbf{E}$ of encryption would correspond to a functionality $\mathcal{F}_{\mathsf{e}}$. IBE for example corresponds to the functionality $\mathcal{F}_{\mathsf{ibe}}$ which regards a as an identity and parses x as a pair (a', m) consisting

M. Abdalla, C. Nita-Rotaru, and R. Dahab (Eds.): CANS 2013, LNCS 8257, pp. 218–234, 2013.

of another identity a' and a message m, returning m if $a = a'$ and $\perp$ otherwise. PE generalizes to functionalities $\mathcal{F}$ for which there is a relation $\mathcal{P}$ such that $\mathcal{F}$, given a and $x = (a', m)$, returns m if $\mathcal{P}(a, a')$ is true and $\perp$ otherwise, IBE being the case where $\mathcal{P}(a, a')$ is true iff $a = a'$. ABE schemes are a subclass of PE schemes where a' is revealed to anyone by the ciphertext.

The works [14,35] sought a general definition of security that applied to an arbitrary functionality. They first provide an indistinguishability-based one (IND). It had the attractive feature of coinciding, for the IBE and PE functionalities, with the the existing definitions of these notions from the literature. But both BSW [14] and O'Neill [35] point to inherent deficiencies of IND when it comes to capturing security of general functionalities. The "main" definition of BSW was accordingly a simulation-based semantic-security one that we call SS1.[1] We may now speak of the SS1-security of an FE scheme FE for *any* functionality $\mathcal{F}$.

The FE framework is elegant and the goals are laudable. A proliferating number of notions of encryption are now put under a single umbrella, seen as special cases of a single primitive. Ad hoc, notion-specific security definitions need not be given. One only has to specify the functionality and SS1 security would return a suitable definition.

Impossibility of SS1 in the NPROM. However, having introduced SS1, BSW [14] claim that it can't be achieved in the standard model, even for IBE, which is the most basic functionality in this area. This is a strong and disappointing claim. Before we delve into its implications, we take a closer look at it. We point out that BSW don't actually prove this. What they prove is that SS1-secure IBE cannot be achieved in the NPROM (Non-Programmable Random Oracle Model). At a first glance, this only sounds like a stronger claim. Every standard model scheme is a NPROM scheme and every standard-model adversary is a NPROM one, so if NPROM achievability is ruled out, isn't standard model achievability ruled out as well? The answer is no. BSW [14] establish their claim by providing an adversary for which they prove that there is no simulator. But their adversary makes calls to the RO, and this is exploited crucially in the proof of non-existence of a simulator. Their proof does not rule out the existence of a simulator for adversaries that do not call the RO, meaning for standard-model adversaries, and thus it does not rule out standard-model achievability of SS1, even for IBE.

This gives a ray of hope. Perhaps SS1-security can be achieved in the standard model after all. This would be interesting even for IBE and certainly beyond. This hope is fueled by a look at the technique underlying the negative result of BSW [14]. It is not a priori clear how to extend this technique to rule out simulators for standard-model adversaries.

A new impossibility result for SS1. We fill the gap by showing that SS1-secure IBE is not achievable even in the standard model. The result is actually

[1] Following [35] we use the terminology "semantic security" throughout the paper to refer to this style of definition. However, [14] and some other works call it "simulation based." They mean the same thing.

more general, ruling out SS1-security for *any non-trivial functionality*, IBE being covered as a special case. Non-triviality essentially means the functionality is not a constant function. The only assumption made is the existence of collision-resistant hash functions.

Our result exploits the recent technique of Bellare, Dowsley, Waters and Yilek (BDWY) [5], used to prove the impossibility of SOA-secure commitment, in combination with techniques from Nielsen's proof of impossibility of non-committing encryption (NCE) [32]. We are able to present a *standard model* adversary for which we can prove that there is no simulator.

Taking a closer look, our result, as is the case with those of Nielsen and BSW, is actually a trade-off. It shows that SS1-security requires long keys, this meaning that the total number of bits in messages securely encrypted must be bounded by the length of a secret key. However, it does this in the standard model.

AN EXPLANATION. This paper offers an explanation for this anamoly that seeds further contributions in a natural way. We contend that SS1 does not capture "plain" FE security. Instead, it captures FE security in the presence of key-revealing selective-opening attacks (SOA-Ks). These are attacks where the adversary may adaptively corrupt some users and obtain their decryption keys *without restrictions.*[2] The revealing fact is that, if we were to write down a definition of SOA-K-security for IBE, what emanates is *exactly* SS1-secure IBE. We now have a natural explanation of why SS1 is subject to such broad unachievability and also why SS1-secure IBE is not the same as the classical IND-secure IBE from [13]. Namely, the former incorporates SOA-K security and the latter does not.

Why is SOA-K-security part of SS1? BSW [14] did not throw it in "on purpose." (Their work has no explicit recognition of the fact that their definition incorporates security against SOA-K. They do however comment on the relation to NCE and [32], which is only a step removed.) Rather, the natural approach to defining semantic security for a general functionality, which is the one followed by BSW [14], leads to the inadvertent incorporation of SOA-K security.

While it is usually easier to define "plain" security than security against SOA-K, with FE, it seems to be the opposite. It is not clear how to define semantically-secure FE in a way that "decouples" basic and SOA-K security. This, in our view, is rather interesting.

SS2 AND SS3. As indicated above, we believe that unifying different existing forms of encryption under a general definition for FE is a highly worthwhile goal. SS1 has not achieved this, capturing instead the SOA-K-secure versions of these goals and thence being subject to strong impossibility results. We move towards

[2] In the standard formulation of IBE, the adversary has a key-derivation oracle via which it may obtain decryption keys for identities of its choice, but use of the oracle is restricted to identities not underlying challenge ciphertexts. An SOA-K results when there are many challenge ciphertexts and *this restriction is dropped.* This is exactly what happens in SS1-secure FE. The interesting thing is that in the context of semantic security for general FE it is not clear how to make appropriate restrictions to exclude the SOA-K. We will elaborate in a bit.

the just-stated goal with two new notions that we call SS2 and SS3. Definining "sans SOA-K" FE security in forms of varying strength, they are able to meet many of the broad goals in this domain and open the door to further efforts.

Our main result about SS2 is that it is equivalent to IND for *all* functionalities. This equivalence has its plusses and its minuses. Let us begin with the former. IND-secure IBE as per [13] is a well established definition, targeted in thousands of papers and proven to work for applications, and IND-secure PE as per [28] is also accepted. The SS2=IND equivalence provides a semantic-security based backing for this IND definition which has so far been absent. Conceptually, it mirrors in the FE setting the classic equivalence between semantic-security and indistinguishability in the PKE setting [23] that is a cornerstone of our understanding of, and faith in, these definitions. More pragmatically, it immediately yields possibility results for semantically-secure FE which were absent under SS1. This is because IND-secure IBE is well-known to be achievable in the standard model [11,42,40], and various possibility results for ABE and PE are known as well (e.g. [26,36,28,33,39,29,2,31,30,34]).[3]

We believe this is progress towards bringing semantically-secure FE closer. But, while the equivalence of SS2 with IND is a plus for common functionalities like ABE, PE and IBE, it is a minus when looking further, for we already know that IND is *not* a good definition of FE security in general [35]. Thus, we would like another definition to complement SS2. We suggest SS3, a strengthening of SS2. We believe SS3 is a good candidate for a general definition of FE for arbitrary functionalties. One reason is that it does not appear to have the drawbacks of IND for beyond-PE functionalities. (BSW [14] and O'Neill [35] present IND-secure FE schemes that are intuitively insecure. However, their schemes will correctly be SS3-insecure.) Another reason is that our impossibility result for SS1 does not extend to SS3. (So in particular, SS3-secure IBE is not ruled out.)

In support of SS3 we show that it is equivalent to IND for "re-sampleable" functionalities. Unfortunately, re-sampleable functionalities does not seem to include common functionalities of interest such as IBE. Indeed, we have not been able to either prove or disprove the equivalence of SS3 with IND for PE functionalities. We suggest that IBE and PE schemes may be directly proven to meet SS3 and leave this as an interesting subject for future work.

Due to space constraints, details about all results concerning SS2 and SS3 can be found in the full version [7].

A CLOSER LOOK. Recall that in IBE, the adversary is given a key-derivation oracle, allowing it to obtain a secret key for any identity of its choice. This does *not* by itself constitute a SOA-K because the adversary is not allowed to call this oracle for the identities underlying challenge ciphertexts. In the SS1 definition, the adversary also gets a key-derivation oracle to obtain a secret key for any

[3] Indeed, a starting point for our work was to posit that existing IND-secure such schemes *should* be deemed secure under whatever SS-type definition one proposes to use. This makes our approach philosophically different from BSW and some concurrent and subsequent works, discussed later.

functionality index a of its choice. But there seems no simple or natural way to make a rule disallowing querying this oracle on "challenge" ciphertexts because there is no general way to "match" indexes with ciphertexts. Indeed, any key allows the adversary to learn, in principle, something from *all* challenge ciphertexts and we can hardly disallow all queries. Instead, SS1 allows unrestricted key-derivation queries and gives a compensating ability to the simulator. But now it incorporates SOA-K and is thus rarely achievable.

Roughly, the idea for SS2 is to run in parallel to the real game a "shadow" game where the inputs are independently generated as per the adversary-provided distributions. Key-derivation queries remain unrestricted. But at the end of the game, we check that the revealed keys don't "differentiate" the real and shadow games. We disallow adversaries who create such differentiation. In essence, this means that we require that the functionality take *predictable* values on the challenge messages when evaluated with the adversary's key derivation queries. One can compare this to the IND definition where the adversary is required to make key derivation queries that take the same value on the (known) challenge messages, so the adversary knows these values. Our definition may be written quite modularly relative to SS1, by adding appropriate boxed statements and checks in the games for the latter.

Our SS3 definition strengthens SS2 by dropping the restriction put by SS2 on key-derivation queries made by an adversary *before* seeing a challenge ciphertext. As such, we believe the SS3 definition is an essentially as-strong-as-possible security definition for FE subject to the constraint that it be achievable without any unnatural restrictions on the adversary or message space. To see why, note the definition of "unpredictable functionalities" used for our impossibility result in Section 4 and the fact that the latter crucially uses the adversary's ability to make "adaptive" key-derivation queries—i.e., depending on a challenge ciphertext. In essence, the SS3 definition demands that the functionality restricted to the adversary's adaptive key derivation queries be *predictable* wrt. the message space.

STANDARD-MODEL POSSIBILITY OF SS1. Returning to SS1, the negative results discussed above imply that we will need long keys, but we do not know that this is sufficient. There exists only one positive result, and this is in the PROM. Namely, BSW [14] provide a long-key, SS1-secure FE scheme for any functionality $\mathcal{F}$ where the space of functionality indexes on which $\mathcal{F}$ is non-trivial has polynomial size. We extend their result to the standard model. We do this by (again) exploiting the SOA-K connection. Namely we establish the same conclusion as BSW but assuming only the existence of a SOA-K-secure PKE scheme, which we know exists in the standard model because we are allowing keys to be long [15,17].

SUMMARY OF CONTRIBUTIONS. We make a connection between selective-opening attacks (SOA-K) and FE by observing the implicit presence of the former in SS1, an observation that seeds all the further contributions of this paper, summarized as follows. (1) We show impossibility of SS1-secure FE in the standard model by exploiting techniques underlying negative results for SOA-K [5]. (2) We present the SS2 definition for sans-SOA-K FE and prove it equivalent to IND for all functionalties, thus obtaining a slew of possibility results for SS2 via known possibility results for IBE and PE. (3) We present the stronger SS3 definition to function as a potential target for functionalites beyond PE and prove a possibility result for it. (4) We extend the only known positive result for a general functionality, namely one from BSW [14] for the case that the the set of indexes on which the functionality is non-trivial has polynomial size, from the PROM (Programmable Random Oracle Model) to the standard model, by using as starting point a SOA-K-secure PKE scheme with large keys, which exists in the standard model [15,17].

Discussion and Related work. The observation underlying BSW's impossibility proof is that SS1-secure IBE must achieve something similar to NCE. O'Neill [35] had the same intuitive observation but did not take it to a result or proof. Our work can be viewed as taking this intuition further to say that SS1-secure IBE must be exactly SOA-K-secure IBE, and similarly for other functionalities.

The difference between NCE and SOA-K is subtle but important, and underrecognized by the community. For example, some works say (for the PKE case) that SOA-K security is impossible with short keys, citing [32]. But, in ruling out NCE, the latter does not rule out SOA-K-security because there are potentially non-NCE ways to achieve SOA-K-security. Our techniques, however, rule out SOA-K-secure PKE with short keys. Although we have known an impossibility result for NCE for a decade, one for SOA-K has only emerged now.

SOAs have so far mainly been considered in the public-key setting. The adversary gets a number of challenge ciphertexts, "opens" a subset of them, and aims to discover something about the messages underlying the rest. There are two kinds of SOAs. In a coin-revealing SOA (SOA-C) the ciphertexts are encrypted under a single public key and opening reveals the coins. Achieving security is challenging but has been done [6,18,27]. SOA-C-security was also considered and achieved for IBE [9]. SOA-C is not relevant to our present concerns. In a key-revealing SOA (SOA-K) for PKE, the ciphertexts are encrypted under different public keys and opening reveals the corresponding decryption keys. But SOA-K has not been defined or considered for IBE, let alone for FE. We claim SS1 is, implicitly, defining SOA-K secure FE.

O'Neill [35] considers non-adaptive adversaries (meaning ones that don't make any key-derivation queries after seeing the challenge ciphertexts). He provides a non-adaptive version of SS1 and shows it equivalent to a non-adaptive version of IND for preimage sampleable functionalities. Most PE functionalities considered in the literature have this property.

Concurrent and subsequent work. A number of concurrent and subsequent works make progress on broadening the class of functionalities for which we have constructions of FE [24,41,20,25,22,21,19]. In particular, the recent breakthrough work of [19] constructs IND-secure FE for the class of all polynomial-time circuits, which can be bootstrapped to SS1-security against a bounded number of non-adaptive key-derivation and encryption queries using the recent work of De Caro et al. [16]. We note that a downside of studying achievability of SS1-security against a bounded number queries is that well-established IND-secure schemes (e.g. Waters' IBE [42]) do not meet it since SOA-K is still present.

Regarding concurrent work on the definitional front, Agrawal, Gorbunov, Vaikuntanathan and Wee (AGVW) [3] present impossibility results for a wPRF-based functionality under SS1 against an unbounded number of non-adaptive key-derivation queries. AGVW also propose a variant of SS1 that allows an *unbounded simulator*, which they call USIM. Interestingly, while they adapt BSW's impossibility proof to rule out USIM, this adaptation assumes "black-box" simulation. Moreover, our improved impossibility result for SS1 assumes collision-resistant hash functions so does not to rule out USIM (because an unbounded simulator can break collision-resistance). Thus, to the best of our knowledge, whether USIM can be achieved using "non-blackbox" simulation is still open.

Additionally, Barbosa and Farshim (BF) [4] point to weaknesses in the BSW definition having to do with "set-up" security. Our definition of SS1 and its variants do not appear to inherit these weaknesses because the simulator is not allowed to choose the auxilliary input. (See the body of the paper for further explanation.) BF also propose a definition that is the same in spirit as our SS3, but with the difference that the "ε-key" (which encodes the information about the message that is publicly computable from the ciphertext) is, like keys queried after seeing the challenge ciphertext, not allowed to differentiate between the real and shadow games, despite the fact that this key is implicitly queried at the beginning of the game by the adversary. (There are not real and shadow games in the BF formalization, but we describe it this way for simplicity.) This modification allows them to show equivalence between (their version of) SS3 and SS1 for a broader class of functionalities than in our result, such as IBE.

2 Preliminaries

NOTATION AND CONVENTIONS. If A is an algorithm then $y \leftarrow A(x_1, \ldots, x_n; r)$ means we run A on inputs $x_1, \ldots, x_n$ and coins r and denote the output by y. By $y \leftarrow\!\!\$\; A(x_1, \ldots, x_n)$ we denote the operation of picking r at random and letting $y \leftarrow A(x_1, \ldots, x_n; r)$. By $[A(x_1, \ldots, x_n)]$ we denote the set of all y that have positive probability of being output by A on inputs $x_1, \ldots, x_n$. Unless otherwise indicated, an algorithm may be randomized. "PT" stands for "polynomial time." The security parameter is denoted $\lambda \in \mathbb{N}$ and whenever λ is input to an algorithm it is understood that it is encoded in unary.

If s is a string then $|s|$ denotes its length, $s[i]$ denotes its ith bit, and $s[i \ldots j]$ denotes the substring consisting of its ith through jth bits. If $\mathbf{x}$ is a vector then $|\mathbf{x}|$ denotes the number of its components, $\mathbf{x}[i]$ denotes its ith component, and $\mathbf{x}[i \ldots j]$ denotes the subvector consisting of its ith through jth components. We write $\mathsf{El}(\mathbf{x})$ to mean $\{\mathbf{x}[i] : 1 \leq i \leq |\mathbf{x}|\}$. If f is a function and $\mathbf{x}$ is a vector then $f(x_1, \ldots, x_{i-1}, \mathbf{x}, x_{i+1}, \ldots, x_n)$ denotes the vector whose i-th component is $f(x_1, \ldots, x_{i-1}, \mathbf{x}[i], x_{i+1}, \ldots, x_n)$ for $1 \leq i \leq |\mathbf{x}|$. A predicate is a function with boolean output.

GAMES. We use the language of code-based game-playing [8]. A game has an INITIALIZE procedure, procedures to respond to adversary oracle queries, and a FINALIZE procedure. A game G is executed with an adversary A and security parameter λ as follows. A is given input λ and can then call game procedures. Its first oracle query must be INITIALIZE(λ) and its last oracle query must be to FINALIZE, and it must make exactly one query to each of these oracles. In between it can query the other procedures as oracles as it wishes. The output of FINALIZE, denoted $\mathrm{G}^A(\lambda)$, is called the output of the game. Let $A^{\mathrm{G}}(\lambda)$ denote the output of the adversary and $T(\mathrm{G}, A, \lambda)$ denote $\Pr\left[\mathrm{G}^A(\lambda) \text{ outputs true}\right]$.

PUBLIC-KEY ENCRYPTION SCHEMES. An *public-key encryption scheme* $\Pi = (\mathcal{G}, \mathcal{E}, \mathcal{D})$ is specified by three PT algorithms. Via $(pk, sk) \leftarrow\$ \mathcal{G}(\lambda)$ the key-generation algorithm $\mathcal{G}$ generates a public key and matching secret key. Via $c \leftarrow\$ \mathcal{E}(pk, m)$ the encryption algorithm $\mathcal{E}$ takes pk and message m and returns a ciphertext $c \in \{0,1\}^* \cup \{\bot\}$. Via $m \leftarrow \mathcal{D}(sk, c)$, the deterministic decryption algorithm $\mathcal{V}$ returns a message m. We require that $\mathcal{D}(sk, \mathcal{E}(pk, m)) = m$ for all $\lambda \in \mathbb{N}$, all $(pk, sk) \in [\mathcal{G}(\lambda)]$, and all $m \in \{0,1\}^*$

HASH FUNCTIONS. A hash function $\mathcal{H} = (K, H)$ is a tuple of PT algorithms. Via $hk \leftarrow\$ K(\lambda)$ the key-generation algorithm K produces a key hk. Via $y \leftarrow H(hk, x)$ the deterministic hashing algorithm H produces the hash of a string x under key hk. Collision-resistance is defined via game CR_Γ whose INITIALIZE(λ) procedure returns $hk \leftarrow\$ K(\lambda)$ and whose FINALIZE procedure on input (x, x') returns $(x \neq x') \wedge (H(hk, x) = H(hk, x'))$. There are no other procedures. The advantage of an adversary C is defined by $\mathbf{Adv}^{\mathrm{col}}_{\mathcal{H},C}(\lambda) = \Pr\left[\mathrm{CR}^C_{\mathcal{H}}(\lambda)\right]$. We say that $\mathcal{H}$ is collision-resistant (CR) if $\mathbf{Adv}^{\mathrm{col}}_{\mathcal{H},C}(\cdot)$ is negligible for every PT C.

3 Functional Encryption and Its Security

FUNCTIONALITIES AND FE SCHEMES. A *functionality* $\mathcal{F}$: $\mathbb{N} \times \{0,1\}^* \times \{0,1\}^* \to \{0,1\}^* \cup \{\bot\}$ is a deterministic PT algorithm. The first input is the security parameter. The second input is called the index and the third input is called the payload. A *functional encryption (FE) scheme* is a tuple of algorithms $\mathsf{FE} = (\mathsf{Setup}, \mathsf{KDer}, \mathsf{Enc}, \mathsf{Dec})$. The setup algorithm Setup on input λ returns a key-pair (pk, sk), the master public and secret keys. The key-derivation algorithm KDer on inputs sk, a returns a secret key dk for a. The encryption algorithm Enc on inputs pk, x returns a ciphertext c. The deterministic decryption algorithm Dec on inputs dk, c returns a string y. We say that an FE scheme $\mathsf{FE} = (\mathsf{Setup}, \mathsf{KDer}, \mathsf{Enc}, \mathsf{Dec})$ is $\mathcal{F}$-correct, or simply an $\mathcal{F}$-FE scheme, if $\mathsf{Dec}(dk, \mathsf{Enc}(pk, x; r)) = \mathcal{F}(\lambda, a, x)$ for all λ, a, x, r satisfying $\mathcal{F}(\lambda, a, x) \neq \bot$, all $(pk, sk) \in [\mathsf{Setup}(\lambda)]$ and all $dk \in [\mathsf{KDer}(sk, a)]$. We stress that correctness makes no requirements when $\mathcal{F}(\lambda, a, x) = \bot$. (We do not mandate that $\mathsf{Dec}(dk, \mathsf{Enc}(pk, x; r)) = \mathcal{F}(\lambda, a, x)$ in this case, but we do not disallow it either.)

SYNTAX AND CORRECTNESS IN BSW. The range of a functionality in the formal definition of BSW [14] does not include $\bot$, and correctness asks that $\mathsf{Dec}(dk, \mathsf{Enc}(pk, x; r)) = \mathcal{F}(\lambda, a, x)$ for all λ, a, x, r, all $(pk, sk) \in [\mathsf{Setup}(\lambda)]$ and all $dk \in [\mathsf{KDer}(sk, a)]$. However, specific functionalites given in BSW (such as that for IBE, $\mathcal{F}_{\mathrm{ibe}}^{\mathsf{P},\mathsf{p}}$ in our notation) do return $\perp$. So it would appear that the formal syntax ought to be amended to add $\perp$ to the range of $\mathcal{F}$. Once this is done, the correctness condition of BSW must be revisited. If left unchanged, it would be asking that $\mathsf{Dec}(dk, \mathsf{Enc}(pk, x; r)) = \mathcal{F}(\lambda, a, x)$ even when $\mathcal{F}(\lambda, a, x) = \perp$. This, however, would be incorrect. Attacks from [1] show that BB-style IBE schemes [10], including the BB IBE scheme [10] and Waters's IBE scheme [42], fail to meet this correctness condition relative to $\mathcal{F}_{\mathrm{ibe}}^{\mathsf{P},\mathsf{p}}$.[4] It was not clear to us exactly what BSW intended but we expect they did intend for existing IBE schemes to meet the correctness condition, and accordingly we have relaxed it to only hold when $\mathcal{F}(\lambda, a, x) \neq \perp$.

PARTICULAR FUNCTIONALITIES. The most important special case of FE in the literature is predicate encryption (PE). We say that $\mathcal{F}$ is a *predicate encryption functionality* if there is a predicate $\mathcal{P}$ such that $\mathcal{F}$ is $\mathcal{P}$-induced. This means that for all λ, all $a \neq \varepsilon$ and all (a', m) we have $\mathcal{F}(\lambda, a, (a', m)) = m$ if $\mathcal{P}(\lambda, a, a') = \mathsf{true}$ and $\perp$ otherwise. (We also require that $\mathcal{F}(\lambda, a, x)$ returns $\perp$ if x is not a pair. Note that no requirement is made on $\mathcal{F}(\lambda, \varepsilon, (a', m))$, so a single predicate could induce many different functionalities which vary in what is revealed under $a = \varepsilon$.) We call m the message. The IBE predicate $\mathcal{P}_{\mathrm{ibe}}$ is defined by $\mathcal{P}_{\mathrm{ibe}}(\lambda, a, a') = (a = a')$, and we say that $\mathcal{F}$ is an IBE functionality if it is $\mathcal{P}_{\mathrm{ibe}}$-induced. (So, again, there may be many different IBE functionalities.) Within the class of PE functionalities, we distinguish whether the index, the message, or both are to be kept private, with corresponding IBE functionalities as canonical examples:

- Public index, private message: We say that $\mathcal{F}$ is a (P, p)-PE functionality if $\mathcal{F}(\lambda, \varepsilon, (a', m)) = (a', |m|)$. Called PE with public index in the literature. The canonical example is the IBE functionality $\mathcal{F}_{\mathrm{ibe}}^{\mathsf{P},\mathsf{p}}$ which sets $\mathcal{F}_{\mathrm{ibe}}^{\mathsf{P},\mathsf{p}}(\lambda, \varepsilon, (a', m)) = (a', |m|)$, corresponding to IBE that hides the message but not necessarily the identity.
- Private index, private message: We say that $\mathcal{F}$ is a (p, p)-PE functionality if $\mathcal{F}(\lambda, \varepsilon, (a', m)) = |m|$. Called PE with private index in the literature. The canonical example is the IBE functionality $\mathcal{F}_{\mathrm{ibe}}^{\mathsf{p},\mathsf{p}}$ which sets $\mathcal{F}_{\mathrm{ibe}}^{\mathsf{p},\mathsf{p}}(\lambda, \varepsilon, (a', m)) = |m|$, corresponding to IBE that hides both the message and the identity (i.e. is anonymous).
- Private index, public message: We say that $\mathcal{F}$ is a (p, P)-PE functionality if $\mathcal{F}(\lambda, \varepsilon, (a', m)) = m$. Called predicate-only PE in the literature. The canonical example is the IBE functionality $\mathcal{F}_{\mathrm{ibe}}^{\mathsf{p},\mathsf{P}}$ which sets $\mathcal{F}_{\mathrm{ibe}}^{\mathsf{p},\mathsf{P}}(\lambda, \varepsilon, (a', m)) = m$, corresponding to IBE that hides the identity but not necessarily the message. PEKS [12] is a (p, P)-PE functionality that additionally satisfies robustness [1].

[4] The difficulty is that correctness is required for all x, a and thus when $x = (a', m)$ with $a' \neq a$, it is required that $\mathsf{Dec}(dk, \mathsf{Enc}(pk, (a', m); r)) = \perp$ when $dk \in [\mathsf{KDer}(sk, a)]$. This is a form of robustness as defined in [1] and, as indicated there, often useful, but it is not a standard requirement for IBE schemes and most don't meet it.

PROC INITIALIZE(λ):	PROC INITIALIZE(λ):
$(pk, sk) \leftarrow\$ \mathsf{Setup}(\lambda)$	$i, j \leftarrow 0$; $St \leftarrow \varepsilon$
$z \leftarrow\$ Z(\lambda)$	$z \leftarrow\$ Z(\lambda)$
$i, j \leftarrow 0$; $St \leftarrow \varepsilon$	Return z
Return (pk, z)	PROC MSG(α):
PROC ENC(α):	$i \leftarrow i + 1$
$i \leftarrow i + 1$	$\mathbf{q}[i] \leftarrow \alpha$; $\mathbf{t}[i] \leftarrow \mathsf{enc}$
$\mathbf{q}[i] \leftarrow \alpha$; $\mathbf{t}[i] \leftarrow \mathsf{enc}$	$(St, \mathbf{x}[i]) \leftarrow\$ D(St, \alpha)$
$(St, \mathbf{x}[i]) \leftarrow\$ D(St, \alpha)$	Return $\mathcal{F}(\lambda, \varepsilon, \mathbf{x}[i])$
$\mathbf{c}[i] \leftarrow\$ \mathsf{Enc}(pk, \mathbf{x}[i])$	PROC OP(a):
Return $(\mathbf{c}[i], \mathcal{F}(\lambda, \varepsilon, \mathbf{x}[i]))$	$i \leftarrow i + 1$
PROC KD(a):	$\mathbf{q}[i] \leftarrow a$; $\mathbf{t}[i] \leftarrow \mathsf{kd}$
$i \leftarrow i + 1$	Return ε
$\mathbf{q}[i] \leftarrow a$; $\mathbf{t}[i] \leftarrow \mathsf{kd}$	PROC F(a, s):
$dk \leftarrow\$ \mathsf{KDer}(sk, a)$	If $a \in \mathsf{El}(\mathbf{a})$ and $1 \le s \le i$ then
Return dk	Return $\mathcal{F}(\lambda, a, \mathbf{x}[s])$
PROC FINALIZE(w):	Else return $\perp$
Return $R(\lambda, z, \mathbf{x}, \mathbf{q}, \mathbf{t}, St, w)$	PROC FINALIZE(w):
	Return $R(\lambda, z, \mathbf{x}, \mathbf{q}, \mathbf{t}, St, w)$

Fig. 1. Left: "Real world" game $\mathrm{RSS1}_{\mathsf{FE},\mathcal{F},Z,D,R}$ for the SS1 definition. Right: "Ideal world" game $\mathrm{ISS1}_{\mathcal{F},Z,D,R}$ for the SS1 definition.

We don't discuss (P, P)-PE because it reveals everything and is uninteresting.

SS1 DEFINITION. The following definition is adapted from [14]. Let $\mathsf{FE} = (\mathsf{Setup}, \mathsf{KDer}, \mathsf{Enc}, \mathsf{Dec})$ be an $\mathcal{F}$-FE scheme. The definition uses games $\mathrm{RSS1}_{\mathsf{FE},\mathcal{F},Z,D,R}$ and $\mathrm{ISS1}_{\mathcal{F},Z,D,R}$ of Fig. 1. We provide some intuition for these games below. We say that FE is *SS1-secure* if for every auxiliary input generator Z, every PT message sampler D, every PT relation R and every PT adversary A, there is a PT simulator S such that

$$\mathbf{Adv}^{\mathrm{ss1}}_{\mathsf{FE},\mathcal{F},A,S,Z,D,R}(\cdot) = T(\mathrm{RSS1}_{\mathsf{FE},\mathcal{F},Z,D,R}, A, \cdot) - T(\mathrm{ISS1}_{\mathcal{F},Z,D,R}, S, \cdot)$$

is negligible. We note that the auxiliary input will be used in our impossibility result in Section 4 (where it contains a key for a collision-resistant hash function). Although we omit to do this for simplicity because it does not affect our results, it can also be given as an additional argument to a functionality itself. For example, in the case of the inner-product functionality introduced in [28] it can then contain the modulus N of unknown factorization.

INTUITIVE OVERVIEW OF THE DEFINITION. To gain some intuition for the games, let us first look at the "real world" game with the adversary. It has access to two main oracles, an encryption oracle ENC and key-derivation oracle KD. The former takes input α, which describes a message-space from which to sample, proc Initialize(λ):

$(pk, sk) \leftarrow\$ \mathsf{Setup}(\lambda)$; $i, j \leftarrow 0$
Return pk

proc LR(x_0, x_1)

$i \leftarrow i + 1$; $(\mathbf{x}_0[i], \mathbf{x}_1[i]) \leftarrow (x_0, x_1)$
$\mathbf{c}[i] \leftarrow\$ \mathsf{Enc}(pk, x_b)$
Return $\mathbf{c}[i]$

proc Kd(a):

$j \leftarrow j + 1$; $\mathbf{a}[j] \leftarrow a$
$dk \leftarrow\$ \mathsf{KDer}(sk, a)$
Return dk

proc Finalize(b'):

$\mathbf{a}[j+1] \leftarrow \varepsilon$
For $j' = 1, \ldots, j+1$ do
  If $\mathcal{F}(\lambda, \mathbf{a}[j'], \mathbf{x}_0) \neq \mathcal{F}(\lambda, \mathbf{a}[j'], \mathbf{x}_1)$ then
    return false
Return $(b' = 1)$

Fig. 2. Game $\mathrm{IND}_{\mathsf{FE},\mathcal{F},b}$ for the IND definition

and outputs the encryption of a sampled message x. The latter takes as input a functionality index a and returns a corresponding secret key. Note that the game records the queries made to these oracles, in order, and provides this as input to the relation R. Now let us look at the "ideal world" game with the simulator. The simulator has access to not two but three main oracles, a message sampling oracle Msg, an operation oracle Op, and a functionality oracle F. The first on input α, which again describes a message-space from which to sample, samples a message x but simply returns $\mathcal{F}(\lambda, \varepsilon, x)$. (We follow BSW [14] in using the value under index ε to describe what information about the message is publicly computable from a ciphertext.) The second records that an input functionality index a is "legal to be used" by the last oracle. The last oracle takes such an index a and a position s to return $\mathcal{F}(\lambda, a, x_s)$ where x_s is the sth sampled message by Msg. Intuitively, Op queries of the simulator correspond to Kd queries of the adversary, and indeed they are input to the relation R in the analogous manner. F queries can always be made "for free" by the simulator (they are not input to R).

Discussion of SS1. We have discussed SS1 as being the BSW [14] definition, which it is in spirit, but there are some differences in detail. BSW indicate that there are several dimensions of choice. They choose to formalize a non-adaptive version with blackbox simulators, saying that variants may be formalized similarly. We have chosen to formalize the variant with adaptive security and non-blackbox simulation. BSW give pk as input to the relation and we do not, but this choice does not matter. However, a novelty of our definition is the introduction of auxiliary inputs. Besides what is noted above in their regard, we note that our use of auxiliary inputs rescues our definitions from the weaknesses of the BSW definition pointed out in BF [4]. The issue raised by the latter arises with a functionality, such as inner-product PE [28], that depends on a parameter, such as a hard-to-factor modulus, that must be generated in a setup phase. Under BSW [14] and O'Neill [35], this would have to be done by the Setup algorithm of the FE scheme and the modulus would be part of *pk*. The problem raised by BF [4] then occurs because the simulator can pick *pk*. We, however, do not give *pk* as input to $\mathcal{F}$ and would capture setup-based functionalities by having the setup done by the auxiliary input generator algorithm Z, so that the modulus, in our example, would be part of the output z of this algorithm. However, the simulator is *not* allowed to pick z, and thus the attack of BF [4] would not appear to apply.

IND DEFINITION. Let $\mathsf{FE} = (\mathsf{Setup}, \mathsf{KDer}, \mathsf{Enc}, \mathsf{Dec})$ be an $\mathcal{F}$-FE scheme. The definition uses game $\mathrm{IND}_{\mathsf{FE},\mathcal{F},b}$ of Fig. 2 for $b \in \{0,1\}$. We say that FE is *IND-secure* if for every adversary B,

$$\mathbf{Adv}^{\mathrm{ind}}_{\mathsf{FE},\mathcal{F},B}(\cdot) \;=\; T(\mathrm{IND}_{\mathsf{FE},\mathcal{F},1}, B, \cdot) - T(\mathrm{IND}_{\mathsf{FE},\mathcal{F},0}, B, \cdot)$$

is negligible.

ROBUSTNESS. Robustness, introduced for IBE and PKE in [1], seems important more generally for FE, particularly for predicate-only predicate encryption. To explain the issue, recall that correctness was mute in the case that $\mathcal{F}(\lambda, a, x) = \bot$, meaning in this case no requirement was put on the output of $\mathsf{Dec}(dk, \mathsf{Enc}(pk, x))$ when $dk \in [\mathsf{KDer}(sk, a)]$. Roughly, robustness asks that $\mathsf{Dec}(dk, \mathsf{Enc}(pk, x)) = \bot$ in this case. In the case of PEKS this is important to avoid false positives in the testing.

The reason it is not quite so simple is that asking for the above condition globally and unconditionally seems to yield something that is hard to achieve. Instead, one can ask for various computational relaxations in the style of [1]. To exemplify, here is one that is very strong but attractive due to its simplicity: procedure INITIALIZE(λ) of game $\mathrm{ROB}_{\mathsf{FE},\mathcal{F}}$ lets $(pk, sk) \leftarrow\!\!\$\; \mathsf{Setup}(\lambda)$ and returns *both* keys, meaning the adversary gets *sk*. FINALIZE(a, x) returns $((\mathcal{F}(\lambda, a, x) = \bot) \wedge (\mathsf{Dec}(\mathsf{KDer}(sk, a), \mathsf{Enc}(pk, x)) \neq \bot)$.

4 Impossibility Results

We show that the SS1 notion is *impossible* to achieve in the *standard model*, so long as the functionality is reasonably likely to take more than one possible value on a challenge message. This result only assumes the existence of a collision-resistant hash function.

Following [14] we also consider a relaxation of the SS1 notion where vectors $\mathbf{a}, \boldsymbol{\alpha}$ are replaced by *unordered sets*, thus giving the simulator more power (since it can make its queries in a different order than the adversary). We obtain a similar but more restrictive impossibility result in this case. Here we present the ordered case. The unordered case is given in the full version [7].

UNPREDICTABLE FUNCTIONALITIES. In the ordered case our result applies to any *unpredictable functionality.* Let $\mathcal{F}$ be a functionality, $\mathcal{A} = \{a_\lambda\}_{\lambda \in \mathbb{N}}$ be a family of functionality indices (strings), and $\mathcal{X} = \{X_\lambda\}_{\lambda \in \mathbb{N}}$ be a family of payload distributions. We say that $\mathcal{F}$ is $p(\cdot)$*-unpredictable wrt.* $\mathcal{A}, \mathcal{X}$ if for all $\lambda \in \mathbb{N}$ and all $y \in \{0,1\}^* \cup \{\bot\}$, $\Pr[x \leftarrow\!\!\$\; X_\lambda : y = \mathcal{F}(\lambda, a_\lambda, x)] \le 1 - 1/p(\lambda)$.

For example, the functionality $\mathcal{F}^{\mathsf{P},\mathsf{p}}_{\text{bit-ibe}}$ for a one-bit IBE scheme, which parses x as (a', b), and returns b if $a = a'$ and $\bot$ otherwise, is a 2-unpredictable function wrt. $\mathcal{A}, \mathcal{X}$ where, for all $\lambda \in \mathbb{N}$, we let a_λ be a fixed but arbitrary identity and $\mathcal{X}_\lambda$ return (a_λ, d) where the message $d \in \{0,1\}$ is random. As another example, the functionality $\mathcal{F}^{\mathsf{p},\mathsf{P}}_{\text{peks}}$for a PEKS scheme, which returns 1 if $a = x$ and $\bot$ otherwise, is a 2-unpredictable function wrt. $\mathcal{A}, \mathcal{X}$ where for all $\lambda \in \mathbb{N}$, we again let a_λ be fixed but arbitrary keyword and $\mathcal{X}_\lambda$ return a random keyword $x \in \{a_\lambda, a'_\lambda\}$ for some also fixed but arbitrary $a'_\lambda \neq a_\lambda$. Indeed, unpredictability with respect to *some* family of input distributions and functionality indices is a minimal requirement for a functionality to be interesting; otherwise, it is trivial to build an FE scheme for it because anyone can decrypt correctly without even using the ciphertext. In this sense, our result below rules out an SS1-secure FE scheme for any non-trivial functionality.

SECRET-KEY LENGTH. we say that an FE scheme $\mathsf{FE} = (\mathsf{Setup}, \mathsf{KDer}, \mathsf{Enc}, \mathsf{Dec})$ has *secret-key length* $\ell(\cdot)$ if $|dk| \le \ell(\lambda) = \mathcal{F}(\lambda, a, x)$ for all λ, a, x, r, all $(pk, sk) \in [\mathsf{Setup}(\lambda)]$, and all $dk \in [\mathsf{KDer}(sk, a)]$. Note that every FE scheme must have some polynomial $\ell(\cdot)$ secret-key length in order to be efficient.

Theorem 1. *Let $p(\cdot) > 1$ be a polynomial. Suppose $\mathcal{F}$ is a $p(\cdot)$-unpredictable functionality wrt. $\mathcal{A} = \{a_\lambda\}_{\lambda \in \mathbb{N}}, \mathcal{X} = \{X_\lambda\}_{\lambda \in \mathbb{N}},$. Furthermore, suppose that for every $\lambda \in N$, $\mathcal{F}(\lambda, \varepsilon, x)$ is the same for all $x \in [X_\lambda]$. Let $\mathcal{H} = (K, H)$ be a collision-resistant hash function. Then there does not exist an SS1-secure $\mathcal{F}$-FE scheme. More precisely, suppose* FE *is a $\mathcal{F}$-FE scheme with secret-key length $\ell(\cdot)$. Then for any function $\mu(\cdot)$ there exists a PT auxiliary input generator Z, message sampler D, PT adversary A, PT relation R, and CR-adversary C such that for every simulator S*

$$\mathbf{Adv}^{\mathrm{ss}}_{\mathsf{FE},\mathcal{F},A,S,Z,D,R}(\cdot) \ \ge \ 1 - \sqrt{\mathbf{Adv}^{\mathrm{col}}_{\mathcal{H},C}(\cdot) + 1/\mu(\cdot)}\,.$$

Adversary A makes $p(\cdot)(\ell(\cdot) + \log \mu(\cdot))$ encryption queries and two key-derivation queries.

The proof is in the full version [7].

To compare, BSW [14] ruled out SS1-secure IBE against adversaries with access to a non-programmable random oracle, so our result improves theirs in two respects: to applies to any non-trivial functionality and standard-model adversaries. It also reveals a trade-off between secret-key length and the total number of bits encrypted. Namely, when the difference is even one bit (i.e., the total number of bits encrypted is one more than the secret-key length) our adversary's advantage is non-negligible. We also note that, while for technical reasons we require $\mathcal{F}(\lambda, \varepsilon, x)$ to take the same value on every possible challenge payload x, this is not a major restriction in practice since typically $\mathcal{F}(\lambda, \varepsilon, x) = |x|$; then we are just requiring as usual that possible challenge messages have the same length.

5 Brute-Force Construction Revisited

We now revisit the "brute-force" scheme defined by BSW [14], which provides a way to construct FE for any functionality with a polynomially-sized index space.

Let $\mathcal{F}$ be a functionality. We say that $\mathcal{F}$ has *polynomially-sized index space* if $\mathcal{F}(\lambda, a, x) = \bot$ if $a \notin \mathcal{A}_\lambda$ where $\mathcal{A}_\lambda = \{\varepsilon, a_1, a_2, \ldots, a_{p(\lambda)}\}$ for a polynomial $p(\cdot)$. Let $(\mathcal{G}, \mathcal{E}, \mathcal{D})$ be a PKE scheme. Then we define a the *brute-force FE scheme* for $\mathcal{F}$ as follows:

$\underline{\text{SETUP}(\lambda)}$	$\underline{\text{ENC}(\mathbf{pk}, m)}$
For $i = 1, \ldots p(\lambda)$ do	For $i = 1, \ldots, p(\lambda)$ do
$\quad (\mathbf{pk}[i], \mathbf{sk}[i]) \leftarrow \mathcal{G}(\lambda)$	$\quad \mathbf{c}[i] \leftarrow_{\$} \mathcal{E}(\mathbf{pk}[i], \mathcal{F}(\lambda, a_i, m))$
Return $(\mathbf{pk}, \mathbf{sk})$	Return $\mathbf{c}$
$\underline{\text{KDER}(sk, a)}$	$\underline{\text{DEC}((i, \mathbf{sk}[i]), \mathbf{c}))}$
For $i = 1, \ldots, p(\lambda)$ do	If $(\mathbf{sk}[i] = \varepsilon)$ then return $\|m\|$
$\quad$ If $a_i = a$ then return $(i, \mathbf{sk}[i])$	Return $\mathcal{D}(\mathbf{sk}[i], \mathbf{c}[i])$

BSW [14] show that this construction is IND-secure (and hence, by our results detailed in the full version [7], SS2-secure) provided that the underlying PKE scheme is semantically secure. Moreover, they show a slightly decorated construction which is SS1-secure in the random oracle model. What we show is that it suffices for the underlying PKE scheme to be secure against *key-revealing SOAs* (SOA-K) for this FE scheme to be SS1-secure. In fact, for their result BSW implicitly use the non-committing (which implies SOA-K) PKE scheme of Nielsen [32] in the random oracle model as the underlying PKE scheme, so our result is a generalization of theirs. In particular, it allows us to obtain instantiations in the standard model by (necessarily) allowing long keys, meaning longer than the total number of bits encrypted; SOA-K secure PKE is known to exist in this setting [15,17].

Details are given in the full version [7].

Acknowledgements. We thank the anonymous reviewers for their comments. Mihir Bellare was supported in part by NSF grants CNS 1228890 and CNS 1116800. Adam O'Neill was supported in part by NSF grants CNS-0915361, CNS-0952692, CNS-1012910, and CNS-0546614.

References

1. Abdalla, M., Bellare, M., Neven, G.: Robust encryption. In: Micciancio, D. (ed.) TCC 2010. LNCS, vol. 5978, pp. 480–497. Springer, Heidelberg (2010)
2. Agrawal, S., Freeman, D.M., Vaikuntanathan, V.: Functional encryption for inner product predicates from learning with errors. In: Lee, D.H., Wang, X. (eds.) ASIACRYPT 2011. LNCS, vol. 7073, pp. 21–40. Springer, Heidelberg (2011)
3. Agrawal, S., Gorbunov, S., Vaikuntanathan, V., Wee, H.: Functional encryption: New perspectives and lower bounds. In: Canetti, R., Garay, J.A. (eds.) CRYPTO 2013, Part II. LNCS, vol. 8043, pp. 500–518. Springer, Heidelberg (2013)
4. Barbosa, M., Farshim, P.: On the semantic security of functional encryption schemes. In: Public Key Cryptography, pp. 143–161 (2013)
5. Bellare, M., Dowsley, R., Waters, B., Yilek, S.: Standard security does not imply security against selective-opening. In: Pointcheval, D., Johansson, T. (eds.) EUROCRYPT 2012. LNCS, vol. 7237, pp. 645–662. Springer, Heidelberg (2012)
6. Bellare, M., Hofheinz, D., Yilek, S.: Possibility and impossibility results for encryption and commitment secure under selective opening. In: Joux, A. (ed.) EUROCRYPT 2009. LNCS, vol. 5479, pp. 1–35. Springer, Heidelberg (2009)
7. Bellare, M., O'Neill, A.: Semantically-secure functional encryption: Possibility results, impossibility results and the quest for a general definition. Cryptology ePrint Archive, Report 2012/515 (2012), `http://eprint.iacr.org/`
8. Bellare, M., Rogaway, P.: The security of triple encryption and a framework for code-based game-playing proofs. In: Vaudenay, S. (ed.) EUROCRYPT 2006. LNCS, vol. 4004, pp. 409–426. Springer, Heidelberg (2006)
9. Bellare, M., Waters, B., Yilek, S.: Identity-based encryption secure against selective opening attack. In: Ishai, Y. (ed.) TCC 2011. LNCS, vol. 6597, pp. 235–252. Springer, Heidelberg (2011)
10. Boneh, D., Boyen, X.: Efficient selective-ID secure identity-based encryption without random oracles. In: Cachin, C., Camenisch, J.L. (eds.) EUROCRYPT 2004. LNCS, vol. 3027, pp. 223–238. Springer, Heidelberg (2004)
11. Boneh, D., Boyen, X.: Secure identity based encryption without random oracles. In: Franklin, M. (ed.) CRYPTO 2004. LNCS, vol. 3152, pp. 443–459. Springer, Heidelberg (2004)
12. Boneh, D., Di Crescenzo, G., Ostrovsky, R., Persiano, G.: Public key encryption with keyword search. In: Cachin, C., Camenisch, J.L. (eds.) EUROCRYPT 2004. LNCS, vol. 3027, pp. 506–522. Springer, Heidelberg (2004)
13. Boneh, D., Franklin, M.K.: Identity based encryption from the Weil pairing. SIAM Journal on Computing 32(3), 586–615 (2003)
14. Boneh, D., Sahai, A., Waters, B.: Functional encryption: Definitions and challenges. In: Ishai, Y. (ed.) TCC 2011. LNCS, vol. 6597, pp. 253–273. Springer, Heidelberg (2011)
15. Canetti, R., Feige, U., Goldreich, O., Naor, M.: Adaptively secure multi-party computation. In: 28th ACM STOC, pp. 639–648. ACM Press (May 1996)
16. De Caro, A., Iovino, V., Jain, A., O'Neill, A., Paneth, O., Persiano, G.: On the achievability of simulation-based security for functional encryption. In: Canetti, R., Garay, J.A. (eds.) CRYPTO 2013, Part II. LNCS, vol. 8043, pp. 519–535. Springer, Heidelberg (2013)
17. Damgård, I.B., Nielsen, J.B.: Improved non-committing encryption schemes based on a general complexity assumption. In: Bellare, M. (ed.) CRYPTO 2000. LNCS, vol. 1880, pp. 432–450. Springer, Heidelberg (2000)

18. Fehr, S., Hofheinz, D., Kiltz, E., Wee, H.: Encryption schemes secure against chosen-ciphertext selective opening attacks. In: Gilbert, H. (ed.) EUROCRYPT 2010. LNCS, vol. 6110, pp. 381–402. Springer, Heidelberg (2010)
19. Garg, S., Gentry, C., Halevi, S., Raykova, M., Sahai, A., Waters, B.: Candidate indistinguishability obfuscation and functional encryption for all circuits. In: FOCS (2013)
20. Garg, S., Gentry, C., Halevi, S., Sahai, A., Waters, B.: Attribute-based encryption for circuits from multilinear map. In: Canetti, R., Garay, J.A. (eds.) CRYPTO 2013, Part II. LNCS, vol. 8043, pp. 479–499. Springer, Heidelberg (2013)
21. Goldwasser, S., Kalai, Y.T., Popa, R.A., Vaikuntanathan, V., Zeldovich, N.: How to run turing machines on encrypted data. In: Canetti, R., Garay, J.A. (eds.) CRYPTO 2013, Part II. LNCS, vol. 8043, pp. 536–553. Springer, Heidelberg (2013)
22. Goldwasser, S., Kalai, Y.T., Popa, R.A., Vaikuntanathan, V., Zeldovich, N.: Reusable garbled circuits and succinct functional encryption. In: STOC, pp. 555–564 (2013)
23. Goldwasser, S., Micali, S.: Probabilistic encryption. Journal of Computer and System Sciences 28(2), 270–299 (1984)
24. Gorbunov, S., Vaikuntanathan, V., Wee, H.: Functional encryption with bounded collusions via multi-party computation. In: Safavi-Naini, R., Canetti, R. (eds.) CRYPTO 2012. LNCS, vol. 7417, pp. 162–179. Springer, Heidelberg (2012)
25. Gorbunov, S., Vaikuntanathan, V., Wee, H.: Attribute-based encryption for circuits. In: STOC, pp. 545–554 (2013)
26. Goyal, V., Pandey, O., Sahai, A., Waters, B.: Attribute-based encryption for fine-grained access control of encrypted data. In: Juels, A., Wright, R.N., Vimercati, S. (eds.) ACM CCS 2006, pp. 89–98. ACM Press (October/November 2006); Available as Cryptology ePrint Archive Report 2006/309
27. Hemenway, B., Libert, B., Ostrovsky, R., Vergnaud, D.: Lossy encryption: Constructions from general assumptions and efficient selective opening chosen ciphertext security. In: Lee, D.H., Wang, X. (eds.) ASIACRYPT 2011. LNCS, vol. 7073, pp. 70–88. Springer, Heidelberg (2011)
28. Katz, J., Sahai, A., Waters, B.: Predicate encryption supporting disjunctions, polynomial equations, and inner products. In: Smart, N.P. (ed.) EUROCRYPT 2008. LNCS, vol. 4965, pp. 146–162. Springer, Heidelberg (2008)
29. Lewko, A., Okamoto, T., Sahai, A., Takashima, K., Waters, B.: Fully secure functional encryption: Attribute-based encryption and (Hierarchical) inner product encryption. In: Gilbert, H. (ed.) EUROCRYPT 2010. LNCS, vol. 6110, pp. 62–91. Springer, Heidelberg (2010)
30. Lewko, A., Waters, B.: Decentralizing attribute-based encryption. In: Paterson, K.G. (ed.) EUROCRYPT 2011. LNCS, vol. 6632, pp. 568–588. Springer, Heidelberg (2011)
31. Lewko, A., Waters, B.: Unbounded HIBE and attribute-based encryption. In: Paterson, K.G. (ed.) EUROCRYPT 2011. LNCS, vol. 6632, pp. 547–567. Springer, Heidelberg (2011)
32. Nielsen, J.B.: Separating random oracle proofs from complexity theoretic proofs: The non-committing encryption case. In: Yung, M. (ed.) CRYPTO 2002. LNCS, vol. 2442, pp. 111–126. Springer, Heidelberg (2002)
33. Okamoto, T., Takashima, K.: Hierarchical predicate encryption for inner-products. In: Matsui, M. (ed.) ASIACRYPT 2009. LNCS, vol. 5912, pp. 214–231. Springer, Heidelberg (2009)

34. Okamoto, T., Takashima, K.: Efficient attribute-based signatures for non-monotone predicates in the standard model. In: Catalano, D., Fazio, N., Gennaro, R., Nicolosi, A. (eds.) PKC 2011. LNCS, vol. 6571, pp. 35–52. Springer, Heidelberg (2011)
35. O'Neill, A.: Definitional issues in functional encryption. Cryptology ePrint Archive, Report 2010/556 (2010), http://eprint.iacr.org/
36. Ostrovsky, R., Sahai, A., Waters, B.: Attribute-based encryption with non-monotonic access structures. In: Ning, P., di Vimercati, S.D.C., Syverson, P.F. (eds.) ACM CCS 2007, pp. 195–203. ACM Press (October 2007)
37. Sahai, A., Waters, B.: Fuzzy identity-based encryption. In: Cramer, R. (ed.) EUROCRYPT 2005. LNCS, vol. 3494, pp. 457–473. Springer, Heidelberg (2005)
38. Shamir, A.: Identity-based cryptosystems and signature schemes. In: Blakely, G.R., Chaum, D. (eds.) CRYPTO 1984. LNCS, vol. 196, pp. 47–53. Springer, Heidelberg (1985)
39. Shen, E., Shi, E., Waters, B.: Predicate privacy in encryption systems. In: Reingold, O. (ed.) TCC 2009. LNCS, vol. 5444, pp. 457–473. Springer, Heidelberg (2009)
40. Waters, B.: Dual system encryption: Realizing fully secure IBE and HIBE under simple assumptions. In: Halevi, S. (ed.) CRYPTO 2009. LNCS, vol. 5677, pp. 619–636. Springer, Heidelberg (2009)
41. Waters, B.: Functional encryption for regular languages. In: Safavi-Naini, R., Canetti, R. (eds.) CRYPTO 2012. LNCS, vol. 7417, pp. 218–235. Springer, Heidelberg (2012)
42. Waters, B.: Efficient identity-based encryption without random oracles. In: Cramer, R. (ed.) EUROCRYPT 2005. LNCS, vol. 3494, pp. 114–127. Springer, Heidelberg (2005)

Efficient Lossy Trapdoor Functions Based on Subgroup Membership Assumptions*

Haiyang Xue[1,2], Bao Li[1,2], Xianhui Lu[1,2], Dingding Jia[1,2], and Yamin Liu[1,2]

[1] Institute of Information Engineering of Chinese Academy of Science, Beijing, China

[2] The Data Assurance and Communication Security Research Center of Chinese Academy of Sciences, Beijing, China

{hyxue12,lb,xhlu,ddjia,ymliu}@is.ac.cn

Abstract. We propose a generic construction of lossy trapdoor function from the subgroup membership assumption. We present three concrete constructions based on the k-DCR assumption over $\mathbb{Z}_{N^2}^*$, the extended p-subgroup assumption over $\mathbb{Z}_{N^2}^*$, and the decisional RSA subgroup membership assumption over $\mathbb{Z}_N^*$. Our constructions are more efficient than the previous construction from the DCR assumption over $\mathbb{Z}_{N^s}^*(s \geq 3)$.

Keywords: Lossy Trapdoor Functions, DCR Assumption, p-subgroup Assumption, Decisional RSA Assumption.

1 Introduction

Peikert and Waters [1] proposed the notion of lossy trapdoor function (LTDF) in STOC 2008. LTDF implies cryptographic primitives such as classic one-way trapdoor function [2], collision resistant hash function [3], oblivious transfer protocol [4], chosen ciphertext secure (CCA) public key encryption scheme[1], deterministic public key encryption scheme [5], OAEP based public key encryption scheme [6], and selective opening secure public key encryption scheme [7]. LTDFs can be constructed based on many assumptions, especially lattice-based assumptions.

Peikert and Waters [1] proposed two constructions of LTDFs, based on the Decisional Diffie-Hellman (DDH) assumption and the Learning with Errors assumption respectively. But the two constructions are not efficient since they both require a function index of size $\mathcal{O}(n^2)$. Boyen *et al.* [8] shrank the function index of the DDH-based construction from $\mathcal{O}(n^2)$ to $\mathcal{O}(n)$ with common reference string and pairing. But their method can only be applied to bilinear groups and their algorithm requires computing pairing, which is an expensive operation. Freeman *et al.* [9], [10] proposed a construction based on the d-linear

* Supported by the National Basic Research Program of China (973 project)(No.2013CB338002), the National Nature Science Foundation of China (No.61070171, No.61272534, No.61272035), the Strategic Priority Research Program of Chinese Academy of Sciences under Grant XDA06010702 and IIE's Cryptography Research Project (No. Y3Z0027103, No.Y3Z0024103, No. Y3Z002A103).

M. Abdalla, C. Nita-Rotaru, and R. Dahab (Eds.): CANS 2013, LNCS 8257, pp. 235–250, 2013.

assumption which is a generalization of the DDH assumption. This construction is not efficient since the size of the function index is $\mathcal{O}(n^2)$.

Under the quadratic residuosity (QR) assumption, two distinct constructions of LTDFs were given in [9], [11]. The construction of [9] only loses one bit of the input information. In the construction of [11], the inversion algorithm does not use the factorization of N but performs a coordinated ElGamal decryption and learns one bit at one time. Joye *et al.* [12] proposed the 2^k-QR assumption, which is a generalization of the QR assumption, and proved that it is implied by the QR assumption. They proposed a LTDF based on DDH and 2^k-QR assumptions which is slightly different from Hemenway-Ostrovsky's [11] method. In their construction, the factorization of N is the trapdoor and the inversion algorithm processes k bits at one time. With a well-chosen k, only a 18×18 matrix over $\mathbb{Z}_N^*$ is needed which highly reduces the length of the output. But the length of output and the function index is also too long for practical application.

The constructions above belong to the matrix based framework proposed by Peikert and Waters [1]. More efficient constructions of LTDFs based on different techniques were proposed. Kiltz *et al.* [6] showed that the RSA permutation provides a lossy property under the Φ-hiding assumption. A efficient LTDF based on the decisional composite residuosity (DCR) assumption over $\mathbb{Z}_{N^s}^*$, for $s \geq 3$, was proposed in [9], [10] and Wee [13] described a generic construction of LTDFs by using dual hash proof systems.

In the construction of Freeman *et al.* [9], the message is embeded into a subgroup generated by $(1 + N) \bmod N^s$ with order N^{s-1} and the image is the group of N-th residuosity with order $\phi(N)$ in lossy mode, s must be larger than 2 in order to make lossiness. It is a very interesting question if we could make lossiness when $s \leq 2$.

1.1 Our Contribution

We propose a generic construction of LTDFs based on the subgroup membership assumption. For a finite cyclic group G with a non-trivial subgroup K, the subgroup membership problem asserts that it is difficult to decide whether an element is in K or $G \backslash K$. To construct LTDFs, two special properties are needed. Firstly, the subgroup discrete logarithm over G/K is easy to compute with the help of a trapdoor. Secondly, the size of G/K is significantly larger than that of K. The construction in [9] based on the DCR assumption over $\mathbb{Z}_{N^s}^*(s \geq 3)$ can be seen as a concrete example of our generic construction. According to our generic construction, $G = Z_{N^s}^*$ and K is the group of N^{s-1}-th residuosity.

We also present three concrete constructions over $\mathbb{Z}_{N^2}^*$ or $\mathbb{Z}_N^*$ which are more efficient. The main idea is to shrink the size of K. Briefly, our constructions can be described as follows.

- **k-DCR based construction.** We extend the 2^k-QR problem from $\mathbb{Z}_N^*$ to $\mathbb{Z}_{N^2}^*$ and get a new assumption named as k-DCR assumption. We prove that the k-DCR assumption over $\mathbb{Z}_{N^2}^*$ is implied by the DCR assumption and the QR assumption. We propose an efficient construction of $(\log N + k, 3k)$-LTDF based on the k-DCR assumption. This construction is more efficient

than the DCR based construction [9] and the 2^k-QR based construction [12]. With a well-chosen parameter k, we can get a $(\frac{9}{8}\log N, \frac{3}{8}\log N)$-LTDF. To our best knowledge, this is the first index independent LTDF over $\mathbb{Z}_{N^2}^*$. We can generalize this construction and get $((s-1)\log N + k, (s-2)\log N + 3k)$-LTDFs over $\mathbb{Z}_{N^s}^*$, for $s \geq 2$.
- **Extended p-subgroup based construction.** We extend the p-subgroup problem from $\mathbb{Z}_N^*$ to $\mathbb{Z}_{N^2}^*$ and get an extended p-subgroup assumption. We propose a construction of $(\log N, \frac{2}{3}\log N)$-LTDF over $\mathbb{Z}_{N^2}^*$. This construction can also be generalized to $\mathbb{Z}_{N^s}^*$, for $s \geq 2$.
- **Decisional RSA subgroup based construction.** The decisional RSA subgroup assumption over Z_N^* for $N = (2p'r_p + 1)(2q'r_q + 1)$ was proposed by Groth [14], where p', q' are primes and r_p, r_q consist of distinct odd prime factors smaller than some low bound B. According to our generic construction, we get a LTDF based on the decisional RSA subgroup assumption.

Kiltz *et al.* [6] proposed an efficient LTDF based on the Φ-hiding assumption over $\mathbb{Z}_N^*$. They utilized a factor of $\phi(N)$ as the public key e in lossy mode. It seems difficult to construct an ALL-But-One (ABO) LTDF for CCA application following their steps. Our generic construction can easily be extended to the ABO LTDF. We will describe the extension in section 3.

1.2 Outline

This paper is organized as follows. In Sect. 2, we introduce the notations and recall the definition of lossy trapdoor function and subgroup membership problem. In Sect. 3, we present the generic construction of LTDF. In Sect. 4, we present concrete constructions of LTDF based on the k-DCR assumption, the extended p-subgroup assumption, and the decisional RSA subgroup assumption, respectively. In Sect. 5, we compare our work with the precious constructions. In Sect. 6, we conclude this paper.

2 Preliminaries

2.1 Notation

If S is a set, we denote its size by $|S|$ and denote by $x \leftarrow S$ the process of sampling x uniformly from S. If A is an algorithm, we denote by $z \leftarrow A(x, y, \cdots)$ the process of running A with input $x, y, \cdots$ and output z. For an integer n, we denote by $[n]$ the set of $\{0, 1, \cdots, n-1\}$. A function is *negligible* if for every $c > 0$ there exists a λ_c such that $f(\lambda) < 1/\lambda^c$ for all $\lambda > \lambda_c$.

2.2 Lossy Trapdoor Function

A collection of lossy trapdoor functions consists of two families of functions. Functions in the first family are injective and can be inverted with the trapdoor, while functions in the second are lossy, meaning that the size of their image is significantly smaller than the size of their preimage. For CCA applications, it is convenient to work with the All-But-One lossy trapdoor function. In the following, we recall the definition of lossy trapdoor functions and All-But-One lossy trapdoor function.

Definition 1 (Lossy Trapdoor Functions). *A collection of (m, l)-lossy trapdoor functions are 4-tuple of probabilistic polynomial time (PPT) algorithms $(S_{inj}, S_{loss}, F_{ltdf}, F_{ltdf}^{-1})$ such that:*

1. Sample Lossy Function $S_{loss}(1^n)$. *Output a function index $\sigma \in \{0,1\}^*$.*
2. Sample Injective Function $S_{inj}(1^n)$. *Output a pair $(\sigma, \tau) \in \{0,1\}^* \times \{0,1\}^*$ where σ is a function index and τ is a trapdoor.*
3. Evaluation algorithm F_{ltdf}. *For every function index σ produced by either S_{loss} or S_{inj}, the algorithm $F_{ltdf}(\sigma, \cdot)$ computes a function $f_\sigma : \{0,1\}^m \to \{0,1\}^*$ with one of the two following properties:*
   - *Lossy: If σ is produced by S_{loss}, then the image of f_σ has size at most 2^{m-l}.*
   - *Injective: If σ is produced by S_{inj}, then the function f_σ is injective.*
4. Inversion algorithm F_{ltdf}^{-1}. *For every pair (σ, τ) produced by S_{inj} and every $x \in \{0,1\}^m$, we have $F_{ltdf}^{-1}(\tau, F_{ltdf}(\sigma, x)) = x$.*

In the above algorithms, the two ensembles $\{\sigma, \sigma \leftarrow S_{loss}(1^n)\}$ and $\{\sigma, (\sigma, \tau) \leftarrow S_{inj}(1^n)\}$ are computationally indistinguishable.

Definition 2 (All-But-One Lossy Trapdoor Functions). *A collection of (m, l)-All-But-One lossy trapdoor functions are 4-tuple of PPT algorithms $(B, S, F_{ltdf}, F_{ltdf}^{-1})$ such that:*

1. Sample a branch B. *On input 1^n, B outputs a value $b \in \{0,1\}^*$.*
2. Sample a function S. *For every value b produced by B, the algorithm S outputs a triple $(\sigma, \tau, \beta) \in \{0,1\}^* \times \{0,1\}^* \times \{0,1\}^*$ where σ is a function index, τ is a trapdoor, and β is a set of lossy branch.*
3. Evaluation algorithm F_{ltdf}. *For any b^* and b produced by $B(1^n)$, every σ, τ, β produced by $S(1^n, b^*)$, the algorithm $F_{ltdf}(\sigma, b, \cdot)$ computes a function $f_{\sigma,b} : \{0,1\}^m \to \{0,1\}^*$ with one of the two following properties:*
   - *Lossy: If $b = b^*$, then the image of f_σ has size at most 2^{m-l}.*
   - *Injective: If $b \neq b^*$, then the function f_σ is injective.*
4. Inversion algorithm F_{ltdf}^{-1}. *For any b^* and b produced by $B(1^n)$ and every (σ, τ, β) produced by $S(1^n, b^*)$ and every $x \in \{0,1\}^m$, we have*

$$F_{ltdf}^{-1}(\tau, F_{ltdf}(\sigma, b, x)) = x.$$

- *In the above algorithms, the two ensembles $\{\sigma, (\sigma, \tau, \beta) \leftarrow S(1^n, b)\}$ and $\{\sigma, (\sigma, \tau, \beta) \leftarrow S(1^n, b^*)\}$ are computationally indistinguishable.*
- *Any PPT algorithm A that receives as input (σ, b^*), where $b^* \leftarrow B(1^n)$ and $(\sigma, \tau, \beta) \leftarrow S(1^n, b^*)$, has only a negligible probability of outputting an element $b \in \beta \setminus \{b^*\}$.*

2.3 Subgroup Membership Assumption

Gjϕsteen [15] discussed the subgroup membership problem. A subgroup membership problem considers a group G with a non-trivial subgroup K. The problem asserts that it is hard to distinguish elements of K from elements of $G \backslash K$. Brown [16] analysed instances of subgroup membership problems and concrete schemes obtained by following the Cramer-Shoup framework [17]. Brown gave the constructions of CCA secure scheme based on the GBD subgroup membership assumption [18] , the r-th residuosity assumption [19], and the p-subgroup assumption [20]. Groth [14] proposed another example of the subgroup membership assumption, the decisional RSA subgroup assumption. Paillier and Pointcheval [21] discussed the subgroup variant of DCR-based encryption. The DCR assumption over this subgroup variant is also a subgroup membership assumption.

Definition 3 (Subgroup Membership Assumption). *Let G be a finite cyclic group G with subgroup K. Let g (resp. h) be a generator of group G (resp. K). The subgroup membership problem $SM_{(G,K)}$ asserts that, for any PPT distinguisher D, the adavantage*

$$Adv_D^{SM_{(G,K)}} = |\Pr[A(G,K,x) = 1 | x \leftarrow K] - \Pr[A(G,K,x) = 1 | x \leftarrow G \setminus K]|.$$

is negligible, where the probability is taken over coin tosses.

There are three interesting subgroup membership problems. We illustrate them here since they are useful for our construction of LTDFs.

The 2^k-QR assumption. Joye *et al.* [12] proposed the 2^k-QR assumption. Let $N = pq$ be the product of two large primes p and q with $p = 2^k p' + 1, q = 2^k q' + 1$, where p', q' are primes. The internal direct product of $\mathbb{Z}_N^*$ is: $\mathbb{Z}_N^* \cong G_{p'q'} \cdot G_{2^k} \cdot K_{2K}$. The decomposition is unique except for the choice of K_{2^k}. Let $G = G_{p'q'} \cdot G_{2^k}$ and $K = G_{p'q'}$, the 2^k-QR assumption asserts that it is infeasible to distinguish elements of $G \setminus K$ from that of K.

The p-subgroup membership assumption. Okamoto and Uchiyama [20] proposed the p-subgroup assumption. Let p, q be primes and set $N = p^2 q$. Let g be a random element of $\mathbb{Z}_N^*$ such that the order of $g_p = g^{p-1} \mod p^2$ is p. Let $h = g^N \mod N$ and $G = \{x = g^m h^r \mod N | m \in \mathbb{Z}_p, r \in \mathbb{Z}_N\}$, $K = \{x = h^r \mod N | r \in \mathbb{Z}_N\}$. The p-subgroup assumption is that it is infeasible to distinguish elements of K from that of $G \setminus K$ given N and g.

The decisional RSA subgroup assumption. Groth [14] described a decisional RSA subgroup assumption over $\mathbb{Z}_N^*$ with semi-smooth order. Let $N = pq = (2p'r_p + 1)(2q'r_q + 1)$, with p, q, p', q' primes and r_p, r_q consists of distinct odd prime factors smaller than some bound B. The internal direct product of $\mathbb{Z}_N^*$ is: $\mathbb{Z}_N^* \cong G_{r_p r_q} \cdot G_{p'q'} \cdot G_2 \cdot T$. Let G be $G_{r_p r_q} \cdot G_{p'q'}$ and $K = G_{p'q'}$. The decisional RSA subgroup assumption asserts the hardness of distinguishing elements in $G \setminus K$ from K.

Gjϕsteen also gave the definition of subgroup discrete logarithm problem which is a generalization of Paillier's [22] partial discrete logarithm problem. In their definition, g is a group element such that its residue class generates

G/K and $\lambda : G \to \mathbb{Z}_{|G/K|}$ is the group homomorphism defined by $\lambda(g) = 1$ with $ker(\lambda) = K$. The subgroup discrete logarithm problem is: given a random $x \in G$, compute $\lambda(x)$. The formal definition follows.

Definition 4 (Subgroup Discrete Logarithm Problem). *Assume that group G has a non-trivial subgroup K and let g be a generator of G. If $\varphi : G \to G/K$ is the canonical epimorphism, then the subgroup discrete logarithm problem $SDL_{(G,K,g)}$ is: given a random $x \in G$, to compute $\log_{\varphi(g)}(\varphi(x))$.*

3 A Generic Construction of LTDF

In order to make lossiness in LTDFs, we assume a generic subgroup assumption having two special properties. The first property (namely SDL property) we assume is that the subgroup discrete logarithm problem is solvable with a trapdoor. For a subgroup membership problem $SM_{(G,K)}$, let τ be the corresponding trapdoor, there is a PPT algorithm to solve $SDL_{(G,K,g)}$ with the trapdoor τ. The second property (namely lossy property) we require is that the length of G/K's order is significantly larger than that of K's order. The input message in $[|G/K|]$ can be embeded into G by computing a pre-image of the map ψ. In the lossy mode, we just compute a pre-image falling into subgroup K. The length of G/K's order should be significantly larger than that of K in order to get lossiness.

In this subsection, we give the generic construction of LTDF based on the subgroup membership assumption with special property. We assume that there is a PPT generator *Gen* of groups with the subgroup membership assumption. The generator *Gen* takes the security parameter n and outputs (G, K, g, h, τ), where g (resp. h) is the generator of G (resp. K) and τ is the corresponding trapdoor. The order of G is a polynomial of n.

We construct a $(\log|G/K|, \log|G/K| - \log|K|)$-lossy trapdoor function $LTDF_{SM} = (S_{inj}, S_{loss}, F_{ltdf}, F_{ltdf}^{-1})$ as follows:

1. *Sample Injective Function S_{inj}.* On input 1^n, S_{inj} chooses a random $r \in \mathbb{Z}_{|K|}$ and computes $c := gh^r$. The function index is $\sigma = (G, g, h, c)$. The trapdoor is $t = \tau$.
2. *Sample Lossy Function S_{loss}.* On input 1^n, S_{loss} chooses a random $r \in \mathbb{Z}_{|K|}$ and computes $c := h^r$. The function index is $\sigma = (G, g, h, c)$.
3. *Evaluation algorithm F_{ltdf}.* Given a function index $\sigma = (N, g, h, c)$ and input $x \in \{0, 1\}^l$ where l is the length of $|G/K|$, the algorithm computes and outputs $z = c^x$.
4. *Inversion algorithm F_{ltdf}^{-1}.* Given a function index (N, g, h, c), the trapdoor $t = \tau$ and a message z, the algorithm recovers x with the algorithm of solving $SDL_{(G,K,g)}(z)$ problem.

Theorem 1. *If the membership assumption holds and the group G has the SDL property and the lossy property, then $LTDF_{SM}$ is an $(\log|G/K|, \log|G/K| - \log|K|)$-lossy trapdoor function.*

Proof. The algorithm to solve $SDL_{(G,K,g)}$ guarantees the correctness of inversion algorithm F_{ltdf}^{-1}. The subgroup membership assumption implies that the indices of injective and lossy functions are computationally indistinguishable. The output of the lossy function falls in subgroup K. The size of the lossy function's image is at most $\log|K|$. Consequently, the lossiness is $\log|G/K| - \log|K|$. □

Remark 1. The construction [9] based on the DCR assumption is a concrete example of this generic construction. The DCR construction is over $\mathbb{Z}_{N^s}^*$, where $N = (2p'+1)(2q'+1)$. The group structure of $\mathbb{Z}_{N^s}^*$ is

$$\mathbb{Z}_{N^s}^* \cong G_{N^{s-1}} \cdot G_{n'} \cdot G_2 \cdot T,$$

where G_t is the group of order t, T is a group with $\{-1, 1\}$ and $n' = p'q'$. The decomposition is unique except for the choice of G_2. In their construction, $G = G_{N^{s-1}} \cdot G_{n'} \cdot G_2 \cdot T$, $K = G_{n'} \cdot G_2 \cdot T$ with $(N+1)$ be the generator of $G_{N^{s-1}}$. The injective (resp. lossy) function index is $(1+N)r^{N^{s-1}} \mod N^s$ (resp. $r^{N^{s-1}} \mod N^s$) for randomly chosen $r \in \mathbb{Z}_N^*$. For a randomly chosen $g_0 \in K$, let g be $(1+N)g_0$ and h be a random element in K, then $LTDF_{SM}$ is exactly the DCR construction. The $SDL_{(G,K,(1+N)g_0)}$ problem can be solved with decryption algorithm of [23] and the lossiness property is satisfied. The disadvantage of the DCR construction is that s should be larger than 2.

The generic construction can easily be extended to a ABO LTDF. We describe the extension here and the security proof is similar with that of Theorem 5.4 in [9] and is therefore omitted. We also assume that there is a PPT generator *Gen* of groups with the subgroup membership assumption. The construction of $LTDF_{SM}^{ABO} = (B, S, F_{ltdf}, F_{ltdf}^{-1})$ follows:

1. *Sample a branch B.* On input 1^n, the algorithm B outputs a uniformly distributed $b \in \{0, 1, \ldots, |G|\}$.
2. *Sample a function S.* On input 1^n and a lossy branch b^*, S chooses a random $r \in \mathbb{Z}_{|K|}$ and computes $c := g^{-b^*}h^r$. The function index is $\sigma = (G, g, h, c)$.
3. *Evaluation algorithm F_{ltdf}.* Given a function index $\sigma = (N, g, h, c)$, a branch b and input $x \in \{0,1\}^l$ where l is the length of $|G/K|$, the algorithm computes and outputs $z = (g^b c)^x$.
4. *Inversion algorithm F_{ltdf}^{-1}.* Given a function index (N, g, h, c), the trapdoor $t = \tau$, a branch $b \neq b^*$ and a message z, the algorithm recovers x with the algorithm of solving $SDL_{(G,K,g^{b-b^*})}(z)$ problem.

Theorem 2. *If the membership assumption holds and the group G has the SDL property and the lossy property, then $LTDF_{SM}^{ABO}$ is an* $(\log|G/K|, \log|G/K| - \log|K|)$*-All But One lossy trapdoor function.*

4 Concrete Constructions of LTDF

This section shows new efficient concrete constructions of LTDFs based on three reasonable assumptions: the k-DCR assumption (implied by DCR and QR assumptions), the extended p-subgroup assumption, and the decisional RSA subgroup membership assumption.

4.1 LTDF Based on k-DCR Assumption

Joye *et al.* [12] proposed the 2^k-QR assumption and proved that it is implied by the classical QR assumption. We first review 2^k-QR assumption and DCR assumption, then give the formal definition of k-DCR assumption.

Definition 5 ([12] Definition 1). *Let p be an odd prime and $2^k | p-1$. Then the symbol*

$$\left(\frac{a}{p}\right)_{2^k} := a^{\frac{p-1}{2^k}} \mod p,$$

is called the 2^k-th power residue symbol modulo p, where $a^{\frac{p-1}{2^k}} \mod p$ are in $[-(p-1)/2, (p-1)/2]$.

Let $N = pq$ be the product of two prime numbers, and $p = 2^k p'+1$, $q = 2^k q'+1$ with p', q' be primes. Let $J_N := \{a \in Z_N^* | (\frac{a}{N})_2 = 1\}$, $QR_N := \{a \in Z_N^* | (\frac{a}{p})_2 = (\frac{a}{q})_2 = 1\}$ and $QNR_N := J_N \setminus QR_N$.

Definition 6. *Let $N = pq$ be the product of two large primes p and q with $p, q \equiv 1 \mod 2^k$. Define two sets*

$$W_0 := \{x \in QNR_N\},$$

$$W_1 := \{y^{2^k} \mod N | y \in Z_N^*\}.$$

The Gap 2^k Residuosity assumption (2^k-QR) asserts that, for any PPT distinguisher D, the advantage

$$\mathrm{Adv}_D^{2^k\text{-}QR} = |\Pr[D(x,N) = 1 | x \leftarrow W_0] - \Pr[D(x,N) = 1 | x \leftarrow W_1]|$$

is negligible, where the probability is taken over coin tosses.

Definition 7. *Let $N = pq$ be the product of two large primes p and q. Define two sets*

$$P := \{a = x^N \mod N^2 | x \in \mathbb{Z}_N^*\},$$

$$M := \{a = (1+N)^y x^N \mod N^2 | x \in \mathbb{Z}_N^*, y \in \mathbb{Z}_N\}.$$

The Decisional Composite Residuosity (DCR) assumption asserts that, for any PPT distinguisher D, the advantage

$$\mathrm{Adv}_D^{DCR} = |\Pr[D(x,N) = 1 | x \leftarrow P] - \Pr[D(x,N) = 1 | x \leftarrow \mathbb{Z}_{N^2}^*]|$$

is negligible, where the probability is taken over coin tosses.

The 2^k-QR assumption is over the group $\mathbb{Z}_N^*$. We embed $\mathbb{Z}_N^*$ into the group $\mathbb{Z}_{N^2}^*$ and get a k-DCR assumption by combining 2^k-QR and DCR assumptions. We also prove that the k-DCR assumption is implied by QR and DCR assumptions.

Definition 8. *Let $N = pq$ be the product of two large primes p and q with $p = 2^k p' + 1, q = 2^k q' + 1$. For random element $y \in QNR_N$, define two sets*

$$W_0 := \{a = r^{2^k N} \mod N^2 | r \in \mathbb{Z}_N^*\},$$

$$W_1 := \{a = (1+N)^z y^{tN} r^{2^k N} \mod N^2 | r \in \mathbb{Z}_N^*, t \in [2^k], z \in \mathbb{Z}_N\}.$$

The k Decisional Composite Residuosity (k-DCR) assumption asserts that, for any PPT distinguisher D, the advantage

$$Adv_D^{k\text{-}DCR} := |\Pr[D(x,y,N) = 1 | x \leftarrow W_0, y \leftarrow QNR_N] - \Pr[D(x,y,N) = 1 | x \leftarrow W_1, y \leftarrow QNR_N].$$

is negligible, where the probability is taken over coin tosses.

With overwhelming probability, random element $y \in QNR_N$ has order $2^k p'q'$ in $\mathbb{Z}_N^*$. In detail, let d_1 be the order of y modulo p, we have that d_1 equals to $2^k p'$ or 2^k since that $(\frac{y}{p})_2 \equiv y^{2^{(k-1)}p} \equiv -1 \mod p$. Similarly, the order of y modulo q, d_2, is $2^k q'$ or 2^k. Consequently, the order of random element y in $\mathbb{Z}_N^*$ is $2^k p'q'$ with probability $1 - \frac{1}{p'} - \frac{1}{q'} + \frac{1}{p'q'}$. We decompose $\mathbb{Z}_{N^2}^*$ as an inner direct product

$$\mathbb{Z}_{N^2}^* \cong G_N \cdot G_{2^k} \cdot G_{p'q'} \cdot K_{2^k},$$

where each group G_t is a group of order t. The decomposition is not unique, but if given an element $y^N \mod N^2$ where $y \in QNR_N$ has order $2^k p'q'$, the subgroup $G_N \cdot G_{2^k} \cdot G_{p'q'}$ is unique. Note that the element $(1+N)$ has order N in $\mathbb{Z}_{N^2}^*$, i.e. it generates G_N while $y^N \mod N^2$ has order $2^k p'q'$, i.e. it generates $G_{2^k} \cdot G_{p'q'}$. We have that $(1+N)y^N$ generates the group $G_N \cdot G_{2^k} \cdot G_{p'q'}$ which is actually W_1 in Definition 8. And W_0 in Definition 8 is actually group $G_{p'q'}$.

Theorem 3. *The k-DCR assumption is implied by the 2^k-QR assumption and QR assumption. It satisfies that,*

$$\mathrm{Adv}_D^{k\text{-}DCR} \leq 2\mathrm{Adv}_B^{2^k\text{-}QR} + \mathrm{Adv}_C^{DCR} \leq 8k\mathrm{Adv}_A^{QR} + \mathrm{Adv}_C^{DCR}.$$

Proof. The complete proof of the theorem can be found in Appendix.

Now, we show a construction of LTDF based on the k-DCR assumption over $\mathbb{Z}_{N^2}^*$. The output of our construction is much shorter, as compared with construction based on the DCR assumption [9] and Joye *et al.*'s construction based on the 2^k-QR assumption [12]. Specifically, the DCR based construction is over $\mathbb{Z}_{N^s}^*$ for $s \geq 3$. The output has $s \log N$ bits for $s \geq 3$. For well-chosen parameters, the output of 2^k-QR construction is a 18×18 matrix over $\mathbb{Z}_N$ with $234 \log N$ bits. Our construction is computed over $\mathbb{Z}_{N^2}^*$. We define $LTDF_{k\text{-}DCR} = (S_{inj}, S_{loss}, F_{ltdf}, F_{ltdf}^{-1})$ as follows

1. *Sample Injective Function* S_{inj}. On input 1^n, S_{inj} chooses an n-bits $N = pq$ where $p = 2^k p' + 1, q = 2^k q' + 1$ and p, q, p', q' are prime numbers. It chooses a random $y \in QNR_N$ and computes $g = y^N \mod N^2$. Then it chooses a random $h_1 \in \mathbb{Z}_N^*$ and compute $h = h_1^{2^k N} \mod N^2$. It chooses a random $r \in [\frac{N}{4^k}]$ and let $c = (1+N)gh^r \mod N^2$. The function index is $\sigma = (N, g, h, c)$. Let $\lambda = (p-1, q-1)$ then the trapdoor is $t = \{\lambda, p\}$.
2. *Sample Lossy Function* S_{loss}. On input 1^n, S_{loss} chooses an n-bits $N = pq$ where $p = 2^k p' + 1, q = 2^k q' + 1$ and p, q, p', q' are prime numbers. It chooses a random $y \in QNR_N$ and computes $g = y^N \mod N^2$. Then it chooses a random $h_1 \in \mathbb{Z}_N^*$ and compute $h = h_1^{2^k N} \mod N^2$. It chooses a random $r \in [\frac{N}{4^k}]$ and let $c = h^r \mod N^2$. The function index is $\sigma = (N, g, h, c)$.
3. *Evaluation algorithm* F_{ltdf}. Given a function index $\sigma = (N, g, h, c)$ and input $x \in [2^k N]$ the algorithm outputs $z = c^x$.
4. *Inversion algorithm* F_{ltdf}^{-1}. Given the function index (N, g, h, c), trapdoor $t = \{\lambda, p\}$ and a message z, the algorithm first computes $x_1 = \frac{z^\lambda - 1}{N}\lambda^{-1} \mod N$, then finds an $x_2 \in [2^k]$ such that the following holds,

$$\left[\left(\frac{g}{p}\right)_{2^k}\right]^{x_2} = \left(\frac{z}{p}\right)_{2^k} \mod p.$$

Finally, it computes x with the Chinese Reminder Theorem:

$$\begin{cases} x = x_1 \mod N, \\ x = x_2 \mod 2^k. \end{cases}$$

Theorem 4. *Under the k-DCR assumption, it holds that $LTDF_{k\text{-}DCR}$ is an $(n+k, 3k)$-lossy trapdoor function.*

Proof. Let $G = G_N \cdot G_{2^k} \cdot G_{p'q'}$ and $G = G_{2^k} \cdot G_{p'q'}$, the $SM_{G,K}$ is the k-DCR assumption. The decryption algorithms of Paillier's scheme [22] and Joye's scheme [12] solve the $SDL_{(G,K,(1+N)g)}$ problem correctly with the trapdoor. The order of G/K here is $2^k N$ and the order of K is $p'q'$. It's a direct result of Theorem 1. □

Remark 2. Joye *et al.* pointed out that for security parameters n, we can choose $k \leq \frac{1}{4}\log N - n$. If $k = n$, it is sufficient to set $k = \frac{1}{8}\log N$. This construction can be generalized to groups over $Z_{N^s}^*, s \geq 2$ by following the step of [23]. We note that if g is omitted, then $LTDF_{k\text{-DCR}}$ has less lossiness.

4.2 LTDF Based on Extended p-Subgroup Assumption

Okamoto and Uchiyama [20] proposed the p-subgroup assumption. with $N = p^2 q$. We restrict p, q to be safe primes for technical reasons. Now we consider the group $\mathbb{Z}_{N^2}^*$ with $N = p^2 q$. The element $(1+N)$ has order N in $\mathbb{Z}_{N^2}^*$. Consider the integer $(1+N)^i \equiv \sum_{j=0}^{i} C_i^j N^j \mod N^2$. The number is 1 modulo N^2 for some i

if and only if $(1+iN) \equiv 1 \mod N^2$. Clearly this is the case $i = aN$ for $a \in \mathbb{N}$, so it follows that the order of $(1+N) \mod N^2$ is N. For random element $y \in Z_N^*$, $g = y^{2N^2}$ has order $p'q'$ modulo N^2 with overwhelming probability. Indeed the order of g modulo p^4 (resp. q^2) is p' (resp. q') with probability $1 - \frac{1}{p'}$ (resp. $1 - \frac{1}{q'}$). The above g has order $p'q'$ modulo N^2 with probability $1 - \frac{1}{p'} - \frac{1}{q'} + \frac{1}{p'q'}$. If the inner direct product of $\mathbb{Z}_{N^2}^*$ is

$$\mathbb{Z}_{N^2}^* \cong G_N \cdot G_p \cdot G_{n'} \cdot K_4,$$

then $(1+N)$ is a generator of G_N and g is a generator of $G_{n'}$ with overwhelming probability. Consequently, $(1+N)g$ is a generator of $G_N \cdot G_{n'}$ with overwhelming probability.

Next, we consider the subgroup problem $SM_{(G_N G_{n'}, G_{n'})}$ over $\mathbb{Z}_{N^2}^*$ and propose another example of the subgroup membership assumption.

Definition 9 (Extended p-subgroup assumption). *With the notions above, let $G = G_N \cdot G_{n'}$ and $K = G_{n'}$. The extended p-subgroup assumption asserts that the subgroup membership problem $SM(G, K)$ is difficult.*

Now, we construct a LTDF based on the extended p-subgroup assumption. We define $LTDF_{E\ p\text{-}sub} = (S_{inj}, S_{loss}, F_{ltdf}, F_{ltdf}^{-1})$ as follows.

1. *Sample Injective Function S_{inj}.* On input security parameter 1^n, S_{inj} chooses $N = p^2 q$ where $p = 2p' + 1, q = 2q' + 1$ and p, q, p', q' are prime numbers. It chooses y randomly in $\mathbb{Z}_N^*$ and computes $h = y^{2N^2} \mod N^2$. S_{inj} chooses a random $r \in \mathbb{Z}_N$ and computes $c = (1+N)h^r \mod N^2$. The function index is $\sigma = (N, h, c)$. The trapdoor is $t = p'q'$.
2. *Sample Lossy Function S_{loss}.* On input security parameter 1^n, S_{loss} chooses $N = p^2 q$ where $p = 2p' + 1, q = 2q' + 1$ and p, q, p', q' are prime numbers. It chooses y randomly in $\mathbb{Z}_N^*$ and computes $h = y^{2N^2} \mod N^2$. S_{loss} chooses a random $r \in \mathbb{Z}_N$ and computes $c = h^r \mod N^2$. The function index is $\sigma = (N, h, c)$.
3. *Evaluation algorithm F_{ltdf}.* Given a function index $\sigma = (N, h, c)$ and input $x \in \mathbb{Z}_N$ the algorithm outputs $z = c^x$.
4. *Inversion algorithm F_{ltdf}^{-1}.* Given the function index (N, g, h, c), trapdoor t and a message z, the algorithm computes $x = \frac{z^t - 1}{N} t^{-1} \mod N$.

Theorem 5. *Under the extended p-subgroup assumption, it holds that $LTDF_{E\ p\text{-}sub}$ is an $(\log N, \frac{1}{3}\log N)$-lossy trapdoor function.*

Proof. Let $G = G_N \cdot G_{n'}$ and $K = G_{n'}$, the inversion algorithm solve the $SDL_{(G, K(1+N)h)}$ correctly. The order of G/K is N and the order of K is n'. It is a direct result of Theorem 1. □

4.3 LTDF Based on the Decisional RSA Subgroup Assumption

Groth [14] described a decisional RSA subgroup assumption over $\mathbb{Z}_N^*$ with semi-smooth order and gave a chosen plaintext secure encryption scheme over this group. Let $N = pq = (2p'r_p + 1)(2q'r_q + 1)$, where p, q, p', q' are primes and r_p, r_q consist of distinct odd prime factors smaller than some low bound B. The internal direct product of $\mathbb{Z}_N^*$ is:

$$\mathbb{Z}_N^* \cong G_{r_p r_q} \cdot G_{p'q'} \cdot G_2 \cdot T.$$

In fact, $G_{r_p r_q} \cdot G_{p'q'}$ is the quadratic residue group QR_N of $\mathbb{Z}_N^*$. Let g be a generator of QR_N then $h = g^{r_p r_q}$ is a generator of $G_{p'q'}$. The decisional RSA subgroup assumption asserts that it is hard to distinguish elements drawn randomly from QR_N or from $G_{p'q'}$. Let $G = G_{p'q'} \cdot G_{r_p r_q}$ and $K = G_{p'q'}$, then the decisional RSA subgroup assumption is another instance of the subgroup membership assumption.

Let t be the number of distinct primes of $r_p r_q$, and we assume the length l of the prime factors is about $\log B$. Lemma 2 in [14] shows that a randomly chosen g in QR_N has order larger than $p'q'2^{(t-d)(l-1)}$ with overwhelming probability. To encrypt a message with length $(t-d)(l-1)$, where d is an integer smaller than t, we can encrypt m as $c = g^m h^r$. To decrypt c, we compute $c^{p'q'} = g^{p'q'm}$ mod N. The message m can be derived since the order of $g^{p'q'}$ has only small prime factors. The decryption algorithm is efficient with the help of a storage list. Groth gave an example of parameters, where $l_N = 1280$, $l_{p'} = l_{q'} = 160$, $B = 2^{15}$, $t = 64$, $d = 7$. The length of message space is no smaller than 698 with probability higher than $1 - 2^{-80}$. With well chosen parameters, this decisional RSA subgroup assumption can be used to construct efficient LTDF.

Next, we construct a LTDF based on the decisional RSA subgroup assumption. We define $LTDF_{RSA} = (S_{inj}, S_{loss}, F_{ltdf}, F_{ltdf}^{-1})$ as follows.

1. *Sample Injective Function* S_{inj}. On input 1^n, S_{inj} chooses $N = pq$ with $p = 2p'r_p + 1, q = 2q'r_q + 1$ where p, q, p', q' are prime numbers. Let r_p, r_q be B-smooth with distinct prime factors. It chooses $g \in QR_N$ randomly, and chooses a generator h of $G_{p'q'}$. It chooses proper parameters t and d and denotes $l_x = (t-d)(l-1)$. It chooses a random $r \in \mathbb{Z}_N$ and computes $c = gh^r \mod N$. The function index is $\sigma = (N, g, h, c)$. The trapdoor is the factorization of $\varphi(N)$.
2. *Sample Lossy Function* S_{loss}. On input 1^n, S_{loss} chooses $N = pq$ with $p = 2p'r_p + 1, q = 2q'r_q + 1$ where p, q, p', q' are prime numbers. Let r_p, r_q be B-smooth with distinct prime factors. It chooses $g \in QR_N$ randomly, and chooses a generator h of $G_{p'q'}$. It chooses proper parameters t and d and denotes $l_x = (t-d)(l-1)$. It chooses a random $r \in \mathbb{Z}_N$ and computes $c = h^r \mod N$. The function index is $\sigma = (N, g, h, c)$.
3. *Evaluation algorithm* F_{ltdf}. Given a function index $\sigma = (N, g, h, c)$ and the input $x \in \{0,1\}^{l_x}$ the algorithm outputs $z = c^x$.
4. *Inversion algorithm* F_{ltdf}^{-1}. Given the function index (N, g, h, c), the factorization of $\psi(N)$ and the message z, the algorithm invokes the inversion algorithm provided by the decryption algorithm of Groth's scheme. We compute $C_p = z^{p'q'} = (g^{p'q'})^x \mod N$. Since the order of $g^{p'q'}$ is B-smooth, we can derive x by computing discrete log of C_p base $g^{p'q'}$.

Theorem 6. *Under the decisional RSA subgroup assumption, it holds that $LTDF_{RSA}$ is an $(l_x, l_x - (l_{p'} + l_{q'}))$-lossy trapdoor function.*

Proof. Let G be the group generated by g and K be the group generated by h, this is a direct result of Theorem 1. □

5 Comparison

In the Table 1, we compare the three constructions instantiated with the generic construction in Section 3 with previous LTDFs. The second column lists the basic number-theoretic assumptions used for guaranteeing the security. The third and fourth columns show the size of a input message in bits and that of lossiness, respectively. The fifth column lists the size of the function index. The last column indicates if there there a direct extension to ABO-LTDF from the construction of LTDF or not.

Table 1. Comparison with existing LTDFs

	Assumption	Input size	Lossiness	Index size	Efficiency	ABO?
[1]	DDH	n	$n - \lvert\mathbb{G}\rvert$	$n^2\mathbb{G}$	n^2 Multi	Yes
[1]	LWE	n	cn	$n(d+w)\mathbb{Z}_q$	$n(d+w)$ Multi	Yes
[9], [10]	d-linear	n	$n - d\lvert\mathbb{G}\rvert$	$n^2\mathbb{G}$	n^2 Multi	Yes
[9], [10]	DCR	$(s-1)\log N$	$(s-2)\log N$	$\mathbb{Z}^*_{N^s}$	1 Modular Exp	Yes
[9], [10]	QR	$\log N$	1	$\mathbb{Z}^*_N$	1 Multi	Yes
[12]	DDH& QR	n	$n - \log N$	$(\frac{n}{k})^2\mathbb{Z}^*_N$	$(\frac{n}{k})^2$ Multi	Yes
[6]	Φ-hiding	$\log N$	$\log e$	$\mathbb{Z}^*_N$	1 Modular Exp	No
Sect.4.1	QR & DCR	$\log N + k$	$3k$	$\mathbb{Z}^*_{N^2}$	1 Modular Exp	Yes
Sect.4.2	E p-sub	$\log N$	$\frac{3}{4}\log N$	$\mathbb{Z}^*_{N^2}$	1 Modular Exp	Yes
Sect.4.3	D RSA	l_x	$l_x - l_{p'} - l_{q'}$	$\mathbb{Z}^*_N$	1 Modular Exp	Yes

In the first and third line, n is the number of rows used in the matrix. It has to be larger than $\lvert\mathbb{G}\rvert$. In the second line, $0 < C < 1$, n is the rows used in the matrix, $w = \frac{n}{\log p}$ with $p^2 \geq q$ and $d < w$. In the forth line, s has to be larger than 2. In the sixth line and the construction in Sect. 4.1, k is less than $\frac{1}{4}\log N - \kappa$ where κ is the security parameter. In the seventh line, e is the factor of $\phi(n)$. In the last line, l_x is the length of the semi-smooth subgroup's order and $l_{p'}$ (resp. $l_{q'}$) is the length of p' (resp. q').

The LTDFs based on the QR, DCR and Φ-hiding assumptions are efficient. The QR based LTDF in [9], [10] has only one bit lossiness which is useless for some applications. Compared with the DCR based LTDF in [9], [10], our construction in Sect. 4.1 is computed over $\mathbb{Z}^*_{N^2}$ and the LTDF in Sect. 4.3 is computed over $\mathbb{Z}^*_N$. Compared with the Φ-hiding based LTDF in [6], our constructions have a direct extension to ABO-LTDFs.

6 Conclusion

We proposed a generic construction of lossy trapdoor function from the subgroup membership assumption. We presented three concrete constructions based on the k-DCR assumption over $\mathbb{Z}_{N^2}^*$, the extended p-subgroup assumption over $\mathbb{Z}_{N^2}^*$, and the decisional RSA subgroup membership assumption over $\mathbb{Z}_N^*$. Our constructions are more efficient than the previous construction from the DCR assumption over $\mathbb{Z}_{N^s}^*(s \geq 3)$.

Acknowledgments. The authors would like to thank anonymous reviewers for their helpful comments and suggestions.

References

[1] Peikert, C., Waters, B.: Lossy trapdoor functions and their applications. In: STOC, pp. 187–196 (2008)
[2] Diffie, W., Hellman, M.E.: New directions in cryptography. IEEE Transactions on Information Theory 22(6), 644–654 (1976)
[3] Goldreich, O.: The Foundations of Cryptography, Basic Techniques, vol. 1. Cambridge University Press (2001)
[4] Goldreich, O.: The Foundations of Cryptography, Basic Applications, vol. 2. Cambridge University Press (2004)
[5] Boldyreva, A., Fehr, S., O'Neill, A.: On notions of security for deterministic encryption, and efficient constructions without random oracles. In: Wagner, D. (ed.) CRYPTO 2008. LNCS, vol. 5157, pp. 335–359. Springer, Heidelberg (2008)
[6] Kiltz, E., O'Neill, A., Smith, A.: Instantiability of RSA-OAEP under chosen-plaintext attack. In: Rabin, T. (ed.) CRYPTO 2010. LNCS, vol. 6223, pp. 295–313. Springer, Heidelberg (2010)
[7] Hofheinz, D.: Possibility and impossibility results for selective decommitments. J. Cryptology 24(3), 470–516 (2011)
[8] Boyen, X., Waters, B.: Shrinking the keys of discrete-log-type lossy trapdoor functions. In: Zhou, J., Yung, M. (eds.) ACNS 2010. LNCS, vol. 6123, pp. 35–52. Springer, Heidelberg (2010)
[9] Freeman, D.M., Goldreich, O., Kiltz, E., Rosen, A., Segev, G.: More constructions of lossy and correlation-secure trapdoor functions. In: Nguyen, P.Q., Pointcheval, D. (eds.) PKC 2010. LNCS, vol. 6056, pp. 279–295. Springer, Heidelberg (2010)
[10] Freeman, D.M., Goldreich, O., Kiltz, E., Rosen, A., Segev, G.: More constructions of lossy and correlation-secure trapdoor functions. J. Cryptology 26(1), 39–74 (2013)
[11] Hemenway, B., Ostrovsky, R.: Lossy trapdoor functions from smooth homomorphic hash proof systems. Electronic Colloquium on Computational Complexity (ECCC) 16, 127 (2009)
[12] Joye, M., Libert, B.: Efficient cryptosystems from 2^k-th power residue symbols. In: Johansson, T., Nguyen, P.Q. (eds.) EUROCRYPT 2013. LNCS, vol. 7881, pp. 76–92. Springer, Heidelberg (2013)
[13] Wee, H.: Dual projective hashing and its applications — lossy trapdoor functions and more. In: Pointcheval, D., Johansson, T. (eds.) EUROCRYPT 2012. LNCS, vol. 7237, pp. 246–262. Springer, Heidelberg (2012)

[14] Groth, J.: Cryptography in subgroups of Z_n^*. In: Kilian, J. (ed.) TCC 2005. LNCS, vol. 3378, pp. 50–65. Springer, Heidelberg (2005)

[15] Gjøsteen, K.: Symmetric subgroup membership problems. In: Vaudenay, S. (ed.) PKC 2005. LNCS, vol. 3386, pp. 104–119. Springer, Heidelberg (2005)

[16] Brown, J., González Nieto, J.M., Boyd, C.: Concrete chosen-ciphertext secure encryption from subgroup membership problems. In: Pointcheval, D., Mu, Y., Chen, K. (eds.) CANS 2006. LNCS, vol. 4301, pp. 1–18. Springer, Heidelberg (2006)

[17] Cramer, R., Shoup, V.: A practical public key cryptosystem provably secure against adaptive chosen ciphertext attack. In: Krawczyk, H. (ed.) CRYPTO 1998. LNCS, vol. 1462, pp. 13–25. Springer, Heidelberg (1998)

[18] Nieto, J.M.G., Boyd, C., Dawson, E.: A public key cryptosystem based on a subgroup membership problem. Des. Codes Cryptography 36(3), 301–316 (2005)

[19] Kurosawa, K., Katayama, Y., Ogata, W., Tsujii, S.: General public key residue cryptosystems and mental poker protocols. In: Damgård, I.B. (ed.) EUROCRYPT 1990. LNCS, vol. 473, pp. 374–388. Springer, Heidelberg (1991)

[20] Okamoto, T., Uchiyama, S.: A new public-key cryptosystem as secure as factoring. In: Nyberg, K. (ed.) EUROCRYPT 1998. LNCS, vol. 1403, pp. 308–318. Springer, Heidelberg (1998)

[21] Paillier, P., Pointcheval, D.: Efficient public-key cryptosystems provably secure against active adversaries. In: Lam, K.-Y., Okamoto, E., Xing, C. (eds.) ASIACRYPT 1999. LNCS, vol. 1716, pp. 165–179. Springer, Heidelberg (1999)

[22] Paillier, P.: Public-key cryptosystems based on composite degree residuosity classes. In: Stern, J. (ed.) EUROCRYPT 1999. LNCS, vol. 1592, pp. 223–238. Springer, Heidelberg (1999)

[23] Damgård, I., Jurik, M.: A generalisation, a simplification and some applications of paillier's probabilistic public key system. Public Key Cryptography (1), 119–136 (2001)

Appendix: Proof of Theorem 3

Proof. Denote by V_0 the set $\{a = r^{2^k} \bmod N | r \in \mathbb{Z}_N^*\}$. D is an algorithm which takes x, y, N as input and returns 0 or 1. We shall need the following experiments, **Experiment** i for $i = 1, 2, 3, 4$.

Experiment 1 :
Input: D, N, $y \in QNR_N$

1. $t \leftarrow [2^k]$, $z \leftarrow \mathbb{Z}_N$.
2. $r \leftarrow \mathbb{Z}_N^*$.
3. $b \leftarrow \{0, 1\}$.
4. If $b = 1$, then $x = r^{2^k N} \bmod N^2$, otherwise $x = r^{2^k N} y^{tN} (1 + N)^z \bmod N^2$.
5. $b' \leftarrow D(N, x, y)$.

Output: If $b' = b$ output 1, otherwise 0.

Experiment 2 :
Input: D, N, $y \in V_0$

1. $t \leftarrow [2^k]$, $z \leftarrow \mathbb{Z}_N$.
2. $r \leftarrow \mathbb{Z}_N^*$.
3. $b \leftarrow \{0, 1\}$.
4. If $b = 1$, then $x = r^{2^k N} \bmod N^2$, otherwise $x = r^{2^k N} y^{tN} (1 + N)^z \bmod N^2$.
5. $b' \leftarrow D(N, x, y)$.

Output: If $b' = b$ output 1, otherwise 0.

Experiment 3 :
Input: D, N, $y \in V_0$

1. $z \leftarrow \mathbb{Z}_N$.
2. $r \leftarrow \mathbb{Z}_N^*$.
3. $b \leftarrow \{0,1\}$.
4. If $b=1$, then $x = r^{2^k N} \mod N^2$, otherwise $x = r^{2^k N}(1+N)^z \mod N^2$.
5. $b' \leftarrow D(N,x,y)$.

Output: If $b' = b$ output 1, otherwise 0.

Experiment 4 :
Input: D, N, $y \in QNR_N$

1. $r \leftarrow \mathbb{Z}_N^*$.
2. $b \leftarrow \{0,1\}$.
3. Set $x = r^{2^k N} \mod N^2$.
4. $b' \leftarrow D(N,x,y)$.

Output: If $b' = b$ output 1, otherwise 0.

Let $T_i, i = 1,2,3,4$ denote the event that the Experiment i returns 1. By the definition of k-DCR, Experiment 1 is exactly the k-DCR experiment, and we have

$$\mathrm{Adv}_D^{k-DCR} \leq |2\Pr[T_1] - 1|.$$

Now we consider the Experiment 2, the only difference between Experiment 1 and 2 is that y is sampled from V_0 instead of QNR_N. We have,

$$2|\Pr[T_1] - \Pr[T_2]| \leq \mathrm{Adv}_B^{2^k\text{-}QR}.$$

In Experiment 3, if y is chosen from V_0 uniformly, then Experiment 2 and 3 are identical. We have that, $\Pr[T_2] = \Pr[T_3]$.

Now we consider Experiment 4. The difference between Experiment 4 and 3 is the choice of x and y. Define $X := \{r^{2^k N}(1+N)^z \mod N^2 | r \leftarrow \mathbb{Z}_N^*, z \leftarrow \mathbb{Z}_N\}$ and $L := \{r^{2^k N} \mod N^2 | r \leftarrow \mathbb{Z}_N^*\}$. Given input x of classical DCR problem, if x is chosen uniformly from M (resp. P), then x^{2^k} is uniformly distributed over X (resp. L). The indistinguishability of y in Experiment 3 and 4 is implied by 2^k-QR assumption. Consequently, the difference between Experiment 4 and 3 is bounded by DCR and 2^k-QR assumptions.

$$2|\Pr[T_3] - \Pr[T_4]| \leq \mathrm{Adv}_B^{DCR} + \mathrm{Adv}_B^{2^k\text{-}QR}.$$

The input of D in Experiment 4 includes no information of b, we have that $Pr[T_4] = \frac{1}{2}$. Combining the above, we have

$$\begin{aligned}
\mathrm{Adv}_D^{k\text{-}DCR} &\leq |2\Pr[T_1] - 1| \\
&\leq 2|\Pr[T_1] - \Pr[T_4]| \\
&\leq 2|\Pr[T_1] - \Pr[T_2]| + 2|\Pr[T_2] - \Pr[T_3]| + 2|\Pr[T_3] - \Pr[T_4]| \\
&\leq 2\mathrm{Adv}_B^{2^k\text{-}QR} + \mathrm{Adv}_C^{DCR}.
\end{aligned}$$

With the result of Theorem 2 in [12], $\mathrm{Adv}_B^{2^k\text{-}QR} \leq 4k\mathrm{Adv}_A^{QR}$, we have that

$$\mathrm{Adv}_D^{k\text{-}DCR} \leq 8k\mathrm{Adv}_A^{QR} + \mathrm{Adv}_C^{DCR}.$$

□

Unique Aggregate Signatures with Applications to Distributed Verifiable Random Functions

Veronika Kuchta and Mark Manulis

Department of Computing, University of Surrey, United Kingdom
v.kuchta@surrey.ac.uk, mark@manulis.eu

Abstract. The computation process of a Distributed Verifiable Random Function (DVRF) on some input specified by the user involves multiple, possibly malicious servers, and results in a publicly verifiable pseudorandom output to the user. Previous DVRF constructions assumed trusted generation of secret keys for the servers and imposed a threshold on the number of corrupted servers.

In this paper we propose the first generic approach for building DVRFs, under much weaker setup assumptions, where we only require existence of a shared random string. More precisely, we first aim at constructions of Distributed Verifiable Unpredictable Functions (DVUF) that can then be converted to DVRF using inner products with a random string as specified by Micali, Rabin, and Vadhan (FOCS'99) for the non-distributed VUF/VRF case.

Our main contribution are generic DVUF constructions from aggregate signatures that satisfy the property of *uniqueness*. We define uniqueness for two flavors of aggregate signatures (with public and sequential aggregation) and show that both flavors can be used to obtain DVUF. By proving uniqueness of existing pairing-based aggregate signature schemes we immediately obtain several concrete communication-efficient DVUF/DVRF instantiations.

1 Introduction

Unique Signatures and VRFs. The uniqueness property for digital signatures, introduced by Goldwasser and Ostrovsky [19], guarantees that all signatures produced by one signer on the same message remain "similar" in that there exists an efficient publicly computable function that yields the same unpredictable value on input of any such signature. This property has been explored for traditional signature schemes [19,24] and more recently in the context of advanced schemes such as group signatures [14] and ring signatures [15] where it enabled more efficient anonymity revocation resp. linkability procedures. The uniqueness property doesn't require all signatures to be identical as it is the case for deterministic schemes. In fact, it is sufficient for an unique signature to contain some unique component that can be used to link different signatures of the same signer on the same message.

M. Abdalla, C. Nita-Rotaru, and R. Dahab (Eds.): CANS 2013, LNCS 8257, pp. 251–270, 2013.

Goldwasser and Ostrovsky [19] established the equivalence between unique signatures and non-interactive zero-knowledge proofs (NIZK) for hard-to-predict languages. The main application of unique signatures, e.g. in [24,12], has been the construction of Verifiable Random Functions (VRF) [25] — these are pseudorandom functions with a corresponding private/public key pair (sk, pk) that on some input x output a pair $(F(sk, x), \pi(sk, x))$ where $F(sk, x)$ is pseudorandom and $\pi(sk, x)$ represents a proof for the correctness of the computation that can be verified in a public fashion using pk. In order to construct VRFs from unique signatures one first needs to construct a so-called Verifiable Unpredictable Function (VUF) and then apply the transformation from [25] to convert VUF into VRF. For the actual construction of VUF out of a unique signature scheme one simply considers the signer's secret key as a secret seed and treats the resulting unique signature (or its unique component) as a VUF output, whose correctness can be checked publicly using the verification procedure of the signature scheme and the signer's public key. As observed in [1], who constructed VRFs in the identity-based setting, VRFs turned out to be very useful for many applications, including resettable zero-knowledge proofs [26], micropayment schemes [28], updatable zero-knowledge databases [21], and verifiable transaction escrow schemes [20].

Distributed VRFs. In a distributed VRF (DVRF) setting, considered by Dodis [11], there are multiple parties (servers), each in possession of its own secret and public key such that any subset of n servers can participate in the computation process. The approach taken in [11] to build a DVRF scheme was to first propose a concrete VRF construction and then turn it into DVRF by using the $(t+1, n)$-secret sharing technique [30] to equip servers with individual shares sk_i of the private VRF key sk. In addition, for each party i an individual public key pk_i is derived from sk_i. In order to compute the DVRF output $(F(sk, x), \pi(sk, x))$ the input x is communicated by the user to each of the n parties that reply with their intermediate VRF outputs $(F(sk_i, x), \pi(sk_i, x))$. If at least $t+1$ intermediate VRF proofs $\pi(sk_i, x)$ are valid (which is checked using corresponding public keys pk_i) then the final DVRF output $(F(sk, x), \pi(sk, x))$ can be computed by the user through polynomial interpolation. The validity of the resulting DVRF proof $\pi(sk, x)$ can be checked publicly using the original pk of the underlying VRF scheme.

The DVRF construction from [11] is reasonably efficient, yet has a few limitations, as discussed in the following. One consequence of using $(t+1, n)$-secret sharing is that in order to guarantee pseudorandomness of $F(sk, x)$ at least $t+1$ parties involved in its computation process must remain honest. The DVRF scheme from [11] requires a trusted setup procedure for the generation and distribution of shares sk_i, which is a strong assumption. The assumption on trusted setup could possibly be removed by adopting a matching Distributed Key Generation (DKG) protocol, e.g. [16], yet at the cost of reduced efficiency and possibly further restrictions on the ratio between the threshold value $t+1$ and n.

We observe that the approach taken in [11] to apply threshold cryptography on top of a non-distributed VRF scheme is so far the only known way to construct DVRF schemes.

The original motivation for DVRF schemes given in [11] is the practical realization of random oracles, a theoretical construct introduced in [4] that is frequently used in security proofs of cryptographic schemes. In a nutshell, random oracle is a mathematical function that on any new input outputs a random string from the output domain. Goldreich, Goldwasser and Micali [17] were the first who showed how to simulate a random oracle for fixed-length input and output strings by using a PRF. Canetti et al. [10] showed that no fixed public function can generically replace the random oracle. They demonstrated that a PRF should not be expected to offer a general solution for realizing random oracles. Micali, Rabin, and Vadhan [25] suggested that a random oracle can be realized using VRF schemes. Dodis observed that this would require a significant amount of trust put into a single party that computes VRF outputs and argued that it is desirable to distribute this trust across multiple, ideally independent parties.

Our DVRF Approach: Unique (Sequential) Aggregate Signatures. In this work we propose another approach for building DVRF schemes without imposing trust assumptions on the generation of secrets keys sk_i for the involved servers and without requiring any particular threshold on the number of honest servers. Our main contribution is to build DVRF schemes generically from different flavors of aggregate signatures [7,23,22] where each signer i has its own private/public key pair (sk_i, pk_i) and a set of n signers contributes to the computation of an aggregate signature $\bar{\sigma}$ on some set of (possibly different) messages $\mathbf{m} = \{m_1, \ldots, m_n\}$ where the size of resulting $\bar{\sigma}$ is independent of n. The signature can be verified using the set of public keys $\mathbf{pk} = \{pk_1, \ldots, pk_n\}$.

Just as in case of a VRF that can be obtained from a VUF we show that different flavors of aggregate signatures can be used to build a distributed VUF (DVUF), which can then be converted to a DVRF using the techniques from [25]. In order to construct DVUFs from aggregate signatures the latter require some sort of uniqueness. Since the property of uniqueness in the context of aggregate signatures has not been considered so far, we first need to define it. We define uniqueness for aggregate signatures with public aggregation (cf. [7]) and denote such schemes by UAS, and for sequential aggregate signatures (cf. [23,22]), denoted by USAS. Our definition of uniqueness in both cases roughly means that for any aggregate signature $\bar{\sigma}$ produced on the same set of messages $\mathbf{m}$ using the same set of private keys $\mathbf{sk} = \{sk_1, \ldots, sk_n\}$ there exists no other aggregate signature $\bar{\bar{\sigma}}$ such that $\mathtt{Verify}(\mathbf{pk}, \mathbf{m}, \bar{\sigma}) = \mathtt{Verify}(\mathbf{pk}, \mathbf{m}, \bar{\bar{\sigma}}) = 1$.

At a high level, our DVUF construction from any UAS/USAS scheme proceeds as follows: the DVUF public key $\mathbf{pk}$ consists of all UAS/USAS public keys pk_i while each UAS/USAS secret key sk_i is generated individually by the respective DVUF server i. The DVUF output $(F(\mathbf{sk}, x), \pi(\mathbf{sk}, x))$ is essentially given by $(\mathtt{unq}(\bar{\sigma}), \bar{\sigma})$ where $\mathtt{unq}(\bar{\sigma})$ determines the *unique* component of aggregate signature $\bar{\sigma}$, which in turn plays the role of the proof. Note that each server signs the same message x that is specified by the user as input to DVUF. The actual computation process and interaction differs for UAS and USAS schemes. Our most efficient UAS-based DVUF construction requires only one communication round in which the user sends x to each of the n servers, obtains their individual signatures and then aggregates them locally to obtain the DVUF output. In the USAS-based DVUF construction the user needs to contact n servers sequentially and obtains the resulting DVUF output and the proof upon contacting the last server in the sequence.

Our UAS/USAS-based approach for constructing DVUF and consequently DVRF has two advantages over [11]: (1) the uniqueness and unforgeability properties of UAS/USAS schemes will guarantee that the DVRF output $F(\mathbf{sk}, x)$ is pseudorandom even if the adversary corrupts up to $n-1$ servers; (2) since each server i can generate her own UAS/USAS key pair (sk_i, pk_i) independently, our DVUF construction doesn't require any trusted setup procedure for the distribution of sk_i. When using the inner product-based technique from [25] to convert out DVUF outputs into DVRF outputs we need to impose existence of a shared random string [13] as an additional, albeit much weaker setup assumption than the trustworthy generation of secret keys adopted in [11].

DVUF/DVRF Instantiations. We obtain several concrete DVUF/DVRF instantiations from existing (sequential) aggregate signatures schemes by proving the uniqueness property for the (pairing-based) aggregate signature schemes by Boneh et al. [7], Lu et al. [22], and Schröder [31]. The scheme from [7] is a very efficient random oracle-based construction that supports public aggregation of signatures. The schemes from [22,31] offer sequential aggregation in the standard model and are based on two popular signature schemes; in particular, [22] offers aggregation of Waters signatures [32], while [31] shows how to aggregate Camenisch-Lysyanskaya [9] signatures.

A Note on Multisignatures. In our generic DVUF constructions parties compute aggregate signatures on the same input message, specified by the user. This step can also be realized using multisignatures [5] that represent a special case of aggregate signatures in that all signers are required to use the same message in the execution of the signing protocol. Our generic DVUF constructions can therefore be analysed from the perspective of unique multisignatures, yet their instantiations may not necessarily be more communication-efficient than those presented in our work. This is because all existing aggregate signatures are non-interactive in that at most one message needs to be exchanged between the signers, which is not the general case for multisignatures. For instance, the signing process of multisignature schemes from [27,3,2] requires several rounds of interaction amongst the participating signers. Those schemes, if unique, can be possibly used to realize a DVUF but at the cost if the increased communication overhead, in comparison to non-interactive aggregate signature schemes used in our constructions. On the other hand, there exist several multisignature schemes where the signing process is non-interactive, e.g. [5,22,6,33]. These schemes seem to satisfy the uniqueness property and could possibly be used to obtain communication-efficient DVUF constructions. For instance, Boldyreva's scheme [5] that uses Gap Diffie-Hellman groups and is based on BLS signatures [8], when realized using pairings, would offer a similar performance for a DVUF, in the random oracle model, as the aggregate signature scheme from [7] that is used in our work. Similarly, the multisignature scheme from [22], which is based on the signature scheme by Waters [32], could be used to build DVUF in the standard model. The resulting scheme would offer similar communication performance to the DVUF construction that we obtain by using their aggregate signature scheme. One advantage of using these non-interactive multisignatures in comparison to corresponding aggregate signatures is that by adding further "proofs of secret key possession" from [29] one could obtain a higher level of security against rogue key attacks that is notoriously difficult to achieve for the more general case of aggregate signatures.

2 Preliminaries

All concrete constructions used in this paper are in the setting of bilinear groups, defined in the following.

Definition 1 (Bilinear Groups). *Let $\mathcal{G}(1^\lambda)$, $\lambda \in \mathbb{N}$ be an algorithm that on input a security parameter 1^λ outputs the description of two cyclic groups $\mathbb{G}_1 = \langle g_1 \rangle$ and $\mathbb{G}_2 = \langle g_2 \rangle$ of prime order q with $|q| = 1^\lambda$, where possibly $\mathbb{G}_1 = \mathbb{G}_2$, and an efficiently computable $e : \mathbb{G}_1 \times \mathbb{G}_2 \to \mathbb{G}_T$ with $\mathbb{G}_T$ being another cyclic group of order q. The group pair $(\mathbb{G}_1, \mathbb{G}_2)$ is called* bilinear *if $e(g_1, g_2) \neq 1$ and $\forall u \in \mathbb{G}_1,\ v \in \mathbb{G}_2,\ \forall a, b \in \mathbb{Z} :\ e(u^a, v^b) = e(u, v)^{ab}$.*

3 Unique Aggregate Signatures

In this section we recall definitions of aggregate signatures with public aggregation and define their uniqueness property. We adopt the syntax and the security model from [7].

Definition 2 (AS scheme). *An* aggregate signature *scheme AS consists of the following algorithms:*

ParGen(1^λ) *is a PPT algorithm that takes as input the security parameter 1^λ and outputs public system parameters I.*

KeyGen(I) *is a PPT algorithm that takes as input I and generates a private/public key pair (sk_i, pk_i) for an user i.*

Sign(sk_i, m_i) *is a possibly deterministic algorithm that takes as input a secret key sk_i and a message m_i and outputs a signature σ_i.*

Verify(pk_i, m_i, σ_i) *is a deterministic algorithm that takes as input a candidate signature σ_i, a public key pk_i, and a message m_i, and outputs 1 if the signature is valid and 0 otherwise.*

Aggregate$(\mathbf{pk}, \mathbf{m}, \boldsymbol{\sigma})$ *is an algorithm that takes as input a set of signatures $\boldsymbol{\sigma} = (\sigma_1, ..., \sigma_n)$, public keys $\mathbf{pk} = (pk_1, \ldots, pk_n)$, and messages $\mathbf{m} = (m_1, \ldots, m_n)$, and outputs an aggregate signature $\bar{\sigma}$.*

AggVerify$(\mathbf{pk}, \mathbf{m}, \bar{\sigma})$ *is a deterministic algorithm that takes as input a candidate aggregate signature* $\bar{\sigma}$*, a set of messages* $\mathbf{m}$ *and public keys* $\mathbf{pk}$*, and outputs 1 if the signature is valid, or 0 otherwise.*

Definition 3 (Unforgeability of AS). *An aggregate signature scheme is* unforgeable *if for any PPT adversary* $\mathcal{A}$*, running in time at most t and invoking the signing oracle at most* q_S *times, the probability that the following experiment outputs* 1 *remains negligible in the security parameter* λ.

Experiment $\mathtt{Forge}_{\mathcal{A}}^{AS}(\lambda)$
$I \leftarrow \mathtt{ParGen}(1^\lambda)$
$(sk_c, pk_c) \leftarrow \mathtt{KeyGen}(I)$
$(\mathbf{m}^*, \mathbf{pk}^*, \sigma^*) \leftarrow \mathcal{A}^{\mathtt{OSign}(sk_c,\cdot)}(I, pk_c)$
Let m_c *be the message those index in* $\mathbf{m}^*$ *corresponds to the index of* pk_c *in* $\mathbf{pk}^*$.
Output 1 if all of the following holds:
- $\mathtt{AggVrfy}(\sigma^*, \mathbf{m}^*, \mathbf{pk}^*) = 1$,
- $m_c \in \mathbf{m}^*$ *was never submitted to* $\mathtt{OSign}(sk_c, \cdot)$

where $\mathcal{A}$ *is given access to the following aggregate signing oracle:*

$\mathtt{OSign}(sk_c \cdot)$: *The adversarial input to the oracle contains a message* m_i *under the public key* pk_c*, the oracle computes the signature* σ_i *on* m_i *using* sk_c *and gives the signature to* $\mathcal{A}$.

Our definition of uniqueness for aggregate signatures with public aggregation is given in Definition 4. This definition fits likewise probabilistic and deterministic schemes due to the use of function $\mathtt{unq}$, even though we are not aware of any (non-interactive) probabilistic scheme that supports public aggregation.

Definition 4 (Unique AS). *An unforgeable AS scheme is said to be unique, denoted by UAS, if there exists an efficient deterministic function* $\mathtt{unq}$ *which on input an aggregate signature* $\bar{\sigma}$ *outputs a string of polynomial-size in the security parameter of the scheme such that for any ordered sequence of messages* $\mathbf{m} = (m_1, \ldots, m_n)$ *and public keys* $\mathbf{pk} = (pk_1, \ldots, pk_n)$ *there exist no two aggregate signatures* $\bar{\sigma}$ *and* $\bar{\bar{\sigma}}$ *for which it holds that* $\mathtt{Verify}(\mathbf{pk}, \mathbf{m}, \bar{\sigma}) = \mathtt{Verify}(\mathbf{pk}, \mathbf{m}, \bar{\bar{\sigma}}) = 1$*, and* $\mathtt{unq}(\bar{\sigma}) \neq \mathtt{unq}(\bar{\bar{\sigma}})$.

3.1 Uniqueness of Boneh-Gentry-Lynn-Shacham AS Scheme

We recall the aggregate signature scheme with public aggregation from [7] where the hash function $H : \{0,1\}^* \to \mathbb{G}_1$ is modeled as a random oracle.

$\mathtt{ParGen}(1^\lambda)$. On input of the security parameter 1^λ this algorithm outputs public parameters $I = (\mathbb{G}_1, \mathbb{G}_2, g_1, g_2, \psi, e, \mathbb{G}_T, q)$, with $\psi(g_2) = g_1$, where ψ is a computable isomorphism from $\mathbb{G}_2$ to $\mathbb{G}_1$.

$\mathtt{KeyGen}(I)$. For an user i, choose randomly $x_i \xleftarrow{r} \mathbb{Z}_q$ and compute $v_i \leftarrow g_2^{x_i}$. It outputs $(sk_i, pk_i) = (x_i, v_i)$.

Sign(m_i, sk_i). For all i, it takes as input sk_i and a message $m_i \in \{0,1\}^*$. The algorithm computes $h_i \leftarrow H(m_i)$, where $h_i \leftarrow \mathbb{G}_1$ and $\sigma_i \leftarrow h_i^{x_i}$. Output is $\sigma_i \in \mathbb{G}_1$.

Verify(m_i, pk_i, σ_i). For all $i \in [n]$ the algorithm takes as input m_i and σ_i. It outputs 1 if $e(\sigma_i, g_2) = e(h_i, v_i)$ and 0 otherwise.

Aggregate$(\mathbf{pk}, \mathbf{m}, \boldsymbol{\sigma})$. On the input $\mathbf{pk}, \mathbf{m}, \boldsymbol{\sigma}$ the algorithm computes $\bar{\sigma} \leftarrow \prod_{i=1}^{n} \sigma_i$. The aggregate signature is $\bar{\sigma} \in \mathbb{G}_1$.

AggVerify$(\mathbf{pk}, \mathbf{m}, \bar{\sigma})$. This algorithm takes as input an aggregate signature $\bar{\sigma}$,a sequence of messages $\mathbf{m} = (m_1, ..., m_n)$ and a sequence of pubic keys $\mathbf{pk} = (v_1, \ldots, v_n) \in \mathbb{G}_2$, for all users u_i. The algorithm outputs 1 if the messages m_i are all distinct and $e(\bar{\sigma}, g_2) = \prod_{i=1}^{n} e(h_i, v_i)$. Otherwise the algorithm outputs 0.

The above scheme offers unforgeability in the random oracle model, as already proven in [7]. Interestingly, our Theorem 1 shows that this scheme is unique without imposing the random oracle assumption on H.

Theorem 1. *The Boneh-Gentry-Lynn-Shacham AS scheme is unique according to Definition 4.*

Proof. Assume that there exist two valid aggregate signatures $\bar{\sigma}$ and $\bar{\bar{\sigma}}$ on an ordered sequence of messages $\mathbf{m} = (m_1, ..., m_i)$ such that the equation ***Verify***$(\mathbf{pk}, \mathbf{m}, \bar{\sigma}) =$ ***Verify***$(\mathbf{pk}, \mathbf{m}, \bar{\bar{\sigma}}) = 1$. We define ***unq***$(\bar{\sigma})$ as an identity function. That is, ***unq***$(\bar{\sigma}) = \bar{\sigma}$ and ***unq***$(\bar{\bar{\sigma}}) = \bar{\bar{\sigma}}$. We know that $\bar{\sigma} = \prod_{j=1}^{i} h_j^{x_j}$. In the following we prove by induction on i that $\bar{\bar{\sigma}} = \bar{\sigma}$:

Base step: $i = 1$. The signature $\bar{\bar{\sigma}}$ must satisfy the verification process $e(\sigma, g_2) = e(h, v)$, i.e. $e(\bar{\bar{\sigma}}, g_2) = e(h, g_2^x) = e(h^x, g_2)$. It holds only if $\bar{\bar{\sigma}} = h^x = \bar{\sigma}$.

Induction step: $i - 1 \mapsto i$. Let the theorem hold for $i - 1$. The verification algorithm will accept $\bar{\bar{\sigma}}_i$ if it satisfies the verification equation $e(\bar{\bar{\sigma}}_i, g_2) = \prod_{j=1}^{i} e(h_j, v_j)$. By the induction hypothesis we have the validity for $i - 1$ aggregated signatures, i.e. $\bar{\bar{\sigma}}_{i-1} = \prod_{j=1}^{i-1} h_j^{x_j}$ and $\bar{\bar{\sigma}}_i = \bar{\bar{\sigma}}_{i-1} \cdot \tilde{\sigma}_i$. We put this value into the verification equation such that:

$$e\left(\left(\prod_{j=1}^{i-1} h_j^{x_j}\right) \cdot \tilde{\sigma}_i, g_2\right) = \prod_{j=1}^{i} e(h_j, v_j) = \prod_{j=1}^{i} (h_j, g_2^{x_j})$$

$$\Leftrightarrow e\left(\prod_{j=1}^{i-1} h_j^{x_j}, g_2\right) e(\tilde{\sigma}_i, g_2) = \prod_{j=1}^{i-1} e(h_j, g_2^{x_j}) e(h_i, g_2^{x_i})$$

$$\Leftrightarrow e(\tilde{\sigma}_i, g_2) = e(h_i, g_2^{x_i}) = e(h_i^{x_i}, g_2) \Leftrightarrow \tilde{\sigma}_i = h_i^{x_i}$$

Therefore we have $\bar{\bar{\sigma}}_i = \bar{\bar{\sigma}}_{i-1} \cdot \tilde{\sigma}_i = \prod_{j=1}^{i-1} h_j^{x_j} \cdot h_i^{x_i} = \bar{\sigma}_i$. □

4 Unique Sequential Aggregate Signatures

In the following we recall definitions of sequential aggregate signatures using the syntax and security model from [23,22] and define their uniqueness.

Definition 5 (SAS scheme). *A* sequential aggregate signature *scheme SAS consists of the following algorithms:*

$\mathtt{ParGen}(1^\lambda)$ is a PPT algorithm that takes as input the security parameter 1^λ and outputs public system parameters I.

$\mathtt{KeyGen}(I)$ is a PPT algorithm that takes as input I and outputs a private/public key pair (sk_i, pk_i) for an user i.

$\mathtt{AggSign}(sk_i, m_i, \bar{\sigma}_{i-1}, \mathbf{m}_{i-1}, \mathbf{pk}_{i-1})$ is a PPT algorithm that on input a private key sk_i, a message $m_i \in \{0,1\}^*$, an aggregate-so-far signature $\bar{\sigma}_{i-1}$, a sequence of messages $\mathbf{m}_{i-1} = (m_1, \ldots, m_{i-1})$ and public keys $\mathbf{pk}_{i-1} = (pk_1, \ldots, pk_{i-1})$, outputs the aggregate-so-far signature $\bar{\sigma}_i$ for the updated sequences $\mathbf{m}_i = (m_1, \ldots, m_i)$ and $\mathbf{pk}_i = (pk_1, \ldots, pk_i)$.

$\mathtt{AggVerify}(\bar{\sigma}_i, \mathbf{m}_i, \mathbf{pk}_i)$ takes as input an aggregate-so-far signature σ_i, a sequence of messages $\mathbf{m}_i$ and public keys $\mathbf{pk}_i$ and outputs 1 if the signature is valid, or 0 otherwise.

An SAS scheme is said to be complete, *if for any sequence $(sk_1, pk_1), \ldots, (sk_n, pk_n)$ with each $(sk_i, pk_i) \leftarrow \mathtt{KeyGen}(I)$, $(m_1, ..., m_n)$ with each $m_i \in \{0,1\}^*$, and some non-empty $\bar{\sigma}_{i-1}$ for which $\mathtt{AggVerify}(\bar{\sigma}_{i-1}, \mathbf{m}_{i-1}, \mathbf{pk}_{i-1}) = 1$, for any $\bar{\sigma}_i \leftarrow \mathtt{AggSign}(sk_i, m_i, \bar{\sigma}_{i-1}, \mathbf{m}_{i-1}, \mathbf{pk}_{i-1})$: $\mathtt{AggVerify}(\bar{\sigma}_i, \mathbf{m}_i, \mathbf{pk}_i) = 1$.*

Definition 6 (Unforgeability of SAS). *An SAS scheme is unforgeable if for any PPT adversary $\mathcal{A}$, running in time at most t and invoking the signing oracle at most q_S times, the probability that the following experiment outputs 1 remains negligible in the security parameter λ.*

Experiment $\mathtt{Forge}_{\mathcal{A}}^{SAS}(\lambda)$
$I \leftarrow \mathtt{ParGen}(1^\lambda)$
$(sk_c, pk_c) \leftarrow \mathtt{KeyGen}(I)$
$(\mathbf{m}^*, \mathbf{pk}^*, \sigma^*) \leftarrow \mathcal{A}^{\mathtt{OSeqAgg}(sk_c, \cdot)}(I, pk_c)$
Let C denote the list of all registered key pairs (sk_i, pk_i) and m_c be the message those index in $\mathbf{m}^*$ corresponds to the index of pk_c in $\mathbf{pk}^*$.
Output 1 if all of the following holds:
- *for any pair $pk_i, pk_j \in \mathbf{pk}^*$ with $i \neq j$: $pk_i \neq pk_j$*
- *$\mathtt{AggVerify}(\sigma^*, \mathbf{m}^*, \mathbf{pk}^*) = 1$,*
- *$m_c \in \mathbf{m}^*$ was never amongst the inputs to $\mathtt{OSeqAgg}(sk_c, \cdot)$*

where $\mathcal{A}$ is given access to the following sequential aggregate signing oracle and the key registration oracle:

OSeqAgg$(sk_c, \cdot)$: *The adversarial input to the signing oracle consists of a message* m, *an aggregate-so-far signature* $\bar{\sigma}_{i-1}$, *a sequence of messages* $\mathbf{m}_{i-1}$ *and public keys* $\mathbf{pk}_{i-1}$. *The oracle computes* $\bar{\sigma}_i \leftarrow$ *AggSign*$(sk_c, m, \bar{\sigma}_{i-1}, \mathbf{m}_{i-1}||m, \mathbf{pk}_{i-1}||pk_c)$ *and returns* $\bar{\sigma}_i$ *to* $\mathcal{A}$.

Our definition of uniqueness for unforgeable SAS schemes is given in Definition 7. Note that by requiring the existence of an appropriate deterministic function *unq* we can cover uniqueness in deterministic and probabilistic SAS schemes. For example, USAS instantiations that we focus on later are all probabilistic SAS schemes that output signatures consisting of multiple components from which one component remains unique. We will prove the uniqueness property of those schemes by using appropriate *unq* functions for each scheme.

Definition 7 (Unique SAS). *An unforgeable SAS scheme is said to be* unique, *denoted by USAS, if there exists an efficient deterministic function* ***unq*** *which on input the aggregate-so-far signature* σ_i *outputs a string of polynomial-size in the security parameter of the scheme such that for any ordered sequence of messages* $\mathbf{m}_i$ *and public keys* $\mathbf{pk}_i$ *there exist no two aggregate-so-far signatures* $\bar{\sigma}_i$ *and* $\bar{\bar{\sigma}}_i$ *for which it holds that* *AggVerify*$(\bar{\sigma}_i, \mathbf{m}_i, \mathbf{pk}_i) = 1$, *AggVerify*$(\bar{\bar{\sigma}}_i, \mathbf{m}_i, \mathbf{pk}_i) = 1$, *and* ***unq***$(\bar{\sigma}_i) \neq$ ***unq***$(\bar{\bar{\sigma}}_i)$.

Note that the uniqueness property of an SAS scheme as defined above respects the order of messages in $\mathbf{m} = (m_1, ..., m_n)$. That is, the resulting aggregate signatures output on permuted sequences of messages in $\mathbf{m}$ for the same set of public keys $\mathbf{pk}$ will differ from each other.

4.1 Uniqueness of Lu-Ostrovsky-Sahai-Shacham-Waters SAS Scheme

The SAS scheme proposed by Lu et al. [22] offers sequential aggregation of Waters signatures [32]. We breifly recall their scheme and explore its uniqueness property.

ParGen(1^λ). On input the security parameter 1^λ output $I = (q, \mathbb{G}, \mathbb{G}_T, g, e)$ for the bilinear group setting according to Definition 1.

KeyGen(I). Pick random $\alpha, y \xleftarrow{r} \mathbb{Z}_q$ and a random vector $\mathbf{y} = (y_1, ..., y_k) \xleftarrow{r} \mathbb{Z}_q^k$. Compute:

$$u' \leftarrow g^{y'}, \quad \mathbf{u} = (u_1, ..., u_k) \leftarrow (g^{y_1}, ..., g^{y_k}), \quad A \leftarrow e(g, g)^\alpha.$$

The private key is set to $sk = (\alpha, y', \mathbf{y}) \in \mathbb{Z}_q^{k+2}$, while the the public key is set to $pk = (A, u', \mathbf{u}) \in \mathbb{G}_T \times \mathbb{G}^{k+1}$. The algorithm outputs (sk, pk).

AggSign$(sk_i, m_i, \bar{\sigma}_{i-1}, \mathbf{m}_{i-1}, \mathbf{pk}_{i-1})$. If ***AggVerify***$(\bar{\sigma}_{i-1}, \mathbf{m}_{i-1}, \mathbf{pk}_{i-1}) = 1$ proceed; else output 0. Parse $\bar{\sigma}_{i-1}$ as $(S_1', S_2') \in \mathbb{G}^2$. For each $1 \le i \le n$ and $1 \le l \le k$ set $m_i = (m_{i,1}, ..., m_{i,k}) \in \{0,1\}^k$ as k-bit message of user i and $pk_i = (A_i, u_i', u_{i,1}, ..., u_i^k) \in \mathbb{G}_T \times \mathbb{G}^{k+1}$ as public key of user i. Compute:

$$w_1 \leftarrow S_1' g^\alpha \left(S_2'\right)^{y' + \sum_{l=1}^{k} y_l m_l}, \quad w_2 \leftarrow S_2'.$$

Proceed with the re-randomization step, i.e. pick random $\tilde{r} \in \mathbb{Z}_q$ and output $\bar{\sigma}_i = (S_1, S_2)$ where

$$S_1 \leftarrow w_1 \cdot \left(u' \prod_{l=1}^{k} u_l^{m_l}\right)^{\tilde{r}} \cdot \prod_{j=1}^{i} \left(u_j' \prod_{l=1}^{k} u_{j,l}^{m_{j,l}}\right)^{\tilde{r}} \quad \text{and} \quad S_2 \leftarrow w_2 g^{\tilde{r}}.$$

(Note that $\bar{\sigma}_i = (S_1, S_2)$ is an aggregate-so-far signature on an updated list of messages $\mathbf{m}_{i-1}||m_i$ and corresponding public keys $\mathbf{pk}_{i-1}||pk_i$. The re-randomization step results in randomness update to $r + \tilde{r}$.)

AggVerify$(\bar{\sigma}_i, \mathbf{m}_i, \mathbf{pk}_i)$. The input is a candidate aggregate signature $\bar{\sigma}_i$ on messages $\mathbf{m}_i$ under public keys $\mathbf{pk}_i$. Set $\bar{\sigma}_i = (S_1, S_2) \in \mathbb{G}$. Check the following equation:

$$e(S_1, g) \cdot e\left(S_2, \prod_{j=1}^{i} \left(u_j' \prod_{l=1}^{k} u_{j,l}^{m_{j,l}}\right)\right)^{-1} = \prod_{j=1}^{i} A_j$$

If the above equation holds output 1, else output 0.

Theorem 2. *The Lu-Ostrovsky-Sahai-Shacham-Waters SAS Scheme is unique according to Definition 7.*

Proof. Let *unq* be a function that outputs the first component of the aggregate signature $\bar{\sigma} = (S_1, S_2)$, i.e. $unq(\bar{\sigma}) = S_1$. Assume that there exists another signature $\bar{\bar{\sigma}}$ that passes the verification process for the same set of messages and public keys as $\bar{\sigma}$ and for which $unq(\bar{\bar{\sigma}}) = \hat{S}_1$. In the following we prove that $\hat{S}_1 = S_1$ by induction on i:

Base step: $i = 1$. The verification algorithm will accept the signature $\bar{\bar{\sigma}} = (\hat{S}_1, S_2)$ if it satisfies the following verification equation

$$e(\hat{S}_1, g) \cdot e\left(S_2, u' \prod_{l=1}^{k} u_l^{m_l}\right)^{-1} = e(g, g)^{\alpha}$$

$$\Leftrightarrow \quad e(\hat{S}_1, g) \cdot e\left(g, \left(u' \prod_{l=1}^{k} u_l^{m_l}\right)^{r}\right)^{-1} = e(g, g)^{\alpha}.$$

It holds only if $\hat{S}_1 = g^{\alpha} \left(u' \prod_{l=1}^{k} u_l^{m_l}\right)^{r}$, because we have then:

$$e(\hat{S}_1, g) \cdot e\left(g, \left(u' \prod_{l=1}^{k} u_l^{m_l}\right)^{r}\right)^{-1} = e(g, g)^{\alpha}$$

$$\Leftrightarrow \quad e\left(g^{\alpha}\left(u' \prod_{l=1}^{k} u_l^{m_l}\right)^{r}, g\right) \cdot e\left(g, \left(u' \prod_{l=1}^{k} u_l^{m_l}\right)^{r}\right)^{-1} = e(g, g)^{\alpha}$$

$$\Leftrightarrow \quad e(g^{\alpha}, g) e\left(\left(u' \prod_{l=1}^{k} u_l^{m_l}\right)^{r}, g\right) e\left(g, \left(u' \prod_{l=1}^{k} u_l^{m_l}\right)^{r}\right)^{-1} = e(g, g)^{\alpha}.$$

Induction step: $i-1 \mapsto i$. Let the theorem hold for $i-1$. The verification algorithm will accept $\textbf{\textit{unq}}(\bar{\bar{\sigma}}_i) = (\hat{S}_1)_i$ if it satisfies the verification equation:

$$e((\hat{S}_1)_i, g) \cdot e\left(S_2, \prod_{j=1}^{i}(u_j^{'}\prod_{l=1}^{k}u_{j,l}^{m_{j,l}})\right)^{-1} = \prod_{j=1}^{i} A_j$$

$$\Leftrightarrow e((\hat{S}_1)_i, g) \cdot e\left(g, \prod_{j=1}^{i}(u_j^{'}\prod_{l=1}^{k}u_{j,l}^{m_{j,l}})^r\right)^{-1} = \prod_{j=1}^{i} e(g,g)^{\alpha_j}$$

By induction hypothesis we have $(\hat{S}_1)_{i-1} = \prod_{j=1}^{i-1} g^{\alpha_j} \prod_{j=1}^{i-1}(u_j^{'}\prod_{l=1}^{k}u_{j,l}^{m_{j,l}})^r$, such that $(\hat{S}_1)_i = (\hat{S}_1)_{i-1} \cdot \delta$. We obtain the following equation:

$$e\left((\hat{S}_1)_{i-1} \cdot \delta, g\right) \cdot e\left(S_2, \prod_{j=1}^{i}(u_j^{'}\prod_{l=1}^{k}u_{j,l}^{m_{j,l}})\right)^{-1} = \prod_{j=1}^{i} A_j$$

$$\Leftrightarrow e\left((\hat{S}_1)_{i-1} \cdot \delta, g\right) \cdot e\left(g, \prod_{j=1}^{i-1}(u_j^{'}\prod_{l=1}^{k}u_{j,l}^{m_{j,l}})^r \cdot \left(u_i^{'}\prod_{l=1}^{k}u_{i,l}^{m_{i,l}}\right)^r\right)^{-1}$$

$$= \prod_{j=1}^{i} e(g,g)^{\alpha_j} \Leftrightarrow \prod_{j=1}^{i-1} e(g,g)^{\alpha_j} e(g,\delta) e\left(g, \left(u_i^{'}\prod_{l=1}^{k}u_{i,l}^{m_{i,l}}\right)^r\right)^{-1} = \prod_{j=1}^{i} e(g,g)^{\alpha_j}$$

The last equation holds if $\delta = g^{\alpha_i}\left(u_i^{'}\prod_{l=1}^{k}u_{i,l}^{m_{i,l}}\right)^r$. This implies the desired equality

$$(\hat{S}_1)_i = (\hat{S}_1)_{i-1} \cdot \delta = \prod_{j=1}^{i} g^{\alpha_j}\left(u_j^{'}\prod_{l=1}^{k}u_{j,l}^{m_{j,l}}\right)^r = S_1 = \textbf{\textit{unq}}(\bar{\sigma}).$$

□

4.2 Uniqueness of Schröder SAS Scheme

The SAS scheme proposed by Schröder [31] offers sequential aggregation for Camenisch-Lysyanskaya (CL) signatures [9]. The SAS scheme slightly modifies the original CL signatures by introducing an additional signature component, denoted in the following by D. We will essentially rely on this new component when proving the uniqueness property of the scheme.

ParGen(1^λ). Output the public parameters $I = (\mathbb{G}, \mathbb{G}_T, g, e)$ for the bilinear group setting according to Definition 1.

KeyGen(I). For each signer i choose $x_i \leftarrow \mathbb{Z}_q$ and $y_i \leftarrow \mathbb{Z}_q$ and sets $X_i = g^{x_i}$, $Y_i = g^{x_i}$ for $i \in [n]$. The algorithm returns $sk_i = (x_i, y_i)$ and $pk_i = (X_i, Y_i)$.

$\mathtt{AggSign}(sk_i, m_i, \bar{\sigma}_{i-1}, \mathbf{m}_{i-1}, \mathbf{pk}_{i-1})$. The algorithm takes as input a secret signing key sk_i, a message $m_i \in \mathbb{Z}_q$, an aggregate-so-far $\bar{\sigma}_{i-1}$ a sequence of messages $\mathbf{m}_{i-1} = (m_1, ..., m_{i-1})$ and a sequence of public keys $\mathbf{pk}_{i-1} = (pk_1, ..., pk_{i-1})$. The algorithm first checks that $|\mathbf{m}| = |\mathbf{pk}|$ and that the sequential verification $\mathtt{AggVerify}(\bar{\sigma}_{i-1}, \mathbf{m}_{i-1}, \mathbf{pk}_{i-1}) = 1$. If the verification holds, than it parses $\bar{\sigma}_{i-1} = (A', B', C', D')$, where $\mathtt{unq}(\bar{\sigma}_{i-1}) = D'$ is the unique component.

$$A' = g^r, \quad B' = \prod_{j=1}^{i} g^{ry_j}, \quad C' = \prod_{j=1}^{i} g^{r(x_j + m_j x_j y_j)}, \quad D' = \prod_{j \neq k}^{i} g^{m_j x_j y_k},$$

and it computes the signature $\bar{\sigma}_i = (A, B, C, D)$:

$$A = g^r, \quad B = B' \cdot A'^{y_i} = \prod_{j=1}^{i} g^{ry_j}, \quad C = C'(A')^{x_i + m_i x_i y_i} = \prod_{j=1}^{i} g^{x_j + m_j x_j y_j},$$

$$D = D' \cdot \left(\prod_{j=1}^{i-1} g^{x_j m_j y_i} g^{y_j x_i m_i} \right) = \prod_{j \neq k}^{i} g^{x_j m_j y_k}$$

$\mathtt{AggVerify}(\bar{\sigma}_i, \mathbf{pk}_i, \mathbf{m}_i)$: On input of a sequence of public keys $\mathbf{pk}_i$, sequence of messages $\mathbf{m}_i$ and $\bar{\sigma}_i = (A, B, C, D)$. The verification algorithm first checks if $|\mathbf{m}| = |\mathbf{pk}|$. It then validates the structure of the elements A, B, D:

$$e(A, \prod_{j=1}^{i} Y_j) = e\left(g, \prod_{j=1}^{i} g^{ry_j}\right) \text{ and } \prod_{j \neq k}^{i} e\left(X_k, Y_j\right)^{m_k} = e(g, D)$$

and checks that C is also formed correctly:

$$\prod_{j=1}^{i} \left(e\left(X_j, A\right) \cdot e\left(X_j, B\right)^{m_j}\right) e(A, D)^{-1} = e(g, C).$$

If all equations are valid, then the algorithm outputs 1; otherwise it returns 0.

Theorem 3. *Schröder SAS Scheme is unique according to Definition 7.*

Proof. Let $\mathtt{unq}$ be a function that outputs the fourth component of the aggregate signature $\bar{\sigma} = (A, B, C, D)$, i.e. $\mathtt{unq}(\bar{\sigma}) = D$. Assume that there exists another aggregate signature $\bar{\bar{\sigma}}$ that passes the verification procedure on the same set of messages and public keys as $\bar{\sigma}$ such that $\mathtt{unq}(\bar{\bar{\sigma}}) = \tilde{D}$. We prove by induction on i that in this case $\tilde{D} = D$ must hold. We use $\bar{\bar{\sigma}}$ to check the verification equations.

Base step: $i = 2$. The verification algorithm will accept $\bar{\bar{\sigma}}$, if $\tilde{D}$ satisfies the verification equations.

We check first the second equation $\prod_{j\neq k}^{2} e(X_j, Y_k)^{m_j} = e(g, \tilde{D})$ and compute:

$$\begin{aligned} & e(X_1, Y_2)^{m_1} e(X_2, Y_1)^{m_2} = e(g, \tilde{D}) \\ \Leftrightarrow\ & e(g^{x_1}, g^{y_2})^{m_1} \cdot e(g^{x_2}, g^{y_1})^{m_2} = e(g, \tilde{D}) \\ \Leftrightarrow\ & e(g, g)^{m_1 x_1 y_2} \cdot e(g, g)^{m_2 x_2 y_1} = e(g, \tilde{D}) \\ \Leftrightarrow\ & e(g, g)^{m_1 x_1 y_2 + m_2 x_2 y_1} = e(g, \tilde{D}) \\ \Leftrightarrow\ & e(g, g^{m_1 x_1 y_2 + m_2 x_2 y_1}) = e(g, \tilde{D}) \end{aligned}$$

The last equation holds only if $\tilde{D} = g^{m_1 x_1 y_2 + m_2 x_2 y_1} = D$.

Induction step: $i - 1 \mapsto i$. Let the theorem hold for $i - 1$. The verification algorithm will accept $\boldsymbol{unq}(\bar{\sigma}_i) = \tilde{D}_i$ if it satisfies the verification equation $\prod_{j\neq k}^{i} (X_j, Y_k)^{m_j} = e(g, \tilde{D}_i)$. By the induction hypothesis we have $\tilde{D}_{i-1} = \prod_{j\neq k}^{i-1} g^{m_j x_j y_k}$ such that $\tilde{D}_i = \tilde{D}_{i-1} \cdot \delta$. Considering the following verification equation we get:

$$\prod_{j\neq k}^{i} e(X_j, Y_k)^{m_j} = e(g, \tilde{D}_i) \quad \Leftrightarrow \quad \prod_{j\neq k}^{i} e(g^{x_j}, g^{y_k})^{m_j} = e(g, \tilde{D}_i)$$

$$\Leftrightarrow \prod_{j\neq k}^{i-1} (g, g)^{m_j x_j y_k} \prod_{j=1}^{i-1} e(g, g)^{m_i x_i y_j + m_j x_j y_i} = e(g, \prod_{j\neq k}^{i-1} g^{m_j x_j y_k} \cdot \delta)$$

$$= \prod_{j\neq k}^{i-1} e(g, g)^{m_j x_j y_k} e(g, \delta) \Leftrightarrow \prod_{j=1}^{i-1} e\left(g, g^{m_i x_i y_j + m_j x_j y_i}\right) = e(g, \delta)$$

The last equation holds if $\delta = \prod_{j=1}^{i-1} g^{m_i x_i y_j + m_j x_j y_i}$. We therefore obtain the desired equality $\tilde{D}_i = D_i = \boldsymbol{unq}(\bar{\sigma}_i)$.

□

5 Distributed Verifiable Random Functions

Distributed Verifiable Random Functions (DVRF) were introduced by Dodis [11]. The so-far only DVRF construction in [11] was obtained by first constructing a non-distributed VRF scheme (based on a variant of the well-known Decisional Diffie-Hellman assumption) and then by making it distributed using threshold secret sharing techniques; more precisely by issuing secret shares of the VRF secret key *sk* to the n servers and then by combining their individual VRF outputs into the DVRF output, whose validity could be checked publicly using the original VRF public key *pk*. This approach, however, imposed undesirable trust assumptions on the trustworthy generation of secret keys (shares) for the n servers and resulted in a threshold on the number of corrupted servers.

In contrast, our approach for building DVRF is generic, proceeds under much weaker setup assumptions, and requires only one server to remain uncorrupted. As a guideline we adopt the approach by Micali, Rabin, and Vadhan [25] that has been used in a non-distributed VRF case, namely to first focus on a weaker family of functions those outputs are unpredictable but not necessarily pseudorandom, the so-called Verifiable Unpredictable Functions (VUF). We observe that the generic transformation from [25] for converting VUF outputs into VRF outputs — by adding a random string r to the VUF public key pk and then computing VRF outputs as inner products of VUF outputs and r (which takes its roots in [18]) — works just fine for the case where the VUF output has been previously obtained in a distributed way. In a distributed VUF setting the required random string r can be made part of a *shared random string (SRS)* [13], which we consider as the only setup assumption in our DVRF schemes. Note that the SRS model is much weaker than the assumed trustworthy generation of secret keys in [11] and belongs to standard cryptographic assumptions.

Following the above approach we thus need to define the notion of Distributed VUF (DVUF). Our Definition 8 essentially tweaks the original definition of VUF from [25] to the distributed setting.

Definition 8 (Distributed Verifiable Unpredictable Function (DVUF)). *Let* $F_{(\cdot)}(\cdot) : \{0,1\}^{a(\lambda)} \rightarrow \{0,1\}^{b(\lambda)}$ *denote a family of functions with associated algorithms:*

$\mathtt{Gen}(1^\lambda)$ *is a PPT algorithm that takes as input the security parameter* 1^λ *and outputs a private/public key pair* (sk_i, pk_i) *for a server* $i \in \{1, \dots, n\}$*. Let* $\mathbf{sk} = \{sk_1, \dots, sk_n\}$ *and* $\mathbf{pk} = \{pk_1, \dots, pk_n\}$*.*

$\mathtt{Prove}(\mathbf{sk}, \mathbf{pk}, x)$ *is an interactive protocol executed between an user and* n *servers with common input* x *chosen by the user and* $\mathbf{pk} = (pk_1, \dots, pk_n)$ *such that at the end of the execution the user obtains a VUF value* $F(\mathbf{sk}, x) = y$ *and the corresponding proof* π*.*

$\mathtt{Verify}(\mathbf{pk}, x, y, \pi)$ *is a deterministic algorithm that takes as input* $\mathbf{pk}, x, y$ *and a candidate proof* π*, and outputs 1 if* π *is a valid proof for* $y = F(\mathbf{sk}, x)$ *and 0 otherwise.*

F is a family of Distributed Verifiable Unpredictable Functions (DVUF) *if it satisfies:*

- Uniqueness: *The DVUF value* $y = F(\mathbf{sk}, m)$ *with proof of correctness* π *is unique if there exists no tuple* $(\mathbf{pk}, x, y_1, y_2, \pi)$ *with* $y_1 \neq y_2$ *but* $\mathtt{Verify}(\mathbf{pk}, x, y_1, \pi) = \mathtt{Verify}(\mathbf{pk}, x, y_2, \pi) = 1$*.*
- Provability: *For all* $(y, \pi) \leftarrow \mathtt{Prove}(\mathbf{sk}, x)$*:* $\mathtt{Verify}(\mathbf{pk}, x, y, \pi) = 1$*.*
- Residual Unpredictability: *For any PPT algorithm* $\mathcal{A} = (\mathcal{A}_1, \mathcal{A}_2)$ *the probability that* $\mathcal{A}$ *succeeds in the following experiment is negligible in the security parameter* 1^λ *:*
  1. $(sk_i, pk_i) \leftarrow \mathtt{Gen}(1^\lambda)$ *for all* $i \in [n]$*.*

2. $[n] \ni c \leftarrow \mathcal{A}_1(\mathbf{pk})$
3. $(x^*, y^*, \pi^*) \leftarrow \mathcal{A}_2^{\mathtt{OProve}(sk_c,\cdot)}(\mathbf{sk} \setminus \{sk_c\})$.
4. *$\mathcal{A}$ succeeds if $x^* \in \{0,1\}^{a(\lambda)}$, $\mathtt{Verify}(\mathbf{pk}, x^*, y^*, \pi^*) = 1$ and x^* was not queried to the $\mathtt{OProve}(sk_c, \cdot)$ oracle by $\mathcal{A}$,*

where

$\mathtt{OProve}(sk_c, \cdot)$: The adversarial input to the oracle is a DVUF input $x \in \{0,1\}^{a(\lambda)}$. The oracle responds on behalf of server c according to the specification of the $\mathtt{Prove}$ protocol.

The following lemma from [25] when applied to the distributed setting shows how to convert DVUF outputs into DVRF outputs. The resulting transformation holds in the shared random string model that provides involved parties with the random string r. Lemma 1 essentially allows us to focus on DVUF constructions in the remaining part of this work.

Lemma 1 (From DVUF to DVRF [25]). *For any DVUF ($\mathtt{Gen}$, $\mathtt{Prove}$, $\mathtt{Verify}$) with input length $a(\lambda)$, output length $b(\lambda)$, and security $s(\lambda)$, there exists a DVRF in the shared random string model with the following three algorithms: ($\overline{\mathtt{Gen}}$, $\overline{\mathtt{Prove}}$, $\overline{\mathtt{Verify}}$) with input length $a'(\lambda) \leq a(\lambda)$, output length $b'(\lambda) = 1$, and security $s'(\lambda) = s(\lambda)^{1/3}/(poly(\lambda) \cdot 2^{a'(\lambda)})$:*

- *$\overline{\mathtt{Gen}}(1^\lambda, r)$ where $r \leftarrow \{0,1\}^{b(\lambda)}$ is shared random string computes public/private keys $(sk_i, pk_i) \leftarrow \mathtt{Gen}(1^\lambda)$ and outputs $(\overline{\mathbf{sk}}, \overline{\mathbf{pk}}) = (\mathbf{sk}, (\mathbf{pk}, r))$.*
- *$\overline{\mathtt{Prove}}(\mathbf{sk}, x, r)$ computes $(y, \pi) \leftarrow \mathtt{Prove}(\mathbf{sk}, x)$, $\overline{y} = \langle y, r \rangle$ as inner product of y and r, $\overline{\pi} := (y, \pi)$ and outputs $(\overline{y}, \overline{\pi})$.*
- *$\overline{\mathtt{Verify}}(\mathbf{pk}, x, \overline{y}, \overline{\pi})$ outputs 1 if $\mathtt{Verify}(\mathbf{pk}, x, y, \pi) = 1$ and $\overline{y} = \langle y, r \rangle$. Otherwise it outputs 0.*

Proof. Since any DVUF/DVRF family F is also a VUF/VRF family the proof of this lemma is implied by the result from [25, Section 5].

5.1 Generic Construction of DVUF from UAS Schemes

We obtain our first generic DVUF construction from UAS schemes where the aggregation process is public. The major benefit of this construction is that it requires only one communication round between the user and the n servers and is thus as efficient in terms of communication as the approach in [11]. The algorithms of our UAS-based DVUF construction are detailed in the following using the UAS syntax from Definition 2:

$\mathtt{Gen}(1^\lambda)$ computes public parameters $I \leftarrow \mathtt{ParGen}(1^\lambda)$ of the UAS scheme. Each server S_i, $i \in [n]$ computes its private/public UAS key pair $(sk_i, pk_i) \leftarrow \mathtt{KeyGen}(I)$. Let $\mathbf{sk} = (sk_1, ..., sk_n)$ and $\mathbf{pk} = (pk_1, \ldots, pk_n)$.

$\mathtt{Prove}(\mathbf{sk}, x)$ *Protocol:* This is a protocol between user U and servers S_i, $i = 1, \ldots, n$ with each server in possession of $sk_i \in \mathbf{sk}$. The common input is x and $\mathbf{pk}$. Each server S_i computes $\sigma_i \leftarrow \mathtt{Sign}(sk_i, x)$ and sends it to U. For all $i \in [n]$, U checks whether $\mathtt{Verify}(pk_i, x, \sigma_i) = 1$ using the verification algorithm of the UAS scheme. If so U computes $\bar{\sigma} \leftarrow \mathtt{Aggregate}(\mathbf{pk}, x, \boldsymbol{\sigma})$ and outputs $(y, \pi) = (\mathtt{unq}(\bar{\sigma}), \bar{\sigma})$.

$\mathit{Verify}(\mathbf{pk}, x, y, \pi)$: Parse π as $\bar{\sigma}$. If $\mathit{AggVerify}(\mathbf{pk}, x, \bar{\sigma}) = 1$ and $y = \mathtt{unq}(\bar{\sigma})$ then output 1, else output 0.

Theorem 4. *Let UAS be a unique aggregate signature scheme according to Definitions 3 and 4. Then our DVUF construction from UAS fulfills the properties of Definition 8.*

Proof. The uniqueness of UAS scheme implies the uniqueness property of DVUF. Because individual UAS signatures σ_i, which pass the UAS verification procedure Verify from Definition 2 can be aggregated into a signature $\bar{\sigma}$, which satisfies the UAS $\mathit{AggVerify}$ algorithm, we can conclude that for all $(y, \pi) \leftarrow \mathit{Prove}(\mathbf{sk}, x)$ we have $\mathit{Verify}(\mathbf{pk}, m, y, \pi) = 1$, where $y = \mathtt{unq}(\bar{\sigma})$, $\pi = \bar{\sigma}$ and x is a value to be signed. This implies the provability of our DVUF scheme.

In the following we thus focus on the residual unpredictability of our DVUF construction. Assuming an adversary $\mathcal{A}$ which breaks the unpredictability of the DVUF scheme, i.e. outputs a valid tuple (x^*, y^*, π^*) according to the experiment in Definition 8, we construct an adversary $\mathcal{B}$ that simulates the environment of $\mathcal{A}$ and breaks the unforgeability of the underlying UAS scheme by outputting a valid tuple $(\mathbf{m}^*, \mathbf{pk}^*, \sigma^*)$ according to the experiment in Definition 3.

The UAS forger $\mathcal{B}$ is initialized with system parameters I and the challenge public key pk_c. For all $i \in [n]$, $i \neq c$, where c is treated as a random index in $[n]$ it computes $(sk_i, pk_i) \leftarrow \mathit{KeyGen}(I)$ using the key generation algorithm of the UAS scheme and invokes the two-stage DVUF adversary $\mathcal{A} = (\mathcal{A}_1, \mathcal{A}_2)$. First it invokes $\mathcal{A}_1(\mathbf{pk})$ where $\mathbf{pk}$ is comprised of all generated pk_i and pk_c whereby index c for pk_c in $\mathbf{pk}$ is assigned randomly by $\mathcal{B}$. If the index c output by $\mathcal{A}_1(\mathbf{pk})$ doesn't match that of pk_c the simulation aborts. The probability that the index matches is given by $1/n$. Otherwise, $\mathcal{B}$ invokes $\mathcal{A}_2(\mathbf{sk}')$, where $\mathbf{sk}'$ is comprised of all generated sk_i (i.e. doesn't include sk_c which is unknown to $\mathcal{B}$) and answers the $\mathit{OProve}(sk_c, \cdot)$ oracle queries of $\mathcal{A}_2$ using its own oracle $\mathit{OSign}(sk_c, \cdot)$. That is, $\mathcal{B}$ performs the computation step of the protocol Prove on behalf of server S_c by obtaining individual signatures σ_c on a given DVUF input x from its own signing oracle. At some point, $\mathcal{A}_2$ outputs a tuple (x^*, y^*, π^*) aiming to break the unpredictability property of the DVUF scheme. This tuple is valid if $\mathcal{A}_2$ never queried x^* to its $\mathit{OProve}(sk_c, \cdot)$ oracle and $\mathit{Verify}(\mathbf{pk}, x^*, y^*, \pi^*) = 1$. $\mathcal{B}$ checks the validity of the tuple and if valid outputs $(\mathbf{m}^*, \mathbf{pk}^*, \sigma^*) = (\mathbf{x}^*, \mathbf{pk}, \pi^*)$ where $\mathbf{x}^*$ is a set consisting of n values x^* as its own forgery.

Let $\mathtt{Succ}_{\mathcal{B}}$ denote the probability that $\mathcal{B}$ outputs a valid forgery for the UAS scheme and $\mathtt{Succ}_{\mathcal{A}}$ denote the probability that $\mathcal{A} = (\mathcal{A}_1, \mathcal{A}_2)$ breaks the DVUF construction. If the index c assigned by $\mathcal{B}$ matches the one output by $\mathcal{A}_1$ then its simulation for $\mathcal{A}$ is perfect. It is easy to see that in this case the resulting tuple $(\mathbf{x}^*, \mathbf{pk}, \pi^*)$ constitutes a valid forgery for the UAS scheme since $\mathcal{B}$ never queried the message x^* to its $\mathit{OSign}(sk_c, \cdot)$ oracle. Considering that indices match with probability $1/n$ we get $\mathtt{Succ}_{\mathcal{A}} \leq n \cdot \mathtt{Succ}_{\mathcal{B}}$. □

5.2 Generic Construction of DVUF from USAS Schemes

Our second generic DVUF construction is based on an USAS scheme where the aggregation process is sequential. This implies that the user must approach each server one-by-one until it obtains the resulting DVUF output from the last server in the sequence. The algorithms of our USAS-based DVUF are detailed in the following using the USAS syntax from Definition 5:

$\mathit{Gen}(1^\lambda)$ computes public parameters $I \leftarrow \mathit{ParGen}(1^\lambda)$ of the USAS scheme. Each server S_i, $i \in [n]$ computes its private/public USAS key pair $(sk_i, pk_i) \leftarrow \mathit{KeyGen}(I)$. Let $\mathbf{sk} = (sk_1, ..., sk_n)$ and $\mathbf{pk} = (pk_1, \ldots, pk_n)$.

$\mathit{Prove}(\mathbf{sk}, x)$ *Protocol:* This is a protocol between user U and servers S_i, $i = 1, \ldots, n$ with each server in possession of $sk_i \in \mathbf{sk}$. The common input is x and $\mathbf{pk}$. Each server S_i computes $\bar{\sigma}_i \leftarrow \mathit{AggSign}(sk_i, x, \bar{\sigma}_{i-1}, \mathbf{pk}_{i-1})$ and sends it to U. For all $i \in [n]$, U checks whether $\mathit{AggVerify}(\bar{\sigma}_i, x, \mathbf{pk}_i) = 1$ using the verification algorithm of the USAS scheme. If so U gives as input to server S_{i+1} an aggregate-so-far $\bar{\sigma}_i$ and value x. Finally it outputs $(y, \pi) = (\mathit{unq}(\bar{\sigma}), \bar{\sigma})$.

$\mathit{Verify}(\mathbf{pk}, x, y, \pi)$: Parse π as $\bar{\sigma}$. If $\mathit{AggVerify}(\mathbf{pk}, x, \bar{\sigma}) = 1$ and $y = \mathbf{unq}(\bar{\sigma})$ then output 1, else output 0.

Theorem 5. *Let USAS be a unique sequential aggregate signature scheme according to Definitions 6 and 7. Then our DVUF construction from USAS fulfills the properties of Definition 8.*

Proof. The uniqueness of USAS scheme implies the uniqueness property of DVUF. Because each aggregate-so-far signature $\bar{\sigma}_{i-1}$ from USAS scheme, which pass the USAS verification procedure $\mathit{AggVerify}$ from Definition 5 can be aggregated into an aggregate signature $\bar{\sigma}_i$ by adding the signature σ_i on message m signed by signer i, we can conclude that for all $(y, \pi) \leftarrow \mathit{Prove}(\mathbf{sk}, x)$ we have $\mathit{Verify}(\mathbf{pk}, m, y, \pi) = 1$, where $y = \mathbf{unq}(\bar{\sigma}_i)$, $\pi = \bar{\sigma}_i$ and x is a value to be signed. This implies the provability of our DVUF scheme.

Similar to the last construction we thus focus here on the residual unpredictability of our DVUF construction. Assuming an adversary $\mathcal{A}$ which breaks the unpredictability of the DVUF scheme, i.e. outputs a valid tuple (x^*, y^*, π^*) according to the experiment in Definition 8, we construct an adversary $\mathcal{B}$ that simulates the environment of $\mathcal{A}$ and breaks the unforgeability of the underlying USAS scheme by outputting a valid tuple $(\mathbf{m}^*, \mathbf{pk}^*, \sigma^*)$ according to the experiment in Definition 6.

The USAS forger $\mathcal{B}$ is initialized with system parameters I and the challenge public key pk_c. For all $i \in [n]$, $i \neq c$, where c is treated as a random index in $[n]$ it computes $(sk_i, pk_i) \leftarrow \mathit{KeyGen}(I)$ using the key generation algorithm of the USAS scheme and invokes the two-stage DVUF adversary $\mathcal{A} = (\mathcal{A}_1, \mathcal{A}_2)$. Because the first stage adversary $\mathcal{A}_1(\mathbf{pk})$ with $\mathbf{pk}$ being comprised of all generated pk_i and given pk_c with a randomly assigned index $c \in [n]$ runs in analogue way to the proof of Theorem 4, we skip here its description and proceed with the invocation of $\mathcal{A}_2(\mathbf{sk}')$, where $\mathbf{sk}'$ is comprised of all generated sk_i, i.e. $\mathbf{sk}'$ doesn't include sk_c which is unknown to $\mathcal{B}$. $\mathcal{B}$ answers the *OProve*$(sk_c, \cdot)$ oracle queries of $\mathcal{A}_2$ on input $(x, \bar{\sigma}_{c-1})$ where x is the provided DVUF input and $\bar{\sigma}_{c-1}$ is the aggregate-so-far signature that is expected by the server S_c during the execution of the ***Prove*** protocol as follows. Upon receiving such query from $\mathcal{A}_2$ it queries its own oracle *OAggSign*$(sk_c, \cdot)$ on input $(x, \bar{\sigma}_{c-1}, \mathbf{x}_{c-1}, \mathbf{pk}_{c-1})$ where $\mathbf{x}_{c-1}$ is a set of $c-1$ messages all of which are equal to x and $\mathbf{pk}_{c-1}$ is comprised of all pk_i, $i = 1, \ldots, c-1$. Recall that the entire set of DVUF public keys $\mathbf{pk}$ is considered as common input to the ***Prove*** protocol. In response to its query, $\mathcal{B}$ obtains the aggregate-so-far signature $\bar{\sigma}_c$ that it forwards on to $\mathcal{A}_2$ which is inline with the specification of the ***Prove*** protocol. At some point, $\mathcal{A}_2$ outputs a tuple (x^*, y^*, π^*) aiming to break the unpredictability property of the DVUF scheme. This tuple is valid if $\mathcal{A}_2$ never queried x^* to its *OProve*$(sk_c, \cdot)$ oracle and ***Verify***$(\mathbf{pk}, x^*, y^*, \pi^*) = 1$. $\mathcal{B}$ checks the validity of the tuple and if valid outputs $(\mathbf{m}^*, \mathbf{pk}^*, \bar{\sigma}^*) = (\mathbf{x}^*, \mathbf{pk}, \pi^*)$ where $\mathbf{x}^*$ is a set consisting of n values x^* as its own forgery.

Let $\mathtt{Succ}_{\mathcal{B}}$ denote the probability that $\mathcal{B}$ outputs a valid forgery for the USAS scheme and $\mathtt{Succ}_{\mathcal{A}}$ denote the probability that $\mathcal{A} = (\mathcal{A}_1, \mathcal{A}_2)$ breaks the DVUF construction. If the index c assigned by $\mathcal{B}$ for pk_c matches the one output by $\mathcal{A}_1$ then its simulation for $\mathcal{A}$ is perfect. It is easy to see that in this case the resulting tuple $(\mathbf{x}^*, \mathbf{pk}, \pi^*)$ constitutes a valid forgery for the USAS scheme since $\mathcal{B}$ never queried the message x^* to its *OAggSign*$(sk_c, \cdot)$ oracle. Considering that indices match with probability $1/n$ we get $\mathtt{Succ}_{\mathcal{A}} \leq n \cdot \mathtt{Succ}_{\mathcal{B}}$. □

6 Conclusion

We explored the uniqueness property of aggregate signatures and showed that it gives rise to generic DVUF constructions, whose outputs can be made pseudorandom in the shared random string model using the techniques from [25]. This gives us first generic DVRF constructions that do not impose assumptions on trusted generation of secret keys and those outputs remain pseudorandom even in presence of up to $n-1$ corrupted servers. A number of concrete DVRF constructions follows immediately from our proofs of uniqueness for the aggregate signature schemes from [7,22,31].

Acknowledgements. This research was supported by the German Science Foundation (DFG) through the project PRIMAKE (MA 4957).

References

1. Abdalla, M., Catalano, D., Fiore, D.: Verifiable Random Functions from Identity-Based Key Encapsulation. In: Joux, A. (ed.) EUROCRYPT 2009. LNCS, vol. 5479, pp. 554–571. Springer, Heidelberg (2009)
2. Bagherzandi, A., Cheon, J.H., Jarecki, S.: Multisignatures Secure under the Discrete Logarithm Assumption and a Generalized Forking Lemma. In: ACM CCS 2008, pp. 449–458. ACM (2008)

3. Bellare, M., Neven, G.: Multi-Signatures in the Plain Public-Key Model and a General Forking Lemma. In: ACM CCS 2006, pp. 390–399. ACM (2006)
4. Bellare, M., Rogaway, P.: Random Oracles are Practical: A Paradigm for Designing Efficient Protocols. In: ACM CCS 1993, pp. 62–73. ACM (1993)
5. Boldyreva, A.: Threshold Signatures, Multisignatures and Blind Signatures Based on the Gap-Diffie-Hellman-Group Signature Scheme. In: Desmedt, Y.G. (ed.) PKC 2003. LNCS, vol. 2567, pp. 31–46. Springer, Heidelberg (2002)
6. Boldyreva, A., Gentry, C., O'Neill, A., Yum, D.H.: Ordered Multisignatures and Identity-Based Sequential Aggregate Signatures, with Applications to Secure Routing. In: ACM CCS 2007, pp. 276–285. ACM (2007)
7. Boneh, D., Gentry, C., Lynn, B., Shacham, H.: Aggregate and Verifiably Encrypted Signatures from Bilinear Maps. In: Biham, E. (ed.) EUROCRYPT 2003. LNCS, vol. 2656, pp. 416–432. Springer, Heidelberg (2003)
8. Boneh, D., Lynn, B., Shacham, H.: Short Signatures from the Weil Pairing. Journal of Cryptology 17, 297–319 (2004)
9. Camenisch, J.L., Lysyanskaya, A.: Signature Schemes and Anonymous Credentials from Bilinear Maps. In: Franklin, M. (ed.) CRYPTO 2004. LNCS, vol. 3152, pp. 56–72. Springer, Heidelberg (2004)
10. Canetti, R., Goldreich, O., Halevi, S.: The Random Oracle Methodology, Revisited. In: ACM STOC 1998, pp. 209–218 (1998)
11. Dodis, Y.: Efficient Construction of (Distributed) Verifiable Random Functions. In: Desmedt, Y.G. (ed.) PKC 2003. LNCS, vol. 2567, pp. 1–17. Springer, Heidelberg (2002)
12. Dodis, Y., Yampolskiy, A.: A Verifiable Random Function with Short Proofs and Keys. In: Vaudenay, S. (ed.) PKC 2005. LNCS, vol. 3386, pp. 416–431. Springer, Heidelberg (2005)
13. Feige, U., Killian, J., Naor, M.: A Minimal Model for Secure Computation. In: ACM STOC 1994, pp. 554–563. ACM (1994)
14. Franklin, M., Zhang, H.: Unique Group Signatures. In: Foresti, S., Yung, M., Martinelli, F. (eds.) ESORICS 2012. LNCS, vol. 7459, pp. 643–660. Springer, Heidelberg (2012)
15. Franklin, M., Zhang, H.: A Framework for Unique Ring Signatures. In: IACR Cryptology ePrint Archive, Report 2012/577 (2012)
16. Gennaro, R., Jarecki, S., Krawczyk, H., Rabin, T.: Secure Distributed Key Generation for Discrete-Log Based Cryptosystems. In: Stern, J. (ed.) EUROCRYPT 1999. LNCS, vol. 1592, pp. 295–310. Springer, Heidelberg (1999)
17. Goldreich, O., Goldwasser, S., Micali, S.: How to construct random functions. Journal of ACM 33(4), 792–807 (1986)
18. Goldreich, O., Levin, L.A.: A Hard-Core Predicate for All One-Way Functions. In: ACM STOC 1989, pp. 25–32. ACM (1989)
19. Goldwasser, S., Ostrovsky, R.: Invariant Signatures and Non-Interactive Zero-Knowledge Proofs are Equivalent. In: Brickell, E.F. (ed.) CRYPTO 1992. LNCS, vol. 740, pp. 228–245. Springer, Heidelberg (1993)
20. Jarecki, S., Shmatikov, V.: Handcuffing Big Brother: An Abuse-Resilient Transaction Escrow Scheme. In: Cachin, C., Camenisch, J.L. (eds.) EUROCRYPT 2004. LNCS, vol. 3027, pp. 590–608. Springer, Heidelberg (2004)
21. Liskov, M.: Updatable Zero-Knowledge Databases. In: Roy, B. (ed.) ASIACRYPT 2005. LNCS, vol. 3788, pp. 174–198. Springer, Heidelberg (2005)
22. Lu, S., Ostrovsky, R., Sahai, A., Shacham, H., Waters, B.: Sequential Aggregate Signatures and Multisignatures Without Random Oracles. In: Vaudenay, S. (ed.) EUROCRYPT 2006. LNCS, vol. 4004, pp. 465–485. Springer, Heidelberg (2006)

23. Lysyanskaya, A., Micali, S., Reyzin, L., Shacham, H.: Sequential Aggregate Signatures from Trapdoor Permutations. In: Cachin, C., Camenisch, J.L. (eds.) EUROCRYPT 2004. LNCS, vol. 3027, pp. 74–90. Springer, Heidelberg (2004)
24. Lysyanskaya, A.: Unique Signatures and Verifiable Random Functions from the DH-DDH Separation. In: Yung, M. (ed.) CRYPTO 2002. LNCS, vol. 2442, pp. 597–612. Springer, Heidelberg (2002)
25. Micali, S., Rabin, M., Vadhan, S.: Verifiable Random Functions. In: IEEE FOCS 1999, pp. 120–130. IEEE Computer Society (1999)
26. Micali, S., Reyzin, L.: Soundness in the Public-Key Model. In: Kilian, J. (ed.) CRYPTO 2001. LNCS, vol. 2139, pp. 542–565. Springer, Heidelberg (2001)
27. Micali, S., Ohta, K., Reyzin, L.: Accountable-subgroup multisignatures: extended abstract. In: ACM CCS 2001, pp. 245–254. ACM (2001)
28. Micali, S., Rivest, R.L.: Micropayments Revisited. In: Preneel, B. (ed.) CT-RSA 2002. LNCS, vol. 2271, pp. 149–163. Springer, Heidelberg (2002)
29. Ristenpart, T., Yilek, S.: The Power of Proofs-of-Possession: Securing Multiparty Signatures against Rogue-Key Attacks. In: Naor, M. (ed.) EUROCRYPT 2007. LNCS, vol. 4515, pp. 228–245. Springer, Heidelberg (2007)
30. Shamir, A.: How to Share a Secret. Communications of the ACM 22(11), 612–613 (1979)
31. Schröder, D.: How to aggregate the CL signature scheme. In: Atluri, V., Diaz, C. (eds.) ESORICS 2011. LNCS, vol. 6879, pp. 298–314. Springer, Heidelberg (2011)
32. Waters, B.: Efficient Identity-Based Encryption without Random Oracles. In: Cramer, R. (ed.) EUROCRYPT 2005. LNCS, vol. 3494, pp. 114–127. Springer, Heidelberg (2005)
33. Zhou, Y., Qian, H., Li, X.: Non-Interactive CDH-Based Multisignature Scheme in the Plain Public Key Model with Tighter Security. In: Lai, X., Zhou, J., Li, H. (eds.) ISC 2011. LNCS, vol. 7001, pp. 341–354. Springer, Heidelberg (2011)

A Practical Related-Key Boomerang Attack for the Full MMB Block Cipher

Tomer Ashur[1] and Orr Dunkelman[2]

[1] Department of Electrical Engineering and iMinds
ESAT/COSIC, KU Leuven, Belgium
tashur@esat.kuleuven.be
[2] Computer Science Department
University of Haifa
Haifa 31905, Israel
orrd@cs.haifa.ac.il

Abstract. The MMB block cipher (Modular Multiplication-based Block cipher) is an iterative block cipher designed by Daemen, Govaerts, and Vandewalle in 1993 as an improvement of the PES and IPES ciphers.

In this paper we present several new related-key differential characteristics of MMB. These characteristics can be used to form several related-key boomerangs to attack the full MMB. Using 2^{20} adaptive chosen plaintexts and ciphertexts we recover all key bits in $2^{35.2}$ time for the full MMB. Our attack was experimentally verified, and it takes less than 15 minutes on a standard Intel i5 machine to recover the full MMB key.

After showing this practical attack on the full key of the full MMB, we present attacks on extended versions of MMB with up to 8 rounds (which is two more rounds than in the full MMB). We recover 64 out of the 128 key in time of $2^{32.2}$ for 7-round MMB, and time of 2^{32} for 8-round MMB using 2^{20} plaintexts.

Keywords: MMB, Differential Cryptanalysis, Related-Key Boomerang Attack.

1 Introduction

The MMB block cipher (Modular Multiplication-based Block cipher) is an iterative block cipher designed by Daemen, Govaerts, and Vandewalle [5] as an improvement of the PES and IPES ciphers [10,11]. The cipher works with blocks of 128 bits and an equal key length. The cipher's non-linearity comes from multiplication mod $2^{32} - 1$ (hence the cipher's name). The cipher consists of 6 rounds without any initialization or finalization steps.

Previously published work on MMB includes two papers in the single-key model [7, 13]. Both papers were able to recover the full key of the full MMB. In [13] Wang et al. use a 5-round differential in a 1R attack in $2^{95.91}$ time, 2^{118} chosen plaintexts, and 2^{65} 32-bit memory words to break the full MMB. In [7] Jia et al. present several attacks, the best of which is a sandwich attack using $2^{13.4}$

M. Abdalla, C. Nita-Rotaru, and R. Dahab (Eds.): CANS 2013, LNCS 8257, pp. 271–290, 2013.

time, 2^{40} adaptive chosen plaintexts and ciphertexts, and $2^{20.6}$ 32-bit memory words. We summarize these results in Table 2.

In this paper we present a related-key attack that allows an adversary to recover all key bits in time of $2^{35.2}$ using 2^{20} adaptive chosen plaintexts and ciphertexts encrypted under 4 related-keys. We first present two related-key differential characteristics of two and three rounds, respectively, and use them to construct two boomerangs covering 5 rounds of MMB. We then use these 5-round boomerangs to attack the full (6 rounds) MMB. Each of the boomerangs can be used to recover 32 bits of the key. The 64 recovered bits are then further used to recover another 32 bits of the key using a 1R related-key differential attack. The remaining 32 bits are then found by a simple exhaustive search.

To verify our results experimentally, we implemented the attack on the full (6-round) MMB using a C program. The program generates the required data, encrypts and decrypts it through the presented related-key boomerangs, identifies the right quartets, and recovers the key bits in about 15 minutes on a home PC.

After presenting our results, we show that even if MMB was extended to 7 or 8 rounds, it would still be insecure. To prove this claim, we extend the first phase of our attack to extended 7-round and 8-round variants of MMB with similar complexity. In other words, we show that using $2^{20.6}$ adaptive chosen plaintexts and ciphertexts, encrypted under 4 related keys for the 7-round variant, and 6 related keys for the 8-round variant, in time of about 2^{32} encryptions, an adversary can recover 64 bits out of the 128-bit key.

This paper is organized as follows: In Section 2 we give a brief description of the MMB block cipher; Section 3 describes some of the previous work done to analyze MMB; in Section 4 we describe the cryptanalytic techniques we use in the paper. In Section 5 we describe the related-key differential characteristics we use and how we use them to create the related-key boomerangs; Section 6 explains how to use the related-key boomerangs to recover the entire key of the full MMB; Section 7 discusses an extended variants of MMB with 7 and 8 rounds and how to attack them, and Section 8 concludes the paper.

2 A Brief Description of MMB and Our Notations

As mentioned before, MMB is an iterative block cipher with a 128-bit block and a 128-bit key. The message and key are each divided into four 32-bit words x_0, x_1, x_2, x_3, and k_0, k_1, k_2, k_3, respectively. In each round, four operations, $\sigma[k^j], \gamma, \eta$, and θ are performed over the state words. Three of the four operations, namely, $\sigma[k^j], \eta$, and θ are involutions (i.e., they are their own inverse).

The key injection operation, $\sigma[k^j]$, XORs the subkey into the message such that $\sigma[k^j](x_0, x_1, x_2, x_3) = (x_0 \oplus k_0^j, x_1 \oplus k_1^j, x_2 \oplus k_2^j, x_3 \oplus k_3^j)$ where $\oplus$ denotes the exclusive-or operation and j denotes the round number. The key injection operation is done 7 times, once at the beginning of the each round and once more after the last round.

The modular multiplication operation, γ, is the only non-linear operation in the cipher. In each encryption round, each of the 32-bit words is multiplied by a fixed constant such that the result y_i is

$$y_i = \begin{cases} x_i & \text{if } x_i = 2^{32}-1 \\ x_i \otimes G_i & \text{if } x_i \neq 2^{32}-1 \end{cases}$$

Where the operator $\otimes$ is the modular multiplication operator (i.e., $a \otimes b = (a * b) \ mod \ (2^{32}-1)$) and $G_0 = 025F1CDB_x, G_1 = 2 \otimes G_0 = 04BE39B6_x, G_2 = 8 \otimes G_0 = 12F8E6D8_x$, and $G_3 = 128 \otimes G_0 = 2F8E6D81_x$. The result of the γ operation is therefore $(y_0, y_1, y_2, y_3) = \gamma(x_0, x_1, x_2, x_3)$.

Inverting γ is done by multiplying the ciphertext with G_i^{-1} such that

$$x_i = \begin{cases} y_i & \text{if } y_i = 2^{32}-1 \\ y_i \otimes G_i^{-1} & \text{if } y_i \neq 2^{32}-1 \end{cases}$$

where $G_0^{-1} = 0DAD4694_x, G_1^{-1} = 06D6A34A_x, G_2^{-1} = 81B5A8D2_x$ and $G_3^{-1} = 281B5A8D_x$.

For every word entering γ, the trivial differential transition $0 \rightarrow 0$ holds with probability 1. Another interesting property that was mentioned in [5] is that the differential transition $FFFFFFFF_x \rightarrow FFFFFFFF_x$ through γ also holds with probability 1. The use of these transitions is described in Section 5.

The η operation is a data-dependent operation on the leftmost and rightmost words of the state. If the LSB of the word is 1 it XORs a predefined constant δ into the word, otherwise it does nothing. Namely, $\eta(x_0, x_1, x_2, x_3) = (x_0 \oplus (lsb(x_0) \cdot \delta), x_1, x_2, x_3 \oplus (lsb(x_3) \cdot \delta))$ where $\delta = 2AAAAAAA_x$.

The diffusion between words comes from the θ operation that mixes the round's words such that every change in any word affects three words in the output. Namely, $\theta(x_0, x_1, x_2, x_3) = (x_0 \oplus x_1 \oplus x_3, x_0 \oplus x_1 \oplus x_2, x_1 \oplus x_2 \oplus x_3, x_0 \oplus x_2 \oplus x_3)$.

The jth round of MMB over the block $X = (x_0, x_1, x_2, x_3)$ is: $\rho[k^j](X) = \theta(\eta(\gamma(\sigma[k^j](X))))$. A full description of MMB with plaintext P is:

$$\sigma[k^6](\rho[k^5](\rho[k^4](\rho[k^3](\rho[k^2](\rho[k^1](\rho[k^0](P)))))))$$

A schematic view of MMB's round function can be found on Figure 1.

2.1 Key Schedule

The original version of MMB used a simple key schedule algorithm that rotates the key words one position to the left (e.g. the key for round 0 is (k_0, k_1, k_2, k_3), the key for round 1 is (k_1, k_2, k_3, k_0) etc.). The key schedule is cyclic and repeats every 4 rounds [5]. To avoid exploitable symmetry properties a new version of MMB was published where in each round, in addition to the position change, each key word is XORed with a round-dependent constant. Therefore, the key word i for round j is $k_i^j = k_{i+j \ mod \ 4} \oplus (2^j \cdot B)$ with $B = DAE_x$ [4].[1]

[1] We note that the change in the key schedule algorithm does not affect our attack which is differential in nature. In other words, all the attacks reported in this paper work for both key schedules, i.e., the original one and the tweaked one.

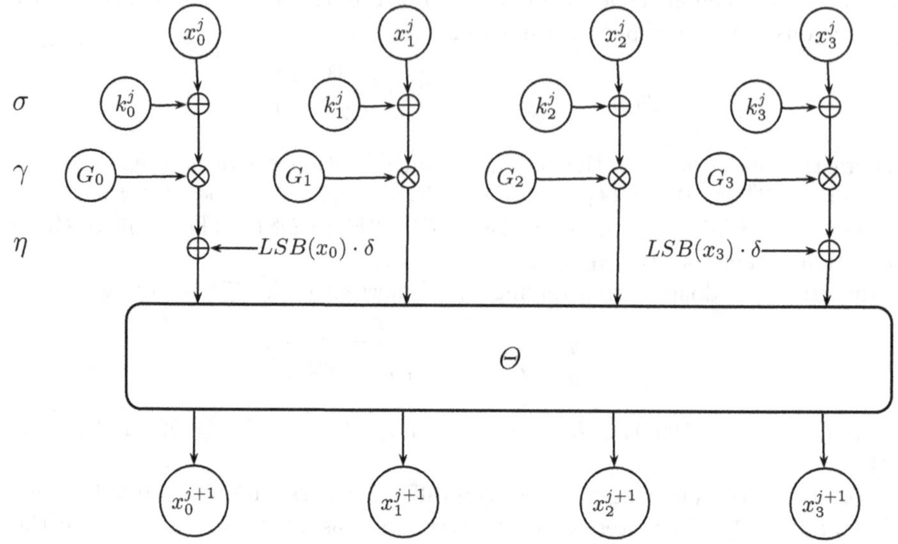

Fig. 1. MMB's Round Function in Round j

2.2 Notations

The notations used throughout the paper are described in Table 1 for the readers' convenience.

Table 1. Notations Used Throughout this Paper

Symbol	Meaning/Value
$\oplus$	Exclusive-or
$\otimes$	Multiplication modulo $2^{32}-1$
$X \rightarrow Y$	Differential transition from X to Y
0	00000000_x
$\bar{0}$	$FFFFFFFF_x$
δ	$2AAAAAAA_x$
$\bar{\delta}$	$\delta \oplus FFFFFFFF_x$
G_0	$025F1CDB_x$
G_1	$04BE39B6_x$
G_2	$12F8E6D8_x$
G_3	$2F8E6D81_x$

Table 2. Summary of the Attacks on MMB

Rounds	Attack	Time*	Data	Memory†	Keys	Source
6	Differential Cryptanalysis	$2^{95.91}$	2^{118} CP**	2^{64}	1	[13]
6	Rectangle-like sandwich	2^{64}	$2^{66.5}$ CP	$2^{70.5}$	1	[7]
6	Sandwich attack	$2^{13.4}$	2^{40} ACPC***	2^{16}	1	[7]
6	Related-key boomerang	$2^{35.2}$	2^{20} ACPC	$2^{20.3}$	4	Section 6
7	Related-key boomerang	$2^{35.3}$	$2^{20.6}$ ACPC	$2^{20.3}$	4	Section 7
8	Related-key boomerang	$2^{35.2}$	$2^{20.6}$ ACPC	$2^{20.3}$	6	Section 7

* The time complexity reported in [7, 13] does not take into account the time needed for generating the data.

** Chosen plaintexts.

*** Adaptive chosen plaintexts and ciphertexts.

† Memory is measured in 32-bit memory words.

3 Previous Attacks on MMB

Wang et al. identified for MMB a 2-round differential characteristic with probability 1 [13]. This 2-round differential characteristic, described in Equation (1) was extended into a 5-round differential characteristic with probability of 2^{-110}. This 5-round differential characteristic can be used in an attack that recovers all of MMB's key bits with data complexity of 2^{118} chosen plaintexts, time complexity of $2^{95.91}$ encryptions, and memory requirements of 2^{65} 32-bit blocks. We note that the time complexity described in [13] does not take into account the fact that the time required to encrypt 2^{118} plaintexts cannot be less than 2^{118}.

$$\begin{aligned}(0,\bar{0},\bar{0},0) &\xrightarrow{\sigma[k^0]} (0,\bar{0},\bar{0},0) \xrightarrow{\gamma} (0,\bar{0},\bar{0},0) \xrightarrow{\eta} (0,\bar{0},\bar{0},0) \xrightarrow{\theta} (\bar{0},0,0,\bar{0}) \\ &\xrightarrow{\sigma[k^1]} (\bar{0},0,0,\bar{0}) \xrightarrow{\gamma} (\bar{0},0,0,\bar{0}) \xrightarrow{\eta} (\bar{\delta},0,0,\bar{\delta}) \xrightarrow{\theta} (0,\bar{\delta},\bar{\delta},0)\end{aligned} \quad (1)$$

Jia et al. [7] improved Wang's analysis to build a 5-round sandwich distinguisher (an extension of the boomerang distinguisher) with probability 1. This attack exploits the 2-round differential characteristic identified in [13] to construct a 5-round sandwich that is then used to recover the full key of the full MMB with 2^{40} adaptive plaintexts and ciphertexts, $2^{13.4}$ time, and 2^{16} memory bytes. They also showed how to transform their attack into a rectangle-like sandwich that can recover the full key of MMB in 2^{64} time, $2^{66.5}$ memory, and $2^{70.5}$ chosen plaintexts.

Table 2 summarizes all previous results on MMB and compares them with ours.

4 Cryptanalytic Techniques for Block Ciphers Used in This Paper

4.1 Differential Cryptanalysis

One of the most notable techniques in cryptanalysis is differential cryptanalysis. Developed by Biham and Shamir [3], differential cryptanalysis examines the evolution of differences between two inputs. An input difference is the difference between two inputs entering a cryptosystem, usually with respect to the exclusive-or operation. The output difference is the difference between the outputs of two such inputs. We say that an input difference Δ can cause an output difference Δ^* under the function f with probability p if a portion p of the possible pairs of messages having a difference Δ result in outputs having a difference Δ^* after applying f. If these conditions hold we write that $\Delta \xrightarrow{f} \Delta^*$ with probability p.

A differential characteristic that describes a single encryption round is called a 1-round differential characteristic. Biham and Shamir showed that two or more differential characteristics can be concatenated to form a longer differential characteristics if the output difference of one differential characteristic is the input difference of the other differential characteristic.

Once a good long differential characteristic is identified, the adversary tries to find a pair of messages that satisfies it. By examining many plaintext pairs, the adversary tries to distinguish the wrong pairs (i.e., those pairs which do not satisfy the differential characteristic) from the right pairs (i.e., those pairs which satisfy the differential characteristic). The amount of data needed to find a right pair is proportional to the inverse of the probability of the differential characteristic used and can be somewhat reduced by various techniques. Once a right pair is found, it can be used to recover the keys used in the cryptosystem by examining which keys cause the messages to satisfy the required differences.

4.2 Related-Key Differential Attack

Since its publication in 1990, differential cryptanalysis received a great deal of attention in the cryptographic community. Several researchers published extensions for the core technique. One of these extensions is the related-key differential attack published by Kelsey et al. in 1997 [8]. In a related-key differential attack the adversary is allowed, in addition to examining the evolution of differences between inputs, to introduce differences to the key. Namely, in the attack, two plaintexts are encrypted using two keys that have some difference chosen by the adversary. This difference is injected into the intermediate encryption values by the key injection operation and sometimes cancel previous differences. Modulo some small technical issues, the remainder of the attack is the same as in regular differential attacks.

4.3 The Boomerang Attack

Another extension to differential cryptanalysis is the boomerang attack suggested by Wagner in 1999 [12]. A boomerang attack uses two differential characteristics of relatively small number of rounds n and m with probabilities p and q, respectively, to construct a distinguisher for $m+n$ rounds.

A boomerang is composed of two differential characteristics $\triangle \rightarrow \triangle^*$ for n rounds and $\bigtriangledown^* \rightarrow \bigtriangledown$ for m rounds with probabilities p and q, respectively.

The adversary chooses two plaintexts P_1 and P_2 such that $P_1 \oplus P_2 = \triangle$ and asks for their respective values C_1 and C_2 after $m+n$ encryption rounds. The adversary then XORs these ciphertexts with ∇ to obtain the ciphertexts C_3 and C_4, respectively, and asks for their decrypted values P_3 and P_4. The boomerang suggests that $P_1 \oplus P_2 = P_3 \oplus P_4 = \triangle$ with probability $p^2 \cdot q^2$.

4.4 Related-Key Boomerang Attack

The related-key boomerang attack is an extension of the boomerang attack first suggested in 2004 by Kim et al. [2,6,9]. The idea of a related-key boomerang is to use two related-key differentials to construct the boomerang. After constructing this boomerang, the attack is then carried in the same way as with regular boomerangs (again, modulo a few small differences).

5 A Related-Key Boomerang Attack for the Full MMB

Before we describe the related-key differential characteristics used to construct the boomerangs we observe that for any plaintext, and any operation, the trivial differential transition $0 \to 0$ holds with probability 1. Another interesting property which is described in [5] is that an input difference $FFFFFFFF_x$ between two input words to $\otimes$ cause an output difference of $FFFFFFFF_x$ with probability 1 (independent of G_i).

Another point worth mentioning is that if the difference between the leftmost or the rightmost words entering η is $\bar{0}$, the output difference must be $\delta \oplus FFFFFFFF_x$. The η operation XORs the constant $\delta = 2AAAAAAA_x$ to the leftmost and rightmost words if their least significant bit is 1. In the event that the difference between two input words is $FFFFFFFF_x$, one of them must have 1 as its least significant bit while the other must have 0, thus, δ is XORed only to one of them, causing the transition.

We present three related-key differentials: The 3-round related key differential $\triangle \to \triangle^*$ with input difference $(0,0,\bar{0},\bar{0})$ and key difference $(0,0,\bar{0},\bar{0})$. This differential is an extension of Equation (1) where we use the key difference to control the propagation of the difference. The related-key differential

$$\begin{aligned}
\triangle = (0,0,\bar{0},\bar{0}) &\xrightarrow[(0,0,\bar{0},\bar{0})]{\sigma[k^1]} (0,0,0,0) \xrightarrow{\gamma} (0,0,0,0) \xrightarrow{\eta} (0,0,0,0) \xrightarrow{\theta} (0,0,0,0) \\
&\xrightarrow[(0,\bar{0},\bar{0},0)]{\sigma[k^2]} (0,\bar{0},\bar{0},0) \xrightarrow{\gamma} (0,\bar{0},\bar{0},0) \xrightarrow{\eta} (0,\bar{0},\bar{0},0) \xrightarrow{\theta} (\bar{0},0,0,\bar{0}) \\
&\xrightarrow[(\bar{0},\bar{0},0,0)]{\sigma[k^3]} (0,\bar{0},0,\bar{0}) \xrightarrow{\gamma} (0,\bar{0},0,\bar{0}) \xrightarrow{\eta} (0,\bar{0},0,\bar{\delta}) \xrightarrow{\theta} (\delta,\bar{0},\delta,\bar{\delta}) = \triangle^*
\end{aligned}$$

holds with probability 1. We can extend this related-key differential by prepending an additional round

$$(\bar{X},\bar{0},0,\bar{0}) \xrightarrow[(\bar{0},0,0,\bar{0})]{\sigma[k^0]} (X,\bar{0},0,0) \xrightarrow{\gamma} (\bar{\delta},\bar{0},0,0) \xrightarrow{\eta} (\bar{0},\bar{0},0,0) \xrightarrow{\theta} (0,0,\bar{0},\bar{0}) = \triangle, \tag{2}$$

where $\bar{X}$ is some undetermined difference satisfying $\bar{X} \xrightarrow{\oplus k_0^0} X$ and $X \xrightarrow{\otimes G_0} \bar{\delta}$.

The second related-key differential we use is a 4-round related-key differential $\nabla^* \to \nabla$ with input difference $(0,0,\bar{0},0)$ and key difference $(0,0,\bar{0},0)$

$$\begin{aligned}\nabla^* = (0,0,\bar{0},0) &\xrightarrow[(0,0,\bar{0},0)]{\sigma[k^1]} (0,0,0,0) \xrightarrow{\gamma} (0,0,0,0) \xrightarrow{\eta} (0,0,0,0) \xrightarrow{\theta} (0,0,0,0)\\ &\xrightarrow[(0,\bar{0},0,0)]{\sigma[k^2]} (0,\bar{0},0,0) \xrightarrow{\gamma} (0,\bar{0},0,0) \xrightarrow{\eta} (0,\bar{0},0,0) \xrightarrow{\theta} (\bar{0},\bar{0},\bar{0},0)\\ &\xrightarrow[(\bar{0},0,0,0)]{\sigma[k^3]} (0,\bar{0},\bar{0},0) \xrightarrow{\gamma} (0,\bar{0},\bar{0},0) \xrightarrow{\eta} (0,\bar{0},\bar{0},0) \xrightarrow{\theta} (\bar{0},0,0,\bar{0})\\ &\xrightarrow[(0,0,0,\bar{0})]{\sigma[k^4]} (\bar{0},0,0,0) \xrightarrow{\gamma} (\bar{0},0,0,0) \xrightarrow{\eta} (\bar{\delta},0,0,0) \xrightarrow{\theta} (\bar{\delta},\bar{\delta},0,\bar{\delta}) = \nabla\end{aligned}$$

that also holds with probability 1. This differential can also be extended by prepending an additional round:

$$(0,\bar{0},\bar{0},\bar{Y}) \xrightarrow[(0,0,0,\bar{0})]{\sigma[k^0]} (0,\bar{0},\bar{0},Y) \xrightarrow{\gamma} (0,\bar{0},\bar{0},\bar{\delta}) \xrightarrow{\eta} (0,\bar{0},\bar{0},\bar{0}) \xrightarrow{\theta} (0,0,\bar{0},0) = \nabla^*, \tag{3}$$

where like in the case of $\bar{X}$, $\bar{Y}$ is an undetermined difference satisfying $\bar{Y} \xrightarrow{\oplus k_3^0} Y$ and $Y \xrightarrow{\otimes G_3} \bar{\delta}$. We list the most probable values of Y's and X's (with their probability) in Appendix A. In Section 6 we show how to use the birthday paradox to construct pairs which satisfy these differences regardless of the exact probabilities.

The third related-key differential we use is a 2-round related-key differential $\tau \to \tau^*$ with input difference $(0,0,0,\bar{0})$ and key difference $(0,0,0,\bar{0})$ that holds with probability[2] 1:

$$\begin{aligned}\tau = (0,0,0,\bar{0}) &\xrightarrow[(0,0,0,\bar{0})]{\sigma[k^4]} (0,0,0,0) \xrightarrow{\gamma} (0,0,0,0) \xrightarrow{\eta} (0,0,0,0) \xrightarrow{\theta} (0,0,0,0)\\ &\xrightarrow[(0,0,\bar{0},0)]{\sigma[k^5]} \xrightarrow{\gamma} (0,0,\bar{0},0) \xrightarrow{\eta} (0,0,\bar{0},0) \xrightarrow{\theta} (0,\bar{0},\bar{0},\bar{0}) = \tau^*\end{aligned}$$

We construct two boomerangs. The first 5-round related-key boomerang is the concatenation of $\tau \to \tau$ after $\Delta \to \Delta^*$ without the additional round presented in Equation (2). This boomerang has probability 1 and can only be used as a distinguisher. Prepending one more round (as specified in Equation (2)) to $\Delta \to \Delta^*$ forms a 6-round related-key boomerang we denote by B_0. This boomerang is depicted in Figure 2.

The second boomerang, which we denote by B_1 is constructed by concatenating the first round of $\Delta \to \Delta^*$ after $\nabla^* \to \nabla$ to form a 5-round boomerang

[2] Note that the key difference for the differential for $\nabla^* \to \nabla$ is the same as for the differential $\tau \to \tau^*$

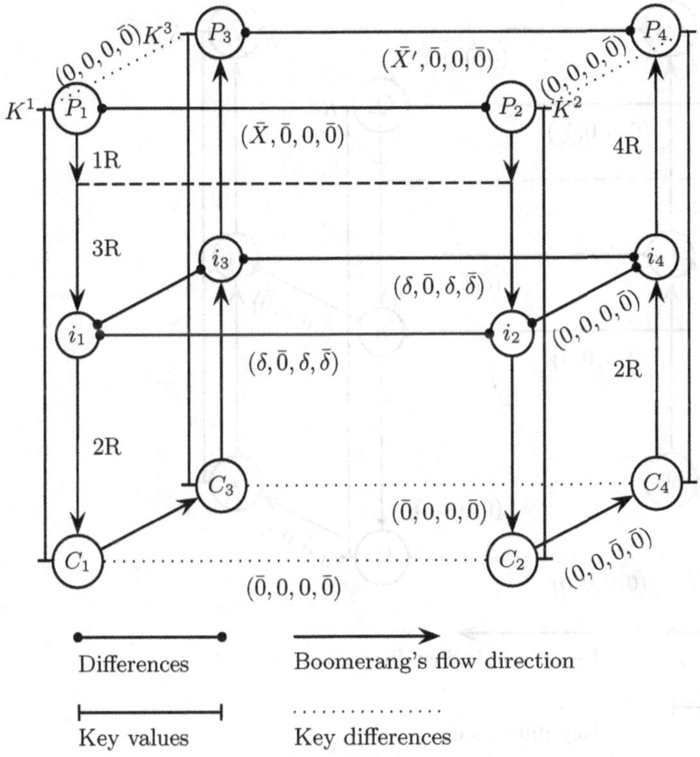

Fig. 2. The Description of B_0

with probability 1. We then prepend one more round (as specified in Equation (3)) to $\nabla \to \nabla^*$ to form a 6-round boomerang that can be used in a 1R attack. The second boomerang is depicted in Figure 3.

6 Description of the Key Recovery Attack

In this section we describe our related-key boomerang attack on MMB and the key recovery phase that is used to recover 64 bits out of the 128-bit key. We then show how to efficiently recover the remaining 64 key bits given the knowledge of the previous 64, for the full MMB. We conclude the section with a description of our experimental verification of this attack.

6.1 Related-Key Boomerang Attack

We recall that the 128-bit key is composed of four 32-bit key words (k_0, k_1, k_2, k_3). We recover each of these words separately. The first 32 key bits (those of k_0)

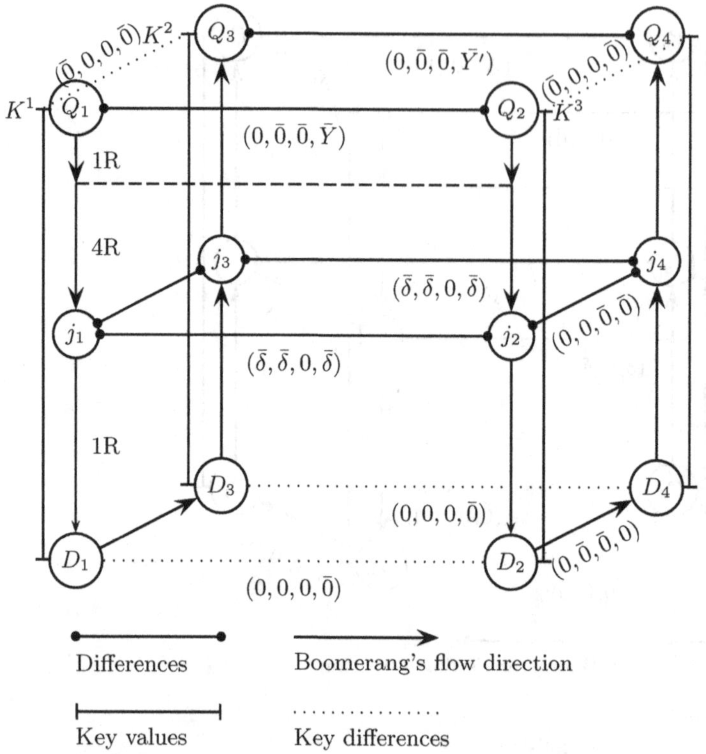

Fig. 3. The Description of B_1

are recovered using the boomerang B_0 and the last 32 key bits (those of k_3) are recovered using the boomerang B_1.

In order to use B_0 we need 4 related-keys. Two of them, namely

$$K^1 = (k_0, k_1, k_2, k_3); K^2 = K^1 \oplus (\bar{0}, 0, 0, \bar{0})$$

are used for encryption and the other two, namely

$$K^3 = K^1 \oplus (0, 0, 0, \bar{0}); K^4 = K^2 \oplus (0, 0, 0, \bar{0}) = K^1 \oplus (\bar{0}, 0, 0, 0),$$

are used for decryption.

We pick a set of 2^{17} random plaintexts $\mathcal{P}^1 = \{P_0^1, ..., P_{2^{17}-1}^1\}$ all having the same value in bits 32–127 and different values in bits 0–31. Then, we generate another set of 2^{17} plaintexts $\mathcal{P}^2 = \{P_0^2, ..., P_{2^{17}-1}^2\}$ where $P_i^2 = P_i^1 \oplus (0, \bar{0}, 0, \bar{0})$. We then ask for the encryption of all the values in $\mathcal{P}^1$ under K^1 to obtain the set of respective ciphertexts, $\mathcal{C}^1 = \{C_0^1, ..., C_{2^{17}-1}^1\}$, and ask for the encryption of all values in $\mathcal{P}^2$ under K^2 to obtain the respective set of ciphertexts $\mathcal{C}^2 = \{C_0^2, ..., C_{2^{17}-1}^2\}$.

We XOR all values of $\mathcal{C}^1$ and $\mathcal{C}^2$ with $(0,0,\bar{0},\bar{0})$ to obtain $\mathcal{C}^3 = \mathcal{C}^1 \oplus (0,0,\bar{0},\bar{0}) = \{C_0^3, ..., C_{2^{17}-1}^3\}$ and $\mathcal{C}^4 = \mathcal{C}^2 \oplus (0,0,\bar{0},\bar{0}) = \{C_0^4, ..., C_{2^{17}-1}^4\}$. We ask for the decryption of the ciphertexts in $\mathcal{C}^3$ under K^3 to obtain a set of plaintexts $\mathcal{P}^3 = \{P_0^3, ..., P_{2^{17}-1}^3\}$, and the decryption of the ciphertexts in $\mathcal{C}^4$ under K^4 to obtain a set of plaintexts $\mathcal{P}^4 = \{P_0^4, ..., P_{2^{17}-1}^4\}$.

We expect, due to the birthday paradox, that two plaintexts P_i^1 and P_j^2, taken from $\mathcal{P}^1$ and $\mathcal{P}^2$, respectively, will collide (i.e., have a zero difference) in bits 0–31 after a single round of $\sigma[k^0], \gamma$, and η with a non-negligible probability.[3] Such two colliding plaintexts form a pair with input difference $\triangle$ as required by the differential characteristic $\triangle \rightarrow \triangle^*$ (the difference in the remaining words is set with probability 1). Since both differentials used in the boomerang hold with probability 1, the encryption, XOR by $(0,0,\bar{0},\bar{0})$ and 5-round decryption of it will inevitably result with a difference of Δ causing its respective P_i^3 and P_j^4 to also have a difference of the form $(\bar{X}',\bar{0},0,\bar{0})$ after the decryption.

Analyzing the expected number of right pairs is straightforward using the birthday paradox framework. The values of $\mathcal{P}_1$ occupy 2^{17} bins out of the 2^{32} possible bins. Therefore, each of the 2^{17} possible values of $\mathcal{P}_2$ has a chance of $\frac{2^{17}}{2^{32}} = 2^{-15}$ to collide with a value from $\mathcal{P}_1$. Hence, the expected number of right pairs (which lead to right quartets with probability 1) is $2^{17} \cdot \frac{2^{17}}{2^{32}} = 4$. In Section 6.4 we test this prediction empirically.

We store all values of $\mathcal{P}_3$ in a hash table using bits 32–127 as the hash key. Then, once obtaining the values of $\mathcal{P}_4$ we search for "collisions" in these bits (taking into account the expected difference between them) to identify a candidate pair (and thus, a candidate quartet). The probability that among all the possible 2^{34} pairs, two plaintexts form a wrong pair (i.e., agreeing on bits 32–127 without following the boomerang) is $2^{34} \cdot 2^{-96} = 2^{-62}$. Thus, we can safely assume that all candidate quartets are right quartets. Note that we do not need to store the plaintexts with their respective ciphertexts, hence, reducing the memory complexity.

Once we identify the four plaintexts forming a right quartet, $((P_i^1,P_j^2),(P_i^3,P_j^4))$, we try all the 2^{32} possible values for $k_0^1 = k_0^3$ and $k_0^2 = k_0^4 = k_0^1 \oplus \bar{0}$ (the first 32 bits of K^1, K^2, K^3, and K^4) to see which of them causes both pairs to have a zero difference in the first word after one round. These 2^{32} trials suggest two possible values as the key word, either k_0^1 or $\bar{k_0^1}$. Note that usually in related-key attacks we expect **one** solution for these cases. However, in the specific case of $\otimes$, complementing the entire input necessarily complements the entire output. Hence, if the two inputs to $\otimes$ are x and x', and a 32-bit key word k satisfies $((x \oplus k) \otimes G_0) \oplus (x' \oplus \bar{k}) \otimes G_0 = \bar{0}$, then $\bar{k}$ also satisfies this relation, as both results are complemented when the value of k_0 is complemented. At the last part of the attack, we encrypt a plaintext using all

[3] As we discuss later, we actually expect four such pairs. Given that the actual number of such pairs follows a Poisson distribution with a mean value of 4, we expect at least one such pair to exist with probability of 98.2%.

key combinations to determine which value is the right key and which value is its complementary.

To recover bits 96–127 of the key we use the same method. We pick 2^{17} random plaintexts $\mathcal{Q}^1 = \{Q_0^1, ..., Q_{2^{17}-1}^1\}$ all having the same value in bits 0–95 and different values in bits 96–127. Then, we generate another 2^{17} plaintexts $\mathcal{Q}^2 = \{Q_0^2, ..., Q_{2^{17}-1}^2\}$, where $Q_i^2 = Q_i^1 \oplus (0, \bar{0}, \bar{0}, 0)$ and use the same algorithm to encrypt the plaintexts under K^1 and K^3, XOR the ciphertexts with Δ^* and decrypt them under K^2 and K^4, respectively. The key word k_3 is then recovered by 2^{32} trials in a similar way to the one described for recovering k_0.

6.2 Recovering the Remaining Key Bits

Recovering Bits 32–63 of the Key. Once we obtained key bits 0–31 and 96–127, we use an extension of the related-key differential $\nabla^* \rightarrow \nabla$ to recover key bits 32–63 with a simple 1R attack. The 4-round related-key differential characteristic

$$\nabla^* = (0,0,\bar{0},0) \xrightarrow[(0,0,\bar{0},0)]{\sigma[k^1]} (0,0,0,0) \xrightarrow{\gamma} (0,0,0,0) \xrightarrow{\eta} (0,0,0,0) \xrightarrow{\theta} (0,0,0,0)$$

$$\xrightarrow[(0,\bar{0},0,0)]{\sigma[k^2]} (0,\bar{0},0,0) \xrightarrow{\gamma} (0,\bar{0},0,0) \xrightarrow{\eta} (0,\bar{0},0,0) \xrightarrow{\theta} (\bar{0},\bar{0},\bar{0},0)$$

$$\xrightarrow[(\bar{0},0,0,0)]{\sigma[k^3]} (0,\bar{0},\bar{0},0) \xrightarrow{\gamma} (0,\bar{0},\bar{0},0) \xrightarrow{\eta} (0,\bar{0},\bar{0},0) \xrightarrow{\theta} (\bar{0},0,0,\bar{0})$$

$$\xrightarrow[(0,0,0,\bar{0})]{\sigma[k^4]} (\bar{0},0,0,0) \xrightarrow{\gamma} (\bar{0},0,0,0) \xrightarrow{\eta} (\bar{\delta},0,0,0) \xrightarrow{\theta} (\bar{\delta},\bar{\delta},0,\bar{\delta}) = \nabla$$

holds with probability 1. With the extension in Equation (3) it forms a 5-round related-key differential characteristic for MMB. i.e., once we know a quartet of values which satisfy Equation (3) (for example, as part of a right quartet in B_1) we can use it as two right pairs with respect to this 5-round related-key differential characteristic.

Let $Q_i^1 \in \mathcal{Q}^1$ and $Q_j^2 \in \mathcal{Q}^2$ be two plaintexts forming a right pair, and let $D_i^1 = (w_6 \oplus k_0^6, x_6 \oplus k_1^6, y_6 \oplus k_2^6, z_6 \oplus k_3^6)$ and $D_j^2 = (w_6^* \oplus k_0^6, x_6^* \oplus k_1^6, y_6^* \oplus k_2^6, z_6^* \oplus k_3^6)$ be their respective ciphertexts. We observe that each of the words $w, x, y, z, w^*, x^*, y^*$, and z^* is the result of the θ operation which XORs three intermediate values. We denote these intermediate values as $a, b, c, d, a^*, b^*, c^*$, and d^*, i.e.,

$$w_6 = a_6 \oplus b_6 \oplus d_6; w_6^* = a_6^* \oplus b_6^* \oplus d_6^*$$

$$x_6 = a_6 \oplus b_6 \oplus c_6; x_6^* = a_6^* \oplus b_6^* \oplus c_6^*$$

$$y_6 = b_6 \oplus c_6 \oplus d_6; y_6^* = b_6^* \oplus c_6^* \oplus d_6^*$$

$$z_6 = a_6 \oplus c_6 \oplus d_6; z_6^* = a_6^* \oplus c_6^* \oplus d_6^*.$$

To recover k_2 we simply XOR the first three words of each ciphertext

$$w_6 \oplus k_0^6 \oplus x_6 \oplus k_1^6 \oplus y_6 \oplus k_2^6 = a_6 \oplus b_6 \oplus d_6 \oplus k_0^6 \oplus a_6 \oplus b_6 \oplus c_6 \oplus k_1^6 \oplus b_6 \oplus c_6 \oplus d_6 \oplus k_2^6 = b_6 \oplus k_0^6 \oplus k_1^6 \oplus k_2^6$$

and

$$w_6^* \oplus k_0^6 \oplus x_6^* \oplus k_1^6 \oplus y_6^* \oplus \bar{k}_2^6 = a_6^* \oplus b_6^* \oplus d_6^* \oplus k_0^6 \oplus a_6^* \oplus b_6^* \oplus c_6^* \oplus k_1^6 \oplus b_6^* \oplus c_6^* \oplus d_6^* \oplus \bar{k}_2^6 = b_6^* \oplus k_0^6 \oplus k_1^6 \oplus \bar{k}_2^6$$

where the values of k_0^6 and k_1^6 are the 64 key bits previously recovered. The adversary then searches for the values of k_2^6 and $\bar{k}_2^6$ that satisfy the equation $((b^* \oplus \bar{k}_2^6 \oplus k_0^6 \oplus k_1^6) \otimes G_2^{-1}) \oplus ((b \oplus k_2^6 \oplus k_0^6 \oplus k_1^6) \otimes G_2^{-1}) = \bar{\delta}$. Taking the second pair of a right boomerang quartet allows discarding a few more of the remaining wrong options.

Recovering Bits 64–95 of the Key. After recovering k_0, k_2, and k_3, the remaining k_1 (32 bits) is recovered by exhaustive search (i.e., brute force).

Analysis of the Full Attack. The first part of the attack allows recovering 64 key bits in $2^{32.4}$ time, using 4 related keys, $2^{20.3}$ memory,[4] and 2^{20} adaptive chosen plaintexts and ciphertexts. The second part of the attack requires running 2^{32} round operations (which are about $\frac{1}{6} \cdot 2^{32} = 2^{29.4}$ full MMB encryptions) with no additional memory and data requirements. The third part of the attack requires running $8 \cdot 2^{32} = 2^{35}$ full MMB encryptions, again, with no additional memory and data requirements. Thus, the overall complexity of this attack is $2^{35.2}$ time, $2^{20.3}$ memory, and 2^{20} adaptive chosen plaintexts and ciphertexts encrypted under 4 related-keys.

6.3 Experimental Verification

The low time, data, and memory complexities of the attack allow verifying it experimentally. The implementation of the attack uses two programming languages: C and Python. The C program was used to implement the cryptographic parts of the attack (i.e. the boomerangs and the key search). Python was used to invoke different modules of the attack and collect data for statistical analysis.

The C program was compiled and ran on a Debian Linux machine using GCC 4.4.5 with the -O3 optimization flag. The program starts by generating a random 128-bit plaintext and a random 128-bit key. It then forks into two processes, one implementing B_0 and the other implementing B_1. The first process generates a second plaintext and a second key with the appropriate differences and replaces the first word of both plaintexts with a random one. It then saves the two plaintexts and encrypts them under the related-keys to obtain their respective ciphertexts. The ciphertexts and the keys are then XORed with the appropriate values and decrypted to obtain new plaintexts. For each such new plaintext, the

[4] We alert the reader that in each boomerang we need to store 2^{18} 128-bit plaintexts from P^3 and P^4, and 2^{18} 32-bit representations of the plaintexts from P^1 and P^2. The ciphertexts themselves are not used in the key recovery part, and thus are not stored.

program stores it for later use. Once all plaintexts are decrypted, the program searches for right quartets. This is done by searching for pairs in which bits 32–127 of the decrypted plaintexts have difference of $(\bar{0}, 0, \bar{0})$.[5]

Once a right quartet is found, the key recovery is done by trying all possible values as the key for the first plaintext word in both pairs and checking which value leads to a zero difference after a single round of $\sigma[k^0], \gamma$, and η. All such values are written into the output file as possible keys. This process is repeated for all quartets satisfying the conditions (i.e., the candidate quartets). The second process does the same with the minor change that it searches for decrypted pairs in which bits 0–95 has difference of $(0, \bar{0}, \bar{0})$ and searches for the forth key word instead of the first.

The Python program was written in Python 2.6.6 over GCC 4.4.5. Once the C program finishes its execution the Python program reads the two output files and invokes another C program that uses the results of the previous phase to recover key bits 32–63 by iterating over all possible key values which satisfy the conditions in Subsection 6.2. The python program then runs another C program that exhaustively searches for the last key word. The program tries in parallel all 8 possible key words combinations with all 2^{32} possible values for the remaining key word. Once the full key is identified in one of the subprograms, the program outputs it and terminates.

6.4 Results of the Experimental Verification

Our experiment included running the program 100 times. Out of these 100 trials, recovering k_0 was successful 98 times (98%), Recovering k_3 was successful 98 times (98%). In 98 of the trials (98%), both k_0 and k_3 were recovered successfully. The key word k_2 was recovered successfully 98 times (98%), i.e., whenever k_0 and k_3 were both recovered, so was k_2. We consider the experiment to be successful in recovering a key word when the Python program returns exactly 2 possible values for that word: the correct one and its complement.

We also tested the actual amount of quartets. Out of the 100 trials, the program found on average 4.06 candidate quartets for B_0 and 4.01 candidate quartets for B_1. This result is perfectly aligned with the calculation we presented in Section 6.1.

The average running time of the program on an i5 personal computer with 4 GBs RAM, running Debian Linux is 196.56 seconds for the first phase and 106.38 seconds for the second phase with standard deviations of 61.47 seconds and 52.19 seconds, respectively. Executing 2^{32} encryptions of the full MMB requires 341.57 seconds. When parallelized over an i5 CPU with 4 cores and terminated on key detection, the average running time of this stage is 504.40 seconds with a standard deviation of 329.01 seconds. Hence, the average total time required for the recovery of the full key is 13.5 minutes with a standard deviation of 4.19 minutes.

[5] Although an implementation using a hash-table is faster in theory, we found out that in practice, the required bookkeeping induces higher overhead than a simple list of values.

Our implementation of the attack presented in Section 5 is available upon request from the authors (via the program chairs, to maintain anonymity). [1]

7 Attacking More Rounds of MMB

In this section we expand our attack to show that even if MMB was extended to 7 or 8 rounds our attack could still be used to recover 64 bits of the key, namely, k_0 and k_3. We first show how to extend the existing boomerangs to cover 6 rounds of MMB, and recover 64 key bits of the 7-round variant. Then, we use the same related-key differentials in different settings to construct related-key boomerangs for the 8-round variant of MMB. Both attacks have been verified experimentally, and can recover the key bits in only a few minutes using a home PC.

7.1 Attacking 7 Rounds of MMB

We start by showing that the related-key differential characteristic $\tau \to \tau^*$ can be extended by one more round and thus, B_0 can be extended to cover 7 rounds of MMB. This extended boomerang can be used to recover k_0 as before.

To attack the 7-round variant of MMB we reuse the previously used differential $\triangle \to \triangle^*$

$$\triangle = (0,0,\bar{0},\bar{0}) \xrightarrow[(0,0,\bar{0},\bar{0})]{\sigma[k^1]} (0,0,0,0) \xrightarrow{\gamma} (0,0,0,0) \xrightarrow{\eta} (0,0,0,0) \xrightarrow{\theta} (0,0,0,0)$$

$$\xrightarrow[(0,\bar{0},\bar{0},0)]{\sigma[k^2]} (0,\bar{0},\bar{0},0) \xrightarrow{\gamma} (0,\bar{0},\bar{0},0) \xrightarrow{\eta} (0,\bar{0},\bar{0},0) \xrightarrow{\theta} (\bar{0},0,0,\bar{0})$$

$$\xrightarrow[(\bar{0},\bar{0},0,0)]{\sigma[k^3]} (0,\bar{0},0,\bar{0}) \xrightarrow{\gamma} (0,\bar{0},0,\bar{0}) \xrightarrow{\eta} (0,\bar{0},0,\bar{\delta}) \xrightarrow{\theta} (\delta,\bar{0},\delta,\bar{\delta}) = \triangle^*$$

which holds with probability 1 by

$$(\bar{X},\bar{0},0,\bar{0}) \xrightarrow[(\bar{0},0,0,\bar{0})]{\sigma[k^0]} (X,\bar{0},0,0) \xrightarrow{\gamma} (\bar{\delta},\bar{0},0,0) \xrightarrow{\eta} (\bar{0},\bar{0},0,0) \xrightarrow{\theta} (0,0,\bar{0},\bar{0}) = \triangle$$

to form a 4-round related-key differential which is used as the basis of the boomerang. We also append one more round to the related-key differential characteristic $\tau \to \tau^*$ presented in Section 5 to form a 3-round related-key differential characteristic $\tau \to \tau_e^*$ with probability 1:

$$\tau = (0,0,0,\bar{0}) \xrightarrow[(0,0,0,\bar{0})]{\sigma[k^4]} (0,0,0,0) \xrightarrow{\gamma} (0,0,0,0) \xrightarrow{\eta} (0,0,0,0) \xrightarrow{\theta} (0,0,0,0)$$

$$\xrightarrow[(0,0,\bar{0},0)]{\sigma[k^5]} (0,0,\bar{0},0) \xrightarrow{\gamma} (0,0,\bar{0},0) \xrightarrow{\eta} (0,0,\bar{0},0) \xrightarrow{\theta} (0,\bar{0},\bar{0},\bar{0})$$

$$\xrightarrow[(0,\bar{0},0,0)]{\sigma[k^6]} (0,0,\bar{0},\bar{0}) \xrightarrow{\gamma} (0,0,\bar{0},\bar{0}) \xrightarrow{\eta} (0,0,\bar{0},\bar{\delta}) \xrightarrow{\theta} (\bar{\delta},\bar{0},\delta,\delta) = \tau_e^*.$$

Using this extended differential, the extended B_0 (namely B_0^e) is constructed by appending the 3 rounds of $\tau \to \tau_e^*$ after the 3 rounds of $\triangle \to \triangle^*$ and prepending the additional input rounds of Equation (2) to form a 7-round boomerang with keys $K^1 = (k_0, k_1, k_2, k_3)$ and $K^2 = K^1 \oplus (\bar{0}, 0, 0, \bar{0})$, which are used for encryption, and $K^3 = K^1 \oplus (0, 0, 0, \bar{0})$ and $K^4 = K^2 \oplus (0, 0, 0, \bar{0}) = K^3 \oplus (\bar{0}, 0, 0, \bar{0})$ which are used for decryption.

The extended B_1 is constructed by appending the first 2 rounds of $\triangle \to \triangle^*$ after the 4 rounds of $\nabla^* \to \nabla$

$$\nabla^* = (0,0,\bar{0},0) \xrightarrow[(0,0,\bar{0},0)]{\sigma[k^1]} (0,0,0,0) \xrightarrow{\gamma} (0,0,0,0) \xrightarrow{\eta} (0,0,0,0) \xrightarrow{\theta} (0,0,0,0)$$
$$\xrightarrow[(0,\bar{0},0,0)]{\sigma[k^2]} (0,\bar{0},0,0) \xrightarrow{\gamma} (0,\bar{0},0,0) \xrightarrow{\eta} (0,\bar{0},0,0) \xrightarrow{\theta} (\bar{0},\bar{0},\bar{0},0)$$
$$\xrightarrow[(\bar{0},0,0,0)]{\sigma[k^3]} (0,\bar{0},\bar{0},0) \xrightarrow{\gamma} (0,\bar{0},\bar{0},0) \xrightarrow{\eta} (0,\bar{0},\bar{0},0) \xrightarrow{\theta} (\bar{0},0,0,\bar{0})$$
$$\xrightarrow[(0,0,0,\bar{0})]{\sigma[k^4]} (\bar{0},0,0,0) \xrightarrow{\gamma} (\bar{0},0,0,0) \xrightarrow{\eta} (\bar{\delta},0,0,0) \xrightarrow{\theta} (\bar{\delta},\bar{\delta},0,\bar{\delta}) = \nabla$$

and prepending the additional input round

$$(0,\bar{0},\bar{0},\bar{Y}) \xrightarrow[(0,0,0,\bar{0})]{\sigma[k^0]} (0,\bar{0},\bar{0},Y) \xrightarrow{\gamma} (0,\bar{0},\bar{0},\bar{\delta}) \xrightarrow{\eta} (0,\bar{0},\bar{0},\bar{0}) \xrightarrow{\theta} (0,0,\bar{0},0) = \nabla^*,$$

thus, forming the 7-round boomerang B_1^e which uses K^1 and K^3 for encryption, and K^2 and K^4 for decryption.

We use the same method as in Section 6 to generate two sets of plaintexts of size 2^{17} each, that differ only in bits 0–31, and another two sets of plaintexts of size 2^{17} each, that differ only in bits 96–127. Then, we encrypt the plaintexts under the appropriate related-keys, XOR them with the required differences and decrypt under the appropriate keys to find right quartets with respect to B_0^e and B_1^e. As in Section 6 we expect two plaintexts, one of each set to collide with non-negligible probability, thus, satisfying the required input differences for $\triangle \to \triangle^*$ and $\nabla^* \to \nabla$. The 32 bits of k_0 are then recovered by 2^{32} trials and the bits of k_3 are recovered by another 2^{32} trials.

This attack uses an overall time of $2^{32.2}$, $2^{20.3}$ memory, and 2^{20} adaptive chosen plaintexts and ciphertexts encrypted under four related-keys.

7.2 Attacking 8 Rounds of MMB

To attack the 8-round variant of MMB we use the related-key differentials in a different setting. We build another boomerang, B_2, which is constructed by appending the 4 rounds of $\nabla^* \to \nabla$

$$\nabla^* = (0,0,\bar{0},0) \xrightarrow[(0,0,\bar{0},0)]{\sigma[k^1]} (0,0,0,0) \xrightarrow{\gamma} (0,0,0,0) \xrightarrow{\eta} (0,0,0,0) \xrightarrow{\theta} (0,0,0,0)$$
$$\xrightarrow[(0,\bar{0},0,0)]{\sigma[k^2]} (0,\bar{0},0,0) \xrightarrow{\gamma} (0,\bar{0},0,0) \xrightarrow{\eta} (0,\bar{0},0,0) \xrightarrow{\theta} (\bar{0},\bar{0},\bar{0},0)$$
$$\xrightarrow[(\bar{0},0,0,0)]{\sigma[k^3]} (0,\bar{0},\bar{0},0) \xrightarrow{\gamma} (0,\bar{0},\bar{0},0) \xrightarrow{\eta} (0,\bar{0},\bar{0},0) \xrightarrow{\theta} (\bar{0},0,0,\bar{0})$$
$$\xrightarrow[(0,0,0,\bar{0})]{\sigma[k^4]} (\bar{0},0,0,0) \xrightarrow{\gamma} (\bar{0},0,0,0) \xrightarrow{\eta} (\bar{\delta},0,0,0) \xrightarrow{\theta} (\bar{\delta},\bar{\delta},0,\bar{\delta}) = \nabla$$

after the 3 rounds of $\Delta \to \Delta^*$

$$\Delta = (0,0,\bar{0},\bar{0}) \xrightarrow[(0,0,\bar{0},\bar{0})]{\sigma[k^1]} (0,0,0,0) \xrightarrow{\gamma} (0,0,0,0) \xrightarrow{\eta} (0,0,0,0) \xrightarrow{\theta} (0,0,0,0)$$
$$\xrightarrow[(0,\bar{0},\bar{0},0)]{\sigma[k^2]} (0,\bar{0},\bar{0},0) \xrightarrow{\gamma} (0,\bar{0},\bar{0},0) \xrightarrow{\eta} (0,\bar{0},\bar{0},0) \xrightarrow{\theta} (\bar{0},0,0,\bar{0})$$
$$\xrightarrow[(\bar{0},\bar{0},0,0)]{\sigma[k^3]} (0,\bar{0},0,\bar{0}) \xrightarrow{\gamma} (0,\bar{0},0,\bar{0}) \xrightarrow{\eta} (0,\bar{0},0,\bar{\delta}) \xrightarrow{\theta} (\delta,\bar{0},\delta,\bar{\delta}) = \Delta^*$$

and prepend the extra input round

$$(\bar{X},\bar{0},0,\bar{0}) \xrightarrow[(\bar{0},0,0,\bar{0})]{\sigma[k^0]} (X,\bar{0},0,0) \xrightarrow{\gamma} (\bar{\delta},\bar{0},0,0) \xrightarrow{\eta} (\bar{0},\bar{0},0,0) \xrightarrow{\theta} (0,0,\bar{0},\bar{0}) = \Delta.$$

The new boomerang, B_2, uses $K^1 = (k_0, k_1, k_2, k_3)$ and $K^2 = K^1 \oplus (\bar{0},0,0,\bar{0})$, for encryption, and $K^3 = K^1 \oplus (0,0,\bar{0},0)$ and $K^4 = K^2 \oplus (0,0,\bar{0},0) = K^3 \oplus (\bar{0},0,0,\bar{0})$ for decryption.

The second boomerang is the extension of B_1^e (namely, B_1^{ee}) where the 3 rounds of $\Delta \to \Delta^*$ are concatenated after the 4 rounds of $\nabla^* \to \nabla$, and the additional input round

$$(0,\bar{0},\bar{0},\bar{Y}) \xrightarrow[(0,0,0,\bar{0})]{\sigma[k^0]} (0,\bar{0},\bar{0},Y) \xrightarrow{\gamma} (0,\bar{0},\bar{0},\bar{\delta}) \xrightarrow{\eta} (0,\bar{0},\bar{0},\bar{0}) \xrightarrow{\theta} (0,0,\bar{0},0) = \nabla^*,$$

is prepended. This boomerang uses K^1 and $K^5 = K^1 \oplus (0,0,0,\bar{0})$ for encryption, and K^2 and $K^6 = K^5 \oplus (\bar{0},0,0,\bar{0}) = K^1 \oplus (\bar{0},0,0,0)$ for decryption.

The same method as before is used when we generate two sets of plaintexts of size 2^{17} each, that differ only in bits 0–31, and another two sets of plaintexts of size 2^{17} each, that differ only in bits 96–127. Then, we encrypt the plaintexts under the appropriate related-keys, XOR them with the required differences and decrypt under the appropriate keys to find right quartets with respect to B_0^{ee} and B_1^{ee}. As in Section 6 we expect two plaintexts, one of each set to collide with non-negligible probability, thus, satisfying the required input differences for $\Delta \to \Delta^*$ and $\nabla^* \to \nabla$. The 32 bits of k_0 are then recovered by 2^{32} trials and the bits of k_3 are recovered by another 2^{32} trials.

This part of the attack uses an overall time of 2^{32}, $2^{20.3}$ memory, and 2^{20} adaptive chosen plaintexts and ciphertexts encrypted under six related-keys.

7.3 Attacking 9 Rounds of MMB

We note that one can use our 4-round related-key differential characteristic $\nabla^* \to \nabla$ twice, to obtain a related-key boomerang distinguisher with probability 1 for 8-round MMB. We note that this distinguisher requires only two keys as the same key differences are needed for the two differentials. Using the techniques mentioned before, it can be easily transformed into a 9-round key recovery attack that retrieves 32 bits of the key in time of about 2^{32} encryptions. At the moment, we are not aware of methods to extract more key bits.

8 Conclusions

In this paper we have used various techniques from the differential cryptanalysis family to break the MMB block cipher. By extending previous results along with a new related-key differential we discovered, we were able to identify three related-key differentials that allowed us to construct two 5-round related-key distinguishers with probability 1. We then used each of these distinguishers as the basis for a 6-round boomerang that is able to recover 32 key bits using 2^{19} data in $2^{19.22}$ time using four related keys. We then used the already recovered key bits to recover another 32 key bits using a simple 1R attack. The last 32 bits are recovered by exhaustive search. The suggested attack can recover all the key bits in $2^{35.2}$ time using 2^{20} adaptive chosen plaintexts and ciphertexts and $2^{20.3}$ memory.

We verified our results experimentally by writing a program that recovers the required key bits in about 15 minutes on a home PC. To the best of our knowledge, though it has been many years since MMB was presented, this is the first practical time attack that recovers its full key.

Finally, we showed that even if MMB had been extended to include 7 or 8 rounds an adversary can still recover half of its key bits using the same techniques, with similar time, data and memory complexities.

Acknowledgement. The authors thank Nathan Keller for his insights and comments, Atul Luykx and Elmar Tischhauser for reading and commenting on early versions of this paper, and Idan Dorfman for his mental support. The authors also thank the anonymous referees for their comments and suggestions. The generous support of the Israeli Ministry of Science and Technology of the first author is acknowledged.

References

1. Ashur, T., Dunkelman, O.: Source Code of the Attack. Available Upon Request (2013)
2. Biham, E., Dunkelman, O., Keller, N.: Related-Key Boomerang and Rectangle Attacks. In: Cramer, R. (ed.) EUROCRYPT 2005. LNCS, vol. 3494, pp. 507–525. Springer, Heidelberg (2005)

3. Biham, E., Shamir, A.: Differential Cryptanalysis of DES-like Cryptosystems. J. Cryptology 4(1), 3–72 (1991)
4. Daemen, J.: Cipher and Hash Function Design. Strategies based on linear and differential cryptanalysis. PhD thesis, Katholieke Universiteit Leuven, Govaerts, R., Vandewalle, J. (promotors) (1995)
5. Daemen, J., Govaerts, R., Vandewalle, J.: Block ciphers based on modular arithmetic. In: Wolfowicz, W. (ed.) Proceedings of the 3rd Symposium on State and Progress of Research in Cryptography, Rome, IT, Fondazione Ugo Bordoni, pp. 80–89 (1993)
6. Hong, S., Kim, J., Lee, S., Preneel, B.: Related-Key Rectangle Attacks on Reduced Versions of SHACAL-1 and AES-192. In: Gilbert, H., Handschuh, H. (eds.) FSE 2005. LNCS, vol. 3557, pp. 368–383. Springer, Heidelberg (2005)
7. Jia, K., Chen, J., Wang, M., Wang, X.: Practical Attack on the Full MMB Block Cipher. In: Miri, A., Vaudenay, S. (eds.) SAC 2011. LNCS, vol. 7118, pp. 185–199. Springer, Heidelberg (2012)
8. Kelsey, J., Schneier, B., Wagner, D.: Related-key Cryptanalysis of 3-WAY, Biham-DES, CAST, DES-X, NewDES, RC2, and TEA. In: Han, Y., Okamoto, T., Quing, S. (eds.) ICICS 1997. LNCS, vol. 1334, pp. 233–246. Springer, Heidelberg (1997)
9. Kim, J., Kim, G., Hong, S., Lee, S., Hong, D.: The Related-Key Rectangle Attack - Application to SHACAL-1. In: Wang, H., Pieprzyk, J., Varadharajan, V. (eds.) ACISP 2004. LNCS, vol. 3108, pp. 123–136. Springer, Heidelberg (2004)
10. Lai, X., Massey, J.L.: A Proposal for a New Block Encryption Standard. In: Damgård, I.B. (ed.) EUROCRYPT 1990. LNCS, vol. 473, pp. 389–404. Springer, Heidelberg (1991)
11. Lai, X., Massey, J.L.: Markov Ciphers and Differential Cryptanalysis. In: Davies, D.W. (ed.) EUROCRYPT 1991. LNCS, vol. 547, pp. 17–38. Springer, Heidelberg (1991)
12. Wagner, D.: The Boomerang Attack. In: Knudsen, L.R. (ed.) FSE 1999. LNCS, vol. 1636, pp. 156–170. Springer, Heidelberg (1999)
13. Wang, M., Nakahara Jr., J., Sun, Y.: Cryptanalysis of the Full MMB Block Cipher. In: Jacobson Jr., M.J., Rijmen, V., Safavi-Naini, R. (eds.) SAC 2009. LNCS, vol. 5867, pp. 231–248. Springer, Heidelberg (2009)

A Probabilities for the Transitions $X \xrightarrow{\otimes G_0} \bar{\delta}$ and $Y \xrightarrow{\otimes G_3} \bar{\delta}$

In this Appendix we present a list of transitions from some input differences to δ with respect to modular multiplication by G_0 and G_3, and their probabilities:

Table 3. Most Probable Transitions for Multiplications in MMB

Input Difference (X)	Probability	$-log_2(p)$
7FBFFB64$_x$	$32768 \cdot 2^{-32}$	17
45440164$_x$	$31872 \cdot 2^{-32}$	17.03
7F3FFB64$_x$	$31744 \cdot 2^{-32}$	17.04
C5440164$_x$	$28032 \cdot 2^{-32}$	17.22
4000C164$_x$	$26912 \cdot 2^{-32}$	17.28
C000C164$_x$	$26336 \cdot 2^{-32}$	17.31
90440164$_x$	$26112 \cdot 2^{-32}$	17.32
88240164$_x$	$26112 \cdot 2^{-32}$	17.32
08240164$_x$	$26112 \cdot 2^{-32}$	17.32
80240164$_x$	$26112 \cdot 2^{-32}$	17.32
00240164$_x$	$26112 \cdot 2^{-32}$	17.32
10440164$_x$	$26112 \cdot 2^{-32}$	17.32
90C40164$_x$	$25344 \cdot 2^{-32}$	17.37
10C40164$_x$	$25344 \cdot 2^{-32}$	17.37
C0014404$_x$	$25024 \cdot 2^{-32}$	17.38
C0014164$_x$	$24992 \cdot 2^{-32}$	17.39
C00A0164$_x$	$24960 \cdot 2^{-32}$	17.39
80012404$_x$	$24576 \cdot 2^{-32}$	17.41
80011C04$_x$	$24576 \cdot 2^{-32}$	17.41
00012404$_x$	$24576 \cdot 2^{-32}$	17.41
00011C04$_x$	$24576 \cdot 2^{-32}$	17.41
400A0164$_x$	$24192 \cdot 2^{-32}$	17.43
40014164$_x$	$24160 \cdot 2^{-32}$	17.43
40014404$_x$	$24128 \cdot 2^{-32}$	17.44
D77FFB64$_x$	$23328 \cdot 2^{-32}$	17.49

25 Most Probable Transitions for $X \xrightarrow{\otimes G_0} \bar{\delta}$

Input Difference (Y)	Probability	$-log_2(p)$
7FFD7FF1$_x$	$17920 \cdot 2^{-32}$	17.87
FFF7FED1$_x$	$16640 \cdot 2^{-32}$	17.97
7FFD7FF9$_x$	$16384 \cdot 2^{-32}$	18
409004D1$_x$	$14848 \cdot 2^{-32}$	18.14
C09004D1$_x$	$14336 \cdot 2^{-32}$	18.19
7FFBF9D1$_x$	$14336 \cdot 2^{-32}$	18.19
5FDED9D1$_x$	$12480 \cdot 2^{-32}$	18.39
400801C9$_x$	$12304 \cdot 2^{-32}$	18.41
7FFBFDD9$_x$	$12288 \cdot 2^{-32}$	18.41
C00801C9$_x$	$12272 \cdot 2^{-32}$	18.41
5FFD79D1$_x$	$12032 \cdot 2^{-32}$	18.44
D41004D1$_x$	$11400 \cdot 2^{-32}$	18.52
775F7FF9$_x$	$11280 \cdot 2^{-32}$	18.53
775F7FF1$_x$	$11280 \cdot 2^{-32}$	18.53
541004D1$_x$	$10632 \cdot 2^{-32}$	18.62
77FDFE51$_x$	$10016 \cdot 2^{-32}$	18.70
FFF7D9D1$_x$	$9984 \cdot 2^{-32}$	18.71
7FDFD851$_x$	$9984 \cdot 2^{-32}$	18.71
C30011D1$_x$	$9760 \cdot 2^{-32}$	18.74
508011D1$_x$	$9632 \cdot 2^{-32}$	18.76
430011D1$_x$	$9504 \cdot 2^{-32}$	18.78
805041D1$_x$	$9472 \cdot 2^{-32}$	18.79
005041D1$_x$	$9472 \cdot 2^{-32}$	18.79
C41111D1$_x$	$9456 \cdot 2^{-32}$	18.79
908011D1$_x$	$9440 \cdot 2^{-32}$	18.79

25 Most Probable Transitions for $Y \xrightarrow{\otimes G_3} \bar{\delta}$

Truncated Differential Analysis of Reduced-Round LBlock*

Sareh Emami[1,2], Cameron McDonald[2], Josef Pieprzyk[1], and Ron Steinfeld[3]

[1] Macquarie University, Australia
[2] Qualcomm Incorporated, Australia
[3] Monash University, Australia

Abstract. In this paper we present truncated differential analysis of reduced-round LBlock by computing the differential distribution of every nibble of the state. LLR statistical test is used as a tool to apply the distinguishing and key-recovery attacks. To build the distinguisher, all possible differences are traced through the cipher and the truncated differential probability distribution is determined for every output nibble. We concatenate additional rounds to the beginning and end of the truncated differential distribution to apply the key-recovery attack. By exploiting properties of the key schedule, we obtain a large overlap of key bits used in the beginning and final rounds. This allows us to significantly increase the differential probabilities and hence reduce the attack complexity. We validate the analysis by implementing the attack on LBlock reduced to 12 rounds. Finally, we apply single-key and related-key attacks on 18 and 21-round LBlock, respectively.

Keywords: Block cipher, LBlock, Truncated differetial analysis, Probability distribution, Log-likelihood ratio, Key-recovery attack.

1 Introduction

With the advent of RFID technology in communication applications, traditional block ciphers are generally not suitable for resource constrained devices. Lightweight block ciphers (with smaller block and key size) are a new class of ciphers designed for such environments. Recently there have been a lot of new lightweight designs, examples include: HIGHT [8], PRESENT [5], PRINTcipher [9], and LBlock [17]. Security analysis of lightweight primitives is currently receiving considerable attention.

Similarly to the other lightweight block ciphers, LBlock has attracted a significant amount of cryptanalysis. For instance, related-key impossible differential attacks were successfully applied to 21 and 22-round LBlock [13,14]. A 16-round related-key truncated differential is exploited to launch an attack on 22-round LBlock [12]. In [15], a 15-round distinguisher is proposed, allowing an integral

* Sareh Emami is supported by the Macquarie University MQRES scholarship. Josef Pieprzyk and Ron Steinfeld are supported by the ARC grant DP0987734. Ron Steinfeld is also supported by ARC Australian Research Fellowship (ARF).

M. Abdalla, C. Nita-Rotaru, and R. Dahab (Eds.): CANS 2013, LNCS 8257, pp. 291–308, 2013.

attack for up to 22 rounds. Zero-correlation linear cryptanalysis of 22-round LBlock is presented in [16]. All attacks published so far require high amount of memory and data.

The standard differential analysis and its derivatives usually follow a differential trail and compute probabilities for known expected differences. Recently differential distribution analysis got high attention in the analysis of block ciphers. These type of attacks typically require lower amount of data in comparision to the standard differential. In the case of lightweight block ciphers, Albrecht and Leander explained in [1], that it is feasible to find the probability distribution of all output differences from one (or more) input difference. In a similar work, multiple differential cryptanalysis using the LLR and χ^2 statistical tests discussed in [3]. However in [1,3] the differential distribution is found for the whole state, which makes the attack possible only on a cipher with a *small* block size. The link between differential analysis and correlations of linear approximations, was exploited in [4] to compute truncated differential probabilities. This method combined with LLR test used to apply multiple differential cryptanalysis on PRESENT.

In this paper we present the truncated differential analysis of LBlock by looking at the difference distributions of the state nibbles independently. After finding a distribution that significantly differs from that of a random permutation, we use LLR statistical test to build the distinguisher. The way we find the truncated differential distribution in the markov model, makes our attack possible on the ciphers with relatively larger states than [1,3]. Additional rounds are added to the end of the distinguisher to be used in a partial key recovery phase. Moreover, by exploiting related key bits in the key schedule, we concatenate additional rounds to the beginning of the distinguisher. Differentials through these beginning rounds have high probability, allowing us to extend the attack without significantly increasing the complexity. We apply the attack on a reduced round LBlock and construct single key and related key attacks up to 18 and 21 rounds, respectively. A comparison with attack complexities from prior work is given in Table 1.

The rest of the paper is structured as follows. Preliminaries are explained in Section 2. A framework to apply the key-recovery attack using the truncated differential distribution, while benefiting the key schedule properties is introduced in Section 3. Section 4 discusses the complexity of the attack and includes the empirical results. Section 5 presents a single-key attack on 18 rounds as well as related-key attacks on 20 and 21 rounds of LBlock. Finally, we conclude the paper in Section 6.

2 Preliminaries

2.1 LBlock Description

LBlock [17] is a lightweight block cipher with a block size of 64 bits and a key size of 80 bits. The design is a 32 round balanced Feistel where the input block is divided into two 32-bit halves, denoted the *left-hand* half (most significant

Table 1. Attacks on LBlock

Type of Attack	rounds	Data	Time	Reference
Related-key impossible differential	22	2^{68}	2^{70}	[14]
Related-key differential	22	$2^{64.1}$	2^{67}	[12]
Integral	18	$2^{62} + 2^{20}$ memory	2^{36}	[17]
Integral	22	$2^{61} + 2^{63}$ memory	2^{70}	[15]
Zero-correlation linear	22	$2^{60} + 2^{64}$ memory	2^{79}	[16]
Truncated differential	18	2^{23}	$2^{68.71}$	This paper
Related-key truncated differential	20	2^{27}	$2^{74.55}$	This paper
Related-key truncated differential	21	2^{30}	$2^{77.56}$	This paper

bits) and the *right-hand* half (least significant bits). Each round includes a key addition, where the round sub-keys are 32-bit values denoted by $SK[i]$. The structure of LBlock is shown in Fig. 1a.

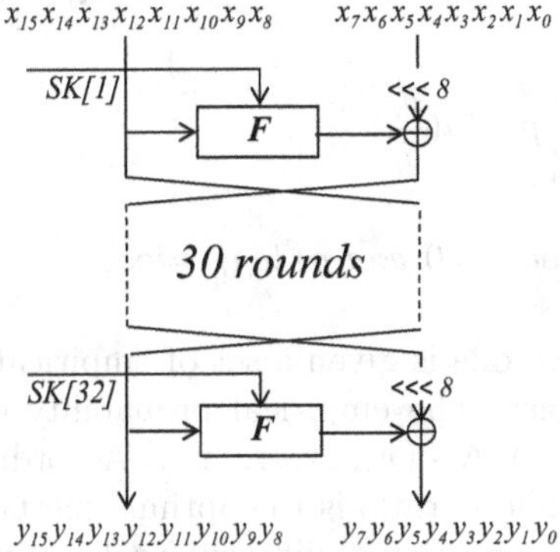

(a) Feistel network

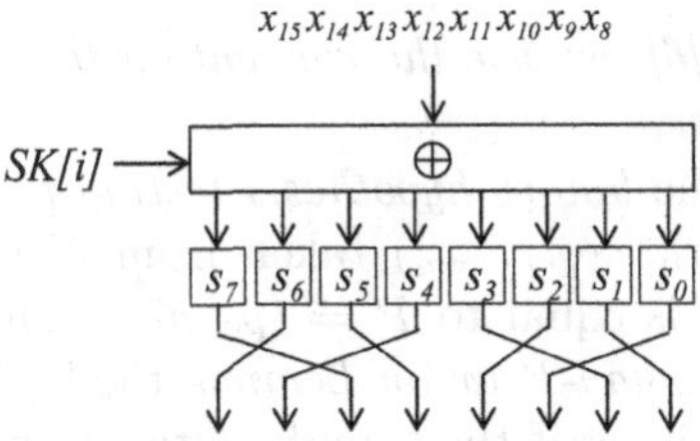

(b) The round function

Fig. 1. LBlock structure

The round function includes a XOR key addition, a nonlinear S-box layer (S) and a linear permutation layer (P). The S-box layer S applies 8 different S-boxes (s_i) in parallel. The linear layer P simply reorders the 8 nibbles in the state. The round function is show in Fig. 1b. Since all the state functions operate on 4 bits, it is convenient to represent the state as a sequence of nibbles using the following notation $\boldsymbol{x} = (x_{15}, \ldots, x_1, x_0)$. LBlock uses a key scheduling function to expand the 80 bit master key K into 32 round sub-keys $SK[i]$, each being 32 bits in size. The master key K is stored in a register, denoted by the sequence of

bits $k_{79}k_{78}k_{77}k_{76}\dots k_1k_0$. The key register is updated by the scheduling process and the 32 most significant bits of the register become the round sub-key. The key scheduling process is as follows:
For $i = 1, 2, \dots, 31$:

1. $K \lll 29$
2. $[k_{79}k_{78}k_{77}k_{76}] = s_9[k_{79}k_{78}k_{77}k_{76}]$ and $[k_{75}k_{74}k_{73}k_{72}] = s_8[k_{75}k_{74}k_{73}k_{72}]$
3. $[k_{50}k_{49}k_{48}k_{47}k_{46}] \oplus [i]_2$
4. Output the leftmost 32 bits of the current content of register K as the round sub-key $SK[i+1]$.

where s_8 and s_9 are two 4-bit S-boxes.

2.2 Likelihood Test

Let $P = (p_0, p_1, \dots, p_n)$ and $Q = (q_0, q_1, \dots, q_n)$ denote two discrete probability distributions of random variables X and Y, respectively. The relative entropy, or Kullback-Leibler divergence, is a measure between two distributions, see [2,6].

Definition 1. *The Kullback-Leibler (KL) divergence between P and Q is defined as follows:*

$$D(P||Q) = \sum_{i=0}^{n} p_i \cdot ln(\frac{p_i}{q_i}) \tag{1}$$

As in [6], we use the convention that $0 \cdot log\frac{0}{q} = 0$ *and* $p \cdot log\frac{p}{0} = \infty$.

In the *binary hypothesis testing problem*, one is given a set of empirical data $x = (x_0, x_1, \dots, x_n)$ taken from N samples. The empirical probability distribution is equal to $\hat{P} = (\hat{p}_0, \hat{p}_1, \dots, \hat{p}_n) = 1/N \cdot (x_0, x_1, \dots, x_n)$. According to the *Neyman-Pearson Lemma*, the log-likelihood ratio is the optimal method for determining if the sample data belongs to one of two different probability distributions P or Q, see [6,7].

Definition 2. *The log-likelihood ratio (LLR) is defined as*

$$LLR(\hat{P}, P, Q) = N \sum_{i=0}^{n} \hat{p}_i \cdot ln(\frac{p_i}{q_i}) \tag{2}$$

If $LLR(\hat{P}, P, Q) \geq \Theta$ (Θ is a threshold parameter), the empirical data is accepted as a sample from the distribution P (rejecting Q as the hypothesis). Otherwise, P is rejected in favour of Q. In our analysis, we use this to distinguish between distributions representing the *right* key and the *wrong* keys which is explained in later sections.

3 Truncated Differential Analysis

The analysis is structured in to the following three phases: Standard Differential phase (SD), Truncated Differential Distribution (TDD), and Partial-Key Recovery phase (PKR). Fig. 2 depicts the range of each phase. SD phase starts from state S_0 with a known input difference $\boldsymbol{\alpha}$, and follows a standard differential trail through SD-rounds up to state S_1 with specific output difference $\boldsymbol{\beta}$. TDD phase calculates the truncated differential distribution from input $\boldsymbol{\beta}$ through TDD-rounds to state S_2 with output $\boldsymbol{\Gamma}$. The output $\boldsymbol{\Gamma}$ here is not a specific difference but a probability distribution over all possible differences. PKR phase involves partial decryption of the ciphertext to determine S_2 from the observed output state S_3. The difference in state S_2 is measured and compared against the expected distribution $\boldsymbol{\Gamma}$.

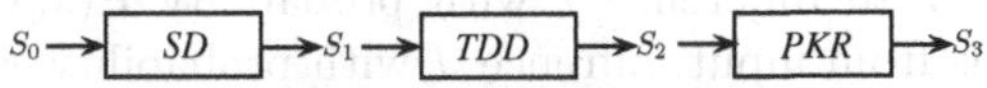

Fig. 2. The attack model

3.1 Standard Differential Phase

The Standard Differential (SD) phase involves finding a high probability differential characteristic through some number of rounds. The XOR-difference between two states $\boldsymbol{x}$ and $\boldsymbol{x}'$ is denoted by $\boldsymbol{\alpha} = (\alpha_{15} \ldots \alpha_1 \alpha_0) = (x_{15} \oplus x'_{15}, \ldots, x_1 \oplus x'_1, x_0 \oplus x'_0)$. Note that α_i represents exact difference of 4-bits, hence $\alpha_i \in \{0, \ldots, 15\}$. The differential trail maps a specific input difference $\boldsymbol{\alpha}$ to a specific output difference $\boldsymbol{\beta}$ with probability denoted $\mathbf{P_{SD}}(\boldsymbol{\alpha} \to \boldsymbol{\beta})$.

For example, let the input difference be $\boldsymbol{\alpha} = (10000000\ \ 00002000)$. A possible output difference, after one round, is $\boldsymbol{\beta} = (00000000\ \ 10000000)$. The probability of this differential is 2^{-2}.

$$\mathbf{SD} : (10000000\ \ 00002000) \to (00000000\ \ 10000000) \qquad (3)$$

The probability is computed under the assumption that the input values of S-box s_7 are not known. If the inputs to the S-box are known, we can detect (with probability 1) whether the differential trail is followed. This requires knowledge of nibble 7 of $SK[0]$. Conversely, given the values of the state, we can find solutions to the sub-key $SK[0]_7$ such that the differential trail is followed.

3.2 Truncated Differetial Distribution Phase

In this phase, we model the difference distribution of *all* possible output differences for every nibble based on a chosen distribution of input differences. This generalisation is the fundamental idea behind truncated differential analysis [10] and all-in-one differential analysis [1].

Computing Truncated Differential Distribution. The round function consists of two components that affect the probability distribution, S-box transformation and XOR addition. Proposition 1, describes probability of differences for each nibble after an S-box transformation, and Proposition 2 shows how XOR addition affect the difference probability distribution.

Proposition 1. *For an S-box $s_n : \mathbb{F}_2^4 \rightarrow \mathbb{F}_2^4$ and input difference probability distribution $\boldsymbol{x} = (x^0 x^1 \ldots x^{15})$, where x^i is the probability of difference i for nibble n, the output difference probability y^i after S-box transformation s_n is calculated as*

$$y^i = \sum_{j=0}^{15} x^j \cdot \mathbf{P}(s_n(j) = i) \tag{4}$$

Proof. Assume the difference J occurs with probability x^J and 4-bit S-box s_n transfers difference J to difference I with probability $\mathbf{P}(s_n(J) = I)$. Hence, difference I happens from input diffrence J with probability $x^J \cdot \mathbf{P}(s_n(J) = I)$. However, difference I might occur from s-box transformation of the other 15 input differences; therefore output difference I happens with probability y^I as $y^I = \sum_{j=0}^{15} x^j \cdot \mathbf{P}(s_n(j) = I)$. The same way is used to calculate probability y^i for every output difference $0 \leq i \leq 15$. □

Proposition 2. *For two input difference probabilities $\boldsymbol{x} = (x^0 x^1 \ldots x^{15})$ and $\boldsymbol{y} = (y^0 y^1 \ldots y^{15})$, the output XOR-difference probability z^i is*

$$z^i = \sum_{j=0}^{15} x^j \cdot y^{i \oplus j} \tag{5}$$

Proof. Assume nibble Z is the XOR-additoion of nibbles X and Y. Difference J at nibble X happens with probability x^J; while, in nibble Y, difference $K = I \oplus J$ happens with probability y^K. By XORing differences J and K, nibble Z has difference I with probability $z^I = x^J \cdot y^{I \oplus J}$. However, difference I might be the result of XORing other 15 differences $0 \leq j \leq 15$ of nibble X with difference $k = I \oplus j$ of nibble Y. Thus, overall difference I happens with probability $z^I = \sum_{j=0}^{15} x^j \cdot y^{I \oplus j}$. For every difference $0 \leq i \leq 15$ of nibble Z probability z^i is calculated with the same way. □

These propositions allow us to construct the differential transformation matrix for the round function; and, given an input distribution, obtain the output truncated differential distribution after a number of rounds. Thus, the TDD phase maps a difference vector $\boldsymbol{\beta}$ to a distribution matrix $\boldsymbol{\Gamma}$. We denote the probability distribution matrix $\mathbf{P_{TDD}}(\boldsymbol{\beta} \rightarrow \boldsymbol{\Gamma})$. For example, let the input difference vector be $\boldsymbol{\beta} = (00000000\ 10000000)$. Table 2 lists the output truncated differential distribution $\mathbf{P_{TDD}}(\boldsymbol{\beta} \rightarrow \boldsymbol{\Gamma})$ for the right-hand half nibbles after 8 rounds of LBlock, calculated using Propositions 1 and 2.

The analysis is more effective if a differential distribution profile is chosen in a way that is easiest to distinguish. More specifically, a distribution that

Table 2. Example truncated differential distribution after 8 rounds

Diff\Nibble	7	6	5	4	3	2	1	0
0	0.0610	0.0654	0.0000	0.0000	0.0667	0.0667	0.0000	0.0000
1	0.0000	0.0592	0.0312	0.0693	0.0625	0.0625	0.0625	0.0645
2	0.0649	0.0620	0.1562	0.0732	0.0626	0.0624	0.0312	0.0635
3	0.0649	0.0619	0.0312	0.0684	0.0623	0.0626	0.0938	0.0649
4	0.0610	0.0608	0.0469	0.0698	0.0620	0.0625	0.0625	0.0654
5	0.0732	0.0646	0.0469	0.0610	0.0626	0.0625	0.0625	0.0664
6	0.0703	0.0657	0.0781	0.0649	0.0622	0.0624	0.1250	0.0654
7	0.0684	0.0604	0.1094	0.0698	0.0625	0.0625	0.0625	0.0688
8	0.0703	0.0588	0.0625	0.0635	0.0617	0.0646	0.0625	0.0649
9	0.0679	0.0663	0.0625	0.0649	0.0618	0.0583	0.0625	0.0757
A	0.0659	0.0627	0.0469	0.0635	0.0623	0.0604	0.0312	0.0659
B	0.0649	0.0626	0.0469	0.0728	0.0619	0.0626	0.0312	0.0684
C	0.0615	0.0615	0.0781	0.0659	0.0621	0.0646	0.0625	0.0649
D	0.0679	0.0634	0.1094	0.0654	0.0619	0.0583	0.0625	0.0728
E	0.0693	0.0591	0.0625	0.0620	0.0626	0.0645	0.1250	0.0630
F	0.0684	0.0656	0.0312	0.0654	0.0623	0.0626	0.0625	0.0654
D(P||U)	**6.59e-2**	**7.37e-4**	**1.81e-1**	**6.59e-2**	**1.55e-4**	**5.6e-4**	**1.46e-1**	**6.57e-2**

is significantly different from uniformly random. As described in Section 2.2, KL-divergence is the most accurate way to measure the distance between two distributions [2]. The last row in Table 2 lists the KL-divergence between calculated probability distribution and uniform distribution for every nibble. Here, U denotes the uniform probability distribution with equal probability $\mathbf{P}_\mathrm{U} = 1/16$. Note, from Table 2, there are impossible differentials in nibbles 0, 1, 4, 5 and 7. This is due to the short number of rounds used in the sample and does not generally occur in longer trails.

3.3 Partial Key Recovery Phase

Similar to a classical differential attack, additional rounds are added to the end of the truncated differential distinguisher. In this analysis, the method for distinguishing is based on the variance between a differential distribution P and the uniform distribution U. From the truncated differential distribution table, we choose one (or more) nibbles with significantly large KL-divergence. This nibble we term the *target* nibble and set P equal to the probability distribution for this nibble. By guessing a subset of the round keys and decrypting ciphertext pairs through the final rounds, we observe the target nibble differential distribution. For LBlock, it is not required that the entire sub-key be known to determine nibbles from previous rounds. For example, we choose nibble 3 (of the right-hand half) as the target nibble. Table 3 lists the nibbles required to decrypt 3 rounds and determine nibble 3. The X signifies nibbles that must be calculated in order to decrypt back to the target nibble. The master key bits are the key bits used relative to the master encryption key at round $n-3$.

Table 3. Nibbles required to decrypt 3 rounds

Round	Left nibbles	Right nibbles	sub-key nibbles	Master Key bits
n-3	- - - - - - - -	- - - - X - - -	X - - - - - - -	79-78-77-76
n-2	- - X - - - - -	X - - - - - - -	- - - - X - - -	34-33-32-31
n-1	- - - - - - X -	- - X - X - - -	X X - - - - - -	21-20-19-18 17-16-15-14
n	X - X - - - - -	X X - - - - X -	- - - - - - - -	

For every partial key guess, we decrypt N ciphertext pairs and count the frequency of each difference in the target nibble. The difference frequency is stored in an array of 16 counters $\boldsymbol{c} = (c_0 c_1 \dots c_{15})$. The corresponding probability distribution $\hat{P}$ for this sample is $\hat{P} = 1/N \cdot \boldsymbol{c}$ which allows us to calculate the LLR for each key guess. The LLR is used to determine if the observed data most likely belongs to distribution P or U. If P is chosen in favour of U, the guessed key is considered a potential solution for the real key. Otherwise, it is discarded.

3.4 Combining SD and TDD Phases

We can combine the standard differential trail of SD with the truncated differential distribution of TDD to achieve a differential profile over an extended number of rounds. However, the expected output difference probabilities of TDD change due to the success probability of each possible SD differential output. The probability distribution of differences resulting from the input difference α can be computed as follows:

$$\begin{aligned} \mathbf{P_{TDD}}(\boldsymbol{\alpha} \to \boldsymbol{\Gamma}) &= \sum_i \mathbf{P_{SD}}(\boldsymbol{\alpha} \to \boldsymbol{\beta}_i) \cdot \mathbf{P_{TDD}}(\boldsymbol{\beta}_i \to \boldsymbol{\Gamma}_i) \\ &= \mathbf{P_{SD}}(\boldsymbol{\alpha} \to \boldsymbol{\beta}_j) \cdot \mathbf{P_{TDD}}(\boldsymbol{\beta}_j \to \boldsymbol{\Gamma}_j) \\ &\quad + \sum_{i \neq j} \mathbf{P_{SD}}(\boldsymbol{\alpha} \to \boldsymbol{\beta}_i) \cdot \mathbf{P_{TDD}}(\boldsymbol{\beta}_i \to \boldsymbol{\Gamma}_i), \end{aligned} \tag{6}$$

where $\boldsymbol{\beta}_i$ are all possible output difference vectors of the SD phase. In Equation (6), $\boldsymbol{\beta}_j$ is the input difference for the truncated differential distribution TDD that has the most distinguishable profile (highest KL-divergence). Usually, $\boldsymbol{\beta}_j$ is the difference with the lowest hamming weight. Also, in practice, all other $\boldsymbol{\beta}_i$ lead to probability distributions that are much closer to uniform (in comparison to $\boldsymbol{\beta}_j$). That is,

$$\sum_{i \neq j} \mathbf{P_{SD}}(\boldsymbol{\alpha} \to \boldsymbol{\beta}_i) \cdot \mathbf{P_{TDD}}(\boldsymbol{\beta}_i \to \boldsymbol{\Gamma}_i) \approx (1 - \mathbf{P_{SD}}(\boldsymbol{\alpha} \to \boldsymbol{\beta}_j)) \cdot \mathbf{P_U} \tag{7}$$

From (6) and (7), the output probability distribution is approximated by

$$\mathbf{P_{TDD}}(\boldsymbol{\alpha} \to \boldsymbol{\Gamma}) \approx \mathbf{P_{SD}}(\boldsymbol{\alpha} \to \boldsymbol{\beta}_j) \cdot \mathbf{P_{TDD}}(\boldsymbol{\beta}_j \to \boldsymbol{\Gamma}_j) + (1 - \mathbf{P_{SD}}(\boldsymbol{\alpha} \to \boldsymbol{\beta}_j)) \cdot \mathbf{P_U} \tag{8}$$

3.5 Dependencies between SD and PKR Phases

From the key schedule, there is a strong dependency between the sub-key bits guessed in PKR and the sub-key bits affecting SD. This changes the success probability $\mathbf{P_{SD}}$. Note there are two S-boxes s_8 and s_9 used in the key scheduling. These S-boxes introduce nonlinear relationships between sub-keys, meaning the PKR key bits are not always directly obtained from SD key bits. We select the SD and PKR phases in a way such that there are as many common bits as possible for the key bits used in the PKR and SD phases.

3.6 12-Round Example

This section gives details about how the analysis is applied to a 12-round version of LBlock. We construct a 9-round differential distinguisher by combining the 1-round $\mathbf{SD}(\boldsymbol{\alpha} \to \boldsymbol{\beta})$ (from (3)) with 8-round $\mathbf{TDD}(\boldsymbol{\beta} \to \boldsymbol{\Gamma})$ (from Section 3.2). An additional 3 rounds are added for the PKR phase (described in Section 3.3). The entire attack structure is depicted in Fig. 3.

To cover the general application of the analysis, we choose nibble 3 as the target nibble for the PKR phase, which does not benefit from the impossible differential. The sub-keys required to decrypt the ciphertext in the PKR phase (i.e. The underlined sub-key nibbles in Fig. 3c) include $SK[11]_7, SK[11]_6, SK[10]_5$ and $SK[9]_2$, a total of 16 unique bits. The sub-key used in SD phase is $SK[0]_7$. From the key schedule we get

$$SK[0]_7 = ((s_9^{-1}(SK[11]_7) \ \& \ \texttt{0x7}) \ll 1) \mid (s_8^{-1}(SK[11]_6) \ \& \ \texttt{0x1}).$$

That is, for a given guess in PKR phase, we determine the sub-key used in the SD phase.

For a chosen input plaintext pair (with difference $\boldsymbol{\alpha}$), we say it is a *right-pair* if it follows the differential SD. Otherwise, the pair is termed a *wrong-pair*. Note that the attacker does not have access to the internal differential states, he only sees the ciphertext pair. For random input pairs, $\mathbf{P_{SD}}(\boldsymbol{\alpha} \to \boldsymbol{\beta}) = 2^{-2}$, and we expect $1/4$ right-pairs on average. Henceforth, we denote the total number of plaintext pairs N_p and the number of right-pairs N. For every guess of key bits in PKR, we determine $SK[0]_7$ and distinguish right-pairs from wrong-pairs (with respect to the key guess). By disregarding wrong-pairs we can increase the probability of the SD phase such that $\mathbf{P_{SD}}(\boldsymbol{\alpha} \to \boldsymbol{\beta}) = 1$. Therefore, from Equation (8), $\mathbf{P_{TDD}}(\boldsymbol{\alpha} \to \boldsymbol{\Gamma}) = \mathbf{P_{TDD}}(\boldsymbol{\beta} \to \boldsymbol{\Gamma})$.

When $SK[0]_7$ is incorrect (due to an incorrect guess in PKR), we mistake a wrong-pair for a right-pair. This false-positive results in the addition of noise to the observed probability distribution. The noise is assumed to be uniformly

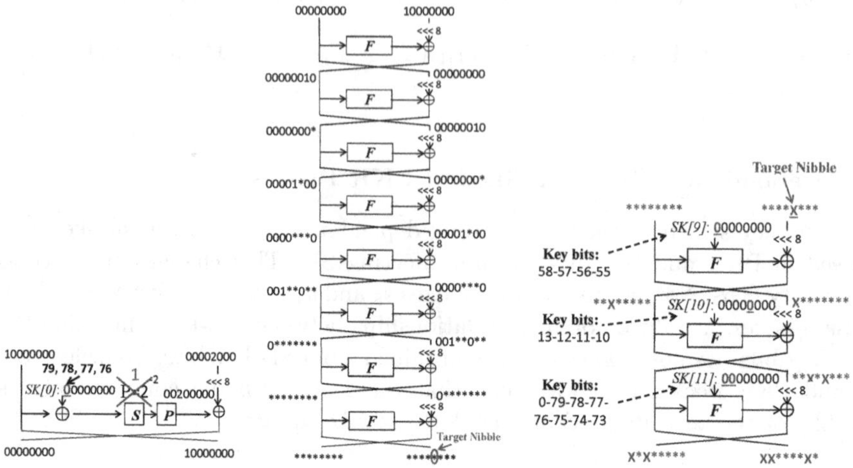

(a) SD phase (b) TDD phase (c) PKR phase

Fig. 3. 3 phases of the 12-round example

random, a similar assumption to the Wrong Key Randomization Hypothesis [11] (explained later). However, this false-positive only occurs for incorrect guesses and does not affect the correct guess distribution.

4 Complexity Analysis

For each key guessed in the PKR phase, we calculate the LLR between the observed truncated differetial distribution and the expected one. If the LLR is above some threshold (Θ), we consider the guessed key a candidate for the right key. The resulting list of candidate keys are checked for correctness. The attack is successful *if* the right key is among the list of candidate keys, we call this the *attack success rate.* In [1], the "gain" of the attack is the fraction of wrong keys ranked above the expected rank of the right key. We extend this concept and determine the expected number of candidate keys and the effort required to find the right key among them.

Assume R is a random variable for the LLR of the right candidate. After decrypting N pairs of ciphertexts, the expected count for the right candidate is defined by $E(R)$ in Equation (9). Likewise, random variable W is defined for the wrong candidates. The value $E(W)$ gives the expected count of the wrong candidate, defined in Equation (10).

$$E(R) = N \sum_i p_i \, ln(\frac{p_i}{q_i}) \tag{9}$$

$$E(W) = N \sum_i q_i \, ln(\frac{p_i}{q_i}) \tag{10}$$

Here N is the number of right-pairs, p_i is the probability of the expected right key that gives the difference i (which is found in the TDD phase), and q_i is the probability of getting the difference by a wrong key. According to the *Wrong Key Randomization Hypothesis* [11], difference probabilities after decryption by a wrong key candidate are distributed as for a random permutation. Our experiments on LBlock confirm the hypothesis for two or more rounds of decryption.

It is shown in [1] that LLR distribution of the right key is approximated by a normal distribution with a mean of $E(R)$ and variance of $Var(R)$ defined in Equation (11). Likewise, the average distribution of the wrong keys, is approximated by another normal distribution with a mean of $E(W)$ and variance of $Var(W)$, given in Equation (12).

$$Var(R) = N\left(\left(\sum_i p_i\left(ln(\frac{p_i}{q_i})\right)^2\right) - \left(\sum_i p_i ln(\frac{p_i}{q_i})\right)^2\right) \tag{11}$$

$$Var(W) = N\left(\left(\sum_i q_i\left(ln(\frac{p_i}{q_i})\right)^2\right) - \left(\sum_i q_i ln(\frac{p_i}{q_i})\right)^2\right) \tag{12}$$

To verify the theoretical findings by experiments, we implemented the analysis on the 12-round example of Section 3.6. We ran the analysis 1000 times with $N = 2^{16}$ right-pairs each, and found the LLR distribution for random variables R and W. Note in this example we guess 16 key bits in the PKR phase, therefore there are 2^{16} candidate keys. Fig. 4b shows the LLR distribution for the right key from the experiments. Likewise, Fig. 4a shows the average LLR distribution of all the wrong keys. The theoretical values describing these distributions are, $E(R) = 10.2242$, $E(W) = -10.0356$, $Var(R) = 20.8225$, and $Var(W) = 19.7064$.

Assume random variable X follows a normal distribution $\mathcal{N}(\mu, \sigma^2)$, where μ and σ^2 are the mean and variance, respectively. According to the cumulative distribution function (CDF), the probability of the random variable X falling into the interval $[x, \infty)$ is (erf is the error function of the distribution):

$$\mathbf{P}(X \geq x) = \frac{1}{2}\left(1 - \text{erf}\left(\frac{x-\mu}{\sigma\sqrt{2}}\right)\right) \tag{13}$$

If Θ represents a threshold for the LLR, $\mathbf{P}(R \geq \Theta)$ gives the probability that the right key LLR is greater than the threshold. Likewise, $\mathbf{P}(W \geq \Theta)$ gives the probability of a wrong key LLR greater than the threshold Θ. Both probabilities are calculated from Equation (13). Since $E(R)$ is the mean for the normal distribution of the expected right key, the right key LLR is higher than $E(R)$ with probability $\frac{1}{2}$. While $\mathbf{P}(W \geq E(R))$ gives the probability of a wrong key being ranked higher than the expected right key. If there are N_K key candidates in the test, N_{wk} denotes the wrong keys ranked higher than the threshold. The expected value of N_{wk} is

$$N_{wk} = N_K \cdot \mathbf{P}(W \geq \Theta) \tag{14}$$

The attack success rate for finding the right key is related to the threshold Θ and N the number of right-pairs (accounting for the SD phase) used in the

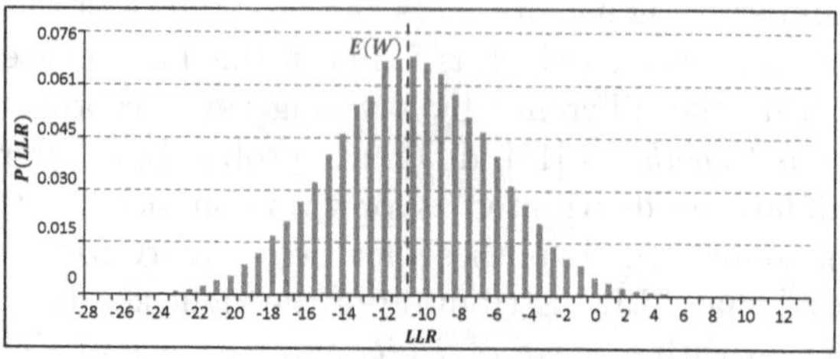

(a) Average LLR distribution of the wrong keys

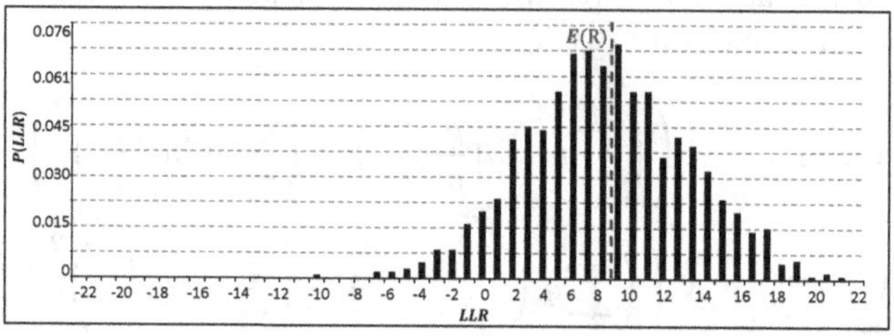

(b) LLR distribution of the right key

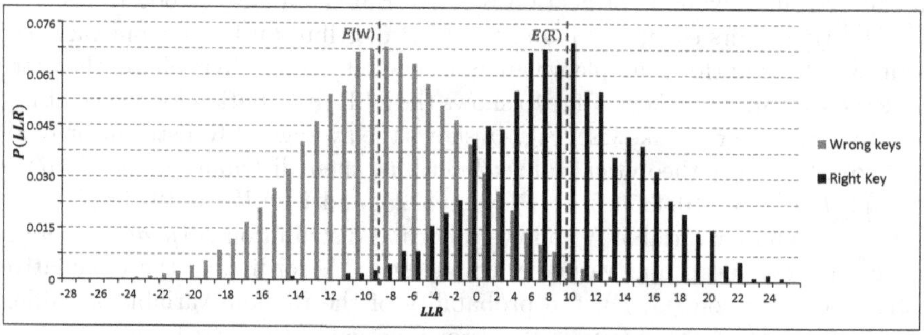

(c) Combined diagrams

Fig. 4. Empirical diagrams of the LLR distributions for the 12-round example

attack. By adjusting Θ and N, the attacker is able to find a higher success rate or a lower N_{wk}.

In the 12-round example attack, we choose $N_p = 2^{18}$ chosen plaintext/ciphertext pairs and expect to get $N = 2^{16}$ right-pairs from the SD phase. We ran the experiments 100 times for each chosen threshold. Table 4 shows the results for different success rates by selecting various LLR thresholds. It is clear in Table 4 that the experiments confirm the theory.

After the partial key-recovery, each candidate key should be checked for correctness to do the full key-recovery. One naive method is to guess the remaining unknown key bits by exhaustive search. Assume b_P is the number of PKR-key bits, then the key-recovery attack complexity is

$$C = N\,2^{b_P} + (N_{wk} + 1)\,2^{80-b_P} \qquad (15)$$

Table 4. 12-round LBlock results for $N = 2^{16}$ right-pairs

Θ	$\mathbf{P}(R \geq \Theta)$	$\mathbf{P}(W \geq \Theta)$	N_{wk}	Empirical $\mathbf{P}(R \geq \Theta)$	Average empirical N_{wk}
2.6189	0.95	0.0021	143	0.94	154.07
5.6610	0.84	0.0002	14	0.87	15.16
7.1821	0.74	5.25e-05	4	0.73	3.68
8.7032	0.63	1.21e-05	0.79	0.61	0.92
10.2242	0.5	2.51e-06	0.16	0.45	0.19

By choosing $N_p = 2^{18}$ plaintext pairs (results in 2^{16} right-pairs) in the 12-round attack, the distinguisher complexity is $2^{16} \times 2^{16} = 2^{32}$. While the whole key recovery attack time complexity is $C = 2^{16} \times 2^{16} + 2^{64} \simeq 2^{64}$ encryptions. Note here, exhaustive key search of the remaining bits dominates the complexity. There are more efficient methods for recovering the remaining bits. In cases where the initial phase is the dominant task, the exhaustive search may be used as it does not significantly increase the total complexity.

5 Key-Recovery Attack on LBlock

5.1 Single-Key Attack on 18 Rounds

Fig. 5 describes the truncated differential distribution attack on 18-round LBlock. We divide the 18 rounds into 3 parts to apply the attack. The SD phase takes the first 4 rounds, the TDD phase consists of the next 8 rounds, and the PKR phase includes the 6 final rounds.

The input state of the 4-round SD phase includes 3 nibbles with non-zero differences in the left-hand half and 5 nibbles with non-zero differences in the right-hand half as shown in Fig. 5a. Through the 4-round standard differential almost all the differences are cancelled. So the output state has difference zero in all the nibbles except nibble 7 of the right-hand half. The TDD phase is very similar to that explained in the 12-round attack. It starts with a low weight state (with only difference 4 at nibble 7). Calculating the truncated differential distribution for the right-hand half nibbles at the output state after 8 rounds, the highest KL-divergence occurs with nibble 5 (i.e. $D(P||Q) = 2.184e-01$). Therefore, nibble 5 is chosen as the target nibble for the 6-round PKR phase. To find the LLR distribution for the target nibble, the attacker needs to guess 52 key-bits in the PKR phase. Observing the SD phase, if the attacker knows the values of 3 sub-key nibbles $SK[0]_1$, $SK[0]_2$ and $SK[0]_3$, he is able to find the output of the 3 active S-boxes in the first round with no extra effort. Likewise, by knowing the values of sub-key nibbles $SK[0]_6$, $SK[0]_7$, $SK[1]_5$ and $SK[1]_7$, he finds the output of 2 active S-boxes in the second round. Overall, he needs to know the values of 28 key bits. These bits are guessed in PKR phase, however going through the key scheduling process the values of bits 73 and 72 are lost.

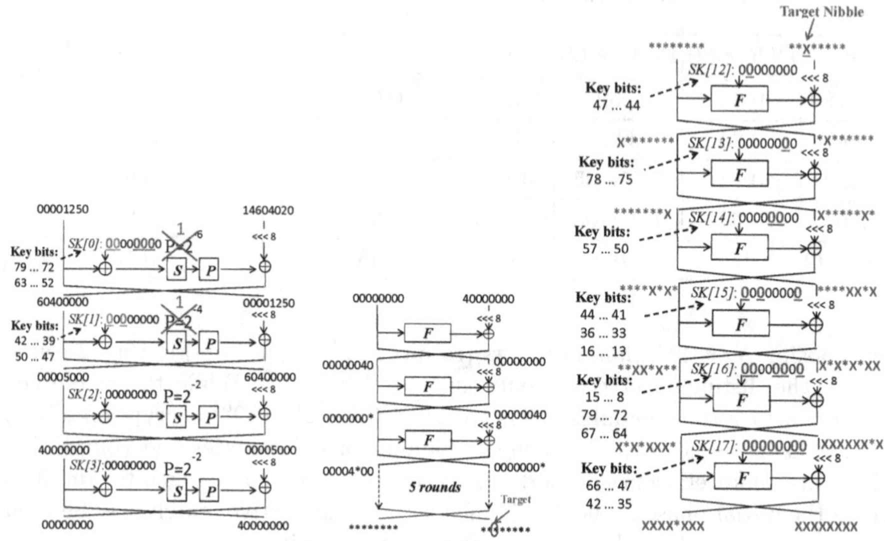

(a) SD phase (b) TDD phase (c) PKR phase

Fig. 5. Truncated differential distribution attack on 18-round LBlock

By re-guessing these key bits and guessing one more (bit 0), all the required 28 bit values are revealed for the SD phase. Therefore, the probability of the SD phase is increased to $\mathbf{P_{SD}} = 2^{-4}$. As mentioned in Section 3.4, difference probability distribution is updated after combining the SD and TDD phases estimated by Equation (6). Probability distribution of the target nibble 5, is shown in Table 5 before and after combining with the SD phase ($\mathbf{P_T}$ and $\mathbf{P_{ST}}$, respectively).

Adjusting N in Equations (9) and (10), the attacker finds $N = 2^{13}$ as the value with the best trade off between success rate and complexity. The statistical characteristic of the right key and the wrong key distributions are as follows: $E(R) = 6.44$, $E(W) = -6.40$, $Var(R) = 12.99$, and $Var(W) = 12.71$. Table 6 shows the result on 18-round key-recovery attack with different chosen thresholds. Note, the number of plaintext pairs includes those satisfying the first two rounds of the SD phase. Therefore, we need $N_p = 2^{13+10} = 2^{23}$ pairs of plaintext/ciphertext to apply the attack. If the attacker chooses the threshold $\Theta = E(R)$, the probability that he finds the right key is 50% and the attack complexity is $2^{68.71}$.

Table 5. Difference probability distribution of the target nibble

Diff	0	1	2	3	4	5	6	7	8	9	A	B	C	D	E	F
$\mathbf{P_T}$	0.000	0.156	0.031	0.093	0.046	0.046	0.015	0.109	0.078	0.109	0.031	0.062	0.093	0.031	0.046	0.046
$\mathbf{P_{ST}}$	0.058	0.068	0.060	0.064	0.061	0.061	0.059	0.065	0.063	0.065	0.060	0.062	0.064	0.060	0.061	0.061

Table 6. Analysis results of 18-round LBlock for 2^{23} plaintext pairs

Θ	$\mathbf{P}(R \geq \Theta)$	$\mathbf{P}(W \geq \Theta)$	N_{wk}	Time Complexity
1.043	0.93	0.018	6.62e+14	$2^{74.25}$
2.245	0.87	0.007	2.75e+14	$2^{73.01}$
3.446	0.79	0.002	1.033e+14	$2^{71.67}$
4.647	0.69	0.0009	3.49e+13	$2^{70.31}$
6.449	0.5	0.0001	5.63e+12	$2^{68.71}$

5.2 Related-Key Attack on 20 and 21 Rounds

The related key truncated differential distribution attack applies to LBlock reduced to 20 and 21 rounds. Considering the key scheduling process, when the key difference goes through the S-boxes s_8 or s_9 the output difference is unknown. However, due to the slow avalanche effect of the key schedule, it takes multiple rounds for key differences to reach these S-boxes. Therefore, it is easy to find the truncated difference probability distribution for all the possible key differentials.

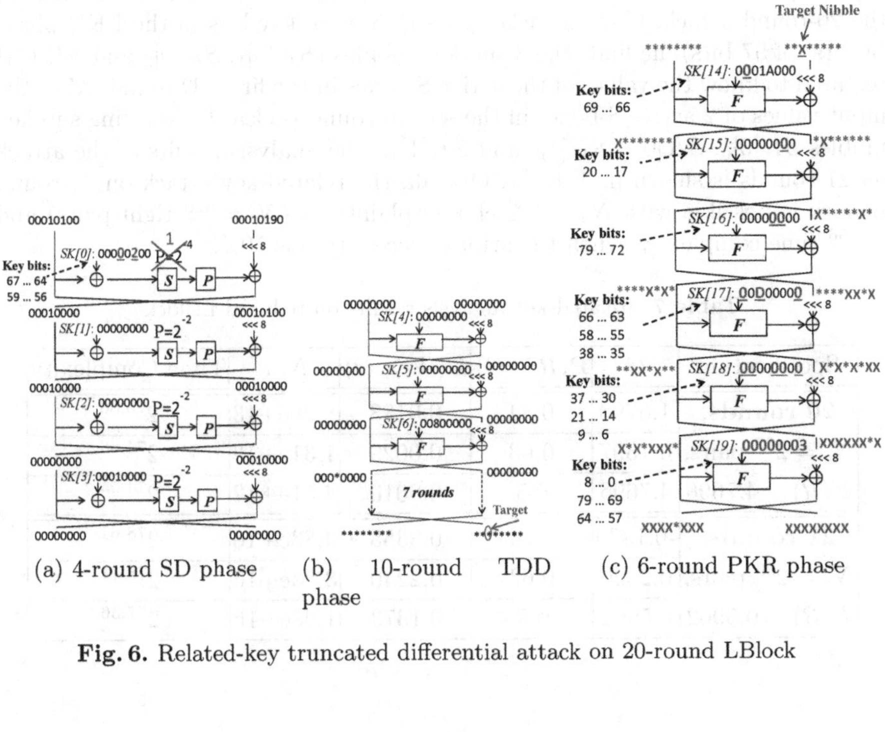

(a) 4-round SD phase (b) 10-round TDD phase (c) 6-round PKR phase

Fig. 6. Related-key truncated differential attack on 20-round LBlock

During the attack, we test each expected key differential in parallel to determine the correct key differential path.

The related key attack on 20 rounds consists of a 4-round SD phase, 10-round TDD, and 6-round PKR phase (see Fig. 6). The SD phase starts with 5 non-zero differences which are all cancelled through the 4 rounds differential trail, finishing with no difference in the output state. The key-register at the first round of the TDD phase has difference in just one bit (the 13th least significant bit). The key difference does not affect the round sub-keys for two rounds. The truncated differential distribution is calculated for the 10-round TDD phase. Nibble 5 (of the output right-hand half) has the highest KL-divergence $D(P||Q) = 2.189429e{-}03$ and is chosen as the target nibble. Finally, 6 final rounds are added as the PKR phase, requiring 52 key bits be guessed to reach the target nibble. From these key bits, two sub-key nibbles $SK[0]_2$ and $SK[0]_4$ are determined for the first round of the SD phase. Consequently, the input values of the active S-boxes are known in the first round and the overall probability of the SD phase increases to $\mathbf{P_{SD}} = 2^{-6}$.

Table 7, shows the results for the 20-round related key attack with different success rates. Note that the number of plaintext/ciphertext pairs includes the amount required to follow the SD phase. Considering the LLR threshold equal to the expected value of the right key ($E(R)$), with 2^{27} chosen plaintexts ($N = 2^{23}$ right-pairs), the complexity of the key recovery attack is $2^{74.55}$.

The related-key attack is extended to 21 rounds by adding one more round to the beginning of the SD phase in the above 20-round attack. Fig. 7 shows the SD phase in 21-round attack. The other phases are similar to the ones in the 20-round attack. If the attacker guesses 5 more key bits in the PKR phase (a total of 57 bits), he finds the 3 sub-key nibbles ($SK[0]_1$, $SK[0]_2$ and $SK[0]_4$) required to know the values of the active S-boxes in the first SD round. Also, the input values of 2 active S-boxes in the second round is clear by knowing sub-key nibbles $SK[0]_0$, $SK[0]_5$, $SK[1]_2$ and $SK[1]_4$. The analysis results of the attack on 21 rounds is shown in Table 7. Overall, the related-key attack on 21-round LBlock is possible with $N_p = 2^{30}$ chosen plaintexts ($N = 2^{20}$ right-pairs) and $2^{77.56}$ time complexity, when the attack success rate is 50%.

Table 7. Related-key analysis results on reduced LBlock

Specification	Θ	$\mathbf{P}(R \geq \Theta)$	$\mathbf{P}(W \geq \Theta)$	N_{wk}	Time Complexity
20 rounds,	1.6798	0.84	0.0183	8.28e+13	$2^{75.36}$
$N_p = 2^{27}$ pairs,	3.7397	0.63	0.0029	1.31e+13	$2^{74.66}$
$E(R) = 4.7696$	4.7696	0.5	0.0010	4.51e+12	$2^{74.55}$
21 rounds,	-0.1320	0.74	0.3355	4.83e+16	$2^{78.61}$
$N_p = 2^{30}$ pairs,	0.2320	0.63	0.2240	3.23e+16	$2^{78.11}$
$E(R) = 0.5962$	0.5962	0.5	0.1373	1.98e+16	$2^{77.56}$

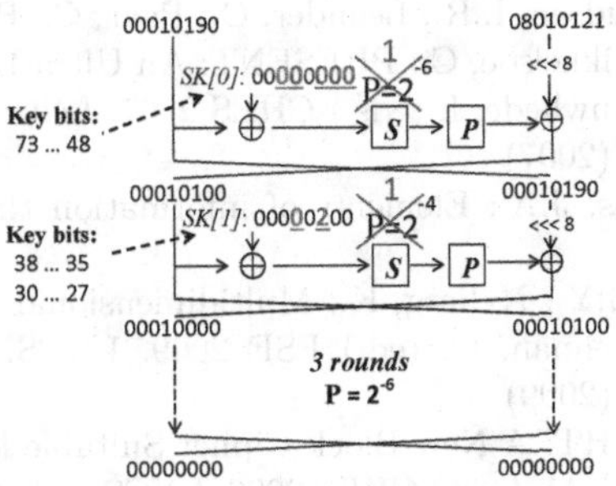

Fig. 7. The SD phase of the 21-round related-key attack

6 Conclusion

In this paper we presented truncated differential analysis of block cipher LBlock by analysing probability distribution of the truncated differences. Also we used LLR statistical test to employ the key-recovery attacks. The attack uses a distinguisher based on truncated differential distribution that are significantly different from a random permutation. Candidate sub-keys are guessed over several final rounds and the observed differences are measured against the expected distribution. We extend the distinguisher by concatenating additional rounds to the beginning which follow a classical differential characteristic. By exploiting the properties of the key schedule, we greatly increase the probabilities of differentials passing through the beginning rounds. We verified the analysis by implementing an example attack on 12-round LBlock and provide empirical data conforming the theory. Finally, we describe single-key and related-key attacks on LBlock reduced to 18 and 21 rounds, respectively. Finding probability distribution of the truncated differential, our attack can be applied on the ciphers with relatively large block size.

References

1. Albrecht, M.R., Leander, G.: An all-in-one approach to differential cryptanalysis for small block ciphers. In: Knudsen, L.R., Wu, H. (eds.) SAC 2012. LNCS, vol. 7707, pp. 1–15. Springer, Heidelberg (2013)
2. Baignères, T., Junod, P., Vaudenay, S.: How far can we go beyond linear cryptanalysis? In: Lee, P.J. (ed.) ASIACRYPT 2004. LNCS, vol. 3329, pp. 432–450. Springer, Heidelberg (2004)
3. Blondeau, C., Gérard, B., Nyberg, K.: Multiple differential cryptanalysis using LLR and χ^2 statistics. In: Visconti, I., De Prisco, R. (eds.) SCN 2012. LNCS, vol. 7485, pp. 343–360. Springer, Heidelberg (2012)
4. Blondeau, C., Nyberg, K.: New links between differential and linear cryptanalysis. In: Johansson, T., Nguyen, P.Q. (eds.) EUROCRYPT 2013. LNCS, vol. 7881, pp. 388–404. Springer, Heidelberg (2013)

5. Bogdanov, A.A., Knudsen, L.R., Leander, G., Paar, C., Poschmann, A., Robshaw, M.J.B., Seurin, Y., Vikkelsoe, C.: PRESENT: An Ultra-Lightweight Block Cipher. In: Paillier, P., Verbauwhede, I. (eds.) CHES 2007. LNCS, vol. 4727, pp. 450–466. Springer, Heidelberg (2007)
6. Cover, T.M., Thomas, J.A.: Elements of information theory. Wiley-Interscience, New York (1991)
7. Hermelin, M., Cho, J.Y., Nyberg, K.: Multidimensional extension of Matsui's algorithm 2. In: Dunkelman, O. (ed.) FSE 2009. LNCS, vol. 5665, pp. 209–227. Springer, Heidelberg (2009)
8. Hong, D., et al.: HIGHT: A New Block Cipher Suitable for Low-Resource Device. In: Goubin, L., Matsui, M. (eds.) CHES 2006. LNCS, vol. 4249, pp. 46–59. Springer, Heidelberg (2006)
9. Knudsen, L., Leander, G., Poschmann, A., Robshaw, M.J.B.: PRINTcipher: A Block Cipher for IC-Printing. In: Mangard, S., Standaert, F.-X. (eds.) CHES 2010. LNCS, vol. 6225, pp. 16–32. Springer, Heidelberg (2010)
10. Knudsen, L.R.: Truncated and higher order differentials. In: Preneel, B. (ed.) FSE 1994. LNCS, vol. 1008, pp. 196–211. Springer, Heidelberg (1995)
11. Lai, X., Massey, J.L., Murphy, S.: Markov ciphers and differential cryptanalysis. In: Davies, D.W. (ed.) EUROCRYPT 1991. LNCS, vol. 547, pp. 17–38. Springer, Heidelberg (1991)
12. Liu, S., Gong, Z., Wang, L.: Improved related-key differential attacks on reduced-round LBlock. In: Chim, T.W., Yuen, T.H. (eds.) ICICS 2012. LNCS, vol. 7618, pp. 58–69. Springer, Heidelberg (2012)
13. Liu, Y., Gu, D., Liu, Z., Li, W.: Impossible differential attacks on reduced-round LBlock. In: Ryan, M.D., Smyth, B., Wang, G. (eds.) ISPEC 2012. LNCS, vol. 7232, pp. 97–108. Springer, Heidelberg (2012)
14. Minier, M., Naya-Plasencia, M.: A related key impossible differential attack against 22 rounds of the lightweight block cipher LBlock. Information Processing Letters 112(16), 624–629 (2012)
15. Sasaki, Y., Wang, L.: Comprehensive study of integral analysis on 22-round LBlock. In: Kwon, T., Lee, M.-K., Kwon, D. (eds.) ICISC 2012. LNCS, vol. 7839, pp. 156–169. Springer, Heidelberg (2013)
16. Soleimany, H., Nyberg, K.: Zero-correlation linear cryptanalysis of reduced-round LBlock. In: International Workshop on Coding and Cryptography, WCC 2013 (2013)
17. Wu, W., Zhang, L.: LBlock: A Lightweight Block Cipher. In: Lopez, J., Tsudik, G. (eds.) ACNS 2011. LNCS, vol. 6715, pp. 327–344. Springer, Heidelberg (2011)

How to Update Documents *Verifiably* in Searchable Symmetric Encryption

Kaoru Kurosawa and Yasuhiro Ohtaki

Ibaraki University, Japan
{kurosawa,y.ohtaki}@mx.ibaraki.ac.jp

Abstract. In a searchable symmetric encryption (SSE) scheme, a client can store encrypted documents to a server in such way that he can later retrieve the encrypted documents which contain a specific keyword, keeping the keyword and the documents secret. In this paper, we show how to update (modify, delete and add) documents in a *verifiable* way. Namely the client can detect any cheating behavior of malicious servers. We then prove that our scheme is UC-secure in the standard model.

Keywords: keyword search, searchable symmetric encryption, update, verifiable.

1 Introduction

We consider a scheme such as follows [15]: a client stores some files D_i in an encrypted form C_i on a remote server in the store phase. Later, in the search phase, the client can efficiently retrieve the encrypted files containing specific keywords w, keeping the keywords themselves secret and not jeopardizing the security of the remotely stored files. Such a scheme is called a searchable symmetric encryption (SSE) scheme because a symmetric key encryption scheme is used to encrypt files. (For example, a client may want to store old email messages encrypted on a server managed by Google or another large vendor, and later retrieve certain messages while traveling with a mobile device.)

The notion of SSE schemes was introduced by Song et al. [25]. Then after a series of works [25, 17, 1, 15], Curtmola, et al. [10, 11] gave a rigorous definition of privacy against passive adversaries. Namely a server is an advresary who is honest but curious. They then showed two schemes, SSE-1 and SSE2-2, where SSE-1 is more efficient than SSE-2, and SSE-2 is more secure than SSE-1. In particular, SSE-2 is secure against adaptive chosen keyword attacks.

On the other hand, Kurosawa et al. [21] considered a case such that the server is malicious. A malicious server may delete some encrypted files to save her memory space, for example. Even if the server is honest, a virus, worm, trojan horse or a software bug may delete, forge or swap some encrypted files. An adversary would then make a profit if the files are related to bank accounts, tax or some critical information. They [21] then showed a *verifiable* SSE scheme in which the client can detect any cheating behavior of malicious servers.

M. Abdalla, C. Nita-Rotaru, and R. Dahab (Eds.): CANS 2013, LNCS 8257, pp. 309–328, 2013.

In fact, Kurosawa et al. [21] proved that their scheme is UC-secure, where UC (universal composability) is a very strong notion of security. In the UC framework [7–9], the security of a protocol is maintained under a general protocol composition. Therefore their SSE scheme [21] is secure even when it is composed with itself and/or other cryptographic protocols and primitives.

Recently Kamara et al. [23] constructed a *dynamic* SSE scheme such that the client can add and delete documents. They then proved that their scheme is secure against adaptive chosen keyword attacks. Further the search time is sublinear. Subsequently Kamara et al. [22] showed a parallel and dynamic SSE scheme. However, these dynamic schemes [23, 22] are not verifiable. Namely the client cannot detect cheating behavior of malicious servers. (Also the security holds in the random oracle model only.)

In this paper, we first show a more efficient verifiable SSE scheme than Kurosawa et al. [21]. In this scheme, the client sends only $n + 128$ bits in the search phase while $(\log n + \ell + 1) \times n$ bits must be sent in [21], where n is the number of documents and ℓ is the bit length of each keyword.

Table 1. Comparison with The Previous Works

	Curtmola et al. [10]	Kurosawa et al. [21]	Kamara et al. [23, 22]	This paper
Verifiability	×	○	×	○
Dynamic (Update)	×	×	○	○

We next extend our verifiable SSE scheme to a *verifiable dynamic* SSE scheme. Namely the client can update (modify, delete and add) documents, and he can detect any cheating behavior of malicious servers. See Table 1 for the comparison with the previous works.

We illustrate our idea of the construction by using an example. Suppose that the client wants to search on a keyword *Austin*, and *Austin* is included in three documents D_1, D_3, D_5 whose ciphetexts are C_1, C_3, C_5. In the verifiable SSE scheme of [21], the client sends a query $t(Austin)$ to the server, and the server returns (C_1, C_3, C_5) together with $tag = \mathtt{MAC}(t(Austin), (C_1, C_3, C_5))$, where $t(Austin)$ is some trapdoor information. Namely the client authenticates the whole communication sequence, $t(Austin)$ and (C_1, C_3, C_5). He then stores the authenticator, tag, on the server in the store phase.

In this scheme, however, the client cannot modify C_i efficiently. For example, suppose that C_1 includes two keywords, *Austin* and *Washington*. To modify C_1 to C_1', the client must store two updated authenticators, $\mathtt{MAC}(t(Austin), (C_1', C_3, C_5))$ and $\mathtt{MAC}(t(Washington), (C_1', \cdots))$, to the server in the update phase. If C_1 includes more keywords, then the client must updates more authenticators.

Now our idea is that the client authenticates only $(t(Austin), 1, 3, 5)$. He separately authenticates each (i, C_i) also. Then to update C_1 to C_1', the client stores just an authenticator on $(1, C_1')$ to the server. The update cost is only this no matter how many keywords are included in C_1. Thus the client can update each C_i efficiently.

To delete a document C_1, the client updates it to a special symbol $C_1' = delete$ similarly. To add a new document D_6 which includes *Austin*, the client updates the authenticator on $(t(Austin), 1, 3, 5)$ to that on $(t(Austin), 1, 3, 5, 6)$.

Finally, we prove that our verifiable dynamic SSE scheme is UC-secure in the standard model.

1.1 Related Work

Conjunctive keyword search in the SSE setting was first considered by Golle et al. [19]. In their scheme, a client specifies at most one keyword in each keyword field. This framework was followed up by [3, 4]. Wang et al. [26] gave a scheme which does not have such a structure. Recently Cash et al. [12] showed a keyword field free scheme which can support general Boolean queries.

Chase et al. [13] extended and generalized the security model of SSE schemes to complex data (e.g., graphs) and introduced the notion of associated data that allows to compose different components of the protocol.

2 Verifiable Searchable Symmetric Encryption

If X is a string, then $|X|$ denotes the bit length of X. $[X]_{1..u}$ denotes the first u bits of X, and $[X]_u$ denotes the uth bit of X. If X is a set, then $|X|$ denotes the cardinality of X. PPT means probabilistic polynomial time.

2.1 Verifiable SSE Scheme

Let $\mathcal{D} = \{D_1, \cdots, D_n\}$ be a set of documents and $\mathcal{W} = \{w_1, \cdots, w_m\}$ be a set of keywords. Let $\texttt{Index} = \{e_{i,j}\}$ be an $m \times n$ binary matrix such that

$$e_{i,j} = \begin{cases} 1 \text{ if } w_i \text{ is contained in } D_j \\ 0 \text{ } otherwise \end{cases}. \tag{1}$$

Let $\texttt{D}(w)$ denote the set of documents which contain a keyword $w \in \mathcal{W}$. Also let $\texttt{List}(w) = \{i \mid D_i \text{ contains } w\}$.

A verifiable SSE scheme is a protocol between a client and a server as follows.

(Store phase)

On input $(\mathcal{D}, \mathcal{W}, \texttt{Index})$, the client sends $(\mathcal{C}, \mathcal{I})$ to the server, where $\mathcal{C} = (C_1, \cdots, C_n)$ is the set of encrypted documents, and $\mathcal{I}$ is an encrypted Index.

(Search phase)

1. On input a keyword $w \in \mathcal{W}$, the client sends a trapdoor information $t(w)$ to the server.
2. The server somehow computes $\texttt{C}(w) = \{C_i \mid D_i \text{ contains } w\}$, and returns $(\texttt{C}(w), Tag)$ to the client, where Tag is an authenticator.

Real Game ($\texttt{Game}_{real}$)

- In the store phase, an adversary **A** chooses $(\mathcal{D}, \mathcal{W}, \texttt{Index})$ and sends them to the challenger. The challenger returns $(\mathcal{I}, \mathcal{C})$.
- In the search phase, for $i = 1, \cdots, q$,
  1. **A** chooses a keyword $w_{a_i} \in \mathcal{W}$ and sends it to the challenger.
  2. The challenger returns a trapdoor information $t(w_{a_i})$ to **A**.
- Finally **A** outputs a bit b.

Fig. 1. Real Game: $\texttt{Game}_{real}$

3. The client verifies the validity of $(\texttt{C}(w), Tag)$. If he accepts, then he decrypts each $C_i \in \texttt{C}(w)$, and outputs $\texttt{D}(w) = \{D_i \mid D_i \text{ contains } w\}$. Otherwise he outputs `reject`.

The definition of usual searchable symmetric encryption (SSE) schemes [10, 11] is obtained by deleting Tag from the verifiable SSE schemes.

2.2 Privacy

Suppose that the server (who is an adversary **A**) is honest but curious. In any SSE scheme, the server learns $|D_1|, \cdots, |D_n|$ and $|\mathcal{W}|$ in the store phase. Also in the search phase, she learns $\texttt{List}(w) = \{i \mid D_i \text{ contains } w\}$ for the search keyword w because she must be able to return $\texttt{C}(w)$. Now the server should not be able to learn any more information. Curtmola, Garay, Kamara and Ostrovsky [10, 11] formulated this security notion as follows.

We consider a real game $\texttt{Game}_{real}$ and a simulation game $\texttt{Game}_{sim}$. $\texttt{Game}_{real}$ is played by a challenger and an adversary **A** as shown in Fig.1. $\texttt{Game}_{sim}$ is played by a challenger, an adversary **A** and a simulator **Sim** as shown in Fig.2.

Let

$$p_0 = \Pr(\mathbf{A} \text{ outputs } b = 1 \text{ in } \texttt{Game}_{real}),$$
$$p_1 = \Pr(\mathbf{A} \text{ outputs } b = 1 \text{ in } \texttt{Game}_{sim}).$$

Definition 1. *We say that a (verifiable) SSE scheme satisfies privacy if there exists a PPT simulator* **Sim** *such that* $|p_0 - p_1|$ *is negligible for any PPT adversary* **A**.

2.3 Reliability (Verifiability)

Suppose that the server (who is an adversary **A**) is malicious. In verifiable SSE schemes, the server should not be able to forge a search result $(\texttt{C}(w), Tag)$ in the search phase. This security notion is formulated as follows [21].

Fix $(\mathcal{D}, \mathcal{W}, \texttt{Index})$ and search queries $w_1, \cdots, w_q \in \mathcal{W}$ arbitrarily. We say that **A** wins if she can return $(\texttt{C}(w_i)^*, Tag^*)$ for some query $t(w_i)$ such that $\texttt{C}(w_i)^* \neq \texttt{C}(w_i)$ and the client accepts $(\texttt{C}(w_i)^*, Tag^*)$.

Simulation Game ($\texttt{Game}_{sim}$)

In the store phase,

- **A** chooses $(\mathcal{D}, \mathcal{W}, \texttt{Index})$ and sends them to the challenger.
- The challenger sends $|D_1|, \cdots, |D_n|$ and $|\mathcal{W}|$ to simulator **Sim**, where $\texttt{D} = \{D_1, \cdots, D_n\}$.
- **Sim** returns $(\mathcal{I}', \texttt{C}')$ to the challenger, and he replays them to **A**.

In the search phase, for $i = 1, \cdots, q$,

1. **A** chooses a keyword $w_{a_i} \in \mathcal{W}$ and sends it to the challenger.
2. The challenger sends $\texttt{List}(w_{a_i}) = \{j \mid D_j \text{ contains } w_{a_i}\}$ to **Sim**.
3. **Sim** returns t' to the challenger, and he relays it to **A**.

Finally **A** outputs a bit b.

Fig. 2. Simulation Game: $\texttt{Game}_{sim}$

Definition 2. *We say that a verifiable SSE satisfies reliability if for any PPT adversary* **A**, Pr(**A** *wins*) *is negligible for any* $(\mathcal{D}, \mathcal{W}, \texttt{Index})$ *and any search queries* $w_1, \cdots, w_q$.

Kurosawa et al. [21] proved the following proposition.

Proposition 1. *A verifiable SSE scheme satisfies privacy and reliability if and only if the corresponding protocol is UC-secure against non-adaptive adversaries.*

3 Our Efficient Verifiable SSE Scheme

In this section, we show a more efficient verifiable SSE scheme than the previous one [21]. In this scheme, the client sends only $n + 128$ bits in the search phase while $(\log n + \ell + 1) \times n$ bits must be sent in [21], where n is the number of documents and ℓ is the bit length of each keyword.

Remember that $\mathcal{D} = \{D_1, \cdots, D_n\}$ is a set of documents, $\mathcal{W} = \{w_1, \cdots, w_m\}$ is a set of keywords and $\texttt{Index} = \{e_{i,j}\}$ is an $m \times n$ binary matrix such that

$$e_{i,j} = \begin{cases} 1 \text{ if } w_i \text{ is contained in } D_j \\ 0 \textit{ otherwise} \end{cases}.$$

Let $\texttt{index}_i$ denote the ith row of $\texttt{Index}$.

3.1 Our Efficient SSE Scheme

In this subsection, we assume that the server is honest but curious. Let $\texttt{PRF}_k : \{0,1\}^\ell \times \{0,1\}^*$ be a pseudorandom function, where k is a key. Let $\texttt{SKE} = (G, E, E^{-1})$ be a symmetric-key encryption scheme, where G is a key generation algorithm, E is an encryption algorithm and E^{-1} is a decryption algorithm. We assume that SKE is CPA-secure in the left-or right sense [2].

Now our SSE scheme is as follows.

(Store phase)

1. The client generates (k_e, k_0, k_1) randomly, where k_e is a key of SKE, and k_0, k_1 are keys of PRF. He then keeps (k_e, k_0, k_1) secret.
2. The client computes $C_i = E_{k_e}(D_i)$ for each document $D_i \in \mathcal{D}$. He also computes

$$\mathtt{label}_i = [\mathtt{PRF}_{k_0}(w_i)]_{1..128}$$
$$\overline{\mathtt{index}_i} = \mathtt{index}_i \oplus [\mathtt{PRF}_{k_1}(w_i)]_{1..n}$$

for each keyword $w_i \in \mathcal{W}$. He also chooses a random permutation σ on $\{1, \cdots, m\}$. He then stores

$$\mathcal{C} = (C_1, \cdots, C_n) \text{ and } \mathcal{I} = \{(\mathtt{label}_{\sigma(i)}, \overline{\mathtt{index}_{\sigma(i)}}) \mid i = 1, \cdots, m\}$$

to the server.

(Search phase) Suppose that the client wants to search on a keyword w_a.

1. The client computes $\mathtt{label}_a$ and $\mathtt{pad}_a = [\mathtt{PRF}_{k_1}(w_a)]_{1..n}$. He then sends $t(w_a) = (\mathtt{label}_a, \mathtt{pad}_a)$ to the server.
2. The server finds $(\mathtt{label}_a, \overline{\mathtt{index}_a}) \in \mathcal{I}$ by using $\mathtt{label}_a$. She then computes

$$\mathtt{index}_a = \overline{\mathtt{index}_a} \oplus \mathtt{pad}_a$$

Let $\mathtt{index}_a = (e_1, \cdots, e_n)$. She returns $\mathtt{C}(w) = \{C_i \mid e_i = 1\}$ to the client.
3. The client decrypts all C_i such that $C_i \in \mathtt{C}(w)$, and outputs $\{D_i \mid C_i \in \mathtt{C}(w)\}$.

Suppose that there are 5 documents $\mathcal{D} = \{D_1, \cdots, D_5\}$ and 2 keywords $\mathcal{W} = \{w_1, w_2\}$ such that $D(w_1) = \{D_1, D_3, D_5\}$ and $D(w_2) = \{D_2, D_4\}$. Then

$$\overline{\mathtt{index}_1} = (1, 0, 1, 0, 1) \oplus [\mathtt{PRF}_{k_1}(w_1)]_{1..5}$$
$$\overline{\mathtt{index}_2} = (0, 1, 0, 1, 0) \oplus [\mathtt{PRF}_{k_1}(w_2)]_{1..5}$$

Theorem 1. *The above scheme satisfies privacy if* SKE *is CPA-secure and* PRF *is a pseudorandom function.*

Proof. (Sketch) In $\mathtt{Game}_{sim}$, our simulator **Sim** behaves as follows.

(Store phase) **Sim** receives $|D_1|, \cdots, |D_n|$ and $m = |\mathcal{W}|$ from the challenger.

1. **Sim** generates a key k_e of SKE randomly. It also chooses a random permutation σ on $\{1, \cdots, m\}$.
2. **Sim** computes $C_i = E_{k_e}(0^{|D_i|})$ for $i = 1, \cdots, n$. **Sim** also chooses $\mathtt{label}_i \in \{0, 1\}^{128}$ and $\overline{\mathtt{index}_i} \in \{0, 1\}^n$ randomly for $i = 1, \cdots, m$.

3. Finally **Sim** returns $\mathcal{C}' = (C_1, \cdots, C_n)$ and $\mathcal{I}' = \{(\mathtt{label}_{\sigma(i)}, \overline{\mathtt{index}_{\sigma(i)}}) \mid i = 1, \cdots, m\}$ to the challenger.

(Search phase) **Sim** receives $\mathtt{List}(w_{a_i}) = \{j \mid D_j \text{ contains } w_{a_i}\}$ from the challenger for $i = 1, \cdots, q$. For each i, let

$$e_j = \begin{cases} 1 \text{ if } j \in \mathtt{List}(w_{a_i}) \\ 0 \; otherwise \end{cases}.$$

Sim then computes $\mathtt{pad}^* = \overline{\mathtt{index}_{\sigma(i)}} \oplus (e_1, \cdots, e_n)$ and returns $t' = (\mathtt{label}_{\sigma(i)}, \mathtt{pad}^*)$ to the challenger.

Now the adversary **A** has $(\mathcal{D}, \mathcal{W}, \mathtt{Index})$. Still in the store phase, **A** cannot distinguish $\mathcal{C}'$ from $\mathcal{C}$ because SKE is CPA-secure. Also **A** cannot distinguish $\mathcal{I}'$ from $\mathcal{I}$ because PRF (which is used in $\mathtt{Game}_{real}$) is a pseudorandom function.

In the search phase, **A** cannot distinguish $t' = (\mathtt{label}_{\sigma(i)}, \mathtt{pad}^*)$ from $t(w_a) = (\mathtt{label}_a, \mathtt{pad}_a)$ because PRF is a pseudorandom function and σ is a random permutation. Therefore **A** cannot distinguish $\mathtt{Game}_{sim}$ from $\mathtt{Game}_{real}$. □

3.2 Our Efficient Verifiable SSE Scheme

In this subsection, we assume that the server is malicious, and extend the above SSE scheme to a verifiable SSE scheme. (It is more efficient than the previous verifiable SSE scheme [21].) Let $\mathtt{MAC}_{k_m}$ be a tag generation algorithm of MAC, where k_m is a key. We assume that MAC is a pseudorandom function. (This means that it is unforgeable against chosen message attack.)

For keyword w_1, a malicious server may return $(\underline{C_2}, C_3, C_5)$ instead of (C_1, C_3, C_5). A naive approach to prevent such active attacks would be to replace each C_i with $(C_i, \mathtt{MAC}_{k_m}(C_i))$. However, this method does not work because $(\underline{C_2}, \mathtt{MAC}_{k_m}(\underline{C_2}))$ is a valid pair. In our verifiable SSE scheme, the server returns $\mathtt{MAC}_{k_m}(\mathtt{label}_1, (C_1, C_3, C_5))$. This method can prevent the above attack because the server must forge
$\mathtt{MAC}_{k_m}(\mathtt{label}_1, (\underline{C_2}, C_3, C_5))$.

Now our verifiable SSE scheme is obtained by modifying the SSE scheme of Sec.3.1 as follows.

(Store phase)

1' The client generates a MAC key k_m randomly, and keeps it secret together with (k_e, k_0, k_1).

2' The client computes $tag_i = \mathtt{MAC}_{k_m}(\mathtt{label}_i, C(w_i))$ for each keyword $w_i \in \mathcal{W}$, and stores

$$\mathcal{I} = \{(\mathtt{label}_{\sigma(i)}, \overline{\mathtt{index}_{\sigma(i)}}, tag_{\sigma(i)}) \mid i = 1, \cdots, m\} \tag{2}$$

to the server, where $\mathtt{label}_i$ and $\overline{\mathtt{index}_i}$ are computed in the same way as in Sec.3.1, and σ is a random permutation on $\{1, \cdots, m\}$.

(Search phase) Suppose that the client wants to search on a keyword w_a.

1' The client sends $(\mathtt{label}_a, \mathtt{pad}_a)$ to the server in the same way as in Sec.3.1.
2' The server finds $(\mathtt{label}_a, \overline{\mathtt{index}_a}, tag_a) \in \mathcal{I}$ by using $\mathtt{label}_a$. She then returns tag_a and $\mathtt{C}(w)$ to the client.
3' If $tag_a = \mathtt{MAC}_{k_m}(\mathtt{label}_a, \mathtt{C}(w))$, then the client decrypts all C_i such that $C_i \in \mathtt{C}(w)$, and outputs them. Otherwise he outputs `reject`.

In the example of Sec.3.1,

$$tag_1 = \mathtt{MAC}_{k_m}(\mathtt{label}_1, (C_1, C_3, C_5)),\ tag_2 = \mathtt{MAC}_{k_m}(\mathtt{label}_2, (C_2, C_4)),$$

Theorem 2. *The above scheme satisfies privacy and reliability if* SKE *is CPA-secure, and* PRF *and* MAC *are pseudorandom functions.*

Proof. (Sketch) We can prove the privacy similarly to the proof of Theorem 1. Hence will will prove the reliability.

Suppose that there exists an adversary **A** who breaks the reliability for some $(\mathcal{D}, \mathcal{W}, \mathtt{Index})$ and some search queries $w_1, \cdots, w_q$. We will show a forger **B** for the underlying MAC. **B** runs **A** by playing the role of a client with $(\mathcal{D}, \mathcal{W}, \mathtt{Index})$ and $w_1, \cdots, w_q$ as an input.

In the store phase, to compute $\mathcal{I}$, **B** obtains each $tag_i = \mathtt{MAC}_{k_m}(\mathtt{label}_i, C(w_i))$ from his MAC oracle, where k_m is randomly chosen by the MAC oracle. That is, for $i = 1, \cdots, q$, **B** queries $(\mathtt{label}_i, C(w_i))$ to the MAC oracle, and receives tag_i.

In the search phase, if **A** returns $(\mathtt{C}(w_i)^*, tag_i^*)$ such that $\mathtt{C}(w_i)^* \neq \mathtt{C}(w_i)$ for some $(\mathtt{label}_i, \mathtt{pad}_i)$, then **B** outputs $(\mathtt{label}_i, C(w_i)^*)$ and tag_i^* as a forgery.

From our assumption, **A** returns such $(\mathtt{C}(w_i)^*, tag_i^*)$ with non-negligible probability. It also holds that

$$tag_i^* = \mathtt{MAC}_{k_m}(\mathtt{label}_i, C(w_i)^*)$$

with non-negligible probability from our assumption. Finally note that **B** never queried $(\mathtt{label}_i, C(w_i)^*) \neq (\mathtt{label}_i, C(w_i))$ to the MAC oracle.

Therefore **B** succeeds in forgery with non-negligible probability. This is against our assumption on MAC. Hence our scheme satisfies reliability. □

4 How to Update Documents

4.1 Our Idea

In the scheme of Sec.3.2, the client stores $tag_1 = \mathtt{MAC}_{k_m}(\mathtt{label}_1, (C_1, C_3, C_5))$ for a keyword w_1. In this scheme, however, the client cannot modify each C_i efficiently. For example, suppose that C_1 includes two keywords, w_1 and w_2. To modify C_1 to C_1', the client must store two updated authenticators, $\mathtt{MAC}(\mathtt{label}_1, (C_1', C_3, C_5))$ and $\mathtt{MAC}(\mathtt{label}_2, (C_1', \cdots))$, to the server in the update phase. If C_1 includes more keywords, then the client must updates more authenticators.

Now our idea is that the client authenticates only $(\mathtt{label}_1, 1, 3, 5)$. He separately authenticates each (i, C_i) also. Then to update C_1 to C_1', the client stores just an authenticator on $(1, C'_1)$. The update cost is only this no matter how many keywords are included in C_1. Thus the client can update each C_i efficiently.

To delete a document C_1, the client updates it to a special symbol $C'_1 = delete$ similarly. To add a new document D_6 which includes w_1, the client updates the authenticator on $(\texttt{label}_1, 1, 3, 5)$ to that on $(\texttt{label}_1, 1, 3, 5, 6)$.

4.2 How to Time Stamp

The last problem is how to times tamp on the current (i, C_i), and how to time stamp on the current/updated $(\texttt{label}_1, 1, 3, 5, 6)$.

We can solve this problem by using an authentication scheme which posses the timestamp functionality such as Merkle hash tree [24], or authenticated skiplist [18] or the RSA accumulator [5, 14]. Such a scheme allows one to hash a set of inputs into one short accumulation value, such that there is a witness that a given input was incorporated into the accumulator, and at the same time, it is infeasible to find a witness for a value that was not accumulated.

The size of witness is $O(\log n)$ in the Merkle hash tree and the authenticated skiplist, where n is the number of documents. It is $O(\lambda)$ in the RSA accumulator, where λ is the security parameter. We can use any one of them. In what follows, we present our scheme based on the RSA accumulator.

4.3 RSA Accumulator

Let $p = 2p' + 1$ and $q = 2q' + 1$ be two large primes such that p' and q' are also primes and $|pq| > 3\lambda$. Let $N = pq$ and let

$$QR_N = \{a \mid a = x^2 \bmod N \text{ for some } x \in Z_N^*\}.$$

Then QR_N is a cyclic group of size $(p-1)(q-1)/4$. Let g be a generator of QR_N. We say that a family of functions $F = \{f : A \to B\}$ is two-universal if $Pr[f(x_1) = f(x_2)] = 1/|B|$ for all $x_1 \neq x_2$ and for a randomly chosen function $f \in F$.

Proposition 2. *[16] For any $y \in \{0,1\}^\lambda$, we can compute a prime $x \in \{0,1\}^{3\lambda}$ such that $f(x) = y$ by sampling $O(\lambda^2)$ times with overwhelming probability from the set of inverses $f^{-1}(y)$, where the probability is taken over $f \in F$.*

Let $F = \{f_a : \{0,1\}^{3\lambda} \to \{0,1\}^\lambda\}$ be a two-universal family of functions and choose $f \in F$ randomly. (Such functions can be built easily. For instance, view a and x as members of $GF(2^{3\lambda})$, and let $f_a(x)$ be the λ least significant bits of $a \times x$.)

For a set $E = \{y_1, \cdots, y_n\}$ with $y_i \in \{0,1\}^\lambda$, the RSA accumulator works as follows.

1. For each y_i, Alice chooses a prime x_i such that $f(x_i) = y_i$ randomly. Let $prime(y_i)$ denote such a prime x_i. She then computes the accumulated value of $E = \{y_1, \cdots, y_n\}$ as
$$\texttt{Acc}(E) = g^{\prod_{i=1}^n prime(y_i)} \bmod N$$
and sends $\texttt{Acc}(E)$ to Bob.

2. Later Alice proves that $y_j \in E$ to Bob as follows. She computes

$$\pi_j = g^{\prod_{i \neq j} prime(y_i)} \bmod N$$

and sends π_j and $prime(y_j)$ to Bob.
3. Bob verifies that

$$\texttt{Acc}(E) = (\pi_j)^{prime(y_j)} \bmod N.$$

Definition 3. *[6] (Strong RSA assumption) Given $N = pq$ and a random element $y \in Z_N$, it is hard to find x and $e > 1$ such that $y = x^e \bmod N$.*

Proposition 3. *Given N, g, f and $E = \{y_1, \cdots, y_n\}$, it is hard to find $y \notin E$ and π such that*

$$\pi^{prime(y)} = \texttt{Acc}(E) \bmod N \tag{3}$$

under the strong RSA assumption.

If we want to apply the above protocol to a set $A = \{a_1, \cdots, a_n\}$ with $a_i \notin \{0,1\}^\lambda$ for some i, then we define the accumulated value of A as

$$\texttt{Acc}(A) = g^{\prod_{i=1}^{n} prime(H(a_i))} \bmod N,$$

where $H : \{0,1\}^* \to \{0,1\}^\lambda$ is a collision resistant hash function. Namely we apply the above protocol to the set $\{H(a_1), \cdots, H(a_n)\}$.

Note that $prime(H(a_i))$ is a prime $x_i \in \{0,1\}^{3\lambda}$ such that $f(x_i) = H(a_i)$, where $f : \{0,1\}^{3\lambda} \to \{0,1\}^\lambda$ is a two-universal hash function. We can compute such a prime x_i efficiently for any $H(a_i) \in \{0,1\}^\lambda$ from Proposition 2.

5 Proposed Verifiable Dynamic SSE Scheme

In this section, we show the details of our idea, i.e., how to *modify*, *delete* and *add* documents efficiently in a verifiable SSE scheme, where the server is a malicious adversary. We call such a scheme a verifiable dynamic SSE scheme.

5.1 Scheme

In the proposed scheme,

- The client applies the RSA accumulator to the sets

$$E_C = \{(i, C_i) \mid i = 1, \cdots, n\},$$
$$E_I = \{(\texttt{label}_i, j, [\boxed{\texttt{index}_i}]_j) \mid i = 1, \cdots, m, j = 1, \cdots, n\},$$

  and compute their accumulated values $\texttt{Acc}(E_C)$ and $\texttt{Acc}(E_I)$.
- He updates $\texttt{Acc}(E_C)$ each time when he modifies or deletes a document, and updates $\texttt{Acc}(E_I)$ each time when he adds a document.
- In the search phase, the client checks if a server returned the valid (updated) ciphertexts based on $\texttt{Acc}(E_C)$ and $\texttt{Acc}(E_I)$.

A subtle problem is how the client and the server compute the same $prime(y)$ locally, where $y = (i, C_i)$ or $(\mathtt{label}_i, j, [\overline{\mathtt{index}_i}]_j)$. Remember that $prime(y)$ is a prime x such that $f(x) = y$. and such x is chosen *randomly*. In the proposed scheme, the client chooses k_a randomly, and sends it to the server at the beginning of the protocol. Then they use $\mathtt{PRF}_{k_a}(y)$ as the randomness when computing $prime(y)$. Thus they can compute the same $prime(y)$ locally.

Let $F = \{f : \{0,1\}^{3\lambda} \to \{0,1\}^{\lambda}\}$ be a two-universal family of functions, and $H : \{0,1\}^* \to \{0,1\}^{\lambda}$ be a collision-resistant hash function. Let $[\overline{\mathtt{index}_i}]_j$ denote the jth bit of $\overline{\mathtt{index}_i}$.

(Store phase)

1. The client generates $(N(= pq), g)$ as shown in Sec. 4.3 and chooses $f \in F$ randomly. He also generates (k_e, k_0, k_1, k_a) randomly, where k_e is a key of SKE, and k_0, k_1, k_a are keys of PRF. He further chooses a random permutation σ on $\{1, \cdots, m\}$. He then sends (N, g, f, k_a) to the server and keeps $(p, q, k_e, k_0, k_1, \sigma)$ secret.
2. The client computes $C_i = E_{k_e}(D_i)$ for each document $D_i \in \mathcal{D}$. He also computes

$$\mathtt{label}_i = [\mathtt{PRF}_{k_0}(w_i)]_{1..128}, \ \mathtt{pad}_i = [\mathtt{PRF}_{k_1}(w_i)]_{1..n}, \ \overline{\mathtt{index}_i} = \mathtt{pad}_i \oplus (e_{i,1}, \cdots, e_{i,n})$$

for each keyword $w_i \in \mathcal{W}$. He then stores $\mathcal{C} = (C_1, \cdots, C_n)$ and

$$\mathcal{I} = \{(\mathtt{label}_{\sigma(i)}, \overline{\mathtt{index}_{\sigma(i)}}) \mid i = 1, \cdots, m\} \tag{4}$$

to the server.
3. He also computes

$$A_C = g^{\prod_{i=1}^{n} prime(H(i, H(C_i)))} \bmod N,$$
$$A_I = g^{\prod_{i=1}^{m} \prod_{j=1}^{n} prime(H(\mathtt{label}_i, j, [\overline{\mathtt{index}_i}]_j))} \bmod N.$$

He then keeps n, A_C and A_I.

(Search phase) Suppose that the client wants to search on a keyword w_a.

1. The client computes $(\mathtt{label}_a, \mathtt{pad}_a)$ and sends them to the server.
2. The server finds $(\mathtt{label}_a, \overline{\mathtt{index}_a}) \in \mathcal{I}$ by using $\mathtt{label}_a$. She computes

$$(e_1, \cdots, e_n) = \mathtt{pad}_a \oplus \overline{\mathtt{index}_a}$$

and sets $\mathtt{C}'(w) = \{(i, C_i) \mid e_i = 1\}$. She next computes

$$\pi_C = g^{\prod_{e_i=0} prime(H(i, H(C_i)))} \bmod N,$$
$$\pi_I = g^{\prod_{i \neq a} \{\prod_{j=1}^{n} prime(H(\mathtt{label}_i, j, [\overline{\mathtt{index}_i}]_j))\}} \bmod N.$$

Finally she returns $(\mathtt{C}'(w), \pi_C, \pi_I)$ to the client.

3. The client first computes $x_i = prime(H(i, H(C_i)))$ for each $(i, C_i) \in \mathtt{C}'(w)$, and checks if

$$A_C = (\pi_C)^{\prod_{e_i=1} x_i} \bmod N \tag{5}$$

The client next reconstructs $(e_1, \cdots, e_n)$ from $\mathtt{C}'(w)$ and computes $\overline{\mathtt{index}_a} = \mathtt{pad}_a \oplus (e_1, \cdots, e_n)$. He then computes $z_j = prime(H(\mathtt{label}_a, j, [\overline{\mathtt{index}_a}]_j))$ for $j = 1, \cdots, n$, and checks if

$$A_I = (\pi_I)^{\prod_{j=1}^{n} z_j} \bmod N \tag{6}$$

If all the checks succeed, then the client decrypts all C_i such that $e_i = 1$ and outputs the documents $\{D_i \mid e_i = 1\}$. Otherwise he outputs `reject`.

(Remark.)

- Eq.(5) verifies the correctness of $\mathtt{C}'(w_a) = \{(i, C_i) \mid D_i \text{ contains } w_a\}$. Eq.(6) verifies the correctness of $\overline{\mathtt{index}_a}$. Hence it verifies the correctness of $(e_1, \cdots, e_n)$.
- For example, if both $(e_1, \cdots, e_5) = (1, 0, 1, 0, 1)$ and $(1, C_1), (3, C_3), (5, C_5)$ are valid, then it is clear that (C_1, C_3, C_5) are the correct ciphertexts.

(Modify) Suppose that the client wants to modify C_i to C_i'.

1. The client send (i, C_i') to the server.
2. The server computes

$$\pi_i = g^{\prod_{j \neq i} prime(H(j, H(C_j)))} \bmod N$$

and returns $(H(C_i), \pi_i)$ to the client.
3. The client computes $x_i = prime(H(i, H(C_i)))$ and checks if

$$A_C = (\pi_i)^{x_i} \bmod N. \tag{7}$$

If the check fails, then he outputs `reject`. Otherwise he computes

$$\begin{aligned} x_i' &= prime(H(i, H(C_i'))), \\ d &= x_i'/x_i \bmod (p-1)(q-1), \\ A_C' &= (A_C)^d = g^{x_1 \cdots x_i' \cdots x_n} \bmod N. \end{aligned}$$

He finally updates A_C to A_C'.

(Delete) Suppose that the client wants to delete C_i. He frist sends $(i, delete)$ to the server. Then apply (Modify) to $C_i' = delete$.

(Add) Suppose that the client wants to add a document D_{n+1}. Let

$$e_{i,n+1} = \begin{cases} 1 \text{ if } w_i \text{ is contained in } D_{n+1} \\ 0 \; otherwise \end{cases}. \tag{8}$$

1. The client computes $C_{n+1} = E_{k_e}(D_{n+1})$, and sends C_{n+1} to the server. He also updates A_C to

$$A'_C = (A_C)^{prime(H(n+1,H(C_{n+1})))} \bmod N.$$

2. The client also computes $a_i = [\mathtt{PRF}_{k_1}(w_i)]_{n+1} \oplus e_{i,n+1}$ for $i = 1, \cdots, m$, where $[\mathtt{PRF}_{k_1}(w_i)]_{n+1}$ denotes the $(n+1)$th bit of $\mathtt{PRF}_{k_1}(w_i)$.
He then sends $(a_{\sigma(1)}, \cdots, a_{\sigma(m)})$ to the server.
3. The server updates $\overline{\mathtt{index}_{\sigma(i)}}$ to $\overline{\mathtt{index}'_{\sigma(i)}} = \overline{\mathtt{index}_{\sigma(i)}} || a_{\sigma(i)}$ for $i = 1, \cdots, m$, where $||$ denotes concatenation.
4. The client computes $z_i = prime(H(\mathtt{label}_i, n+1, a_i))$ for $i = 1, \cdots, m$, and updates A_I to

$$A'_I = (A_I)^{z_1 \cdots z_m} \bmod N.$$

Finally he updates n to $n + 1$.

5.2 Example

Consider the example shown in Sec.3.1. In the store phase, the client computes

$$A_C = g^{\prod_{i=1}^{5} prime(H(i,H(C_i)))} \bmod N,$$
$$A_I = g^{\prod_{i=1}^{2} \prod_{j=1}^{5} prime(H(\mathtt{label}_i, j, [\overline{\mathtt{index}_i}]_j))} \bmod N$$

and keeps $n = 5$, A_C and A_I.

(Search phase) Suppose that the client wants to search on w_1. He then sends $(\mathtt{label}_1, \mathtt{pad}_1)$ to the server.

1. The server finds $\overline{\mathtt{index}_1}$ from $\mathcal{I}$, and computes $\mathtt{pad}_1 \oplus \overline{\mathtt{index}_1} = (1,0,1,0,1)$. From this $(1,0,1,0,1)$, she sets $\mathtt{C}'(w_1) = \{(1, C_1), (3, C_3), (5, C_5)\}$. She then computes

$$\pi_C = g^{\prod_{i=2,4} prime(H(i,H(C_i)))} \bmod N,$$
$$\pi_I = g^{\prod_{j=1}^{5} prime(H(\mathtt{label}_2, j, [\overline{\mathtt{index}_2}]_j))} \bmod N.$$

Finally she returns $(\mathtt{C}'(w_1), \pi_C, \pi_I)$ to the client.
2. The client computes $x_i = prime(H(i, H(C_i)))$ for $i = 1, 3, 5$, and checks if

$$A_C = (\pi_C)^{\prod_{i=1,3,5} x_i} \bmod N. \tag{9}$$

Also he reconstructs $\overline{\mathtt{index}_1} = \mathtt{pad}_1 \oplus (1,0,1,0,1)$ from $\mathtt{C}'(w_1)$. He then computes $z_j = prime(H(\mathtt{label}_1, j, [\overline{\mathtt{index}_1}]_j))$ for $j = 1, \cdots, 5$, and checks if

$$A_I = (\pi_I)^{\prod_{j=1}^{5} z_j} \bmod N. \tag{10}$$

If all the checks succeed, then the client decrypts (C_1, C_3, C_5), and outputs the documents (D_1, D_3, D_5). Otherwise he outputs `reject`.

(Modify) Suppose that the client wants to modify C_1 to C_1'.

1. The client sends $(1, C_1')$ to the server.
2. The server computes

$$\pi_1 = g^{\prod_{j=2}^{5} prime(H(j,H(C_j)))} \bmod N$$

   and returns $(H(C_1), \pi_1)$ to the client.
3. The client computes $x_1 = prime(H(1, H(C_1)))$ and checks if

$$A_C = (\pi_1)^{x_1} \bmod N.$$

   If the check fails, then he outputs `reject`. Otherwise he computes

$$x_1' = prime(H(1, H(C_1'))),$$
$$d = x_1'/x_1 \bmod (p-1)(q-1),$$
$$A_C' = (A_C)^d = g^{x_1' x_2 \cdots x_5} \bmod N.$$

   He finally updates A_C to A_C'.

(Delete) Suppose that the client wants to delete C_2. He first sends $(2, delete)$ to the server. Then apply (Modify) to $C_2' = delete$.

(Add) Suppose that the client wants to add a document D_6 which contains w_1 as a keyword.

1. The client computes $C_6 = E_{k_e}(D_6)$, and sends C_6 to the server. He also updates A_C to $A_C' = (A_C)^{prime(H(6,H(C_6)))} \bmod N$.
2. The client also computes $a_1 = [\mathtt{PRF}_{k_1}(w_1)]_6 \oplus 1$ and $a_2 = [\mathtt{PRF}_{k_1}(w_2)]_6 \oplus 0$. He then sends $(a_{\sigma(1)}, a_{\sigma(2)})$ to the server.
3. The server updates $\overline{\mathtt{index}}_{\sigma(i)}$ to $\overline{\mathtt{index}}'_{\sigma(i)} = \overline{\mathtt{index}}_{\sigma(i)} || a_{\sigma(i)}$ for $i = 1, 2$.
4. The client computes $z_i = prime(H(\mathtt{label}_i, 6, a_i))$ for $i = 1, 2$, and updates A_I to $A_I' = (A_I)^{z_1 \cdot z_2} \bmod N$. Finally he updates $n = 5$ to $n = 6$.

6 Security

In this section, we prove that the proposed verifiable dynamic SSE scheme is UC-secure. If a protocol Σ is secure in the universally composable (UC) security framework, its security is maintained under a general protocol composition [7–9].

In the UC framework, there exists an environment $\mathcal{Z}$ which generates the input to all parties, reads all outputs, and in addition interacts with an adversary **A** in an arbitrary way throughout the computation.

A protocol Σ is said to securely realize a given functionality $\mathcal{F}$ if for any adversary **A**, there exists an ideal world adversary **S** such that no environment $\mathcal{Z}$ can tell whether it is interacting with **A** and parties running the protocol, or with **S** and parties that interact with $\mathcal{F}$ in the ideal world.

6.1 Ideal Functionality

We describe the ideal functionality $\mathcal{F}$ of verifiable dynamic SSE schemes in Fig.3. In the ideal world, $\mathcal{Z}$ interacts with the dummy client and the dummy server, where the dummy players communicate with $\mathcal{F}$.

Our $\mathcal{F}$ provides an ideal world because the ideal world adversary **S** (i.e., a malicious server) learns only $|D_1|, \cdots, |D_n|$ and $|\mathcal{W}|$ for the store command of $\mathcal{Z}$, only $\texttt{List}(w)$ for a search command on keyword w, only $(i, |D'_i|)$ for a modify command on (i, D'_i), only i for a delete command on i, and only $|D|$ for an add command on D. (See the beginning of Sec.2.2.)

We say that a protocol (client, server) is UC-secure if it securely realizes the ideal functionality $\mathcal{F}$.

Ideal Functionality $\mathcal{F}$

Running with the dummy client P_1, the dummy server P_2 and an adversary **S**.

- Upon receiving (**store**, $sid, \mathcal{D}, \mathcal{W}$, $\texttt{Index}$) from P_1, verify that this is the first input from P_1 with (**store**, sid). If so, store $(n, \mathcal{D}, \mathcal{W}, \texttt{Index})$, and send $|D_1|, \cdots, |D_n|$ and $|\mathcal{W}|$ to **S**. Otherwise ignore this input.
- Upon receiving (**search**, sid, w_a) from P_1, send $\texttt{List}(w_a)$ to **S**, where $w_a \in \mathcal{W}$.
  1. If **S** returns OK, then send $\texttt{D}(w_a)$ to P_1.
  2. If **S** returns `reject`, then send `reject` to P_1.
- Upon receiving (**modify**, sid, i, D'_i) from P_1, send $(i, |D'_i|)$ to **S**.
  1. If **S** returns OK, then replace D_i with D'_i.
  2. If **S** returns `reject`, then send `reject` to P_1.
- Upon receiving (**delete**, sid, i) from P_1, send i to **S**.
  1. If **S** returns OK, then let $D_i :=$ *delete*.
  2. If **S** returns `reject`, then send `reject` to P_1.
- Upon receiving (**add**, sid, D) from P_1, add D to $\mathcal{D}$, and send $|D|$ to **S**.

Fig. 3. Ideal Functionality of Dynamic SSE

6.2 UC-Security of Our Scheme

Theorem 3. *The proposed scheme is UC-secure against non-adaptive adversaries under the strong RSA assumption if* SKE *is CPA-secure,* PRF *is a pseudorandom function and* H *is a collision-resistant hash function.*

A proof is given in Appendix A.

7 Efficiency

7.1 Efficiency of the Proposed Verifiable Dynamic SSE Scheme

Table 2 shows the communication overheads and the computation costs of the proposed verifiable dynamic SSE scheme. For example, in the search phase, to search on a keyword w_a, the client sends $(\mathtt{label}_a, \mathtt{pad}_a)$ to the server, and the server returns $(\mathtt{C}'(w), \pi_C, \pi_I)$, where $\mathtt{C}'(w) = \{(i, C_i) \mid D_i \text{ contains } w\}$. Therefore the total communication cost is

$$T_s = |\mathtt{label}_a| + |\mathtt{pad}_a| + |\mathtt{C}'(w)| + |\pi_C| + |\pi_I|.$$

Hence the communication overhead is

$$T_s - |\mathtt{C}'(w)| = |\mathtt{label}_a| + |\mathtt{pad}_a| + |\pi_C| + |\pi_I| = n + O(\lambda),$$

where λ is the security parameter of the RSA accumulator.

Table 2. Efficiency of the Proposed Verifiable Dynamic SSE Scheme

	search	modify	delete	add
communication overhead	$n + O(\lambda)$	$O(\lambda)$	$O(\lambda)$	m
computation cost of the server	$O(nm)$	$O(n)$	$O(n)$	$O(m)$
computation cost of the client	$O(n)$	$O(1)$	$O(1)$	$O(m)$

The storage overhead is $n(m + 128)$.

7.2 More Efficient Variant with No *Add*

Suppose that the client does not add new documents. Then we can consider a more efficient variant of the proposed scheme such that the RSA accumulator is not used to authenticate $\mathtt{Index}$.

Instead, the client computes $tag_i = \mathtt{MAC}_{k_m}(\mathtt{label}_i, \mathtt{List}(w_i))$ for each keyword $w_i \in \mathcal{W}$, and stores

$$\mathcal{I} = \{(\mathtt{label}_{\sigma(i)}, \overline{\mathtt{index}_{\sigma(i)}}, tag_{\sigma(i)}) \mid i = 1, \cdots, m\} \tag{11}$$

to the server in the store phase.

In the search phase, the server returns tag_a to the client for a search keyword w_a instead of π_I. Then the computation cost of the server is reduced from $O(nm)$ to $O(n)$ in the search phase. The computation cost of the client is reduced from $O(n)$ to $O(n_a)$, where n_a is the number of documents which contain w_a. See Table 3.

Table 3. A Variant with No Add

	search	modify	delete
communication overhead	$n + O(\lambda)$	$O(\lambda)$	$O(\lambda)$
computation cost of the server	$O(n)$	$O(n)$	$O(n)$
computation cost of the client	$O(n_a)$	$O(1)$	$O(1)$

References

1. Bellovin, S., Cheswick, W.: Privacy-Enhanced Searches Using Encrypted Bloom Filters, Cryptology ePrint Archive, Report 2006/210 (2006), `http://eprint.iacr.org/`
2. Bellare, M., Desai, A., Jokipii, E., Rogaway, P.: A Concrete Security Treatment of Symmetric Encryption. In: FOCS 1997, pp. 394–403 (1997)
3. Ballard, L., Kamara, S., Monrose, F.: Achieving Efficient Conjunctive Keyword Searches over Encrypted Data. In: Qing, S., Mao, W., López, J., Wang, G. (eds.) ICICS 2005. LNCS, vol. 3783, pp. 414–426. Springer, Heidelberg (2005)
4. Byun, J.W., Lee, D.-H., Lim, J.: Efficient conjunctive keyword search on encrypted data storage system. In: Atzeni, A.S., Lioy, A. (eds.) EuroPKI 2006. LNCS, vol. 4043, pp. 184–196. Springer, Heidelberg (2006)
5. Benaloh, J., de Mare, M.: One-way accumulators: A decentralized alternative to digital signatures. In: Helleseth, T. (ed.) EUROCRYPT 1993. LNCS, vol. 765, pp. 274–285. Springer, Heidelberg (1994)
6. Barić, N., Pfitzmann, B.: Collision-free accumulators and fail-stop signature schemes without trees. In: Fumy, W. (ed.) EUROCRYPT 1997. LNCS, vol. 1233, pp. 480–494. Springer, Heidelberg (1997)
7. Canetti, R.: Universally Composable Security: A New Paradigm for Cryptographic Protocols, Revision 1 of ECCC Report TR01-016 (2001)
8. Canetti, R.: Universally Composable Signatures, Certification and Authentication, Cryptology ePrint Archive, Report 2003/239 (2003), `http://eprint.iacr.org/`
9. Canetti, R.: Universally Composable Security: A New Paradigm for Cryptographic Protocols, Cryptology ePrint Archive, Report 2000/067 (2005), `http://eprint.iacr.org/`
10. Curtmola, R., Garay, J.A., Kamara, S., Ostrovsky, R.: Searchable symmetric encryption: improved definitions and efficient constructions. In: ACM Conference on Computer and Communications Security, pp. 79–88 (2006)
11. Full version of the above: Cryptology ePrint Archive, Report 2006/210 (2006), `http://eprint.iacr.org/`
12. Cash, D., Jarecki, S., Jutla, C., Krawczyk, H., Roşu, M.-C., Steiner, M.: Highly-Scalable Searchable Symmetric Encryption with Support for Boolean Queries. In: Canetti, R., Garay, J.A. (eds.) CRYPTO 2013, Part I. LNCS, vol. 8042, pp. 353–373. Springer, Heidelberg (2013)
13. Chase, M., Kamara, S.: Structured encryption and controlled disclosure. In: Abe, M. (ed.) ASIACRYPT 2010. LNCS, vol. 6477, pp. 577–594. Springer, Heidelberg (2010)
14. Camenisch, J., Lysyanskaya, A.: Dynamic accumulators and application to efficient revocation of anonymous credentials. In: Yung, M. (ed.) CRYPTO 2002. LNCS, vol. 2442, pp. 61–76. Springer, Heidelberg (2002)
15. Chang, Y.-C., Mitzenmacher, M.: Privacy Preserving Keyword Searches on Remote Encrypted Data. In: Ioannidis, J., Keromytis, A.D., Yung, M. (eds.) ACNS 2005. LNCS, vol. 3531, pp. 442–455. Springer, Heidelberg (2005)
16. Gennaro, R., Halevi, S., Rabin, T.: Secure hash-and-sign signatures without the random oracle. In: Stern, J. (ed.) EUROCRYPT 1999. LNCS, vol. 1592, pp. 123–139. Springer, Heidelberg (1999)
17. Goh, E.-J.: Secure Indexes. Cryptology ePrint Archive, Report 2003/216 (2003), `http://eprint.iacr.org/`
18. Goodrich, M.T., Papamanthou, C., Tamassia, R.: On the Cost of Persistence and Authentication in Skip Lists. In: Demetrescu, C. (ed.) WEA 2007. LNCS, vol. 4525, pp. 94–107. Springer, Heidelberg (2007)

19. Golle, P., Staddon, J., Waters, B.: Secure Conjunctive Keyword Search over Encrypted Data. In: Jakobsson, M., Yung, M., Zhou, J. (eds.) ACNS 2004. LNCS, vol. 3089, pp. 31–45. Springer, Heidelberg (2004)
20. Kirsch, A., Mitzenmacher, M., Wieder, U.: More Robust Hashing: Cuckoo Hashing with a Stash. SIAM J. Comput. 39(4), 1543–1561 (2009)
21. Kurosawa, K., Ohtaki, Y.: UC-Secure Searchable Symmetric Encryption. In: Keromytis, A.D. (ed.) FC 2012. LNCS, vol. 7397, pp. 285–298. Springer, Heidelberg (2012)
22. Kamara, S., Papamanthou, C.: Parallel and Dynamic Searchable Symmetric Encryption. In: Sadeghi, A.-R. (ed.) FC 2013. LNCS, vol. 7859, pp. 258–274. Springer, Heidelberg (2013)
23. Kamara, S., Papamanthou, C., Roeder, T.: Dynamic searchable symmetric encryption. In: ACM Conference on Computer and Communications Security, pp. 965–976 (2012)
24. Merkle Tree, `http://en.wikipedia.org/wiki/Merkle~tree`
25. Song, D., Wagner, D., Perrig, A.: Practical Techniques for Searches on Encrypted Data. In: IEEE Symposium on Security and Privacy 2000, pp. 44–55 (2000)
26. Wang, P., Wang, H., Pieprzyk, J.: Keyword Field-Free Conjunctive Keyword Searches on Encrypted Data and Extension for Dynamic Groups. In: Franklin, M.K., Hui, L.C.K., Wong, D.S. (eds.) CANS 2008. LNCS, vol. 5339, pp. 178–195. Springer, Heidelberg (2008)

A Proof of Theorem 3

(1) Suppose that the real world adversary **A** does not corrupt any party in our protocol. Then it is easy to see that the client outputs the correct documents for each search keyword. Further $\mathcal{Z}$ interacts only with the client ($= P_1$). Therefore no $\mathcal{Z}$ can distinguish the real world from the ideal world.

(2) Suppose that $\mathcal{Z}$ asks **A** to corrupt the client ($= P_1$) in our protocol. In this case, **A** may report the communication pattern of the client to $\mathcal{Z}$. Consider an ideal world adversary **S** who runs **A** internally by playing the role of the server ($= P_2$), forwarding all messages from $\mathcal{Z}$ to **A** and vice versa. Note that **S** can play the role of the server faithfully because it has no interaction with $\mathcal{Z}$. This means that no $\mathcal{Z}$ can distinguish the real world from the ideal world.

(3) Suppose that $\mathcal{Z}$ asks **A** to corrupt the server ($= P_2$). In this case, our ideal world adversary **S** runs **A** internally by playing the role of the client ($= P_1$), forwarding all messages from $\mathcal{Z}$ to **A** and vice versa.

(Store) Suppose that $\mathcal{Z}$ sends a store command to P_1. P_1 relays it to $\mathcal{F}$. $\mathcal{F}$ then sends $|D_1|, \cdots, |D_n|$ and $|\mathcal{W}|$ to **S**.

1. **S** runs the client's algorithm on input $\mathcal{D}' = \{D'_i = 0^{|D_i|} \mid i = 1, \cdots, n\}$, $\mathcal{W}' = \{1, \cdots, m\}$ and $\texttt{Index}' = \{e'_{i,j}\}$ with $e'_{i,j} = 0$ for all (i, j).
2. By doing so, **S** sends (N, g, f, k_a) and $(\mathcal{I}, \mathcal{C})$ to **A**, and keeps
$$sk = (p, q, k_e, k_0, k_1, \sigma)$$
secret, where $\mathcal{C} = (C_1, \cdots, C_n)$ and $\mathcal{I} = \{(\texttt{label}_{\sigma(i)}, \overline{\texttt{index}_{\sigma(i)}})\}$.

(Search) Suppose that $\mathcal{Z}$ sends the ith search command on a keyword $w_a \in \mathcal{W}$ to P_1. P_1 relays it to $\mathcal{F}$. $\mathcal{F}$ then sends $\mathtt{List}(w_a) = \{j \mid D_j \text{ contains } w_a\}$ to **S**.

1. Let
$$e_j = \begin{cases} 1 \text{ if } j \in \mathtt{List}(w_a) \\ 0 \text{ } otherwise \end{cases}.$$
S computes $\mathtt{pad}^* = \overline{\mathtt{index}_{\sigma(i)}} \oplus (e_1, \cdots, e_n)$ and sends $(\mathtt{label}_{\sigma(i)}, \mathtt{pad}^*)$ to **A**.
2. **A** returns $(\mathtt{C}'(w_a), \pi_C, \pi_I)$.
3. **S** runs the client's algorithm on input $(\mathtt{C}'(w_a), \pi_C, \pi_I)$ and sk. If the client outputs `reject`, then **S** sends `reject` to $\mathcal{F}$. Otherwise **S** sends OK to $\mathcal{F}$.

(Modify) Suppose that $\mathcal{Z}$ sends a modify command (i, D_i') to P_1. Then **S** is given $|D_i'|$ by $\mathcal{F}$.

1. **S** first computes $C_i' = E_{k_e}(0^{|D_i'|})$.
2. Then **S** runs our protocol (Modify) with **A** by playing the role of the client.
3. If the client outputs `reject`, then **S** sends `reject` to $\mathcal{F}$. Otherwise **S** sends OK to $\mathcal{F}$.

(Delete) Suppose that $\mathcal{Z}$ sends a modify command i to P_1. Then **S** is given i by $\mathcal{F}$. **S** runs our protocol (Delete) with **A** by playing the role of the client. If the client outputs `reject`, then **S** sends `reject` to $\mathcal{F}$. Otherwise **S** sends OK to $\mathcal{F}$.

(Add) Suppose that $\mathcal{Z}$ sends an add command D to P_1. Then **S** is given $|D|$ by $\mathcal{F}$. **S** first computes $C_{n+1} = E_{k_e}(0^{|D|})$. **S** then runs our protocol (Add) with **A** by playing the role of the client. If the client outputs `reject`, then **S** sends `reject` to $\mathcal{F}$. Otherwise **S** sends OK to $\mathcal{F}$.

Now because SKE is CPA-secure, each $E_{k_e}(D)$ and $E_{k_e}(0^{|D|})$ are indistinguishable in the store phase, in the search phase, when modifying a document, and when adding a document. Further because PRF is a pseudo-random function, we can see that:

- The real $\mathcal{I}$ and the simulated one are indistinguishable.
- In the search phase, the real pad and the simulated $\mathtt{pad}^*$ are indistinguishable.
- When adding a document, the real $(a_1, \cdots, a_m)$ and the simulated one are indistinguishable.

Therefore the inputs to **A** inside of **S** are indistinguishable from those in the real world. This means that inside of **S**, **A** behaves in the same way as in the real world.

We next show that the outputs of the client (which $\mathcal{Z}$ receives) in the real world are indistinguishable from those in the ideal world. Remember that **A** inside of **S** behaves in the same way as in the real world.

For a modify query (i, D_i'),

1. the client sends (i, C_i') to the server, and
2. the server returns $(H(C_i), \pi_i)$ to the client.

First suppose that **A** returns $(H(C_i), \pi_i)$ correctly.

- In the real world, the client updates A_C correctly, and outputs nothing.
- In the ideal world, **S** returns OK to $\mathcal{F}$, and $\mathcal{F}$ replaces D_i with D_i'.

Next suppose that **A** returns an invalid $(H(C_i), \pi_i)$. Then eq.(7) does not hold with overwhelming probability from Proposition 3. Hence

- In the real world, the client outputs `reject`, and $\mathcal{Z}$ receives `reject`.
- In the ideal world, **S** returns `reject` to $\mathcal{F}$, $\mathcal{F}$ sends it to P_1, and P_1 relays it to $\mathcal{Z}$.

Therefore the real world and the ideal world are indistinguishable.

Similarly, for a delete query, the real world and the ideal world are indistinguishable.

For an add query D, the client receives nothing from the server (= **A**). Hence he always updates A_C and A_I correctly, and outputs nothing.

Finally for a search query on a keyword w,

1. the client sends $(\texttt{label}, \texttt{pad})$ to the server, and
2. the server returns $(\texttt{C}'(w), \pi_C, \pi_I)$ to the client, where $\texttt{C}'(w) = \{(i, C_i) \mid D_i \text{ contains } w\}$.

First suppose that **A** returns $(\texttt{C}'(w), \pi_C, \pi_I)$ correctly.

- In the real world, the client outputs $\texttt{D}(w) = \{D_i \mid D_i \text{ contains } w\}$ correctly.
- In the ideal world, **S** returns OK to $\mathcal{F}$, and $\mathcal{F}$ sends $\texttt{D}(w)$ to P_1.

Next suppose that **A** returns an invalid $(\texttt{C}''(w), \pi_C', \pi_I')$ such that

$$(\texttt{C}''(w), \pi_C', \pi_I') \neq (\texttt{C}'(w), \pi_C, \pi_I).$$

We will show that eq.(6) or eq.(5) does not hold with overwhelming probability.

- (Case 1) $\texttt{C}''(w) = \texttt{C}'(w)$ and $(\pi_C', \pi_I') \neq (\pi_C, \pi_I)$. In this case, the client computes $\{z_j\}$ and $\{x_i\}$ correctly. Hence eq.(6) or eq.(5) does not hold clearly because $(\pi_C', \pi_I') \neq (\pi_C, \pi_I)$.
- (Case 2) $\texttt{C}''(w) \neq \texttt{C}'(w)$. If the client does not compute $\{z_j\}$ correctly, then we can see that eq.(6) does not hold from Proposition 3.
  Suppose that the client computes $\{z_j\}$ correctly. Then he reconstructed $(e_1, \cdots, e_n)$ and $\overline{\texttt{index}}_a$ correctly. This means that there exist some $(i, C_i') \in \texttt{C}''(w)$ and $(i, C_i) \in \texttt{C}'(w)$ such that $C_i' \neq C_i$ because $\texttt{C}''(w) \neq \texttt{C}'(w)$. For such i, $H(i, H(C_i')) \neq H(i, H(C_i))$ because H is collision-resistant. Hence eq.(5) does not hold from Proposition 3 because $prime(H(i, H(C_i'))) \neq prime(H(i, H(C_i)))$.

Therefore in the real world, the client outputs `reject`, and $\mathcal{Z}$ receives `reject`. In the ideal world, **S** returns `reject` to $\mathcal{F}$, $\mathcal{F}$ sends it to P_1, and P_1 relays it to $\mathcal{Z}$. Consequently, we can see that $\mathcal{Z}$ cannot distinguish the real world from the ideal world.

Q.E.D.

Private Outsourcing of Polynomial Evaluation and Matrix Multiplication Using Multilinear Maps

Liang Feng Zhang and Reihaneh Safavi-Naini

Institute for Security, Privacy and Information Assurance
Department of Computer Science
University of Calgary

Abstract. *Verifiable computation* (VC) allows a computationally weak client to outsource evaluation of a function on many inputs to a powerful but untrusted server. The client invests a large amount of off-line computation to obtain an encoding of its function which is then given to the server. The server returns both the evaluation of the function on the client's input and a proof with which the client can verify the correctness of the evaluation using substantially less effort than doing the evaluation on its own. We consider *privacy preserving* VC schemes whose executions reveal no information on the client's input or function to the server. We construct VC schemes with input privacy for univariate polynomial evaluation and matrix multiplication and then extend them to achieve function privacy. Our main tool is the recently proposed *mutilinear maps*. We show that the proposed VC schemes can be used to implement verifiable outsourcing of private information retrieval (PIR).

1 Introduction

The rise of cloud computing in recent years has made outsourcing of storage and computation a reality. There are many scenarios where outsourcing computation will provide an attractive solution to the problem at hand. For example, large computations have a severe impact on resources (e.g. battery) of weak clients and outsourcing computation will provide an ideal way of freeing up the resources of the client. A natural question however is how to trust the computation result without trusting the server. The required assurance is not only against malicious behavior of the server but also random faults in the server infrastructure that can result in undetectable error in computation results. Verifiable computation (VC) systems [16] provide such assurance for many scenarios where computation must be delegated. The client in this model invests a large amount of off-line computation and generates an encoding of its function f. Given this encoding and any input α, the server computes and responds with y and a proof that $y = f(\alpha)$. With the server's response, the client can verify if the computation has been carried out correctly using substantially less effort than computing $f(\alpha)$ on its own. The client's off-line computation cost is *amortized* over the evaluations

M. Abdalla, C. Nita-Rotaru, and R. Dahab (Eds.): CANS 2013, LNCS 8257, pp. 329–348, 2013.

of f on multiple inputs α and will become negligible when computations of the same function is required.

VC schemes were formally defined by Gennaro, Gentry and Parno [16] and then constructed for a variety of computations [11,3,25,2,23,13,12]. We say that a VC scheme is *privacy preserving* if its execution reveals no information on the client's input or function to the server. Protecting the client's input and function from the server is an essential requirement in many real-life scenarios. For example, a health professional querying a database of medical records may need to protect both the identity and the record of his patient. VC schemes with input privacy have been considered in [16,2] where a generic function is written as a circuit, and each gate is evaluated using a fully homomorphic encryption scheme (FHE). These VC schemes evaluate the outsourced functions as circuits and are costly in practice. However, the outsourced function is given to the server in clear and so function privacy is not provided. Benabbas, Gennaro and Vahlis [3] and several other works [13,12,23] design VC schemes for specific functions without using FHE. One scheme of [3] even achieves function privacy. However, they do not consider the input privacy.

1.1 Results and Techniques

In this paper, we consider privacy preserving VC schemes for specific function evaluations without using FHE. The function evaluations we study include univariate polynomial evaluation and matrix multiplication. Our privacy definition is indistinguishability based and guarantees no untrusted server can distinguish between different inputs or functions of the client. In privacy preserving VC schemes both the client's input and function must be hidden (e.g., encrypted) from the server and the server must evaluate the hidden function on the hidden input and then generate a proof that the evaluation has been carried out correctly. We note that such a proof can be generated using the non-interactive proof or argument systems from [22,4] but they require the use of either random oracle or knowledge of exponent (KoE) type assumptions, both of which are considered as strong [23] and have been carefully avoided in VC literatures [16,3,25].

We construct VC schemes for univariate polynomial evaluation and matrix multiplication that achieve input privacy and then extend them such that the function privacy is also achieved. Our main tool is the multilinear maps [14,15]. Recently, Garg, Gentry, and Halvei [14] proposed a candidate mechanism that would approximate multilinear maps for many applications. The proposed instantiation has generated much interest and promise of studying new constructions using a multilinear map abstraction [15]. We use a framework of leveled multilinear maps where one can call a group generator $\mathcal{G}(1^\lambda, k)$ to obtain a sequence of groups $G_1, \ldots, G_k$ of order N along with their generators $g_1, \ldots, g_k$, where $N = pq$ for two λ-bit primes p and q. Slightly abusing notation, if $i+j \leq k$, we can compute a bilinear map operation on $g_i^a \in G_i, g_j^b \in G_j$ as $e(g_i^a, g_j^b) = g_{i+j}^{ab}$. These maps can be seen as implementing a *k-multilinear map*. We denote by

$$\Gamma_k = (N, G_1, \ldots, G_k, e, g_1, \ldots, g_k) \leftarrow \mathcal{G}(1^\lambda, k) \tag{1}$$

a random k-multilinear map instance, where $N = pq$ for two λ-bit primes p and q. We start with the BGN encryption scheme (denoted by BGN_2) of Boneh, Goh and Nissim [6] which is based on Γ_2 and semantically secure when the subgroup decision assumption (abbreviated as SDA, see Definition 1) for Γ_2 holds. It is well-known that BGN_2 is both additively homomorphic and multiplicatively homomorphic, i.e., given BGN_2 ciphertexts $\mathsf{Enc}(m_1)$ and $\mathsf{Enc}(m_2)$ one can easily compute $\mathsf{Enc}(m_1+m_2)$ and $\mathsf{Enc}(m_1 m_2)$. Furthermore, BGN_2 supports an unlimited number of additive homomorphic operations: for any integer $k \geq 2$, given BGN_2 ciphertexts $\mathsf{Enc}(m_1), \ldots, \mathsf{Enc}(m_k)$ one can easily compute $\mathsf{Enc}(m_1 + \cdots + m_k)$. This means one can easily compute $\mathsf{Enc}(f(\alpha))$ from $\mathsf{Enc}(\alpha)$ for any quadratic polynomial $f(x)$. On the other hand, BGN_2 supports only one multiplicative homomorphic operation: one cannot compute $\mathsf{Enc}(m_1 m_2 m_3)$ from $\mathsf{Enc}(m_1), \mathsf{Enc}(m_2)$ and $\mathsf{Enc}(m_3)$. In particular, one cannot compute $\mathsf{Enc}(f(\alpha))$ from $\mathsf{Enc}(\alpha)$ for any polynomial $f(x)$ of degree ≥ 3. In Section 2.2, we introduce BGN_k, which is a generalization of BGN_2 over Γ_k and semantically secure under the SDA for Γ_k. BGN_k supports both an unlimited number of additive homomorphic operations and up to $k-1$ multiplicative homomorphic operations. As a result, it allows us to compute $\mathsf{Enc}(f(\alpha))$ from $\mathsf{Enc}(\alpha)$ for any degree-k polynomial $f(x)$. In our VC schemes, the client's input and function are encrypted using BGN_k for a suitable k and the server computes on the ciphertexts.

Polynomial Evaluation. In Section 3.1 we propose a VC scheme Π_{pe} with input privacy (see Fig. 2) that allows the client to outsource the evaluation of a degree n polynomial $f(x)$ on any input α from a polynomial size domain $\mathbb{D}$. We use a polynomial commitment scheme proposed in [20] to construct a basic VC scheme and then show how to convert it into a privacy preserving scheme. The polynomial commitment scheme uses the algebraic property that there is a polynomial $c(x)$ of degree $n-1$ such that $f(x)-f(\alpha) = (x-\alpha)c(x)$. The basic VC scheme works as follows. Let $e : G_1 \times G_1 \to G_2$ be a bilinear map, where G_1 and G_2 are cyclic groups of prime order p and G_1 is generated by g_1. In the basic VC scheme, the client makes public $t = g_1^{f(s)}$ and gives $pk = (g_1, g_1^s, \ldots, g_1^{s^n}, f(x))$ to the server, where s is uniformly chosen from $\mathbb{Z}_p$. To verifiably compute $f(\alpha)$, the client gives α to the server and the server returns $\rho = f(\alpha)$ along with a proof $\pi = g_1^{c(s)}$. Finally the client verifies if $e(t/g_1^{\rho}, g_1) = e(g_1^s/g_1^{\alpha}, \pi)$. The basic VC scheme is secure under the SBDH assumption [20]. It is the univariate case of the VC schemes for multivariate polynomial evaluation of [23].

In Π_{pe}, the α should be hidden from the server (e.g., the client gives $\mathsf{Enc}(\alpha)$ to the server) which makes the server's computation of ρ and π (as in the basic VC scheme) impossible. Instead, the best one can expect is to compute a ciphertext $\rho = \mathsf{Enc}(f(\alpha))$ from $\mathsf{Enc}(\alpha)$ and $f(x)$. This can be achieved if the underlying encryption scheme Enc is an FHE which we want to avoid. On the other hand, a proof π that the computation of ρ has been carried out correctly should be given to the client. To the best of our knowledge, for generating such a proof π, one may adopt the non-interactive proofs or arguments of [22,4] but those constructions require the use of either random oracles or KoE type assumptions which we want to avoid as well. Our idea is to adopt the multilinear maps [14,15] which allow the server to homomorphically compute on $\mathsf{Enc}(\alpha)$ and $f(x)$ and then generate $\rho = \mathsf{Enc}(f(\alpha))$. In $\Pi_{\rm pe}$, the client picks a $(2k+1)$-multilinear map instance Γ as in (1). It stores $t = g_1^{f(s)}$ and gives $\boldsymbol{\xi} = (g_1, g_1^s, g_1^{s^2} \ldots, g_1^{s^{2^{k-1}}})$ and $f(x)$ to the server, where $k = \log\lceil n+1 \rceil$. It also sets up BGN_{2k+1}. In order to verifiably compute $f(\alpha)$, the client gives k ciphertexts $\sigma = (\sigma_1, \ldots, \sigma_k)$ to the server and the server returns $\rho = \mathsf{Enc}(f(\alpha))$ along with a proof $\pi = \mathsf{Enc}(c(s))$, where $\sigma_\ell = \mathsf{Enc}(\alpha^{2^{\ell-1}})$ for every $\ell \in [k]$. Note that $f(\alpha)$ and $c(s) = (f(s)-f(\alpha))/(s-\alpha)$ are both polynomials in α and s. In Section 2.2, we show how the server can compute ρ and π from $f(x), \sigma$ and $\boldsymbol{\xi}$. Upon receiving (ρ, π), the client decrypts ρ to y and verifies if $e(t/g_1^y, g_{2k}^p) = e(g_1^s/g_1^\alpha, \pi^p)$. We can show the security and privacy of $\Pi_{\rm pe}$ under the assumptions $(2k+1, n)$-MSDHS (see Definition 2) and SDA (see Definition 1).

Matrix Multiplication. In Section 3.2 we propose a VC scheme $\Pi_{\rm mm}$ with input privacy (see Fig. 3) that allows the client to outsource the computation of Mx for any $n \times n$ matrix $M = (M_{ij})$ and vector $x = (x_1, \ldots, x_n)$. It is based on the algebraic PRFs with closed form efficiency (firstly defined by [3]). In Section 2.3, we present an algebraic PRF with closed form efficiency $\mathsf{PRF}_{\rm dlin} = (\mathsf{KG}, \mathsf{F})$ over a trilinear map instance Γ, where for any secret key K generated by KG, F_K is a function with domain $[n]^2$ and range G_1. In $\Pi_{\rm mm}$, the client gives both M and its blinded version $T = (T_{ij})$ to the server, where $T_{ij} = g_1^{p^2 a M_{ij}} \cdot \mathsf{F}_K(i,j)$ for every $(i,j) \in [n]^2$ and a is randomly chosen from $\mathbb{Z}_N$ and is fixed for any $(i,j) \in [n]^2$. It also sets up BGN_3. In order to verifiably compute Mx, the client stores $\tau_i = \prod_{j=1}^n e(\mathsf{F}_K(i,j), g_2^{px_j})$ for every $i \in [n]$, where τ_i can be efficiently computed using the closed form efficiency property of $\mathsf{PRF}_{\rm dlin}$. It gives the ciphertexts $\sigma = (\mathsf{Enc}(x_1), \ldots, \mathsf{Enc}(x_n))$ to the server and the server returns $\rho_i = \mathsf{Enc}(\sum_{j=1}^n M_{ij}x_j)$ along with a proof $\pi_i = \prod_{j=1}^n e(T_{ij}, \mathsf{Enc}(x_j))$ for every $i \in [n]$. Upon receiving $\rho = (\rho_1, \ldots, \rho_n)$ and $\pi = (\pi_1, \ldots, \pi_n)$, the client can decrypt ρ_i to y_i and verify if $e(\pi_i, g_1^p) = \eta^{py_i} \cdot \tau_i$ for every $i \in [n]$, where $\eta = g_3^{p^2 a}$. Finally, we can show the security and privacy of $\Pi_{\rm mm}$ under the assumptions 3-co-CDHS (see Definition 5), DLIN (see Definition 5) and SDA.

Applications. Our VC schemes can be used to implement verifiable outsourcing of private information retrieval (PIR) where a client stores a large database w (which is modeled as a bit string $w = w_1 \cdots w_n \in \{0,1\}^n$) with the cloud and later retrieves a bit without revealing which bit he is interested in. This is a scenario that is well motivated by real life applications. For example a health professional that stores a database of medical records with the cloud may want to privately retrieve the record of a certain patient. Our VC schemes provide easy solutions for outsourcing PIR. A client with database w can outsource a polynomial $f(x)$ to the cloud using $\Pi_{\rm pe}$, where $f(i) = w_i$ for every $i \in [n]$. The client can also represent its database as a $\sqrt{n} \times \sqrt{n}$ matrix $M = (M_{ij})$ and outsource it to the cloud using $\Pi_{\rm mm}$. Retrieving any bit M_{ij} can be reduced to computing Mx for a 0-1 vector $x \in \{0,1\}^{\sqrt{n}}$ whose j-th bit is 1 and all other bits are 0. Our indistinguishability based definition of input privacy (see Fig. 1) guarantees that the server cannot learn which bit the client is interested in.

Discussions. We note that decrypting $\rho = \mathsf{Enc}(f(\alpha))$ in $\Pi_{\rm pe}$ requires computing discrete logarithms (see Section 2.2). Hence, the $f(\alpha)$ should be from a polynomial-size domain $\mathbb{M}$ since otherwise the client will not be able to decrypt ρ and then verify its correctness. In fact, this is an inherent limitation of [6] and inherited by the generalized BGN encryption schemes. However, in Section 3.3 we shall see that in many applications such as outsourcing PIR where $f(\alpha) \in \{0,1\}$, the limitation does not affect the applicability of our VC schemes in practice. One may also argue that with $f(x)$ and the knowledge of "$f(\alpha) \in \mathbb{M}$", the server may learn a polynomial size domain $\mathbb{D}$ where α is drawn from and therefore guess α with non-negligible probability. We note that the input privacy (see Definition 9) achieved by $\Pi_{\rm pe}$ is indistinguishability based and does not contradict to the above argument. In Section 3.4, we show how to modify $\Pi_{\rm pe}$ such that $f(x)$ is also hidden and therefore prevent the cloud from learning any information about α. Discussions similar to above are also applicable to $\Pi_{\rm mm}$.

Extensions. In Section 3.4, we modify $\Pi_{\rm pe}$ and $\Pi_{\rm mm}$ such that the function privacy is also achieved. In the modified schemes $\Pi'_{\rm pe}$ (see Fig. 4) and $\Pi'_{\rm mm}$ (see Fig. 5), the outsourced functions are encrypted and then given to the server. The basic approach is to increase the multi-linearity by 1 such that both the server and the client can compute on encrypted inputs and functions with one more application of the multilinear map e. The modified schemes $\Pi'_{\rm pe}$ and $\Pi'_{\rm mm}$ achieve both input and function privacy.

1.2 Related Work

Verifiable computation can be traced back to the work on *interactive* proofs or arguments [19,22]. In the context of VC, the *non-interactive* proofs or arguments are much more desirable and have been considered in [22,4] for various computations. However, they use either random oracles or KoE type assumptions.

Gennaro, Gentry and Parno [16] constructed the first non-interactive VC schemes without using random oracles or KoE type assumptions. Their construction is based on the FHE and garbled circuits. Using FHE, Chung et al. [11] proposed a VC scheme that requires no public key. Applebaum et al. [1] reduced VC to suitable variants of secure multiparty computation protocols. Barbosa et al. [2] also obtained VC schemes using delegatable homomorphic encryption. Although the input privacy has been explicitly considered in [16,2], those schemes evaluate the outsourced functions as circuits and are not efficient. None of them provides function privacy.

Benabbas et al. [3] initiated a line of research on efficient VC schemes for specific function (polynomial) evaluations based on algebraic PRFs with closed form efficiency. In particular, one of their VC schemes achieves function privacy but not input privacy. Parno et al. [25] initiated a line of research on public VC schemes for evaluating Boolean formulas, where the correctness of the server's computation can be verified by any client. Using algebraic PRFs with closed form efficiency, Fiore et al. [13,12] constructed public VC schemes for both polynomial evaluation and matrix multiplication. Using the idea of polynomial commitments [20], Papamanthou et al. [23] constructed public VC schemes that enable *efficient updates.* The schemes of [3,25,13,12,23] do not provide input privacy. Extensions of VC schemes to other different models have also been constructed in [18,22,10,4,8,9]. However, none of them is privacy preserving.

Organization. In Section 2, we firstly review several cryptographic assumptions related to multilinear maps; then introduce a generalization of the BGN encryption scheme [6]; we also recall algebraic PRFs with closed form efficiency and the formal definition of VC. In Section 3, we present our VC schemes for univariate polynomial evaluation and matrix multiplication. In Section 4, we show applications of our VC schemes in outsourcing PIR. Section 5 contains some concluding remarks.

2 Preliminaries

For any finite set A, the notation $\omega \leftarrow A$ means that ω is uniformly chosen from A. Let λ be a security parameter. We denote by $\mathsf{neg}(\lambda)$ the class of functions $\epsilon(\cdot)$ that are negligible in λ, i.e., for every constant $c > 0$, $\epsilon(\lambda) < \lambda^{-c}$ as long as λ is large enough. We denote by $\mathsf{poly}(\lambda)$ the class of polynomial functions in λ.

2.1 Multilinear Maps and Assumptions

In this section, we review several cryptographic assumptions concerning multilinear maps. Given the Γ_k in (1) and $x \in G_i$, the subgroup decision problem in G_i is deciding whether x is of order p or not, where $i \in [k]$. When $k = 2$, Boneh et al. [6] suggested the Subgroup Decision Assumption (SDA) which says that the subgroup decision problems in G_1 and G_2 are intractable. In this paper, we make the same assumption but for a general integer $k \geq 2$.

Definition 1. (SDA) *We say that* SDA_i *holds if for any probabilistic polynomial time* (PPT) *algorithm* $\mathcal{A}$, $|\Pr[\mathcal{A}(\Gamma_k, u) = 1] - \Pr[\mathcal{A}(\Gamma_k, u^q) = 1]| < \mathsf{neg}(\lambda)$, *where the probabilities are taken over* $\Gamma_k \leftarrow \mathcal{G}(1^\lambda, k)$, $u \leftarrow G_i$ *and* $\mathcal{A}$*'s random coins. We say that* SDA *holds if* SDA_i *holds for every* $i \in [k]$.

The k-Multilinear n-Strong Diffie-Hellman assumption ((k,n)-MSDH) was suggested in [24]: Given $g_1^s, g_1^{s^2}, \ldots, g_1^{s^n}$ for some $s \leftarrow \mathbb{Z}_N$, it is difficult for any PPT algorithm to find $\alpha \in \mathbb{Z}_N \setminus \{-s\}$ and output $g_k^{1/(s+\alpha)}$.

Definition 2. ((k,n)-MSDH) *For any PPT algorithm* $\mathcal{A}$, $\Pr\left[\mathcal{A}(p, q, \Gamma_k, g_1, g_1^s, \ldots, g_1^{s^n}) = (\alpha, g_k^{\frac{1}{s+\alpha}})\right] < \mathsf{neg}(\lambda)$, *where* $\alpha \in \mathbb{Z}_N \setminus \{-s\}$ *and the probability is taken over* $\Gamma_k \leftarrow \mathcal{G}(1^\lambda, k)$, $s \leftarrow \mathbb{Z}_N$ *and* $\mathcal{A}$*'s random coins.*

In the full version [26], we are able to construct a privacy preserving VC scheme for univariate polynomial evaluation which is secure based on (k,n)-MSDH. Under the (k,n)-MSDH assumption, the following lemma (see [26] for the proof) shows that either one of the following two problems is difficult for any PPT algorithm: (i) given $g_1, g_1^s, \ldots, g_1^{s^n}$ for some $s \leftarrow \mathbb{Z}_N$, compute $g_k^{p/s}$; (ii) given $g_1, g_1^s, \ldots, g_1^{s^n}$ for some $s \leftarrow \mathbb{Z}_N$, compute $g_k^{q/s}$.

Lemma 1. *If (k, n)-MSDH holds, then except for a negligible fraction of the k-multilinear map instances $\Gamma_k \leftarrow \mathcal{G}(1^\lambda, k)$, either* $\Pr[\mathcal{A}(p, q, \Gamma_k, g_1, g_1^s, \ldots, g_1^{s^n}) = g_k^{p/s}] < \mathsf{neg}(\lambda)$ *for any PPT algorithm $\mathcal{A}$ or* $\Pr[\mathcal{A}(p, q, \Gamma_k, g_1, g_1^s, \cdots, g_1^{s^n}) = g_k^{q/s}] < \mathsf{neg}(\lambda)$ *for any PPT algorithm $\mathcal{A}$, where the probabilities are taken over $s \leftarrow \mathbb{Z}_N$ and $\mathcal{A}$'s random coins.*

Due to Lemma 1, it looks reasonable to assume that (i) (resp. (ii)) is difficult. Furthermore, under this slightly stronger assumption (i.e., (i) is difficult, called (k, n)-MSDHS from now on), we can construct a VC scheme Π_{pe} (see Fig. 2) that is more efficient than the one based on (k, n)-MSDH. In this version, we only present the scheme Π_{pe} based on (k, n)-MSDHS.

Definition 3. ((k, n)-MSDHS) *For any PPT algorithm $\mathcal{A}$,* $\Pr[\mathcal{A}(p, q, \Gamma_k, g_1, g_1^s, \ldots, g_1^{s^n}) = g_k^{p/s}] < \mathsf{neg}(\lambda)$*, where the probability is taken over $\Gamma_k \leftarrow \mathcal{G}(1^\lambda, k)$, $s \leftarrow \mathbb{Z}_N$ and $\mathcal{A}$'s random coins.*

The k-Multilinear Decision Diffie-Hellman assumption (k-MDDH) was suggested in [14,15]: Given $g_1^s, g_1^{a_1}, \ldots, g_1^{a_k} \leftarrow G_1$, it is difficult for any PPT algorithm to distinguish between $g_k^{sa_1 \cdots a_k}$ and $h \leftarrow G_k$.

Definition 4. (k-MDDH) *For any PPT algorithm $\mathcal{A}$,* $|\Pr[\mathcal{A}(p, q, \Gamma_k, g_1^s, g_1^{a_1}, \ldots, g_1^{a_k}, g_k^{sa_1 \cdots a_k}) = 1] - \Pr[\mathcal{A}(p, q, \Gamma_k, g_1^s, g_1^{a_1}, \ldots, g_1^{a_k}, h) = 1]| < \mathsf{neg}(\lambda)$*, where the probabilities are taken over $\Gamma_k \leftarrow \mathcal{G}(1^\lambda, k)$, $s, a_1, \ldots, a_k \leftarrow \mathbb{Z}_N, h \leftarrow G_k$ and $\mathcal{A}$'s random coins.*

Let $\Gamma_3 = (N, G_1, G_2, G_3, e, g_1, g_2, g_3) \leftarrow \mathcal{G}(1^\lambda, 3)$ be a random trilinear map instance. Let $h_1 = g_1^p$ and $h_2 = g_2^p$. The trilinear co-Computational Diffie-Hellman assumption for the order q Subgroups (3-co-CDHS) says that given $h_1^a \leftarrow G_1$ and $h_2^b \leftarrow G_2$, it is difficult for any PPT algorithm to compute h_2^{ab}.

Definition 5. (3-co-CDHS) *For any PPT algorithm $\mathcal{A}$,* $\Pr[\mathcal{A}(p, q, \Gamma_3, h_1^a, h_2^b) = h_2^{ab}] < \mathsf{neg}(\lambda)$*, where the probability is taken over $\Gamma_3 \leftarrow \mathcal{G}(1^\lambda, 3)$, $a, b \leftarrow \mathbb{Z}_N$ and $\mathcal{A}$'s random coins.*

The following lemma shows that 3-co-CDHS is not a new assumption but weaker than 3-MDDH (see [26] for the proof).

Lemma 2. *If 3-MDDH holds, then 3-co-CDHS holds.*

The Decision LINear assumption (DLIN) has been suggested in [5] for cyclic groups that admit bilinear maps. In this paper, we use the DLIN assumption on the groups of Γ_3.

Definition 6. (DLIN) *Let G be a cyclic group of order $N = pq$, where p, q are λ-bit primes. For any PPT algorithm $\mathcal{A}$,* $|\Pr[\mathcal{A}(p, q, u, v, w, u^a, v^b, w^{a+b}) = 1] - \Pr[\mathcal{A}(p, q, u, v, w, u^a, v^b, w^c) = 1]| < \mathsf{neg}(\lambda)$*, where the probabilities are taken over $u, v, w \leftarrow G$, $a, b, c \leftarrow \mathbb{Z}_N$ and $\mathcal{A}$'s random coins.*

2.2 Generalized BGN Encryption

BGN_2 [6] allows one to evaluate quadratic polynomials on encrypted inputs (see Section 1.1). Boneh et al. [6] noted that this property arises from the bilinear map and a k-multilinear map would enable the evaluation of degree-k polynomials on encrypted inputs. Let $\mathbb{M}$ be a polynomial size domain, i.e. $|\mathbb{M}| = \mathsf{poly}(\lambda)$. Below we generalize BGN_2 and define $\mathrm{BGN}_k = (\mathsf{Gen}, \mathsf{Enc}, \mathsf{Dec})$ for any $k \geq 2$, where

- $(pk, sk) \leftarrow \mathsf{Gen}(1^\lambda, k)$ is a key generation algorithm. It picks Γ_k as in (1) and then outputs both a public key $pk = (\Gamma_k, g_1, h)$ and a secret key $sk = p$, where $h = u^q$ for $u \leftarrow G_1$.
- $c \leftarrow \mathsf{Enc}(pk, m)$ is an encryption algorithm which encrypts any message $m \in \mathbb{M}$ as a ciphertext $c = g_1^m h^r \in G_1$, where $r \leftarrow \mathbb{Z}_N$.
- $m \leftarrow \mathsf{Dec}(sk, c)$ is a decryption algorithm which takes as input sk and a ciphertext c, and outputs a message $m \in \mathbb{M}$ such that $c^p = (g_1^p)^m$.

Note that all algorithms above are defined over G_1 but in general they can be defined over G_i for any $i \in [k]$. This can be done by setting $pk = (\Gamma_k, g_i, h)$ and replacing any occurrence of g_1 with g_i, where $h = u^q$ for $u \leftarrow G_i$. Similar to [6], one can show that BGN_k is semantically secure under the SDA.

Below we discuss useful properties of BGN_k. For every integer $2 \leq i \leq k$, we define a map $e_i : G_1 \times \cdots \times G_1 \to G_i$ such that $e_i(g_1^{a_1}, \ldots, g_1^{a_i}) = g_i^{a_1 \cdots a_i}$ for any $a_1, \ldots, a_i \in \mathbb{Z}_N$. Firstly, we shall see that BGN_k allows us to compute $\mathsf{Enc}(m_1 \cdots m_k)$ from $\mathsf{Enc}(m_1), \ldots, \mathsf{Enc}(m_k)$. Suppose $\mathsf{Enc}(m_\ell) = g_1^{m_\ell} h^{r_\ell}$ for every $\ell \in [k]$, where $h = g_1^{q\delta}$ for some $\delta \in \mathbb{Z}_N$ and $r_\ell \leftarrow \mathbb{Z}_N$. Let $h_k = e_k(h, g_1, \ldots, g_1) = g_k^{q\delta}$. Then $e_k(\mathsf{Enc}(m_1), \ldots, \mathsf{Enc}(m_k)) = g_k^m h_k^r$ is a ciphertext of $m = m_1 \cdots m_k$ in G_k, where $r = \frac{1}{q\delta}(\prod_{\ell=1}^k (m_\ell + q\delta r_\ell) - m)$.

Computing ρ with Reduced Multi-linearity Level. In Π_{pe}, the client gives a polynomial $f(x) = f_0 + f_1 x + \cdots + f_n x^n$ and k ciphertexts $\sigma = (\sigma_1, \sigma_2, \ldots, \sigma_k)$ of $\alpha, \alpha^2, \ldots, \alpha^{2^{k-1}}$ under BGN_{2k+1} to the server and the server returns $\rho = \mathsf{Enc}(f(\alpha))$, where $k = \lceil \log(n+1) \rceil$. Below we show how to compute the ρ using σ and $f(x)$. Suppose $\sigma_\ell = g_1^{\alpha^{2^{\ell-1}}} h^{r_\ell}$ for every $\ell \in [k]$, where $h = g_1^{q\delta}$ for some $\delta \in \mathbb{Z}_N$ and $r_\ell \leftarrow \mathbb{Z}_N$. Clearly, any $i \in \{0, 1, \ldots, n\}$ has a binary representation $(i_1, \ldots, i_k)$ such that $i = \sum_{\ell=1}^k i_\ell 2^{\ell-1}$. Then $\alpha^i = \alpha^{i_1} \cdot (\alpha^2)^{i_2} \cdots (\alpha^{2^{k-1}})^{i_k}$ is the product of $i_1 + \cdots + i_k$ elements of $\{\alpha, \alpha^2, \ldots, \alpha^{2^{k-1}}\}$. For every $\ell \in [k]$, let $\phi_\ell = \sigma_\ell$ if $i_\ell = 1$ and $\phi_\ell = g_1$ otherwise. Then $\rho_i \triangleq e_k(\phi_1, \ldots, \phi_k) = g_k^{\mu_i} = g_k^m h_k^r$ is a ciphertext of $m = \alpha^i$ under BGN_{2k+1}, where $\mu_i = \prod_{\ell=1}^k (\alpha^{2^{\ell-1}} + q\delta r_\ell)^{i_\ell}$ and $r = \frac{1}{q\delta}(\mu_i - m)$. Thus, $\rho = \prod_{i=0}^n \rho_i^{f_i}$ is a ciphertext of $f(\alpha)$ under BGN_{2k+1}.

Computing π with Reduced Multi-linearity Level. In Π_{pe}, $k+1$ group elements $\boldsymbol{\xi} = (g_1, g_1^s, \ldots, g_1^{s^{2^{k-1}}})$ are also known to the server as part of the public key, where $s \leftarrow \mathbb{Z}_N$. The server must return $\pi = \mathsf{Enc}(c(s))$ as the proof that $\rho = \mathsf{Enc}(f(\alpha))$ has been correctly computed. Below we show how to compute π using $\boldsymbol{\xi}$ and σ. Note that $c(s) = (f(s) - f(\alpha))/(s - \alpha) = \sum_{i=0}^{n-1} \sum_{j=0}^i f_{i+1} \alpha^j s^{i-j}$.

It suffices to show how to compute $\pi_{ij} \triangleq \mathsf{Enc}(f_{i+1}\alpha^j s^{i-j})$ for every $i \in \{0,1,\ldots,n-1\}$ and $j \in \{0,1,\ldots,i\}$. Let $(j_1,\ldots,j_k)$, $(i_1,\ldots,i_k) \in \{0,1\}^k$ be the binary representations of j and $i-j$, respectively. Let $\phi_\ell = \sigma_\ell$ if $j_\ell = 1$ and $\phi_\ell = g_1$ otherwise. Let $\psi_\ell = g_1^{s^{2^{\ell-1}}}$ if $i_\ell = 1$ and $\psi_\ell = g_1$ otherwise. Then it is easy to see that $\pi_{ij} = e(e_k(\phi_1,\ldots,\phi_k), e_k(\psi_1,\ldots,\psi_k)) = g_{2k}^{\nu_{ij}} = g_{2k}^m h_{2k}^r$ is a ciphertext of $m = \alpha^j s^{i-j}$, where $\nu_{ij} = s^{i-j}\prod_{\ell=1}^k(\alpha^{2^{\ell-1}} + q\delta r_\ell)^{j_\ell}$, $h_{2k} = g_{2k}^{q\delta}$ and $r = \frac{1}{q\delta}(\nu_{ij} - m)$. Let $\nu = \sum_{i=0}^{n-1}\sum_{j=0}^{i} f_{i+1}\nu_{ij}$. Thus, $\pi \triangleq g_{2k}^{\nu} = \prod_{i=0}^{n-1}\prod_{j=0}^{i}\pi_{ij}^{f_{i+1}} = \mathsf{Enc}(c(s))$.

2.3 Algebraic PRFs with Closed Form Efficiency

In Π_{mm}, the client gives both a square matrix $M = (M_{ij})$ of order n and its blinded version $T = (T_{ij})$ to the server. The computation of T requires an algebraic PRF with closed form efficiency, which has very efficient algorithms for certain computations on large data. Formally, an algebraic PRF with closed form efficiency is a pair $\mathsf{PRF} = (\mathsf{KG}, \mathsf{F})$, where $\mathsf{KG}(1^\lambda, \mathsf{pp})$ generates a secret key K from any public parameter pp and $\mathsf{F}_K : I \to G$ is a function with domain I and range G (both specified by pp). We say that PRF has pseudorandom property if for any pp and any PPT algorithm $\mathcal{A}$, it holds that $|\Pr[\mathcal{A}^{\mathsf{F}_K(\cdot)}(1^\lambda,\mathsf{pp}) = 1] - \Pr[\mathcal{A}^{\mathsf{R}(\cdot)}(1^\lambda,\mathsf{pp}) = 1]| < \mathsf{neg}(\lambda)$, where the probabilities are taken over the randomness of $\mathsf{KG}, \mathcal{A}$ and the random function $\mathsf{R} : I \to G$. Consider an arbitrary computation Comp that takes as input $R = (R_1,\ldots,R_n) \in G^n$ and $x = (x_1,\ldots,x_n)$, and assume that the best algorithm to compute $\mathsf{Comp}(R_1,\ldots,R_n,x_1,\ldots,x_n)$ takes time t. Let $z = (z_1,\ldots,z_n) \in I^n$. We say that PRF has closed form efficiency for (Comp, z) if there is an efficient algorithm CFE such that $\mathsf{CFE}_{\mathsf{Comp},z}(K,x) = \mathsf{Comp}(\mathsf{F}_K(z_1),\ldots,\mathsf{F}_K(z_n),x_1,\ldots,x_n)$ and its running time is $o(t)$.

A PRF with Closed Form Efficiency. Fiore et al. [13] constructed an algebraic PRF with closed form efficiency $\mathsf{PRF}_{\mathsf{dlin}}$ based on the DLIN assumption for the bilinear groups. We generalize it over trilinear groups. In the generalized setting, KG generates $\Gamma_3 \leftarrow \mathcal{G}(1^\lambda, 3)$, picks $\alpha_i, \beta_i \leftarrow \mathbb{Z}_N$, $A_i, B_i \leftarrow G_1$ for every $i \in [n]$, and outputs $K = \{\alpha_i, \beta_i, A_i, B_i : i \in [n]\}$. The function F_K maps any pair $(i,j) \in [n]^2$ to $\mathsf{F}_K(i,j) = A_j^{\alpha_i} B_j^{\beta_i}$. The closed form efficiency of $\mathsf{PRF}_{\mathsf{dlin}}$ is described as below. Let $x = (x_1,\ldots,x_n) \in \mathbb{Z}_N^n$. The computation Comp we consider is computing $\prod_{j=1}^n \mathsf{F}_K(i,j)^{x_j}$ for all $i \in [n]$. Clearly, it requires $\Omega(n^2)$ exponentiations if no CFE is available. However, one can precompute $A = A_1^{x_1}\cdots A_n^{x_n}$ and $B = B_1^{x_1}\cdots B_n^{x_n}$ and have that $\prod_{j=1}^n \mathsf{F}_K(i,j)^{x_j} = A^{\alpha_i}B^{\beta_i}$ for every $i \in [n]$. Computing $A^{\alpha_i}B^{\beta_i}$ requires 2 exponentiations and hence the $\mathsf{PRF}_{\mathsf{dlin}}$ has closed form efficiency for (Comp, z), where $z = \{(i,j) : i,j \in [n]\}$. The $\mathsf{PRF}_{\mathsf{dlin}}$ in [13] is pseudorandom merely based on the DLIN for bilinear groups. Similarly, the generalized $\mathsf{PRF}_{\mathsf{dlin}}$ is also pseudorandom based on the DLIN assumption for trilinear groups. Consequently, we have the following lemma.

Lemma 3. *If DLIN holds in the trilinear setting, then* $\mathsf{PRF}_{\mathsf{dlin}}$ *is an algebraic PRF with closed form efficiency.*

2.4 Verifiable Computation

Verifiable computation [16,3,13] is a two-party protocol between a client and a server, where the client gives encodings of its function f and input x to the server, the server returns an encoding of $f(x)$ along with a proof, and finally the client efficiently verifies the server's computation. Formally, a VC scheme $\Pi = (\mathsf{KeyGen}, \mathsf{ProbGen}, \mathsf{Compute}, \mathsf{Verify})$ is defined by four algorithms, where

- $(pk, sk) \leftarrow \mathsf{KeyGen}(1^\lambda, f)$ takes as input a security parameter λ and a function f, and generates both a public key pk and a secret key sk;
- $(\sigma, \tau) \leftarrow \mathsf{ProbGen}(sk, x)$ takes as input the secret key sk and an input x, and generates both an encoded input σ and a verification key τ;
- $(\rho, \pi) \leftarrow \mathsf{Compute}(pk, \sigma)$ takes as input the public key pk and an encoded input σ, and produces both an encoded output ρ and a proof π;
- $\{f(x), \perp\} \leftarrow \mathsf{Verify}(sk, \tau, \rho, \pi)$ takes as input the secret key sk, the verification key τ, the encoded output ρ and a proof π, and outputs either $f(x)$ or $\perp$ (which indicates that ρ is not valid).

Correctness. The scheme Π should be correct. Intuitively, the scheme Π is correct if an honest server always outputs a pair (ρ, π) that gives the correct computation result. Let $\mathcal{F}$ be a family of functions.

Definition 7. *The scheme Π is said to be $\mathcal{F}$-*correct *if for any $f \in \mathcal{F}$, any $(pk, sk) \leftarrow \mathsf{KeyGen}(1^\lambda, f)$, any input x to f, any $(\sigma, \tau) \leftarrow \mathsf{ProbGen}(sk, x)$, any $(\rho, \pi) \leftarrow \mathsf{Compute}(pk, \sigma)$, it holds that $f(x) = \mathsf{Verify}(sk, \tau, \rho, \pi)$.*

Experiment $\mathsf{Exp}_{\mathcal{A}}^{\mathsf{Ver}}(\Pi, f, \lambda)$	Experiment $\mathsf{Exp}_{\mathcal{A}}^{\mathsf{Pri}}(\Pi, f, \lambda)$
1. $(pk, sk) \leftarrow \mathsf{KeyGen}(1^\lambda, f)$;	1. $(pk, sk) \leftarrow \mathsf{KeyGen}(1^\lambda, f)$;
2. for $i = 1$ to $l = \mathsf{poly}(\lambda)$ do	2. $(x_0, x_1) \leftarrow \mathcal{A}^{\mathsf{PubProbGen}(sk,\cdot)}(pk)$;
3. $x_i \leftarrow \mathcal{A}(pk, x_1, \sigma_1, \ldots, x_{i-1}, \sigma_{i-1})$;	3. $b \leftarrow \{0, 1\}$;
4. $(\sigma_i, \tau_i) \leftarrow \mathsf{ProbGen}(sk, x_i)$;	4. $(\sigma, \tau) \leftarrow \mathsf{ProbGen}(sk, x_b)$;
5. $\hat{x} \leftarrow \mathcal{A}(pk, x_1, \sigma_1, \ldots, x_l, \sigma_l)$	5. $b' \leftarrow \mathcal{A}^{\mathsf{PubProbGen}(sk,\cdot)}(pk, x_0, x_1, \sigma)$
6. $(\hat{\sigma}, \hat{\tau}) \leftarrow \mathsf{ProbGen}(sk, \hat{x})$;	6. output 1 if $b' = b$ and 0 otherwise.
7. $(\bar{\rho}, \bar{\pi}) \leftarrow \mathcal{A}(pk, x_1, \sigma_1, \ldots, x_l, \sigma_l, \hat{\sigma})$	Remark: $\mathsf{PubProbGen}(sk, \cdot)$ takes as input x, runs $(\sigma, \tau) \leftarrow \mathsf{ProbGen}(sk, x)$ and returns σ.
8. $\bar{y} \leftarrow \mathsf{Verify}(sk, \hat{\tau}, \bar{\rho}, \bar{\pi})$;	
9. output 1 if $\bar{y} \notin \{f(\hat{x}), \perp\}$ and 0 otherwise.	

Fig. 1. Experiments for security and privacy [16]

Security. The scheme Π should be secure. As in [16], we say that the scheme Π is secure if no untrusted server can cause the client to accept an incorrect computation result with a forged proof. This intuition can be formalized by an experiment $\mathsf{Exp}_{\mathcal{A}}^{\mathsf{Ver}}(\Pi, f, \lambda)$ (see Fig. 1) where the challenger plays the role of the client and the adversary $\mathcal{A}$ plays the role of the untrusted server.

Definition 8. *The scheme Π is said to be $\mathcal{F}$-*secure *if for any $f \in \mathcal{F}$ and any PPT adversary $\mathcal{A}$, it holds that $\Pr[\mathsf{Exp}_{\mathcal{A}}^{\mathsf{Ver}}(\Pi, f, \lambda) = 1] < \mathsf{neg}(\lambda)$.*

Privacy. The client's input should be hidden from the server in Π. As in [16], we define input privacy based on the intuition that no untrusted server can distinguish between different inputs of the client. This is formalized by an experiment $\mathsf{Exp}_{\mathcal{A}}^{\mathsf{Pri}}(\Pi, f, \lambda)$ (see Fig. 1) where the challenger plays the role of the client and the adversary $\mathcal{A}$ plays the role of the untrusted server.

Definition 9. *The scheme Π is said to achieve* input privacy *if for any function $f \in \mathcal{F}$, any PPT algorithm $\mathcal{A}$, it holds that* $\Pr[\mathsf{Exp}_{\mathcal{A}}^{\mathsf{Pri}}(\Pi, f, \lambda) = 1] < \mathsf{neg}(\lambda)$.

Efficiency. The algorithms ProbGen and Verify will be run by the client for each evaluation of the outsourced function f. Their running time should be substantially less than evaluating f.

Definition 10. *The scheme Π is said to be* outsourced *if for any $f \in \mathcal{F}$ and any input x to f, the running time of* ProbGen *and* Verify *is $o(t)$, where t is the time required to compute $f(x)$.*

3 Our Schemes

3.1 Univariate Polynomial Evaluation

In this section, we present our VC scheme $\Pi_{\rm pe}$ with input privacy (see Fig. 2) for univariate polynomial evaluation. In $\Pi_{\rm pe}$, the client outsources a degree n polynomial $f(x) = f_0 + f_1 x + \cdots + f_n x^n \in \mathbb{Z}_q[x]$ to the server and may evaluate $f(\alpha)$ for any input $\alpha \in \mathbb{D} \subseteq \mathbb{Z}_q$, where q is a λ-bit prime not known to the server and $|\mathbb{D}| = \mathsf{poly}(\lambda)$. Our scheme uses a $(2k+1)$-multilinear map instance Γ with groups of order $N = pq$, where $k = \lceil \log(n+1) \rceil$ and p is also a λ-bit prime not known to the server. The client stores $t = g_1^{f(s)}$ and gives $(g_1^s, g_1^{s^2} \ldots, g_1^{s^{2^{k-1}}}, f)$ to the server, where $s \leftarrow \mathbb{Z}_N$. It also sets up BGN_{2k+1} based on Γ. In order to verifiably compute $f(\alpha)$, the client gives $\sigma = (\sigma_1, \ldots, \sigma_k)$ to the server and the server returns $\rho = \mathsf{Enc}(f(\alpha))$ along with $\pi = \mathsf{Enc}(c(s))$, where $\sigma_\ell = \mathsf{Enc}(\alpha^{2^{\ell-1}})$ for every $\ell \in [k]$ and (ρ, π) is computed using the techniques in Section 2.2. At last, the client decrypts ρ to y and verifies if the equation (2) holds.

Correctness. The correctness of $\Pi_{\rm pe}$ requires that the client always outputs $f(\alpha)$ as long as the server is honest, i.e., $y = f(\alpha)$ and (2) holds. It is shown by the following lemma (see [26] for the proof).

Lemma 4. *If the server is honest, then $y = f(\alpha)$ and (2) holds.*

Security. The security of $\Pi_{\rm pe}$ requires that no untrusted server can cause the client to accept a value $\bar{y} \neq f(\alpha)$ with a forged proof. It is based on the $(2k+1, n)$-MSDHS assumption (see Definition 2).

Lemma 5. *If $(2k+1, n)$-MSDHS holds for Γ, then the scheme $\Pi_{\rm pe}$ is secure.*

Proof. Suppose that $\Pi_{\rm pe}$ is not secure. Then there is a PPT adversary $\mathcal{A}$ that breaks its security with non-negligible probability ϵ_1. We shall construct a PPT simulator $\mathcal{B}$ that simulates $\mathcal{A}$ and breaks the $(2k+1, n)$-MSDHS for Γ.

- KeyGen$(1^\lambda, f(x))$: Pick $\Gamma = (N, G_1, \ldots, G_{2k+1}, e, g_1, \ldots, g_{2k+1}) \leftarrow \mathcal{G}(1^\lambda, 2k+1)$. Pick $s \leftarrow \mathbb{Z}_N$ and compute $t = g_1^{f(s)}$. Pick $u \leftarrow G_1$ and compute $h = u^q$, where $u = g_1^\delta$ for an integer $\delta \in \mathbb{Z}_N$. Set up BGN_{2k+1} with public key (Γ, g_1, h) and secret key p. Output $sk = (p, q, s, t)$ and $pk = (\Gamma, g_1, h; g_1^s, g_1^{s^2}, \ldots, g_1^{s^{2^k-1}}; f)$.
- ProbGen(sk, α): For every $\ell \in [k]$, pick $r_\ell \leftarrow \mathbb{Z}_N$ and compute $\sigma_\ell = g_1^{\alpha^{2^{\ell-1}}} h^{r_\ell}$. Output $\sigma = (\sigma_1, \ldots, \sigma_k)$ and $\tau = \perp$ (τ is not used).
- Compute(pk, σ): Compute $\rho_i = g_k^{\mu_i}$ for every $i \in \{0, 1, \ldots, n\}$ using the technique in Section 2.2. Compute $\rho = \prod_{i=0}^n \rho_i^{f_i}$. Compute $\pi_{ij} = g_{2k}^{\nu_{ij}}$ for every $i \in \{0, 1, \ldots, n-1\}$ and $j \in \{0, 1, \ldots, i\}$ using the technique in Section 2.2. Compute $\pi = \prod_{i=0}^{n-1} \prod_{j=0}^i \pi_{ij}^{f_{i+1}}$. Output ρ and π.
- Verify(sk, τ, ρ, π): Compute the $y \in \mathbb{Z}_q$ such that $\rho^p = (g_k^p)^y$. If
$$e\left(t/g_1^y, g_{2k}^p\right) = e\left(g_1^s/g_1^\alpha, \pi^p\right), \tag{2}$$
then output y; otherwise, output $\perp$.

Fig. 2. Univariate polynomial evaluation (Π_{pe})

The simulator $\mathcal{B}$ takes as input $(p, q, \Gamma, g_1, g_1^s, \ldots, g_1^{s^n})$, where $s \leftarrow \mathbb{Z}_N$. The simulator $\mathcal{B}$ is required to output $g_{2k+1}^{p/s}$. In order to do so, $\mathcal{B}$ simulates $\mathcal{A}$ as below:

(A) Pick a polynomial $f(x) = f_0 + f_1 x + \cdots + f_n x^n \in \mathbb{Z}_q[x]$. Pick $u \leftarrow G_1$, compute $h = u^q$ and set up BGN_{2k+1} with public key (Γ, g_1, h) and secret key p. Pick $\beta \leftarrow \mathbb{D}$ and implicitly set $\hat{s} = s + \beta$ ($\hat{s}$ is not known to $\mathcal{B}$). Mimic KeyGen by sending $pk = (\Gamma, g_1, h, g_1^{\hat{s}}, g_1^{\hat{s}^2} \ldots, g_1^{\hat{s}^{2^k-1}}, f)$ to $\mathcal{A}$ (note that $\mathcal{B}$ can compute $g_1^{\hat{s}^{2^{\ell-1}}}$ for every $\ell \in [k]$ based on the knowledge of β and $g_1, g_1^s, \ldots, g_1^{s^n}$). Set $sk = (p, q, t)$, where $t = g_1^{f(\hat{s})}$ (note that sk does not include $\hat{s}$ as a component because $\hat{s}$ is neither known to $\mathcal{B}$ nor used by $\mathcal{B}$);

(B) Upon receiving $\alpha \in \mathbb{D}$ from $\mathcal{A}$, mimic ProbGen as below: pick $r_\ell \leftarrow \mathbb{Z}_N$ and compute $\sigma_\ell = g_1^{\alpha^{2^{\ell-1}}} h^{r_\ell}$ for every $\ell \in [k]$; send $\sigma = (\sigma_1, \ldots, \sigma_k)$ to $\mathcal{A}$.

It is trivial to verify that the pk and σ generated by $\mathcal{B}$ are identically distributed to those generated by the client in an execution of Π_{pe}. We remark that (A) is the step 1 in $\mathsf{Exp}_{\mathcal{A}}^{\mathsf{Ver}}(\Pi, f, \lambda)$ (see Fig. 1) and (B) consists of steps 3 and 4 in $\mathsf{Exp}_{\mathcal{A}}^{\mathsf{Ver}}(\Pi, f, \lambda)$. Furthermore, (B) may be run $l = \mathsf{poly}(\lambda)$ times as described by step 2 of $\mathsf{Exp}_{\mathcal{A}}^{\mathsf{Ver}}(\Pi, f, \lambda)$. After l executions of (B), the adversary $\mathcal{A}$ will provide an input $\hat{\alpha}$ on which he is willing to be challenged. If $\hat{\alpha} \neq \beta$, then the simulator $\mathcal{B}$ aborts; otherwise, it continues. Note that both β and $\hat{\alpha}$ are from the same polynomial size domain $\mathbb{D}$, the event that $\hat{\alpha} = \beta$ will occur with probability $\epsilon_2 \geq 1/|\mathbb{D}|$, which is non-negligible. If the simulator $\mathcal{B}$ does not abort, it next runs $(\hat{\sigma}, \hat{\tau}) \leftarrow \mathsf{ProbGen}(sk, \hat{\alpha})$ and gives $\mathcal{A}$ an encoded input $\hat{\sigma}$. Then the adversary $\mathcal{A}$ may maliciously reply with $(\bar{\rho}, \bar{\pi})$ such that $\mathsf{Verify}(sk, \hat{\tau}, \bar{\rho}, \bar{\pi}) \triangleq \bar{y} \notin \{f(\hat{\alpha}), \perp\}$. On the other hand, an honest server in Π_{pe} will reply with $(\hat{\rho}, \hat{\pi})$. Due to Theorem 4, it must be the case that $\mathsf{Verify}(sk, \hat{\tau}, \hat{\rho}, \hat{\pi}) \triangleq \hat{y} = f(\hat{\alpha})$. Note that the event that $\bar{y} \notin \{f(\hat{\alpha}), \perp\}$ occurs with probability ϵ_1. Suppose the event $\bar{y} \notin \{f(\hat{\alpha}), \perp\}$ occurs, then the equation (2) is satisfied by both $(\bar{y}, \bar{\pi})$ and $(\hat{y}, \hat{\pi})$, i.e.,

$$e\left(t/g_1^{\bar{y}}, g_{2k}^p\right) = e\left(g_1^{\hat{s}}/g_1^{\hat{\alpha}}, \bar{\pi}^p\right) \text{ and } e\left(t/g_1^{\hat{y}}, g_{2k}^p\right) = e\left(g_1^{\hat{s}}/g_1^{\hat{\alpha}}, \hat{\pi}^p\right). \quad (3)$$

The equalities in (3) imply that $e\left(g_1^{\bar{y}-\hat{y}}, g_{2k}^p\right) = e\left(g_1^{\hat{s}-\hat{\alpha}}, \left(\hat{\pi}/\bar{\pi}\right)^p\right)$. Hence,

$$g_{2k+1}^{\frac{p}{\hat{s}-\hat{\alpha}}} = e\left(g_1, \left(\hat{\pi}/\bar{\pi}\right)^p\right)^{\frac{1}{\bar{y}-\hat{y}}}. \quad (4)$$

Note that the left hand side of (4) is $g_{2k+1}^{p/s}$ due to $\beta = \hat{\alpha}$. Therefore, (4) means that the simulator $\mathcal{B}$ can break the $(2k+1, n)$-MSDHS assumption (Definition 3) with probability $\epsilon = \epsilon_1\epsilon_2$, which is non-negligible and contradicts to the $(2k+1, n)$-MSDHS assumption. Hence, under the $(2k+1, n)$-MSDHS assumption, ϵ_1 must be negligible in λ, i.e., the scheme Π_{pe} is secure.

Privacy. The input privacy of Π_{pe} requires that no untrusted server can distinguish between different inputs of the client. This is formally defined by the experiment $\mathsf{Exp}_{\mathcal{A}}^{\mathsf{Pri}}(\Pi, f, \lambda)$ in Fig. 1. The client in our VC scheme encrypts its input α using BGN_{2k+1} which is semantically secure under SDA for Γ. As a result, our VC scheme achieves input privacy under SDA for Γ (see [26] for the proof of the following lemma).

Lemma 6. *If SDA holds for Γ, then the scheme Π_{pe} achieves the input privacy.*

Efficiency. In order to verifiably compute $f(\alpha)$ with the cloud, the client computes $k = \lceil \log(n+1) \rceil$ ciphertexts $\sigma_1, \ldots, \sigma_k$ under BGN_{2k+1} in the execution of $\mathsf{ProbGen}$; it also decrypts one ciphertext $\rho = \mathsf{Enc}(f(\alpha))$ under BGN_{2k+1} and then verifies the equation (2). The overall computation of the client will be $O(\log n) = o(n)$ and therefore Π_{pe} is outsourced. On the other hand, the server needs to perform $O(n^2 \log n)$ multilinear map computations and $O(n^2)$ exponentiations in each execution of $\mathsf{Compute}$, which is comparable with the VC schemes based on FHE. Based on Lemmas 4, 5, 6 and the efficiency analysis, we have the following theorem.

Theorem 1. *If the $(2k+1, n)$-MSDHS and SDA assumptions for Γ both hold, then Π_{pe} is a VC scheme with input privacy.*

3.2 Matrix Multiplication

In this section, we present our VC scheme Π_{mm} with input privacy (see Fig. 3) for matrix multiplication. In Π_{mm}, the client outsources an $n \times n$ matrix $M = (M_{ij})$ over $\mathbb{Z}_q$ to the server and may compute Mx for an input vector $x = (x_1, \ldots, x_n) \in \mathbb{D} \subseteq \mathbb{Z}_q^n$, where q is a λ-bit prime not known to the server and $|\mathbb{D}| = \mathsf{poly}(\lambda)$. Our scheme uses a trilinear map instance Γ with groups of order $N = pq$, where p is also a λ-bit prime not known to the server. In Π_{mm}, the client gives both M and its blinded version $T = (T_{ij})$ to the server, where T is computed using the $\mathsf{PRF}_{\mathrm{dlin}}$. It also sets up BGN_3. In order to verifiably compute

- $\mathsf{KeyGen}(1^\lambda, M)$: Pick a trilinear map instance $\Gamma = (N, G_1, G_2, G_3, e, g_1, g_2, g_3) \leftarrow \mathcal{G}(1^\lambda, 3)$. Consider the $\mathsf{PRF}_{\text{dlin}}$ in Section 2.3. Run $\mathsf{KG}(1^\lambda, n)$ and pick a secret key K. Pick $a \leftarrow \mathbb{Z}_N$ and compute $T_{ij} = g_1^{p^2 a M_{ij}} \cdot \mathsf{F}_K(i,j)$ for every $(i,j) \in [n]^2$. Pick $u \leftarrow G_1$ and compute $h = u^q$. Set up BGN$_3$ with public key (Γ, g_1, h) and secret key p. Output $sk = (p, q, K, a, \eta)$ and $pk = (\Gamma, g_1, h, M, T)$, where $\eta = g_3^{p^2 a}$.
- $\mathsf{ProbGen}(sk, x)$: For every $j \in [n]$, pick $r_j \leftarrow \mathbb{Z}_N$ and compute $\sigma_j = g_1^{x_j} h^{r_j}$. For every $i \in [n]$, compute $\tau_i = e(\prod_{j=1}^n \mathsf{F}_K(i,j)^{x_j}, g_2^p)$ using the efficient CFE algorithm in Section 2.3. Output $\sigma = (\sigma_1, \ldots, \sigma_n)$ and $\tau = (\tau_1, \ldots, \tau_n)$.
- $\mathsf{Compute}(pk, \sigma)$: Compute $\rho_i = \prod_{j=1}^n \sigma_j^{M_{ij}}$ and $\pi_i = \prod_{j=1}^n e(T_{ij}, \sigma_j)$ for every $i \in [n]$. Output $\rho = (\rho_1, \ldots, \rho_n)$ and $\pi = (\pi_1, \ldots, \pi_n)$.
- $\mathsf{Verify}(sk, \tau, \rho, \pi)$: For every $i \in [n]$, compute y_i such that $\rho_i^p = (g_1^p)^{y_i}$. If
$$e(\pi_i, g_1^p) = \eta^{p y_i} \cdot \tau_i \quad (5)$$
for every $i \in [n]$, then output $y = (y_1, \ldots, y_n)$; otherwise output $\perp$.

Fig. 3. Matrix multiplication (Π_{mm})

Mx, the client stores $\tau = (\tau_1, \ldots, \tau_n)$, where each τ_i is efficiently computed using the closed form efficiency property of $\mathsf{PRF}_{\text{dlin}}$. It gives $\sigma = (\mathsf{Enc}(x_1), \ldots, \mathsf{Enc}(x_n))$ to the server and the server returns $\rho = (\rho_1, \ldots, \rho_n) = \mathsf{Enc}(Mx)$ along with $\pi = (\pi_1, \ldots, \pi_n)$. At last, the client decrypts ρ_i to y_i and verify if (5) holds for every $i \in [n]$.

Correctness. The correctness of Π_{mm} requires that the client always outputs Mx as long as the server is honest, i.e., $y = Mx$ and (5) holds for every $i \in [n]$. It is shown by the following lemma (see [26] for the proof).

Lemma 7. *If the server is honest, then $y = Mx$ and (5) holds for every $i \in [n]$.*

Security. The security of Π_{mm} requires that no untrusted server can cause the client to accept $\bar{y} \notin \{Mx, \perp\}$ with a forged proof. It is based on the 3-co-CDHS assumption for Γ (Lemma 2) and the DLIN assumption (Definition 6).

Lemma 8. *If the 3-co-CDHS assumption for Γ and the DLIN assumption both hold, then the scheme Π_{mm} is secure.*

Proof. We define three games G_0, G_1 and G_2 as below:

G_0 : this is the standard security game $\mathsf{Exp}_{\mathcal{A}}^{\mathsf{Ver}}(\Pi, M, \lambda)$ defined in Fig. 1.

G_1 : the only difference between this game and G_0 is a change to $\mathsf{ProbGen}$. For any $(x_1, \ldots, x_n)$ queried by the adversary, instead of computing τ using the efficient CFE algorithm, the inefficient evaluation of τ_i is used, i.e., $\tau_i = \prod_{j=1}^n e(\mathsf{F}_K(i,j)^{x_j}, g_2^p)$ for every $i \in [n]$.

G_2 : the only difference between this game and G_1 is that the matrix T is computed as $T_{ij} = g_1^{p^2 a M_{ij}} \cdot R_{ij}$, where $R_{ij} \leftarrow G_1$ for every $i, j \in [n]$.

For every $i \in \{0,1,2\}$, we denote by $\mathsf{G}_i(\mathcal{A})$ the output of game i when it is run with an adversary $\mathcal{A}$. The proof of the theorem proceeds by a standard hybrid argument, and is obtained by combining the proofs of the following three claims.

Claim 1. We have that $\Pr[\mathsf{G}_0(\mathcal{A}) = 1] = \Pr[\mathsf{G}_1(\mathcal{A}) = 1]$.

The only difference between G_1 and G_0 is in the computation of τ. Due to the correctness of the CFE algorithm, such difference does not change the distribution of the values τ returned to the adversary. Therefore, the probabilities that $\mathcal{A}$ wins in both games are identical.

Claim 2. We have that $|\Pr[\mathsf{G}_1(\mathcal{A}) = 1] - \Pr[\mathsf{G}_2(\mathcal{A}) = 1]| < \mathsf{neg}(\lambda)$.

The only difference between G_2 and G_1 is that we replace the pseudorandom group elements $\mathsf{F}_K(i,j)$ with truly random group elements $R_{ij} \leftarrow G_1$ for every $i,j \in [n]$. Clearly, if $|\Pr[\mathsf{G}_1(\mathcal{A}) = 1] - \Pr[\mathsf{G}_2(\mathcal{A}) = 1]|$ is non-negligible, we can construct an simulator $\mathcal{B}$ that simulates $\mathcal{A}$ and breaks the pseudorandom property of PRF with a non-negligible advantage.

Claim 3. We have that $\Pr[\mathsf{G}_2(\mathcal{A}) = 1] < \mathsf{neg}(\lambda)$.

Suppose that there is a PPT adversary $\mathcal{A}$ that wins with non-negligible probability ϵ in G_2. We want to construct a PPT simulator $\mathcal{B}$ that simulates $\mathcal{A}$ and breaks the 3-co-CDHS assumption (see Definition 5) with non-negligible probability. The adversary $\mathcal{B}$ takes as input a tuple $(p, q, \Gamma, h_1^\alpha, h_2^\beta)$, where $h_1 = g_1^p, h_2 = g_2^p$ and $\alpha, \beta \leftarrow \mathbb{Z}_N$. The adversary $\mathcal{B}$ is required to output $h_2^{\alpha\beta}$. In order to do so, $\mathcal{B}$ simulates $\mathcal{A}$ as below:

(A) Pick an $n \times n$ matrix M and mimic the KeyGen of game G_2 as below:
  - implicitly set $a = \alpha\beta$ by computing $\eta = e(h_1^\alpha, h_2^\beta) = g_3^{p^2\alpha\beta}$;
  - pick $u \leftarrow G_1$, compute $h = u^q$ and set up BGN_3 with public key (Γ, g_1, h) and secret key p;
  - pick $T_{ij} \leftarrow G_1$ for every $i,j \in [n]$ and send $pk = (\Gamma, g_1, h, M, T)$ to $\mathcal{A}$, where $T = (T_{ij})$;

(B) Upon receiving a query $x = (x_1, \ldots, x_n)$ from $\mathcal{A}$, mimic ProbGen as below:
  - for every $j \in [n]$, pick $r_j \leftarrow \mathbb{Z}_N$ and compute $\sigma_j = g_1^{x_j} h^{r_j}$;
  - for every $i,j \in [n]$, compute $Z_{ij} = e(T_{ij}, g_2^{px_j})/\eta^{pM_{ij}x_j}$;
  - for every $i \in [n]$, compute $\tau_i = \prod_{j=1}^n Z_{ij}$;
  - send $\sigma = (\sigma_1, \ldots, \sigma_n)$ to $\mathcal{A}$.

It is straightforward to verify that the pk, σ and τ generated by $\mathcal{B}$ are identically distributed to those generated by the client in game G_2. We remark that (A) is the step 1 in $\mathsf{Exp}_{\mathcal{A}}^{\mathsf{Ver}}(\Pi, M, \lambda)$ (see Fig. 1) and (B) consists of steps 3 and 4 in $\mathsf{Exp}_{\mathcal{A}}^{\mathsf{Ver}}(\Pi, M, \lambda)$. Furthermore, (B) may be run $l = \mathsf{poly}(\lambda)$ times as described by step 2 of $\mathsf{Exp}_{\mathcal{A}}^{\mathsf{Ver}}(\Pi, M, \lambda)$. After l executions of (B), the adversary $\mathcal{A}$ will provide an input $\hat{x} = (\hat{x}_1, \ldots, \hat{x}_n)$ on which he is willing to be challenged. Upon receiving $\hat{x}$, the simulator $\mathcal{B}$ mimics ProbGen as (B) and gives $\mathcal{A}$ an encoded input $\hat{\sigma}$. Then the adversary $\mathcal{A}$ may maliciously reply with $\bar{\rho} = (\bar{\rho}_1, \ldots, \bar{\rho}_n)$ and $\bar{\pi} = (\bar{\pi}_1, \ldots, \bar{\pi}_n)$ such that $\mathsf{Verify}(sk, \hat{\tau}, \bar{\rho}, \bar{\pi}) \triangleq \bar{y} \notin \{M\hat{x}, \perp\}$. On the other hand, an honest server in our VC scheme will reply with $\hat{\rho} = (\hat{\rho}_1, \ldots, \hat{\rho}_n)$ and $\hat{\pi} = (\hat{\pi}_1, \ldots, \hat{\pi}_n)$. Due to Lemma 7, it must be the case that $\mathsf{Verify}(sk, \hat{\tau}, \hat{\rho}, \hat{\pi}) \triangleq$

$\hat{y} = M\hat{x}$. Note that the event $\bar{y} \notin \{M\hat{x}, \perp\}$ occurs with probability ϵ. Suppose it occurs. Then there is an integer $i \in [n]$ such that $\bar{y}_i \neq \hat{y}_i$. Note that neither $\bar{y}$ nor $\hat{y}$ is $\perp$, the equation (5) must be satisfied by both $(\bar{y}, \bar{\pi})$ and $(\hat{y}, \hat{\pi})$, which translates into $e(\bar{\pi}_i, g_1^p) = \eta^{p\bar{y}_i} \cdot \hat{\tau}_i$ and $e(\hat{\pi}_i, g_1^p) = \eta^{p\hat{y}_i} \cdot \hat{\tau}_i$, we have that

$$e(\hat{\pi}_i/\bar{\pi}_i, g_1^p) = \eta^{p(\hat{y}_i - \bar{y}_i)} = e(g_2^{p^2\alpha\beta(\hat{y}_i - \bar{y}_i)}, g_1^p),$$

which in turn implies that $\hat{\pi}_i/\bar{\pi}_i = g_2^{p\alpha\beta \cdot p(\hat{y}_i - \bar{y}_i)}$. Let $\phi \in \mathbb{Z}_q^*$ be the multiplicative inverse of $p(\hat{y}_i - \bar{y}_i) \in \mathbb{Z}_q^*$. Then $g_2^{p\alpha\beta} = (\hat{\pi}_i/\bar{\pi}_i)^\phi$, i.e., $h_2^{\alpha\beta} = (\hat{\pi}_i/\bar{\pi}_i)^\phi$, which implies that $\mathcal{B}$ can break the 3-co-CDHS with probability at least ϵ. Therefore, this ϵ must be negligible in λ, i.e., $\Pr[\mathsf{G}_2(\mathcal{A}) = 1] < \mathsf{neg}(\lambda)$.

Privacy. The input privacy of $\Pi_{\rm mm}$ requires that no untrusted server can distinguish between different inputs of the client. This is formally defined by the experiment $\mathsf{Exp}_{\mathcal{A}}^{\mathsf{Pri}}(\Pi, f, \lambda)$ in Fig. 1. The client in our VC scheme encrypts its input x using BGN_3 which is semantically secure under SDA for Γ. As a result, $\Pi_{\rm mm}$ achieves input privacy under SDA for Γ (see [26] for the proof).

Lemma 9. *If the SDA for Γ holds, then $\Pi_{\rm mm}$ achieves the input privacy.*

Efficiency. In order to verifiably compute Mx with the cloud, the client computes n ciphertexts $\sigma_1, \ldots, \sigma_k$ under BGN_3 and n verification keys $\tau_1, \ldots, \tau_n$ in the execution of $\mathsf{ProbGen}$; it also decrypts n ciphertext $\rho = \mathsf{Enc}(Mx)$ under BGN_3 and then verifies the equation (5). The overall computation of the client will be $O(n) = o(n^2)$ and therefore $\Pi_{\rm pe}$ is outsourced. On the other hand, the server needs to perform $O(n^2)$ multilinear map computations and $O(n)$ exponentiations in each execution of $\mathsf{Compute}$, which is comparable with the VC schemes based on FHE. Based on Lemmas 7, 8, 9 and the efficiency analysis, we have the following theorem.

Theorem 2. *If the 3-co-CDHS, DLIN and SDA assumptions for Γ all hold, then $\Pi_{\rm mm}$ is a VC scheme with input privacy.*

3.3 Discussions

A theoretical limitation of our VC schemes $\Pi_{\rm pe}$ and $\Pi_{\rm mm}$ is that the computation results (i.e., $f(\alpha)$ and Mx) must belong to a polynomial size domain $\mathbb{M}$ since otherwise the client will not be able to decrypt ρ and then verify its correctness. However, we stress that this is not a real limitation when we apply both schemes in outsourcing PIR (see Section 4) where the computation results are either 0 or 1. On the other hand, with $f(x)$ and the knowledge "$f(\alpha) \in \mathbb{M}$" (resp. M and the knowledge "$Mx \subseteq \mathbb{M}$"), one may argue that the cloud can also learn a polynomial size domain $\mathbb{D}$ where α (resp. Mx) is drawn from and therefore guess the actual value of α (resp. x) with non-negligible probability. However, recall that our privacy experiment $\mathsf{Exp}_{\mathcal{A}}^{\mathsf{Pri}}(\Pi, f, \lambda)$ in Fig. 1 only requires the indistinguishability of different inputs. This is achieved by $\Pi_{\rm pe}$ and $\Pi_{\rm mm}$ (though for polynomial size domains) and suffices for our applications. Furthermore, in

Section 3.4, we shall show how to modify $\Pi_{\rm pe}$ and $\Pi_{\rm mm}$ such that the functions (i.e., $f(x)$ and M) are encrypted and then given to the cloud. As a consequence, the cloud learns no information on either the outsourced function or input unless it can break the underlying encryption scheme.

3.4 Function Privacy

Note that $\Pi_{\rm pe}$ and $\Pi_{\rm mm}$ only achieve input privacy. We say that a VC scheme achieves *function privacy* if the server cannot learn any information about the outsourced function. A formal definition of function privacy can be given using an experiment similar to $\mathsf{Exp}_{\mathcal{A}}^{\mathsf{Pri}}(\Pi, f, \lambda)$. Both $\Pi_{\rm pe}$ and $\Pi_{\rm mm}$ can be modified such that function privacy is also achieved. In the modified VC scheme $\Pi'_{\rm pe}$ (see Fig. 4 in Appendix A), the client gives BGN_{2k+2} ciphertexts $\mathsf{Enc}(f) = (\mathsf{Enc}(f_0), \ldots, \mathsf{Enc}(f_n))$ and $\sigma = (\mathsf{Enc}(\alpha), \ldots, \mathsf{Enc}(\alpha^{2^{k-1}}))$ to the server. Then the server can compute $\rho = \mathsf{Enc}(f(\alpha))$ along with a proof $\pi = \mathsf{Enc}(c(s))$ using $\mathsf{Enc}(f)$ and σ. In the modified VC scheme $\Pi'_{\rm mm}$ (see Fig. 5 in Appendix A), the client gives BGN_3 ciphertexts $\mathsf{Enc}(M) = (\mathsf{Enc}(M_{ij}))$ and $\sigma = (\mathsf{Enc}(x_1), \ldots, \mathsf{Enc}(x_n))$ to the server. Then the server can compute $\mathsf{Enc}(\sum_{j=1}^{n} M_{ij}x_j)$ along with a proof π_i using $\mathsf{Enc}(M)$ and σ for every $i \in [n]$. It is not hard to prove that the schemes $\Pi'_{\rm pe}$ and $\Pi'_{\rm mm}$ are secure and achieve both input and function privacy.

4 Applications

Our VC schemes have application in outsourcing private information retrieval (PIR). PIR [21] allows a client to retrieve any bit w_i of a database $w = w_1 \cdots w_n \in \{0,1\}^n$ from a remote server without revealing i to the server. In a trivial solution of PIR, the client simply downloads w and extracts w_i. The main drawback of this solution is its prohibitive communication cost (i.e. n). In [21,7,17], PIR schemes with non-trivial communication complexity $o(n)$ have been constructed based on various cryptographic assumptions. However, all of them assume that the server is *honest-but-curious*. In real-life scenarios, the server may have strong incentive to give the client an incorrect response. Such malicious behaviors may cause the client to make completely wrong decisions in its economic activities (say the client is retrieving price information from a stock database and deciding in which stock it is going to invest). Therefore, PIR schemes that are secure against malicious severs are very interesting. In particular, outsourcing PIR to untrusted clouds in the modern age of cloud computing is very interesting. Both of our VC schemes can provide easy solutions in outsourcing PIR. Using $\Pi_{\rm pe}$, the client can outsource a degree n polynomial $f(x)$ to the cloud, where $f(i) = w_i$ for every $i \in [n]$. To privately retrieve w_i, the client can execute $\Pi_{\rm pe}$ with input i. In this solution, the communication cost consists of $O(\log n)$ group elements. Using $\Pi_{\rm mm}$, the client can represent the w as a square matrix $M = (M_{ij})$ of order $\sqrt{n}$ and delegate M to the cloud. To privately retrieve a bit M_{ij}, the client can execute $\Pi_{\rm mm}$ with input $x \in \{0,1\}^{\sqrt{n}}$, where $x_j = 1$ and all the other bits are 0. In this solution, the communication cost consists of $O(\sqrt{n})$ group elements.

Note that in our outsourced PIR schemes, the computation results always belong to $\{0, 1\} \subseteq \mathbb{M}$. Therefore, the theoretical limitation we discussed in Section 3.3 does not really affect the application of our VC schemes in outsourcing PIR.

5 Conclusions

In this paper, we constructed privacy preserving VC schemes for both univariate polynomial evaluation and matrix multiplication, which have useful applications in outsourcing PIR. Our main tools are the recently developed multilinear maps. A theoretical limitation of our constructions is that the results of the computations should belong to a polynomial-size domain. Although this limitation does not really affect their applications in outsourcing PIR, it is still interesting to remove it in the future works. We also note that our VC schemes are only privately verifiable. It is also interesting to construct privacy preserving VC schemes that are publicly verifiable.

Acknowledgement. This research was in part supported by Alberta Innovates Technology Future, Alberta, Canada.

References

1. Applebaum, B., Ishai, Y., Kushilevitz, E.: From Secrecy to Soundness: Efficient Verification via Secure Computation. In: Abramsky, S., Gavoille, C., Kirchner, C., Meyer auf der Heide, F., Spirakis, P.G. (eds.) ICALP 2010. LNCS, vol. 6198, pp. 152–163. Springer, Heidelberg (2010)
2. Barbosa, M., Farshim, P.: Delegatable Homomorphic Encryption with Applications to Secure Outsourcing of Computation. In: Dunkelman, O. (ed.) CT-RSA 2012. LNCS, vol. 7178, pp. 296–312. Springer, Heidelberg (2012)
3. Benabbas, S., Gennaro, R., Vahlis, Y.: Verifiable Delegation of Computation over Large Datasets. In: Rogaway, P. (ed.) CRYPTO 2011. LNCS, vol. 6841, pp. 111–131. Springer, Heidelberg (2011)
4. Bitansky, N., Canetti, R., Chiesa, A., Tromer, E.: From Extractable Collision Resistance to Succinct Non-Interactive Arguments of Knowledge, and Back Again. In: ITCS 2012, pp. 326–349 (2012)
5. Boneh, D., Boyen, X., Shacham, H.: Short Group Signatures. In: Franklin, M. (ed.) CRYPTO 2004. LNCS, vol. 3152, pp. 41–55. Springer, Heidelberg (2004)
6. Boneh, D., Goh, E.-J., Nissim, K.: Evaluating 2-DNF Formulas on Ciphertexts. In: Kilian, J. (ed.) TCC 2005. LNCS, vol. 3378, pp. 325–341. Springer, Heidelberg (2005)
7. Cachin, C., Micali, S., Stadler, M.A.: Computationally Private Information Retrieval with Polylogarithmic Communication. In: Stern, J. (ed.) EUROCRYPT 1999. LNCS, vol. 1592, pp. 402–414. Springer, Heidelberg (1999)
8. Canetti, R., Riva, B., Rothblum, G.: Practical Delegation of Computation Using Multiple Servers. In: CCS 2011, pp. 445–454 (2011)
9. Choi, S.G., Katz, J., Kumaresan, R., Cid, C.: Multi-Client Non-Interactive Verifiable Computation. In: Sahai, A. (ed.) TCC 2013. LNCS, vol. 7785, pp. 499–518. Springer, Heidelberg (2013)

10. Chung, K.-M., Kalai, Y.T., Liu, F.-H., Raz, R.: Memory Delegation. In: Rogaway, P. (ed.) CRYPTO 2011. LNCS, vol. 6841, pp. 151–168. Springer, Heidelberg (2011)
11. Chung, K.-M., Kalai, Y., Vadhan, S.: Improved Delegation of Computation Using Fully Homomorphic Encryption. In: Rabin, T. (ed.) CRYPTO 2010. LNCS, vol. 6223, pp. 483–501. Springer, Heidelberg (2010)
12. Catalano, D., Fiore, D., Gennaro, R., Vamvourellis, K.: Algebraic (Trapdoor) One Way Functions and Their Applications. In: Sahai, A. (ed.) TCC 2013. LNCS, vol. 7785, pp. 680–699. Springer, Heidelberg (2013)
13. Fiore, D., Gennaro, R.: Publicly Verifiable Delegation of Large Polynomials and Matrix Computations, with Applications. In: CCS 2012, pp. 501–512 (2012)
14. Garg, S., Gentry, C., Halevi, S.: Candidate Multilinear Maps from Ideal Lattices. In: Johansson, T., Nguyen, P.Q. (eds.) EUROCRYPT 2013. LNCS, vol. 7881, pp. 1–17. Springer, Heidelberg (2013)
15. Garg, S., Gentry, C., Halevi, S., Sahai, A., Waters, B.: Attribute-Based Encryption for Circuits from Multilinear Maps. In: Canetti, R., Garay, J.A. (eds.) CRYPTO 2013, Part II. LNCS, vol. 8043, pp. 479–499. Springer, Heidelberg (2013)
16. Gennaro, R., Gentry, C., Parno, B.: Non-Interactive Verifiable Computing: Outsourcing Computation to Untrusted Workers. In: Rabin, T. (ed.) CRYPTO 2010. LNCS, vol. 6223, pp. 465–482. Springer, Heidelberg (2010)
17. Gentry, C., Ramzan, Z.: Single-Database Private Information Retrieval with Constant Communication Rate. In: Caires, L., Italiano, G.F., Monteiro, L., Palamidessi, C., Yung, M. (eds.) ICALP 2005. LNCS, vol. 3580, pp. 803–815. Springer, Heidelberg (2005)
18. Goldwasser, S., Kalai, Y.T., Rothblum, G.N.: Delegating Computation: Interactive Proofs for Muggles. In: STOC 2008, pp. 113–122 (2008)
19. Goldwasser, S., Micali, S., Rackoff, C.: The Knowledge Complexity of Interactive Proof Systems. In: STOC 1985, pp. 186–208 (1985)
20. Kate, A., Zaverucha, G.M., Goldberg, I.: Constant-Size Commitments to Polynomials and Their Applications. In: Abe, M. (ed.) ASIACRYPT 2010. LNCS, vol. 6477, pp. 177–194. Springer, Heidelberg (2010)
21. Kushilevitz, E., Ostrovsky, R.: Replication Is Not Needed: Single Database, Computationally-Private Information Retrieval. In: FOCS 1997, pp. 364–373 (1997)
22. Micali, S.: Computationally Sound Proofs. SIAM Journal of Computing 30(4), 1253–1298 (2000)
23. Papamanthou, C., Shi, E., Tamassia, R.: Signatures of Correct Computation. In: Sahai, A. (ed.) TCC 2013. LNCS, vol. 7785, pp. 222–242. Springer, Heidelberg (2013)
24. Papamanthou, C., Tamassia, R., Triandopoulos, N.: Optimal Authenticated Data Structures with Multilinear Forms. In: Joye, M., Miyaji, A., Otsuka, A. (eds.) Pairing 2010. LNCS, vol. 6487, pp. 246–264. Springer, Heidelberg (2010)
25. Parno, B., Raykova, M., Vaikuntanathan, V.: How to Delegate and Verify in Public: Verifiable Computation from Attribute-Based Encryption. In: Cramer, R. (ed.) TCC 2012. LNCS, vol. 7194, pp. 422–439. Springer, Heidelberg (2012)
26. Zhang, L.F., Safavi-Naini, R.: Private Outsourcing of Polynomial Evaluation and Matrix Multiplication using Multilinear Maps? (Full Version of this Paper), `http://arxiv.org/abs/1308.4218`

A Privacy Preserving VC Schemes

- KeyGen$(1^\lambda, f(x))$: Pick $\Gamma = (N, G_1, \ldots, G_{2k+2}, e, g_1, \ldots, g_{2k+2}) \leftarrow \mathcal{G}(1^\lambda, 2k+2)$. Pick $s \leftarrow \mathbb{Z}_N$ and compute $t = g_1^{f(s)}$. Pick $u \leftarrow G_1$ and compute $h = u^q$, where $u = g_1^\delta$ for an integer $\delta \in \mathbb{Z}_N$. Set up BGN$_{2k+2}$ with public key (Γ, g_1, h) and secret key p. For every $i \in \{0, 1, \ldots, n\}$, pick $v_i \leftarrow \mathbb{Z}_N$ and compute $\gamma_i = g_1^{f_i} h^{v_i}$. Output $sk = (p, q, s, t)$ and $pk = (\Gamma, g_1, h, g_1^s, g_1^{s^2}, \ldots, g_1^{s^{2^{k-1}}}, \gamma)$, where $\gamma = (\gamma_0, \ldots, \gamma_n)$.
- ProbGen(sk, α): For every $\ell \in [k]$, pick $r_\ell \leftarrow \mathbb{Z}_N$ and compute $\sigma_\ell = g_1^{\alpha^{2^{\ell-1}}} h^{r_\ell}$. Output $\sigma = (\sigma_1, \ldots, \sigma_k)$ and $\tau = \perp$ (τ is not used).
- Compute(pk, σ): Compute $\rho_i = g_k^{\mu_i}$ for every $i \in \{0, 1, \ldots, n\}$ using the technique in Section 2.2. Compute $\rho_i' = e(\gamma_i, \rho_i) = g_{k+1}^{\mu_i'}$, where $\mu_i' = (f_i + q\delta v_i)\mu_i$. Compute $\rho = \prod_{i=0}^n \rho_i'$. Compute $\pi_{ij} = g_{2k}^{\nu_{ij}}$ using the technique in Section 2.2 for every $i \in \{0, 1, \ldots, n-1\}$ and $j \in \{0, 1, \ldots, i\}$. Compute $\pi_{ij}' = e(\gamma_{i+1}, \pi_{ij}) = g_{2k+1}^{\nu_{ij}'}$, where $\nu_{ij}' = (f_{i+1} + q\delta v_{i+1})\nu_{ij}$. Set $\pi = \prod_{i=0}^{n-1} \prod_{j=0}^{i} \pi_{ij}'$.Output ρ and π.
- Verify(sk, τ, ρ, π): Compute the $y \in \mathbb{Z}_q$ such that $\rho^p = (g_{k+1}^p)^y$. If the equality $e\big(t/g_1^y, g_{2k+1}^p\big) = e\big(g_1^s/g_1^\alpha, \pi^p\big)$ holds, output y; otherwise, output $\perp$.

Fig. 4. Univariate polynomial evaluation ($\Pi_{\rm pe}'$)

- KeyGen$(1^\lambda, M)$: Pick $\Gamma = (N, G_1, G_2, G_3, e, g_1, g_2, g_3) \leftarrow \mathcal{G}(1^\lambda, 3)$. Consider the PRF$_{\rm dlin}$ in Section 2.3. Run KG$(1^\lambda, n)$ and pick a secret key K. Pick $a \leftarrow \mathbb{Z}_N$ and compute $T_{ij} = g_1^{p^2 a M_{ij}} \cdot \mathsf{F}_K(i, j)$ for every $(i, j) \in [n]^2$. Pick $u \leftarrow G_1$ and compute $h = u^q$, where $u = g_1^\delta$ for an integer $\delta \in \mathbb{Z}_N$. Set up BGN$_3$ with public key (Γ, g_1, h) and secret key p. For every $(i, j) \in [n]^2$, pick $v_{ij} \leftarrow \mathbb{Z}_N$ and compute $\gamma_{ij} = g_1^{M_{ij}} h^{v_{ij}}$. Output $sk = (p, q, K, a, \eta)$ and $pk = (\Gamma, g_1, h, \gamma, T)$, where $\eta = g_3^{p^2 a}$ and $\gamma = (\gamma_{ij})$.
- ProbGen(sk, x): For every $j \in [n]$, pick $r_j \leftarrow \mathbb{Z}_N$ and compute $\sigma_j = g_1^{x_j} h^{r_j}$. For every $i \in [n]$, compute $\tau_i = e(\prod_{j=1}^n \mathsf{F}_K(i, j)^{x_j}, g_2^p)$ using the efficient CFE algorithm in Section 2.3. Output $\sigma = (\sigma_1, \ldots, \sigma_n)$ and $\tau = (\tau_1, \ldots, \tau_n)$.
- Compute(pk, σ): Compute $\rho_i = \prod_{j=1}^n e(\gamma_{ij}, \sigma_j)$ and $\pi_i = \prod_{j=1}^n e(T_{ij}, \sigma_j)$ for every $i \in [n]$. Output $\rho = (\rho_1, \ldots, \rho_n)$ and $\pi = (\pi_1, \ldots, \pi_n)$.
- Verify(sk, τ, ρ, π): For every $i \in [n]$, compute y_i such that $\rho_i^p = (g_2^p)^{y_i}$. If $e(\pi_i, g_1^p) = \eta^{p y_i} \cdot \tau_i$ for every $i \in [n]$, then output $y = (y_1, \ldots, y_n)$; otherwise, output $\perp$.

Fig. 5. Matrix multiplication ($\Pi_{\rm mm}'$)

Author Index